THE SEX OFFENDER

CURRENT TREATMENT MODALITIES

AND SYSTEMS ISSUES

VOLUME IV

Edited by
Barbara K. Schwartz, Ph.D.

CRI Civic Research Institute
4478 U.S. Route 27 • P.O. Box 585 • Kingston, NJ 08528

Copyright © 2002

By Civic Research Institute, Inc.
Kingston, New Jersey 08528

Printed in the United States of America

Library of Congress Cataloging in Publication Data
The sex offender: Volume IV: Current treatment modalities and systems issues/Barbara K. Schwartz

ISBN 1-887554-23-8

Library of Congress Catalog Card Number 95-70893

Acknowledgments

The editor wishes to thank the authors who agreed to share their work and research for this volume. Without exception they were totally cooperative and timely. National organizations such as the Association for the Treatment of Sexual Abusers and the Massachusetts Association for the Treatment of Sexual Abusers as well as others have provided the initial impetus for the preparation of these works for public consumption. Without the support of my employer, Justice Resource Institute, Susan Wayne, M.S.W. and Greg Canfield, M.S.W., this volume would not have been possible. As ever my husband, Ed, has provided unqualified sustenance as have my children, Betsy and Benjamin, and Thomas, Cedey, and Roger have helped to preserve my sanity.

This volume in dedicated to the memory of

Theoharis K. Seghorn, Ph.D.
1939–2001
"People like you help people like me go on. . . ."
Si Kahn

About the Authors

Vicki MacIntyre Agee, Ph.D.

Vicki MacIntyre Agee, a clinical psychologist, has many years of experience designing and implementing treatment programs for adolescent sexual offenders and for serious juvenile offenders. She had particular expertise in designing cognitive behavioral programs with therapeutic milieus. Another area of specialty is quality control monitoring keyed to achieving high standards in treatment. Dr. Agee is clinical director of Twin Cedars Youth Services, Inc., in LaGrange, Georgia. She is a member of the National Task Force on Standards for Juvenile Sex Offender Treatment for the National Adolescent Perpetrator Network and is Tennessee State Representative to the Public Policy Board of the Association for the Treatment of Sexual Abusers. She has also consulted widely in the United States and Canada.

Dana Anderson, M.A.

Dana Anderson earned her B.A. (Hons) at the University of Waterloo and her M.A. at Queen's University at Kingston. She is completing her Ph.D. in clinical psychology at Queen's University under the supervision of Dr. W. L. Marshall. She is currently the clinical director of the Tupiq program for Inuit Offenders at Fenbrook Institution in Gravenhurst, Ontario. She has treated sexual offenders of all levels of security within the Canadian federal penitentiary system, has made several conference presentations, has published articles in refereed journals and books, and has coauthored a book on the treatment of sexual offenders. Her research interests include substance abuse in sexual offenders, self-esteem, interpersonal theory, and the psychotherapeutic process.

Steven M. Bengis, Ed.D., L.C.S.W.

Steven Bengis is a nationally recognized trainer in the field of juvenile sexual offending. He has offered workshops and keynoted conferences in more than twenty-five states, in Israel and New Zealand, and throughout Canada. He is a former member of the National Task Force on Juvenile Sexual Offending and president of the Massachusetts Adolescent Sexual Offender Coalition, Inc. He is author of several articles and book chapters and a monograph titled "A Comprehensive Service Delivery System with a Continuum of Care for Adolescent Sexual Offenders," published by Safer Society Press. Together with his wife, Penny Cuninggim, Ed.D., he founded and directs the New England Adolescent Research Institute, Inc. (NEARI) in Holyoke, Massachusetts. NEARI administers a day school that provides special education services to severely emotionally disturbed and behaviorally disordered youth, an early intervention program, "Jumpstart," for severely at-risk youth, the NEARI Press, a publishing house specializing in education and intervention with "at-risk youth," and a training and consulting center.

Dr. Bengis, holds a doctorate in counseling psychology from the University of Massachusetts and has worked as a therapist both privately and in outpatient, residential, and school settings.

David Bright, B.S.

David Bright completed a B.S. (Hons.) in psychology at the University of New South Wales in 1994. He is currently enrolled in the combined Master of Psychology (Forensic)/Ph.D. program at the University of New South Wales. In addition to his studies, he is a psychologist with Sex Offender Programmes, New South Wales Department of Corrective Services. He has worked for Sex Offender Programmes since 1998 and is currently providing assessment and treatment services to moderate- and high-risk sexual offenders in the Custody-Based Intensive Treatment (CUBIT) program at the Malabar Special Programmes Centre located in Long Bay Correctional Centre, Sydney, Australia. He worked from 1994 to 1998 for the New South Wales Department of Health and in private practice.

Kirk A. Brunswig, M.S.

Kirk A. Brunswig is currently working as a psychologist with civilly committed, sexually violent predators at the Special Commitment Center, McNeil Island, Washington. He is also an advanced doctoral student completing his Ph.D. in clinical psychology at the University of Nevada, Reno. Mr. Brunswig has coauthored a body of work in the areas of sexual harassment and sexual abuse/sexual offending and has made several conference presentations in these areas. He earned his master's degree at Western Washington University, with an emphasis on measurement, evaluation, and statistical analysis.

Julie Campbell, M.S.W., L.S.W.

Julie Campbell is a licensed social worker in Philadelphia, PA. Ms. Campbell received a Master's Degree in Social Work from the University of Pennsylvania and received Post-graduate Certification in Marital and Family Therapy from the Penn Council for Relationships. Ms. Campbell has specialized in the area of sexual abuse treatment with children, adults, and families for the past twelve years. Currently, Ms. Campbell provides treatment to children who have experienced traumatic events including sexual trauma. Ms. Campbell has provided clinical training and supervision in the area of sexual abuse treatment and has presented at local and national conferences.

Gayle E. Christensen, L.C.S.W., B.C.D.

Gayle E. Christensen is co-founder and clinical supervisor at The Family Center of Colorado Springs, P.C. The Family Center provides comprehensive treatment services for all members of families who have experienced sexual abuse within the family. Mr. Christensen is also a Full Operating Level Treatment Provider with the Colorado Sex Offender Management Board.

Franca Cortoni, Ph.D., R. Psych.

Franca Cortoni obtained her Ph.D. in clinical and forensic psychology at Queen's University at Kingston in 1998. Since 1989, she has worked with or conducted research on sexual offenders in a variety of institutional and community settings. In 1997, Dr. Cortoni became the director of the Sex Offender Program in Kingston Penitentiary, a maximum-security federal penitentiary located in Kingston, Ontario, Canada. She was on leave in 1999 and 2000 to provide consultation services on program implementation and staff training to Sex Offender Programmes of the

Department of Corrective Services, New South Wales, Australia. During that time, she also was an Honorary Associate in the School of Psychology, University of New South Wales. Her research interests include coping, developmental factors, and thinking patterns in sexual offenders, as well as sexual violence within correctional settings. Dr. Cortoni has made several presentations at national and international conferences and published on these topics.

Kathleen Davis, M.Ed.

Kathleen Davis is an award-winning student from the Department of Counselor Education at Florida Atlantic University. Her interests include the clinical dynamics related to domestic violence and the treatment of child and adolescent sexual offenders and their victims.

Melissa P. DelBello, M.D.

Melissa P. DelBello received her M.D. from the University of Rochester School of Medicine, Rochester, New York in 1995 and served her Residency in Psychiatry at Payne Whitney Clinic New York Hospital, Cornell Medical Center, New York City, in 1995–1996 and then at the University of Cincinnati College of Medicine in Cincinnati, Ohio from 1996 to 1998. Dr. DelBello completed her Clinical Child and Adolescent Psychiatry Fellowship at Cincinnati Children's Hospital Medical Center, Cincinnati, Ohio, and Research Fellowship in the Bipolar and Psychotic Disorders Research Program, Department of Psychiatry, University of Cincinnati College of Medicine from 1998 to 2000. Her academic appointments include assistant professor of psychiatry and pediatrics, University of Cincinnati College of Medicine and director, Child and Adolescent Psychiatry Division, Psychotic and Bipolar Disorder Research Program. In 2000, Dr. DelBello was appointed attending psychiatrist as well as co-director of the Mood Disorders Program at Children's Hospital Medical Center in Cincinnati. In addition to teaching and lecturing, she has received numerous awards and honors. She has authored or coauthored some seventy reports, abstracts, peer-reviewed articles, reviews, and publications. Her primary research interests include the developmental psychopathology of bipolar disorder.

Dennis M. Doren, Ph.D., DABPS, ABAP

Dennis M. Doren is the Evaluation Director at the Sand Ridge Secure Treatment Center in Mauston, Wisconsin, where he supervises and conducts sex offender civil commitment assessments. He has written a soon-to-be-published book concerning sex offender civil commitment assessments, as well as numerous professional articles on related topics. His evaluation work in this regard has occurred in most U.S. states with such commitment laws. Likewise, he has been called to give court testimony in most of those states concerning risk assessment procedures. Dr. Doren has also conducted consultations and training concerning sex offender risk assessments across the country and at national and international conferences.

Yolanda M. Fernandez, Ph.D.

Yolanda Fernandez was born in Toronto, Canada. She graduated with a B.A. (Hons.) in 1994, an M.A. in 1996, and a Ph.D. in clinical/forensic psychology in 2001 from Queen's University in Kingston Ontario. She is currently working with Dr. W .L. Marshall at Rockwood Psychological Services as the clinical director of the Sexual

Offender Treatment Program located at Bath Institution (a medium-security federal penitentiary). In addition to her clinical work, Dr. Fernandez is an active researcher who currently has made several presentations at international conferences and contributed to twenty publications. Her publications include one coauthored book and one coedited book. Dr. Fernandez"s research interests include therapeutic process in sexual offender treatment, empathy deficits in sexual offenders, and phallometric testing with sexual offenders.

Timothy P. Foley, Ph.D.

Timothy P. Foley is a licensed psychologist in New Jersey and Pennsylvania with a primary emphasis on forensic and therapeutic issues related to sexual misconduct. He testifies frequently in state and federal courts on a wide variety of issues related to sex crimes. One of his particular areas of interest and expertise is Internet pornography.

Laurie Guidry, Psy.D.

Laurie Guidry is a native New Orleanian who moved to New England to pursue her graduate studies. Dr. Guidry has done clinical work with both victims and perpetrators of sexual abuse. She is the coauthor of *Addictions and Trauma Recovery: Healing the Mind, Body and Spirit* (June 2001, Norton), a treatment manual for survivors of trauma who struggle with issues of addictions. Currently, Dr. Guidry is employed by the University of Massachusetts Medical School and the Massachusetts Department of Mental Health (DMH) as program director for DMH's statewide initiative to develop assessment and treatment programming for psychiatric inpatients who present with co-occurring major mental illness and sexual behavior disorders. She also works as a clinical consultant and lectures on issues related to trauma and sexual violence.

Bert Harris, M.A., L.P.

Bert Harris is a licensed clinical psychologist and certified psychodramatist working in Philadelphia. Mr. Harris received his master's degree in clinical psychology from West Chester University. He has specialized in forensic psychology with adult and juvenile sex offenders for the past eleven years. He has assisted in the development of risk assessments for juvenile sex offender's and published research in this area. Mr. Harris is a member of the Pennsylvania Sexual Offenders Assessment Board and the Association for the Treatment of Sexual Abuse. He has conducted training and presentations in the area of sexual offending at the local and national level. Currently, Mr. Harris treats adolescent and adult sex offenders and evaluates adolescent sexual offender services for the city of Philadelphia.

Fran Henry, M.B.A.

Fran Henry earned a master's degree in business administration from Harvard University Graduate School of Business Administration and earned her undergraduate degree at the New School for Social Research in New York. She is the author of *Toughing It Out at Harvard: The Making of a Woman MBA* (G.P. Putnams's Sons, 1983) and *Dangerous Journey, Safe Passage: The Sexual Abuse of Children and Its Remedy* (in press).

Ms. Henry founded and has served as president of STOP IT NOW! since 1992. The organization uses public health messages to prevent child sexual abuse by reaching abusers and those who know them through media and community action campaigns. STOP IT NOW! conducts public education and research and advocates for change in policies.

Ms. Henry serves on the board of directors of the Association for the Treatment of Sexual Abusers (ATSA). She co-chairs ATSA's Public Policy Committee and represents ATSA on the National Resource Group of the Center for Sex Offender Management. She also serves on the editorial board of *Crime Victims Report*.

Ms. Henry is a survivor of child sexual abuse.

Charles E. Hodges, Jr., M.S.W., M.Div.

Charles E. Hodges, Jr. holds a Master of Divinity and a master's degree in clinical social work. He is a licensed clinical social worker (Virginia), a certified sex offender treatment provider (Virginia), and a juvenile forensic evaluator (Virginia). He has many years experience as a treatment program administrator, sex offender clinician, staff trainer, and author. Work settings include both community and residential sexual offender treatment.

Brian J. Holmgren, J.D.

Brian J. Holmgren is currently an assistant district attorney general with the Davidson County District Attorney General's Office in Nashville, Tennessee, where he is assigned to the child abuse unit. Mr. Holmgren served for four years as a senior attorney with the American Prosecutors Research Institute's National Center for Prosecution of Child Abuse. Prior to that he was an assistant district attorney in Kenosha County, Wisconsin, for ten years, where he directed the sensitive crimes unit. He currently serves on the board of directors for the American Professional Society on the Abuse of Children and is a former board member of the Wisconsin chapter. Mr. Holmgren received his undergraduate degree from the University of Chicago in 1981 and his law degree from Vanderbilt University in 1985.

Robin C. Hubbell, M.S.W., L.I.C.S.W.

Robin Hubbell has been involved in the sexual offender field for fifteen years working with adolescents and adults, male and female: as a family therapist, individual therapist, group facilitator, assessor, and program director. She has worked in private practice, foster care, residential treatment, and school districts. She designed and implemented a program to train and supervise foster parents in the dynamics of sexual abuse/perpetration, which allows foster homes to specialize in the adolescent sex offender population within the foster care arena. Ms. Hubbell has written a curriculum to educate friends, families, and the community in understanding sexual offenders within the restorative justice concepts and a curriculum used to train court-approved supervisors to supervise the behaviors of sexual offenders within a community. In addition, Ms. Hubbell is an adjunct college professor.

Denise Hughes-Conlon, M.S., L.M.H.C.

Denise Hughes-Conlon is a licensed mental health counselor in the state of Florida, an associate trainer in neurolinguistic programming, and a licensed hypnotherapist. Ms. Hughes-Conlon works actively with the Pinellas County Domestic Violence Task Force and is a member of the Steering Committee. She is a Certified Batterers Intervention Provider/Assessor and is also approved by the state of Florida to train facilitators for the Batterer's Programs. Ms. Hughes-Conlon has been a CBIBF member for approximately five years. She is a member of the Association for the Treatment of Sexual Abusers and Secretary for FATSA, the ATSA Florida chapter. She and her partner of thirteen years, Don Sweeney, have a private practice working with domestic batterers and adult sex offenders in St. Petersburg, Florida., "A Better Solution." Currently they run nine batterer's groups and six sex offender groups in the Pinellas County area.

Alejandro Leguizamo, Ph.D.

Alejandro Leguizamo received his undergraduate degree in psychology from Boston University and his doctoral degree in clinical psychology from the University of Michigan. The focus of his dissertation was the study of factors associated with sexual aggression using a multivariate method based on an ecological model. He completed a postdoctoral fellow in forensic psychology at the University of Massachusetts Medical School. He is currently working at Bridgewater State Hospital and Bedford Policy Institute, both in Massachusetts.

Robert E. Longo, M.R.C., L.P.C.

Robert E. Longo is corporate director of special programming and clinical training for New Hope Treatment Centers in South Carolina. He also serves as a consultant, educator, trainer, and author dedicated to sexual abuse prevention and treatment. Mr. Longo's focus is on public policy, public relations, and sexual abuse prevention and treatment and he is an international consultant in the field of sexual abuser assessment, treatment and program development. He is co-founder and first president of the Association for the Treatment of Sexual Abusers. Mr. Longo was previously director of the Safer Society Foundation, Inc., and the Safer Society Press from 1993 through 1998. He is a member of the National Offense-Specific Residential Standards Task Force and an Advisory Board member of the National Adolescent Perpetrator Network. He has specialized in the sexual abuse field and has worked with victims and with juvenile and adult sex abusers in residential hospital, prison, and community-based settings since 1978.

Liam Marshall, B.A.(Hons.)

Liam is the lead therapist for the Millhaven Sexual Offenders' Preparatory Program. He is also a graduate student in psychology at Queen's University at Kingston, Canada. Liam has published and presented papers on a variety of sexual offender topics including attachment, excessive sexual desire disorder, mood, and the etiology of sexual offending.

W. L. Marshall

Bill Marshall is an Emeritus Professor of Psychology and Psychiatry at Queen's University in Canada and the director of Rockwood Psychological Services, which provides treatment for incarcerated sexual offenders. He has been treating and doing work with sexual offenders for thirty-three years and has more than 240 publications, including nine books. Bill was the 1999 recipient of the Santiago Grisolia Prize for his worldwide contributions to the reduction of violence, and in 2000 he was elected a Fellow of the Royal Society of Canada. Bill is currently president of the Association for the Treatment of Sexual Abusers.

Susan L. McElroy, M.D.

Susan L. McElroy received her M.D. from Cornell University Medical School. Following her residency in Internal Medicine at Columbia Presbyterian Hospital, New York, she completed a residency in Psychiatry at McLean Hospital in Belmont, Massachusetts, where she was a Clinical Fellow in Psychiatry at Harvard Medical School. Dr. McElroy served as director of the Psychopharmacologic Services, Adult Outpatient Clinic at McLean Hospital from 1988 to 1991 and was an assistant professor of psychiatry at Harvard Medical School.

In 1991, Dr. McElroy became associate professor of psychiatry at the University of Cincinnati College of Medicine, where she is director of the Biological Psychiatry Program. Dr. McElroy became a full professor of psychiatry in 1998.

Dr. McElroy has published more than 100 original articles, 1 book, 59 reviews and book chapters, 10 letters, and 80 original abstracts, most regarding the treatment of bipolar disorder. She lectures extensively on this subject both nationally and internationally.

Dr. McElroy's research interests include bipolar disorder, depression, paraphilia, obsessive-compulsive disorder, and the various impulse control disorders (e.g., compulsive shopping, binge eating disorder, kleptomania, and intermittent explosive disorder).

Alexis O. Miranda, Ph.D.

Alexis O. Miranda is a psychologist and an associate professor in the Department of Counselor Education at Florida Atlantic University. Among other areas, he studies the treatment of child and adolescent sexual offenders. His most recent publications include "Comparison of Sexual Abuse Perpetration Characteristics between Male Juvenile and Adult Sexual Offenders Against Minors," published in the *Sexual Abuse: A Journal of Research and Treatment*.

Erik B. Nelson, M.D.

Erik B. Nelson received his M.D. degree from the University of Cincinnati College of Medicine in 1992. He served as chief resident during his subspecialty training in psychiatry at the University of Cincinnati Hospital. After completing his psychiatry residency in 1996, he joined the faculty of the Department of Psychiatry at the University of Cincinnati, where he currently holds the title of assistant professor. He was the clinical director of the Biological Psychiatry Center, an outpatient psychopharmacology clinic, from 1996 to 2000. He has also served as assistant director of the Biological Psychiatry Research Program and has been actively involved in a number of research projects associated with this group. He has been involved in the medical treatment of sex offenders since 1996 and has authored or coauthored several papers and abstracts in this area. Dr. Nelson's other research interests include major depression, bipolar disorder and antidepressant-induced sexual dysfunction.

Terry Nicholaichuk, Ph.D.

Terry Nicholaichuk received his Ph.D. in psychology from the University of Saskatchewan in 1987. During his career, he has worked as a psychologist, director of a high-intensity sex offender program, and national administrator of sex offender programs for the Correctional Service of Canada (CSC). He has also been involved in the development of the National Sex Offender program for CSC. He was an adjunct professor at the University of Saskatchewan and carries an Order in Council appointment to the Saskatchewan Public Disclosure Committee. In addition to his private practice, Dr. Nicholaichuk is the regional administrator of psychologists and sex offender treatment programs for the CSC, Prairie Region. His publications and research interests are in the areas of sex offender assessment, sex offender treatment outcome, and dynamic predictors of sex offender risk.

Michael J. Nilan, Ph.D., L.M.F.T.

Michael Nilan has twenty years of experience conducting evaluations and assessments in settings to include crisis intervention, outpatient treatment, inpatient treatment, residential treatment, and private practice. His experience includes working with both adults and adolescent male and female sexual offenders. He has court testimony experience relative to these evaluations and assessments. Dr. Nilan cofacilitated and further developed the first outpatient services available for recalcitrant offenders in a group setting within the state of Minnesota. He has designed a curriculum specifically for the offender/abuser charged with sexual harassment and others demonstrating inappropriate sexual behaviors who do not require an intensive sex offender program. He is also an adjunct college professor.

William T. O'Donohue, Ph.D.

William T. O'Donohue is the Nicholas Cummings Professor of Organized Behavioral Healthcare Delivery at the University of Nevada, Reno. He has a doctoral in clinical psychology from the State University of New York at Stony Brook and a master's degree in philosophy from Indiana University. He is the editor of *Sexual Harassment: Theory and Treatment* (Allyn & Bacon, 1997).

Erin M. Oksol, M.A.

Erin M. Oksol is a graduate student in the clinical psychology program at the University of Reno, Nevada. She is the program coordinator and therapist for the Victims of Crime Treatment Center, a program which offers individual therapy to children who have been sexually abused and their nonoffending parents, as well as adult victims of sexual assault. Mrs. Oksol's research interests include mental health service delivery, human sexuality (sexual harassment, assessment and treatment of victims of sexual abuse, and pedophiles), forensic psychology, prevention, psychoeducational programs, management and administration, and behavior therapy.

Heather Cramer Reu, M.S.S.W., C.I.C.S.W.

Heather Cramer Reu is a psychotherapist in private practice in Madison, Wisconsin. She is a clinician, consultant and trainer specializing in working with adult and juvenile sex offenders and their families. She has presented in various locations throughout the United States on topics including nonoffending parents, family reunification and resolution following incest, sexualized children and youth who sexually offend, and community management of sex offenders.

Steven Sawyer, L.I.C.S.W., C.G.P.

Steven Sawyer received his M.S.S.W. from the University of Wisconsin-Madison. He is a clinical social worker and certified group psychotherapist. He has provided evaluation and treatment services to adult sex offenders since 1983. He is a founding board member and executive director of Project Pathfinder, Inc. in St. Paul, Minnesota. He is past president of the Minnesota chapter of the Association for the Treatment of Sexual Abusers (ATSA) and a clinical member of the American Group Psychotherapy Association (AGPA). He has presented locally, nationally, and internationally on the treatment of sex offenders, treatment outcome, and original research on men who use prostitutes.

Barbara K. Schwartz, Ph.D.

Barbara K. Schwartz received her degrees from the University of New Mexico and the New School for Social Research in New York City. She has been treating sex offenders since 1971 and has directed statewide sex offender treatment programs for Departments of Correction in New Mexico, Washington State, and Massachusetts. She is currently the clinical director of justice programs for Justice Resource Institute of Boston; in that capacity she directs programs for involuntarily committed sexually dangerous persons as well as incarcerated offenders throughout Massachusetts. Dr. Schwartz is the clinical consultant to Cliff House School, a residential program for adolescent sex offenders. She has consulted throughout the country for the National Institute of Corrections and the Center for Sex Offender Management as well as in Canada and Israel. She has authored, edited, and co-edited five major books in the field of sex offender treatment, as well as numerous articles and conference presentations.

Carl Schwartz, Ph.D., J.D., M.C.

Carl Schwartz has worked with juvenile sex offenders and conduct-disordered youth for twenty-two years. He specializes in merging behavioral and transpersonal models for change. His work emphasizes "discovery as process," "personality as defense," and success as "navigating challenge." Dr. Schwartz works for Prehab of Arizona.

Geris Serran, B.A.

Geris Serran was born in Kincardine, Canada. She graduated with a B.A. (Hons.) Psychology in 1998 from Queen's University in Kingston, Ontario and is currently completing a Ph.D. in clinical psychology at the University of Ottawa in Ottawa, Ontario. She has been working with Dr. W .L. Marshall at Rockwood Psychological Services as a therapist in the Sexual Offenders Treatment Program at Bath Institution (a medium-security fFederal Institution). In addition, Ms. Serran is an active researcher who has a number of publications. Her research interests include therapeutic process in sexual offender treatment, coping and sexual offending, and mood state and sexual offending.

Cesar A. Soutullo, M.D.

Cesar A. Soutullo graduated from the Complutense University of Madrid, Spain. After two years of general training (internal medicine, surgery, and emergency medicine) in Great Britain, he completed his residency in psychiatry and fellowships in biological psychiatry and child and adolescent psychiatry at the University of Cincinnati, Ohio. During his residency training, Dr. Soutello worked with Drs. Susan McElroy and Erik Nelson at the Volunteers of America New Life Program for Sex Offenders. He continued working at the University of Cincinnati as assistant professor in clinical psychiatry, and then moved to his current position as assistant professor of psychiatry at the University of Navarra, in Pamplona, Spain. He is now director of the Child and Adolescent

Psychiatry Program in the university clinic at this prestigious Spanish university. His main interests are bipolar and psychotic disorders in children and adolescents, impulse control disorders, and pediatric psychopharmacology.

Charlene Steen, Ph.D., J.D.

Charlene Steenis a licensed psychologist and retired attorney, who provides assessments and expert testimony for the courts, evaluates sexually violent predators for the state of California, provides outpatient treatment for sex offenders, has directed a family sexual abuse treatment program, and presents workshops throughout the United States, Canada, and Europe. She has written *The Adult Relapse Prevention Workbook* (Safer Society Press, 2000), *The Relapse Prevention Workbook for Youth in Treatment* (Safer Society Press, 1993), *Treating Adolescent Sex Offenders in the Community* (Charles C. Thomas, 1989), "Case Management of Sexual Abuse Victims" in *The Handbook of Forensic Sexology* (Plenum Press, 1994), and a number of articles, including "Treating Denying Offenders" in the *California Coalition on Sex Offending Newsletter*.

Joan Tabachnik, M.B.A.

Joan Tabachnick received an M.B.A. from the Yale School of Management. Currently she is the director of public education for STOP IT NOW! As director, she designs the organization's public education programs and authors the publications associated with this project. These publications includes the well-received guidebook titled *Because There Is a Way to Prevent Child Sexual Abuse: Facts About Abuse and Those Who Commit It*.

Ms. Tabcchnik has worked in nonprofit and social change organizations for twenty years.

Pamela M. Yates, Ph.D., R. Psych.

Pamela Yates is the national manager of sex offender programs for the Correctional Service of Canada. She was formerly a psychologist and clinical director of a high-risk sexual offender treatment unit and senior researcher for the Assessment and Treatment of Sex Offenders Research Team at the Muriel McQueen Fergusson Centre for Family Violence Research at the University of New Brunswick. Dr. Yates received her B.A. degree from St. Mary's University in Halifax, Canada, and her master's and doctoral degrees from Carleton University in Ottawa, Canada. She has researched sex offender risk, recidivism, and treatment and has collaborated on and coauthored reports in the areas of sexual abuse, sex offender assessment, treatment of sex offenders, phallometric assessment, and criminal harassment. She has worked within the Canadian federal and provincial correctional systems and in the community with victims of familial and sexual violence. She has been involved in the development of sex offender treatment and violence prevention programs for the Correctional Service of Canada.

James M. Yokley, Ph.D.

James Yokley is a clinical psychologist on the medical staff in the Department of Psychiatry at MetroHealth Medical Center in Cleveland, Ohio and an assistant professor at Case Western Reserve University School of Medicine. Dr. Yokley is also the consulting psychologist at Quest Recovery Services drug and alcohol treatment center and the supervising psychologist at The Twelve Inc., TASC program. He has behavior therapy expertise in the use of cognitive-behavioral learning experiences with abusive, addictive (self-reinforcing) behavioral problems that are dangerous to self or others and has authored over fifty professional research publications, book chapters, and presentations in his areas of expertise. Dr. Yokley designed the TASC Forensic Foster Care program which employs social responsibility therapy to develop appropriate social behavior control and social-emotional maturity in multiple abusers (i.e., offenders referred for sexual abuse along with other types of abuse requiring treatment). He has a broad base of experience in training, teaching, and supervising mental health professionals. This experience has included psychiatry residents, medical students, psychology, counseling, and social work staff as well as graduate students along with drug and alcohol treatment providers and forensic foster parents.

Introduction

A recent survey of incarcerated sex offenders reveals that there are 154,518 sex offenders in the forty-three states that responded to the survey, ranging from 161 in North Dakota to 25,398 in Texas (West, Hromas, & Wenger, 2000). This represents an average increase of 26% from 1994 to 1999 (West et al., 2000) and between 33% and 77% of the prison population.

In 1996, Massachusetts spent $1.2 billion to support its criminal justice system, with a disproportionate amount going to dealing with 26% who are sex offenders (Criminal Justice Policy Coalition, 2000). This amount is up from $700 million in 1988 and is almost twice as much money as was spent on higher education in 1996. That same year, the Commonwealth authorized 3,000 more prison beds at a cost of $60,000 plus finance charges and interest per bed as well as $30,000 per year to maintain each inmate (Criminal Justice Policy Coalition, 2000).

With this phenomenal amount of money which is replicated in every state, it is imperative that creative solutions be devised to reduce this expenditure. Over the past decade, two different paths have emerged in dealing with sex offenders.

One track is associated with an initiative by the National Academy of Corrections that more than fifteen years ago planted the seeds of a systems approach to the problem of sexual assault by training teams from over thirty states in a method that emphasized a team approach to sex offender treatment. States were taught how to encourage cooperation between supervision and treatment. Some areas, particularly the Pacific Northwest, incorporate polygraphy into this cooperative unit.

In the mid-1990s, English, Pullen, and Jones (1996) studied approaches of the Colorado Department to handling this population in the community throughout the country and determined that the most effective method emphasized the cooperation of the treatment provider, the parole or probation officer, and the polygrapher. This model was dubbed "the Containment Approach."

At the same time, the number of prison-based treatment programs has been growing. Currently thirty-seven states have formal sex offender programs, with nineteen having therapeutic communities (West et al., 2000). An additional four states are attempting to implement programs.

In 1998, the Justice Department funded the Center for Sex offender Management, which has worked with leading experts throughout the country to fund the establishment of mentor sites, technical assistance, and research grants to improve the management of this population.

Groups such as Stop It Now! and the Association for the Treatment of Sexual Abusers have advocated for defining sexual abuse as a public health issue. This paradigm would focus on creating an informed society that proactively works to prevent sexual abuse, to allow individuals who are disturbed by their deviant urges to get help and to support victims.

Effective programs that stress competent treatment coupled with effective supervision can dramatically reduce recidivism (West et al., 2000, included recidivism rates for several programs). In Massachusetts, among treated sex offenders paroled to the intensive Sex Offenders Parole Unit, none have reoffended. Colorado also reported zero recidivism among paroled treated sex offenders. In Kentucky, the recidivism rate is three times higher for untreated offenders. In New Hampshire, treated sex offenders serving shorter sentences reoffend at half the rate of new sex offenders and a quarter of the rate of other crimes than does the nontreated group. Vermont's program showed a 3.8% reoffense rate for treatment completers versus 27% for those not treated (West et al., 2000). Preventing a sex offender from reoffending and being sentenced to a minimum of ten years would save tax payers at least $300,000, to say nothing of the pain and suffering that are avoided.

However, another path has stressed a much more controversial approach featuring public notification of the whereabouts of sex offenders and involuntary civil commitment. In 1994, Congress passed the Jacob Wetterling Crimes Against Children and Sexually Violent Offender Registration Act (42 U.S.C. § 14071), named after an 11-year-old boy who was abducted and has never been found. This law provided for the registration of sex offenders in a community with the police.

However, in 1996, in response to the sexual assault and murder of a young New Jersey girl, the aforementioned law was amended, resulting in "Megan's Law." All states were mandated to release relevant information on registered sex offenders. Failure to adhere to the requirements of this law were subject to a 10% reduction in federal block grant funds for criminal justice purposes under the Byrne Memorial State and Local Law Enforcement Assistance Funding Program.

Because this legislation was passed without any committee hearings, there was no evidence whatsoever presented as to the efficacy of such a program. In the ensuing years, worries about vigilantism have come true. In Great Britain, where there are similar laws, a "pediatrician" was attacked by a person who confused this term with "pedophilia." Addresses have been confused, and innocent persons have been attacked and/or had their homes burned to the ground. To date there is no evidence that sexual assaults have declined or that the public feels safer due to this legislation.

However, some jurisdictions have handled public notification much better than others. Washington State, particularly the Seattle area, has decided to use the introduction of a sex offender into a neighborhood as an opportunity to educate the public, and to perhaps build a support network for the offender. This method appears to resemble a restorative justice approach and could well be emulated by other areas that wish to seriously decrease the risk that the sex offender presents.

This law is expensive to administrate. Most states have had to establish a new agency with lawyers and a professional board to rule on levels of notification. Many states provide for legal appeals, which requires lawyers' fees and court costs as well as using the time of overcrowded courts. In addition, victims may be reluctant to report crimes such as incest for fear that their identities will be revealed through the public notification process. Defense attorneys are refusing to plea bargain or are negotiating pleas for nonsexual offenses for their clients. This makes it difficult to get these individuals into sex offender–specific treatment as both procedures reinforce denial. Therefore, rather than a system that encourages offenders to take responsibility for their actions, seek treatment, receive appropriate supervision, and eventually reconcile with their community and perhaps even their family and victim, a system now exists that encourages deception; victimizes the victims; and precludes treatment, supervision, and reconciliation.

The second prong, which represents a more punitive approach, is the return to the enactment of sexual psychopath/sexually dangerous person/mentally disordered sex offender, now inflammatorily referred to as sexually violent predator laws. These laws follow a tradition that harkens back to defective delinquent legislation, popular at the turn of the century. Those laws were based on the assumption that somewhere between people who are mentally ill and those who are criminals lies a category of individuals who are not suffering from a recognized mental illness but whose antisocial behavior is the by-product of a mental disorder. This belief could have spawned an enlightened approach to understanding many deviant behaviors and treating them in a humane manner respecting the patient's civil rights.

However, what these laws allowed was institutionalization of a variety of social misfits who needed only to be identified by a physician. When the system started to be used to incapacite political dissidents, it was dismantled. However, its ghost lived in on the sexual psychopath laws.

In 1937, Michigan was the first state to pass a law that attempted to identify and confine in a mental hospital, individuals whose sexual acting out was seen as the by-product of a mental aberration rather than an act committed by a criminal. However, their law was judged unconstitutional. In 1938, Illinois passed the first law to meet constitutional muster, and Minnesota passed the legislation that was to become the national model. Eventually thirty states had sexual psychopath programs.

These laws had three basic components that marked them as different from current legislation. The process of identifying, committing, and treating these individuals was invoked at the beginning or in lieu of an individual's criminal sentence. In most states these individuals went to a treatment center rather than a hospital. Finally the condition that set them apart from other sex offenders was clearly identified: They utterly lacked the ability to control their sexual urges.

Certainly there are individuals who meet this last criteria. These are individuals who may be floridly mentally ill, neurologically impaired, or suffering from dementia. Usually they are housed in mental hospitals, facilities for the developmentally disabled, or nursing homes. Rarely but occasionally they will be found in prisons. Multiple offenses are not evidence of an utter lack of control. Moreover, to be unable to control one's impulses is very different from not wishing to control one's impulses. Minimally, the former condition implies that the behavior is ego dystonic. This would dramatically differentiate these two groups and it is a basic tenet of our criminal justice system that individuals whose behavior is the product of a mental illness should not be held criminally responsible for their behavior.

These early laws and related programs operated between the late 1930s until 1975 when half the statutes were repealed (Prentky, 2000). By 1985, only six state programs were in operation. In retrospect the demise of these programs was related to four factors (Prentky, 2000). First, the feminist movement strongly objected to sex offenders, particularly rapists, being defined as mentally ill and placed in treatment rather than incarcerated in prisons. Furthermore, authors such as Susan Brownmiller (1975) argued that sexually aggressive behavior was not deviant for males—it was the norm.

The second factor was dissatisfaction among professionals. These programs had been established before there was any research regarding what types of treatments might be effective. Professionals in these programs were forced to work in isolation without the professional organizations, conferences, or specialized journals that exist today. In 1977, the Second Group for Advancement of Psychiatry recommended abolishing the sexual psychopath laws and programs.

Third, increasing numbers of mental health and legal professionals became concerned about due process issues. They pointed out that these involuntary commitment statutes represented punishment disguised as treatment.

Fourth, the public became disenchanted. Funds for the operation of these programs came out of the budgets of departments of mental health. Advocates for the mentally ill viewed this as criminals depriving legitimate mental patients of resources. In addition, some communities such as Lakeview, Washington became alarmed when sex offenders in community access programs ventured into affluent neighborhoods and sexually assaulted residents.

During 1989, there was a unified opinion that sexual psychopath laws had been a failed experiment. However, in 1990 a released sex offender brutally assaulted a young boy. In the wake of this crime, the second generation of involuntary commitment laws was born. Between 1990 and 1999, nineteen states had passed sexual predator laws, although Texas mandates these individuals to participate in outpatient programs rather than be in institutions. All but Massachusetts house these individuals in facilities operated by the state departments of mental health, although some facilities are located within prisons.

This is meant to ensure that "treatment" rather than "punishment" is the ruling paradigm. In Massachusetts, the Department of Corrections is in charge of the treatment program. Massachusetts was also the last jurisdiction to pass a sexual predator Act.

The major reason for current disenchantment appears to be financial. Civil commitment is tremendously expensive. The state must not only foot the bill for caring for these men (at least $35,000 per year) but must provide them with treatment as well. Washington estimates that cost to be at least $112,000 per year per resident ("Cost of involuntary commitment," 2000). Even with this level of expenditure, Washington is under a consent decree for inadequacy of treatment and has been forced to compensate those civilly committed to the tune of $10,000 apiece.

This is not a revolving population. State prisons may be able to maintain a stable head count, provided there is no major change in legislation. However, experience has shown that civil populations increase. Minnesota has estimated that by 2010, one-fourth of all confined sex offenders will be civilly committed, and by then it will cost $76.9 million. Illinois has estimated that in ten years, there will be 7,650 civil commitments costing roughly $91,000 per year for a total of $703,073,300. Furthermore the state will need to build three new facilities costing $304,646,000 annually just to house and treat this population (Janus, 2000). Add to this cost of confinement the fact that these men are older than the average prisoner and will be confined for a much longer period and estimated medical costs become staggering.

These costs do not reflect legal expenses. There are lawyers and witnesses for both sides which must be paid at the probable cause hearing, the trial, and in some jurisdictions at yearly hearings. Washington has estimated that the cost of initial confinement is $127,750. Furthermore, this is a highly litigious population. As Washington can attest, consent decrees are quite expensive. Courts may also order these men to be placed on less restrictive programs. In Washington, one sex offender ordered by the court to be housed and supervised in the community costs that state $10,000 a month to maintain ("Cost of involuntary commitment," 2000).

So far there is no documented evidence that public policies such as involuntary commitment or public notification decrease the rate of sexual offending. However, there is evidence that innovative approaches do work.

The Center of Sex Offender Management has been working with jurisdictions around the country to set up mentor sites. Model projects range from the Commonwealth of Massachusetts, which has established a collaborative network of services, and the state of Vermont, which has incorporated principles of restorative justice in managing sex offenders in counties such as Jackson County, Oregon; Maricopa County, Arizona; and Westchester County, New York. Several Native American tribes have established model programs. The approaches incorporate a number of state-of-the-art techniques including psychopharmacology, polygraphy, electronic monitoring, intensive community supervision, input from victims and their advocates, plus a range of treatment options. The containment approach previously mentioned has been used in many of these juridictions; is in full operation in Massachusetts, Oregon, Washington, and Colorado; and has significantly reduced recidivism

It is indeed tragic when an effective approach to a major social problem is identified but policymakers choose to ignore it and instead focus on unproven, phenomenally expensive knee-jerk responses. It will be interesting in the future to contrast a state such as Texas, which has chosen to invest resources in prison-based treatment combined with community-based treatment on release for high-risk offenders, with California, which has no prison-based treatment and an ever-growing and highly expensive involuntary commitment process.

This volume, as its predecessor, attempts to present the latest developments in the sex offender management arena. It focuses on emerging theories and techniques for children, adolescents, and adults with sexually inappropriate behavior as well as management approaches and legal issues. It is hoped that the information in this volume will be used to enhance efforts to maintain public safety and return offenders to being fully functioning citizens.

References

Brownmiller, S. (1975). *Against our will: Men, women and rape.* New York: Simon & Schuster.

Cost of involuntary commitment. (2000). *Whitestone Foundation Newsletter*, pp. 2, 3, 6.

Criminal Justice Policy Coalition. (2000). *Education and incarceration.* Boston: Author.

English, K., Pullen, S., & Jones, L. (1996). *Managing adult sex offenders: A containment approach.* Colorado Division of Criminal Justice & American Probation and Parole Association.

Janus, E. (2000). An empirical study of Minnesota's sex offender commitment program. *Sex Offender Law Review, 1*(4), 49–50.

Prentky, R. A. (2000, November 1). *Involuntary commitment.* Paper presented at the international conference of the Association for the Treatment of Sexual Abusers, San Diego.

West, M., Hromas, S., & Wender, P. (2000). *State sex offender treatment programs.* Denver, CO: Department of Corrections.

Table of Contents

PART 1: THEORETICAL ISSUES

Chapter 1: The JRI Model for Treating Varied Populations With Inappropriate Sexual Behvior

Chapter 2: A Holistic/Integrated Approach to Treating Sexual Offenders

Chapter 5: Locus of Control, Coping, and Sexual Offenders

PART 2: SYSTEMS ISSUES

Chapter 6: The Use of Actuarial Risk Assessment

Chapter 7: Treatment Efficacy—Outcomes of the Clearwater Sex Offender Program

Chapter 10: Community-Based Treatment Using the Therapist/Agent Model

PART 3: LEGAL ISSUES

Chapter 11: A Comparative Analysis of State Statutes Providing for the Involuntary Commitment of Sexually Violent Predators

Chapter 12: The Expert Witness in the Sex Offender Case—
A Practical Guide

PART 4: ADULT TREATMENT ISSUES

Chapter 13: The Psychopharmacological Treatment of Sex Offenders

Chapter 14: Group Therapy With Adult Sex Offenders

Chapter 15: Addressing the Victim/Perpetrator Dialectic—Treatment for the Effects of Sexual Victimization on Sex Offenders

Chapter 16: Using Domestice Violence Approaches for Sex Offender Treatment

PART 5: ADOLESCENT SEX OFFENDERS

Chapter 17: Family Therapy in Sibling-on-Sibling Sexual Abuse

Chapter 18: Sexually Abusive Children—Etiological and Treatment Considerations

Chapter 19: Creating Empathic Responses With Adolescent Sex Offenders

Chapter 20: A Model for Therapists to Assess Readiness for and Provide Reunification Treatment to Juvenile Sex Offenders and Their Victims—The S.A.F.E.R. Model

Chapter 21: The Treatment of Multiple Abuser Youth in Forensic Foster Care—A Social Responsibility Therapy Program Description

Chapter 22: Standards of Care for Youth in Sex Offense-Specific Residential Programs

Chapter 23: Creating a Positive Milieu in Residential Treatment for Adolescent Sexual Abusers

Chapter 24: Demonstrating Social Responsibility Through Emotional Restitution—Victim Responsibility Training

PART 6: EMERGING POPULATIONS

Chapter 25: Assessment and Treatment of the Nonoffending Parent for the Benefit of the Victim—A Dynamic Continuum of Reaction and Response

Chapter 26: Forensic Assessment of Internet Child Pornography Offenders

Part 1

Theoretical Issues

There has been a serious disconnection in the sex offender treatment field. In the "hard sciences," theory precedes application—except in the case of purely accidental discoveries. Without a basic understanding of the laws of physics, there would be no mechanical engineering. Without an understanding of chemistry, new drugs could not be formulated. In medicine there should be an understanding of the mechanism of a disease in order for a treatment to work reliably. The process of diabetes is basically understood. Therefore, a sound treatment addressing itself to that process has been devised. However, although a number of cancer treatments have been developed, barring accidental discoveries, conquest of this disease awaits an understanding of its causes and mechanisms.

In the mental health field there is a greater split between theory and practice. The treatment of autism has not depended on whether one believes that the parents were emotionally cold or whether one believes that it is a neurological problem. However, even after the efficacy of the phenothiazenes was clearly demonstrated, professionals were still debating about whether schizophrenia is caused by a chemical imbalance or parents who sent double messages.

There are a number of theories about causes of sexual deviancies. These theories range from physiological to ethnobiological to sociological to addiction. However, rarely have treatment approaches sprung forth from these theories. Physiological and behavioral treatments do derive from theoretical foundations. But cognitive-behavioral treatment does not have its roots in a comprehensive theory of the development of sexual aggression. Why do sex offenders have cognitive distortions anyway?

A number of prominent researchers in the sex offender treatment field have, over the past decade, become interested in the role of attachment theory in the development of sexual deviance. Clearly sexual abuse is a profound violation of an interpersonal relation. To understand how one can so rupture the human connection, it makes sense to explore how the abuser's attachment to others developed or failed to do so. Early treatment specialists including Groth, Cohen, Seghorn, and Prendergast, working with this population, and by and large having a psychodynamic orientation, focused almost exclusively on exploring the sex offender's family dynamics. Although they may not have identified the patterns they discovered as "attachment disorder," they certainly discovered abuse associated with it.

There are multiple theories about why certain individuals behave in a sexually deviant manner. Sociologists point to the "subculture of violence" or cultural norms for socializing males. Psychologists view the problem from their professional orientation, behaviorists focus on reinforcement schedules, cognitive-behaviorists analyze thinking errors, and ego analysts concentrate on object relations. Psychiatrists specialize in psychopharmacological responses.

Sexual assault is a phenomenon with multiple causations. Each discipline brings insights to bear in understanding the dynamics. In the following chapters the authors have chosen to write from their perspectives of a model that analyzes the etiology of sexually inappropriate behaviors according to addictions, attachment, cognitive, developmental, family systems, intrapsychic, learning, and physiological theories. Treatment focuses on unifying mind, body, spiritual, and emotional needs, specifically harnessing needs for generosity, belonging, mastery, and independence to redirect dysfunctional behavior.

The authors in this section have investigated basic theory as to the development of aberrant sexual behavior and in some cases have drawn conclusions about the type of treatment that would be most helpful.

Barbara K. Schwartz advocates for the use of holistic methods that draw from a variety of approaches. Dr. Schwartz's integrative model (see *The Sex Offender*, Vol. I, for a full description) has been adopted for the treatment of adults and individuals with a variety of psychiatric, cognitive, and characterological disabilities. Chapter 1 discusses a system for identifying treatment needs for both individuals and program populations. It then graphs a way of deciding when and how to apply sex offender approaches to these specialized populations.

Robert E. Longo also advocates for a holistic method. In Chapter 2, he hypothesizes that the etiology for sexually deviant behavior is explained by a combination of addiction, attachment, cognitive-behavioral, developmental, family systems, intrapsychic, learning, and physiological theories. He has developed a treatment approach that uses the basic needs for generosity, belonging, mastery, and independence.

Liam E. Marshall and W. L. Marshall discuss attachment theory and its relations. In Chapter 3, they present a dimensional model which describes types of attachment and their relationship to differing forms of sexually inappropriate behavior, specifically a variety of types of "grooming."

Alejandro Leguizamo presents an object relations approach to understanding juvenile sexual offending (Chapter 4). He discusses how the effects of early trauma mold one's world view and may result in the internalization of the abusive interaction. This author explores family characteristics and their relation to types of abusive behavior as well as clinical applications to the treatment of sex offenders.

Franca Cortoni, Dana Anderson, and David Bright, in Chapter 5, discuss possible bases of interpersonal conflicts and their relationship to locus of control. Individuals who have little faith in their ability to control their behaviors will have a difficult time making meaningful decisions. It would be extremely difficult to initiate a relapse prevention plan. This chapter focuses on developing strategies that enhance self-efficacy, thus encouraging an internal locus of control.

Chapter 1

The JRI Model for Treating Varied Populations With Inappropriate Sexual Behavior

by Barbara K. Schwartz, Ph.D.

Overview

Sex offender treatment was developed primarily for adults who do not suffer major cognitive and/or emotional problems and then for adolescents who likewise are not experiencing significant mental illness or developmental disabilities. Therapists and program administrators have traditionally been skeptical that such treatment would work with relatively intact individuals and have been reluctant to develop programs to treat the sexually deviant behavior in clients with severe comorbid conditions. However, program staff have become increasingly aware that when individuals present with inappropriate behavior, eventually that behavior, unless addressed, will prevent the person from being safely released to the community. Consequently, sex offender treatment must be adapted to respond to subpopulations. Justice Resource Institute, which operates a variety of programs for multiply challenged children and adults, has developed a way to treat sexually inappropriate behavior using a uniform but adaptable approach.

Introduction

Justice Resource Institute (JRI), a nonprofit organization based in Boston, Massachusetts, has as its mission the provision of services to the most difficult populations, those individuals whom other agencies avoid as "just too challenging."

In this spirit, JRI has provided services to sex offenders since the 1980s. JRI was among the first agencies in the country to recognize the need for specialized services for adolescent sex offenders. Then, in 1992, JRI was asked to take over the provision of treatment and rehabilitation at the deeply troubled Massachusetts Treatment Center for Sexually Dangerous Persons. Today that program is the cornerstone of an array of services and has been selected as one of two statewide systems designated mentor sites by the Center for Sex Offender Management. A hallmark of all JRI programs, be they services for AIDS mothers, developmentally disabled children, homeless youths or sex offenders, is that the programs strive to provide innovative, individualized services. To this end JRI has developed an array of specialized programs for individuals with sexually inappropriate behavior (ISIBs). This term is being used because many of these individuals have not been adjudicated in connection with their sexual misconduct and therefore are not "sex offenders" in the legal sense of the term. These programs build from a basic cognitive-behavioral model, adding specialized treatment techniques as the population diverges from the norm.

The Multidimensional Approach

Range of Deviance. Individuals who engage in inappropriate sexual behavior come in a wide variety of types. They represent both sexes, all ages, every level of intelligence, every type of mental abnormality as well as a lack thereof, and a tremendous variety of deviancies. Indeed, it is their wide heterogeneity among other characteristics that makes them such a challenging and, yes, interesting population to treat. Some of the most relevant dimensions include the following:

- Age:
  - — Sexually reactive children;
  - — Adolescent sex offenders; and
  - — Adult sex offenders.
- Gender:
  - — Male sex offenders; and
  - — Female sex offenders.
- Range of deviance:
  - — Violence;
  - — Deviant arousal; and
  - — Selection of victim.
- Functional impairments:
  - — Developmental disabilities;
  - — Major mental illness;
  - — Personality disorders;
  - — Behavioral impairments; and
  - — Psychopathy.

JRI currently runs separate programs for the following:

- Incarcerated male sex offenders;
- Incarcerated female sex offenders;
- Civilly committed male sex offenders;
- Developmentally disabled adult male sex offenders living in the community;
- Developmentally disabled, mentally ill adolescent male and female sex offenders in residential settings;
- Mentally ill adolescent male and female sex offenders in residential settings;
- Mentally ill adult male and female sex offenders and nonadjudicated individuals in hospital setting; and
- Adolescent male sex offenders in residential settings.

A basic two-dimensional model has been developed which in turn is applied with some differences to males and females as well as to adults and adolescents (see Figure 1.1).

The two basic dimensions are Range of Deviance and Functional Impairment. Looking at the exact center of the model, one would find a population of ISIBs who do not suffer from any kind of mental illness or cognitive impairment. They do not have prior criminal records and may have lived entirely law-abiding lives. They are not violent and show little or no deviant arousal. They are, in fact, the individuals for whom a high proportion of community-based sex offender treatment programs are designed.

These individuals can be treated in outpatient therapy and need only the basics of sex offender treatment. However, although many ISIBs meet that profile, many do not. For example, a significant proportion of ISIBs are violent, ranging from individuals who verbally threaten violence to those who use instrumental violence to force a victim to comply. Still other sex offenders gratuitously attack their victims—hitting, kicking, strangling, and beating their victims out of anger and/or frustration. Finally, sadists torture and humiliate their victims as a way of achieving sexual gratification.

At the other end of this continuum is the offender who is not violent but sees himself involved in a "relationship" with his victim. These are often the members of organized groups of pedophiles who maintain that their behavior positively benefits the children who are being molesting. This is, of course, couched in the language of a "love affair." They are highly manipulative and need not resort to violence or coercion as they are often able to identify victims who are starved for attention and then use their considerable powers of persuasion as well as material bribery to lure children into their sphere of influence.

Thus the upper range of this dimension ranges from sadism to gratuitous violence to instrumental violence to threats of violence, differentiating between attacks on strangers versus attacks on acquaintances. At the center are individuals who may be involved in opportunistic assaults, which involve neither violence nor active efforts to acquire victims based on deviant sexual attraction. These crimes might involve some types of date rape situations and some interfamilial situations. Progressing along the continuum past the center, one encounters a group of offenders who use coercion or manipulation to obtain victims to gratify deviant arousal

Deviant arousal is found on both ends of the vertical continuum (Table 1.1). The sadist derives his or her sexual gratification from the humiliation, degradation, pain, and suffering of his or her victims. The confirmed pedophile is exclusively aroused by children. As previously discussed, there are also adults who sexually abuse other adults while harboring the delusion that they are somehow benefiting these individuals. Although their deviant arousal may not be measurable on the plethysmograph, their sexual gratification comes from the exploitive nature of their relationships, is compulsive in nature, and is often accompanied by elaborate fantasies and ritualized behavior.

On the lower end of the continuum is the "politically justified" pedophile. As previously mentioned,, such individuals may belong to one of the formal pedophile organizations or may be professionals who have found a way to manipulate their adult victims into compliance by convincing both the victims and themselves that their behavior is in the victim's best interest based on some abstract concept (e.g., "Nude therapy frees up my inhibited clients." "I have found a way to express God's true love to certain members of my congregation." "Children should feel free to express their sexuality.").

Typically one finds rapists on the upper end of the continuum and pedophiles on the lower end of the horizontal axis (see Figure 1.1). However, this is not always true;

Table 1.1
Range of Deviance

Score	Upper Axis	Lower Axis
70–61	Use of intimidation or subtle intimidation of violence	Use of power differential
60–51	Threats of violence aqainst acquaintances	Bribes, manipulation
50–41	Threats of violence against strangers	Mild deviant arousal without violence
40–31	Use of weapons	Moderate deviant arousal without violence
30–21	Instrumental violence	High deviant arousal without violence
20–11	Gratuitous violence	Exclusive deviant arousal without violence, but with repeated pattern
10–1	Sadistic violence	Politically justified

deviant arousal is high at both ends of the continuum but violence decreases as one moves down the axis. Sadistic murderers can certainly attack children. There might be highly deviantly aroused sex offenders who target adults but do not use violence if they are able to trick their victims through the use of positions of power and influence. These individuals would have to be in a relationship with an adult that is comparable in terms of inherent power to that of an adult-child relationship. For example, comparable to the North American Man-Boy Love Association (NAMBLA) member might be the exhibitionist who exposes himself in the guise of being a therapist who conducts nude encounter sessions while having convinced himself that he is doing this in the best interest of his patients

Functional Impairment. ISIBs can range from a severely mental ill, possibly psychotic, developmentally disabled individual to an individual with no significant cognitive or affective disabilities to a person diagnosed as a full-blown psychopath. In analyzing the continuum the first dynamic one encounters involves personal responsibility for one's behavior. The severely mentally ill, developmentally disabled individual is neither legally nor therapeutically responsible for his or her pathology. Certainly the goal of treatment is to develop responsible behavior. However, this is in contrast to treatment for sociopaths or psychopaths, who are assumed for the sake of this model to have no congenital or physiologically based limitation to their control over their behavior but have great difficulty accepting that responsibility (although at some time in the future an underlying neurology or biochemical basis for their behav-

Figure 1.1
JRI Model of Sexual Deviance (Male)

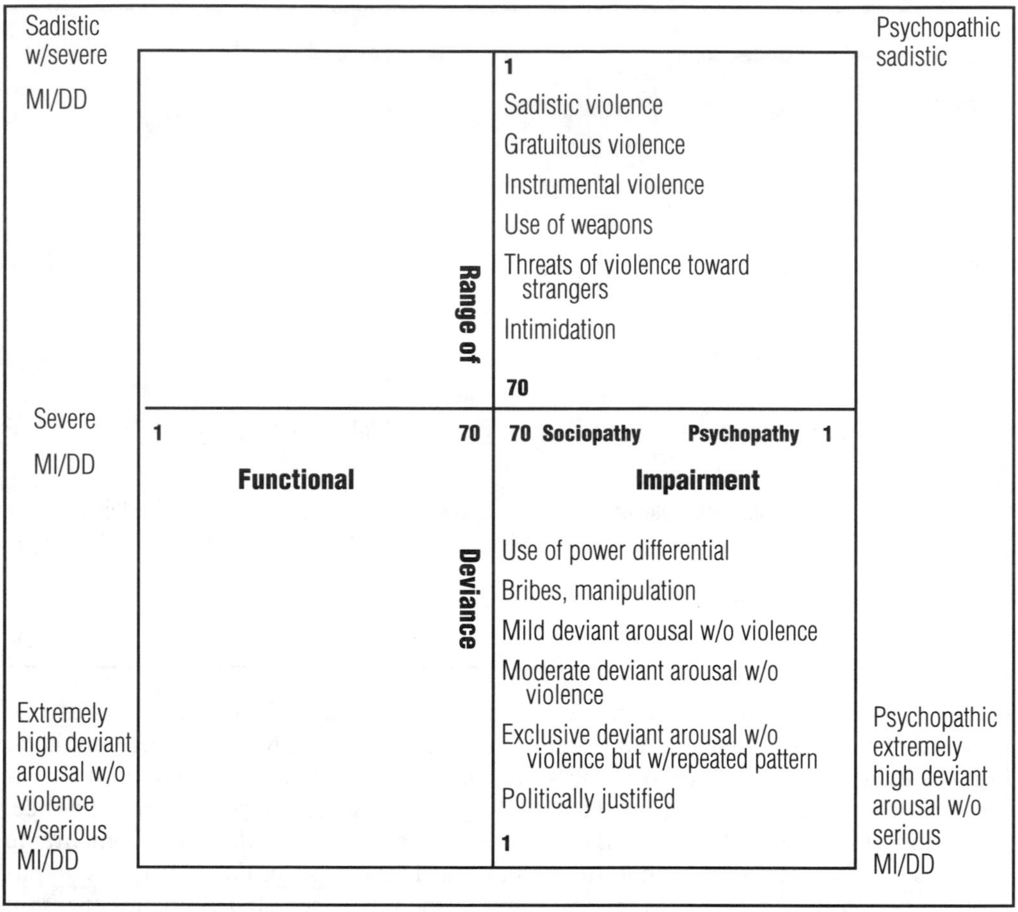

Sadistic w/severe MI/DD			Psychopathic sadistic
		1 Sadistic violence Gratuitous violence Instrumental violence Use of weapons Threats of violence toward strangers Intimidation **70**	
Severe MI/DD	**1** **Functional** **70**	**70 Sociopathy Psychopathy 1** **Impairment** Use of power differential Bribes, manipulation Mild deviant arousal w/o violence Moderate deviant arousal w/o violence Exclusive deviant arousal w/o violence but w/repeated pattern Politically justified **1**	
Extremely high deviant arousal w/o violence w/serious MI/DD			Psychopathic extremely high deviant arousal w/o serious MI/DD

(Range of / Deviance labels on vertical axes)

ior may be identified). In the meanwhile, for the sake of this model, the first group are defined as "not responsible" and the second group as "irresponsible."

At the left side of the horizontal axis is the severely disabled individual whose behavior is largely dictated by organic deficits beyond his or her control but who may be able to learn to cope with his or her problems through a combination of drugs, behavioral interventions, and a structured environment (see Figure 1.1). Other groups are arranged as follows:

- The individual whose behavior is moderately to mildly impaired by psychiatric or cognitive limitations

- The individual who does not suffer from these limitations

- The individual whose behavior may be attributed to a disregard of society's mandates and expectations which is often rooted in sociological factors or having been raised in a criminally oriented family. This individual would be classified as a "sociopath" (Lykkin, 1995).

- The individual whose disregard for others and for society appears to be rooted in a character disorder and who meets the criteria of "psychopath" (Lykkin, 1995).

Therapeutically, these individuals have widely differing treatment needs.

Psychiatrically or cognitively impaired individuals may require a highly individualized treatment program for the following reasons:

1. Much of their treatment may be psychopharmacological and will need to be administered by a psychiatrist.

2. Their symptoms may be so idiosyncratic that they may have little ability to find common ground in a group and may need individual treatment. Although group therapy is the preferred modality for delivering sex offender-specific treatment, psychiatrically or cognitively impaired individuals may need years of pretreatment dealing with their specific symptoms (control of delusions or hallucinations, learning to sit still and attend to others, etc.) before they can benefit from a sex offender group.

3. To understand basic concepts in sex offender treatment, some of these individuals will need individual tutoring.

4. These individuals may be so behaviorally disordered secondary to their condition that they would totally disrupt a group.

On the other end of the continuum are the psychopaths who should never be given individual therapy. These individuals are highly sophisticated, highly manipulative, and highly dangerous. They are easily able to fool therapists, especially in one-on-one situations. Sociopathic and Psychopathic individuals need group confrontation by peers who can identify their manipulative tactics far more readily than therapists can, because such behavior mirrors that of their peers.

The middle range of offenders will profit most from group therapy, but individual therapy would not necessarily worsen their condition or place the therapist in danger. However, individual therapy for these midrange individuals would probably not qualify as sex offender-specific treatment.

This range of offenders also varies in the degree of emphasis placed on accepting responsibility for behavior. Many of these individuals may have been declared legally "not responsible" for their behavior. There is little point in demanding that an actively delusional individual with an IQ of 50 take responsibility for a sexual assault committed several years previously. More constructive use of his therapy would be to focus on controlling his mental illness and improving his cognitive skills so that he may be better able to control all his behavior in the future. At the point at which that behavior is under control, sex offender-specific treatment can be offered.

On the other hand, the sociopath or the psychopath must be held responsible not only for his past behavior but for his current behavior as well. One of his trademarks is that he has been "irresponsible" in contrast to being "not responsible." His behavior while in treatment will reflect an ongoing need to manipulate, control, and abuse others and will require continuous intervention.

It is hotly contested whether substance abuse is a mental illness or a personality disorder, a genetically determined condition, or a moral failing. This model does not place substance abuse in any one place on the continuum. It is a comorbid condition that can at times be associated with a mental illness, as when an individual seeks relief from the symptoms of an emotional disorder by self-medicating, or with criminal behavior, as when an antisocial individual abuses substances as a by-product of gang affiliation, subcultural mores, desire for stimulation, or genetics.

Global Assessment of Functioning Scale. All the individuals along the horizontal axis show functional impairments, which can be rated along the continuum used in the fourth edition of the *Diagnostic and Statistical Manual of Mental Disorders* (DSM-IV; American Psychiatric Association, 1994). Individuals are rated from 1 to 100 on the Global Assessment of Functioning (GAF) Scale defined by DSM-IV. However, because it is unlikely that an individual charged with a sex offense could continue to be defined in terms of superior functioning, the rating has been cut off at 70 (Table 1.2).

The GAF Scale can be used to assess the degree to which both one's functional level and one's range of deviance determine the type of sexual acting out one will engage in and the treatments that may be used. The scale quantifies the range of impairment as follows: The vertical axis rates the individual on the extent to which his sexual deviance affects his life. Both the sadist and the "politically justified" offender present a persistent danger to others. Although their style might be completely different and the degree to which they would inflict gratuitous violence on their victims would differ markedly, they would both present a persistent danger to others.

On the other hand, some ISIBs are situational offenders without deviant sexual arousal whose behavior represents an aberration in their normal pattern. These individuals might range from being seriously mentally impaired to being hardened criminals, or they may be fairly functional individuals but are not patterned sex offenders.

In positioning a given individual on this graph, one would first look at his overall functional level on the horizontal axis. If this individual's behavior were primarily attributable to an identifiable disability, then he would be scored on the left side of the axis. If his behavior was primarily a by-product of a sociopathic or psychopathic personality structure, he would fall along the right side of the axis.

This rating defines how one's comorbid condition impairs one's life. Thus a mentally ill individual may act out sexually in a nonviolent manner but due to his psychiatric condition may be physically violent to others in a nonsexual content. This individual would be given a rating between 1 and 10 on the horizontal axis, as his violent behavior is a product of his illness rather than a manifestation of his sexual problems. A criminal may violently attack a fellow inmate but this would be separate from his sexual proclivities. Thus he would be rated between 1 and 10 on the right side of the horizontal axis.

Next one would analyze the individual's position on the vertical axis. The upper level focuses more on the use of violence while the lower level focuses more on behavior which is marked by the presence of deviant arousal without the use of extraneous violence. As previously stated, this does not imply that deviant arousal is absent in violent sex offenders. In fact, at the upper ranges, which are marked by gratuitous or sadistic violence, it is indeed present.

The position of an individual on these two axes will place the individual in one of four quadrants, which will determine the overall treatment approach.

Table 1.2
Functional Ability

Score	Disabled (Left Axis)	Antisocial (Right Axis)
70–61	Mild symptoms or some difficulty in social, occupational, or school functioning, but generally functioning pretty well, has some meaningful personal relationships	Lack of history of antisocial behavior other than minor offenses (e.g., traffic, minor misdemeanors)
60–51	Moderate symptom or moderate difficulty (e.g., few friends, conflict with peers)	History of minor offenses or antisocial behavior that affected at least on major function (work, inter-personal relations)
50–41	Serious symptoms (severe OCD, frequent shoplifting) or any serious impairment in social, occupational, or school functions (e.g., no friends, can't hold a job)	Conviction of at least one nonsexual felony
40–31	Some impairment in reality testing or communication or major impairment in several areas such as work or school, family relations, judgment, thinking, or mood	History of nonsexual convictions
30–21	Behavior is considerably influenced by delusion or hallucinations or serious impairment in communication or judgment or inability to function in almost all areas	Significant history of nonsexual animal behavior with little to no history of appropriate functioning in community
20–11	Some danger of hurting self or others (e.g., frequently violent) or occasionally fails to maintain minimal personal hygiene (e.g., smears feces) or gross impairment in communication	Convictions of violent felony (e.g., assault and battery) or history of nonsexual physical assaults against others
10–1	Persistent danger of severely hurting self or others (e.g., recurring violence) or persistent inability to maintain minimal personal hygiene	Convictions of nonsexual violent felonies (e.g., murder or crimes) with clear intent to kill victim) or presents ongoing physical danger to caretakers

This method can also be used to design an overall treatment program. One could analyze a given population and plot all members on a single graph. By studying the pattern of a given group of individuals, treatment parameters can be easily identified.

Some programs have the luxury of designing a treatment regime and controlling

Figure 1.2
JRI Model for Treatment of Sexual Deviance (Male)

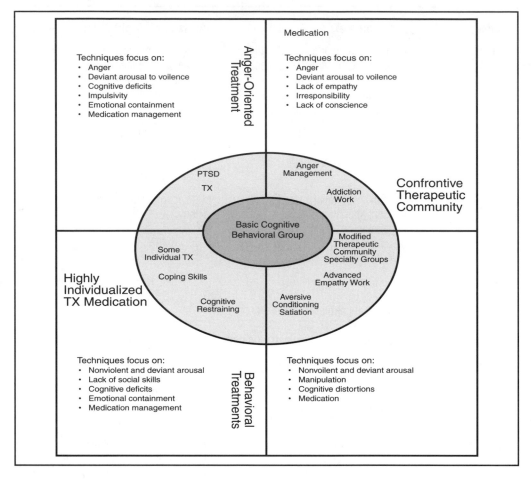

the admission of participants who can benefit from that design. The parameters can be outlined on the graph and applicants can be assessed to see whether they fit within those parameters. For example, JRI programs are designed to fit the following subpopulations:

Butler Center	Mixed population of adolescent male ISIBs
Centerpoint	Emotionally disturbed juvenile male ISIBs
Cliff House	Mixed population of adolescent male ISIBs
Cresson Secure	Mixed population of juvenile male ISIBs
Integrated Clinical Services	Developmentally disabled adult male ISIBs
Massachusetts Treatment Center	Adult male and female ISIBs

Meadowridge	Emotionally disturbed adolescent male ISIBs
Metropolitan Treatment Center	Mixed population of adolescent male ISIBs*
NFI	Mixed population of adolescent male ISIBs
Swansea Wood School	Developmentally disabled male and female adolescent ISIBs
Southbridge Center	Emotionally disturbed adolescent male ISIBs

*Mixed population includes individuals with mental illness and/or developmental disabilities as well as those with characterologically based antisocial conduct.

Matching Treatment to Individual Needs

Sex. Although females with sexually inappropriate behavior have been incorporated into this model, their treatment needs and dynamics are sufficiently different to be outside the scope of this chapter.

Age. Unfortunately, ISIBs come in all ages. Sexually reactive children can be toddlers. Senior citizens with neurological damage can suddenly begin acting out. Sex offender treatment needs to take age into account in at least two areas:

1. Accounting for the offender's developmental stage; and

2. Dealing with the changing role of the family.

Sexually reactive children need treatment techniques different from those for middle-age psychopaths, although both may need to do the following:

1. Make a commitment to change their behavior;

2. Develop empathy for others;

3. Identify their high-risk situations and develop interventions; and

4. Address the roots of their behaviors.

Clearly, materials must be relevant to age. Activity levels of therapy need to be geared to age. For example, adolescents need active, multisensory modalities more than do adults, who can tolerate more traditional group and classroom settings. Treatment for the elderly as well as the physically challenged must take into account such issues as visual or hearing problems, seating arrangements, or access to restroom facilities.

Family involvement differs across the age spectrum. With children and adolescent offenders, the question of appropriate custody is critical. Many, if not most, of these young offenders have been sexually abused themselves, often by family members. Furthermore, many young offenders have violated family members. Whether the family can provide protection for the offender and/or the victim(s) is the first question that must be asked. Once that issue is decided, the therapist can begin working with those who are or will be the primary caretakers (e.g., family, friends, foster parents, and group home staff).

The more effort devoted to this task the better. Caretakers of juvenile sex offenders must be able to do the following:

- Provide adequate twenty-four-hour protection and supervision;
- Develop an in-depth understanding of the offender's relapse prevention plan, particularly high-risk situations and interventions; and
- Be willing and able to confront the offender over failure to follow his plan and, if need be, report lapses to the authorities.

Not only must families of adult offenders be able to provide appropriate emotional support and helpful confrontation, but they must decide how much public exposure they can cope with without compromising the well-being of the rest of the family.

Surrounding the center of the JRI model at the point at which the axis intersects are the least pathological offenders. They do not suffer from mental illness, developmental disabilities, or antisocial attitudes. Concurrently, they also do not show the use of violence or deviant sexual arousal. These are the individuals who are often placed on probation and whose therapy may be limited to a weekly group that focuses on the most basic elements of sex offender treatment, including the following:

- Relapse prevention;
- Recognizing cognitive distortions;
- Developing basic victim empathy; and
- Simple behavioral techniques (e.g., covert sensitization).

Expanding outward from this core group are individuals with more serious pathology whose global functioning is impaired to a moderate degree by either a cognitive or emotional disability or antisocial traits and who may have used instrumental violence and/or show deviant arousal. These individuals would belong in a comprehensive institutional or residential sex offender treatment program that would address the full range of dynamics which contribute to sexual assault (see discussion of integrative model, later in this chapter).

These individuals often are dually diagnosed with substance abuse problems, posttraumatic stress disorder (PTSD), and/or a variety of personality disorders. Although the comprehensive sex offender program is designed to treat these combined disorders, the focus remains on sexual deviancy rather than the concomitant psychopathologies.

However, as individuals move to the far ends of the axes, treatment may need to become more specialized. For example, on the deviancy axis the sadistic murderer and the confirmed NAMBLA member present major challenges within the traditional sex offender program. Most programs would exclude these individuals. However, we will never learn anything about treating them until some program tackles the challenge.

Severely psychotic sex offenders may need individualized treatment, primarily focused on controlling their mental illness. However, their tendency to act out sexually may preclude their being housed in the traditional coed dorm usually found in state hospitals. Thus, even the most floridly mentally ill individual may need a specialized setting which understands his sexual impulsivity. Furthermore, once that individual is stabilized, dealing with his sexual deviancy becomes a prerequisite to his release into the community.

The developmentally disabled individual with sexual control issues also presents a challenge to the treatment provider. This individual may be able to return to his family and/or community once some internal or external controls are in place, or he may need lifelong care in a special facility. In any case, the treatment provider will be challenged to develop ways of presenting complex material in an easily understood format, and some concepts, which are taken for granted, are actually very complex. For example, what is involved in the concept of "consent"?

1. One must address how one's partner gives consent and what does one consent to. Must consent be verbal or can it be nonverbal? How does one know what behaviors are being consented to?

2. A person must be a certain age to give consent, but that age varies depending on the context of the relationship. How does one convey this to a developmentally disabled individual who cannot understand the concept of numbers, much less the concept of chronological age?

3. If one's prospective partner is developmentally disabled or otherwise incompetent to give consent, age does not matter. How would a developmentally delayed individual evaluate whether his prospective partner is competent to give consent?

4. Current practice dictates that developmentally disabled individuals have a right to be treated in the "least restrictive environment." They have a right to express their sexuality in a safe and healthy way. How does that fit with a situation in which the prospective partner is probably incompetent to give consent? This is a particularly complicated area when one member of the couple has a history of inappropriate sexual behavior.

Analyzing the types of individuals who are described along each axis, it becomes obvious that as one moves from the center to the extremes treatment becomes more focused on providing a highly structured environment. The seriously mentally ill individual needs a residential psychiatric placement.

It is important that the dynamic nature of this model be stressed. Individuals will constantly move along these axes as they improve or regress. A client whose mental condition improves significantly may move away from needing the special treatments provided in a specific quadrant to being able to profit from a more traditional sex offender-specific program. Likewise a person may regress to the point at which a therapist may need to move that individual into a more specialized and perhaps restrictive environment. This becomes critical when an ISIB who may be receiving treatment in the community becomes less functional and needs to be referred either to inpatient care or, if on probation or parole, back to the correctional institution.

Quadrant 1 (Sexually Violent MI/DD Sex Offenders). Individuals who fall into the sexually violent mentally ill/developmentally disabled (MI/DD) sex offender category suffer from significant mental illness or developmental disability and use violence to procure sex, either instrumentally to force their victim's compliance or because their sexual arousal depends on inflicting pain and degradation. These individuals clearly need a variety of treatments aimed at enhancing their global functioning. Such treatment could include the following:

- Medication management;
- Social skills training;
- Life skills training;
- Cognitive skills training;
- Emotions containment training; and
- Educational/vocational training (where indicated).

Moreover, their sex offender treatment needs to be geared to their specialized needs. Not only may members of this subgroup resort to the use of aggression with their victims, they may act out on the staff and their peers as well. Consequently, this must be taken into account when designing the physical setting for the treatment.

Initial treatment should focus on the following:

- Anger management;
- Emotional control;
- Impulse control;
- Management of symptoms of major mental illness, if applicable;
- Social skills; and
- Basic communication skills.

When the individual is able to contain his behavior so that he can function in the therapeutic milieu, and he is able to begin to discuss his sexual behavior without losing emotional control, he is ready to progress to sex offender-specific treatment. For this group, basic sex offender treatment needs to be specialized to include attention to the following:

- Deviant and possibly sadistic sexual arousal associated with anger and violence;
- Inability to relate to women secondary to mental illness or developmental disability which feeds the anger;
- Cognitive distortions which are further twisted by psychotic thought processes or developmental disability; and
- Sexual impulsivity which may be physiologically based and secondary to mental illness, developmental disabilities, and/or neurological impairment.

Quadrant 2 (Violent Sociopathic/Psychopathic Sex Offenders). Lykken (1995) has described a range of antisocial personalities which extend from the psychologically normal offender who may be persons who are actually innocent of the charge against them or are victims of circumstance (the individual who is charged as a codefendant for simply being there at the time of a crime) to persons who are sociopathic to the full-blown psychopath.

In this typology, Lykken (1995) describes sociopaths as follows: "[those individuals] who were simply never adequately socialized during childhood and adolescence. Many members of this genus also possess impulse peculiarities or habit patterns that are traceable to deviant learning histories interacting, perhaps, with deviant genetic predilections" (p. 22). The defining feature of these individuals is their lack of socialization which can be understood as a product of their upbringing.

In contrast, Lykken (1995) describes the psychopath as an individual whose problems lie "in his psyche rather than his situation" (p. 31). These individuals are not mentally ill in the classic sense. Someday we may come to understand that there is some underlying mental or physiological pathology that accounts for their behavior, but for this model they are defined as individuals whose behavior is a manifestation of their character rather than a recognized disease process.

Hare (1991) has defined these individuals by the following characteristics:

- Glibness/superficial charm

- Egocentric/grandiose sense of self-worth

- Need for stimulation/proness to boredom

- Pathological lying and deception

- Conning/manipulative

- Lack of remorse or guilt

- Shallow affect

- Callous/lack of empathy

- Parasitic lifestyle

- Poor behavioral controls

- Promiscuous sexual relations

- Early behavior problems

- Lack of realistic, long-term plans

- Impulsivity

- Irresponsibility

- Failure to accept responsibility for own actions

- Many short-term marital relationships

- Juvenile delinquency

- Revocation of conditional release

- Criminal versatility. (Hare, 1991, p. 2)

Hare (1991) states the following:

Psychopathy can be differentiated from other personality disorders on the basis of its characteristic pattern of interpersonal, affective and behavioral symptoms. Interpersonally, psychopaths are grandiose, egocentric, manipulative, dominant, forceful and cold-hearted. Affectivity, they display shallow and labile emotions, are unable to form long-lasting bonds to people, principles or goals, and are lacking in empathy, anxiety and genuine guilt and remorse. Behaviorally, psychopaths are impulsive and sensation seeking, and they readily violate social norms. The most obvious expressions of these predispositions involve criminality, substance abuse, and a failure to fulfill social obligations and responsibilities. (p. 3)

Most of the sex offenders in Quadrant 2 are either rapists or individuals who have used gratuitous violence against children. The treatment needs of these individuals center around their inability to take responsibility for their behavior and their exploitive relations with others. Whether they meet the criteria for sociopathy or psychopathy, they are likely to have problems with authority, difficulty following rules and norms, and problems with empathy. They tend to be impulsive and to put their needs and desires before anything else. They also crave excitement and may violate rules and boundaries for the "thrill of it."

These individuals do not respond well to individual therapy. In fact, it is believed that individual therapy can actually make these individuals worse (Prendergast, 1991) Those at the extreme end of the continuum tend to be socially sophisticated and able to easily manipulate others. They can present a real threat to staff who can be taken in by them and may either find themselves in physical danger or be lured into a "romance" or into colluding in some type of illegal behavior or both. The most effective treatment for these individuals is the therapeutic community (Gendreau, 1998). In this forum, other like-minded individuals can confront their fellow residents about patterns of behaviors to which the staff may be oblivious.

There are some individuals in this category who may be unable initially to function in a sex offender-specific treatment program because of the following:

- Their behavior is so impulsive that they spend most of their time in some type of segregation.

- Their substance abuse problems are so great that they are under the influence of drugs or alcohol most of the time.

- Their hostility prevents them from being able to participate in any type of group activity.

These individuals need help in resolving such issues prior to beginning sex offender-specific treatment. Such treatment might include an anger management program, a substance abuse therapeutic community, or programs focused on criminal thinking patterns. When they are able to participate in sex offender-specific treatment, special attention should be paid to the following:

- Anger management;

- Deviant, possibly sadistic, sexual arousal;

- Lack of empathy;

- Failure to take responsibility for sexual assault;

- Misogynistic attitudes; and

- Culturally reinforced attitudes toward women and violence.

Quadrant 3 (Nonviolent, Sociopathic/Psychopathic Sex Offenders). This group of sex offenders can range from fairly lightweight offenders who do not have a significant amount of deviant arousal, and whose crimes are basically opportunistic in nature, to individuals with high levels of deviant arousal accompanied by psychopathic personalities. At the extreme, these individuals are totally convinced of the legitimacy of their sexual relations with children and are actively attempting to change laws outlawing child sexual abuse.

The more psychopathic of these offenders are clever manipulators who expend a great deal of energy planning their crimes and grooming their victims. They may have entered careers that give them access to children or volunteered to sponsor youth-center events. On the other hand, some individuals with deviant arousal do not have the social skills to engage in elaborate grooming rituals and may just grab children and assault them.

This is the group of offenders for whom most sex offender treatment has been devised. Therefore, the core treatment program will satisfy the majority of these individuals' needs. However, the highly psychopathic personalities will need the type of treatment described for the Quadrant 2 psychopaths.

Individuals who are aligned with national pedophile organizations such as NAMBLA are extremely challenging to treat. They have organized on an international level to undermine treatment (e.g., publishing handbooks that give instructions for faking the plethysmograph). Therapists should realize that these individuals are often highly litigious and are looking for ways to discredit both sex offender treatment and those who treat sex offenders.

Many of these individuals do have a history of personal victimization that needs to be addressed in order to do the following:

- Dissuade these individuals of the notion that "it happened to me and nothing bad resulted";

- Release the emotion that may be bound to that experience so that it can be used to develop empathy for their victims;

- Deal with the repetition compulsion that sometimes is evident; and

- Treat the underlying symptoms of the childhood abuse that may have contributed to the need for tension-relieving mechanisms such as substance abuse and deviant sexuality.

Quadrant 4 (Nonviolent, MI/DD Individuals). Quadrant 4 individuals have at least one comorbid condition, mental illness, or developmental disabilities, or both. Although being mentally ill or developmentally disabled is not correlated with having deviant sexual arousal, it does make the treatment more challenging. Therefore, sex offender treatment needs to be offered within the context of the other disorder. Developmentally disabled individuals need their treatment modified so that it is presented in understandable manner. Mentally ill individuals need to have treatment presented in such a way as to not aggravate their mental illness (e.g., one would not use highly confrontive techniques with psychotic individuals).

There is, of course, some overlap. Increasing the social skills and self-esteem of these individuals will enhance their functioning in a variety of other areas. Most of these individuals will need much more focus on basic skills, including the following:

- Communication skills;
- Stress management;
- Sex education; and
- Social skills.

For the less deviant individuals, enhancing their ability to acquire an appropriate sex partner may replace their need to choose children, who are less threatening than adults, as their sexual partners. Individuals with deviant arousal will need behavioral treatment

The Integrative Model

Initiation of Various Stages of Treatment. Sex offender treatment consists of many components. However, not all ISIBs need all these modalities. Furthermore, not all ISIBs can cope cognitively or psychologically with all techniques. The following section deals with the timing of the presentation of different modalities. Because the basic model assumes that individuals can move along the continuum, a person might not be ready for a certain treatment at one time but might be ready later on in his therapy.

Various Domains. The integrative model addresses the following domains:

- Physiological;
- Behavioral;
- Cognitive;
- Affective;
- Interpersonal;
- Familial;
- Societal; and
- Spiritual.

Physiological. Those clients with serious mental illness or neurological problems often associated with developmental disabilities are frequently on complicated psychopharmacological regimes from the time they enter treatment. In some cases medications can over time be decreased and even eliminated. In other cases these individuals will have to learn to manage their medications on a long-term basis. Proper psychopharmacological treatment can assist the individual with maintaining contact with reality, controlling mood swings, helping to lessen impulsively and assist with anger control (Figure 1.3). All of these effects will enhance sex offender treatment.

In addition, individuals with a history of sexually assaulting others may have special medication needs. Many of these individuals suffer from obsessive compulsive disorder, often manifested as intrusive fantasies or compulsive masturbation. This condition often responds well to medication. Proper use of drugs to control this condition may make the client more psychologically available for treatment. Moreover, drugs may help to control some highly repetitive types of offending behavior, such as exhibitionism.

For those individuals whose behavior appears to be related to heightened testosterone levels, anti-androgen treatment is a possibility. However, this type of treatment may best be initiated shortly before the client enters the community, thereby minimizing any possible dangers associated with long-term use and maximizing the benefits of decreasing arousal while in the community. Of course, if an individual is acting out in the program, the use of medication may be required.

Caution should always be exercised when using medications with antisocial types. Substance abuse is a major problem with this population, and many of these individuals will do anything to acquire drugs of almost any type. Furthermore they may already believe in "better living through chemistry"—that they can only manage life with the help of drugs or alcohol. Therefore, any legitimate use of psychopharmacology with this population must be balanced by efforts to psychologically separate the legitimate use of medication from substance abuse.

Figure 1.3
Physiological Treatment

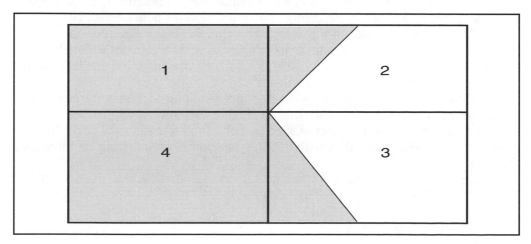

Figure 1.4
General Behavioral Techniques

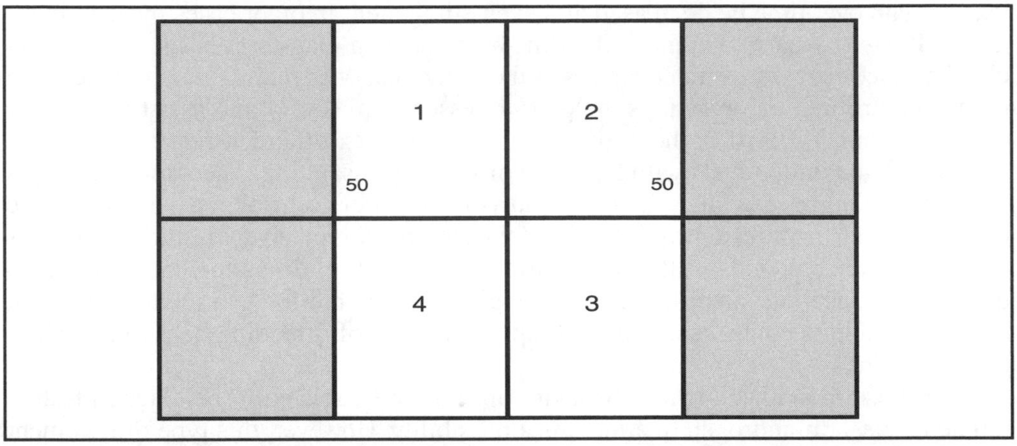

Of course, no medication has been shown to address antisocial behavior unless one counts some of the drugs prescribed through substance abuse programs, which by decreasing the need for the illegal drug lowers the need to engage in crime.

This model proposes that the further the individual falls along the "irresponsible" continuum, the less likely it is that medication can be helpful. The individual with psychopathic characteristics may be much more driven by his character pathology than by his neurotransmitters or his hormonal level. However, there is always the possibility that a biological basis for his condition will be discovered. Psychopharmacological treatment should always be considered for individuals in Quadrants 1 and 4. Medication to lower deviant arousal would be useful for individuals in Quadrants 2 and 3 as long as their deviance is not considered a by-product of their antisocial attitudes.

Behavioral. Behavioral treatments can be helpful with all these groups on a variety of different levels. Token economies and the informed use of positive and negative reinforcement can be helpful to mold behavior in a variety of populations. These techniques have long been used in managing the mentally ill and developmentally disabled. Prison systems have used these techniques to contain inmates with behavioral problems. They may even be helpful with psychopaths who may find that less disruptive, less predatory behavior is more self-serving.

Structured behavioral management programs would be necessary for individuals on the far ends of the functional dimension (Figure 1.4). As one approaches the center, a therapist might use a number of specific behavioral techniques to deal with specific issues (flooding for dealing with PTSD, systematically reinforcing assertiveness, etc.)

Specific behaviorally based techniques for sex offenders include a variety of different approaches:

- Covert sensitization;
- Assisted covert;

Figure 1.5
Specific Sex Offender Behavioral Treatment

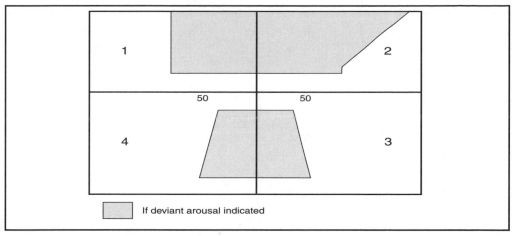

If deviant arousal indicated

- Olfactory aversion; and

- Masturbatory satiation.

Covert and assertive techniques are used to lessen deviant arousal by pairing it with negative associations while positively reinforcing appropriate arousal. The techniques require a good deal of motivation, as they are often embarrassing, intrusive, or boring. Satiation techniques involve pairing deviant arousal with a boring or aversive situation created by overindulging the deviant urge. Individuals are required to either masturbate for prolonged periods when they are not sexually aroused or recite the deviant fantasies repeatedly until it becomes boring. From Figure 1.5 it is apparent that specific behavioral techniques can be used with individuals in Quadrants 1 and 4 whose functional level allows them to engage in behavioral treatments that require a significant amount of motivation and concentration. In Quadrant 2, specific behavioral techniques would be used with individuals who show deviant arousal and sufficient motivation to seriously engage in this work. Highly sadistic individuals who are not severely psychopathic could be offered this treatment, as any technique that might help with these dangerous individuals should be tried.

It is doubtful that the seriously mentally ill or severely developmentally disabled individual could concentrate long enough to successfully participate in this treatment In addition, it might be impossible to find stimulus aversive enough to combat sadistic arousal or to challenge the politically justified child molester. These methods are best suited to highly motivated individuals who do show deviant arousal. Individuals who do not show deviant arousal are not candidates for this technique.

Cognitive. The function of cognitive-behavioral treatment is to address the thought patterns that reinforce maladaptive behavior. This treatment has been found to be helpful with a wide variety of problems from depression to borderline personality disorder to PTSD and, of course, to sexual deviancy. The basic paradigm is that thoughts produce feelings, which in turn produce behaviors. If one can change the thoughts, the negative feelings will be dissipated, and the maladaptive behaviors aborted.

Figure 1.6
Cognitive-Behavioral Techniques

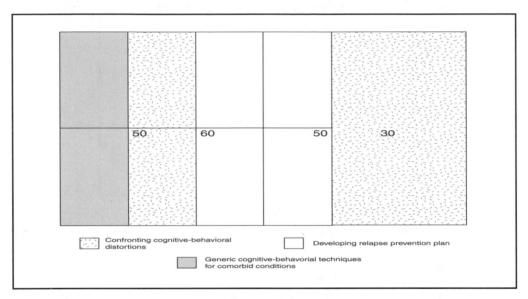

Relapse prevention is also classified as a cognitive-behavioral technique as it focuses on the maladaptive thoughts, feelings, and behaviors that begin and continue the deviant cycle.

Cognitive-behavioral treatment can be used with all populations to deal with a variety of problems. Dialectical behavior therapy, developed by Marsha Linehan (1993), has been found to be highly useful in helping people to deal with the overwhelming emotional responses often found in borderline personalities. It has also been successfully used with developmentally disabled sex offenders (Figure 1.6).

Individuals who manifest sociopathic and psychopathic traits can benefit from analyzing their thought patterns and recognizing those thoughts that promote feelings of entitlement, anger, revenge, and so on. This may not be sufficient to change their behavior, but unless they recognize these distortions they will experience a great deal of discomfort with the way they perceive and interact with the world.

Therapeutic communities such as Delancey Street that deal successfully with the worst of the antisocials are based on confronting these flawed thoughts, beliefs, and values. Substance abuse programs dating back to the founding of Alcoholics Anonymous have recognized the role played by "stinkin' thinkin'." Yochelson and Samenow (1976) did pioneering work with criminals by meticulously analyzing their thought patterns.

Currently it would be hard to find a sex offender treatment program that (1) does not confront the cognitive distortions that perpetuate offending behavior, and (2) does not have the offender prepare a relapse prevention plan. However, these individuals must have sufficient insight into their behaviors to make such a plan useful. Therefore, this task is often one of the last goals achieved.

For those individuals whose mental illness or development disability renders them (1) incapable or recognizing distorted thinking and/or (2) too fragile to deal with any type of confrontation, more general cognitive-behavioral techniques can be introduced to deal with depression or anger. The long-range goal is to move them to the point at which they can begin to deal with their "stinkin' thinkin'" and its contribution to their sexually assaultive behavior.

Affective. A crucial factor in motivating individuals to control their sexually offensive behavior is the development of empathy for others. Empathy is an emotion—you "feel for" others. However, most sexually assaultive individuals have become numbed to their emotions. There are a variety of techniques to help ISIBs reconnect with their feelings. Sometimes simply talking about their offense or a trauma that may have happened to them may elicit feelings. For other individuals, experiential therapy, including art, music, or drama therapy, will reawaken an emotional response (Figure 1.7).

This type of treatment is quite intense and may evoke emotional responses in other members of the treatment group. Consequently, it must be used with caution with MI/DD individuals. Such treatment may produce deep feelings of guilt and shame, which may be valuable in helping an individual face the harm he may have done to others but may be overwhelming for a seriously mentally ill individual. It may even arouse suicidal impulses. However, all ISIBs must face the reality of the damage they have done by sexually acting out. If they are too fragile to deal with this reality in a treatment setting, they are probably too unstable to function safely in the community.

Depending on one's primary diagnosis, healing from past traumas may be a significant treatment goal. If it is not, the therapist will have to determine which traumas are involved in the individual's sexual deviance. For example, sexual victimization as a child may contribute to a compulsion to reenact that trauma. The therapist may need to find a way to work with these issues that does not result in decompensation, or he

Figure 1.7
Affective Techniques

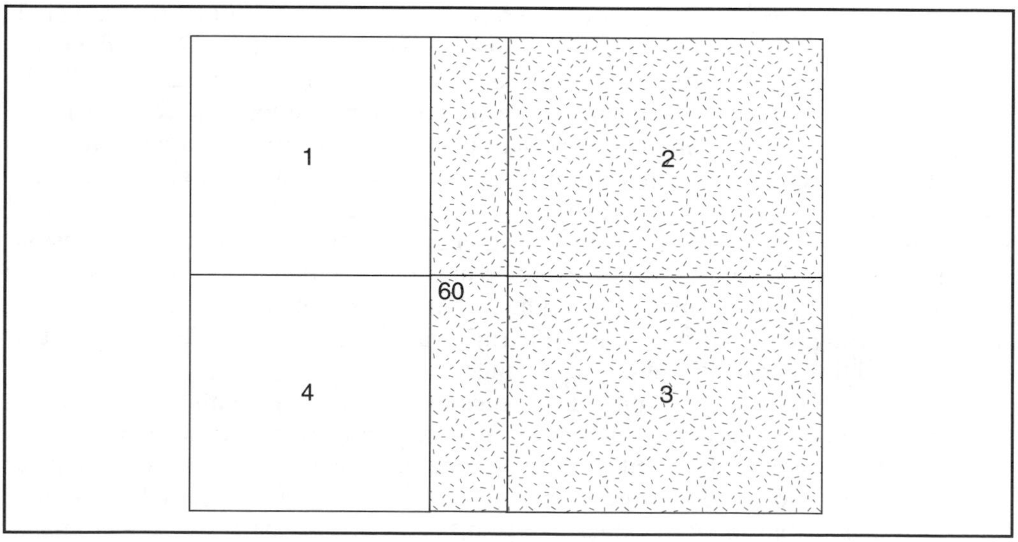

may need to be able to time this intervention so that the material is not presented prematurely.

Developmentally disabled individuals are probably not at risk to psychologically decompensate but may not know how to handle strong feelings. They may also experience neurologically based impulsivity that manifests itself during periods of affective arousal. These individuals need to learn how to express their feelings of guilt, shame, anger, and humiliation in appropriate ways by talking about the emotions rather than by acting on them.

Interpersonal. The more a person's problems effect his interpersonal relationships, the more society feels compelled to do something about them. Throughout time a reclusive old woman living isolated from others could be regarded as odd but basically ignored until she was accused of affecting others. At such a time the reaction of society would be swift and often lethal.

Adults and children are in institutions, be they prisons or treatment centers, because their behaviors have had an impact on others. Individuals are usually placed in nursing homes or long-term care facilities because their needs exceed the capabilities of those around them to care for them. Clearly this varies greatly from situation to situation.

All the individuals being discussed in this chapter have demonstrated behaviors which have had a negative influence on those around them. Even those who are developmentally disabled and are in residential treatment programs have had needs that exceeded their families' ability to provide for them. The mentally ill who are in residential care also demonstrate behaviors that have led to their being removed from their homes and the community. Of course, all individuals who commit sexual assaults have a negative impact on others. The abuse of interpersonal relations is the core of their problem.

All these individuals bring their patterns of relations to others into the treatment. Being able to observe the manifestation of these abusive patterns is the strength of residential programs and therapeutic communities.

Improving the way one relates to others is a primary goal for all these individuals from the moment they begin whatever treatment they are in (Figure 1.8). As the client progresses in treatment, more and more is demanded of him in this area. Initially the goal for some would just be to be able to be around others without attacking them. As treatment continues, the individual must start to deal with the impact of his sexual acting out, develop empathy for his victim, and then be able to act in a responsible and empathic manner around everyone. A number of different techniques would be used to address these issues but it must be an ongoing treatment goal on every dimension.

In this model the further one goes out on any axis, the more likely one's behavior will influence a larger number of individuals. On the functional dimension any score of 30 or less suggests that others are in harm's way. Scores of 20 or less suggest that those around this person are in physical danger.

Every sexually assaultive individual needs to come to grips with how his behavior has affected others. Barring the existence of certain comorbid conditions, such as those discussed previously, eliciting an emotional appreciation for the consequences of his behaviors should be a priority. This applies to all sex offenders, including those on the "irresponsible axis." Whether those on the far end of the right axis can really

Figure 1.8
Improving Interpersonal Relations

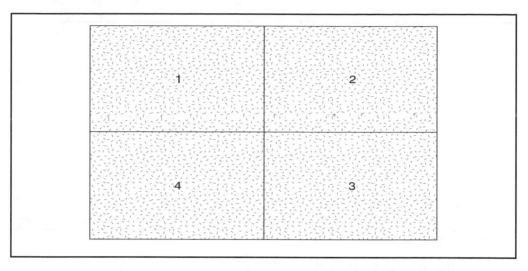

gain an emotional understanding of the harm they have done or whether they can connect with emotions other than anger remains to be seen. Certainly every effort should
be made to encourage this understanding.

Familial. There are two issues concerning the role of the family in the treatment of
these individuals: (1) untangling the role of the family of origin in the current pathology and helping the individual resolve it and (2) encouraging every family member or
friend to become part of an effective support network for the client.

Dealing with trauma that originated in the family is a fairly advanced treatment
goal (Figure 1.9). Individuals whose behavior is out of control have more pressing
here-and-now matters to focus on. However, these old family issues may be continuing to serve as triggers for one's sexual-acting-out cycle. Thus, to be able to exercise
maximum control over one's behavior, one should work on resolving these old traumas. This work, however, should not overshadow one's work on one's own abusive
behavior. It is far too easy to get sidetracked into blaming one's family for one's problems and failing to take control of one's actions.

Enlisting the current family and friends as a responsible support network working
to reinforce treatment is something that should be done throughout therapy at all
stages (Figure 1.10). At any point in treatment, it is possible for other individuals to
collude with the client to the detriment of all. In the worst-case scenarios one sees a
wife or girlfriend who helps the offender escape from prison. At the other end is the
parent who removed his or her seriously mentally ill offspring from a treatment facility. A family member might actively oppose a certain kind of treatment or may simply insist on remaining in denial. Thus it is important in every case in which a significant other(s) has influence over the client to enlist those individuals in support of the
treatment program. This is important with adult clients but absolutely crucial with
children and adolescents.

In the early stages of treatment, support for the course of treatment is vital. In the

Figure 1.9
Family-of-Origin Trauma Issues

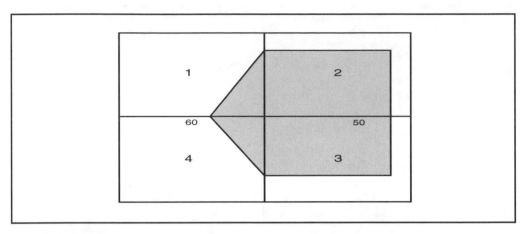

Figure 1.10
Training of Support System

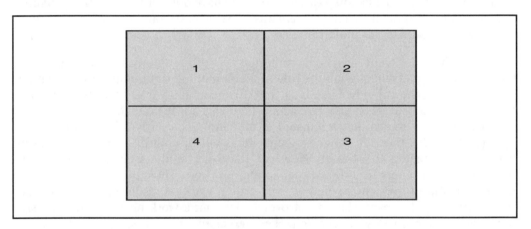

later stages the family can assist the client in overcoming denial, understanding motivators and disinhibitors, and preparing the relapse prevention plan. In the final stages of treatment, the support network will be an important source of strength in maintaining recovery. Support persons must be willing to assist the client in intervening in his deviant cycle and in some cases to call in others (e.g., probation and parole law enforcement) should the individual progress too far in that cycle.

Societal. One's society, whether it is defined as one's physical community, one's subculture, or one's ethnic or national origin, can act as a source of strength or a source of problems. And because it probably acts as all at the same time, everyone is constantly learning to draw on its strengths and ignore the weaknesses. Society certainly has an impact on the way one's emotions are expressed, and the way one's beliefs develop. Individuals who act out sexually have usually been exposed to negative messages about how to deal with their emotions as well as numerous cognitive distortions that contribute to their proclivity to assault others.

For example, individuals who have trouble controlling their anger have frequently been socialized to believe that anger is the only emotion a "real man" can experience and express. Consequently, all negative emotions, including depression, sorrow, and frustration, are channeled into anger. With this population it is further complicated by the fact that many men are raised with negative stereotypes about women which fuel and direct their anger.

In deciding the groups on which one needs to focus efforts at resocialization, it is probably true that severely mentally ill and developmentally disabled individuals experience fewer problems in this area because they are less amenable to outside influences. Thus, just as their condition makes them less accessible to normal socialization, they are also less susceptible to negative societal influences.

There are three subgroups with which we are dealing that are particularly susceptible to negative societal influences. On the deviance dimension, as one progresses toward the ends of the continuum, the more individuals are at risk due either to the violence being employed or to the exclusivity of the deviant arousal.

Unfortunately our society contributes to the prevalence of sexual assault against women through such myths as "women like it rough," "they really want it," "she's asking for it." These cognitive distortions combine with societal socialization of males to be aggressive, unfeeling, and competitive to handicap males in dealing with emotions, dealing with rejection, and being empathetic.

Movies, books, videos, and musical lyrics all endorse or excuse sexual assault. Several years ago this author saw an ad in a prominent women's magazine geared to homemakers for a collector's music box that featured a scene from *Gone with the Wind*. And which scene did the sculptor choose? The rape scene—Rhett Butler is carrying Scarlett upstairs after he has sexually approached her and been rebuffed. The ad even acknowledged that this scene depicted Rhett's way of overcoming Scarlett's resistance.

The media is notorious for glamorizing men forcibly overcoming a woman's choice not to participate in sex.

Many sadistic offenders draw from stereotypes about women in their choice of victims. They often prey on prostitutes, justifying their behavior with cognitive distortions such as "they're asking for it" or "they deserve it." However, while society's attitude toward prostitutes offer sadists a ready justification, much more than early cultural socialization has contributed to their pathology. The same is true for the psychopath whose behavior is more a product of individual pathology than an antisocial subculture.

However, treatment programs can combat these societal attitudes and stereotypes by addressing basic assumptions to which we expose males (see Figure 1.11). Our treatment program uses a class called Messages in the Media to examine myths and distortions that perpetrate violence.

On the other hand, individuals with sociopathic tendencies usually have been socialized by antisocial peers into accepting a set of values that encourage or facilitate illegal behavior. For example, these individuals often choose unlawful actions to satisfy their sensation seeking needs.

They find illegal drugs readily available. They may engage in assaultive behavior

Figure 1.11
Confronting Societal Support for Female Sterotypes

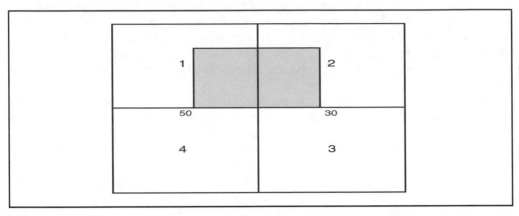

out of gang loyalty rather than any personal anger at their victim. Furthermore their antisocial behavior developed prior to incarceration has been impacted by the "con code," the prison code of conduct. This too must be confronted head on. Treating the person with sociopathic tendencies will involve reteaching him a set of values. In therapeutic communities individuals are taught to live by the "recovery" code rather than the "con" code (see Figure 1.12).

The "recovery " code stresses openly expressing feelings, developing trust, taking responsibility for behavior, being honest and talking rather than acting impulsively. Conflict resolution replaces games such as "Let's You and Him Fight" or "Got Ya". This is difficult to accomplish in a prison but can be done in therapeutic communities.

Individuals in Quadrants 1 and 2 represent those whose negative behavior has been influenced by certain cultural or subcultural attitudes regarding women and violence. It is less likely that individuals in Quadrants 3 and 4 who are more into grooming and manipulating children would find support in societal attitudes.

Figure 1.12
Dealing With Sociopathic Offenders

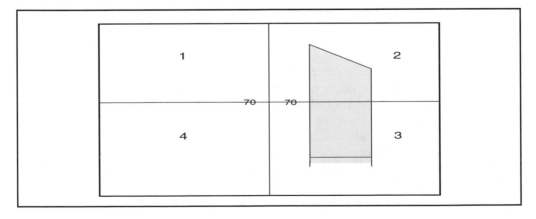

Figure 1.13
Confronting Societal Justication for Pedophilia

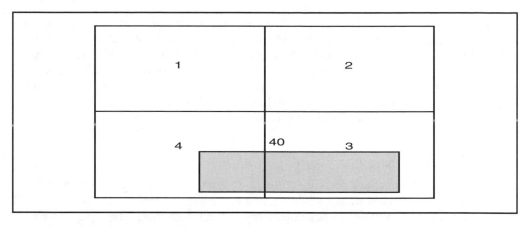

The third group that finds support for their behavior are the "politically justified" pedophiles. These individuals find justification for acting out their deviance in groups such as NAMBLA. In addition, the existence of "kiddie porn" reassures pedophiles that there is an organized subculture that shares their sexual orientation (see Figure 1.13).

Spiritual. All programs should offer all their clients some sort of opportunity to express their spirituality (Figure 1.14). Most institutions have a chaplaincy staff who provide or coordinate formal religious services. However, every residential program should provide opportunities for nondenominational spiritual experiences. This could include classes in and opportunities for meditation or yoga. There should also be arrangements made for the practice of specific religions, attendance at religious services, and celebration of religious holidays.

Figure 1.14
Enhancing Spirituality

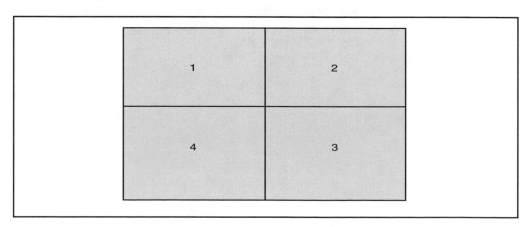

Valuable adjuncts to every therapy program are the 12-Step programs. These groups not only are invaluable in the treatment of a variety of addictions but foster spirituality.

There is one group for which issues around spirituality present a treatment challenge. This group is the sex offenders who demonstrate religiosity rather than spirituality. They have often been raised with a great deal of sexual guilt fostered by some religious groups. They are highly judgmental, seeing the world as "black and white." They are often homophobic and highly anxious over masturbation. These individuals emerge all over the continuum. Their maladaptive religious beliefs can best be dealt with by offering them opportunities to focus on core issues of spirituality.

Conclusion

Individuals who act out sexually come in a variety of types with a variety of distinct problems. The field of sex offender treatment has come a long way in the past thirty years as it has worked to develop effective treatment modalities. It is time now to begin to fine-tune the techniques to fit the heterogeneity of this population. The JRI model was developed to fit a wide range of clients with multiple comorbid disorders but to ensure that all the programs worked under the same theoretical model. This model can be used to develop either an individual treatment plan or a treatment model for an entire program. It begins with a core treatment approach and then modifies the plan as the client or clientele demonstrate more unique problems. It is hoped that this model will prove useful to others in adapting established techniques to individual situations.

References

American Psychiatric Association. (1994). *Diagnostic and statistical manual of mental disorders* (4th ed.). Washington, DC: Author

Gendreau, P. (1998, October 18). *Correctional programs that work.* Paper presented at the annual conference of the Association for the Treatment of Sexual Abusers, Vancouver.

Hare, R. D. (1991). *The Hare PCL-R Rating Booklet.* North Tonowanda, NY: Multi-Health Systems.

Linehan, M. M. (1993). *Cognitive-behavioral treatment of borderline personality disorder.* New York: Guilford Press.

Lykken, D. T. (1995). *The antisocial personality.* Hillsdale, NJ: Erlbaum.

Prendergast, W. E. (1991). *Treating sex offenders in correctional institutions and outpatient clinics: A guide to clinical practice.* New York: Haworth Press.

Yochelson, S,. & Samenow, S. (1976). *The criminal personality: Vol. 1. A profile for change.* New York: Jason Aronson.

Chapter 2

A Holistic/Integrated Approach to Treating Sexual Offenders

by Robert E. Longo, M.R.C., L.P.C.

"Treat patients, clients, and work personnel as they 'could be'—so that they will become that" [if only treated as they currently are, they will stay that way].

— Goethe

Overview

The treatment of juvenile and adult sexual offenders has been developing and growing over the course of the past twenty-five years (Burton et al., 2000). This growth has been influenced primarily by the field of treating adult sexual abusers. Unfortunately, in some ways, the development and maintenance of juvenile sexual offender treatment programs have been heavily influenced by the trickle-down effect from adult sexual offender treatment models without looking at children who sexually abuse as a separate and distinct group of patients with individual differences and treatment needs. In many cases developmental and contextual issues have been ignored in working with this population (Ryan & Associates, 1999).

This chapter explores the use of a holistic treatment model in working with youth with sexual behavior problems, and adult sexual abusers. It addresses ways of blending traditional sexual offender treatment models and modalities with holistic approaches that incorporate developmental issues and humanistic approaches and includes a variety of experiential therapies as a part of the therapeutic and learning process in treatment.

Introduction

The field of assessing and treating juvenile and adult sexual abusers, although not new, is still in a developmental stage. As of the writing of this chapter, there is no literature that defines the "best practice" in treating children and adolescents with sexual behavior problems (Development Services Group, 2000), and the literature is scarce regarding models treating adult sexual abusers that have been proven effective via long-term, replicated research. In fact, the field of treating sex offenders continues to operate with the belief that cognitive-behavioral treatments used within the context of the relapse prevention model are "best practice" when there is little scientific evidence that these approaches are superior or more effective than other treatment methods and models that are in use or might be used to treat people who sexually abuse. Simply put, we cannot say with absolute conviction that we know what works and what does not.

The assessment and treatment of juvenile and adult sexual offenders has been developing over the past twenty-five years (Burton et al., 2000). The growth of specialized programs has been influenced by a variety of factors including networking, political establishment of programs, an increase in the reporting of sex crimes, and increasing numbers of sexual offenders being convicted and required to participate in specific sex-offense treatment programs. To date the criminal justice system has failed to develop laws that take into account developmental and contextual issues in working with this population, and many programs specializing in the treatment of juvenile sexual offenders also fail to address these factors (Freeman-Longo, 2000; Ryan & Associates, 1999). Children and juveniles who sexually abuse should be assessed as a separate and distinct group of patients with individual differences and treatment needs different from those of adults.

The number of identified specialized juvenile and adult sexual abuser programs and treatment providers has mushroomed from 643 identified programs in 1986 to more than 1,391 programs in 1996 (see Table 2.1). Generally, and until recently, juvenile sexual abuser treatment services have grown less rapidly than adult programs which now appear to be declining as more prison-based treatment programs close their doors, diverting funds from programming to prison construction. The Safer Society Foundation (SSF) has maintained files on identified programs and clinicians providing such services to juvenile and adult sex offenders since 1976, and from the first national survey in 1986, the SSF's listings of identified specialized juvenile and adult sex offender programs and treatment providers increased dramatically.

Table 2.1
Comparison of Treatment Provider Responses Since 1986

Year	Adult	Juvenile	Child	Total
1986	297	346	N/A	643
1988	429	573	N/A	1,002
1990	541	626	N/A	1,167
1992	745	755	N/A	1,500
1994	710	684	390	1,784
1996	527	539	314	1,380

The Safer Society national surveys recognized "identified" programs only as those programs whose responders filled out and returned the nationwide surveys. In 1994, the survey was lengthened and only 65% of the programs queried returned the survey. During the 1996 survey, only an estimated 55% of programs receiving the survey questionnaire completed it and returned it to the Safer Society by the specified date. The 2000 survey, which has been under way since the fall of 1999, is showing an even greater decrease in respondents than previous surveys (Burton et al., 2000). Thus the figures in Table 2.1 reflect only identified programs that responded to the surveys and do not accurately represent the total number of specialized programs in existence in the United States.

Programs treating juvenile sexual abusers have, unfortunately, been developed using a trickle-down process from the adult sex offender treatment field. In many programs this trickle-down process has resulted in (1) the misuse of technology, (2) the failure to address children and their treatment needs by taking into account their developmental stage, (3) the use of a language and materials that may not be easily understood by children who have learning disabilities, and (4) highly confrontational approaches that may trigger trauma in youth with histories of child abuse and neglect.

Juvenile Programs Based on Adult Models

The majority of juvenile sexual offender treatment programs have generally adhered to traditional sex offender treatment models and strategies for treating adolescents with sexual behavior problems. These standard treatments usually include cognitive-behavioral/relapse prevention models, and a variety of treatment modalities, such as teaching the sexual abuse cycle, empathy training, anger management, social and interpersonal skills training, cognitive restructuring, emotional development, teaching coping responses and interventions, assertiveness training, journaling, sex education, and communication skills (Burton, Smith-Darden, Levins, Fiske, & Freeman-Longo, 2000; Freeman-Longo, Bird, Stevenson, & Fiske, 1995; Knopp, Freeman-Longo, & Stevenson, 1993; Knopp, Rosenberg, & Stevenson, 1986; Knopp & Stevenson, 1989).

Recently, some of the more traditional approaches to treating adult and juvenile sexual abusers have been criticized, including relapse prevention (RP)—the most widely used model by programs treating both juvenile and adult sexual abusers (Laws, Hudson & Ward, 2000; Ward & Hudson, 1996). These authors have noted that the RP model has limited ways to account for offense behavior. In addition, the model's presentation of the offense chain is overly rigid and leaves no room for individual differences in behavior (there is no flexibility in the chain of behaviors and events leading to sexual assault), it is academic (it intellectualizes sex offending)—with abstract concepts and complex terms and language—and it relies on coping strategies that are not positive goal oriented (i.e., avoidance and escape). Despite its many limitations, RP is a viable model which, when modified, can be used in conjunction with a holistic approach.

Another criticism of sex offender treatment is its use of the sexual abuse cycles, a traditional method of teaching the sexual abuse process, which has also come under fire in recent times (Maletzky, 1998). Maletzky (1998) notes, "If sexual offenders operated in cycles of behavior, they would be perpetually seeking deviant gratification; however, that does not match the reality of most sex offenders" (p. 1). What Maletzky fails to realize, however, is that cycles are not timed in any special way. For some the cycle can take minutes, for other hours or days, and yet for others weeks, or months. Unhealthy cycles can be broken and new healthy behaviors learned. Furthermore, the concept of cycles goes well beyond the field of sexual abuse treatment. From early times to the present many cultures, including those of aboriginal peoples, have used the concept of cycles, life cycles, cycles of life, and so on, to describe human behavior and the progression through the varied stages of human life. Cycles are not absolute or limited. Cycles can have subcycles that can develop and build up over time. As Carich (1999) notes in response to Maletzky, "The definition of a cycle used by Maletzky is very limited when applied to sexual offenders" (p. 249).

Adapting Relapse Prevention to a Holistic Model

Teaching clients about relapse prevention and the cycle of sexual abuse can be readily blended into a holistic model (Freeman-Longo, 2001). The RP model has already been adapted to teaching the sexual abuse cycle for many years (Freeman-Longo & Pithers, 1992). Recent modifications to this model enable the blending of the four universal needs, the four aspects of self, and the use of core values and beliefs (Figure 2.1) to teaching clients about cycles of abuse (Figure 2.2). By developing a four-phase cycle, the four universal needs and the four aspects of self can be readily adapted.

The "pretends-to-be-normal" phase of the cycle represents the universal need for belonging and the spiritual self. When a client is in this phase of the cycle, basic life areas are not being managed and problems are ongoing. The client is likely to be withdrawn from others and his spiritual self is not developed.

In the "build-up" phase of the cycle, the client is engaging in a variety of risk factors, lapses, and maladaptive coping responses. The emotion self is not healthy and the client mismanages emotions, often leaving him- or herself with feelings of anger, rejection, low self-esteem, and so on. The universal need for mastery is malfunctioning as the client continues to lose control of his life, thoughts, feelings, and behaviors. The client is out of control and seeking to gain control over people or situations by acting out.

The "acting out" phase of the cycle is the sexual abuse behavior, or other mal-

Figure 2.1
The Four Universal Needs, Aspects of Self, and Core Values and Beliefs

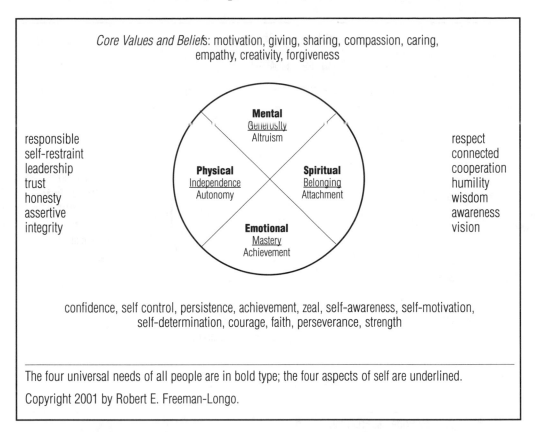

Core Values and Beliefs: motivation, giving, sharing, compassion, caring, empathy, creativity, forgiveness

responsible
self-restraint
leadership
trust
honesty
assertive
integrity

Mental
Generosity
Altruism

Physical
Independence
Autonomy

Spiritual
Belonging
Attachment

Emotional
Mastery
Achievement

respect
connected
cooperation
humility
wisdom
awareness
vision

confidence, self control, persistence, achievement, zeal, self-awareness, self-motivation, self-determination, courage, faith, perseverance, strength

The four universal needs of all people are in bold type; the four aspects of self are underlined.

Copyright 2001 by Robert E. Freeman-Longo.

adaptive/problematic behaviors such as anger/aggression or substance abuse. The universal need for independence is not met as the client needs a victim in order to act out his feelings and problems. The physical self is acting irresponsibly. The ongoing life problems, and the continual engaging in risk factors and lapses ultimately ends up in the client's acting out.

The "justification phase" of the cycle, or the "downward spiral," represents the universal need for generosity and the mental self. During this phase the client is engaging in denial and other defense mechanisms and the mental self is dominated by unhealthy thoughts and cognitive distortions. There is good reason in the mind of the client to defend himself and cover up what he has done. The need for generosity is replaced with a selfish impulse to protect the self and the client takes from others, if he engages others at all; he does not give or share. At this point the client becomes a closed system focusing on self preservation. Communication with others shuts down or the client engages in lying, storytelling, blaming others, and justifying his behavior.

This chapter promotes the use of a holistic model in the assessment and treatment of sexual abuse and its application to juvenile and adult sex offenders. The holistic model described takes into account the fact that (1) people progress through various

Figure 2.2
The Acting-Out or Abuse Cycle

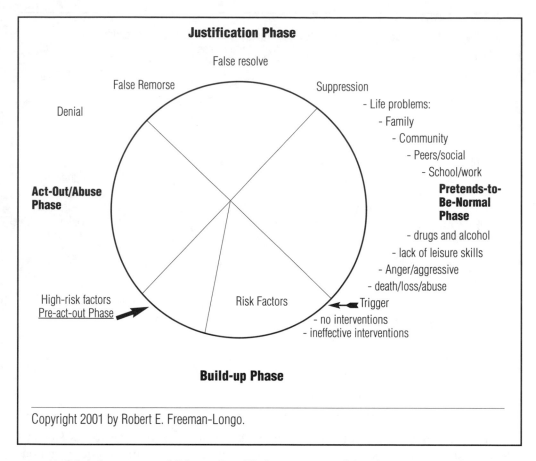

stages of development and life stages, (2) these stages of development are often arrest-ed as a result of trauma, child abuse and neglect, attachment and bonding disorders, and other life issues, (3) humanistic approaches and a focus on developing a thera-peutic relationship with these clients are essential to the healing and recovery process, (4) people learn and work with a variety of learning styles and multiple intelligences, and (5) many traditional assessment and treatment approaches in working with sexu-al abusers can be modified if necessary. Traditional sex offender models and treatment modalities can be blended into a holistic model that addresses the wide variety of problems these clients have when entering treatment as well as the sex-offending problems for which they have been referred.

Etiology of Sexual Aggression and the Use of Holistic Treatment

There are various theories regarding the etiology of sexual aggression. Some are more plausible than others, but each has its case examples. What we do know is that there is no identifiable single cause for sexual aggression, and thus there are no simple solutions for prevention. Sexual abuse is a complex issue that requires a multi-modality approach to treatment. Simply treating sexual abusers by addressing only their sexual behavior will not be effective in addressing the plethora of problems they have which lead to their problematic behavior.

Some of the most widely cited theories regarding the etiology of sexual abuse (Ryan & Lane, 1997) include the following:

1. Addiction theory: that sexually abusive behavior is the result of the addiction process.

2. Attachment disorders: that sexually abusive behavior is the result of unhealthy development and an interruption or failure to attach and/or bond to significant others.

3. Cognitive theory: that sexually abusive behavior is the result of early unhealthy thinking or the development of a criminal personality.

4. Developmental/contextual: that sexually abusive behavior is the result of child abuse/neglect.

5. Family systems theory: that sexually abusive behavior is the result of the family environment and generates sexual misconduct.

6. Intrapsychic conflict: that sexually abusive behavior is the result of childhood trauma that generates intrapsychic conflicts (Freudian theory).

7. Learning theory: that sexually abusive behavior is the result of learned behaviors that result in sexual acting out (the most widely accepted theory within the field).

8. Physiological/neurological/hormonal: that sexually abusive behavior is the result of sexual offenders being born with a disorder that leads to the behavior and that they are raised to be this way.

9. Psychosis: that sexually abusive behavior is the result of a major psychiatric disorder (this accounts for less than 8% of all sexual abusers).

Despite many theories and the absence of psychological literature or proof of these theories, we should acknowledge that for many clients one or more of these theories may play a significant role in the etiology of their sexually abusive and aggressive behaviors.

Holistic Treatment and Wellness

What is holistic treatment? Although many often think otherwise, holistic treatment is not a new age fad but, rather, a traditional approach to healing and wellness. In regard to the treatment of juvenile and adult sex offenders, holistic treatment is a model that incorporates and modifies, yet moves beyond, the traditional cognitive-behavioral and RP models used by the majority of programs. It uses a variety of traditional and alternative treatment methods and techniques that explore and incorporate a variety of models to improve one's overall mental and physical health and recovery.

In addition, it uses a balance of theoretical and humanistic knowledge that embraces the concept that the therapeutic relationship is the focal point of treatment and essential to the treatment process if it is going to influence the client. A holistic model also focuses on cultures and cultural differences. It recognizes that traditional Western mental health models and traditional models and treatment modalities developed to work with sex offenders are important but not exclusive to the treatment process.

Holistic treatment focuses on wellness. When we label others by their behavior or with a particular diagnosis, we potentially brand them for life. We see this most clearly with psychiatric diagnoses. People become know as bipolar, pedophiles, mentally ill, and so on. The clearest example I can think of in regard to the field of treating sexual abusers is the saying "shooting oneself in the foot." In the field of sexual abuse I use a similar analogy that I refer to as "the double barrel shot to the feet." Back in the late 1970s, when I entered this work, I heard two statements that I found problematic: (1) "all victims of sexual abuse are damaged for life," and (2) "sex offenders cannot be cured." Unfortunately, we continue to hear these statements today, even in the face of scientific literature that tells us otherwise. These statements label victims and abusers as people who are damaged for life and not treatable. Both statements and labels are messages of "no hope" for the persons who wear them. In the case of sexual abusers, especially those who have been abused, the labels can be devastating—a message telling them that in addition to being damaged for life, they will not be responsive to treatment.

We know from some sources in the literature that as many as 20 to 25% of child victims of sexual abuse who enter treatment emerge into adulthood with little or no residual trauma. We meet adults who have been sexually abused who are thriving today and have happy healthy and productive lives (D. P. Orcutt, personal communication, November 13, 2000). If we work in this field long enough we are blessed with the opportunities to meet women and men who have been sexually abused and/or brutally raped as children or adults and have worked through the horrific trauma of these experiences and go on to celebrate life.

We know from our clinical experience and the experience of other professionals that many sexual abusers go on to lead productive, happy lives after going through treatment. There are literally hundreds of thousands of sexual offenders who have been through specialized treatment programs and live productively and happily in our communities. Yet when we treat adolescent and adult sexual abusers, we are often guilty of making statements to them that victims are damaged for life and sex offenders cannot be cured. In fact, youth with sexual behavior problems are more likely to reoffend, if they reoffend, in nonsexual offenses (Center for Sex Offender Management, 1999).

Most adolescent sexual abusers and a significant percentage of adult sexual abusers have experienced childhood abuse and/or neglect. Therefore, we must ask ourselves: What messages are we giving them when we talk about lifelong damage and no cure? These powerful statements are debilitating and do not give clients a sense of hope and potential for recovery any more than do the statements we give people with medical problems and illnesses that they have a debilitating or terminal illness. Holistic treatment has a focus on wellness with messages of hope. It gives clients a clear message that they can heal, that they can go forward, and that they are human beings worthy of respect and dignity.

A Return to Basics

Holistic or integrative treatment, in the simplest of terms is a return to basics. It focuses on looking at the four domains or aspects of self: mind, body, spirit, and the emotional self (see Figure 2.1). In addition, a holistic model addresses the four universal needs for generosity, belonging, mastery, and independence (Brendtro, Brokenleg, & Van Bockern, 1990). The need for generosity is the need for people to give and share of themselves. This is not a giving of materialistic goods but, rather, a giving and sharing of time, of one's feelings, and oneself. The need for generosity is our need to give to others unconditionally, to help others, to be supportive, and to offer our help because we care about people. We cannot give that which we do not have (love, empathy, etc.).

The need for belonging transcends all cultures and societies. Human beings are social animals with a need to belong to a family, a community, a society, and a country, and the need to feel connected to the universe. The lack of belonging leaves one feeling isolated and lonely and intimacy suffers. Our spiritual self begins to die. Within our families, communities, and groups to which we may belong (church groups, service organizations, and prosocial organizations) we learn to respect others and we develop many of our core values and beliefs. Even members of gangs who are violent and often engage in acts of violence against others and destruction of property describe their gangs as "family."

The need for mastery is essential for personal growth and learning. Each of us has a need to feel we have the courage and strength to master tasks from the simple to the more complex. We need to feel in control of ourselves and assured that we can master the tasks that will take us through life. As we gain valuable experience in taking on new tasks and challenges, we develop a sense of self-confidence, competency, and completion of projects and tasks that are important to us.

Finally, the need for independence is that need to operate our lives in a fashion in which we are free from dependence on others. This is not to say that we do not need or depend on others from time to time; we all do. However, to depend on others consistently, especially in co-dependent ways, is unhealthy. Assaultive people depend on others, they need a victim. People with healthy, independent selves are being responsible for themselves and assertive in getting their needs met. It is through the achievement of a sense of independence that we learn about trust, honesty, and personal integrity.

The teaching focus of a holistic approach takes into account several core values and beliefs that address the four aspects of self and the four universal needs. These concepts also fit nicely with four leading theories in psychology; altruism, autonomy, attachment, and achievement (see Figure 2.1).

The Core Values

Within the holistic model of treating juvenile and adult sexual abusers, there is a component that teaches clients about core values and beliefs. Sexual abusers enter treatment programs because they have been damaged and need to heal. The damage, often the result of abuse and neglect, leaves these clients lacking a sense of self. They often do not identify strengths but generally are able to recite the many weaknesses they see in themselves. Thus, part of the therapeutic journey entails their learning to recognize their strengths and build on them as well as teaching them healthy values common to cultures and societies and belief systems that reject the notion that they are worthless, that no one cares, that the world is evil and not a safe place.

In Figure 2.1, the characteristics in the outside of the circle are values and beliefs that coincide with the four universal needs and the four aspects of self. Of course, they are not exclusive to each area but represent areas of learning and development to make up the "whole" person. They are not unique to a holistic model and many are concepts taught in programs which treat sexual abusers. For example, inasmuch as trust and honesty are essential for one to develop a healthy sense of independence, these two values are equally important in developing relationships that foster a sense of belonging and connection to others as well as a belief in oneself.

Each value and belief can be used to develop and enhance the client's potential to use the multiple intelligences that help him learn and grow personally. In most cases, the professional is struck with the resistance of clients to adopt these values and beliefs while letting go of the destructive ones they have harbored since their earliest years.

The Danger of Labeling

It is important when looking to a holistic model for treatment to be sensitive to the individual's culture, race, and spirituality. A holistic model addresses and includes *all* life issues and strives for balance and harmony. It sees the whole person as made up of many parts: family, friends, community, work, school, love/care, death and loss, leisure activities and hobbies, anger problems, substance abuse, intimate relationships, and so forth (see Figure 2.3). Holistic treatment sees each person as unique yet does not label. In the field of treating sexual abusers, clients are often called and labeled "sex offenders." Many programs often require clients to open a group by taking turns saying, "My name is _____ and I'm a sex offender. I . . .," similar to addictions models such as Alcoholics Anonymous. Negative labels do not help people heal but, rather, reinforce their staying in the unhealthy state such as "sex offender" for life. A holistic model does not view people as their label or their behavior but, rather, sees them as humans first with a particular problem or problems (Freeman-Longo & Blanchard, 1998).

The Theory of Multiple Intelligences

Holistic treatment seeks to bring a variety of theories and models into the treatment process to enhance a person's potential. For example Gardner (1983), noted for his work on multiple intelligences, teaches us that people have a variety of learning styles and abilities and suggests there are seven learning styles common to people: (1) intrapersonal intelligence, (2) interpersonal intelligence, (3) visual/spacial intelligence, (4) verbal/linguistic intelligence, (5) logical mathematical intelligence, (6) musical /rhythmic intelligence, and (7) body/kinesthetic intelligence.

Intrapersonal intelligence involves knowledge of the internal aspects of the self, such as knowledge of feelings, the range of emotional responses, thinking processes, self-reflection, and metacognition (a sense of our intuition and awareness of spiritual

Figure 2.3
"The Person as a Whole"

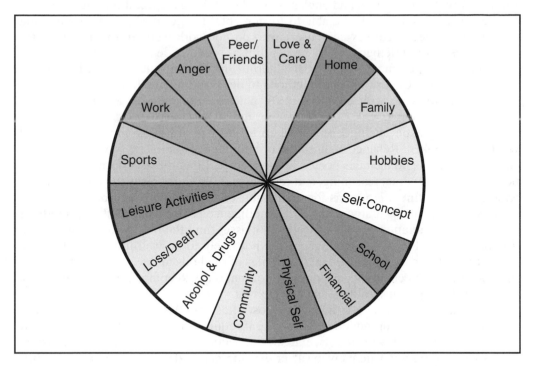

realities). It allows us to step back from ourselves and watch ourselves as outside observers. It involves our capacity to experience wholeness and unity, to discern patterns of connection with the larger order of things, to perceive higher states of consciousness, to experience the lure of the future, and to dream of and actualize the possible. One facet of the treatment of sexual abusers is to develop this intelligence in order to promote the client's ability to cultivate relationships, feel empathy, and work on unhealthy thinking patterns. If this intelligence is not developed as a part of treatment, there is less likelihood that cognitive restructuring and emotional growth will realize their fullest potential as part of the treatment process. Most certainly, the failure to develop this intelligence will affect attachment and the ability to form meaningful relationships. Examples of methods to develop this intelligence include teaching silent meditation/reflection, thinking strategies, emotional processing, focusing/concentration skills, and complex guided imagery.

Interpersonal intelligence involves the ability to work cooperatively with others in a group as well as the ability to communicate verbally and nonverbally with other people. This intelligence builds on the capacity to notice distinctions among others (e.g., contrasts in moods and temperament). Thus, interpersonal intelligence operates primarily through person-to-person relationships and communication. When this intelligence is used, the therapeutic relationship can be extremely powerful in teaching clients and supporting them through the treatment process. Examples of methods to develop this intelligence include giving and receiving feedback, intuiting other's feelings, cooperative learning strategies, practicing empathy, collaboration skills, and group projects.

Visual/spatial intelligence deals with such things as visual arts (including painting, drawing, and sculpture), and games which require the ability to visualize objects from different perspectives and angles (e.g., chess). Visual/special intelligence relies on the sense of sight and being able to form mental images/pictures in the mind and to visualize objects. For sexual abusers who do not work well with verbal/linguistic intelligences, this intelligence can be a primary mode of learning and assimilating information. Experiential therapies are helpful in working with those who use this form of intelligence. Examples of methods to develop this intelligence include guided imagery, working with color schemes, patterns and designs, art therapies, and working with pictures.

Verbal/linguistic intelligence is related to the use of words and language, both written and spoken. Reliance on this kind of intelligence dominates most Western educational systems and includes poetry, humor, storytelling, the use of metaphors, symbolic thinking, abstract reasoning, and reading and writing. This is the intelligence on which most treatment programs for sexual abusers rely, as they incorporate a variety of reading and writing assignments. This intelligence is also used in sit-down individual and group therapies, psychoeducational classes, and the like. Sexual abusers who do not learn well with this intelligence are not likely to do well in treatment or may even drop out of or fail in treatment. Examples of methods to develop this intelligence include reading, vocabulary development, journal/diary keeping, creative writing, use of humor, impromptu speaking, and storytelling.

Logical mathematical intelligence is most often associated with what is known as "scientific thinking," or inductive reasoning. It requires the capacity to recognize patterns, work with abstract symbols, and see connections between separate and distinct pieces of information. Clients who suffer developmental delays and learning disabilities often do not rely on this form of intelligence for learning. Examples of methods to develop this intelligence include outlining, number sequences, calculation, problem solving, and pattern games.

Musical/rhythmic intelligence encompasses such capacities as the recognition of rhythmic and tonal patterns, including sensitivity to various environmental sounds, the human voice, and musical instruments. Of all forms of intelligence, the "consciousness altering" effect of music and rhythm on the brain is probably the greatest. Examples of methods to develop this intelligence include teaching rhythmic patterns, vocal sounds and tones, music composition, percussion vibrations, humming, singing, and music performance.

Body/kinesthetic intelligence is related to physical movement and the knowing/wisdom of the body, including the brain's motor cortex, which controls bodily motion. This intelligence relies on the ability to use the body to express emotions, to play a game, and to create new products. It is "learning by doing." Examples of methods to develop this intelligence include folk/creative dance, martial arts, physical exercise, mime, and experiential therapies such as drama therapy and role playing.

In addition, Daniel Goleman (1995) in his book on emotional intelligence teaches us that EQ (emotional quotient) plays an equal if not greater role than does IQ (intelligence quotient) in the way people relate to and treat each other. Successful people often have an equal or greater level of emotional intelligence than intellectual intelligence.

Wellness as a Whole

Holistic treatment uses a "wellness" approach, and looks at the "whole" person, not at damaged parts. It pushes personal growth while noting that one's problems are a "part" of the whole, not the whole person. Holistic treatment is a strengths-based model that seeks to find what one can do—"approach goals." This model contrasts with a deficit-based model (looking at the person's weaknesses alone), which addresses only what one should not do—"avoidance and escape goals"—from the criminal justice/forensic model, which is often focused on punishment. When treating sex abusers, one often cannot avoid using avoidance strategies, therefore, when we suggest to clients that they need to avoid or escape a risk factor we should couple it with positive approach goals—for example, "You need to avoid being around children, so it makes sense to find ways to spend time with peers your age." While looking at the whole person, the holistic model works with all the various components that comprise a human being. There is a focus on the physical part of self instead of viewing the client as a sex offender and focusing on just the genitals. It sees the connection between a healthy physical self and a balanced whole person including a healthy mental, emotional, and spiritual self.

Unlike most sex offender treatment programs in existence today, a holistic model incorporates spirituality into the treatment process. Incorporating spirituality into treatment does not necessarily mean engaging clients in organized religious activities, although that may be the path many clients choose to develop their spiritual self. In a more global sense, addressing the client's spiritually means that as professionals we need to address the client's need for "belonging," his yearning, sadness, and so on, which are a part of one's spirituality. The spiritual self is one's connection to others, and for many one's feeling connected to all life.

The holistic model recognizes that to be healthy and to maintain a balanced life, the client must also work on developing his mental self and emotional self. These two parts of the whole can only be healthy when the physical self is healthy and the two combined make up a healthy spiritual self. The unhealthy mental self feeds denial systems, and when one is unhealthy these unhealthy thoughts support the client's cognitive distortions and distorted thinking processes. Most programs for sexual abusers address thinking errors, but they must also be sure to develop and enhance the client's healthy thinking process using a strengths-based approach.

The emotional self is probably one of the most difficult aspects of self to heal and maintain in a healthy fashion. Most programs have a treatment component that addresses teaching empathy, but there is more to healthy emotions than the ability to have empathy for victims. In fact, to have empathy for others means one must first have empathy for oneself, an aspect of treatment often overlooked by specific sex-offender treatment programs. A holistic model teaches clients about feelings, how to recognize feelings in oneself and others, and how to express one's feelings and uses a variety of modalities to help clients explore their feeling self.

Transforming Power

We live in a world that is based on personal power Often power and control over others is a dynamic that is apparent in the majority of sex offenses committed by clients. It is a world that at times appears to be divided into two core groups of people, the "oppressors" and the "oppressed." Holistic treatment avoids the "oppressor" and "oppressed" dichotomy. As sexual abusers, and often people who have been abused physically, sexually, and emotionally and neglected, our clients experience both sides of this dichotomy. At the time before offending, they often feel powerless, out of control, and in some cases controlled by others, or assigned the role of the oppressed. During the commission of a sexual offense, the client often feels a sense of being powerful and in control as the oppressor. Upon entering treatment, the client is now placed in a position of being the oppressed once again. The holistic model attempts to level the playing field or relationship between the client, program, and program staff by seeing the client as an equal partner in the treatment process.

Holistic treatment does not ignore societal influences that perpetuate sexual abuse but helps the client understand and manage ways to live with them. Again, our cultures and societies look down on those who commit these crimes and sees them as bad and evil persons deserving of punishment and to be deprived of the rights of others. Holistic treatment is nonjudgmental and nonpunitive. It teaches that respect and empathy are critical components. If professionals do not demonstrate empathy and respect, they serve as poor role models for clients. Empathy in the therapeutic relationship is critical and continues to hold the client accountable and responsible for his or her behavior and choices in life. However, it does so with respect for clients and seeing them as human beings first and then as persons with an unhealthy lifestyle in need of repair. It teaches clients that they are healthiest when they have power and control over their own lives, not the lives of others.

The Therapeutic Relationship in the Holistic Model

Holistic treatment sees a healthy therapeutic relationship as the foundation of good treatment and essential to the healing process. It supports a mutual relationship of give and take and learning. According to Blanchard (1998), a healthy therapeutic relationship consists of the following components: trust, compassion, self-disclosure, humor, respect, congruence, equality, authenticity, vulnerability, warmth, and a willingness to attempt to understand the client's emotional condition and life situation with a concern for his or her growth and happiness.

We live in a world that abhors violence. It is a society that sees others as their behavior, their identity being defined by an image of what they do, and not as humans with problems. Even in the field of mental health we can become calloused to the point of losing respect for the people we treat, and this is more likely to occur when we work with those who are violent and harm others. As professionals we must monitor our own values, beliefs, and biases. We must be vigilant in keeping ourselves free of biased and angry thoughts about those we treat. It does not mean that we accept the behavior of our clients but, rather, that though we may despise their behavior, we respect the person and offer understanding and compassion while holding him accountable for his behavior.

To facilitate the therapeutic relationship and maximize the potential for both therapist and client to learn and grow there must be elements of trust, compassion, and respect for the client. The client must experience the professional as genuine and caring and supportive yet challenging of unhealthy ways. We as professionals must be authentic in the relationship while being ourselves so that warmth and understanding come across. When there is an act of kindness, true healing will occur.

Holistic Treatment as a Process

Holistic treatment is process oriented and looks at the Gestalt. It is interactive and experiential, not something we do *to* clients but rather a process of change, growth and healing that we experience *with* clients. It facilitates change while including goals, and the process/journey is equally as important. Both the client and the therapist grow and learn through the process. It recognizes the client's need for a connection to others and the community. It incorporates a wellness plan focused on wellness activities in each of the four aspects of self—mental, spiritual, emotional, and physical. Traditional sex offender treatment is structured and directive, focuses on target goals (often negative behaviors), and thus is very goal oriented. This type of treatment has the potential to isolate the client. Prevention plans are focused on avoidance, escape, and managing risk factors.

Wellness plans use approach goals with a focus on healing and self-improvement. Although wellness plans may suggest avoidance of certain behaviors or activities, these restrictions are always followed by what the client should do to change the behavior into a healthy one. For example, a wellness plan (Ellerby, 1999) may incorporate the following:

- How to maintain *emotional* health and balance to stay well and manage risk:

  - Be more aware of how you experience feelings, both yours and what you observe in others.

  - Explore your feelings so you can better understand them and where they are coming from.

  - Avoid overreacting to situations. Learn to respond with appropriate assertiveness.

- How to maintain *mental* health and balance to stay well and manage risk:

  - Challenge irrational thoughts.

  - Try to keep in harmony with your head, heart, gut, and environment.

  - Avoid "all or nothing" thinking, be flexible.

- How to maintain *spiritual* health and balance to stay well and manage risk:

  - Participate in spiritually related activity (meditation, church, meetings, etc.) regularly.

  - Take time for yourself.

  - Realize what you can control and what you cannot control. Give what you can't control to God or a higher power.

- How to maintain *physical* health and balance to stay well and manage risk:

  - Continue on medications you are taking.

— Do not isolate or withdraw, seek others for companionship and activities.

— Keep active, spend leisure time wisely, exercise regularly and take care of your physical health.

— Eat on a regular and healthy basis.

It must be noted, however, that holistic treatment recognizes that some individuals are damaged to the point that the holistic method may be difficult for them to use, or they may not be willing to use it. Like any other model in mental health, some clients will offer resistance or be reluctant to engage in any type of therapy. It may be that this model will not work with persons assessed and determined to be psychopathic personalities.

Implementing a Holistic Treatment Approach With Sexual Abusers

This section further suggests areas to address in the treatment process. The first step in treatment is to give the client a general orientation to the treatment program and to review what is expected of the client while in treatment. This section also reviews program rules, homework expectations, general conduct, writing of an autobiography, and so on.

A major component of working with youth with sexual behavior problems is family work. Family work and/or the improvement of peer relationships and intimate relationships is critical for adults as well. Although some clients may have families that are unavailable or unwilling to participate, whenever possible the family should be included in the treatment process and family treatment should be conducted routinely.

Sexual abuse results from a variety of problems that include cognitive distortions and unhealthy thinking. Cognitive restructuring is essential to the treatment process to counter those thoughts that feed low self-esteem, violent impulses, anger, denial, and the many problems with which the client is faced. Cognitive restructuring is critical in the development of empathy. This work should also address dispelling unhealthy family beliefs and values and other myths that may exist about sexual abuse.

Most sexual abusers entering treatment programs suffer from a lack of or deficit of healthy emotions. Like unhealthy thinking, unhealthy emotions serve as a block to developing empathy. Helping clients develop a healthy emotional self should include learning about feelings and how to recognize them in oneself and in others, emotional expression, and empathy training and development.

Personal victimization work is a necessary component of any treatment program for sexual abusers. As noted previously, the majority of sexual abusers entering such programs have experienced childhood abuse that may be psychological, verbal, physical, sexual, or a combination of abuses. More often than not these abusive incidents and periods of a person's life play a direct role in the abuse the person heaps on. Programs should provide clients with the opportunity to work on personal abuse issues with the hope of achieving some level of resolution.

No sexual abuser comes into treatment without anger problems. If one examines the cycle of abuse (Figure 2.2), it is evident that anger is occurring in the pretends-to-be-normal phase of the cycle and continues to be prevalent throughout the cycle.

Anger management and positive assertiveness are critical to developing a healthy self. Anger management should include work with developing self-esteem, teaching situation perception training, and teaching clients relaxation techniques.

Sexual abusers need to learn a variety of techniques that help them cope with problems and intervene in destructive cycles of behavior. This part of treatment should focus on positive goal setting and managing risk factors and should provide clients opportunities to practice the coping responses and interventions they are learning. Interventions and coping responses should be realistic, and there should be a likelihood that the client will use them. The professional should never accept an intervention at face value, no matter how good it looks on paper or sounds, until the client has demonstrated the ability to use the intervention consistently.

The fact that sexual abusers have committed sexually abusive acts is reason to address healthy sexual behavior during the course of treatment. Teaching clients about human sexuality is a more detailed and laborious process than simply providing them with a class in sex education. Healthy sexuality curriculums should include information on sexual anatomy of both men and women, sexually transmitted diseases, contraception and disease prevention, male and female roles in sexual relationships, what constitutes consent (including legal age requirements), what constitutes healthy sexual practices (including foreplay, various forms of intercourse, and the variety of sexual practices in which people engage), deviant sexual practices, fantasy work, and dating skills. The information taught should be age appropriate for youth and adolescents.

As noted earlier, a holistic model includes working with clients to develop healthy values and belief systems that parallel those of society in general.

The majority of programs treating sexual abusers teach clients about cycles of abuse and/or relapse prevention. These models help clients integrate knowledge that sexual abuse is not only about behavior management but also includes emotional and intellectual processes that contribute to the cycle of abuse and the relapse process.

When treating clients in a residential setting, transition planning and community living strategies are essential to the client's eventual success. Transition planning should begin the first day of treatment and should include where the client will live, aftercare treatment, family work, working with the client's work/school, establishing healthy peer relations, and developing a community support system. Many programs require clients to develop a community living plan and wellness plan (Freeman-Longo, 2001).

Integrating Experiential Treatments

Because the holistic model includes a variety of approaches and integrates them within the context of treatment while taking into account individual client differences in development and learning style, various experiential therapies should be used in the treatment process. There are too many experiential treatments and therapies to address given the limited scope of this chapter; however, such treatments and therapies deserve mention and endorsement regarding their use in working with sexual abusers. Only trained and experienced clinicians should engage clients in such therapies; they can be powerful interventions which generate extreme cathartic experiences. Therefore, caution must be exercised when using these therapies, especially in outpatient programs where follow-up care cannot be readily given to clients who are emotionally engaged. A variety of experiential treatments can be used with sexual abusers. The more common ones include role plays, drama therapy, art therapy, music therapy, and exercises to build trust and explore family issues.

Conclusion

Holistic treatment with sexual abusers is quickly growing in its acceptance within the field. We have come to recognize that adult sex-offender-based treatment methods and models have serious shortcomings and potentially negative implications in regard to their application to youth with sexual behavior problems. The adult field is also looking more closely at the work it is doing and looking for more comprehensive approaches while recognizing shortcomings in the RP model and in using strictly cognitive-behavioral techniques.

Youth are resilient and have a tremendous capacity to recover from trauma and childhood experiences and problems that have resulted in serious behavioral problems. In working with youth we must understand that they are not miniature adults and our work with them must take into account developmental and contextual issues as well as learning differences and learning disabilities. Adults are not too old to change, learn, and grow. If we take into account cultures, customs, learning styles, and the use of integrated treatment methods we can be equally if not more effective.

Holistic treatment means treating the whole person not just a particular problem. All too often programs treating sexual abusers view the client in the context of the referring problem. They see the client as a sex offender instead of a person with many parts, of which sexually abusive behavior is only one aspect. Visualize a circle cut into sections much like a pie (see Figure 2.3). If we were to look at the person solely as a sex offender, the circle would have no slices. A holistic approach sees the person as a circle with many parts or slices (as a pie would have) and one of those slices is the sex-offending part of that whole person. The other slices of the pie would include such parts as family, peers, community, school, hobbies and leisuretime interests, sports, dating, and more.

When we see the whole person as a person with many facets, many of which are damaged parts, we are better able to understand the nature of what we must treat and the complexities of doing so. Each part that is damaged needs to be repaired and given the time and opportunity to heal.

References

Blanchard, G. (1998). *The difficult connection:Therapeutic relationship with sex offenders* (rev.). Brandon, VT: Safer Society Press.

Brendtro, L., Brokenleg, M., & Van Bockern, S. (1990). *Reclaiming youth at risk: Our hope for the future.* Bloomington, IN: National Education Service.

Burton, D., Burton, D., Smith-Darden, J., Levins, J., Fiske, J., & Longo, R. E. (2000). *1996 nationwide survey of treatment programs & models: Serving abuse reactive children and adolescent & adult sexual offenders.* Brandon, VT: Safer Society Press.

Carich, M. A. (1999). In defense of the assault cycle: A commentary. *Sexual Abuse: A Journal of Research and Treatment, 11*(3), 249–251.

Center for Sex Offender Management. (1999). *Understanding juvenile sexual offending behavior: Emerging research, treatment approaches and management practices.* Silver Spring, MD: Center for Sex Offender Management.

Development Services Group. (2000). *Understanding treatment and accountability in juvenile sex offending: Results and recommendations from an OJJDP Focus Group.* Paper prepared for Office of Juvenile Justice and Delinquency Prevention Training and Technical Assistance Division, Bethesda, MD 20814.

Ellerby, L. A. (1999, September 24). *Holistic approach to treating sexual abusers.* Workshop at the 18th annual conference of the Association for the Treatment of Sexual Abusers, Lake Buena Vista, FL.

Freeman-Longo, R. E., Bird, S., Stevenson, W. F., & Fiske, J. A. (1995). *1994 nationwide survey of treatment programs & models: Serving abuse reactive children and adolescent & adult sexual offenders.* Brandon, VT: Safer Society Press.

Freeman-Longo, R. E., & Blanchard, G. T. (1998). *Sexual abuse in America: Epidemic of the 21st century.* Brandon, VT: Safer Society Press.

Freeman-Longo, R. E., & Pithers, W. D. (1992). *A structured approach to preventing relapse.* Brandon, VT: Safer Society Press.

Gardner, H. (1983). *Frames of mind: The theory of multiple intelligences.* New York: Basic Books

Goleman, D. (1995). *Emotional intelligence: Why it can matter more than IQ.* New York: Bantam Books.

Knopp, F. H., Freeman-Longo, R. E., & Stevenson, W. F. (1993). *Nationwide survey of juvenile & adult sex offender treatment programs & models, 1992.* Orwell, VT: Safer Society Press.

Knopp, F. H., Rosenberg, J., & Stevenson, W. F. (1986). *Report on nationwide survey of juvenile and adult sex-offender treatment programs and providers, 1986.* Orwell, VT: Safer Society Press.

Knopp, F. H., & Stevenson, W. F. (1989). *Nationwide survey of juvenile & adult sex-offender treatment programs & models, 1988.* Orwell, VT: Safer Society Press.

Laws, D. R., Hudson, S. M., & Ward, T. (Eds.). (2000). *Remaking relapse prevention with sex offenders: A sourcebook.* Thousand Oaks, CA: Sage.

Longo, R. E. (2000, April 6). *Revisiting Megan's law and sex offender registration: Prevention or problem* [On-line]. Available: http://www.appa-net.org.)

Longo, R. E. (2001). *Paths to wellness.* Holyoke, MA: NEARI Press.Maletzky, B. M. (1998). Defining our field II: Cycles, chains, and assorted misnomers. *Sexual Abuse: A Journal of Research and Treatment, 10*(1), 1–3.

Ryan, G., & Associates. (1999). *Web of meaning: A developmental-contextual approach in sexual abuse treatment.* Brandon, VT: Safer Society Press.

Ryan, G., Lane, S., & Rinzler, A. (Eds.). (1997). *Juvenile sexual offending: Cause, consequences, and correction.* San Francisco: Jossey-Bass.

Ward, T., & Hudson, S. M. (1996). Relapse prevention: A critical analysis. *Sexual Abuse: A Journal of Research and Treatment, 8*(3), 177–200.

Chapter 3

The Role of Attachment in Sexual Offending— An Examination of Preoccupied-Attachment-Style Offending Behavior

Liam E. Marshall, B.A.(Hons.) and W. L. Marshall, Ph.D.

Overview

The etiology and maintenance of sexual offending has long been the focus of psychological research. Early psychological theorists such as Freud, Krafft-Ebing, and Ellis have all put forth theories meant to explain rape and child molestation as subsets of deviant sexual behaviors (Smallbone, 1998). More recently, Marshall and Barbaree (1990) presented a comprehensive account of the etiology of sexual offending. They have attempted to explain sexual offending in terms of biological influences, sociocultural factors, and developmental experiences. A critical component of Marshall and Barbaree's theory is the childhood experiences of future sexual offenders that lead to the development of vulnerability. Elsewhere we have outlined a developmental explanation of the etiology of the vulnerability that Marshall and Barbaree see as crucial in explaining sexual offending behavior (Marshall & Marshall, 2000). A key component of this vulnerability is the childhood attachments of future sexual offenders to parents or guardians and subsequent attachment behavior in adult relationships. This chapter explores the role of attachment style in the development of sexually aberrant behavior.

Introduction

Attachment theory describes the propensity of humans to make strong affectionate bonds with others and explains the emotional distress caused by unwanted loss or separation (Bowlby, 1976). Attachment behavior describes the behavior of an individual in relation to an attachment figure. The attachment figure is the person we seek out for comfort when we are distressed, anxious, or frightened. The primary attachment figure in childhood is usually a parent; in adulthood it is a romantic partner or a close friend. These attachment relations are based on who we would most like to be with when we feel distressed, and not necessarily on the attachment figure's ability to help. Attachment behavior is believed to be relatively stable throughout the lifespan (Bretherton, 1985; Scharfe & Bartholomew, 1994). Indirect evidence of attachment stability is generally believed to be shown through reports of similar distribution of percentages of attachment categories in young adults, adolescents, and children.

Development of Attachment Theory

Childhood Attachment. Attachment theory has grown in four stages. The first stage began when John Bowlby identified the importance of mother-child bonds in the 1950s. Bowlby noticed that some of the juvenile thieves with whom he was working lacked feelings for other people. After further investigation, Bowlby found that these juveniles had not had the opportunity to develop any close attachment relationship in their early childhood. At around the same time, Harry Harlow (1958) was examining contact comfort in rhesus monkeys. He found that baby rhesus monkeys sought out their mothers not just for food and warmth, but also for contact-comfort independent of the need for food and warmth. From this it has been assumed that the human child's desire for mother contact-comfort is an innate need and the basis of the infant's first attachment.

Although Harlow only examined monkeys, his research lent credence to Bowlby's claims and created a climate favorable to the acceptance of his theory. Erik Erickson (1950) also understood the importance of caregiver attachment and comfort as evidenced by his belief that an infant's first social achievement is the willingness to let his or her mother out of sight without undue anxiety or anger. A limitation to Bowlby's theory, however, was the lack of a method to empirically validate mother-child attachment. The second stage, then, was the development in the late 1960s of the "Strange Situation" test by Mary Ainsworth (Ainsworth, Blehar, Waters, & Walls, 1978).

The Strange Situation procedure involved putting a mother and child in a playroom. Then, a stranger would enter the room and interact with the mother and then approach and adjust his or her behavior to the child's as the mother inconspicuously left the room. The mother would then reenter the room and comfort the child and then leave again. During the second separation the child is left alone. The stranger then reenters the room and matches his or her behavior to the child's. The mother then returns to the room and interacts and picks up the child while the stranger leaves. The researchers observe the infant's behavior during the experiment and base the quality of the mother-child attachment on the following criteria: (1) active play and exploration in the caregiver's presence; (2) how enthusiastic the greetings are when the child is not distressed; (3) the effectiveness of contact when the infant is distressed; and (4) the presence or absence of anger, petulance, and physical contact when the infant is distressed.

Based on this research, Ainsworth et al. (1978) described three styles of attachment: secure, anxious/ambivalent, and avoidant. A securely attached child is characterized by autonomy and confidence, which reflects a strong attachment bond with the caregiver. Anxious/ambivalent children are characterized by feelings of inadequacy and fears of abandonment. An anxious/ambivalent child has an interpersonal style that is often termed "clingy." Avoidant children's attachment style is characterized by a lack of interest in others and may even be rejecting of their caregiver. A fourth category, disorganized/disoriented, was added in the 1980s to classify maltreated infants who did not fit into the other categories. Research has shown these childhood attachment styles to be highly consistent and predictive of the way individuals will relate to others many years in the future (Ainsworth, 1989).

Adult Attachment. The third stage of attachment research focused on relationships between adults and began with the development of the Adult Attachment Interview. This research resulted in the identification of four principal categories of adult attachment which have been theoretically and empirically related to corresponding infant attachment categories (Main, 1996). Thus researchers were able to examine attachment patterns in adolescents and young adults in a reliable way.

Dimensional Model of Attachment. A fourth stage is the development of a further model of adult attachment by Kim Bartholomew (1990). She conceptualized adult attachment in a two-dimensional four-category typology that is based on the individual's inner-working model of self and others. The inner-working model of others is based on whether others are perceived as likely to respond in times of need; the inner-working model of self is based on whether the person views him- or herself as someone who is likely to elicit assistance from others in times of need. These inner-working models, then, concern whether the person views others as capable of being loving and themselves as worthy of being loved and capable of eliciting love from others. Clearly, a model of this type has implications for the development of relationship skills, intimacy, and self-esteem.

Bartholomew (1990) classifies adult attachment patterns as either secure or insecure. A person with a secure attachment pattern is characterized by a positive view of both self and others. Securely attached persons are comfortable in relationships and typically meet their intimacy and companionship needs satisfactorily.

Bartholomew also describes three insecure attachment categories: fearful, dismissive, and preoccupied. Fearful attachment pattern (also known as Avoidant I) is characterized by a negative view of self and others. These people wish to be in relationships but have a distrust of others and a belief that they are not worthy of another's love. Thus, they attempt to establish somewhat superficial relationships that are devoid of intimacy.

Individuals with a dismissive attachment pattern have a positive view of themselves but a negative view of others. They reject the idea of a need for relationships. If they do have relationships, the relationships are superficial and short-lived and are engaged purely to satisfy the dismissive person's immediate needs, often sexual.

A preoccupied attachment pattern (essentially identical to the anxious/ambivalent pattern described in children) is characterized by a negative view of self and a positive view of others. These individuals desperately seek intimacy but are, at the same time, afraid of closeness. As a result, they tend to rush into relationships without due consideration of their compatibility with their partner. Once in a relationship, they are controlling of the level of intimacy and seek approval and affection from their partner. Preoccupied individuals tend to view their worth through their relationships and be smothering of their partners. They tend to have fluctuating but never satisfactory levels of intimacy.

Attachment and Sexual Offending

Research has provided evidence in support of a relationship between poor quality attachments and sexual offending (Marshall & Mazzucco, 1995; Smallbone & Dadds, 1998; Ward, Hudson, & Marshall, 1996; Ward, Hudson, Marshall, & Siegert, 1995). Ward et al. (1995) have proposed that sexual offenders who have a preoccupied insecure attachment style will offend against children where the offender "courts" the child and treats him or her as a lover. The two avoidant attachment styles (fearful and dismissive), Ward et al. suggest, will be associated with more impersonal and even aggressive offending behavior.

Daniel Siegal (2000) has provided evidence in support of neural adaptation to insecure attachment patterns such that the normal behavioral inhibition processes are bypassed. This has significant implications for research on attachment and the etiology of sexual offending. We have elsewhere outlined a proposed theory that puts attachment behavior as a key component in the etiology of sexual offending (Marshall & Marshall, 2000).

Although a relationship between insecure attachment style and sexual offending has been demonstrated, it remains to be seen whether attachment style is related to the manner in which offenders perpetrate their crimes in the ways suggested by Ward et al. (1995). The following study, then, specifically examines one aspect of Ward et al.'s theory, namely, the proposed link between preoccupied attachment style, grooming behavior, and level of coercion used in committing sexual offenses.

Grooming Behavior Attachment Study

The purpose of this study is to examine the relationship between preoccupied attachment style, grooming behavior, and degree of coercion used by sexual offenders in committing their crimes. Specifically, Ward et al. (1995) proposed that sexual offenders who have a preoccupied attachment style will attempt to seek an affectionate relationship with a child whom they can control and who will admire or approve of them. Grooming their victim over time is expected of these offenders. Thus, these offenders avoid the use of physical coercion although they may use bribes of one kind or another. The expected relationships, then, should apply only to child molesters.

Thirty-two males convicted of sexual offenses who were serving time in a federal, medium-security institution completed paper-and-pencil tests as part of a larger battery of assessments. These sexual offenders included sixteen rapists who ranged in age from 26 years to 49 years ($M = 38.11$, $SD = 7.22$) and sixteen child molesters who ranged in age from 22 years to 73 years ($M = 50.64$ years, $SD = 14.94$). The discrepancies in the ages of these two groups is a direct reflection of the typical age ranges of rapists and child molesters in Canadian penitentiaries and has not in our past research influenced our findings (see Marshall, Anderson, & Fernandez, 1999, for a summary of our earlier research).

Attachment style was assessed by two measures that have been used extensively in attachment research (Feeney, Noller, & Hanrahan, 1994): the Relationship Questionnaire (RQ; Bartholomew & Horowitz, 1991) and the Relationship Scales Questionnaire (RSQ; Griffin & Bartholomew, 1994). The RQ is a five-question measure adapted by Bartholomew and Horowitz (1991) from Hazan and Shaver's (1987) three-category attachment measure. Respondents first choose the best match of four sentences that describe the attachment behaviors of the different attachment styles. Next, they rate the degree to which they believe each attachment style, described by the four sentences, matches their own attachment behavior on a 7-point Likert-type scale. Although scales of this type are normally associated with poor reliability (Fraley & Waller, 1998), the RQ has been shown to have satisfactory reliability and validity (Bartholomew & Shaver, 1998).

The RSQ is a thirty-item instrument that less transparently measures attachment style by embedding eighteen questions related to attachment behavior in a longer instrument. There are five questions relating to secure attachment style, five for dismissive, and four each for preoccupied and fearful. This scale has shown good convergent and divergent validity (Griffin & Bartholomew, 1994).

Classification by Style of Attachment

Distribution of attachment style was based on participants being assigned to one of the four possible attachment categories independently for each measure. This discrete classification was accomplished by summing models of self and others and assigning a category based on the method recommended in Griffin and Bartholomew (1994). The participants' "model of self" is derived by summing scores on the secure and dismissive dimensions and subtracting the result from the sum of the scores on the preoccupied and fearful dimensions. "Model of others" is computed by summing scores on the secure and preoccupied dimensions and subtracting the result from the sum of scores on the dismissive and fearful dimensions. A positive model of self and others classifies participants as secure. A negative model of self and others categorizes participants as fearful. A positive model of self and a negative model of others is taken to indicate a dismissive attachment style, whereas respondents with a negative model of self and a positive model of others are categorized as preoccupied.

The extent of grooming behavior was determined by examining official court and police documentation about the offender's offenses. This examination resulted in classifying offenders as having or not having groomed their victims. Grooming was considered to be present when there was clear evidence that the offender had spent time engaging in preoffending behavior that either matched adult courtship behavior or was meant to entice the victim into cooperating with sexual advances. Ratings of degree of violence (0 = no violence, 1 = threats, 2 = force sufficient for compliance, 3 = gratuitous violence) were obtained from the same sources as the ratings of grooming behavior. Two independent judges made both of these ratings, and agreement in both cases was over 90%.

Attachment Style Related to Grooming

Table 3.1 describes the findings concerning attachment styles and grooming behaviors. Chi-square analyses revealed that the offenders classified as having a preoccupied attachment style on the RQ were more likely to engage in grooming behavior than were those offenders reporting other attachment styles on the RQ, χ^2 (1, $N = 32$) = 7.31, $p < .01$. However, the categorizations based on the RSQ revealed no significant differences, χ^2 (1, $N = 32$) = 2.28, $p = .13$.

Chi-square analyses revealed that child molesters were significantly more likely to groom their victims (9 of 16 groomed) than were rapists (1 of 16 groomed), χ^2 (1, $N = 32$) = 9.31, $p < .01$. Offenders using grooming behavior used less force in the commission of their offenses ($M = 1.3$, $SD = 1.16$) than did those offenders who did not exhibit grooming ($M = 2.27$, $SD = 0.70$), t (30) = 2.95, $p < .01$.

Preoccupied Attachment Style Related to Grooming

The results of this study offer support to one aspect of Wardet al.'s (1995) theory of the relationship between attachment style and sexual offending behavior. The first hypothesis, that sexual offenders reporting a preoccupied attachment style would be more likely to engage in grooming behavior than sexual offenders in the other attachment categories, was supported when the measure of attachment style was the RQ. When the RSQ measure of attachment style was used the results did not reach significance ($p = .13$). This, however, may be a result of the low number of participants used in this study.

The hypothesis that sexual offenders with a preoccupied attachment style would be more likely to be child molesters was also supported by the results of this study. In addition, more than half of the child molesters in this study used grooming behavior whereas only one rapist evidenced grooming behavior. Future research would be useful to examine whether the child molesters who exhibit a preoccupied attachment style, grooming behavior, and low levels of coercion are more likely to be incest offenders.

Groomers Rarely Use Force

The results of this study also support the hypothesis that offenders who exhibit grooming behavior would be more likely to use less force in the commission of their offense than offenders who did not groom their victims. The positive view of others seems to prevent the sexual offenders with a preoccupied style from being aggressive in their offending behavior, and instead they court their victims much like a non-offender would court a prospective romantic partner.

Table 3.1
Number of Offenders in Each Attachment Category by Whether They Groomed Their Victim

| | | Attachment Style Based on RQ | | | |
		Secure	Fearful	Preoccupied	Dismissive
RQ measure					
	No	10	2	3	7
Groomed victim					
	Yes	3	1	6	0
RSQ measure					
	No	9	8	2	3
Groomed victim					
	Yes	4	3	3	0

Conclusion

In this study, grooming behavior, type of victim, and a low level of coercion used in the commission of a sexual offense was associated with a preoccupied attachment style. The features of preoccupied attachment style—negative view of self, positive view of others, need to control the level of intimacy, seeking approval and affection from the partner—seem to be related to the choice of victim (children) and the way in which the preoccupied attachment style-offenders get their victims to comply with their sexual demands (grooming).

These findings have implications for the assessment and treatment of sexual offenders. Further research, however, is needed to replicate these findings and to validate the other hypothesized relationships between attachment style and offending behavior proposed by Ward et al. (1995). It is clear form the results of this study, though, that a preoccupied attachment style is associated with a particular style of offending (i.e., grooming and low level of coercion). This knowledge, then, can guide sexual offender therapists to the important aspects of this type of offender, which can then be addressed in the treatment program. That is, if an offender has used grooming behavior and a low level of coercion in the commission of his offense, the therapist may wish to emphasize the enhancement of self-esteem and enhance understanding of relationship issues such as intimacy and the importance of getting to know a prospective partner before committing to a relationship.

References

Ainsworth, M. D. S. (1989). Attachments beyond infancy. *American Psychologist, 44*, 709–716.

Ainsworth, M. D. S., Blehar, M. C., Waters, E., & Walls, S. (1978). *Patterns of attachment: A psychological study of the Strange Situation.* Hillsdale, NJ: Erlbaum.

Bartholomew, K. (1990). Avoidance of intimacy: An attachment perspective. *Journal of Social and Personal Relationships, 7,* 147–178.

Bartholomew, K., & Horowitz, L. M. (1991). Attachment styles among young adults: A test of a four-category model. *Journal of Personality and Social Psychology, 61,* 226–244.

Bartholomew, K., & Shaver, P. R. (1998). Methods of assessing adult attachment: Do they converge? In J. A. Simpson & W. S. Rholes (Eds.), *Attachment theory and close relationships* (pp. 25–45). New York: Guilford Press.

Bretherton, I. (1985). Attachment theory: Retrospect and prospect. *Monographs of the Society for Research in Child Development, 50,* 3–35.

Bowlby, J. (1944). Forty-four juvenile thieves: Their characters and home-life (II). *International Journal of Psycho-Analysis, 25,* 107–128

Bowlby, J. (1976). Human personality development in an ethological light. In G. Serban & A. Kling (Eds.), *Animal models in human psychobiology* (pp. 27–36). New York: Plenum.

Erikson, E. (1950). *Childhood and society.* New York: Norton.

Feeney, J. A., Noller, P., & Hanrahan, M. (1994). Assessing adult attachment. In M. B. Sperling & W. H. Berman (Eds.), *Attachment in adults: Clinical and developmental perspectives* (pp. 128–152). New York: Guilford Press.

Fraley, R. C., & Waller, N. G. (1998). Adult attachment patterns: A test of the typological model. In J. A. Simpson & W. S. Rholes (Eds.), *Attachment theory and close relationships* (pp. 77–114). New York: Guilford Press.

Griffin, D. W., & Bartholomew, K. (1994). The metaphysics of measurement: The case of adult attachment. In K. Bartholomew & D. Perlman (Eds.), *Advances in personal relationships* (Vol. 5, pp. 17–52). London: Jessica Kingsley.

Harlow, H. F. (1958). The nature of love. *American Psychologist, 13,* 673–685.

Hazan, C., & Shaver, P. (1987). Romantic love conceptualized as an attachment process. *Journal of Personality and Social Psychology, 52,* 511–524.

Main, M. (1996). Introduction to the special section on attachment and psychopathology II: Overview of the field of attachment. *Journal of Consulting and Clinical Psychology, 64,* 237–243.

Marshall, W. L., & Barbaree, H. E. (1990). An integrated theory of the etiology of sexual offending. In W. L. Marshall, D. R. Laws, & H. E. Barbaree (Eds.), *Handbook of sexual assault: Issues, theories, and treatment of the offender* (pp. 257–275) New York: Plenum.

Marshall, W. L., & Marshall, L. E. (2000). The origins of sexual offending. *Trauma, Violence, and Abuse: A Review Journal, 1,* 250–263.

Marshall, W. L., & Mazzucco, A. (1995). Self-esteem and parental attachment in child molesters. *Sexual Abuse: A Journal of Research and Treatment, 7,* 279–285.

Scharfe, E., & Bartholomew, K. (1994). Reliability and stability of adult attachment patterns. *Personal Relationships, 1,* 23–43.

Siegal, D. (2000). *Toward and interpersonal neurobiology of the developing mind: Attachment relationships, mindsight, and neural integration.* Paper presented at the 19th annual treatment and research conference of the Association for the Treatment of Sexual Abusers, San Diego.

Smallbone, S. W. (1998). *The role of attachment insecurity in the development of sexual offending behaviour.* Unpublished doctoral dissertation, Griffith University, Brisbane, Queensland, Australia.

Smallbone, S. W., & Dadds, M. R. (1998). *Attachment and coercive behaviour.* Unpublished report. Griffith University, Brisbane, Queensland, Australia.

Ward, T., Hudson, S. M., & Marshall, W. L. (1996). Attachment style in sex offenders: A preliminary study. *Journal of Sex Research, 33,* 17–26.

Ward, T., Hudson, S. M., Marshall, W. L., & Siegert, R. (1995). Attachment style and intimacy deficits in sex offenders: A theoretical framework. *Sexual Abuse: A Journal of Research and Treatment, 7,* 317–335.

Chapter 4

The Object Relations and Victimization Histories of Juvenile Sex Offenders

by Alejandro Leguizamo, Ph.D.

Overview

    In the past two decades, juvenile sexual offending has increasingly become the focus of empirical study (e.g., Davis & Leitenberg, 1987; Gerber, 1990; Zgourides, Monto, & Harris, 1997). However, the literature has been plagued by poor methodology: small samples, questionable comparison groups, and elusive, poorly defined constructs. Nonetheless, the literature has been able to provide leads regarding the possible etiology of sexually aggressive behaviors. These include, for example, the personal characteristics of juvenile sex offenders (e.g., Davis & Leitenberg, 1987), the role of prior victimization in the life experience of the offender (e.g., Ryan, 1989), and exposure to pornography (e.g., Donnerstein & Malamuth, 1997). Most of the relevant research has been concentrated on male offenders because they constitute the majority of adjudicated sex offenders, roughly 95% to 98% (Camp & Thyer, 1993; Davis & Leitenberg, 1987; Ryan, Miyoshi, Metzner, Krugman, & Fryer, 1996).

    The chapter introduces the reader to object relations theory and its application to sexual victimization and sexual aggression. As an integral aspect of how an individual develops the way in which he or she relates to others, research that considers the attachment styles and social functioning of juvenile sex offenders is also presented. Next, this chapter discusses research on the experience of abuse and neglect of juvenile sex offenders. Subsequently, a research project that explores the object relations and victimization histories of juvenile sex offenders, as compared to non-sexual juvenile delinquents is described. Finally, this chapter considers the utility of applying object relations theory to sexual aggression.

Introduction

Although psychodynamic theory has played an important role in the early conceptualization of sexual behavior and sexual aggression historically, it has not done so in the study or treatment of sex offenders (Gerber, 1990; Schwartz, 1995). The primary criticism of dynamic thought is that it explains sexual offending in terms of fixations, regressions, and identification with the aggressor, concepts that may not have empirical support, and provides no guidance for treatment (Gerber, 1990). Further attempts to use psychodynamic concepts to explain sexual offending have been extremely rare. For example, the only study that could be found in recent years focused on the self-psychology of juvenile sex offenders using qualitative methods (Chorn & Parekh, 1997). However, this study had a sample of only seven sex offenders, some of whom were adjudicated and others who participated in outpatient treatment without having been adjudicated. Nonetheless, other theories derived from psychodynamic thought, such as object relations, may provide a better framework for explaining sexual aggression.

Object Relations Theory Explains Individual's Conceptualization of the World. Object relations theory emphasizes the relationship between the individual and the original object (caretaker) and the influence that relationship has on the individual's social functioning. The relationship between the individual and the caretaker engenders what object relational theorists call object representations. As Blatt, Wiseman, Prince-Gibson, and Gatt (1991) define it:

> Object representations refers to the conscious and unconscious mental structures or schemata—including cognitive, affective, and experiential components—of interpersonal interactions encountered in reality. Object representations can be relatively veridical and reflect consensual reality, or relatively idiosyncratic, expressing unique constructions, or relatively distorted and primitive, suggesting psychopathology. (p. 273)

Initially, the focus of the theory was to think about how the child came to understand and interpret the world. Thinkers in this tradition believed that the child actively gathers information about his or her environment (especially the caretaker) and interprets it in order to understand it the best he or she can, using object representations as templates (Blatt et al., 1991). Later, others emphasized not only the child's view of the caretaker but actually the interaction with the caretaker itself, along with the memories and feelings involved in the interaction (Kernberg, 1976).

Kernberg (1976) argued that as the individual develops, his or her ego becomes more organized. Further, there is a consolidation of structures that forms a sense of continuity of the self, the conception of the world of objects (consistency of interpersonal interactions), and recognition of consistency in interactions in the environment, and environmental recognition (confirmation). Thus, the child begins to have a continuous sense of him- or herself that remains constant through different interactions. Also, the child begins to compile a registry of who other people are and how they interact with him/her. Furthermore, the child is then able to recognize how new people interact with him/her by comparing the essence of the interaction with those encountered before. In other words, as the individual recognizes interactions, these interactions become guideposts for interpersonal relationships, meaning that the individual seeks in the environment what he or she can identify (Stierlin, 1970). Generally, the complexity of these representations of others increases as children develop cognitively; in addition, their understanding of social interactions and social rules become more sophisticated (Westen et al., 1991).

Object Relations Explain Individual's Affective Regulation. Not only does the interaction with the caretaker influence the child's sociocognitive development but it has an impact on his or her affective development as well. Through the interaction with the caretaker, the infant learns to regulate his or her own affective states by responding to the caretaker's encouragement or soothing (Stern, 1985). Infants, Stern argued, develop through affect attunement the knowledge of their own affectivity and sense of self. In other words, the infant depends on the caretaker to regulate the extent to which he or she is exposed to environmental stimulation. Also, the caretaker, being sensitive to the child's needs and responses to the environment, provides soothing when the child becomes overstimulated by the environment and needs to be calmed down. Consequently, the interaction between the caretaker and the child helps the child develop a sense of how to regulate his or her own affective states, when to seek more stimulation, and when to shy away from it to prevent being overwhelmed. That is, the child begins to develop coping mechanisms with which to deal with his or her environment.

Distorted Representations Interact in a Reciprocal Manner. Object relations theory concentrates on what happens to the developing child as the child interacts with his or her caretaker. However, some authors have also considered what the caretaker brings into to the interaction (Fonagy, 1994; Sandler, 1987). Sandler (1987) pointed out that the caretaker's interactions with the child are based on the caretaker's representation of past attachment relationships. In such encounters, the caretaker may modify the representations of the child, making that representation identical to an unwanted aspect of him- or herself. The caretaker may then manipulate the infant to behave in ways that become consistent with the caretaker's own distorted representations of the child. Stern (1985) added that the process works both ways in that the infant may, from time to time, distort his or her representation of the caregiver to deal with unmanageable affect and bring about behavioral reactions in the adult that confirm the accuracy of the mental representation. This model is dynamic in that what children experience as unmanageable is by no means absolute but, rather, strongly dependent on what they perceive to be experienced by their caregiver as overwhelming and unacceptable to them. Gradually, Stern (1985) argued, the child's self-perception may increasingly come to resemble that of his or her caregiver. Consequently, the child's development of representations of others and of the self is shaped by the interactions with the caretaker. However, the caretaker's interactions with the child are in turn shaped by his or her representations of the child and how the child interacted with his or her caretaker.

Trauma Modifies Quality of Object Relations. Throughout the theory, there is an assumption that mental representations of others are the result of the primary relationship and that they are invariant (Fonagy, 1994). However, evidence suggests that representations develop over time (Westen et al., 1991), can change through the course of therapy (Blatt et al., 1991; Schneider, 1990), and may be affected by traumatic events, such as sexual abuse (e.g., Ornduff & Kelsey, 1996). In the case of trauma, it has been noted that the structures which guide perception of events, situations, and people, may become stuck in primitive levels of functioning and may lose their ability to adapt to and change according to the reality encountered in future occasions (Fish-Murray, Koby, & van der Kolk, 1987; Nigg et al., 1991).

Gediman (1991) stated that the victim of abuse must internalize the abuse interaction in order to survive. This internalization may help the child to adapt to the abusive environment, making it as predictable as possible for the child. However, the result is that the survivor's representational world can be seriously affected, for his or her views of him- or herself and others become distorted by dysfunctional scenarios. Consequently, as the child grows up, he or she may continue to perceive and react to situations as if they were potentially abusive, thus distorting the actual perception and interpretation of real events. The key point, then, is that the individual does not internalize the object per se but, rather, the interaction with that object (Bemporad, 1980).

Trauma May Cause Internalization of the Abusive Interaction. Pryor (1996) carried the concept of the internalization of the interaction a step further by writing that, in the case of extreme trauma, the individual internalizes the abusive interaction. His argument, though written with sexually abused children in mind, also seems readily applicable to physically abused and neglected children and adults as well. Pryor (1996) began by stating that there are four basic dynamics that abused children are hypothesized to experience. First, there is a relentless reliving of abusive relationships, either as a victim or as a perpetrator. Second, there is a reliance on identifying with the aggressor as a basic mode of psychological defense, which brings about feelings of guilt. Third, there is an unshakable conviction of being the cause of the abuse, of deserving the abuse, and of being utterly bad. Finally, object contact is sought through physical violence, sexuality, or some combination of the two.

According to Pryor (1996), attempts by the child to integrate the abuse experience engender eight existential dilemmas:

1. I have two choices: to be a victim or a victimizer. Each is unbearable, unlivable.

2. If I am vulnerable, I will live in terror of being abused again. If I identify with the aggressor, I may be safe from retraumatization, but I will have become what I hate most. I will be guilty of doing to others what was done to me, and I will have to take out on myself the rage I feel toward the perpetrator.

3. If I remedy my powerless and passive state by believing I caused and deserved the treatment I received, I have within myself the badness that causes such horrors and the belief that I can make these things happen.

4. I cannot bear to exist alone and unconnected to others. I desperately need human love and contact. But the only way to make real contact with others is through perverse and aggressive ways. My very need for relatedness causes me to be a victim or a victimizer.

5. If I do not internalize the people around me, I am empty. But if I do internalize abusive objects, I have become at the very core of myself that which is evil and destructive. Either I am nothing or I am bad.

6. I originally thought I was good. But since I deserve abuse, I am bad. I do not really know what I am. I do not really know what is real.

7. I hate the abuse. But since the way to have contact with others is through abuse, I want what I hate. I truly am perverse.

8. I am enraged about the abuse I have suffered. But surely this rage is what caused the abuse. And further, people are right to reject or be cruel to me now, because I am so rageful. (pp. 75–76)

Therefore, the child internalizes the abusive interaction and process to play the "role" of either victim or perpetrator. Pryor's (1996) concepts go far beyond the idea of the victimized child identifying with the aggressor only as a way to cope with abuse. For if the child who is abused only identifies with the aggressor, there would be far more female perpetrators, because they are sexually abused more frequently than boys (e.g., Elliot & Briere, 1995). According to Pryor, (1996), an abuse survivor who does not abuse others may play the perpetrator role by further victimizing him- or herself through promiscuous or otherwise risky behavior.

Pryor's (1996) argument applies not only to sexually abused children but also to other forms of child victimization. In physical abuse, there may also be an internalization of the abusive relationship. The nature of the relationship is abusive, regardless of its sexual content. The dynamics of neglect are more difficult to explain using Pryor's concepts. However, it may be possible that the neglected child attempts to connect with the neglecting parent, and the rejection may be internalized as the abusive relationship. Pryor (1996) noted that the child holds on to these "masochistic" attachments for the following reasons:

[They] are so difficult to give up because pain and painful relationships constitute core aspects of the self, without which psychological identity, integrity, and relatedness all dissolve. The child will cleave to his sense of badness and to abusive templates or relationships as a way of preserving that internal pain that conveys the felt presence of the early object. For the child growing up amid pervasive neglect and abuse, the ties to the abusive parent and the bad internal object are paradoxically all the stronger because nothing good has been internalized. Without the tie to the bad object, the child is exposed to near autistic isolation and genuine disintegration of the psyche. (pp. 102–103)

Distinguishing Adaptive From Maladaptive Responses to Trauma. It is unclear, however, how children who have been abused but are asymptomatic function. One could argue that those children do have positive, supportive relationships that ameliorate the impact of the abuse. One also must include the abuse variables here, such as length of abuse, force, and relationship with the perpetrator. It seems that if the child is abused and does not have the chance to make connections with other appropriate attachment figures (relatives, teachers, therapists, etc.), he or she could be at risk of internalizing the abusive relationship. Further, the child's personality must also be taken into account, for perhaps certain personality characteristics could place the child at risk of developing symptoms at a lower level of traumatization. Last, this theory does not explain why the child would develop sexually aggressive behaviors. One would assume that if the child has been sexually abused, he or she would do the same to others to retaliate or to reenact the abusive relationship. However, this is not the case; some sex offenders have not been sexually abused and some non-sex offenders have. Thus, we need to understand what makes the individual aggress sexually.

In sum, object relations theory centers on how individuals internalize their interactions with their caretakers into templates and then apply them to their present relationships. Consequently, to study these templates, we must consider the individual's construction of his or her relationships with caretakers and how the individual perceives his or her interactions with others. To understand how these constructs have been applied to the study of sex offenders, the literature on the attachment styles and social functioning of sex offenders is reviewed. Then, the literature on their victimization history is discussed before the present study is described.

Attachment Theory and Sexual Aggression

This review of the literature regarding the attachment styles of sex offenders concentrates on the adult sex offender literature because there are no studies to date that investigate juvenile sex offenders. Studies about the attachment status of adult sex offenders are reviewed to provide an approximated framework for the present study.

Although the quality of sex offenders' relationships with their caretakers (e.g., parental inconsistency) has been previously studied (Prentky, Knight, Sims-Knight, & Straus, 1989), the nature of the specific attachment styles that adult sex offenders have with their families of origin has not been studied until recently (e.g., Ward, Hudson, & Marshall, 1996). An important aspect of attachment is that it contributes to the individual's ability to regulate his or her emotions (van der Kolk & Fisler, 1994) and its quality may influence the person's interpersonal relationships (Alexander, 1992).

van der Kolk and Fisler (1994) argued that children's ability to regulate their emotions develops as their caregivers help them modulate their physiological arousal by providing a balance between soothing and stimulation, which in turn regulates normal play and exploratory activity. Secure attachments allow children to move back and forth between exploring the environment and returning to their caregivers. As children grow up, they are less likely to become overstimulated or overwhelmed and may be able to tolerate higher levels of arousal. van der Kolk and Fisler (1994) noted that children who have experienced abuse or neglect may lack such coaching and may develop into individuals who are not able to regulate themselves. Thus, when a child is traumatized, his or her ability to identify internal states decreases and may lead to the development of psychosomatic reactions and aggression directed against the self and/or others. Consequently, if the child is not able to use symbolic representations of his or her internal states, it may lead the child to act out those internal states instead of using symbolic representations that would allow for flexible response strategies. In other words, once aroused, traumatized children and adults are presumed unable to postpone their behavioral responses to sensory input by assessing the stimulus appropriately.

Poor attachment can also be the result of prolonged separation, death of a parent, adoption or multiple foster parenting, and emotional rejection (Marshall, 1993). Other authors have also found that insecurely attached children generalize their experience of insecurity in their relationships with others—as expressed by their distrust, suspiciousness, lack of intimacy, and isolation (Cole & Putnam, 1992; Marshall, Hudson, & Hodkinson, 1993), which may persist into adulthood (Marshall, 1993).

Hence, insecurely attached children may grow up unable to regulate their emotions and therefore may be impaired when dealing with strong arousal. They may then act out their emotions, perhaps aggressively, instead of using words to identify and process emotions. Thus, sex offenders with insecure attachments with their families of origin, combined with their own experience of sexual victimization and/or over-sexualized family environments (Becker, 1994; Ryan, 1997), may well become unable to appropriately handle arousal, possibly turning to inappropriate and aggressive sexual expressions.

Marshall (1993) stated that the main vulnerability for offending sexually is alienation resulting from poor attachments. Further, he argues that men who have poor-quality attachments will be poorly equipped to develop relationships with peers. Once they reach adolescence and have to deal with hormonal changes and increased sexual drives, if they do not know how to interact with others, their sexual and aggressive drives may cause frustration and anger. This anger then will cause them to resort to whatever means brings them some degree of relief.

For all these theory-based possibilities, however, the attachment status of juvenile sex offenders has not been studied directly. For example, Koboyashi, Sales, Becker, Figueredo, and Kaplan (1995) found that having a positive bond to mother was negatively associated with adolescent sexual aggression. In addition, Saunders, Awad, and White (1986) found that adolescent rapists experienced more parent-child long-term separations than other youth, which could in turn influence the quality of their attachments. Unfortunately, Saunders et al.'s, (1986) study only did an in-group comparison between adolescent rapists, child molesters, and noncontact sex offenders. Also, the samples used were small, with groups of nineteen, seventeen, and twenty, respectively. Research addressing the attachment status of juvenile sex offenders is clearly needed.

Given the lack of attachment research on juvenile sex offenders, we may look to the sparse research on the attachment status of adult sex offenders (e.g., Ward et al., 1996). The attachment styles of adult sex offenders have primarily been assessed using Bartholomew's adult attachment model (as described in Ward, Hudson, Marshall, & Siegert, 1995). The model includes four types of attachment styles, depending on how the individual views him- or herself and others.

Bartholomew's Attachment Styles. The first is secure attachment, which corresponds to the original secure attachment style (Ainsworth, 1989). Here the individual has a positive regard for him- or herself and for others and thus is able to seek and establish relationships with others.

The second is preoccupied attachment, corresponding to Ainsworth's anxious/ambivalent style. Here the individual has a negative view of the self but a positive view of others and thus seeks approval using a controlling style. These individuals have fluctuating levels of intimacy, which are never satisfactory (Ward et al., 1995). They are typically sexually preoccupied and attempt to meet their strong needs for security and affection through sexual interactions. They can become offenders if they begin to fantasize about a child, see the child as a lover, and think that the child benefits from the relationship and that this relationship is mutual (Ward et al., 1996).

This type of attachment style appears to be more applicable to child molesters who perpetrate against children in the attempt to establish what they believe to be a caring relationship with another person. (For more on the preoccupied attachment style and sexual offenders, see Chapter 3.)

The third category is fearful attachment, corresponding to Ainsworth's avoidant style. Here the individual has a negative view of the self and of others. The individual with this style desires social contact and intimacy but experiences pervasive interpersonal distrust and fear of rejection. The fear of rejection leads these people to seek impersonal contacts with others (Ward et al., 1996).

Finally, the fourth style is dismissive attachment, also corresponding to Ainsworth's avoidant style. Here the individual has a positive view of the self but a negative view of others. These individuals are skeptical of the value of close relationships and place a great deal of value on remaining independent and invulnerable to negative feelings. They are more likely to be actively hostile in their interpersonal style and are likely to seek relationships or social contacts that involve minimal levels of emotional or personal disclosure. Further, they tend to blame others for their lack of intimacy, with their hostility primarily directed toward the gender of their preferred adult partners (Ward et al., 1996). This attachment style appears to be more applicable to rapists, who perpetrate more forcefully against individuals who are of about the same age or older than they are.

Patterns of Attachment Among Sex Offenders. Using Bartholomew's framework, Ward et al. (1996) found that adult sex offenders tend to be insecurely attached. Sixty-nine percent of the rapists and 78% of the child molesters were reported to be insecurely attached. However, violent non-sexual offenders were also insecurely attached (97%). Using the same sample of sex offenders and criminals, Hudson and Ward (1997) studied the relationship between attachment style, intimacy, loneliness, anger, hostility toward women, and acceptance of rape myths. Rape myths refer to those beliefs that place the blame of rape on the victim, such as "no means yes." Hudson and Ward (1997) found significant differences between rapists, child molesters, and violent and nonviolent offenders on all measures. Nevertheless, when group comparisons depended on attachment status, Hudson and Ward (1997) found that subjects with preoccupied and fearful attachments reported feeling lonelier than did other subjects. Further, individuals with fearful and dismissing attachments scored higher on both the expression and suppression of anger than did the other groups. Also, insecurely attached subjects manifested the most hostile attitudes toward women. Further, those who had dismissing attachments were the most accepting of rape myths. The Hudson and Ward (1997) and Ward et al. (1996) studies seem fairly robust insofar as they used a relatively large sample of eighty-five sex offenders and sixty-two non-sex offenders. Further, the measures used in this study were reported to have acceptable psychometrics.

Juvenile Sex Offenders and Social Functioning. Some authors have suggested that emotional loneliness and alienation also may contribute to sexual offending in adult sex offenders (Marshall, 1993; Marshall et al., 1993; Seidman, Marshall, Hudson, & Robertson, 1994). Marshall et al. (1993) theorized that insecure attachment leads to an incapacity for intimacy, which produces painful feelings of emotional loneliness, which may in turn lead to aggressive behavior. Marshall (1993) noted:

> Emotional loneliness sets the stage for aggression and self-serving behaviors to emerge, and make more attractive those social messages (contained, for example, in pornography, but also in other communications) that see other people as objects serving to meet the needs of whoever is willing to abuse them. Sexual offending is one obvious, but not the only consequence of such a history. (p. 114)

Seidman, et al. (1994) conducted two studies of adult sex offenders. They used psychometrically acceptable measures, including a social desirability scale, but had to contend with some missing data. In the first study, Seidman et al. (1994) compared a total of sixty-five outpatient sex offenders with fifteen wife batterers having no history of sexual aggression and eighteen individuals recruited from the community, most of whom were college students. Seidman et al. found that sex offenders reported experiencing less intimacy, more loneliness, and more hostility toward women than did the control groups (batterers and normals). Further, rapists and nonfamily child molesters had the lowest scores on the intimacy measure. These findings were replicated in the second study, using fifty-seven incarcerated sex offenders and forty-one non-sex offenders (twenty-one violent offenders and twenty nonviolent).

This theory may also be extended down the age scale to juvenile sex offenders; they may also be turning to sex in order to fulfill their needs for intimacy and love. Fehrenbach, Smith, Monastersky, and Deisher (1986) reported that 65% of juvenile sexual offenders showed evidence of significant social isolation, 32% reported having no friends, and 34% reported having a couple of friends but none with whom they were close. On the positive side, some evidence suggests that juvenile sex offenders do wish to have better relationships with others; however, they prefer to initiate the interaction and be in control of it, which may lead to lack of acceptance by peers (Ford & Linney, 1995).

These youth may not have the skills to seek appropriate intimate relationships and are afraid of rejection, as that characterized their relationships with their parents. Thus, they may become more interested in impersonal, unaffectionate relationships, beginning with masturbatory fantasies in which the "characters" in the fantasy comply with anything the adolescent wants. Eventually, these youth may cross the line between fantasy and reality and may play out these deviant fantasies with a victim. These experiences may solidify beliefs and attitudes that are self-centered, oblivious to the needs or desires of a partner, and show a preoccupation with physical gratification, which would not foster appropriate intimate relationships and may fail to inhibit tendencies to offend sexually (Marshall et al., 1993).

Adolescent samples of sex offenders have been found to be socially maladapted (e.g., Aljazireh, 1993; Fehrenbach et al., 1986). As noted previously, Fehrenbach et al. (1986) found that two-thirds of juvenile sex offenders in their study showed evidence of significant self-reported social isolation. These children tended to prefer the company of younger peers or adults. One-third reported having no friends, and another third reported having a couple of friends, but none with whom they were close. In fact, rapists reported having no friends more than did any other group. Interestingly, Ford and Linney (1995) found that adolescent child molesters were more likely to initiate interactions in social situations. They preferred to take control of the situations and tried to involve others in interpersonal contact. However, sex offenders may not have the social skills to maintain this contact with others once engaged.

In sum, studies suggest that adult sex offenders are likely to be insecurely attached, which in turn places them at risk of antisocial behavior. In addition, sex offenders exhibit and experience numerous difficulties in social interactions, which leaves them feeling lonely, angry, and not able to establish intimate connections with others. Thus, they may turn to younger, more forgiving peers, who would be willing to accept them despite their social deficits. However, other factors need to be taken into account to understand sexual aggression, particularly those that might have a direct impact on the child's ability to establish nurturing and trusting relationships with others. One such factor is the experience of childhood victimization because it may contribute to (1) a lack of knowledge of appropriate ways to express affection or (2) a recapitulation of traumatic experiences by victimizing another person, particularly younger peers.

Sex Offenders' Experience of Abuse and Neglect. Research on the victimization histories of sex offenders has been prolific (e.g., Fehrenbach et al., 1986; Ryan et al., 1996; Seghorn, Prentky, & Boucher, 1987). The idea that a person who is sexually abused is at risk of becoming a perpetrator has found fertile ground in many theories. Some authors argue that the abused child will repeat what he or she has learned (e.g., Allen et al., 1995). Darke (1990) states that individuals may be seeking the personal power they lost through their own victimization, as aggression may make the perpetrator feel powerful. Other authors note that the individual may be recapitulating his or her own victimization and is identifying with the aggressor (Rogers & Terry, 1984; Ryan, 1989). However, it is difficult to pinpoint what specific consequences the experience of abuse or neglect may have on an individual, as abused individuals tend to experience more than one form of victimization (Friedrich, 1998). Consequently, it becomes imperative to consider sex offenders' histories of sexual abuse, physical abuse, and neglect, for each may be strong a contributor to sexual offending.

Sexual Abuse and Juvenile Sex Offenders. Sexual abuse has been defined as "sexual contact that is accomplished by force or threat of force, regardless of the age of the participants, and all sexual contact between an adult and a child, regardless of whether there is deception or the child understands the sexual nature of the activity" (Berliner & Elliot, 1996, p. 51). Although sexual abuse has been described as common in the history of juvenile sexual offenders (Vizard, Monck, & Misch, 1995), there is a wide variety in the rates reported in the literature. However, most of these rates are higher than those of community samples. For example, Finkelhor, Hotaling, Lewis, and Smith (1990) found that 16% of men in a national telephone survey reported having been sexually abused as children, whereas the rates reported for juvenile sex offenders range from 17% to 57% (mean = 37.36), as presented in Table 4.1.

Generally, it is difficult to approximate the percentage of juvenile sex offenders who have been sexually abused because the problems in the research literature are extensive. Specifically, only three of the studies presented next included a definition

Table 4.1
Rates of Sexual Abuse Among Juvenile Sex Offenders

Study	n of sex off.	Age	Subjects	Comparison group	Comparison group n (% reporting sexual abuse)	Percentage of subjects reporting sexual abuse	Method
Benoit & Kennedy (1992)	100	12–18	Incarcerated sex offenders	In group	—	17	Archival
Fehrenbach et al. (1986)	305	$M=$ 14.8	Outpatient evaluation	None	—	18.8	Self-report
Awad & Saunders (1991)	49	11–16	Rapists (outpatient)	Delinquents Child molesters	24.0 / 45 (.04)	Rapists 2 Molesters 21	Self-report
Cooper et al. (1996)	300	$M=$ 15	Outpatient	None	—	34..2	Self-report, family, or record
Ryan et al. (1996)	1,600	5–21	Various	None	—	39.1	Unknown
Worling (1995b)	29	12–19	Outpatient	None	—	43	Clinical interaction
Truscott (1993)	23	12–18	Court-ordered assessment unit	Violent offender Property offender	51 (13.7) / 79(19)	43.5	Self-report
Spaccarelli et al. (1997)	50	12–17	24 convicted 26 self-reported	Nonviolent delinquents	54 (35.2)	50	Self-report
Zgourides et al. (1997)	80	13–19	Convicted sex offenders	Community Sample	96	57	Self-report

of sexual abuse (Cooper, Murphy, & Haynes, 1996; Spaccarelli, Bowden, Coatsworth, & Kim, 1997; Zgourides et al., 1997). Cooper et al. (1996) and Spaccarelli et al. (1997) provided a thorough definition of sexual abuse that included an age differential between the youth and their abusers and/or instances in which clear force was used. Zgourides et al. (1997), however, only asked subjects whether an adult had touched them sexually. Other studies used small samples (Truscott, 1993; Worling, 1995b). Also, a number of these studies did not include a comparison group (Cooper et al., 1996; Fehrenbach et al., 1986; Ryan et al., 1996 Worling, 1995a), which prevents us from comparing juvenile sex offenders to other populations. In addition, most studies used self-report measures to ascertain whether the subject had been sexually abused (Awad & Saunders, 1991; Fehrenbach et al., 1986; Spaccarelli et al., 1997; Truscott, 1993; Zgourides et al., 1997). Others obtained information about sexual abuse histories through the course of extended evaluations (Worling, 1995a, 1995b). Still others used archival data (Benoit & Kennedy, 1992). Cooper et al. (1996) used a combination of self-reports, family reports, and youth records. Because the accuracy of the rates reported can be affected by the subjects' honesty (in the case of self-report and interviews) and/or the thoroughness of case records, the estimated rates must be regarded with caution. Interestingly, of those studies using self-report measures or interviews, only three included a social desirability scale (Worling, 1995a, 1995b; Zgourides et al., 1997). Nevertheless, studies that had a combination of social desirability measures to control for dishonest answering, used documented cases of abuse, and had an acceptable number of subjects generally report higher prevalence levels of sexual abuse histories.

Aside from poor methodology, other factors may affect these rates. First, the self-reported prevalence of abuse of sexual offenders may increase as these sex offenders undergo treatment, because they may become more comfortable disclosing such information (Worling, 1995a). Thus, rates may vary if the study is done pre-, during, or posttreatment. In addition, the underreporting of sexual abuse by male victims needs to be considered. A number of authors have concluded that males tend not to disclose that they have been victimized (e.g., Black & DeBlasie, 1993), especially when compared to female victims (Finkelhor et al., 1990).

In addition, it is not clear that sex offenders report higher rates of sexual abuse than do other populations because most studies failed to include a comparison group. Of those that did include a comparison sample (Away & Saunders, 1991; Spaccarelli et al., 1997; Truscott, 1993; Worling, 1995b; Zgourides et al., 1997), only Awad and Saunders (1991) and Truscott (1993) found a significant difference in the reported rates of sexual abusers and comparison groups. Specifically, Awad and Saunders (1991) reported that juvenile child molesters had higher sexual abuse rates than did juvenile rapists or delinquents.

In summary, a large percentage of sex offenders do report having been sexually abused in the past. However, not all sex offenders report such histories. In addition, many adolescent non-sexual offenders report having been sexually abused, and they have not committed sexual offenses. Thus, it appears that being sexually abused is not necessarily a precursor or prerequisite for offending sexually. As Watkins and Bentovim (1992) concluded, "current evidence supports the conclusion that the sexual abuse of boys in childhood is an important contributory, but not a necessary, factor in the development of a perpetrator" (p. 221).

Physical Abuse and Juvenile Sex Offenders. The experience of physical abuse in the lives of juvenile sex offenders also varies between studies. Even though it has been given some attention in the literature, physical abuse has taken a secondary role to that of sexual abuse. However, it may play just as important a role in the development of an aggressive style in social interactions. Rates reported range from 21.2% to 43.6%.

Table 4.2
Physical Abuse and Juvenile Sex Offenders

Study	n of sex off.	Age	Subjects	Comparison group	Comparison group n (% reporting sexual abuse)	Percentage of subjects reporting sexual abuse	Method
Cooper et al. (1996)	300	M = 15	Outpatient	None	—	21..2	Self-report, family, or record
Fehrenbach et al. (1986)	305	M = 14.8	Outpatient evaluation	None	—	24.5	Self-report
Awad & Saunders (1991)	49	11–16	Rapists (outpatient)	Delinquents Child molesters	24 (12) 45 (27)	Rapists 33 Molesters 27	Self-report
Benoit & Kennedy (1992)	100	12–18	Incarcerated sex offenders	In group	—	42	Archival
Spaccarelli et al. (1997)	50	12–17	24 convicted 26 self-reported	Nonviolent delinquents	54 (20.8)	43.6	Self-report

Table 4.2 summarizes these rates. Rates of physical abuse in the general population are difficult to obtain, as most studies rely on rates of abuse reported to protective service agencies. Wauchope and Straus (1990), in a study of more than 8,000 families, found that many children experience severe forms of physical punishment (rates peak at 90.5% for 3–4-year-olds; from thereon rates decline steadily).

Studies on the prevalence of physical abuse among sex offenders have many of the same problems as those we reviewed for histories of sexual abuse. Even the task of defining physical abuse is elusive, especially as it is difficult to discern where the boundary between discipline and abuse lies (Kolko, 1996). Most studies of juvenile sex offenders, in fact, do not include a definition of physical abuse. In the present review, only Cooper et al. (1996) and Spaccarelli et al. (1997) included a definition of physical abuse in their studies. The former defined it as any nonaccidental physical injury inflicted on a child by a parent, guardian, or caretaker, whereas the latter defined it as any report of being kicked, bit, hit with a fist, beaten up, choked, threatened with a knife or gun, or actually being assaulted with a knife or a gun. Another common problem in these studies is the exclusion of a comparison group. Thus, it is difficult to know how sex offenders compare to, or differ, from other populations. Further, most studies again relied on self-report measures to ascertain whether the subject had been physically abused.

Of those studies that included a comparison group (Awad & Saunders, 1991;

Benoit & Kennedy, 1992; Spaccarelli et al., 1997), Spaccarelli et al. (1997) found sex offenders to report having been physically abused more frequently than low violence delinquents. However, this difference was not present when sex offenders were compared to high-violence delinquents. The high rate of physical abuse reported by Spaccarelli et al. (1997) is likely due to their detailed definition of what would be considered physical abuse. Studies on the physical abuse of juvenile sex offenders are rare, because most of the sex offender literature has concentrated on adult offenders (who have reported higher rates of physical abuse than do non-sex offenders). For example, Seghorn et al. (1987) indicated that 59% of their sample of adult sex offenders had reported a history of physical abuse.

Neglect and Juvenile Sex Offenders. The childhood experience of neglect in juvenile sex offenders has received little attention in the offender literature. Interestingly, studies of non-sex offenders suggest that neglect might be particularly important in the development of antisocial behavior (e.g., Lemmon, 1996). The most commonly identified form of neglect is physical neglect, which has been defined as a failure to protect from harm or danger and provide for a child's basic physical needs, including adequate shelter, food, or clothing (Erickson & Egeland, 1996). The rates of neglect reported by the literature also vary considerably between studies. Ryan et al. (1996) found that 25.9% of adolescent sex offenders had been neglected. Fifty percent of Seghorn et al.'s (1987) adult sample reported having been neglected when they were children.

Studying Object Relations and Victimization. To assess the object relations and victimization histories of juvenile sex offenders, it is necessary to use as appropriate as possible a comparison group. In the present case, a sample of juvenile delinquents who were adjudicated for nonsexual crimes (hereon, general delinquents) was used as a comparison group.

Three general hypotheses were tested. First, the sex offender group would exhibit more object relations deficits than the general delinquent group. Second, the rates of victimization reported by the sex offender group would be higher than that of the general delinquent group. Third, the relationship between abuse and object relations variables would be explored.

Subjects ($N = 128$) were recruited from the W. J. Maxey Boys Training School, a medium to high security correctional facility in Whitmore Lake, Michigan. The study was explained to the youth in each of their halls. Youth halls at the Maxey Training School are divided into sex offender halls and general delinquent halls. All youth in six sex offender halls and in ten general delinquent halls were invited to participate. For the sex offender sample, only those youth actually adjudicated for sexual offenses were invited to participate.

To screen for nonadjudicated sex offenders in the general delinquent halls, youth were invited to participate only if they were able to provide a positive answer to the following statement: "I'm a person who has never made, forced or coerced anybody to do anything sexual against their will." The statement was presented to the youth when the study was described to the entire hall and individually after they had signed the consent or assent form. Of those invited to participate, seventy-five sex offenders and fifty-three general delinquent youth completed the interview process.

Measures

Interview. Among other things, the interview schedule asked subjects about their general demographic characteristics, the offense for which they were adjudicated, their victimization histories, the number of family disruptions they have experienced, and the extent of their exposure to sexually explicit materials.

Definition of Sexual Abuse, Physical Abuse, and Neglect. To assess whether a subject had been sexually abused as a child, he was asked whether someone forced, coerced, or made him do sexual things when he was under the age of 16. Physical abuse was assessed by asking subjects whether any person or persons had hurt them physically before the age of 16. Neglect was assessed by asking subjects if they had been neglected, as in not having enough food or clothing, before the age of 16.

Bell Object Relations and Reality Testing Inventory. There are only three empirically validated object relations measures to this date: the Social Cognition and Object Relations Scale (SCORS; Westen, Silk, Lohr, & Kerber, 1985), the SCORS–Q (Q-sort version; Westen, 1995), and the Bell Object Relations and Reality Testing Inventory (BORRTI; Bell, 1995). The former assess the object relations and social cognition of individuals using projective narratives. Although it can yield rich findings about the psychological world of an individual, the SCORS–Q requires ten Thematic Apperception Test (TAT) or other narrative responses to work effectively. Although this measure was considered for the present study, it would have been impossible to train interviewers in the administration of the TAT, and further, it would have been extremely impractical to include a method that requires a lengthy testing session to an interview schedule that already took about two to three hours to be completed. On the other hand, the BORRTI is a short questionnaire that takes about twenty minutes to complete and can be scored using a computer scoring program. Consequently, the BORRTI was chosen because it is a short paper-and-pencil measure and thus more practical for our purposes.

The BORRTI (Bell, 1995) is a ninety-item true-false scale designed to assess an individual's object relations and reality testing. It was designed for individual pencil-and-paper administration. The object relations scale was first developed by Bell, Billington, and Becker (1986). It consists of four subscales: Alienation, Insecure Attachment, Egocentricity, and Social Incompetence. The reality testing scale consists of three subscales: Reality Distortion, Uncertainty of Perception, and Hallucinations and Delusions. However, for the purposes of the present study, only the object relations scales were used.

The BORRTI has been able to discriminate between adult clinical samples, both in Axis I and Axis II diagnoses (American Psychiatric Association, 1994) and two nonclinical groups (students and community adults) (Bell et al., 1986). In addition, it has been used successfully with adolescent samples, where it has differentiated physically from sexually abused individuals (Haviland, Sonne, & Woods, 1995). Further, it has shown good correlations with several other measures, including the Brief Psychiatric Rating Scale, the Minnesota Multiphasic Personality Inventory (MMPI), the Symptom Checklist 90-R, and the Millon Clinical Multiaxial Inventory (Bell, 1995).

The scales have acceptable Cronbach's alpha coefficients for internal consistency

(Alienation = .90, Insecure Attachment = .82, Egocentricity = .78, and Social Incompetence = .79) (Bell et al., 1986). The overall internal reliability for the measure obtained in the present study was satisfactory (Cronbach's alpha = .78).

The Alienation Scale. The Alienation scale is intended to measure the individual's experience in relationships. Individuals with high scores on this scale (T score of 60 or higher) often experience a basic lack of trust in relationships. These individuals are presumed to have unstable relationships and an inability to make meaningful, gratifying connections with others.

The Insecure Attachment Scale. The Insecure Attachment scale measures the extent to which subjects are likely to be sensitive to rejection and easily hurt by others. Individuals with high scores on this scale (T score of 60 or higher) are believed to experience an intense desire for closeness with others. However, they are presumed to be hypervigilant to any signs of abandonment and to have relationships filled with anxiety, guilt, and jealousy. These individuals do not tolerate separations, losses, or loneliness well.

The Egocentricity Scale. The Egocentricity scale was designed to measure the extent to which individuals view the existence of others in terms of themselves. Individuals with high scores on this scale (T score of 60 or higher) are assumed to take a self-protective and exploitative attitude toward relationships and are likely to be intrusive, coercive, demanding, manipulative, and controlling.

The Social Incompetence Scale. The Social Incompetence scale is intended to measure the extent to which individuals are shy, nervous, and uncertain about how to interact with members of the opposite sex and have difficulties making friends. Individuals with high scores (T score of 60 or higher) are believed to see themselves as socially incompetent. These individuals may tend to view relationships as bewildering and unpredictable. The resulting anxiety that these individuals may feel is usually relieved by avoidance and escape from the interpersonal field (Bell, 1995).

Childhood Trauma Questionnaire. The Childhood Trauma Questionnaire (CTQ; Bernstein et al., 1994) is a seventy-item self-report, 5-point Likert scale instrument developed to retrospectively assess the experience of abuse and neglect in childhood. The questionnaire has appropriate internal consistencies in its four factors: physical and emotional abuse (.94), emotional neglect (.91), sexual abuse (.92), physical neglect (.79). The overall consistency was found to be .95. The measure also has good test-retest reliability (.88) (Bernstein et al., 1994). The present study used the short form (Bernstein & Fink, 1998), which consists of twenty-eight items. The short version yields six scales: sexual abuse, physical abuse, emotional abuse, physical neglect, emotional neglect, and minimization/denial (Bernstein & Fink, 1998). The short version has acceptable internal consistence, reliability coefficients ranging from .78 for physical neglect to .95 for sexual abuse. The short version was validated using adult substance abusers, adolescent psychiatric inpatients, and female members of a health maintenance organization to confirm the initial factor analysis.

The scales used for this project were sexual abuse, physical abuse, physical neglect, and emotional neglect. The scales included in the analyses obtained acceptable reliability coefficients: sexual abuse (.93), physical abuse (.81), physical neglect (.77), and emotional neglect (.87).

Procedure for Acquiring the Data. Trained interviewers dealt with subjects individually. Interviewers were two doctoral students (one in social work and one in clinical psychology), and eleven master's-level social work students. All interviewers completed two eight-hours training sessions. They were familiarized with the interview protocol, trained in interviewing, and coached on how to behave in a secure juvenile facility in order to ensure their own safety and that of the youth. After completing the training process, interviewers observed one of the two doctoral students conduct an interview, following which the interviewers conducted an interview under the observation of one of the two doctoral students. Interviewers were given feedback and either were observed again or were allowed to conduct interviews on their own. Before the interview took place, all subjects went through a consent process in which a consent form was read to them.

Interviews began with general questions about the youth (demographic information) in order to allow subjects to become as comfortable with the interview and interviewer as possible. The interview consisted of questions that were asked aloud by interviewers and questionnaires that the subject completed with a pencil. Sections of the interview where the youth were asked questions aloud and sections where they completed questionnaires were interchanged to make the process as manageable for the subject as possible. All subjects were given the option of having the questionnaires read to them. After a short break, the final part of the interview was administered. It consisted of questions designed to ease the subjects' transition back to their halls. Subjects were asked what they believed to be the most important thing they had learned while at the training school, what they would like their lives to be like in five years, and how they were feeling after answering all the questions. Then subjects were asked whether they wanted to talk to somebody. Ten sex offenders and one general delinquent indicated the wish to talk to their therapist as soon as that person could be available to them. One subject in the sex offender group indicated the need to talk to somebody immediately. This information was conveyed to the youth's staff to ensure that the youth was safe and the youth's therapist was informed.

Demographic Characteristics of the Samples. The two groups did not differ in age.[1] However, they differed significantly in their ethnic makeup. The sex offender sample was evenly divided between Caucasian and African-American subjects. The general delinquent sample, however, consisted mainly of African-American subjects. Table 4.3 presents the ethnic breakdown for both samples.

The samples were comparable in their socioeconomic status.[2] The two groups did not differ significantly in the amount of time they had spent out of their homes or in the number of facilities in which they had been housed.

The samples differed significantly in their living arrangements at the time of the offense for which they were adjudicated.[3] A greater percentage of sex offenders lived at home at the time of this offense (80% vs. 64.2% of the general delinquent sample).

Offense Characteristics for the Sex Offender Group. First, it is important to note that information was gathered only for the offense for which subjects were adjudicated (the offense that had placed the youth in the current facility). Reporting informa-

Table 4.3
Subjects' Ethnicity

	Sex offenders $n = 75$	%	General delinquent $n = 53$	%	χ^2 (df)	p (two-tailed)
African American or black	33	44	39	73.6	16.34 (4)	.003*
Caucasian or white	35	46.7	7	13.2		
Latino or Hispanic	1	1.3	1	1.9		
Native American or American Indian	2	2.7	3	5.7		
Other	3	4	3	5.7		
Refused to answer	1	1.3	0	0		

* $p < .01$.

tion about an offense that was already public allowed the youth to answer questions about it more openly. In addition, it circumvented the necessity of reporting new crimes to the authorities or to protective services.

At the time of the offense for which they were adjudicated, the sex offender sample was, on average 13.3 years old (with a range from 6 to 18). This offense generally involved only one victim (74%) and the youth tended to act alone (83.8%). Almost half of the victims (47.5%) were related to or living with the offender. Also, sex offenders were significantly more likely to aggress against females (67% vs. 33% males).[4] Male and female victims did not differ significantly in age.[5]

The types of sexual acts that were involved in the sexual offense included exhibition (showing sexual parts), fondling (touching sexual parts), and penetration (oral sex or penetration). Most offenses involved a combination of two or more of the above acts. Table 4.4 presents a description of the type(s) of act(s) in which the sex offender sample was engaged.

More than half of the sexual offenses involved some type of force (59.6%). Table 4.5 presents a more detailed description of the sex offenders' modus operandi. Sex offenders used games or tricks and bribed their victims more frequently than they used other methods. Of those who used force in their offense, holding the victim down and hitting the victim with their hand occurred more frequently than other methods of force.

Object Relations. Table 4.6 presents summaries of scores for the BORRTI scales. A multivariate analysis of variance (MANOVA) was performed to ascertain whether the samples differed significantly from one another. Overall, the samples differed significantly from one another.[6] Table 4. 7 presents the post hoc analysis for the object rela-

Table 4.4
Sexual Acts Included in Offense for Which Sex Offenders
Were Adjudicated

Sexual act	Frequency	Percentage
Exhibition alone	2	2.02
Fondling alone	9	9.09
Penetration alone	9	9.09
Exhibition and fondling	11	11.11
Fondling and penetration	24	24.24
All acts	38	38.38
None of the above	6	6.06
Total acts perpetrated by the sex offenders	99	99.99

Table 4.5
Acts Committed by Sex Offender Sample in Order to Subdue Their
Victim(s)

Action taken by offender	Frequency	%
Played games or tricked victim	60	60.6
Offered victim a favor or bribe	48	48.5
Convinced victim to go along	59	59.6
Threatened to hurt victim or somebody else	33	33.3
Held victim down	31	52.5
Tied victim down	2	3.4
Hit victim with his/her hand	20	33.9
Hit victim with an object	5	8.5
Threatened victim with a weapon	10	16.9
Used a weapon on victim	7	11.9
Total no. of crimes where force was used	**59**	**60**
Total no. of acts committed by sex offenders	**99**	

Notes. Frequencies and percentages based on the total number of offenses. Frequencies and percentages based on a total of 59 offenses where force was used.

Table 4.6
Object Relations Scores

BORRTI scale	Sex offenders n = 75			General delinquents n = 53		
	M	SD	Range	M	SD	Range
Alienation	57.13	10.81	30–80	53.13	8.46	36–71
Insecure Attachment	54.49	10.84	30–78	47.91	11.31	30–75
Egocentricity	59.23	11.54	34–80	57.00	11.07	30–80
Social Incompetence	51.72	10.54	30–77	46.81	8.46	30–66

Table 4.7
Post Hoc Analysis of Object Relations Variables

BORRTI scale	$F(2, 125)$	p
Alienation	3.349	.038*
Insecure Attachment	6.056	.003*
Egocentricity	1.4	.251
Social Incompetence	7.248	.001*

$* p < .05; ** p < .01.$

tions scales. Sex offenders scored significantly higher on all scales with the exception of the Egocentricity scale.

Further analyses were performed to ascertain the rates of scores in the clinical range (> 60) and whether these rates differed between the groups. Table 4.8 presents these findings. Rates of scores in the clinical range differed significantly between groups for the Egocentricity and the Social Incompetence scales. Rates approached significant difference for the Alienation scale.

The first hypothesis was substantively corroborated by the findings. On average, sex offenders were found to have higher scores on all scales with the exception of the Egocentricity scale. In addition, they tended to have more scores in the clinical range for the Egocentricity and Social Incompetence scale.

Victimization Histories. Table 4.9 presents rates of victimization for both samples and a comparison of those rates. Sex offenders were found to report having been abused sexually at significantly higher rates than general delinquent youth; however, no difference was found in their reports of neglect, either physical or emotional. Rates of reported physical abuse presented a mixed picture. When rates of physical abuse

Table 4.8
Rates of Scores in the Clinical Range for the Object Relations Variables

BORRTI scale	Sex offenders $n = 75$	General delinquents $n = 53$	χ^2 (1)	p (2-sided)
	n (%)	n (%)		
Alienation	30 (40)	13 (24.5)	3.332	.07
Insecure Attachment	22 (29.3)	9 (17)	2.582	.11
Egocentricity	45 (60)	18 (34)	8.424	.004*
Social Incompetence	17 (22.7)	5 (9.4)	3.820	.05**

* $p < .01$; ** $p < .05$.

Table 4.9
Victimization Rates

Source of the information	Sex offenders $n = 75$	General delinquents $n = 53$	χ^2 (1)	p (2-tailed)
Interview				
Sexual abuse	50 (67%)	11 (20.8%)	27.112	.000***
Physical abuse	62 (84.9%)	38 (71.7%)	3.284	.070
Physical neglect	27 (37%)	20 (37.7%)	.007	.932
CTQ				
Sexual abuse	52 (69.3%)	21 (39.6%)	11.186	.001***
Physical abuse	67 (89.39%)	40 (75.5%)	4.351	.04*
Physical neglect	47 (62.7%)	34 (64.2%)	.029	.86
Emotional neglect	46 (61.3%)	29 (54.7%)	.56	.45

* $p < .05$; ** $p < .01$; *** $p < .001$.

were obtained from the interview schedule, there was no difference between the samples. However, the information obtained from the CTQ self-report indicates a significant difference between the groups. Using this measure, sex offenders again reported significantly higher rates of physical abuse than did the general delinquent youth.

A secondary analysis was performed to ascertain whether rates using the interview and the CTQ differed significantly from one another. For the sex offender group, the rates of physical neglect reported using the CTQ were significantly higher than those obtained in the interview.[7] For the general delinquent group, the CTQ rates were significantly higher than those obtained in the interview for sexual abuse and for

Table 4.10
Relationship and Gender of the Perpetrator of Abuse to the Subject

Perpetrator was	Sexual Abuse		Physical Abuse		Neglect	
	Sex offenders $n = 50$	General delinquent $n = 11$	Sex offenders $n = 62$	General delinquent $n = 38$	Sex offenders $n = 27$	General delinquent $n = 20$
Not related to or living with the subject*	8 (16.3%)	3 (27.3%)	5 (8.1%)	9 (23.7%)	0 (0%)	1 (5.0%)
Related to or living with the subject	31 (163.3)	6 (54.5)	44 (71.0)	24 (63.2)	25 (92.6)	15 (75.0)
Both in the home and someone outside the home	10 (20.4)	2 (18.2)	13 (21.0)	5 (13.2)	2 (7.4)	4 (20.0)
Male	25 (50.0)	5 (45.5)	34 (54.8)	19 (50.0)	3 (11.1)	1 (5.0)
Female	6 (12.0)	1 (19.1)	2 (3.2)	5 (13.2)	6 (22.2)	5 (25.0)
Was abused by both males and females	19 (38.0)	5 (45.5)	26 (41.9)	14 (36.8)	18 (66.7)	14 (70.0)

* One subject refused to answer whether his abuser was related to or living with him.

physical neglect.[8] These findings suggest that general delinquents felt more comfortable answering sensitive questions about their abuse histories using a questionnaire than a face-to-face interview. Concordance rates between the interview and the CTQ were 82% for sexual abuse, 78% for physical abuse, and 54% for physical neglect.

Consequently, the second hypothesis was corroborated for the most part. Using the interview information, the sex offender sample did report significantly higher rates of sexual abuse than did the general delinquent sample. On the other hand, using the CTQ data, the sex offender sample reported significantly higher rates of both sexual and physical abuse. The rates of reported neglect (both types) were not significantly higher for either group using any of the two methods.

Regarding the severity of the abuse, as measured by the CTQ, significantly more sex offenders attained a score in the severe to extreme range for sexual abuse and for physical abuse than did the general delinquents.[9] Thus, sex offenders not only reported greater incidence of sexual and physical victimization than general delinquents but also tended to be abused more severely.

The next analysis reports the relationship between and the subjects and the person(s) who abused them in their childhood, as well as the gender of the perpetrators. Table 4.10 presents these results. Trends suggest that for the three types of abuse investigated, most subjects were likely to be abused by a person who was related to or living with them. In addition, most were likely abused by either a male or both males

Table 4.11
Sexual Acts Perpetrated on the Subjects

Sexual act	Sexually abused sex offenders $n = 50$	Sexually abused general delinquents $n = 11$	$\chi^2 (1)$	p 2-tailed
Exhibition	34 (68%)	7 (63.6%)	.078	.78
Fondling	44 (88%)	9 (81.8%)	.302	.58
Penetration (including fondling)	46 (92%)	10 (90.9%)	.014	.90

and females, as opposed to a female acting alone. In regard to sexual victimization, there were no significant differences in the kinds of sexual acts that were perpetrated against each group. Table 4.11 presents these results.

In addition, the modus operandi of those who abused the subjects in this study was analyzed. This information was analyzed using chi-squared statistics. This method was used to compare the way in which subjects were overpowered by their abusers and whether sex offenders were subjected to more extreme use of force in their abuse.

Three indices were constructed from the modus operandi of the perpetrators of the sexual abuse against the subjects. These indices were coercion by word (convincing, bribing, playing games, etc.), coercion by hand (holding down, hitting with the hand, etc.), and coercion by object (hitting with an object, using a weapon, etc.). The groups, controlling for race, differed significantly from one another in the form of coercion to which they were subjected.[10] Table 4.12 presents the ways in which subjects were coerced by their victimizers. Sex offenders reported having been coerced by word and hand to a significantly higher extent than did general delinquents.[11] A further analysis was performed to ascertain more specific differences. Sex offenders reported having been convinced to comply with the abuser at a significantly higher rate than did general delinquents (68% vs. 36.4%).[12] On the other hand, a significantly higher percentage of the general delinquents reported that the abuser used a weapon on them (37.5% vs. 8.8%)[13]; however, this finding is probably the result of the small number of subjects included in the analysis, as both percentages reflect three subjects per group reporting having been forced to comply via the use of a weapon.

The sex offender sample in the present study was less likely to experience extreme force in their victimization. Instead, they were cajoled or forced into compliance without the use of objects or weapons.

Next, the ages at which the subjects were abused for the first time and the ages at which the abuse ceased were analyzed and compared for the groups (for sexual abuse, physical abuse, and physical neglect). There were only two significant differences between groups. Sex offenders were younger than general delinquents were when their physical abuse and physical neglect ended.[14] The age at which physical abuse and physical neglect began approaches significance (in both cases, in the direction of sex offenders being younger than the general delinquents).

Table 4.12
Type of Coercion Used Against Sexually Abused Subjects by Their Abusers:
Interview Data

Type of coercion	Sexually abused sex offenders $n = 50$	Sexually abused general delinquents $n = 11$	$F(2, 125)$	p 2-tailed
	$M(SD)$	$M(SD)$		
Coercion by word	1.56 (1.46)	.34 (.81)	23.389	.000*
Coercion by hand	1.33 (1.32)	.34 (.85)	9.942	.000*
Coercion by object	.24 (.67)	.17 (.70)	.732	.48

* $p < .001$.

In the next analysis, the frequencies of the various types of victimization are analyzed. Subjects who reported a particular type of abuse in the interview were asked how frequently they had experienced the abuse: every day, every week, every month, or every year or less often. Sex offenders reported having been physically abused on a daily basis significantly more often than did general delinquents.[15] General delinquents, on the other hand, reported having been physically abused every year or less often, at significantly higher rates than sex offenders.[16] The groups did not differ significantly in their reported frequency of either sexual abuse or physical neglect.

Relationship Between Victimization and Object Relations. Finally, the relationship between the different types of victimizations and object relations constructs must be considered. Although it is not possible to test any causal relationships with the present design, the different tendencies between these variables can be analyzed. Table 4.13 presents the correlations between the victimization and object relations variables for juvenile sex offenders, and Table 4.14 does so for general juvenile delinquents.

The abuse variables were related to the object relations variables to a greater extent for the sex offender sample than for the general delinquent sample. The sex offender sample demonstrated a number of significant correlations between the abuse and object relations scores. Surprisingly, sexual abuse scores were related significantly only with the Alienation scores. Physical abuse scores were correlated significantly with scores on the Alienation, Insecure Attachment, and the Social Incompetence scales. Physical neglect scores were significantly correlated only with the Alienation scores. Emotional neglect scores were significantly correlated with the Alienation, Insecure Attachment, and Social Incompetence scales.

On the other hand, for the general delinquent sample there were only three significant correlations. Physical Neglect was significantly correlated with the Alienation and Insecure Attachment scales, whereas the emotional neglect scores were significantly correlated with the Alienation scale.

Table 4.13
**Correlations Between Object Relations and CTQ Variables for
Juvenile Sex Offender Sample**

	CTQ sexual abuse	CTQ physical abuse	CTQ physical neglect	CTQ emotional neglect
Alienation	.215	.316**	.274**	.401***
Insecure Attachment	.171	.319**	.112	.244*
Egocentricity	.172	.142	.119	-.027
Social Incompetence	.230*	.277*	.119	.393***

$* p < .05;\ ** p < .01;\ p < .001$ (2-tailed).

Table 4.14
**Correlations Between Object Relations and CTQ Variables for
General Delinquent Sample**

	CTQ sexual abuse	CTQ physical abuse	CTQ physical neglect	CTQ emotional neglect
Alienation	.067	.171	.296*	.306*
Insecure Attachment	.015	.135	.280*	.183
Egocentricity	.037	-.037	.147	.165
Social Incompetence	.237	.199	.222	.166

$* p < .05$ (2-tailed).

Object Relations and Its Utility in the Study of Juvenile Sex Offending and Childhood Sexual Abuse

Object relations refer to the ways in which people construe mental representations about social relationships. Even though object relations theory has guided our thinking on the effects of childhood victimization on an individual, the present study was the first to include an empirical measure of object relations in a study of juvenile sexual offenders.

Comparison to Previous Research Using Object Relations Constructs. Even though this study was the first to include a measure of object relations, several of the object relational constructs employed have been studied previously. Findings on the

Alienation scale are consistent with the theoretical framework presented by Marshall (1993) and Marshall et al. (1993) for adult sex offenders. These authors suggest that feeling alienated from others contributes to the development of sexually aggressive behaviors. Further, sex offenders' characteristic feelings of isolation and lack of intimacy have been reported for both adult (Seidman et al., 1994) and juvenile samples (Awad & Saunders, 1991; Fehrenbach et al., 1986). Forty percent of juvenile sex offenders in the present study felt significant alienation from others. Fehrenbach et al. (1986) found that 65% of a sample of juvenile sex offenders was found to exhibit significant social isolation from peers. Awad and Saunders (1991) found that one-third of juvenile sexual assaulters and two-thirds of juvenile child molesters reported being socially isolated. The difference between the present study and that of Fehrenbach et al. (1986) may be that the measure used in the present study is thought to index the individual's ability to trust others and consequently have stable relationships not only with peers but also with other people in general.

It appears that the measure used in the present study was able to discern why some juvenile sex offenders experience social isolation. A subset of these youth have a considerable lack of trust of others, which prevents them from forming stable relationships and in turn would prevent them from having opportunities to alleviate their feelings of isolation.

Almost 30% of juvenile sex offenders in the present study were also found to be extremely sensitive to rejection and to be easily hurt by others, as assessed by the Insecure Attachment scale. To date, there are no studies that assess the attachment status of juvenile sex offenders. Thus, it is difficult to place this finding into an existing research context. Nevertheless, this finding is consistent with findings in the adult sex offender literature (as scarce as it is in this area). Ward et al. (1996) found that 77% of a sample of adult sex offenders was insecurely attached. Even though this is a much larger percentage than the 30% found in the present study of juveniles, the difference disappears when the various types of insecure attachment assessed by Ward and his colleagues are considered.

The type of insecure attachment measured in the present study appears to be similar to the fearful attachment style measured by the Relationship Questionnaire (Griffin & Bartholomew, as described in Ward et al., 1995) used by Ward et al. (1996). Fearfully attached individuals tend to experience pervasive interpersonal distrust and fear of rejection. In their study, Ward et al. (1996) found 30% of adult sex offenders to be fearfully attached. This rate is almost identical to that found in the present study for the Insecure Attachment scale of the BORRTI.

A large percentage of juvenile sex offenders in the present study (60%) were found to use relationships to fulfill their own needs and to lack reciprocity in their interactions with others. Although no other study could be located in which this characteristic of juvenile sex offenders had been considered, other authors (e.g., Ford & Linney, 1995) have found juvenile sex offenders, particularly child molesters, to favor initiation and control in their interpersonal interactions. It seems likely that if individuals prefer to control social interactions, they would be likely to place their own needs before those of others and thus to lack the reciprocity needed for appropriate social exchange.

Finally, almost 23% of juvenile sex offenders were found to report having much difficulty in making friends, as well as feeling nervous or uncomfortable when interacting with members of the opposite sex. This finding may underestimate the problems some of the youth encounter when attempting to establish romantic connection with others as the BORRTI only asks about heterosexual romantic relationships. It is possible that a subset of the sample prefers homosexual relationships, in which case some of the questions asked in this study (e.g., "I do not know how to meet or talk with members of the opposite sex") would not accurately reflect their social functioning. Nevertheless, the aforementioned finding is somewhat consistent with that presented by Fehrenbach et al. (1986). These authors found that a third of a sample of juvenile sex offenders reported having no friends.

Findings Regarding the Childhood Victimization of Juvenile Sex Offenders. The rates of victimization obtained here differed significantly depending on the source of information used. These findings contradict the common clinical assumption that interviews are more effective in gathering information than are questionnaires.

Sexual Abuse. The percentage of sex offenders who reported having been sexually victimized in childhood (69.3) was greater than that reported in the literature. The closest figure found in the literature was 57%, reported by Zgourides et al. (1997). This difference may be a result of subjects being more candid than in previous samples, particularly because they had been in treatment for some time before they participated in the interview. On the other hand, subjects in the present study were recruited from the highest security juvenile facility in the state of Michigan. It is likely that our sample represents not only the most dangerous sex offenders but also the most disturbed and victimized. Interestingly, the rate of sexual victimization among general delinquents was similar to those reported by other authors (e.g., Dembo, Deitke, la Voie, & Borders 1987). This finding suggests that for the samples studied in the present study, sexual abuse played a greater role in the development of youth who engaged in sexual offending.

Contrary to the sexual abuse literature, which has stated that males are more likely to experience extrafamilial sexual abuse (e.g., Faller, 1989; Finkelhor et al., 1990; Watkins & Bentovin, 1992), both samples in the present study were more likely to report having been abused by somebody related to or living with them. The impact of being abused sexually at home has long been considered to be greater than that of being victimized outside the home, particularly when the child is abused by a caretaker (Berliner & Elliot, 1996). Although it cannot be said with certainty, subjects who were abused at home may have felt that other adults at home failed to protect them from the abuser, or the adult may not have been supportive when the youth disclosed having been abused. Further, about 20% of sex offenders and general delinquents reported being victimized both inside and outside their homes. In these cases, the youth may have felt that there were no adults around to prevent, or protect them from, the abuse. Consequently, these individuals probably did not receive help from adults in coping with their experience of victimization.

However, almost a third of general delinquents who reported a history of sexual victimization stated that they had been abused outside their homes. These youth may have had more support from their families than other youth who were abused inside their homes, or both inside and outside their homes. Unfortunately, a careful analysis of what impact these factors may have had on the youths' psychological functioning was beyond the scope of this study.

In addition, sex offenders in the present study reported having been abused more frequently than did general delinquents, though the span of time in which both groups were abused did not differ. Interestingly, both samples experienced similar acts in their abuse. In fact, it appears that their reported experience of sexual victimization differed in that more sex offenders were abused, and that the abuse was more frequent than that reported by general delinquents. Also, more general delinquents may have benefited from familial support because their abuse happened outside their home.

Physical Abuse. The rate of physical abuse found for the sex offender sample in the present study was considerably higher than that reported in the literature (e.g., Spaccarelli et al., 1997). Most subjects reported having been physically abused by someone related to or living with them. Perpetrators tended to be male, or a combination of males and females. However, sex offenders were more likely to be physically abused both inside and outside their homes, and to be younger when the abuse occurred, than were general delinquents. Conversely, more general delinquents were physically abused outside of their homes, or abused exclusively by a female.

Although it was not possible to fully assess the impact of physical abuse in this study, many of the issues raised in the "sexual abuse" section apply here, particularly about the facility from which the samples were recruited. Also, it appears that more general delinquents may have benefited from familial support since their abuse occurred outside their home. In addition, since general delinquents were older when the abuse took place, they may have been better equipped physically and psychologically to cope with it, and may have more time to develop appropriate relationship schemas than were sex offenders.

Physical and Emotional Neglect. Sex offenders' experience of childhood neglect has been overlooked in both the juvenile and the adult sex offender literature, which only allows us to make tentative comparisons between this and other studies. Further, the one study found in the juvenile sex offender literature (Ryan et al., 1996) did not differentiate between physical and emotional neglect. Ryan et al. indicated that 25.9% of a national sample of juvenile sex offenders reported a history of neglect. In contrast, 36–62.7% (interview or CTQ, respectively) of sex offenders in the present study reported a history of physical neglect These findings are more similar to those reported by Seghorn et al. (1987) in a study of adult sex offenders. General delinquents also reported a higher rate of physical neglect than that found in the literature (15%, reported by Famularo, Kinscheff, Fenton, & Bolduc, 1990).

There was a dramatic difference between the rates of neglect reported by the youth during the interview and those obtained from the questionnaire. Either many subjects did not consider their experience neglect or what was meant by neglect was not clear to them during the interview. On the other hand, many of the items about neglect on the questionnaire may also apply to poor families (like the subjects') in which resources are scarce and in which the parent or both parents need to work long hours to provide for the family and may not be present when the child needs them. Such experience would be qualitatively different from that of being ignored, insulted, and/or underfed in a household that was financially and physically capable of providing such nurturance.

Family Characteristics. The family lives of the youth included in this study tended to be chaotic, plagued with inconsistent care, frequent disruptions, and multiple forms of victimization. Sex offenders did report a number of family disruptions similar to general delinquents. However, these experiences were related to different problems for each group. For the sex offender sample, as the number of family disruptions increased, the subjects tended to exhibit more problems (e.g., fearing that people around them would abandon them) and to be considerably more concerned with their own needs (rather than those of others) when it came to interpersonal relationships. For these youth, disruptions in family life are paired with the experience of sexual and physical abuse, and neglect.

It was beyond the scope of this study to evaluate whether such disruptions in family life first placed the youths at risk for abuse or whether such experiences continuously influenced each other in a feedback loop. Nevertheless, we can conclude that these youth come from families that experience considerable instability, where abuse is, in many cases, a frequent event.

Theoretical and Clinical Implications

Theoretical Implications. The study and treatment of sexual offenders have concentrated particularly on the ways in which the offenders' cognitive distortions and experience of childhood victimization lead them to offend for the first time and to continue offending (i.e., the cognitive-based offense cycle; Way & Balthazor, 1990). However, object relations theory may provide the underlying context in which the sexual offender develops his views about himself and others and how he develops his style of relating to others. The present study corroborated previous findings that state that the experience of sexual abuse in childhood affects the ways in which children believe social interactions work and their self-reported ability to establish such relationships. Sexually victimized youth reported intense fears that other people will abandon them and thus are quite sensitive to rejection. Further, these youth also reported having significant problems making friends.

Previous object relations arguments (Pryor, 1996), though immensely helpful, do not specifically address all the possible ramifications of the child's internalization of the image of the aggressor in the abuse relationship. Findings in this study suggest that those youth who indeed identified themselves with the aggressor may experience sexual victimization in a way different from those youth who do not internalize the sexualized aspect of the abuse relationship. In other words, youth who experience sexual abuse in childhood, Pryor (1996) argues, may internalize either or both aspects of the abusive interaction; they can identify with the aggressor's role or with the victim's. However, the identification with the aggressor's role may take on different characteristics depending on how the youth was abused. All youth in the present study had exhibited some type of aggressive behavior, whether it was directed toward another person sexually or nonsexually or toward property.

Nevertheless, it appears that youth who were sexually abused more frequently, and who were convinced to participate in the abuse without the use of overt physical force, were more likely to express that aggression in a sexual way. They may have internalized the perpetrator's role because they may have come to believe that they actively participated in the abuse. As Pryor argued, they may think that if such a horrible event happened to them and they actively participated in it, they must be the type of person that engages in such behavior. However, Pryor did not account for the child who experiences general neglect yet only receives attention when being sexually abused. If this attention is received during abuse that is not physically traumatic for the child (i.e., pleasurable), the child, in turn, may learn that the only way to express and receive attention and affection is through sexual means. Even though the child may be confused by the event, it does not mean that the child necessarily perceives the abusive event as negative. Such children may then perpetrate on others as an attempt to befriend or connect emotionally with them.

Children who are abused in a more traumatic fashion, through threats or physical force, may develop the psychology proposed by Pryor (1996). In these cases the child may internalize both aspects of the abusive relationship and might become a perpetrator in order to regain the power that was lost during the abuse.

On the other hand, children who were victimized infrequently, and who were subject to extreme physical force, may internalize the rage from being helpless under the attack from somebody more powerful than they are. However, the role of the abuser may or may not be internalized in a sexualized manner and may concentrate on the aggression exhibited by the perpetrator. These children may then perpetrate sexually against others in a more forceful manner (e.g., peer or adult rape) or may perpetrate nonsexually against others, as, for example, in the case of assaults.

Even though some authors consider sexual behavior problems (in childhood) to be the most evident behavioral manifestation of sexual abuse (Friedrich, 1998; Kendall-Tackett, Williams, & Finkelhor, 1993), it is still not clear why many children who have been sexually abused do not offend against others, either sexually or at all. To answer this issue, Friedrich (1998) suggests that future studies of conduct-disordered youth may need to include sexual perpetration as a variant of that disorder. Such a suggestion raises the interesting issue of why somebody who has not been sexually abused would sexually abuse another person. Perhaps the concept of power should be added to this type of research. It may be the case that sexually offending youth who have no histories of sexual victimization turn to perpetrating as an expression of their defiance to social norms, or as a way to feel powerful by oppressing another person.

These issues bring us to the discussion of two interesting findings from the present study. First, subjects, contrary to clinical expectations, were more candid about reporting a history of childhood victimization when answering questionnaires than when being asked questions directly by an interviewer. Second, sex offenders who stated they had been sexually abused in childhood reported striking differences in the modus operandi of their abusers from the general delinquents' descriptions.

There are several possible explanations as to why subjects were more comfortable answering questions about their abuse histories in a questionnaire than in the face-to-face interview. First, subjects might have been reluctant to admit to the interviewer that had been abused. Most interviewers were young, female social work students; subjects may have worried about what the interviewer would think of them if they admitted to having been abused. Subjects may have thought that they would appear weak to the interviewer, especially if they admitted to having been sexually abused.

Also, subjects may have been trying to avoid the shame of having to talk about their abuse histories.

Second, subjects may have been protecting themselves by not discussing such personal information with somebody they did not know or trust. Some subjects, when the project was described to them, asked if they were going to get "feedback." This meant that they thought the interviewer would comment on what the subject said during the interview, much like a therapy session. Some subjects, then, may have thought that they were going to get "feedback" and decided to avoid it by denying the experience of abuse during the interview. Then, they would answer honestly about their history in the questionnaire because they knew that the interviewer would not see their answers, making the feared "feedback" impossible.

Third, some subjects, particularly general delinquents, may not have considered their experiences as abusive and thus would answer a direct question negatively; however, when asked about specific behavior displayed by their families, the scores they received in the questionnaire would indicate abuse. It cannot be said, with certainty, why subjects were more candid about their abuse histories on the questionnaire. In fact, there may have been many reasons that a particular subject would choose not to answer questions in the interview, and different subjects may have had different reasons for doing so.

What is clear, however, is that researchers need to use a variety of methods to ascertain whether they are obtaining accurate data. If we had not inquired into the subjects' abuse histories with the questionnaire, the rates of abuse would have been quite different. In addition, researchers need to gather data from as many sources as possible (as recommended, among others, by Friedrich, 1998) to cross-validate the information given by subjects. The use of a variety of methods would ensure a greater accuracy in the data gathered. In addition, researchers need to use empirically validated measures for findings across studies to be comparable.

The second remarkable finding was that for those subjects who reported a history of sexual abuse, more sex offenders reported being convinced or talked into complying with the abuse, whereas more general delinquents reported that the perpetrator used a weapon to force them to comply. It could be hypothesized that sex offenders who reported a history of sexual abuse would have experienced a greater degree of force than general delinquents who reported such history.

However, findings suggest that the sexual abuse using manipulation and covert coercion may have a greater impact on the individual's psychology and self-concept. If a young child (the average age when the abuse began for our subjects was age 6) were to be manipulated into compliance by the perpetrator, he or she would not be prepared cognitively to interpret the older perpetrator's behavior correctly. Young children would not be able to detect the underlying motivation of the perpetrator, and if they agree to participate in the abuse, they may come to believe that they were consensual participants of the event. The confusion and guilt may be paired with a sense of even being responsible for the event. Such confusion and guilt may also be paired with an enjoyment of the event (as in the case of fondling), which may lead the child to perpetrate on others as an attempt to express affection.

On the other hand, if the abusive event was physically traumatic, the child may also feel anger toward the perpetrator. This anger, combined with a sense of powerlessness and weakness, may lead the child to perpetrate against others when he or she feels slighted. In other words, when the child feels attacked and powerless, he or she may lash out sexually in order to "defend" him- or herself, feel powerful, and subjugate the other person.

More research is needed to understand the impact of verbally manipulative abuse and its effects on development of self-concept and object relations victims. Further, we also need to study sex offenders who do not report, or do not have histories of sexual victimization, and general delinquents who do report such history, but do offend sexually. In addition, we need to assess the impact of other types of victimization more carefully. Such thorough analyses were not possible in the present study due to time and resource constraints.

Clinical Implications/Prevention Issues. Juvenile sex offenders exhibit a considerable number of difficulties that need to be addressed in treatment. First and foremost, mental health professionals need to be aware that these youth will not trust them and will resist treatment. Not only will they deny their offense, but also unresolved attachment issues will prevent them from being able to establish trusting relationships with others. Therefore, these youth will act out against treatment and will try to sabotage efforts to establish therapeutic relationships with them. Therapists and others working with sex-offending youth need to keep in mind what purpose the youths' acting-out serves for them (to keep others away) and avoid reacting to the youth in ways that prevent the development of therapeutic relationships (lockdowns, restraints, or other forms of punishments). In other words, the youth's acting out should signal the therapist that he or she is getting very close to the youth, and that the youth is becoming uncomfortable with this closeness. Consequently, the therapist can then aid the youth to explore the reasons for these concerns, which may, in turn, allow the youth to develop a deeper relationship with the clinician.

Treatment approaches that teach individuals how to connect with others in meaningful ways may help these youth establish a relationship with the therapist first and then with other people. For example, social skills training groups may help these youth to develop appropriate ways to approach others and to maintain these social connections. Other approaches that focus on the individual's disordered attachments may also foster the youth's ability to establish relationships with others. Even though these approaches have been used mainly with children (e.g., Hughes, 1997), therapists may benefit from assessing whether these methods are helpful to adolescents. In addition, these youth need help in resolving their childhood traumas, not only due to experiences of sexual abuse but also because they are likely to have experienced physical abuse and/or neglect as well. Also, other types of psychopathology need to be identified and treated, as many of these youth suffer from other psychological disorders (depression, anxiety, etc.).

Because sex offenders exhibit a number of difficulties in their experiences of themselves and others in relationships, and because such difficulties may contribute to sexual offending, it may be possible to develop programs that teach children appropriate social skills, which, in turn, may prevent them from becoming sexually aggressive. In addition, measures such as the BORRTI may then be used to assess the child's progress.

Parents and educators also need to be aware of the behavioral expressions of factors that may contribute to the development of sexual aggression. They have to learn the behavioral signs of sexual abuse (social withdrawal, depression, sexual acting out, etc.) in order to identify children who may have been victimized and are in need of treatment. Further, parents and educators need to be able to recognize children who experience considerable problems relating to children their own age, and who seek the company of younger peers. These children's likely sense of inadequacy may lead them to offend sexually if they are made to feel powerless by the younger peers. Then, they may aggress sexually when they become adolescents and do not have same-age peers with whom to interact. Finally, parents and educators need to be aware of the children with whom they interact to be able to discern whether any of them are experiencing difficulties that may require adult intervention, including professional help.

Limitations of This Study

The present study had a number of important limitations. The total sample size, though larger than that of many of the previous studies, was still small. Second, the nature of the samples included in this study limit the generalizability of the findings to broader populations because all were recruited from one facility. In addition, subjects in this study were volunteers. We were not able to assess how accurately they represented the populations we sought to study. Future research needs significantly larger samples to improve their generalizability and should employ multivariate methods.

Further, the generalizability of the findings would also have improved if other samples were included in the study. The inclusion of a community and a clinical (non-delinquent) sample would have greatly enriched the findings of this study by providing information about those samples and about how the juvenile sex offender may differ from youth in the community and in clinical settings. Another way to maximize not only the candidness of the subjects' responses but also the number of subjects that volunteer for research would be to conduct surveys (administering the questionnaire packet to a large group of individuals at the same time) which would ensure complete confidentiality for subjects. This method proved to be more effective in gathering sensitive information in the present study.

Even though we attempted to make sure that the data gathered were as accurate as possible, we had to rely on the honesty of our subjects. The inclusion of a measure of social desirability did ensure that no response biases significantly influenced the model tested. However, to cross-validate the subjects' answers, data should have been gathered from other sources as well. Such a method would have allowed us to confirm that the information obtained during the interview was candid. Future endeavors need to include data gathered from the youths' clinicians, families, and teachers in order to provide as complete a picture as possible of these youth.

Future research is also needed to corroborate the foregoing findings (i.e. replicate) and to continue the work of investigating the development of sexual aggression. The inclusion of object relations measures is warranted by the foregoing findings. However, future studies of adolescent samples may benefit from using the new adolescent version of the BORRTI, for it separates the Egocentricity scale into two scales (Hostile Dependent Egocentricity and Manipulative Egocentricity) and also includes a scale of Positive Attachment (M. D. Bell, personal communication, January 7, 1998).

Research should use multivariate models that allow the assessment of various aspects of juvenile sex offenders and their experiences and how those characteristics and experiences interact with one another. Also, the use of multivariate models allows researchers to study those individuals who do not fit the model.

The present study raises a number of questions that could be addressed in future studies. For example, we need to compare balanced groups of juvenile sex offenders and general delinquents who report histories of childhood victimization and groups of both types of delinquents (sexual and nonsexual) who do not report such histories. Of course, victimization histories need to be validated by other data (records, therapists, etc.). Then, we need to carefully and thoroughly assess the perpetrators' modus operandi, not only for sexual abuse but also for other forms of childhood victimization.

Further, we need to compare the youths' modus operandi (whether or not the offense was sexual in nature) to the modus operandi of those who abused them when they were children. This would allow us to assess whether the youth learned how to abuse or attack others from those who perpetrated against them. Ideally, we would need an objective record of the abuse (i.e., videotapes); however, it would be extremely difficult to gather a sufficiently large sample of youth who were videotaped while being abused as children. In fact, even if we were able to retain such a sample, it would seriously limit the generalizability of the study given the unique characteristics of the sample being studied.

It is recommended that such a study use questionnaire packets that could be administered in a group setting (as opposed to individual administrations). Once the youth completes the packet, he would be able to place it in a box containing other packets, thus ensuring that the researchers would not be able to identify which packet the youth completed. Also, the anonymous nature of the group survey may allow the youths to answer sensitive questions about their histories of victimization more honestly, for they would not have to feel scrutinized by an individual interviewer or to worry about what the interviewers think of them.

Finally, future research should include a measure of personality and psychopathology because it would allow researchers to assess the impact of various experiences on the individual's psychological functioning. Subsequently, we would be able to test what aspects of the youth's experiences and/or psychological functioning contribute to the development of sexual aggression.

Conclusion

This chapter sought to provide information about the utility of object relations theory in the study of juvenile sexual aggression. Its usefulness stems from the concepts it seeks to explain, the interactions between individuals, the way in which the individual conceptualizes such interactions, and the origin of those conceptualizations. In addition, it sought to provide information about the victimization histories of juvenile sex offenders Findings from a research project offered interesting information about how juvenile sex offenders think and feel about relationships as well as a description of their own victimization. Findings generally corroborated previous conclusions presented in literature using similar constructs and signal the usefulness of applying object relational concepts in the understanding of sexual aggression.

Footnotes

[1] $t = -.982$, 124.8df, $p = .33$.

[2] Hollingshead (1957) method ($t = .788$, 126 df, $p = .216$, 1-tailed).

[3] χ^2 (6, N = 128) = 16.15, $p < .05$, 2-tailed.

[4] χ^2 (1, N = 99) = 11, $p = .001$

[5] Age comparison for male and female victims of the sex offender group, (mean age for males was 7.2, $SD = 3.3$, mean age for females was 10.3, $SD = 7.37$), t (84) = -1.70, $p = .092$, 2-tailed.

[6] Wilk's Lambda = .055, F (4, 122) = 528.5, $p < .001$.

[7] χ^2 (1) = 14.87, $p < .001$.

[8] For sexual abuse χ^2 (1) = 21.15, $p < .001$ and for physical neglect, χ^2 (1) = 17.95, $p < .001$.

[9] For sexual abuse, χ^2 (1, $N = 128$) = 18.335, $p < .001$, and for physical abuse, χ^2 (1, N = 128) = 4.506, $p < .05$.

[10] Wilk's Lambda = .926, F (3, 123) = 3.297, $p < .05$.

[11] Coercion by word or by hand, F (2, 125) = 23.4, $p < 001$ and F (2, 125) = 9.9, $p < 001$, respectively.

[12] χ^2 (1, $N = 61$) = 3.84, $p = .05$.

[13] χ^2 (1, $N = 61$) = 4.35, $p < .05$

[14] Comparison of the age in which the subjects' physical abuse ended, t (80.7) = -2.410, $p < .05$, and physical neglect ended, t (38.1) = -2.582, $p < .05$.

[15] χ^2 (1, $n = 100$) = 3.886, $p < .05$.

[16] χ^2 (1, $n = 100$) = 8.804, $p < .01$.

Acknowledgements

The present study was submitted as partial fulfillment for the author's doctoral degree at the University of Michigan. The author would like to thank Eric Bermann, David Burton, Kathleen C. Faller, and Christopher Peterson for their guidance and help. In addition, this project would not have been possible without the help and openness of the staff at the W. J. Maxey Boys Training School, particularly Stacey Frisinger, and the generous financial support from the Office of the Vice President for Research and the Psychology Department of the University of Michigan.

References

Ainsworth, M. D. S. (1989). Attachments beyond infancy. *American Psychologist, 44*, 709–716.

Alexander, P. (1992). Application of attachment theory to the study of sexual abuse. *Journal of Consulting and Clinical Psychology, 60*, 185–195.

Aljazireh, L. (1993). Historical, environmental, and behavioral correlates of sexual offending by male adolescents: A critical review. *Behavioral Sciences and the Law, 11*, 423–440.

Allen, M., D'Alessio, D., & Brezgel, K. (1995). A meta-analysis summarizing the effects of pornography. II: Aggression after exposure. *Human Communication Research, 22*, 258–283.

American Psychiatric Association. (1994). *Diagnostic and statistical manual of mental disorders* (4th ed). Washington, DC: Author.

Awad, G.A., & Saunders, E. B. (1991). Male adolescent sexual assaulters. *Journal of Interpersonal Violence, 6*, 446–460.

Becker, J. V. (1994). Offenders: Characteristics and treatment. *The Future of Children: Sexual Abuse of Children, 4*, 176–197.

Bell, M. (1995). *Bell Object Relations and Reality Testing Inventory manual.* Los Angeles: Western Psychological Services.

Bell, M., Billington, R., & Becker, B. (1986). A scale for the assessment of object relations: Reliability, validity, and factorial invariance. *Journal of Clinical Psychology, 42,* 733–741.

Bemporad, J. R. (1980). Review of object relations theory in light of cognitive development. *Journal of the American Academy of Psychoanalysis, 8,* 57–75.

Benoit, J. L., & Kennedy, W. A. (1992). The abuse history of male adolescent sex offenders. *Journal of Interpersonal Violence, 7,* 543–548.

Berliner, L., & Elliot, D. M. (1996). Sexual abuse of children. In J. Briere, L. Berliner, J. A. Bulkley, C. Jenny, & T. Reid (Eds.), *The APSAC handbook on child maltreatment* (pp. 51–71). Thousand Oaks, CA: Sage.

Bernstein, D. P., & Fink, L. (1998). *Childhood Trauma Questionnaire: A retrospective self-report manual.* San Antonio, TX: Psychological Corporation.

Bernstein, D. P., Fink, L., Handelsman, L., Foote, J., Lovejoy, M., Wenzel, K., Sapareto, E., & Ruggiero, J. (1994). Initial reliability and validity of a new retrospective measure of child abuse and neglect. *American Journal of Psychiatry, 151,* 1132–1136.

Black, C. A., & DeBlassie, R. R. (1993). Sexual abuse in male children and adolescents: Indicators, effects and treatments. *Adolescence, 28,* 123–133.

Blatt, S. J., Wiseman, H., Prince-Gibson, E., & Gatt, C. (1991). Object representations and change in clinical functioning. *Psychotherapy, 28,* 273–283.

Camp, B. H., & Thyer, B. S. (1993). Treatment of adolescent sex offenders: A review of empirical research. *Journal of Applied Social Sciences, 17,* 191–206.

Chorn, R., & Parekh, A. (1997). Adolescent sexual offenders: A self-psychological perspective. *American Journal of Psychiatry, 51,* 210–228.

Cole, P. M., & Putnam, F. W. (1992). Effect of incest on self and social functioning: A developmental psychophathology perspective. *Journal of Consulting and Clinical Psychology, 60,* 174–184.

Cooper, C. L., Murphy, W. D., & Haynes, M. R. (1996). Characteristics of abused and nonabused adolescent sexual offenders. *Sexual Abuse: A Journal of Research and Treatment, 8,* 105–119.

Darke, J. L. (1990). Sexual aggression—Achieving power through humiliation. In W. L. Marshall, D. R. Laws, & H. E. Barbaree (Eds.), *Handbook of sexual assault* (pp. 55–72). New York: Plenum.

Davis, G. E., & Leitenberg, H. (1987). Adolescent sex offenders. *Psychological Bulletin, 101,* 417–427.

Dembo, P., Deitke, M., la Voie, L., & Borders, S. (1987). Physical abuse, sexual victimization and illicit drug use: A structural analysis among high risk adolescants. *Journal of Adolescence, 10,* 13–34.

Donnerstein, E., & Malamuth, N. (1997). Pornography: Its consequences on the observer. In L. B. Schlesinger & E. Revitch (Eds.), *Sexual dynamics of anti-social behavior* (2nd ed., pp. 30–49). Springfield, IL: Charles C. Thomas.

Elliot, D. M., & Briere, J. (1995). Posttraumatic stress associated with delayed recall of sexual abuse: A general population study. *Journal of Traumatic Stress Studies, 8,* 629–648.

Erickson, M. F,. & Egeland, B. (1996). Child neglect. In J. Briere, L. Berliner, J. A. Bulkley, C. Jenny, & T. Reid (Eds.), *The APSAC handbook on child maltreatment* (pp. 4–20). Thousand Oaks, CA: Sage.

Faller, K. C. (1989). Characteristics of a clinical sample of sexually abused children: How boy and girl victims differ. *Child Abuse and Neglect, 13,* 281–291.

Famularo, R., Kinscheff, R., Fenton, T., & Bolduc, S. M. (1990). Child maltreatment histories among runaway and delinquent children. *Clinical Pediatrics, 29,* 713- 718.

Fehrenbach, P. A., Smith, W., Monastersky, C., & Deisher, R. W. (1986). Adolescent sexual offenders: Offender and offense characteristics. *American Journal of Orthopsychiatry, 56,* 225–233.

Finkelhor, D., Hotaling, G., Lewis, I. A., & Smith, C. (1990). Sexual abuse in a national survey of adult men and women: Prevalence, characteristics and risk factors. *Child Abuse and Neglect, 14,* 19–28.

Fish-Murray, C., Koby, E., & van der Kolk, B. A. (1987). Evolving ideas: The effect of abuse on children's thought. In B. A. van der Kolk (Ed.), *Psychological trauma* (pp. 89–110). Washington, DC: American Psychiatric Press.

Fonagy, P. (1994). Mental representations from an intergenerational cognitive science perspective. *Infant Mental Health Journal, 15*, 57–68.

Ford, M. E., & Linney J. A. (1995). Comparative analysis of juvenile sexual offenders, violent non-sexual offenders, and status offenders. *Journal of Interpersonal Violence, 10*, 56–70.

Friedrich, W. N. (1998). Behavioral manifestations of child sexual abuse. *Child Abuse and Neglect, 17*, 523–531.

Gediman, H. K. (1991, Fall). Seduction trauma: Complemental intrapsychic and interpersonal perspectives on fantasy and reality. *Psychoanalytic Psychology, 8*(4), 381–401.

Gerber, P. N. (1990). Victims becoming offenders: A study of ambiguities. In M. Hunter (Ed.), *The sexually abused male* (Vol. 1, pp. 153–175). Lexington, MA: Lexington Books.

Haviland, M. G., Sonne, J. L., & Woods, L. R. (1995). Beyond post-traumatic stress disorder: Object relations and reality testing disturbances in physically and sexually abused adolescents. *Journal of the American Academy of Child and Adolescent Psychiatry, 34*, 1054–1059.

Hudson, S. M., & Ward, T. (1997). Intimacy, loneliness, and attachment style in sexual offenders. *Journal of Interpersonal Violence, 12*, 323–339.

Hughes, D. A. (1997). *Facilitating developmental attachment.* Northvale, NJ: Jason Aronson.

Kendall-Tackett, K. A., Williams, L. M., & Finkelhor, D. (1993). The impact of sexual abuse on children: A review and synthesis of recent empirical studies. *Psychological Bulletin, 113*, 164–180.

Kernberg, O. F. (1976). *Object-relations theory and clinical psychoanalysis.* New York: Jason Aronson.

Kobayashi, J., Sales, B. D., Becker, J. V., Figueredo, A. J., & Kaplan, M. S. (1995). Perceived parental deviance, parent-child bonding, child abuse and child sexual aggression. *Sexual Abuse: A Journal of Research and Treatment, 7*, 25–44.

Kolko, D. J. (1996). Child physical abuse. In J. Briere, L. Berliner, J. A. Bulkley, C. Jenny, & T. Reid (Eds.), *The APSAC handbook on child maltreament* (pp. 21–50). Thousand Oaks, CA: Sage.

Lemmon, J. H. (1996). The effect of child maltreatment on juvenile delinquency among a cohort of low-income urban males. *Dissertation Abstracts International, 58*(02), 0587A.

Marshall, W. L. (1993). The role of attachments, intimacy and loneliness in the etiology and maintenance of sexual offending. *Sexual and Marital Therapy, 8*, 109–121.

Marshall, W. L., Hudson, S. M., & Hodkinson, S. (1993). The importance of attachment bonds in the development of juvenile sex offending. In H. E. Barbaree, W. L. Marshall, & S. M. Hudson (Eds.), *The juvenile sex offender* (pp. 164–181). New York: Guilford Press.

Nigg, J. T., Silk, K. R., Westen, D., Lohr, N., Gold, L. J., Ogata, S., & Goodrich, S. (1991). Object representations in the early memories of sexually abused borderline patients. *American Journal of Psychiatry, 148*, 864–869.

Ornduff, S. R., & Kelsey, R. M. (1996). Object relations of sexually and physically abused female children: A TAT analysis. *Journal of Personality Assessment, 66*, 91–105.

Prentky, R. A., Knight, R. A., Sims-Knight, J. E., Straus, H., Rokous, F., & Cerce, D. (1989). Developmental antecedents of sexual aggression. *Development and Psychopathology, 1*, 153–169.

Pryor, S. (1996). *Object relations in severe trauma.* London: Jason Aronson.

Ryan, G. (1989). Victim to victimizer. *Journal of Interpersonal Violence, 4*(3), 325–341.

Ryan, G. (1997). Sexually abusive youth: Defining the population. In G. Ryan, S. Lane, & A. Rinzler (Eds.) *Juvenile sexual offending: Causes, connections, and correction* (pp. 3–9). San Francisco: Jossey-Bass.

Ryan, G., Miyoshi, T. J., Metzner, J. L., Krugman, R. D., & Fryer, G. E. (1996). Trends in a national sample of sexually abusive youth. *Journal of the American Academy of Child and Adolescent Psychiatry, 35*, 17–25.

Sandler, J. (Ed.). (1987). *Projection, identification, projective identification.* Madison, CT: International Universities Press.

Saunders, E., Awad, G. A., & White, G. (1986). Male adolescent sexual offenders: The offender and the offense. *Canadian Journal of Psychiatry, 31*, 542–549.

Schneider, E. L. (1990, October). The effects of brief psychotherapy on the level of patient's object relations. *Dissertations Abstracts International, 51*(4-A), 1391.

Schwartz, B. K. (1995). Theories of sex offenses. In B. K. Schwartz & H. R. Cellini (Eds.), *The sex offender: Corrections, treatment and legal practice* (Vol. 1, pp. 2-1–2-32). Kingston, NJ: Civic Research Institute.

Seghorn, T. K., Prentky, R. A., & Boucher, R. J. (1987). Childhood sexual abuse in the lives of sexually aggressive offenders. *Journal of the American Academy of Child and Adolescent Psychiatry, 26*, 262–267.

Seidman, B., Marshall, W. L., Hudson, S. M., & Robertson, P. J. (1994). An examination of intimacy and loneliness in sex offenders. *Journal of Interpersonal Violence, 9*, 518–534.

Spaccarelli, S., Bowden, B., Coatsworth, J. D., & Kim, S. (1997). Psychosocial correlates of male sexual aggression in a chronic delinquent sample. *Criminal Justice and Behavior, 24*, 71–95.

Stern, D. N. (1985). *The interpersonal world of the infant.* New York: Basic Books.

Stierlin, H. (1970). The function of "inner objects." *International Journal of Psychoanalysis, 51*, 321–329.

Truscott, D. (1993). Adolescent offenders: Comparison for sexual, violent, and property offences. *Psychological Reports, 73*, 657–658.

van der Kolk, B. A., & Fisler, R. E. (1994). Childhood abuse and neglect and loss of self-regulation. *Bulletin of the Menninger Clinic, 58*, 145–168.

Vizard, E., Monck, E., & Misch, P. (1995). Child and adolescent sex abuse perpetrators: A review of the research literature. *Journal of Child Psychology and Psychiatry, 36*, 731–756.

Ward, T., Hudson, S. M., & Marshall, W. L. (1996). Attachment style in sex offenders: A preliminaty study. *Journal of Sex Research, 33*, 17–26.

Ward, T., Hudson, S. M., Marshall, W. L., & Siegert, R. (1995). Attachment style and intimacy deficits in sex offenders: A theoretical framework. *Sexual Abuse: A Journal of Research and Treatment, 7*, 317–335.

Watkins, B., & Bentovin, A. (1992). The sexual abuse of male children and adolescents: A review of current research. *Journal of Child Psychology and Psychiatry, 33*, 197–248.

Wauchope, B. A., & Straus, M. A. (1990). Physical punishment and physical abuse of American children: Incidence rates by age, gender, and occupational class. In M. A. Straus & R. J. Gelles (Eds.), *Physical violence in American families: Risk factors and adaptations to violence in 8,145 families* (pp. 133–148). New Brunswick, NJ: Transaction.

Way, I. F., & Balthazor, T. J. (1990). *A manual for structured group treatment with adolescent sexual offenders.* Notre Dame, IN: Jalice.

Westen, D. (1995). *Social Cognition and Object Relations Scale: Q-Sort for Projective Stories (SCORS-Q).* Unpublished manuscript, Cambridge Hospital and Harvard University Medical School, Department of Psychiatry.

Westen, D., Silk, K. R., Lohr, N., & Kerber, K (1985). *Object relations and social cognition: TAT scoring manual.* Unpublished manuscript, University of Michigan, Ann Arbor.

Westen, D., Klempster, J., Ruffins, S., Silverman, M., Lifton, N., & Boekamp, J. (1991). Object relations in childhood and adolescence: The development of working representations. *Journal of Consulting and Clinical Psychology, 59*, 400–409.

Worling, J. R. (1995a). Sexual abuse histories of adolescent male sex offenders: Differences on the basis of the age and gender of their victims. *Journal of Abnormal Psychology, 104*, 610- 613.

Worling, J. R. (1995b). Adolescent sex offenders against females: Differences based on the age of their victims. *International Journal of Offender Therapy and Comparative Criminology, 39*, 276–293.

Zgourides, G., Monto, M., & Harris, R. (1997). Correlates of adolescent male sexual offense: Prior adult sexual contact, sexual attitudes, and use of sexually explicit materials. *International Journal of Offender Therapy and Comparative Criminology, 41*, 272–283.

Chapter 5

Locus of Control, Coping, and Sexual Offenders

by Franca Cortoni, Ph.D., Dana Anderson, M.A., and David Bright, B.Sc. (Hons.)

Overview

In this chapter, the authors suggest that locus of control needs to be considered to expand our understanding of the coping styles of sexual offenders and their ability to effectively cope with the problematic life situations that lead to relapse. In the following review, the authors first provide an overview of the concept of locus of control and distinguish it from self-efficacy. Then they examine how locus of control influences coping and review its applicability within the relapse prevention model. Finally, they discuss the implications of locus of control in relation to the treatment of sexual offenders.

Introduction

In recent years, the treatment of sexual offenders has typically involved a relapse prevention approach (Laws, Hudson, & Ward, 2000) that focuses on helping offenders develop more appropriate and effective coping skills (Eccles & Marshall, 1999).

Marshall (1996a, 1996b; Marshall, Anderson, & Fernandez, 1999) suggests that self-efficacy (the belief that one has the ability to produce a desired outcome) and self-esteem (the appraisal of the self) are inextricably linked to the offenders' ability to develop and use more effective coping skills. To that end, this chapter recommends a number of techniques designed to help offenders enhance their self-esteem and self-efficacy and to promote improved mastery in previously lacking coping skills.

Although enhanced self-efficacy appears to improve the ability to use effective coping skills, it may not be sufficient to help offenders learn to cope effectively with the myriad life factors that trigger the pathways to sexual offending. There now is evidence that though the deficits in specific coping skills of sexual offenders are important, the general coping styles of sexual offenders also need to be considered (Cortoni, 1998; Cortoni & Marshall, 1995, 1996; Marshall, Cripps, Anderson, & Cortoni, 1999; Marshall, Serran, & Cortoni, 2000). self-efficacy appears to be situationally determined, and may not generalize to new, and consequently unlearned and unpracticed, situations (Litt, 1988). In fact, whereas Bandura (1977) maintained that self-efficacy is the determinant of behavior change in specific situations, he also distinguished it from the concept of locus of control. Locus of control refers to people's beliefs in their ability to affect life situations and experiences (Rotter, 1966). It is viewed as a dispositional variable that will interact with self-efficacy to determine, depending on the novelty or familiarity of a situation, appraisal of the situation and subsequent coping efforts (Litt, 1988).

Locus of Control and Social Learning Theory

The locus of control construct developed out of the social learning theory movement of the 1950s and 1960s. Social learning theory (Rotter, 1954; Rotter, Chance, & Phares, 1972) is a theory of personality that attempts to integrate two diverse but important trends in psychological theory: reinforcement theories on the one hand and cognitive theories on the other. There are four classes of variables in social learning theory: behavior, expectancies, reinforcements, and psychological situations. In its most basic form, the general formula is that the potential for a behavior to occur in any specific psychological situation is a function of the expectancy that the behavior will lead to a particular reinforcement in that situation and the value of that reinforcement. Stable personality characteristics arise because human beings are constantly abstracting and generalizing so that similarities develop in their responses to classes of situations. The concept of locus of control (Rotter, 1966) is viewed as acquired through past experience. In many cases, people learn that their control of rewards differs across situations. In those situations in which they are uncertain, it is their locus of control that will predict their beliefs about the effectiveness of their own efforts. Locus of control is considered a stable dispositional characteristic of individuals (Rapee, Craske, Brown, & Barlow, 1996).

Locus of control generally refers to the extent to which an individual believes his or her behavior determines specific life events (Lefcourt, 1981; Rotter, 1966; Rotter et al., 1972). According to Rotter's (1966) conceptualization, individuals differ in the degree to which they perceive reinforcement as being contingent upon their behavior. Individuals who believe that reinforcement is a result of their own actions have a high belief in internal control, whereas individuals who believe that reinforcement is the result of random forces have a high belief in external control. Thus, individuals with an internal locus of control tend to believe they are in control of their destinies and are able to cause or influence certain events. Persons with an external locus of control tend to believe that events are caused by factors beyond their control (fate, luck, or powerful others). It is hypothesized that the individual who views events such as job success or educational achievement as a result of his or her actions or within his or her control has a belief in an internal control over life. Conversely, the individual who views similar life events as independent of his or her own actions and more dependent on luck, chance, fate, or powerful others believes in an external control over life. Locus of control may be affected by powerful external life events such as illness or divorce. Use of locus of control theory helps explain shifts in functioning because it correlates highly with powerful external events in the client's life which may temporarily impact upon behavior (loss of job, divorce, illness etc.). The degree to which people view events as within their control can become a dispositional characteristic (Rapee et al., 1996). It is important to note that the terms "internal" and "external" are simple expressive shortcuts and are not meant to imply that a person is entirely one way or the other.

Differences in Individuals Based on Locus of Control

Empirical research supports the validity of the locus of control construct and reveals differences between those individuals with an internal locus of control and those with an external locus of control. In general, research seems to support the notion that people with more of an internal locus of control are better adjusted than those with more of an external locus of control. For example, Benassi, Sweeney, and Dufour (1988) reviewed research studying the relationship between locus of control and depression and found that an external locus of control was associated with higher levels of depression. In addition, an internal locus of control has been associated with better physical health (e.g., Strickland, 1978), and those who report fewer physical symptoms perceive themselves to be in control of their health (Feeney, 1995). Those with an internal locus of control may be more likely to achieve academically (for a review, see Findley & Cooper, 1983). Finally, Wege and Moller (1995) found that ineffective problem solvers reported a more external control orientation than did more effective problem solvers.

According to Lefcourt (1992), internals (i.e., those who tend toward an internal locus of control) are more cognitively active than are externals (i.e., those who tend toward an external locus of control) when they become engaged in novel tasks. Furthermore, the cognitive activity that characterizes internals seems akin to that of a running internal monologue in which a person considers and chooses among alternative positions and constructs as he or she deals with the realities of daily life. Externals, in contrast, seem to take whatever occurs to them as given, as if there were no other way to regard their circumstances other than from the view that has been provided or is most salient. Being more circumspect about their stressful experiences than externals, internals may be less overwhelmed by these experiences and more prepared to reconstrue their significance so as to better cope with them.

Lefcourt (1992) considers that internals are more flexible than externals and are able to shift perspectives during their encounters with stressful events. According to

this view, the ability to perceive oneself as responsible for one's outcomes and experiences requires the sensitivity to note one's own actions while being attentive to those
of others. That is, individuals would have to perceive both changes in the external
world and variations in their own behaviors, mannerisms, and gestures if they were to
conclude that they were causing or had an effect on the kinds of experiences they were
having.

Locus of Control and Self-Efficacy

The self-efficacy construct represents an individual's belief that he or she can perform a particular behavior. According to Bandura (Bandura, O'Leary, Taylor,
Gauthier, & Gossard, 1987), self-efficacy may mediate the aversiveness of an event in
a variety of ways. Litt (1988) suggested that persons with high self-efficacy may manage stress by persisting longer and devoting more effort to cognitive control strategies.
High levels of efficacy appear to reduce anxiety and therefore attenuate the experienced distress.

Locus of control and self-efficacy are different though related constructs. One
way to conceptualize the relationship between these constructs is to consider "control
beliefs," or the subjective representation of one's capabilities to exercise control
(Flammer, 1995). According to Flammer (1995), control beliefs may be conceptualized as a composite of contingency beliefs and competence beliefs. Contingency
beliefs are beliefs about the probability that a certain action will lead to a certain outcome, whereas competence beliefs refer to the perceived ability to produce these
actions oneself (Flammer, 1995). This distinction is prevalent in several contemporary
lines of research. Bandura (1977) distinguished between self-efficacy and locus of
control by positing that locus of control, also viewed as contingency belief, represents
an outcome expectancy that is defined as a person's estimate that a given behavior will
lead to certain outcomes. He then conceptualized self-efficacy expectancies, or com-
pentency beliefs, as the conviction that one can successfully execute the behavior
required to produce the outcomes (p. 193). Within this framework, self-efficacy
expectations interact with, but are independent of, locus of control.

According to Bandura (1977), although self-efficacy expectancies and outcome
expectancies interact, and although self-efficacy may be the causal factor in behavior
change, the outcome expectancy will influence whether the behavior will initially be
attempted. Bandura asserts that self-efficacy expectancies may vary on several dimensions. The first dimension is the magnitude of the level of self-efficacy. In other
words, what is the person's estimate of his or her best performance level of a given
behavior. The second dimension is the strength of the efficacy belief. This dimension
involves the person's confidence in his or her ability to actually perform at that estimated level. The third dimension relates to the fact that efficacy expectations differ in
generalization in that some experiences create circumscribed mastery expectations
while others instill a sense of efficacy that extends beyond the specific situation.
Consequently, once reasonable outcome expectancies are present, the level and
strength of one's efficacy expectations for a particular behavior will determine
whether or not the behavior will be attempted, how much effort will be expended, and
how long that effort will be sustained.

The implication of this is that both locus of control and self-efficacy should be recognized by practitioners as related though separate constructs. Both should be measured independently, and each should be targeted by therapeutic intervention in order to maximize behavior change. In fact, employing the conceptualizations discussed above, targeting locus of control in treatment may be even more effective than targeting only self-efficacy for reasons that will be discussed later in this chapter

Coping and Locus of Control

Coping. While the concept of coping has its roots in psychoanalytical views of defense, in the late 1970s and early 1980s, coping became reconceptualized as conscious responses to external stressful or upsetting events or situations (Endler & Parker, 1999). Lazarus and Folkman (1984) define coping as "constantly changing cognitive and behavioural efforts to manage specific external and/or internal demands that are appraised as taxing or exceeding the resources of the person" (p. 141). Underlying the concept of coping is the assumption that the need to establish control over the environment is a fundamental human need. Over the years, a wide body of research has been conducted to examine the typical coping strategies of individuals under a given situation or to examine the habitual coping styles of individuals across situations. This dual focus has created a division of the coping research and has also led to confusion for those who seek a better understanding of the utility of coping issues in their relevant clinical area (Parker & Endler, 1996). It is therefore important to clarify the nature of the coping concept and research before examining the impact of the locus of control on coping.

The division in the conceptualization of coping concerns the intraindividual versus the interindividual approach to coping. The intraindividual approach is based on a contextual approach to coping and is concerned with how people cope in a given situation. The argument is that coping is situationally defined, and it is the environment, rather than the person, that determines the coping strategies that are used (Parker & Endler, 1996). This approach focuses on the process of coping and examines how coping changes in response to particular types of stressors. The interindividual approach is based on a trait or dispositional model of coping. It is concerned with the identification of basic coping patterns, or coping styles, used by individuals across situations. The premise of the interindividual approach is that individuals have a preference or a prototypical manner of attempting to cope with problematic situations when a variety of coping responses are feasible (Endler & Parker, 1999). Consequently, people will exhibit consistency in the nature of their coping strategies across situations.

An almost unlimited number of coping strategies are potentially available to an individual, but there is a general agreement in the coping literature that both intraindividual coping strategies and interindividual coping styles cluster on three major dimensions (Parker & Endler, 1996). The first dimension—problem focused or task oriented—involves coping strategies that center on resolving the problem or reconceptualizing it to reduce its stressful effect. The second type of coping—emotion focused or emotion oriented—centers on the person undergoing the stressor and involves affect regulation, including fantasizing reactions, self-preoccupation, and other activities related to mood regulation. The final type of coping—avoidance—involves the use of strategies designed to avoid the problem such as engaging in other tasks or distracting activities (distraction) or seeking out other people (social diversion). Parker and Endler (1992) note that social support is not considered a coping strategy; rather, it is viewed as a resource that facilitates effective coping.

Appraisal Process in Coping. Central to both the intra- and interindividual approaches to coping is the appraisal of the stressor (Lazarus & Folkman, 1984). Lazarus (1966; Lazarus & Folkman, 1984) has posited a two-tier process model of threat appraisal: primary and secondary appraisal. Primary appraisal is the cognitive evaluation of whether the stressful event poses a psychological threat to the individual. In other words, is the aversive event perceived as such by the person? Secondary appraisal concerns the cognitive evaluation of one's ability to respond to the demands of the stressor. At this secondary stage, the process involves how one will choose to deal with the stressor. Together, the appraisal process shapes the quality and intensity of emotions, and influences the coping response (Folkman, 1992). As seen in Figure 5.1, a number of inaccurate appraisals may be present, leading alternatively to poor recognition of stressors or to poor mobilization of resources. Lazarus and Folkman (1984) contend that it is the appraisal process that shapes coping, and within this framework, maladaptive coping is viewed as resulting from inaccurate primary or secondary appraisal.

In the primary appraisal stage, personality characteristics of the individual influence whether the situation is appraised as being one involving harm, loss, threat, or challenge (i.e., identify whether there is a problem and the nature of that problem). This appraisal is formed by generalized beliefs about the situation and its controllability, and general personal beliefs about one's ability to cope. Secondary appraisal involves the evaluation of coping resources and options with respect to the demands of the situation. Locus of control has an immediate impact on these processes, depending on the nature of the stressor.

The Influence of Locus of Control on Coping. Locus of control influences one's personal sense of controllability and thus exerts a clear influence on the type or nature of coping responses, with an external locus of control being associated with maladaptive coping (Folkman, 1984; Litt, 1988). An external locus of control was particularly found to negatively correlate with task-oriented coping (Horner, 1996). Though an external locus of control may at times be associated with increased emotion-focused coping (Lu & Chen, 1996), it appears primarily associated with avoidance coping (Hewitt & Flett, 1996). It is also noted that an external locus of control is associated with negative affect such as depression (Lefcourt, 1992), and depression is associated with increased use of emotion-focused coping (Endler & Parker, 1999).

An internal locus of control, on the other hand, predicts positive adjustment to a wide range of circumstances. These circumstances include dealing with personal crises, caring for sick children, adjusting to medical training, reduced burnout in medical work and marine corps training, commuting to work, and dealing with life-threatening illness and natural disasters and war (Lefcourt, 1992; Parkes, 1986; Solomon, Mikulincer, & Avitzur, 1988). People with a high internal locus of control are more likely to use direct coping strategies to deal with problems, or to engage in cognitive reframing in unsolvable situations (Charlton & Thompson, 1996; Lu & Chen, 1996). In a longitudinal study of college students, Aspinwall and Taylor (1992) found that higher self-esteem, greater optimism, and an internal locus of control predicted less

Figure 5.1
Types of Faulty Appraisals and Their Influence on Coping

Faulty Primary Appraisal

1. Failure to appraise the situation as potentially harmful. This faulty appraisal leads to a lack of necessary anticipatory coping.

2. Inaccurately appraising an event as harmful. This faulty appraisal leads to the unnecessary mobilization of coping resources.

Faulty Secondary Appraisal

3. Overly pessimistic appraisal of coping resources. This faulty appraisal leads individuals to restrict their coping efforts, hence not addressing the stressor.

4. Overly optimistic appraisal of coping resources. This faulty appraisal leads to unsatisfactory outcomes, as the coping resources do not effectively address the stressor.

---

use of avoidant coping. Internally controlled individuals were found to be higher on self-esteem and used more direct coping strategies to deal with feelings of jealousy (McIntosh & Matthews, 1992). Perceived control was also found to be associated with an improved ability to capitalize on positive events (Langston, 1994), an often neglected aspect of people's lives. This improved ability was associated with reduced stress while individuals with low perceived controllability reported increased stress with daily hassles (Langston, 1994). It is also interesting to note that an internal locus of control is associated with increased persistence in a task in mentally disordered offenders lacking in inhibitory control (Kendall, Moses, & Finch, 1980).

It is important to clarify that under some circumstances, emotion-focused and avoidance strategies are adaptive even for one with an internal locus of control (Hewitt & Flett, 1996). For example, seeking some social distraction when faced with work problems provides a pleasurable experience that temporarily relieves the stress. Problems occur when the predominant style is consistently and rigidly applied regardless of the situational demands, as this rigidity can lead to increased stress when the problematic situation is not addressed (Holohan, Moos, & Schaeffer, 1996). For example, persevering in attempts to deal directly with a problem when it is clear that no effective solution is present represents maladaptive coping (Litt, 1988). The key is flexibility, and locus of control influences whether rigidity in coping reactions to stressors will be present. People with a predominant internal locus of control are more likely to demonstrate cognitive flexibility in response to stressors and to use a wider and more effective repertoire of coping strategies (Lefcourt, 1992; Wege & Moller, 1995). The importance of cognitive flexibility is certainly a key issue when dealing with offenders as they overwhelmingly demonstrate a lack of analysis of problems and little anticipation of the consequences of their first coping response (Zamble & Quinsey, 1997).

Differential Effect of Locus of Control and Self-Efficacy on Coping. Overall, then, an internal locus of control is overwhelmingly associated with more effective coping. As Folkman (1992) explained, however, self-efficacy also has a crucial role to play in coping, and therefore both locus of control and self-efficacy must be considered. According to Litt (1988), whether the mechanism of locus of control or the mechanism of self-efficacy comes into play depends heavily on whether the stressor is novel and/or ambiguous or specific and well defined. It must be noted that life-threatening and emergency situations (e.g., the case of a death) present unique considerations in that the available coping responses are severely restricted by the very nature of the situation (Parker & Endler, 1996). Consequently, the selected coping responses are not necessarily contingent on locus of control or self-efficacy.

As discussed earlier, an internal or an external locus of control appears to trigger the use of a particular and predominant coping style in people, with the external locus being associated with less effective coping. According to Litt (1988), and as Figure 5.2 illustrates, when a stressful situation is ambiguous or novel, locus of control governs the choice of a particular coping pattern. self-efficacy does not play a role as the novel or ambiguous nature of the situation precludes its presence. For example, an offender may be well rehearsed in dealing with marital conflicts. He may not, however, have experienced conflict within the context of a friendship, potentially due to a previous lack of intimacy in his social relationships. His coping strategy for this situation would therefore not be well rehearsed. If the offender does not generally believe that his behavior influences how the conflict will be resolved (i.e., he has an external locus of control), he is less likely to engage in a specific coping strategy designed to directly target that problem. Rather, he would engage in his preferred coping pattern. As offenders tend not to have a task-oriented coping style (Cortoni, 1998; Marshall, Cripps, et al., 1999; Marshall et al., 2000), the offender in our example would be more likely to blame himself or the other person for the conflict (i.e., more likely to be emotion oriented) or simply to decide to avoid the person (avoidance coping). Clearly, either situation would not lead to a satisfactory resolution of the problematic situation. In addition, it would serve only to reinforce for the offender that he has no control over interpersonal conflicts, at least those outside his marital relationship.

If the situation is specific and well defined, and the person has well-rehearsed coping strategies for that type of situation, then expectancies of behavioral efficacy, or self-efficacy, for that situation would override the locus of control (Litt, 1988). In other words, in the case of an offender, although he may not generally believe that his behavior influences outcomes, he would know that in a particular situation he has the skills to effectively deal with it. Using our previous example, the offender may have developed clear conflict resolution skills within the context of his romantic relationship. He knows he has the skills to deal with the situation and also the confidence to employ them. This would facilitate problem-focused coping and presumably lead to a resolution of the conflict. Concurrently, he would experience satisfaction with his successful efforts and reinforce his self-esteem. Suppose now that this marital relationship ends and the offender eventually begins a new one. He starts employing his previously effective marital skills but the new partner does not respond. Would this offender, if he does not have an internal sense that his actions influence outcomes, be more likely to directly address the problem or to engage in some cognitive restructuring to reduce the stress associated with the conflict (i.e., task-oriented coping), or would he be more likely to give up on his efforts to maintain a healthy romantic relationship? In this situation, his external locus of control would override this offender's sense of self-efficacy (Litt, 1998) and make this offender more likely to engage in

Figure 5.2
Situational Differences in Coping

Ambiguous, novel situations	Specific, well-defined situations
Generalized expectancies of perceived behavioral control (locus of control; Rotter, 1966)	Situational expectancies of behavioral efficacy (self-efficacy; Bandura, 1977)
General coping that is not contingent upon the situation comes into play.	Specific coping strategies tailored to the situation are used.
That is, the coping pattern preferred by the individual is the available response as no situation-specific coping strategy would be available (interindividual approach; Endler & Parker, 1999)	The general coping style of the individual may not necessarily be consistent with those specific coping strategies (intraindividual approach; Lazarus & Folkman, 1984).
Internal locus of control more likely to lead to task oriented coping.	The coping strategy more likely to take the form of problem focused.
External locus of control more likely to lead to emotion-oriented or avoidance coping.	

ineffective coping (Folkman, 1984). Clearly then, this differential effect of locus of control and self-efficacy on coping has implications for the manner in which we approach the work on the coping abilities of sexual offenders.

Locus of Control and Relapse Prevention

The goals of most relapse prevention work with sexual offenders are to identify well-defined risk situations and to develop relevant appropriate specific coping strategies. A deficit in coping skills is viewed as a fundamental problem with sexual offenders, leading to an increased risk of relapse (Carey & McGrath, 1989: Miner, 2000; Miner, Day, & Nafpaktitis, 1989). Treatment efforts with sexual offenders therefore focus on the intraindividual approach to coping by helping the offender develop tailored coping strategies to effectively manage his specific individual risk factors. In this context, strategies designed to enhance sexual offenders' ability to successfully cope with stressful events should be effective to the extent that they enhance efficacy expectations (Marshall, Anderson, & Fernandez, 1999). Although it is important to understand the situational coping strategies of sexual offenders, their general coping patterns must also be examined to understand the impact of these patterns across a broad range of situations. It is within that context that general outcome expectations, or locus of control, will play a role. This need is particularly important in light of Marshall and Anderson's (2000) contention that it is more useful to provide sexual offenders with a general approach to problems rather than to identify an extensive list of specific risk factors.

In an earlier attempt at examining the coping strategies of child molesters, Neidigh and Tomiko (1991) found that child molesters made more use of self-denigration and avoidance techniques both when dealing with stressors in general and when they attempted to control the temptation to molest. self-denigration clearly falls within the category of emotion-focused strategies, and such strategies, along with avoidance strategies, have been found to be typically ineffective in dealing with stressors over time (Endler & Parker, 1999). More recently, and consistent with the earlier findings by Neidigh and Tomiko, our own investigations examining the coping styles of sexual offenders show that child molesters exhibit a predominant emotion-oriented coping style (Cortoni, 1998, Cortoni, Looman, & Anderson, 1999; Cortoni & Marshall, 1995, 1996; Marshall, Cripps, et al., 1999; Marshall et al., 2000). Though findings are less clear with rapists, preliminary findings indicate that rapists, like child molesters, exhibit more emotion-oriented and avoidance coping styles when compared to the general coping styles of nonoffending males in the community (Cortoni et al., 1999).

It is unrealistic to expect that a relapse prevention program will be able to instill self-efficacy in coping effectively with all possible specific situations that may lead to risk of reoffending for a given sexual offender (Marshall & Anderson, 2000). Litt's (1988) conceptualization of the differential effect of locus of control and self-efficacy on coping is particularly useful in this context. The day-to-day aspects of the sexual offender's life are typically found as precursors to offending (Pithers, Beal, Armstrong, & Petty, 1989; Miner, 2000). These aspects include issues such as general and sexual self-regulation, intimacy deficits, negative emotional states, substance abuse, and access to victims, all of which can lead to sexual offending (Hanson & Harris, 2000). These risk factors are not major life events but, rather, components involving the offender and his environment. Clearly, they also are broad issues that may manifest themselves in a variety of ambiguous or novel situations, as opposed to specific, well-defined situations (Hanson, 2000). Consequently, more work should be devoted to helping offenders develop an increased internal locus of control. This internal control, in turn, will likely improve the ability of offenders to engage in a more effective coping style in novel situations (Litt, 1988) and to maintain the cognitive flexibility required to improve their coping ability (Lefcourt, 1992).

Coping plays a crucial role in the traditional conceptualization of the offense cycle and relapse prevention with sexual offenders (Laws, 1989) as well as in the recent advances in the field (Laws et al., 2000). The traditional model stipulates that it is a failure to cope that leads to eventual offending. Cortoni (1998) and colleagues (Cortoni & Marshall, 1998, 2001; Marshall, Cripps, et al., 1999; Marshall et al., 2000) have argued that offenders do not fail to cope with stressors, but rather habitually cope in inappropriate ways. In either case, the coping processes of sexual offenders are the key. Factors that influence these processes must be taken into account as the aim should be to break the connection between the stressor and its resulting negative emotional states, and the ineffective coping patterns that result in sexual offending (Hanson, 2000).

In their reconceptualization of the relapse model, Ward and Hudson (1998, 2000a) proposed a tri-pathway self-regulation model to the relapse process in sexual offenders. The model is based on the attainment of goals, but its initial phases bear remarkable similarity to the coping process. Specifically, the link between phase 1 (life events) and phase 2 (desire for offensive sex/activities) of the self-regulation model is based on the appraisal of life events. Ward and Hudson (2000a) described life events as either a major life transition such as divorce or simply a daily hassle such as an argument. Another way to describe such life events is to call them stressors, which, if accurately appraised as such, trigger the need for coping. Ward and Hudson (1998, 2000a) posited that this appraisal process is influenced by individual factors such as needs and beliefs, as well as by interpersonal factors. Similarly, the appraisal process of a stressor in the coping literature is viewed as being influenced by individual factors. As locus of control was found to be one such variable (Folkman, 1984), it is reasonable to assume that locus of control would have a similar effect on the appraisal process within the context of the self-regulation model.

Within the self-regulation model, an internal locus of control would likely affect the appraisal process of the stressor by improving the likelihood that task-oriented coping will be employed, therefore breaking the connection between stressors and desire for offensive sex. We have already discussed how an internal locus of control is also associated with increased cognitive flexibility (Lefcourt, 1992). Consequently, an internal locus of control would also contribute to the weakening of the connection by decreasing the likelihood of the triggering of previous specific patterns of thoughts, emotions, and interactions that lead to a resurgence of cues associated with offending (Ward & Hudson, 2000b). Similarly, due to its concomitant increased cognitive flexibility, an increased internal locus of control should also help to reduce the likelihood that an offender will engage in a cognitively deconstructed state (Ward, Hudson, & Marshall, 1995). Hence, whether one views the relapse process as the result of a failure to cope, as the result of inappropriate coping, or as the result of an appraisal process that triggers cognitive cues associated with offending, the concept of locus of control within the context of the general coping abilities of sexual offenders is equally applicable.

Locus of Control and Treatment

Rotter's (1966) conceptualization of locus of control originated from the observation that some clients in psychotherapy "appear to gain from new experiences or to change their behavior as a result of new experiences, while others seem to discount new experiences by attributing them to chance or to others and to their own behavior or characteristics" (p. 2). According to Rotter (1978), the common element in many different therapies that leads to lasting improvement is a feeling on the client's part that he or she has learned to control his or her destiny to some extent.

Empirical research conducted in a range of settings and with a variety of populations attests to the relationship between therapeutic intervention and a shift toward internal locus of control. Smith (1970) found that clients who sought psychotherapy to resolve an immediate, acute life crisis showed a significant decrease in externality as they learned more effective coping techniques in therapy. Dua (1970) compared pre- and posttreatment locus of control across behavior therapy, reeducative therapy (focused on attitudes and beliefs), and a control group. Clients in the behavior therapy group showed increases in internality significantly greater than those in the reeducative therapy or control groups. Studies have also shown that clients in encounter group therapy show significant shifts toward internality and successful therapy has been shown to be associated with increased attitudes of internality (Dua, 1970; Foulds, 1971; Gillis & Jessor, 1970). In a review of locus of control and psychotherapy, Glicken and Glicken (1982) concluded that locus of control, and consequently achievement and adjustment, may be shifted through psychotherapy. They stated that as locus of control correlates with good adjustment and higher achievement, the use of locus of control theory can be a meaningful way of establishing psychotherapeutic gains. According to Lefcourt (1976), more action-oriented therapies that stress the learning of contingent results seem to be the optimal approaches for changing clients perceptions of causality.

Enhancement of self-efficacy was also demonstrated to be associated with therapeutic intervention. Bandura (1977) suggested that an individual's self-efficacy, or the belief in his or her ability to produce a particular behavioral response, can be enhanced in several ways. One way is to directly engage in the relevant behavior so that occasional failures that are later overcome can strengthen self-motivated persistence. However, occasional failures appear beneficial only if the client finds through experience that even the most difficult obstacles can be mastered by sustained effort. An individual also enhances self-efficacy by observing a model engaging successfully in the behavior. Seeing others perform threatening activities without adverse consequences can be beneficial to the client. For such a benefit to occur, however, the client must make inferences from social comparison. Also, clients can be verbally persuaded to engage in the behavior so that they can be led through suggestion into believing that they can cope successfully. Finally, clients must feel calm enough to evaluate their capabilities with optimism. Stressful and taxing situations generally elicit emotional arousal that, depending on the circumstances, might have informative value concerning personal competency.

Simply enhancing self-efficacy, however, is predicted to have a narrower impact on functioning and behavior due to its situation-specific characteristic, compared with the more global dispositional construct of locus of control. In fact, D'Zurilla and Goldfried (1971), in their review of the outcome of behavior modification therapies, suggested that the main ingredient in successful outcome may be clients learning that they can control their own responses and behavior. Clearly, such control is a highly desirable outcome in the treatment of sexual offenders.

Implications for the Treatment of Sexual Offenders

Motivation is an important component of successful relapse prevention (Hanson, 2000; Mann, 2000). According to Marshall, Anderson, and Fernandez (1999), an offender's motivation to practice tasks is related to self-efficacy. That is, the greater the offender's self-efficacy, the more likely he will be to engage in and repeatedly practice particular behaviors designed to reduce his risk to reoffend. As discussed previously, the likelihood that a person will engage in a particular behavior (especially novel behavior) is related to his or her expectancy of success. Due to the situation specificity of self-efficacy, an individual may have enhanced self-efficacy to particular, discrete situations but this enhanced self-efficacy is not expected to transfer to other dissimilar situations. As both Hanson (2000) and Marshall, Anderson, and Fernandez (1999) pointed out, the path to offending does not always involve specific or highly similar situations. In fact, Marshall, Anderson, and Fernandez (1999) stated that the offense chain "may not reflect the offender's typical modus operandi or initial state that triggers all his offences" (p. 140). Marshall, Anderson, and Fernandez (1999) then go on to explain that it is the general issues involved in the offending that must be addressed as "most offenders display variability in their offense chain across different occasions of offending" (p. 140).

Given this situation, then, motivation to produce a behavior designed to manage and reduce the risk of offending may indeed be enhanced if self-efficacy is high, but only in those situations that are identical to or strongly resemble the situation in which self-efficacy beliefs are enhanced. Motivation to produce and practice behavior that targets broader and more general issues, however, will surely be enhanced when the offender believes he can exert an influence on the outcome. That is, the offender must believe that he is in control of what ultimately happens in his life. Without that belief, when facing new challenges and stressors, the client may feel that he has been pushed down the same path that led to his previous offending.

To help improve and maintain motivation in positive coping efforts even in post-treatment situations when the offender is not subject to external controls, an internal locus of control would be useful. In fact, it appears that Marshall and Anderson's (2000) suggestion to provide sexual offenders with a general approach to monitoring their future risk is actually more consistent with helping these offenders to develop an internal locus of control, as opposed to simply improving their sense of self-efficacy.

As discussed earlier in this chapter, an internal locus of control appears to predispose an individual to use a talk-oriented coping style when in novel or ambiguous circumstances. Individuals who engage in task-oriented coping are also found to have higher self-esteem (McIntosh & Matthews, 1992). Marshall, Anderson, and Fernandez (1999) discussed how self-esteem and self-worth improve the motivation and ability (i.e., the self-efficacy) of an offender to engage in successful coping. Weiner (1986), in his theory of motivation and emotions, specifically linked self-esteem to an internal locus of control. In his review of a body of research and as well in his own research, he found that emotions such as pride, competence, confidence, and satisfaction, which he claimed are the foundation of self-esteem, were found in people with an internal locus of control. These findings suggest that while, as posited by Marshall, Anderson, and Fernandez (1999), enhancing situationally specific self-efficacy improves self-esteem, helping the offender to develop a stronger sense of internal causality would actually solidify the offender's self-esteem. In turn, the offender would be better prepared for those inevitable unforeseen stressful circumstances that will arise in his life and the likelihood that he will engage in effective coping will be increased.

The implication is not only that treatment should aim to enhance self-efficacy in particular, discrete situations, as is typically the current practice, but that a more important target should be a shift toward an increased internal locus of control. This shift in locus of control has obvious implications for relapse prevention strategies. When faced with an unrehearsed high-risk situation, an offender with a more external locus of control may not be motivated to engage in constructive strategies that are incompatible with sexual offending. On the one hand, he may not be cognitively prepared to view the situation as high risk as he would have been prepared for and would understand only specific rehearsed high-risk situations. Consequently, that offender would fail to appraise the situation accurately as threatening and would not mobilize his coping resources. On the other hand, that offender may recognize the situation as high risk but feel unprepared for it and fall back to old coping ways, the same coping ways that eventually led to an offense in the past.

An offender with a more internal locus of control may be able to apply strategies learned in treatment to a new context, drawing on the increased cognitive flexibility described earlier. Shifting locus of control toward internality would improve the offender's motivation to practice tasks in a variety of both novel and familiar situations and provide him with more opportunities for success. Of course, in such circumstances, self-esteem would concurrently be enhanced. Recently, Mann (2000) observed that the relapse prevention strategies based on the avoidance of risk situations may actually lead to increased stress in the offender's life. The finding that sexual offenders typically demonstrate poor coping styles, including avoidance coping, reinforces the need to pay more attention to the elements that facilitate increased use of task-oriented coping. Mann (2000) suggested the use of goal-setting theory to improve successful interventions with sexual offenders. To that end, she discusses the use of "approach goals" and a learning orientation during therapy as a way to help offenders persist in the achievement of the overall goal of an offense-free life (see Mann, 2000, for an in-depth discussion of this issue). The point here is that a learning orientation entails the setting of meaningful and achievable goals for the offender, leading to the experience of success early in therapy, and increased motivation for future efforts. Rotter (1966, 1978) pointed out that it is the experience of success due to their own efforts that leads clients to learn that they have control over their destiny to some extent. Mann's recommended therapeutic approach is certainly consistent with Rotter's views. Mann's views are not only consistent with helping the offenders develop an increased internal locus of control but also with helping the offender concurrently develop and practice task-oriented coping: two aims of treatment that should ultimately prove effective in reducing sexual recidivism.

Conclusion

In this chapter, the authors have integrated the construct of locus of control with the coping literature. In doing so, they have highlighted how locus of control plays an integral role in people's coping patterns. In addition, the authors have discussed these issues within the context of relapse prevention and demonstrated the importance of considering locus of control in the treatment of sexual offenders. We have yet much to learn about what contributes to or maintains sexual offending. These authors believe that by integrating locus of control with the current views on sexual offenders, they have added a useful dimension to further effectiveness in reducing recidivism.

References

Aspinwall, L. G., & Taylor, S. E. (1992). Modeling cognitive adaptation: A longitudinal investigation of the impact of individual differences and coping on college adjustment and performance. *Journal of Personality and Social Psychology, 63,* 989–1003.

Bandura, A. (1977). Self-efficacy: Toward a unifying theory of behavioral change. *Psychological Review, 84,* 191–215.

Bandura, A., O'Leary, A., Taylor, C. B., Gauthier, J., & Gossard, D. (1987). Perceived self-efficacy and pain control: Opioid and nonopioid mediators. *Journal of Personality and Social Psychology, 53,* 563–571.

Benassi, V. A., Sweeney, P. D., & Dufour, C. L. (1988). Is there a relation between locus of control orientation and depression? *Journal of Abnormal Psychology, 97,* 357–336

Carey, C. H., & McGrath, R. J. (1989). Coping with urges and cravings. In R. Laws (Ed.), *Relapse prevention with sex offenders* (pp. 188–196). New York: Guilford Press.

Charlton, P. F. C., & Thompson, J. A. (1996). Ways of coping with psychological distress. *British Journal of Clinical Psychology, 35,* 517–530.

Cortoni, F. A. (1998). *The relationship between attachment styles, coping, the use of sex as a coping mechanism, and juvenile sexual history in sexual offenders.* Unpublished doctoral dissertation, Queen's University, Kingston, Ontario.

Cortoni, F. A., Looman, J. A., & Anderson, D. (1999). *Locus of control and coping in sexual offenders.* Paper presented at the 18th annual Research and Treatment Conference of the Association for the Treatment of Sexual Abusers, Orlando, FL.

Cortoni, F. A., & Marshall, W. L. (1995). *Childhood attachments, juvenile sexual history and adult coping skills in sex offenders.* Paper presented at the 14th annual Research and Treatment Conference of the Association for the Treatment of Sexual Abusers, New Orleans.

Cortoni, F. A., & Marshall, W. L. (1996). *Juvenile sexual history, sex and coping strategies: A comparison of sexual and violent offenders.* Paper presented at the International Congress of Psychology, Montreal.

Cortoni, F. A., & Marshall, W. L. (1998). *The relationship between attachment and coping in sexual offenders.* Paper presented at the 17th annual Research and Treatment Conference of the Association for the Treatment of Sexual Abusers, Vancouver.

Cortoni, F. A., & Marshall, W. L. (2001). Sex as a coping strategy and its relationship to juvenile sexual history and intimacy in sexual offenders. *Sexual Abuse: A Journal of Research and Treatment, 13,* 27–44.

D'Zurilla, T. J., & Goldfried, M. R. (1971). Problem-solving and behavior modification. *Journal of Abnormal Psychology, 78,* 107–126.

Dua, P. S. (1970). Comparison of the effects of behaviourally oriented action and psychotherapy re-education on introversion-extroversion, emotionality, and internal-external control. *Journal of Counseling Psychology, 19,* 253–260.

Eccles, A., & Marshall, W. L. (1999). Relapse prevention. In W. L. Marshall, D. Anderson, & Y. Fernandez (Eds.), *Cognitive behavioural treatment of sexual offenders* (pp. 127–146). London: Wiley.

Endler, N. S., & Parker, J. D. A. (1999). *Coping Inventory for Stressful Situations: Manual* (2nd ed.). Toronto: Multi-Health Systems.

Feeney, J. A. (1995). Adult attachment, coping style and health locus of control as predictors of health behavior. *Australian Journal of Psychology, 47,* 171–177.

Findley, M. J., & Cooper, H. M. (1983). Locus of control and academic achievement: A literature review. *Journal of Personality and Social Psychology, 44,* 419–427.

Flammer, A. (1995). Developmental analysis of control beliefs. In A. Bandura (Ed.), *Self-efficacy in changing societies* (pp. 69–113). Melbourne, Australia: Cambridge University Press.

Folkman, S. (1984). Personal control and stress and coping processes: A theoretical analysis. *Journal of Personality and Social Psychology, 46,* 839–852.

Folkman, S. (1992). Making the case for coping. In B. N. Carpenter (Ed.), *Personal coping: Theory, research, and application* (pp. 31–46). Westport, CT: Praeger.

Foulds, M. L. (1971). Changes in locus of control internal-external control. *Comparative Group Studies, 2,* 293–300.

Gillis, J. S., & Jessor, R. (1970). Effects of brief psychotherapy on belief in internal control: An exploratory study. *Psychotherapy: Theory, Research and Practice, 7,* 135–137.

Glicken, V. K., & Glicken, M. D. (1982). The utilization of locus of control theory in treatment. *Indian Journal of Social Work, 43,* 173–185.

Hanson, R. K. (2000). What is so special about relapse prevention? In D. R. Laws, S. M. Hudson, & T. Ward (Eds.), *Remaking relapse prevention with sex offenders: A sourcebook* (pp. 27–38). Thousand Oaks, CA: Sage.

Hanson, R. K., & Harris, A. (2000). *The Sex Offender Needs Assessment Rating (SONAR): A method for measuring change in risk levels* (User Report 2000-1). Ottawa: Solicitor General of Canada.

Hewitt, P. L., & Flett, G. L. (1996). Personality traits and the coping process. In M. Zeidner & N. S. Endler (Eds.), *Handbook of coping: Theory, research, applications* (pp. 410–433). New York: Wiley.

Holohan, C. J., Moos, R. H., & Schaeffer, J. A. (1996). Coping, stress resistance, and growth: Conceptualizing adaptive functioning. In M. Zeidner & N. S. Endler (Eds.), *Handbook of coping: Theory, research, applications* (pp. 410–433). New York: Wiley.

Horner, K. L. (1996). Locus of control, neuroticism, and stressors: Combined influences on reported physical illness. *Personality and Individual Differences, 21,* 195–204.

Kendall, P. C., Moses Jr., J. A., & Finch, A. J. (1980). Impulsivity and persistence in adult inpatient "impulse" offenders. *Journal of Clinical Psychology, 36,* 363–365.

Langston, C. A. (1994). Capitalizing on and coping with daily-life events: Expressive responses to positive events. *Journal of Personality and Social Psychology, 67,* 1112–1125.

Laws, D. R. (Ed.). (1989). *Relapse prevention with sex offenders.* New York: Guilford Press.

Laws, D. R., Hudson, S. M. & Ward, T. (Eds.) (2000). *Remaking relapse prevention with sex offenders: A sourcebook.* Thousand Oaks, CA: Sage Publications.

Lazarus, R. S. (1966). *Psychological stress and the coping process.* New York: McGraw-Hill.

Lazarus, R. S., & Folkman, S. (1984). *Stress, appraisal, and coping.* New York: Springer.

Lefcourt, H. M. (1976). *Locus of control: Current trends in theory and research.* Hillsdale, NJ: Erlbaum.

Lefcourt, H. M. (1981). *Research with the locus of control construct* (Vol. 1). New York: Academic Press.

Lefcourt, H. M. (1992). Perceived control, personal effectiveness, and emotional states. In B. N. Carpenter (Ed.), *Personal coping: Theory, research, and application* (pp. 111–131). Westport, CT: Praeger.

Litt, M. D. (1988). Cognitive mediators of stressful experiences: Self-efficacy and perceived control. *Cognitive Therapy and Research, 12,* 241–260.

Lu, L., & Chen, C. S. (1996). Correlates of coping behaviours: Internal and external resources. *Counselling Psychology Quarterly, 9,* 297–307.

Mann, R. E. (2000). Managing resistance and rebellion in relapse prevention intervention. In D. R. Laws, S. M. Hudson, & T. Ward (Eds.), *Remaking relapse prevention with sex offenders: A sourcebook* (pp. 187–200). Thousand Oaks, CA: Sage.

Marshall, W. L. (1996a). The sexual offender: Monster, victim, or everyman. *Sexual Abuse: A Journal of Research and Treatment, 8,* 317–335.

Marshall, W. L. (1996b). Marshall, W. L. (1996). Assessment, treatment, and theorizing about sex offenders: Developments during the past twenty years and future directions. *Criminal Justice and Behavior, 23,* 162–199.

Marshall, W. L., & Anderson, D. (2000). Do relapse prevention components enhance treatment effectiveness? In D. R. Laws, S. M. Hudson, & T. Ward (Eds.), *Remaking relapse prevention with sex offenders: A sourcebook* (pp. 39–55). Thousand Oaks, CA: Sage.

Marshall, W. L., Anderson, D., & Fernandez, Y. (1999). *Cognitive behavioural treatment of sexual offenders.* London: Wiley.

Marshall, W. L., Cripps, E., Anderson, D., & Cortoni, F. A. (1999). Self-esteem and coping strategies in child molesters. *Journal of Interpersonal Violence, 14,* 955–962.

Marshall, W. L., Serran, G. A., & Cortoni, F. A. (2000). Childhood attachment, sexual abuse, and the relationship to adult coping in child molesters. *Sexual Abuse: A Journal of Research and Treatment, 12,* 17–26.

McIntosh, E. G., & Matthews, C. O. (1992). Use of direct coping resources in dealing with jealousy. *Psychological Reports, 70,* 1037–1038.

Miner, M. H. (2000). Competency-based assessment. In D. R. Laws, S. M. Hudson, & T. Ward (Eds.), *Remaking relapse prevention with sex offenders: A sourcebook* (pp. 213–224). Thousand Oaks, CA: Sage.

Miner, M. H., Day, D. M., & Nafpaktitis, M. K. (1989). Assessment of coping skills: Development of a Situational Competency Test. In D. R. Laws (Ed.), *Relapse prevention with sex offenders* (pp. 127–136). New York: Guilford Press.

Neidigh, L., & Tomiko, R. (1991). The coping strategies of child sexual abusers. *Journal of Sex Education and Therapy, 17,* 103–110.

Parker, J. D. A., & Endler, N. S. (1992). Coping with coping assessment: A critical review. *European Journal of Personality, 6,* 321–344.

Parker, J. D. A., & Endler, N. S. (1996). Coping and defense: A historical overview. In M. Zeidner & N. S. Endler (Eds.), *Handbook of coping: Theory, research, applictions* (pp. 3–23). New York: Wiley.

Parkes, K. R. (1986). Coping in stressful episodes: The role of individual differences, environmental factors, and situational characteristics. *Journal of Personality and Social Psychology, 51,* 1277–1292.

Pithers, W. D., Beal, L. S., Armstrong, J., & Petty, J. (1989). Identification of risk factors through clinical interviews and analysis of records. In D. R. Laws (Ed.), *Relapse prevention with sex offenders* (pp. 77–87). New York: Guilford Press.

Rapee, R. M., Craske, M. G., Brown, T. A., & Barlow, D. H. (1996). Measurement of perceived control over anxiety-related events. *Behavior Therapy, 27,* 279–293.

Rotter, J. B. (1954). *Social learning and clinical psychology.* Englewood Cliffs, NJ: Prentice-Hall, 1954.

Rotter, J. B. (1966). Generalized expectancies for internal versus external control of reinforcement. *Psychological Monographs, 80,* 1–28.

Rotter, J. B. (1978). Generalized expectancies for problem solving psychotherapy. *Cognitive Therapy and Research, 2,* 1–10.

Rotter, J. B., Chance, J., & Phares, E. J. (Eds.). (1972). *Applications of a social learning theory of personality.* New York: Holt, Rinehart & Winston.

Smith, R. E. (1970). Changes in locus of control as a function of life crisis resolution. *Journal of Abnormal Psychology, 75,* 328–332.

Solomon, Z., Mikulincer, M., & Avitzur, E. (1988). Coping, locus of control, social support, and combat-related post traumatic stress disorder: A prospective study. *Journal of Personality and Social Psychology, 55,* 279–285.

Strickland, B. R. (1978). Internal-external expectancies and health-related behaviors. *Journal of Consulting and Clinical Psychology, 46,* 1192–1211.

Ward, T,. & Hudson, S. M. (1998). A model of the relapse process in sexual offenders. *Journal of Interpersonal Violence, 13,* 400–425.

Ward, T., & Hudson, S. M. (2000a). A self-regulation model of relapse prevention. In D. R. Laws, S. M. Hudson, & T. Ward (Eds.), *Remaking relapse prevention with sex offenders: A sourcebook* (pp. 79–101). Thousand Oaks, CA: Sage.

Ward, T., & Hudson, S. M. (2000b). Sexual offenders' implicit planning: A conceptual model. *Sexual Abuse: A Journal of Research and Treatment, 12,* 189–202.

Ward, T., Hudson, S. M., & Marshall, W. L. (1995). Cognitive distortions and affective deficits in sexual offenders: A cognitive deconstructionist approach. *Sexual Abuse: A Journal of Research and Treatment, 7,* 67–83.

Wege, J. W., & Moller, A. T. (1995). Effectiveness of a problem solving training program. *Psychological Reports, 76,* 507–514.

Weiner, B. (1986). An attributional theory of motivation and emotion. New York: Springer.

Zamble, E., & Quinsey, V. L. (1997). *The criminal recidivism process.* Cambridge, UK: Cambridge University Press.

Part 2
Systems Issues

Reference was made earlier in the volume to the widely diverse systems approaches to sexual crimes. From public notification, involuntary commitment, mandatory life sentences, and adult sentences for juveniles to restorative justice, the containment approach, intensive supervision and use of various technologies, and systemic responses vary radically.

Even on a single issue jurisdictions vary widely. One example is public notification. Louisiana makes the offender notify the neighbors of his whereabouts. Oregon has placed placards in front of offenders' homes. However, Washington, having experienced some catastrophic responses to public notification, has taken a much more positive proactive approach. In 1991, Washington State began notifying citizens of the presence of sex offenders in their neighborhoods. Vigilantism was anticipated and indeed became a reality when a house in which a sex offender resided but which belonged to a family member was burnt. In addition, another home, mistakenly identified as the home of a sex offender, was burnt. The state decided that public education was needed to counteract this hysteria. Seattle police officer Bob Shelling took over the process and has developed a system that educates the public and encourages the community to assist sex offenders with their reintegration.

The Center for Sex Offender Management is actively encouraging jurisdictions of all sizes to develop collaborative networks to respond to the problem of sexual abuse. Criminal justice and corrections professionals, supervisory agents, therapists, polygraphers, and victims are cooperating to on these issues. (Check out the website www.csom.org for specifics).

Chapter 6, on risk assessment, is placed in this section because so many different agencies and professionals are now concerned with making these decisions and evaluating using these instruments. In this chapter, Dennis Doren distinguishes between risk assessment, risk management, and risk prediction as well as discussing the different types of risk: risk to be rearrested for anything versus risk to be reconvicted of a sex offense. Dr. Doren also discusses clinical risk assessment as opposed to actuarial risk assessment. Professionals making use of one of the recently developed instruments need to constantly update themselves on the research on these instruments.

In developing systematic approaches to managing sex offenders, it is important to know what works and with whom. In Chapter 7, Terry Nicholaichuk and Pamela Yates present research conducted in Canada on a prison-based program using cognitive-behavioral techniques. This research is particularly important in that it looks at recidivism based on a variety of inmate characteristics, including psychopathy. This latter concept is the focus of a great deal of controversy in the field. Some research indicates that this is a static personality feature that does not change and bodes poorly for treatment response. Others suggest that psychopathy can be modified and that "psychopaths" have always been treated in sex offender programs with a significant percentage responding positively. This chapter presents important findings in this area.

Who says one person cannot make major changes in a system? No one told that to Fran Henry when she developed "STOP IT NOW," a national organization that encourages offenders and their families to stop their behavior by self-reporting and getting help (Henry & Tabachnik, Chapter 8). This relieves the victim of having the sole responsibility of stopping the abuse by reporting it. STOP IT NOW seeks to reach out to individuals who may be offending or are fearful that they might start by bringing them a message of hope, hope that with treatment this behavior can be controlled. A professionally developed public relations campaign featuring newspaper ads, radio, and television has been used in Vermont and most recently in Philadelphia to raise public awareness, not only for offenders but for the public in general. In fact, in Vermont awareness of child sexual abuse went from 44.5% to 84.8% among the state's citizens. This approach treats sex abuse as a public health issues and seeks to evoke the same type of public awareness that Mothers Against Drunk Drivers has promoted.

In Chapter 9, Yolanda Fernandez and Geris Serran challenge the widely held belief that the effective sex offender therapist is either an objective technician applying behavioral methods or an "in your face" confronter. Their research has shown that a motivational approach is associated with the most treatment progress.

Michael Nilan and Robin Hubbell, in Chapter 10, discuss an approach to co-therapy using a therapist and a probation officer. Some professionals have viewed this model with skepticism, but it has a variety of distinct advantages.

Chapter 6

The Use of Actuarial Risk Assessment

by Dennis M. Doren, Ph.D., DABPS, ABAP

Overview

This chapter was designed to facilitate the process of making risk decisions using the greatest degree of current empirical support. Given that the myriad details concerning sex offender risk assessment can fill a book, this chapter needed to be limited in its scope. The following discussion involves three main topic areas. The first describes the process of defining the type of risk evaluation of interest (people often improperly lump together various types of risk and related assessments). The second topic is an explanation of a theoretical structure for understanding the risk to be assessed. Finally, this chapter delineates current procedures for performing a risk assessment based on that theoretical structure.

Introduction

Individuals who work with sex offenders are charged with the awesome responsibility to make a number of important decisions regarding these individuals, most having to do with various types of risks. These risk considerations may involve (1) whether or not to agree to a plea bargain that could put the offender back onto the street sooner, (2) what sentence to give an offender, (3) when to grant a work release,

(4) when to advise a parole or supervised release, (5) when to recommend a sex offender civil commitment, (6) when to alter mandated community supervisory conditions, and (7) when to recommend a change in the subject's treatment. In working with sex offenders, there probably is no way to avoid the issue of risk.

Differentiating Risk Assessment From Risk Management and Prediction

The phrase "risk assessment" has unfortunately been used in a variety of contexts with different meanings as if the single phrase always means the same thing. To ensure clarity in what this chapter has to offer, a short digression seems appropriate to differentiate the phrase from other concepts.

Risk assessment involves an evaluation of either the relative or absolute degree of likelihood someone represents for behaving in specified harmful ways. This definition clearly differentiates risk assessment from another related phrase, "risk management." The latter far more pertains to the implementation of external deterrents and controls over someone in an effort to lower the subject's near-term likelihood for doing undesired behaviors. Risk management can easily incorporate a risk assessment but needs to go beyond it. A risk assessment may take risk management plans into consideration but also may not, this being dependent on the circumstances.

Another term often used interchangeably with "risk assessment" is "prediction." These terms, again, are not the same. Prediction involves a statement that a certain event will or will not happen in the future. There is no "maybe" involved in a prediction. For example, one predicts whether a coin will turn up heads or tails on its next flip. A risk assessment, on the other hand, involves a determination about the degree of likelihood for an event. Nontrivial risk assessments rarely culminate with "100%" or "0%" (i.e., will or will not happen) conclusions but somewhere in between (e.g., an unbiased coin has a 50% likelihood for turning up "heads"). The concepts of prediction and risk assessment can be seen as overlapping, but confusing the two typically leads to errors in how we make conclusions about the accuracy of the risk assessment statement. For example, when meteorologists tell us there is a 60% chance of rain tomorrow, they are giving us the results of a risk assessment, the likelihood for rain. If it then does not rain, many of us say the meteorologists were wrong. In reality, it is we who are the ones making an error by interpreting the meteorologists' "risk" assessment as a prediction of rain. The meteorologists may have been very accurate in their risk assessment—there was 60% likelihood for rain—even though it did not rain. They did not say it would or would not rain; they just stated the degree of likelihood.

Different Types of Risk Assessments

Even when properly defined, risk assessments can still be in three forms, not just one. Each form addresses a different question and hence has different utility within different contexts.

The first type of risk assessment uses the process of rank ordering. Results from this type of evaluation come in the form of "person X is at higher risk than person Y" or "event W is more likely than event Z." This form of assessment does not inform anyone about the ultimate degree of likelihood for the relevant behavior or event, but can nevertheless be useful under certain circumstances. The question being addressed is basically of the following type: "Which is of greater risk?" Applications for this type of risk assessment include, for instance, the process of determining the degree of community notification appropriate for a set of sex offenders. Offenders are typically categorized into low, medium, and high risk to make such notifications differentially based on the risk posed. Similarly, allocations of supervision resources can be appropriately determined through this type of risk assessment.

A second type of risk assessment is of a more absolute form. The question being addressed can be described as follows: "What is the specific percentage of risk?" This type of evaluation results in determinations analogous to that stated previously for the weather: There is 60% likelihood for recidivism. Although some people would be pleased if we could be this exact in sex offender risk assessments, this degree of exactness appears yet to be beyond the state of our science. Currently, this type of evaluation conclusion is made only by those who overinterpret existing data, such as those who are ill informed about the proper interpretation of actuarial risk assessment instruments. In these cases, a percentage attached to an instrument's score is erroneously interpreted as reflecting the subject's specific and exact degree of risk.

Present sex offender civil commitment risk evaluations involve a third type of assessment. These evaluations can be described as "relative to a threshold," with the concomitant addressed issue being as follows: "Is this person's risk above or below a specific degree of risk?" In civil commitment statutes, the determination needs to be made about whether or not the offender's risk is beyond a specific (albeit typically poorly defined) threshold. By way of illustration, evaluators doing this type of assessment do not need to determine whether the person's relevant risk is 25%, 52%, or 87% but, simply, whether or not the subject's risk is beyond the statutory threshold, say, 50%.

Defining the Type of Risk

Within the context of any of the foregoing three forms of risk assessments is the necessity to define the risk being evaluated. There are two main considerations here: (1) the type of behavior of concern and (2) the time period over which the concern lies. The former refers to the process of differentiating risk related to sexual reoffending, violent reoffending, and general criminal reoffending. The latter concern relates to the need to state over what time period one is assessing risk. There is little meaning to a risk assessment without specifying the time context in which the risk exists. These considerations may seem obvious to the reader, but one can frequently find evaluations that conclude that a subject is a "low-" or "high-"risk offender with those categorizations lacking the "obvious" descriptors.

Theoretical Structure for Risk Assessment

An implicitly commonly held view of recidivism risk, even when risk is properly specified in form and type, is that it is composed of only one underlying etiology. Without analyzing their underlying assumption, evaluators performing sex offender assessments often assume that all correlates of the relevant risk are measuring the same phenomenon. Interestingly, we know better than to believe this is true in a wide variety of other applied sciences. Somehow, we forget to apply what we know in evaluating the risk of sex offenders.

For example, when we go to a physician for a general health checkup, we are interested in learning of any threats to our overall health. We would be rather confused, at best, if the physician only checked out one part of our body and then proclaimed we were either in good or bad overall health. Instead, we all know that we need to have many of our body's systems checked out before such a proclamation has any real meaning. There are many relatively independent factors, each of which can lead to "bad health" despite "good health" being indicated from all other considerations. Stated another way, it really will not matter much to us that our heart shows minimal signs of risk when we are also told that we have a malignant brain tumor. Our overall "health" can be seriously at risk as determined from one consideration even though any variety of relatively independent risk factors are not present.

By analogy, the same situation seems to exist within the assessment of recidivism risk for sex offenders. At least two relatively independent pathways (or drives, or dimensions) appear to have both empirical and theoretical support. The first of these pertains to sexual deviancies that are related to illegal behaviors. Examples include sexual interests in children and exposing one's genitals to unsuspecting strangers. The second type of drive stems from generally violent and antisocial personality traits. Knight (1999), in a theoretical summary from his research, labeled these two dimensions "sexual deviancy/preoccupation" and "hypermasculine," "hyperaggressive," or "negative masculinity." Doren and Roberts (1998) found such a structure within a U.S. study of common actuarial risk assessment instruments, where some instruments correlated with deviant sexual interests and some correlated with psychopathy and personality disorders, but they did not correlate as highly with one another. This structure among the instruments was essentially replicated with an Irish sample in a study by Quackenbush (2000). David Thornton (personal communication, June, 2000) effectively also replicated these two dimensions in a factor analytic study using a different set of risk factors with a very different (U.K.) sample.

The evaluator in a sex offender risk assessment needs to examine the evidence for risk along each known pathway or dimension. To do less than this is to be incomplete. Just like the physician who assessed only the patient's heart, proclaimed him in fine health, and totally missed the high risk factor of a malignant brain tumor, evaluators of sex offender risk would be seriously amiss through even a thorough assessment of only one pathway toward recidivism. If any dimension shows significant signs of high risk, the subject represents a potentially high risk despite signs of low risk from a relatively independent dimension. The strongly fixated pedophile with prior sexual convictions involving extrafamilial boys does not need to be a psychopath with a penchant for raping adult women while burglarizing homes to represent a significant risk to reoffend, and vice versa.

General Procedures for a Risk Assessment

Hanson (1998) offered a description of different methodologies in the performing of a risk assessment. The first, clinical judgment not aided by empirical results, used to be the most commonly employed. In the not too distant past, we did not really know how accurate those judgments were, but we believed we had nothing better. From summary studies such as those of Grove and Meehl (1996) and, more recently, Grove, Zald, Lebow, Snitz, and Nelson (2000), however, we learned that subjectively determined predictions of virtually all types are at best only as good as, and many times not as accurate as, more mechanical procedures. Taking these findings to their logical extreme, it would appear that the purely mechanical or actuarial method would offer the greatest promise of accuracy, given assumptions of (1) appropriateness of application and (2) comprehensiveness in scope. Given that sufficiently comprehensive actuarial procedures do not yet appear to exist even for selected populations, however, we can only continue to work to approach this ideal.

One of two moves in this direction has been termed "research-guided clinical judgment." This methodology involves the process of using a research-based enumeration of risk factors to structure one's clinical judgment. The exact relationship among the factors is viewed as unknown, both in terms of their relative weighting and the degree to which they overlap in what they measure. Still, this methodology is clearly a major step above the process of using our own "pet theories" for guiding judgments about people's recidivism risk. The Historical Clinical Risk Management-20 (HCR-20; Webster, Douglas, Eaves, & Hart, 1997) is the apparent leading instrument using this methodology. A web site enumeration of research using this instrument, involving more than twenty-five studies, has documented consistent and significant interrater reliability, predictive validity, and concurrent validity (www.sfu.ca/psychology/groups/mhlpi/hcr-20.htm). Not all such risk factor compilations, however, are as good as the HCR-20. For instance, the validity of the Sexual Violence Risk–20 (SVR-20; Boer, Hart, Kropp, & Webster, 1997) and the Multifactorial Assessment of Sex Offense Recidivism Risk (MASORR; Barbaree & Seto, 1998) have not been clearly supported (e.g., Barbaree, Seto, Langton, & Peacock, 2001; Sjöstedt & Långström, in press).

The other methodology involves the use of actuarial instrumentation but then allows for a limited degree of adjustments to be made based on clinical concerns. These clinically based adjustments reflect the need to consider protective factors and risk factors that are beyond the comprehensiveness of the instruments. The clinically adjusted actuarial approach has been supported through research by authors such as Haynes, Yates, Nicholaichuk, Gu, and Bolton (2000); McGrath, Cumming, Livingston, and Hoke (2000); and Wong, Olver, Wilde, Nicholaichuk, and Gordon (2000).

Apparently, there have never been any direct comparisons of the effectiveness of the research-guided clinical approach and the clinically adjusted actuarial methodology. Comparisons of the research-guided clinical approach with the purely actuarial model have been few, with a resultant varying picture between actuarial superiority and no difference between the two in their predictive accuracy (e.g., Grann, Belfrage, & Tengström, 2000; Polvi, 1999). These findings, coupled with those by Grove et al. (2000) suggest that actuarial instrumentation promises equal or improved risk assessment accuracy compared to any other methodology.

Actuarial Instrumentation

For the reasons stated previously, sex offender risk evaluations should typically involve the employment of empirically derived assessment procedures, at least as the "anchor" for other clinical adjustments (to borrow a term from Webster, Rice, Harris, Cormier, & Quinsey, 1994). The choice to assess violent or sexual offending risk without using any actuarial instrument (or at least a well-supported research-based instrument such as the HCR-20) is becoming virtually indefensible under circumstances involving "typical" sex offenders. Which instruments an evaluator should use, however, depends at least in part on the type of risk one is trying to assess.

For instance, for relatively short-term risk related to general criminality, the Level of Service Inventory—Revised (LSI-R; Andrews & Bonta, 1995) is recommended. This instrument is not specific to sex offenders, but there does not appear to be any reason it cannot be used with this population.

Likewise, if general interpersonal violence within a longer-term period is of primary concern, then either the Violence Risk Appraisal Guide (VRAG; Webster et al., 1994) or the Sex Offender Risk Appraisal Guide (SORAG; Quinsey, Harris, Rice, & Cormier, 1998) apparently represent the best validated and, hence, the best choice for this evaluation. For violence risk assessments with sex offenders, the SORAG shows a slightly higher degree of predictive accuracy than does the VRAG (e.g., Area Under Curve [AUC] = 0.80 vs. 0.76, from their respective developmental research results). To benefit fully from this somewhat higher accuracy, however, one needs to have the subject's results from a penile plethysmograph, something that can be difficult to obtain in many settings. The overlap of these two instruments is quite substantial (ten items are the same, with only two to four items differing between the two scales), with a near perfect correlation of results ($r = 0.93$; Rice & Harris, 1999), such that using the VRAG instead of the SORAG with a sex offender is easily justified. Using both instruments for the same subject, however, is quite redundant.

Risk Assessment for Civil Commitment

In the sex offender civil commitment realm, the issue specifically of the likelihood for sexual reoffending relative to a legal threshold is of sole importance within the risk assessment. Here, there are more than a score of instruments that have been promoted by someone as of use (Doren, 1999). When we restrict ourselves only to those with demonstrated statistical validation and cross-validation, however, there are only a few remaining from which to choose. The most commonly employed in the United States on this short list include (1) the Rapid Risk Assessment for Sex Offense Recidivism (RRASOR; Hanson, 1997), (2) the Minnesota Sex Offender Screening Tool—Revised (MnSOST-R; Epperson et al., 1999), and (3) the Static-99 (Hanson & Thornton, 2000). In contrast to unaided clinical judgment with its mean correlation with sexual recidivism of about .10 (Hanson & Bussière, 1998), these instruments show replicated correlations ranging from 0.27–0.35. (for the RRASOR and MnSOST-R, respectively; Doren, 2000) and AUCs typically in the range of 0.68–0.76 (with some findings both above and below this range) (Doren, 2000).

All the instruments described previously can be used within "relative" risk assessments (i.e., the assessment of which sex offenders are at higher or lower risk than other sex offenders). Within their defined follow-up time periods and type of recidivism outcome measure, they also all can be employed for "relative to a threshold" evaluations. No instrument, however, uses the same outcome time period and outcome measure as described by current sex offender civil commitment laws in the relevant states (i.e., none directly assess lifetime sexual reoffending risk). Some degree of extrapolation from the instrument results can be necessary when applied to the civil commitment realm.

Interpreting Instrument Results

If an evaluator uses solely one of the foregoing actuarial instruments, the assessment of recidivism risk stemming from either of two (or more) sources or pathways seems problematic. Hence, the use of at least one instrument per theorized/known dimension is recommended. For sexual reoffending risk assessments, the RRASOR is the only currently validated actuarial instrument that seems to correlate mostly with the sexual deviancy dimension (Doren & Roberts, 1998; Nicholaichuk, Templeman, & Gu, 1999). Likewise, the RRASOR tends to show only relatively small (though still statistically significant) correlations with the instruments that correlate with the violent/antisocial/hyperaggressive dimension: the MnSOST-R, Static-99, and VRAG (Doren & Roberts, 1998; Quackenbush, 2000). Hence, the use of the RRASOR as part of the assessment of the sexual deviancy dimensionally driven risk is recommended. Evaluations of the hyperaggressive dimension can include any of most of the other actuarial instruments already named.

From the theoretical perspective involving multiple types of drives toward reoffending, it seems clear that a finding of a low score on one scale does not necessarily mean a low-risk finding overall. For instance, if a subject's score on the RRASOR is rather low, the finding of a high set of scores on the Static-99, MnSOST-R, and other related instrumentation still indicates a high degree of sexual recidivism risk. Similarly, all of the foregoing named actuarial instrument scores can be low with the exception of the RRASOR, whose score is high, and one still has rationale for interpreting at least this portion of the risk assessment as indicating high risk for sexual reoffending. As described previously, this is analogous to a physician's finding that one's cardiac and neurological systems are all in fine shape but the single finding one has lung cancer still indicates there is a seriously high risk to his or her overall health.

Significant Combinations of Risk Factors

The fact that none of the actuarial instruments appears to encompass all the known research-supported risk factors for the relevant type of recidivism suggests that there may be reason to go beyond the existing instruments in a limited way.

One empirically and theoretically supported set of factors to consider is the degree to which the individual is psychopathic, as defined by the Psychopathy Checklist—Revised (PCL-R; Hare, 1991). This scale clearly is relevant to the assessment of the violent/antisocial/hyperaggressive dimension. Of importance beyond the actuarial instruments, however, is that the combination of a high degree of psychopathy (defined as 25+ on the PCL-R) with a deviant penile plethysmograph result seems associated to a particularly high degree of recidivism risk. For instance, concerning sexual reoffense risk, Rice and Harris (1997) found a 75% sexual rearrest recidivism rate for such people, much higher than other groups of people sampled. Harris et al. (2001) and Serin, Mailloux, and Malcolm (2001) essentially replicated that finding, with significantly worse sexual and general criminality recidivism rates for the doubly afflicted group.

Similarly, Gretton, McBride, Hare, O'Shaugnessy, and Kumka (2001) found that violent recidivism was significantly greater in adolescents who were both psychopathic and deviant versus those who had only one or neither of these attributes.

The finding that this risk factor combination is associated with particularly high recidivism risk probably should not come as much of a surprise. People who are both psychopathic and sexually deviant are essentially afflicted with high-risk signs on both of the identified pathways for recidivism.

Treatment Benefit

Virtually all items on the current set of actuarial instruments are rather unalterable, or what is considered static in nature. There can, however, be things that change about the individual since his last crime that potentially affect his recidivism risk. These newer and potentially dynamic (i.e., willfully changeable) features of the clinical picture become part of the potential adjustments to the actuarial risk assessment.

The most common consideration of this type is whether the person participates in, and completes a meaningful sex offender treatment program. In general, sex offender treatment programs have shown effectiveness in reducing recidivism rates of people who complete them (e.g., Hanson, 2000). McGrath et al. (2000) and Wong et al. (2000) have gone beyond that general finding with research indicating that treatment benefit can be an important consideration (in reducing assessed recidivism risk) compared to the results from a static actuarial instrument. Concomitantly, McGrath et al. (2000) also demonstrated that subjects' dropping out of treatment was a relevant consideration for increasing assessed risk beyond actuarial results.

All such research results to date, however, have involved a follow-up period of no longer than six years. If one is performing a risk assessment for a time period much beyond six years, one is left without direct research on which to assess the relevance of treatment participation. Though we might all hope that treatment benefit lasts a lifetime, there is at least one piece of research that suggests otherwise, given certain conditions. In the study by Hanson, Steffy, and Gauthier (1993), benefit from treatment during incarceration was demonstrated in the initial follow-up years, but it was found to dissipate over about ten years after incarceration. Notably there was no "maintenance" treatment during that time, a condition we might not find acceptable today. In combination with the foregoing findings, however, we cannot be sure what weight to give sex offender treatment (especially without maintenance follow-up in the community) as compared to the current (static) instruments in assessing long-term recidivism risk.

Other Clinical Considerations

Beyond all of the foregoing, there are some considerations that are clearly related to recidivism risk even though research has not studied them. An obvious "protective" factor is for the subject to be on his deathbed and without access to his types of victims. Another is that the person is going to remain incarcerated and away from all of his potential victims (e.g., children). An apparently clear high-risk factor is the subject's emphatic statement of intent to continue committing sex crimes if and when he is allowed access to potential victims.

The point of these examples is not to instruct the reader about the obvious. The real idea demonstrated here is that there are some clearly relevant considerations that are still beyond any of the risk assessment instrumentation we have. The existence of such factors does not mean that the instruments are seriously flawed. The fact we can name such obvious protective and risk factors just means that when using the best of our risk assessment technology, we all still need to think. The context of our assessment still matters

Conclusion

Until fairly recently, professionals working with sex offenders were forced to make crucial and highly risky decisions based solely on their clinical judgment that has little empirically based validity. Public policies including sex offender registration, public notification, and involuntary commitment have prompted the development of a number of actuarial risk assessment instrument. This chapter has reviewed a number of these tools. The passage of time will help to assess which ones of these are able to effectively identify those sex offenders who reoffend.

References

Andrews, D. A., & Bonta, J. (1995). *LSI-R: The Level of Service Inventory—Revised.* Toronto, Ontario: Multi-Health Systems.

Barbaree, H. E., & Seto, M. C. (1998). *The ongoing follow-up of sex offenders treated at the Warkworth Sexual Behaviour Clinic: Research report.* Toronto: Centre for Addiction and Mental Health.

Barbaree, H. E., Seto, M. C., Langton, C., & Peacock, E. (2001). Evaluating the predictive accuracy of six risk assessment instruments for adult sex offenders. *Criminal Justice and Behavior, 28*(4), 490–521.

Boer, D. P., Hart, S. D., Kropp, P. R., & Webster, C. D. (1997). *Manual for the Sexual Violence Risk— 20: Professional guidelines for assessing risk of sexual violence.* Burnaby, British Columbia: The Mental Health, Law, & Policy Institute, Simon Fraser University.

Doren, D. M. (1999, September). *A comprehensive comparison of risk assessment instruments to determine their relative value within civil commitment evaluations.* Paper presented at the 18th annual Research and Treatment Conference of the Association for the Treatment of Sexual Abusers in Lake Buena Vista, FL.

Doren, D. M. (2000, November). *Being accurate about the accuracy of commonly used risk assessment instruments.* Paper presented at the 19th annual Research and Treatment Conference of the Association for the Treatment of Sexual Abusers, San Diego, CA.

Doren, D. M., & Roberts, C. F. (1998, October). *The proper use and interpretation of actuarial instruments in assessing recidivism risk.* Paper presented at the 17th annual Research and Treatment Conference of the Association for the Treatment of Sexual Abusers, Vancouver.

Epperson, D. L., Kaul, J. D., Huot, S. J., Hesselton, D., Alexander, W., & Goldman, R. (1999). *Minnesota Sex Offender Screening Tool—Revised (MnSOST-R): Development, performance, and recommended risk level cut scores* [On-line]. Available: http://psych-server.iastate.edu/faculty/ epperson/MnSOST-R.htm.

Grann, M., Belfrage, H., & Tengström, A. (2001). Actuarial assessment of risk for violence: Predictive validity of the VRAG and historical part of the HCR-20. *Criminal Justice and Behavior, 27,* 97–114.

Gretton, H. M., McBride, M., Hare, R. D., O'Shaugnessy, R., & Kumka, G. (2001). Psychopathy and recidivism in adolescent sex offenders. *Criminal Justice and Behavior, 28*(4), 427–449.

Grove, W. M., & Meehl, P. E. (1996). Comparative efficiency of informal (subjective, impressionistic) and formal (mechanical, algorithmic) prediction procedures: The clinical-statistical controversy. *Psychology, Public Policy, and Law, 2*, 293–323.

Grove, W. M., Zald, D. H., Lebow, B. S., Snitz, B. E., & Nelson, C. (2000). Clinical versus mechanical prediction: A meta-analysis. *Psychological Assessment, 12*(1), 19–30.

Hanson, R. K. (1997). *The development of a brief Actuarial Risk Scale for Sexual Offense Recidivism* (User Report 97–04). Ottawa: Department of the Solicitor General of Canada.

Hanson, R. K. (1998). What do we know about sex offender risk assessment? *Psychology, Public Policy, and the Law, 4*(1/2) 50–72.

Hanson, R. K. (2000). *The effectiveness of treatment for sexual offenders: Report of the ATSA collaborative data research committee.* Paper presented at the 19th annual Research and Treatment Conference, San Diego.

Hanson, R. K., & Bussière, M. T. (1998). Predicting relapse: A meta-analysis of sexual offender recidivism studies. *Journal of Consulting and Clinical Psychology, 66*(2), 348–362.

Hanson, R. K., Steffy, R. A., & Gauthier, R. (1993). Long-term recidivism of child molesters. *Journal of Consulting and Clinical Psychology, 61*, 646–652.

Hanson, R. K., & Thornton, D. (2000). Improving risk assessments for sex offenders: A comparison of three actuarial scales. *Law and Human Behavior, 24*(1), 119–136.

Hare, R. D. (1991). *The Hare Psychopathy Checklist—Revised.* North Tonowanda, NY: Multi-Health Systems.

Harris, G. T., Rice, M. E., Quinsey, V. L., Lalumière, M. L., Boer, D., & Lang, C. (2001). *A multisite comparison of actuarial risk instruments for sex offenders.* Manuscript submitted for publication.

Haynes, A. K., Yates, P. M., Nicholaichuk, T., Gu, D., & Bolton, R. (2000, June). *Sexual deviancy, risk, and recidivism: The relationship between deviant arousal, the Rapid Risk Assessment for Sexual Offence Recidivism (RRASOR) and sexual recidivism.* Paper presented at annual convention of the Canadian Psychological Association, Ottawa.

Knight, R. (1999, September). *Unified theory of sexual coercion.* Paper presented at the 18th annual Research and Treatment Conference of the Association for the Treatment of Sexual Abusers in Buena Vista, FL.

McGrath, R. J., Cumming, G., Livingston, J. A., & Hoke, S. E. (2000, November). *The Vermont treatment program for sexual aggressors: An evaluation of a prison-based treatment program.* Poster presentation at the 19th annual Research and Treatment Conference of the Association for the Treatment of Sexual Abusers, San Diego, CA.

Nicholaichuk, T., Templeman, R., & Gu, D. (1999, May). *Empirically based screening for sex offender risk.* Paper presented at the Conference of the Correctional Services of Canada, Ottawa.

Polvi, N. (1999). *The prediction of violence in pretrial forensic patients: The relative efficacy of statistical versus clinical predictions of dangerousness.* Unpublished doctoral dissertation, Simon Fraser University Department of Psychology.

Quackenbush, R. (2000). *The assessment of sex offenders in Ireland and the Irish Sex Offender Risk Tool.* Unpublished manuscript.

Quinsey, V. L., Harris, G. T., Rice, M. E., & Cormier, C. A. (1998). *Violent offenders: Appraising and managing risk.* Washington, DC: American Psychological Association.

Rice, M. E., & Harris, G. T. (1997). Cross-validation and extension of the violence risk appraisal guide for child molesters and rapists. *Law and Human Behavior, 21*(2), 231–241.

Rice, M. E., & Harris, G. T. (1999, May). A multi-site follow-up study of sex offenders: The predictive accuracy of risk prediction instruments. Paper presented at the 3rd annual Forensic Psychiatry Program Research Day, University of Toronto, Penetanguishene, Ontario.

Serin, R. C., Mailloux, D. L., & Malcolm, P. B. (2001). Psychopathy, deviant sexual arousal and recidivism among sexual offenders. *Journal of Interpersonal Violence, 16*(3), 234–246.

Sjöstedt, G., & Långström, N. (in press). Assessment of risk for criminal recidivism among rapists in Sweden: A comparison of different procedures. *Psychology, Crime, and Law.*

Webster, C. D., Douglas, K. S., Eaves, S. D., & Hart, S. D. (1997). Assessing risk of violence to others. In C. D. Webster & M. A. Jackson (Eds.), *Impulsivity: Theory, assessment and treatment* (pp.
251–277). New York: Guilford Press.

Webster, C. D., Harris, G. T., Rice, M. E., Cormier, C., & Quinsey, V. L. (1994). *The Violence
Prediction Scheme: Assessing dangerousness in high risk men.* Toronto: Centre of Criminology,
University of Toronto.

Wong, S., Olver, M., Wilde, S., Nicholaichuk, T., & Gordon, A. (2000, June). *Violence Risk Scale
(VRS) and the Violence Risk Scale—Sex Offender Version (VRS-SO).* Paper presented at the annual convention of the Canadian Psychological Association, Ottawa, Ontario.

Chapter 7

Treatment Efficacy— Outcomes of the Clearwater Sex Offender Program

by Terry Nicholaichuk, Ph.D. and Pamela Yates, Ph.D.

Overview

This study of a Canadian prison-based sex offender treatment program presents outcome data which are subdivided to look at level of violence, psychopathy, ethnic origin, sexual deviancy, and age. Treated sex offenders recidivated at a significantly lower rate than untreated. Interesting results were revealed by scores on the Psychopathy Checklist—Revised (PCL-R; Hare, 1991) and the Rapid Risk Assessment for Sexual Recidivism (Hanson, 1997b).

Introduction

Sexual violence is a serious public concern; it has a substantial impact on victims, their families, and the community. There has been a considerable increase during the past decade in the sexual offender population within Canadian (Gordon & Porporino, 1990; Motiuk & Belcourt, 1996), U.S. (Becker, 1994; Becker & Murphy, 1998; Gordon & Porporino, 1990; McGrath, Hoke, & Vojtisek, 1998), and British (Fisher & Beech, 1999) correctional systems. Thus, there is a growing need for interventions demonstrated to reduce the likelihood of the recurrence of sexual offending among convicted sexual offenders. Although sex offender treatment has been in existence for many years (Pithers, 1993), and the availability of treatment interventions for sexual offenders has increased dramatically over the past decade, it is only relatively recently that empirical investigations of the efficacy of treatment have been conducted and even more recently that a sufficient number of studies have been conducted to enable thorough qualitative and meta-analytic reviews.

Controversy Over Efficacy

As the research literature on the effectiveness of interventions with sexual offenders is fraught with theoretical, practical, and methodological limitations, researchers have debated the efficacy of treatment. Though many researchers have concluded that treatment is effective in reducing the recurrence of sexual aggression (e.g., Alexander, 1999; Becker & Murphy, 1998; Grossman, Martis, & Fichtner, 1999; Marshall, Jones, Ward, Johnson, & Barbaree, 1991; Nicholaichuk, Gordon, Gu, & Wong, 2000; Pithers & Cumming, 1989), others have concluded that sexual offenders do not benefit from treatment (Furby, Weinrott, & Blackshaw, 1989; Quinsey, Harris, Rice, & Lalumiere, 1993; Quinsey, Khanna, & Malcolm, 1998). Historically, there have been a wide variety of treatment interventions implemented with adult sexual offenders, including general psychotherapeutic, physical and surgical, pharmacological, behavioral, and cognitive-behavioral approaches. However, cognitive-behavioral interventions have demonstrated the greatest effect in reducing sexual reoffending.

The purpose of this chapter is to evaluate the efficacy of treatment for adult male sexual offenders who were seen for treatment at a Canadian institutional treatment program located at the Regional Psychiatric Centre in Saskatoon, Canada (Nicholaichuk et al., 2000).

Cognitive-Behavioral Intervention With Sexual Offenders

As indicated previously, cognitive-behavioral interventions, based on social learning theory (Bandura, 1973, 1978, 1986), are the most widely accepted type of intervention with offenders generally (Andrews & Bonta, 1998) and with sexual offenders specifically (Becker & Murphy, 1998; Freeman-Longo & Knopp, 1992; Laws, 1989;

Yates, Goguen, & Nicholaichuk, 2000). Cognitive-behavioral treatment is based on the premise that cognitive and affective processes and behavior are linked, and that cognitions, affect, and behavior are mutually influential. Cognitive-behavioral interventions therefore involve skills acquisition and rehearsal, development of effective problem-solving strategies; social and victim perspective taking; sexual and social relationships; examination of the relationship between cognition, affect, and behavior; reducing deviant arousal and fantasy; and self management of behavior (Yates et al., 2000).

In addition to an overall cognitive-behavioral orientation, treatment of sexual offenders also typically incorporates relapse prevention. Relapse prevention as a treatment approach for sexual offenders was originally adapted from addictions research and is designed as a posttreatment intervention to assist in the maintenance of treatment and to prevent a return to sexual offending through the acquisition of self-management skills. Relapse prevention differs from many other approaches to treatment in that other approaches view sexual offending from the perspective of the medical model and, hence, attempt to "cure" or eliminate the problem, whereas relapse prevention focuses on control of behavior and conceptualizes treatment as a continuum or process rather than an end point (Becker & Murphy, 1998; Pithers & Cumming, 1989). Sexual offenders are no longer viewed as suffering from a disease, and it is theorized that they cannot be "cured," referring to a total, permanent alleviation of the condition. This is not unlike alcoholism, drug addiction, or obesity. Thus, behavioral control is regarded as a more realistic goal of treatment (Pithers & Cumming, 1989; Yates et al., 2000).

Qualitative and Quantitative Reviews of Sex Offender Treatment Efficacy

One of the first comprehensive reviews of sex offender treatment was conducted by Furby et al. (1989). This review found that in those studies for which multiple follow-up periods of the same subjects were conducted, there was a tendency for general recidivism (i.e., any reoffense) to increase over time, although there was no corresponding tendency evinced for sexual reoffending.

Furby et al. (1989) concluded that there was no evidence that treatment for sexual offenders reduced recidivism, either generally or differentially for different groups of offenders. This conclusion is regarded by most subsequent reviewers as overly pessimistic (e.g., Marshall et al., 1991; Marshall & Pithers, 1994). Among the problems associated with the Furby et al. (1989) review were the tendency to hold the studies reviewed to overly rigorous, unrealistic methodological standards (Marshall et al., 1991), the finding that many of the interventions applied in the treatment programs were out of date by the time of publication, and the finding that a number of the samples of offenders overlapped between the studies included in the review (Pithers, 1993).

In a subsequent review, Hall (1995) examined twelve studies including approximately 1,300 offenders published subsequent to the Furby et al. (1989) review. Hall's (1995) review examined recidivism of treated sexual offenders in comparison to sexual offenders who had not been treated or who had completed a comparison treatment program. Recidivism was broadly defined as additional sexually aggressive behavior which resulted in official legal charges. Hall (1995) found a small but robust effect size favoring treatment ($r = .12$). The overall recidivism rate for treated sexual offenders was 19% as compared to an overall recidivism rate of 27% for untreated or comparison-treated sexual offenders. However, treatment effect sizes varied considerably across studies, ranging from $r = -.07$ to $r = .55$, with studies with longer follow-up periods demonstrating the strongest effect sizes. Hall (1995) concluded that treatment was effective but that the low base rates of recidivism among sexual offenders likely precludes detecting statistically significant treatment effects.

Differential treatment was also a source of variability in treatment effect sizes. Studies in which either cognitive-behavioral (r = approximately .28) or hormonal (r = approximately .32) treatments were administered yielded significantly greater effect sizes than did studies in which behavioral treatment alone was employed (r = approximately -.10). Effect sizes for cognitive-behavioral and hormonal treatments were not significantly different from each other. These data suggest differential treatment effects on recidivism as a function of treatment type and the superiority of cognitive-behavioral and hormonal treatments relative to behavioral treatments. Cognitive-behavioral treatments may be the treatment of choice given that the refusal and attrition rates for hormonal treatments are considerably greater than those for cognitive-behavioral interventions (Hall, 1995).

Thus, unlike the Furby et al. (1989) review, Hall's (1995) review was considerably more optimistic about the effectiveness of sex offender treatment. Importantly, this meta-analysis identified the potential for differential treatment effects as a function of such factors as type of treatment, location of treatment, and risk or pathology of offenders.

In a recent review, Alexander (1999) conducted a quantitative analysis of seventy-nine sex offender treatment outcome studies, encompassing almost 11,000 treated and untreated sexual offenders. This review found that, overall, treated sexual offenders recidivated at a lower rate than did untreated sexual offenders (13% vs. 18%). This was true for the various subtypes of sexual offenders, including treated and untreated rapists (20.1% vs. 23.7%), child molesters generally (14.4% vs. 25.8%), child molesters whose victims were male (18.2% vs. 34.1%), and exhibitionists (19.7% vs. 57.1%). There were no differences between treated and untreated child molesters with female victims (15.6% vs. 15.7%) or when the type of sex offender was not specified in the original study (13.1% vs. 12%). These findings highlight the importance of examining outcome according to type of sex offender and demonstrate how treatment effects may be masked when recidivism rates are examined collapsing across the heterogeneous sex offender types.

Alexander's (1999) review also found that recidivism was reduced to a greater extent when treatment was provided in outpatient, prison, unspecified, or mixed settings than when provided in hospital settings. However, further analyses indicated that this was only true for child molesters who were treated in outpatient rather than prison settings (13.9% vs. 21.4%). Unfortunately, interactions were not examined by Alexander (1999), so the interaction between treatment type and location, which would be expected to be significant, was not examined. Support for prison settings over hospital settings, for example, may be a result of a greater availability of cognitive-behavioral treatment in prison settings, whereas hospital settings may not provide either cognitive-behavioral or sex offender-specific treatment.

In examining recidivism rates in relation to the date of publication of individual studies, Alexander (1999) found that recidivism rates declined for research published in the 1990s as compared to the 1980s for treated adult rapists (21.9% vs. 13.6%), adult child molesters of female victims (17.2% vs. 10.7%), incest offenders (6.4% vs. 3.1%), and nonincest offenders (17.7% vs. 6.1%). Conversely, recidivism increased from the 1980s to the 1990s among adult offenders against male children (17.6% vs. 21.3%) and among juvenile sexual offenders (2.9% vs. 10.6%). These findings suggest an increased rigor in treatment outcome research as well as a greater likelihood of appropriate treatment in later studies.

Reviews also highlight the importance of looking at treatment outcome as a function of sex offender risk, examining such factors as actuarially measured risk, offense history, and the like. For example, a history of sexual offending has been found to be associated with future sexual recidivism. It has been stated that the best predictor of future behavior is previous behavior (Grubin & Wingate, 1996), although, in some instances, this has not been borne out in outcome research (Yates & Nicholaichuk, 1998). Nonetheless, it has been found, with reasonable consistency, that recidivism is higher among sex offenders with histories of previous sexual offenses than among first-time sexual offenders (Marshall, 1994; Marshall et al., 1991; Nicholaichuk et al., 2000). In short, among sex offenders, a comparatively large number of offenders recidivate at a low rate, while a relatively small number recidivate at a high rate (Grubin & Wingate, 1996), which is also true for offenders generally (Broadhurst & Maller, 1992).

Effectiveness of Cognitive-Behavioral Treatment for Sex Offenders

In addition to the foregoing research pertaining to treatment effectiveness overall, research has also been conducted to examine the efficacy of cognitive-behavioral treatment specifically. Marshall et al. (1991) demonstrated the superiority of cognitive-behavioral intervention relative to behavioral treatment. In a study of treated exhibitionists, results indicated that such behavioral techniques as electrical aversion therapy, desensitization, and orgasmic reconditioning reduced reoffending, although recidivism rates remained substantial. Examining both official and unofficial recidivism rates over a follow-up period of greater than eight years, it was found that treated exhibitionists recidivated at a rate of 39% as compared to a rate of 57% among untreated exhibitionists. Although recidivism was lower among the treated men, the rate of reoffending obviously remained unacceptably high. Marshall et al. (1991) later added cognitive and cognitive-behavioral elements to the behavioral treatment program, including cognitive restructuring, relationship skills, assertiveness training, stress management, and other similar methods. At follow-up (approximately four years), the recidivism rate of the group that received cognitive-behavioral intervention was 23.6%, which, when corrected for the difference in length of follow-up, was significantly lower than that of the treated men who had received only behavioral treatment.

One recent study conducted to assess a specialized cognitive-behavioral intervention (McGrath et al., 1998) illustrates yet another important principle in sex offender treatment. In this study, McGrath et al. (1998) compared the effectiveness of specialized sex offender treatment to nonspecialized treatment and to an untreated control group. Results indicated a low overall recidivism rate of 6.6% for all offenders (treated and untreated). In addition, the data indicated that posttreatment sexual recidivism was lowest among offenders receiving specialized sex offender treatment (1.4%), followed by those receiving no treatment (10.5%), and those receiving nonspecialized treatment (15.6%). Although the untreated comparison group was considered at higher risk at pretreatment, as reflected by significantly more previous convictions for nonsexual violent and nonviolent offenses and a significantly longer period of incarceration, these data illustrate that treatment may, in some cases, be associated with higher rates of recidivism than not providing treatment at all, particularly if the treatment provided is nonspecific or inappropriate.

Methodological Limitations of Treatment Effectiveness Research

Research on the effectiveness of treatment outcome for sex offenders is hampered by a plethora of methodological limitations, including low base rates of reoffending, problems with sample selection, study design, selection of comparison groups, length of follow-up periods, and selection of outcome measures. These are reviewed briefly herein.

One of the most prominent methodological limitations to sex offender treatment outcome research is the low base rate of recidivism among sexual offenders (e.g., Hanson, 1997a; Nicholaichuk et al., 2000). Low base rates of recidivism result in difficulty in detecting treatment effects and consequently in the conclusion that treatment is ineffective. Similarly, the duration of follow-up posttreatment in treatment outcome studies affects conclusions regarding the efficacy of treatment. Specifically, research has found that sexual reoffending can occur after extended periods following treatment (e.g., Hanson, Steffy, & Gauthier, 1993; Marques, Day, Nelson, & Miner, 1989). However, treatment outcome studies frequently do not have lengthy posttreatment follow-up periods. Generally, studies with shorter follow-up periods are more likely to find a treatment effect than those with longer follow-up periods, thereby resulting in the conclusion that treatment may be more effective than is actually the case.

Sample selection has been a particular problem with treatment outcome research. Many treatment programs select participants on the basis of some predetermined criterion, such as motivation for treatment, or exclude participants on the basis of some criterion, such as the existence of denial or previous sexual offenses (Becker, 1994; Furby et al., 1989). As a result, some programs exclude high-risk offenders and treat low-risk offenders, who do not demonstrate a treatment effect due to a floor effect (Nicholaichuk, 1996; Nicholaichuk et al., 2000). These biases result in "evidence" of a lack of a treatment effect or, alternatively, when aggregated with data for higher-risk offenders, attenuate the magnitude of the treatment effect, thus giving the appearance that treatment is ineffective.

Similarly, although heterogeneity among sexual offenders is widely acknowledged among researchers and clinicians, many outcome evaluation studies do not examine reoffending as a function of the type of sex offender but, rather, aggregate findings from different types of offenders, for whom differential recidivism rates are now known to occur (e.g., Alexander, 1999; Marshall et al., 1991; Nicholaichuk et al., 2000). Analyses which do not account for such variation overestimate reoffending among those offenders who recidivate at the lowest rates (e.g., incest offenders) and underestimate reoffending among those offenders who recidivate at higher rates (e.g., exhibitionists and pedophiles who offend against boys).

Similarly, studies of specialized populations, such as mentally disordered, not criminally responsible, certified mentally ill, or offenders committed for pretrial assessment, may not be generalizable to other, less specialized samples of sexual offenders (i.e., those typically found in correctional settings). Such studies have not found a significant positive effect of treatment for such offenders (e.g., Rice, Harris, & Cormier, 1992; Rice, Harris, & Quinsey, 1990; Rice, Quinsey, & Harris, 1991; Webster, Harris, Rice, & Quinsey, 1994). However, given that these sample populations are highly specialized and were not treated using cognitive-behavioral methods, these findings may not be comparable to the general population of sexual offenders. Regardless, findings from research on these populations are frequently generalized to conclude that treatment is ineffective, or these samples are included in studies with other samples of sexual offenders, with the result that treatment effects are masked or attenuated.

Other research which has concluded a lack of treatment effects has been conducted on programs which offered only a single intervention to all offenders, ignoring variability treatment in needs and the multidimensional nature of sexual offending behavior (Gordon & Nicholaichuk, 1996). Each of these problems with sample selection and treatment methods compromises the integrity of the treatment program, the evaluation, or both and, thus, negatively affects conclusions about the effectiveness of treatment.

The lack of appropriate comparison groups is only one of many problems plaguing the search for effective recidivism reduction strategies. Statistical analytic strategies have, to date, largely ignored the qualitative element in recidivism research. For example, in calculating recidivism statistics, all new sexual crimes following treatment are given the same weight and are counted as failures. However, the actual crime could range from indecent exposure to assaults which result in great victim harm. Fortunately, an analytic strategy has become available which captures more information about a criminal career and helps shed some light on the qualitative elements of criminal behavior, the Criminal Career Profile, a concept developed by Wong, Templeman, Gu, Andre, and Leis (1996) with the support of the Correctional Service of Canada.

The Criminal Career Profile

Nicholaichuk et al. (2000) first reported the use of the Criminal Career Profile (CCP) in recidivism research with sexual offenders. The CCP (Wong et al., 1996) is the ratio of the time (years) that an offender has spent incarcerated plotted against time spent in the community. Wong et al. (1998) showed that two measures derived from an offender's CCP, Age of First Conviction (AFC) and Slope, provide an overall measure of the degree of violence of an offender's past criminal convictions. Offenders who have committed more violent crimes tend to receive longer sentences. The more violent the offender's criminal career, the steeper the slope of the CCP. A least-square regression line can be fitted to the slope of the CCP to obtain a measure of angle in degrees. Wong et al. (1998) also reported that the slope of the CCP and the AFC are both highly correlated with the number of past violent convictions (.50 and -.33, respectively) and with PCL-R (Hare, 1991) scores (.40 and -.33, respectively).

There are a number of important benefits to the use of the CCP. First, it is easy to obtain the necessary information, as the data are based on official documentation related to convictions. In Canada, all criminal convictions are captured in a national database. Second, because the slope of the CCP is correlated with the violence of the individual's criminal career, it allows for subjects to be matched according to the degree of violence of their offenses and for their reoffenses to be weighted in terms of severity. It should be noted that this technique may be less appropriate in the United States where sentencing structures between different states are highly heterogeneous and not necessarily correlated with the degree of violence.

The Clearwater Study

Even with the methodological limitations described previously, it is possible to draw conclusions about the efficacy of sex offender treatment. The discussion that follows reviews the outcomes from a Canadian sex offender treatment program with an emphasis on qualitative and quantitative outcome evaluation. The study presents outcome data from the Clearwater Sex Offender Treatment Program operated by the Correctional Service of Canada (CSC) at the Regional Psychiatric Centre in Saskatoon, Canada. The study also incorporated the CCP, which has some advantages over strategies previously employed in that it provides a measure of the degree of violence in the criminal pattern. Finally, additional analyses were conducted to address specific areas of concern. The outcomes of Native versus non-Native offenders were compared and the relationship between psychopathy and sexual recidivism posttreatment was examined. Finally, the effects of sexual deviance in increasing recidivism posttreatment and the effect of aging in reducing recidivism were also studied.

Program Description. The Clearwater Sex Offender Treatment Program is located within the Regional Psychiatric Centre (RPC) in Saskatoon, Canada. The RPC is a stand-alone, multilevel security psychiatric facility which is also an accredited teaching hospital affiliated with the University of Saskatchewan. Clearwater is a forty-eight-bed active treatment unit which serves high-risk and high-need sexual offenders whose treatment needs could not be met in their parent institutions. Historically, these offenders have tended to be men who are recidivistic and criminalized and have high treatment needs. They were ordinarily housed in CSC penitentiaries and transferred to the Clearwater Program for active treatment, after which they were returned to their original institutions. In addition to treating individuals who were exceptionally criminalized or sexually deviant, the program admitted many men who were diagnosed as low functioning for various reasons (e.g., cognitive delay and acquired brain injury).

While at the Clearwater program, clients received both individual and group treatment relating to social skills, human sexuality, and emotions management. Victim awareness/empathy training was also introduced. Deviant arousal was targeted directly using behavioral or, more recently, cognitive-behavioral strategies including covert sensitization, arousal reconditioning, and masturbatory conditioning. In recent years, the Clearwater program also enlisted the assistance of the Aboriginal community. Native Elders became part of the treatment staff and conducted spiritual ceremonies and other cultural practices as part of the program. The remaining treatment personnel consisted of psychologists, parole officers, and nursing staff. The program ordinarily was between six and eight months in duration, with some special-needs clients remaining somewhat longer. Then, the Clearwater program underwent a series of changes. In the later half of the 1980s, relapse prevention (RP) training was formally implemented. Nonetheless, certain continuities have existed throughout the program's history. For example, it has always been based on a social learning model and has always used a multidisciplinary staff team.

Defining the Population. The treated group included sexual offenders who completed the Clearwater program between 1981 and 1996 and who had been released. This group (N = 296) included 168 (57%) rapists, 49 (17%) pedophiles, 47 (15%) mixed offenders (men who offended against both adults and children), and 32 (11%) incest offenders. Twenty-eight percent of the sample were Native and seventy-two (72%) were non-Native.

A stratified matched comparison group was drawn from an archive of approximately 2,600 sexual offenders who had been incarcerated in the Prairie Region of the CSC between 1983 and 1996. A match was created for each treated offender on a number of dimensions: (1) age at data collection, (2) age at first conviction, (3) age at index offense, (4) race, (5) prior criminal history and the number of sexual and non-sexual convictions prior to the index offense, and (6) follow-up period.

After matching, a comparison group of offenders (N = 283) was established. Forty-four percent of the comparison subjects were Native and fifty-six (56%) were non-Native. In addition, an attempt was made to identify offenders in the comparison sample according to whether they were rapists, pedophiles, mixed, or incest offenders. However, due to the lack of electronic records, this was possible in only eighty cases. Between the treated and matched groups, the proportion of mixed offenders was different (15.9 vs. 5%, respectively, z = 2.36, p < .018), but the proportion of rapists, incest offenders, and pedophiles was the same.

There were some preindex offense differences between the treated and comparison groups. The treated group had a greater number of convictions for violent crimes, t (576) = 4.89, p < .001, and all other crimes, t (576) = -2.82, p < .01. The treated group was slightly older, t (576) = 2.53, p < .05 and had a lower proportion of Native to non-Native offenders when compared to the comparison sample, χ^2 = 16.64 (1), p < 001. The follow-up period for the comparison sample was 1.4 years longer than that of the treatment sample (7.3 vs. 5.9 years, respectively); a significant difference, t (576) = 24.51, p < .001. Finally, approximately half of the matched sample subjects for whom records could be obtained had participated in some sort of treatment at other sites. However, none had been seen at the high-intensity Clearwater program (Hanson & Nicholaichuk, 2000).

Subjects were followed from their first release date after the index offense until June 1996, the data collection date, and subsequent analyses were based on official criminal records. Outcomes were coded according to whether there was a new sexual or nonsexual offense, a new violent or nonviolent offense, or no readmission to prison. Outcomes were analyzed by means of tests of proportion which focused on all offenses following treatment regardless of the penalties incurred. Survival analyses were completed comparing survival rates between treated and comparison offenders and

Native versus non-Native offenders. Finally, the CCP was calculated for each subject, pretreatment and posttreatment. Slopes for the CCP for groups were computed as the mean of all individual slopes in the group.

Program Outcomes. The program's outcomes showed that 14.5% of the treated and 33.2% of the untreated offenders committed new sexual offenses during the follow-up period, $z = -5.289$, $p < .001$. However, only 8.8% of treated first-time offenders committed new sexual crimes, whereas 27.3% of untreated first-time offenders reoffended sexually, $z = -5.289$, $p < .001$. Offenders with more than one prior conviction for sexual crimes reoffended at higher rates. For example, 23.5% of treated recidivistic offenders committed new sexual crimes whereas 43% of untreated recidivistic offenders did so, $z = -3.092$, $p < .001$. Men without previous convictions for sexual crimes committed new sexual crimes at lower rates than did repeat offenders (8.8% vs. 23.5%, respectively).

Data were also analyzed by type of offender. A significant reduction in recidivism was observed for all offender types except for incest offenders. Because this was a low-risk group of offenders, a floor effect was encountered, and there was no significant reduction in recidivism posttreatment. Finally, 19% fewer treated offenders did not return to prison for any new crime, sexual or nonsexual. The differences in readmission for any new crime between treated and matched offenders was 33.4% and 44.5%, respectively.

Survival Analysis: Treated vs. Nontreated and Native vs. Non-Native Comparisons. Figure 7.1 presents survival curves for the treated and comparison samples over a maximum period of 14 years. During the study period, the survival rate between treated and comparison groups was significantly different, Wilcoxin (1) = 12.200, $p <$ .001. Between treated and Natives and treated Non-Natives, there were no differences in outcome, Wilcoxin (1) = 0.00, $p = .998$. Further, treated Natives reoffended at lower rates than did untreated Natives, Wilcoxin (1) = 4.78, $p < .05$. Similarly, treated non-Natives reoffended at lower rates than did untreated non-Natives, Wilcoxin (1) = 0.13, $p = .936$. Figure 7.1 also shows that offenders in the comparison group, regardless of ethnicity, began reoffending earlier after their release from prison and continued to reoffend at higher rates throughout the entire follow-up period.

Results From Criminal Career Profile

Nicholaichuk et al. (2000), reported pre- and posttreatment CCP slopes for treated and comparison groups in the original Clearwater outcome study. Their analysis showed that criminal histories of the comparison subjects were not as violent as the treated group in spite of a similar number of preindex offense criminal convictions. This finding was indicated by the lower CCP slope for this group. The mean angle pretreatment for the treated group was 19.90 and the posttreatment angle was 4.70, t (295) = 12.02, $p < .01$, indicating significantly less serious posttreatment offending. For the comparison group, the preindex offense angle was 12.90 and postindex offense angle was 6.80 , t (282) = 5.81, $p < .01$.

It appeared that subjects in the comparison sample received shorter sentences for their crimes and, thus, the slope of the group CCP was less steep than the slope for the

Figure 7.1
Overall Survival Function Treated vs. Untreated by Native vs. Non-Native

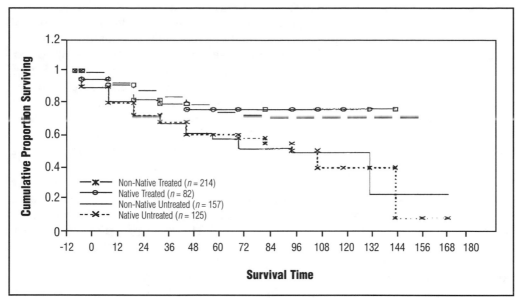

treatment group. Assuming that sentence length reflects the degree of violence of the crime, the lower slope suggests that the offenders in the comparison sample committed less violent crimes and therefore received shorter sentences than did offenders in the treated group. The change in the posttreatment slope of the CCP following the index offense for both groups reflected a reduction in new crime for both groups. However, the reduction in the degree of violence was more pronounced among members of the treated sample.

A repeated measures ANOVA (analysis of variance) was conducted taking pre- and posttreatment slopes of the CCP as dependent measures. The analysis showed a main effect pre- and posttreatment, $F(1,570) = 166.47$, $p < .0001$. There was also a significant effect of the interaction, $F(1, 570) = 30.86$, $p < .0001$. Although there was a reduction in new crime following the index offense in both groups, the interaction indicated that the effect was significantly more pronounced in the treated group.

Differences in CCP slope pre- and posttreatment were also significantly for the different offender groups. Specifically, the treated rapist, mixed, and pedophile groups each demonstrated less steep CCP slopes at posttreatment than at pretreatment [$t(167) = 9.88$ $p < .01$; $t(46) = 5.59$, $p < .01$ and $t(48) = 4.32$, $p < .01$, respectively]. For the incest offenders, the comparison was not significant, $t(31) = 1.82$, $p = .08$. The lack of a treatment effect among incest offenders was not surprising, as these men represent a lower-risk group and, therefore, a floor effect was encountered (Nicholaichuk, 1996).

Relationship Between Psychopathy Checklist—Revised and Sexual Recidivism

Psychopathy (Hare, 1991) has been found to be predictive of general (nonsexual) violence. However, its relationship to treatment outcome specifically with regard to sexual recidivism among sex offenders has not been clearly demonstrated. Nonetheless, the PCL-R (Hare, 1991) is frequently applied to the assessment of sex offenders (Boer, Wilson, Gauthier, & Hart, 1997). In one study (Rice et al., 1990), psychopathy in conjunction with deviant sexual arousal was found to be predictive of sexual recidivism. However, this study has not been replicated and additional studies assessing the usefulness of psychopathy among sexual offenders have not appeared. Furthermore, by its definition as a personality disorder (Hare, 1991), it can be argued that psychopathy represents a static factor which is unlikely to be amenable to change following intervention. As such, its usefulness as a target of treatment interventions is therefore unknown.

A study by Yates and Nicholaichuk (1998) examined the relationship between the CCP, psychopathy as measured by the PCL-R (Hare, 1991), and outcome following the Clearwater Sex Offender Program. The subjects in this study were a subset of seventy-six offenders who had participated in the Clearwater study and for whom we had PCL-R scores. They were 29.5 years old at their index offense, 48.7% were rapists, 14.5 % were pedophiles, 22.4% were mixed offenders, and 14.5% were incest offenders. In addition, 68.4% were non-Native and 31.6 % were Native. Their mean pretreatment CCP Score was 19.80 (SD = 20.15) and their mean PCL-R score was 22.0 (SD = 7.62). The incidence of psychopathy, defined by having a score of greater than 30 on the PCL-R, was 22% (N = 17).

The majority of the offenders in this study (80.3 %) did not recidivate sexually following treatment. Ten of the fifty-nine nonpsychopaths recidivated sexually and five of the seventeen psychopaths recidivated sexually. However, a nonparametric test of proportion revealed that the differences were not significant, z = 1.138, p > .255. Clearly, these conclusions should be accepted with caution due to the small sample size.

PCL-R scores were moderately correlated with pretreatment CCP (r = .38, p < .01); however, the PCL-R score was not significantly correlated with posttreatment CCP (r = .22, p > .05). Thus, the posttreatment CCP correlated with posttreatment recidivism to a greater extent than did PCL-R and the PCL-R score was more strongly positively correlated with previous offense history than with posttreatment recidivism.

The Effect of Sexual Deviance on Outcome

An additional analysis of the Clearwater data (Haynes, Yates, Nicholaichuk, Gu, & Bolton, 2000) was conducted to examine the relationship between risk as measured by the Rapid Risk Assessment for Sexual Recidivism (RRASOR; Hanson, 1997b), deviant sexual arousal assessed through phallometric assessment, and posttreatment recidivism. The subjects were another subset of the Clearwater treated sample (N = 174). Just over half (52.3%) were rapists, 16.7% were pedophiles, 13.2% were incest offenders, and 17.8% were from the mixed offender group. They were divided into deviant and nondeviant groups based on their responses to slide stimuli, using a cutoff of 15% full erection value (% FEV). Using this cutoff, thirty-eight (21.8%) offenders were classified as deviant, defined as showing deviant sexual arousal which they were unable to control. The remainder of the men in the study were classified as nondeviant (N = 136; 78.2%) because they either showed no deviant arousal or were able to control arousal voluntarily. Subjects were rated on the RRASOR and followed

Figure 7.2
Sexual Recidivism by Offender Risk and Deviant Arousal (*N* = 174)

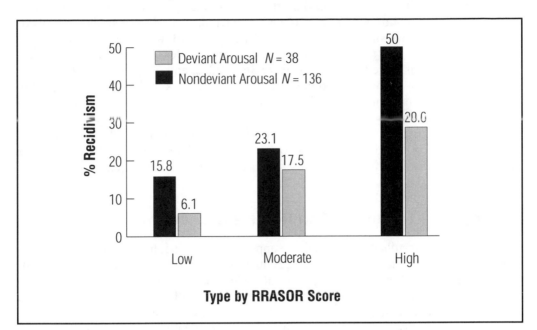

for an average of 5.9 years post-release. Recidivism records were obtained in accordance with the Nicholaichuk et al. (2000) procedure described previously.

Figure 7.2 shows the sexual recidivism rates for the RRASOR score risk categories by deviant and nondeviant arousal groups. It is apparent from Figure 7.2 that sexual deviance increased the risk for new sexual offenses. Specifically, there was a statistically significant interaction between risk and deviant sexual arousal on postrelease sexual recidivism. Within each of the three risk groups, offenders who demonstrated deviant sexual arousal or who were unable to control arousal recidivated sexually at a higher rate postrelease than did offenders who demonstrated no deviant sexual arousal. These results suggest that deviant sexual arousal is a dynamic factor associated with sex offense risk. For example, deviant sexual arousal among sex offenders assessed as low risk using actuarial measures of static variables may serve to elevate that risk to a higher level. Similarly, offenders who are assessed using static measures as high risk but who do not evince deviant sexual arousal, might be regarded as lower risk than offenders assessed as high risk who demonstrate deviant arousal.

The sexually deviant group had significantly more child victims, female victims, and total victims than did the nondeviant group. Contrary to Hanson's (1997b) findings, however, the groups were not significantly different in terms of the number of male victims. However, the deviant group demonstrated greater sexual arousal to males than did the nondeviant group, suggesting that a generalized pattern of arousal may represent a risk factor rather than number of male victims per se. In summary, this study suggested that deviant sexual arousal can add to assessment of risk for sexual recidivism in conjunction with assessment of risk as measured using actuarial tools such as the RRASOR.

The Effect of Aging on Outcome

The final set of analyses focused on the effect of aging on sexual recidivism. The subjects were the 604 offenders from the Nicholaichuk et al. (2000) study. They were grouped according to whether they were under 25 years of age at release ($N = 109$), 25–45 years at release ($N = 424$), or over 45 years at release ($N = 71$). The sexual recidivism rates for these three groups were 36%, 22%, and 7%, respectively. A one-way analysis of covariance was conducted using time at risk and number of preindex sexual offenses (an estimate of risk) as covariates. After controlling for these variables, the effect of aging was significant, $F(2) = 3.617$, $p < .027$. Figure 7.3 presents these results in graphic form. Thus, the process of aging, in and of itself, appears to have had the effect of reducing the risk for new sexual offenses. The finding that aging can mitigate criminal history is consistent with other research (e.g., Hall, 1996; Hanson, 2000).

Appropriate Treatment Can Reduce Recidivism

The primary results of these studies support the conclusion that appropriate treatment can reduce sexual recidivism. The reduction in sexual recidivism posttreatment was more significant in already high-risk offenders and was independent of race. The diagnosis of psychopathy did not appear to be highly related to sexual recidivism. Sexual deviance assessed phallometrically was shown to elevate risk even in actuarially low-risk groups but only among men who were unable to inhibit their arousal when asked to do so. Finally, it was observed that aging, to some extent, appears to mitigate the effect of criminal history. Older men showed low sexual recidivism rates when sex offense history and time at risk were controlled.

Admittedly, there may be some methodological limitations associated with con-

Figure 7.3
Percent Sexual Recidivism Rate by Age at Release

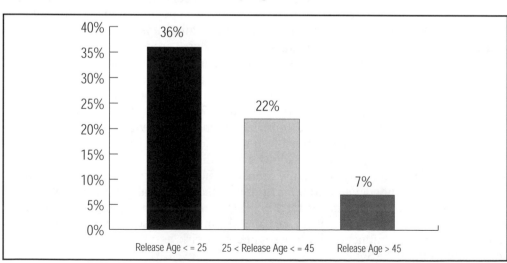

ducting research in this fashion due to attrition of criminal records from the data base in which they are held (cf. Hanson & Nicholaichuk, 2000), but even with these caveats, the effect of treatment was significant. This is consistent with other research (e.g., Alexander, 1999; Hall, 1995; Hanson, 2000; Marques et al., 1989). The 50% reduction in recidivism shown here was thought to be clinically significant. Although a history of previous convictions for sexual offenses is a risk factor for future sexual recidivism (Hanson & Thornton, 1999), the present study suggests that the impact of this risk factor can be mitigated through treatment.

The study also presented a new method for assessing outcome. The CCP includes information about the degree of violence in an offender's criminal history. The AFC and CCP together give important information about the violence inherent in offense patterns as this is reflected in sentence length. More serious offenses usually result in higher slopes pre- and posttreatment. Usual methods of assessing outcomes are not able to capture this dimension as easily and clearly. By employing the CCP as an outcome measure, we were able to investigate the degree to which both the quantity and quality of criminal behavior can be modified by treatment. CCP slope changes at posttreatment indicated a reduction in the number of new crimes as well as a reduction in the degree of violence in these crimes.

Findings from the present study support the relationship of deviant sexual arousal as a risk factor for recidivism (e.g., Hanson & Bussière, 1998). However, the interactional relationship between deviant arousal and risk, which would be expected, has not been investigated in previous research. In the present study, deviant sexual arousal was found to interact with risk as measured by the RRASOR (Hanson, 1997b) in its effect on treatment outcome. Specifically, although risk was associated with increased recidivism, it was so associated only in interaction with deviant sexual arousal. Within each of the three risk categories assessed by the RRASOR (high, moderate, and low), the presence of deviant sexual arousal was associated with increased recidivism, whereas nondeviant arousal or ability to control deviant arousal mitigated the influence of static risk on recidivism of treated sexual offenders. These findings suggest that deviant sexual arousal is a dynamic risk factor which, when treated, may reduce risk for sexual recidivism.

Results from the present study indicated that psychopathy was only moderately correlated with the pretreatment CCPs of incarcerated high-risk sexual offenders and was not significantly correlated with posttreatment CCP. These findings suggest that, although psychopathy may be associated with the commission of violence, it may only be moderately associated with the seriousness of that violence. In addition, psychopathy was found to be more strongly associated with pretreatment violent offense history than with posttreatment violent reoffending, whereas the CCP was more strongly associated with posttreatment recidivism than was psychopathy. Logistic regression analyses indicated that psychopathy did not predict sexual recidivism following treatment, when measured using a variety of recidivism indicators, including federal versus any jurisdictional readmission, first recidivism event posttreatment, or all recidivism occurring following release after treatment. Finally, results indicated no differences in posttreatment sexual recidivism between psychopaths and nonpsychopaths.

These findings suggest that, although previous research demonstrates that psychopathy is a predictor of risk for violent recidivism among nonsexual offenders (e.g., Hare, 1996; Hart, Kropp, & Hare, 1988; Serin, 1996; Serin, Peters, & Barbaree,

1990), psychopathy does not predict sexual recidivism among treated high-risk sex offenders. However, as indicated previously, these findings should be viewed with caution due to the small sample size and the low base rate of recidivism among this subsample of offenders in the study.

The effect of aging on sexual recidivism was another interesting finding which arose out of this series of studies. In our risk prediction equations, we typically assign risk points to younger offenders because of the well-established link between young age and criminal risk (e.g. Hanson & Thornton, 1999). Studies such as this suggest that we should consider subtracting points when offenders are over the age of 45. The exact weight which should be given to the aging variable is as yet undetermined, but clearly, this is variable that needs to be factored into any assessment of sex offender risk. Treatment completion appears to be another variable which deserves consideration as a factor that can mitigate risk.

Conclusion

In summary, the outcome of the Clearwater study supports findings from other research (e.g., Alexander, 1999; Hall, 1995; Hanson, 2000; Marques et al., 1989) that cognitive-behavioral treatment of sexual offenders, applied to appropriate subjects, can reduce the occurrence of posttreatment sexual reoffending. The study also highlights the importance of addressing responsivity in treatment (Andrews & Bonta, 1998). Specifically, our findings indicated that risk for posttreatment recidivism is differentially associated with age, sexual offense history, type of offender, deviant sexual arousal, psychopathy, and severity of pretreatment offense history. Treatment of sexual offenders, therefore, should ensure that factors such as these are taken into account in treatment planning and risk assessment. Future research should ensure that assessment of these various factors, particularly dynamic risk factors, are evaluated with regard to their differential impact on treatment outcome.

References

Alexander, M. A. (1999). Sexual offender treatment efficacy revisited. *Sexual Abuse: A Journal of Research and Treatment, 11*(2), 101–116.

Andrews, D. A., & Bonta, J. (1998). *The psychology of criminal conduct* (2nd ed.). Cincinnati, OH: Anderson Press.

Bandura, A. (1973). *Aggression: A social learning analysis.* Englewood Cliffs, NJ: Prentice-Hall.

Bandura, A. (1978). Social learning theory of aggression. *Journal of Communication, 28,* 12–29.

Bandura, A. (1986). *Social foundations of thought and action: A social cognitive theory.* Englewood Cliffs, NJ: Prentice-Hall.

Becker, J. V. (1994). Offenders: Characteristics and treatment. *The Future of Children, 4,* 176–197.

Becker, J. V., & Murphy, W. D. (1998). What we know and do not know about assessing and treating sex offenders. *Psychology, Public Policy, and Law, 4*(1–2), 116–137.

Boer, D. P., Wilson, R. J., Gauthier, C. M., & Hart, S. D. (1997). Assessing risk of sexual violence: Guidelines for clinical practice. In C. D. Webster & M. A. Jackson (Eds.), *Impulsivity: Theory, assessment, and treatment* (pp. 326–342). New York: Guilford Press.

Broadhurst, R. G., & Maller, R.A. (1992). The recidivism of sex offenders in the Western Australian prison population. *British Journal of Criminology, 32*(1), 54–80.

Fisher, D., & Beech, A. R. (1999). Current practice in Britain with sexual offenders. *Journal of Interpersonal Violence, 14*(3), 240–256.

Freeman-Longo, R. E., & Knopp, H. F. (1992). State-of-the-art sex offender treatment: Outcome and issues. *Annals of Sex Research, 5*(3), 141–160.

Furby, L., Weinrott, M. R., & Blackshaw, L. (1989). Sex offender recidivism: A review. *Psychological Bulletin, 105*, 3–30.

Gordon, A., & Nicholaichuk, T. (1996). Applying the risk principle to sex offender treatment. *Forum on Corrections Research, 8*(2), 36–38.

Gordon, A., & Porporino, F. J. (1990). *Managing the treatment of sexual offenders: A Canadian perspective* (Research Report No. B-05). Ottawa: Correctional Service of Canada.

Grossman, L. S., Martis, B., & Fichtner, C. G. (1999). Are sex offenders treatable? A research review. *Psychiatric Services, 50*(3), 349–361.

Grubin, D., & Wingate, S. (1996). Sexual offence recidivism: Prediction versus understanding. *Criminal Behaviour and Mental Health, 6*, 349–359.

Hall, G. C. N. (1995). Sexual offender recidivism revisited: A meta-analysis of recent treatment studies. *Journal of Consulting and Clinical Psychology, 63*, 802–809.

Hall, G. C. N. (1996). *Theory-based assessment, treatment, and prevention of sexual aggression.* New York: Oxford University Press.

Hanson, R. K. (1997a). How to know what works with sexual offenders. *Sexual Abuse: A Journal of Research and Treatment, 9*, 129–145.

Hanson, R. K. (1997b). *The development of a brief Actuarial Risk Scale for Sexual Offense Recidivism* (User Report 97–04). Ottawa: Solicitor General of Canada.

Hanson, R. K. (2000, November). *The effectiveness of treatment for sexual offenders: Report of the ATSA Collaborative Database Research Committee.* Paper presented at the 19th annual Research and Treatment Conference of the Association for the Treatment of Sexual Abusers, San Diego.

Hanson, R. K., & Bussière, M. T. (1998). Predicting relapse: A meta-analysis of sexual offender recidivism studies. *Journal of Consulting and Clinical Psychology, 66*(2), 348–362.

Hanson, R. K., & Nicholaichuk, T. P. (2000). A cautionary note regarding Nicholaichuk, et al. (2000). *Sexual Abuse: A Journal of Research and Treatment, 12*, 289–293.

Hanson, R. K., Steffy, R. A., & Gauthier, R. (1993). Long-term recidivism of child molesters. *Journal of Consulting and Clinical Psychology, 61*, 646–652.

Hanson, R. K., & Thornton, D. (1999). *Static-99: Improving actuarial risk assessments for sex offenders* (User Report No. 99-02). Ottawa: Solicitor General of Canada.

Hare, R. D. (1991). *The Hare Psychopathy Checklist—Revised.* North Tonowanda, NY: Multihealth Systems.

Hare, R. D. (1996). Psychopathy: A clinical construct whose time has come. *Criminal Justice and Behaviour, 23*, 25–54.

Hart, S. D., Kropp, P. R., & Hare, R. D. (1988). Performance of male psychopaths following conditional release from prison. *Journal of Consulting and Clinical Psychology, 56*, 227–232.

Haynes, A. K., Yates, P. M., Nicholaichuk, T., Gu, D., & Bolton, R. (2000, July). *Sexual deviancy, risk, and recidivism: The relationship between deviant arousal, the Rapid Risk Assessment for Sexual Offence Recidivism (RRASOR), and sexual recidivism.* Paper presented at the 61st annual conference of the Canadian Psychological Association, Ottawa.

Laws, D. R. (1989). *Relapse prevention with sex offenders.* New York: Guilford Press.

Marques, J. K., Day, D. M., Nelson, C., & Miner, M. H. (1989). The sex offender treatment and evaluation project: California's relapse prevention program. In D. R. Laws (Ed.), *Relapse prevention with sex offenders* (pp. 247–267). New York: Guilford Press.

Marshall, W. L. (1994). Treatment effects on denial and minimization in incarcerated sex offenders. *Behaviour Research and Therapy, 5*, 559–564.

Marshall, W. L., Jones, R., Ward, T. Johnson, P., & Barbaree, H. E. (1991). Treatment outcome with sex offenders. *Clinical Psychology Review, 11*, 465–485.

Marshall, W. L., & Pithers, W.D. (1994). A reconsideration of treatment outcome with sex offenders. *Criminal Justice and Behavior, 21*(1), 10–27.

McGrath, R. J., Hoke, S. E., & Vojtisek, J. E. (1998). Cognitive-behavioral treatment of sex offenders. *Criminal Justice and Behavior, 25*(2), 203–225.

Motiuk, L., & Belcourt, R. (1996). Profiling the Canadian federal sex offender population. Research in brief. *Forum on Corrections Research, 8*(2), 3–7.

Nicholaichuk, T. P. (1996). Sex offender treatment priority: An illustration of the risk/need principle. *Forum on Corrections Research, 8*(2), 30–32.

Nicholaichuk, T. P., Gordon, A., Gu, D., & Wong, S. (2000). Outcome of an institutional sexual offender treatment program: A comparison between treated & matched untreated offenders. *Sexual Abuse: A Journal of Research and Treatment, 12*(2), 139–153.

Pithers, W. D. (1993). Treatment of rapists: Reinterpretation of early outcome data and exploratory constructs to enhance therapeutic efficacy. In G. C. N. Hall & R. Hirschman (Eds.), *Sexual aggression: Issues in etiology, assessment, and treatment* [Series in Applied Psychology: Social Issues and Questions] (pp. 167–196). Washington, DC: Taylor & Francis.

Pithers, W. D., & Cumming, G. F. (1989). Can relapse be prevented? Initial outcome data from the Vermont Treatment Program for Sexual Aggressors. In D. R. Laws (Ed.), *Relapse prevention with sex offenders* (pp. 313–325). New York: Guilford Press.

Quinsey, V. L., Harris, G. T., Rice, M. E., & Lalumiere, M. (1993). Assessing the treatment efficacy in outcome studies of sex offenders. *Journal of Interpersonal Violence, 8*(4), 512–523.

Quinsey, V. L., Khanna, A., & Malcolm, P. B. (1998). A retrospective evaluation of the regional treatment centre sex offender treatment program. *Journal of Interpersonal Violence, 13*(5), 621–644.

Rice, M. E., Harris, G. T., & Cormier, C. A. (1992). An evaluation of a maximum security therapeutic community for psychopaths and other mentally disordered offenders. *Law and Human Behavior, 16*(4), 399–412.

Rice, M. E., Harris, G. T., & Quinsey, V. L. (1990). A follow-up of rapists assessed in a maximum security psychiatric facility. *Journal of Interpersonal Violence, 5*, 435–448.

Rice, M. E., Quinsey, V. L., & Harris, G. T. (1991). Sexual recidivism among child molesters released from a maximum security psychiatric institution. *Journal of Consulting and Clinical Psychology, 3*, 381–386.

Serin, R. C. (1996). Violent recidivism in criminal psychopaths. *Law and Human Behaviour, 20*, 207–217.

Serin, R. C., Peters, R. D., & Barbaree, H. E. (1990). Predictors of psychopathy and release outcome in a criminal population. *Psychological Assessment: A Journal of Consulting and Clinical Psychology, 2*, 419–422.

Webster, C. D., Harris, G. T., Rice, M. E., & Quinsey, V. L. (1994). *The Violence Prediction Scheme: Assessing dangerousness in high risk men.* Toronto: Centre of Criminology, University of Toronto.

Wong, S., Templeman, R., Gu, D., Andre, G., & Leis, T. (1996). *Criminal Career Profile: A quantitative index of past violent convictions.* Saskatoon, Canada: Correctional Service of Canada.

Yates, P. M., Goguen, B. C., & Nicholaichuk, T. P. (2000). *National sex offender treatment: Volume II. Moderate intensity treatment.* Ottawa, Canada: Correctional Services of Canada.

Yates, P. M., & Nicholaichuk, T. (1998). *The relationship between Criminal Career Profile, psychopathy, and treatment outcome in the Clearwater sex offender program.* Paper presented at the annual conference of the Canadian Psychological Association, Edmonton, Alberta.

Chapter 8

STOP IT NOW! The Campaign to Prevent Child Sexual Abuse

by Fran Henry, M.B.A. and Joan Tabachnick, M.B.A.

Overview

Until recently there have been two primary responses to child sexual abuse. One approach is to address the offender through the criminal justice system. This approach usually involves a combination of supervision and/or incarceration and, ideally, treatment. The other approach is to educate children to avoid and to report abuse. However, thisapproach lays the responsibility for preventing abuse on those least likely to be able to accomplish it. STOP IT NOW was developed to place the responsibility for the prevention of abuse in the hands of the adults who could be aware of a dangerous situation. In most cases this involves other adults who could be aware of warning signs of abuse. This chapter deals with designing a new paradigm for viewing child sexual assault as the serious community health issue that it is.

Introduction

"Don't trade off the needs of victims for the rights of offenders," said a participant at a STOP IT NOW! policy briefing in Washington, DC. She was right. She named the challenge our whole society wrestles with as it tries to prevent the tragic sexual molestation of so many American children.

Research has shown that one in three to four girls and one is seven to ten boys are sexually abused by the age of 18 (Finkelhor, 1994). STOP IT NOW!'s research has shown that 91% of child sexual abuse has not been reported to authorities (Henry & McMahon, 2000). The research agrees with published studies that show 86% of women not reporting sexual assault (Kilpatrick, 1996). Thus, the child protection and the criminal justice systems do not hear about the vast majority of sexual abuse cases.

Dozens of studies have shown the harm of sexual abuse. Adults who have been sexually victimized as children, compared to those who have not been victimized, suffer multiple times the rates of depression, posttraumatic stress disorder, substance abuse,(Saunders, Kilpatrick, Hanson, Resnick, & Walker, 1999), cognitive problems, emotional distress, impaired sense of self, dissociative disorder, suicide, and social and interpersonal problems (Briere & Elliott,1994).

Most of us do not realize the extent to which society has asked children to prevent their own sexual molestation. Our entire system waits for a child to disclose sexual abuse. But most abuse occurs by a trusted adult and a child's truth telling explodes the family structure. The child protection response and the companion criminal justice procedures have fallen short of meeting the needs of the children who have been abused, their families, and the people who have perpetrated the abuse.

To solve this grievous problem, we need a new solution. More adults need to take responsibility for sexual abuse, including perpetrators and those who know them. We need to amass the tremendous insight and power of our nationwide system of public health and use public health tools in addition to using criminal justice sanctions and child protection services. This is the innovation that STOP IT NOW! has brought to the issue of child sexual abuse. STOP IT NOW! uses methods of primary and secondary prevention, reaching people before the abuse has occurred. Then the needs of victims will not be traded off for offender's rights.

How a Public Health Campaign Could Prevent Sexual Abuse

Public health campaigns have proven successful in eradicating diseases such as smallpox, polio, and tuberculosis. Public health has also led the way to give Americans healthier and longer lives through motivating changes in behavior, such as promoting heart-healthy eating. Injury-prevention campaigns have focused on safety issues such as advocacy for wearing helmets when riding a bicycle.

What all public health campaigns have in common is their focus on what and who causes illness. Interventions take the form of primary campaigns, which target a broad citizenry with messages and information to prevent an occurrence of illness before the fact. Secondary public health campaigns target people who are at risk for unhealthy behaviors or who are at risk to get a disease. Tertiary campaigns seek to limit the spread of an illness or behavior by intervening and containing those who already have it or exhibit it. To prevent and intervene at these three levels public health officials work with the people who have the illness as well as those who might be at risk to get it.

Since 1992, STOP IT NOW! has championed the sexual abuse of children as a preventable social illness. STOP IT NOW! calls on citizens to join with public health officials to prevent sexual abuse.

Breaking Down Barriers and Building Up Benefits to Adults Taking Responsibility

Knowing that we must stop sexual abuse before it starts means we have to know who is doing it and how to change his or her behavior. We need a team that includes survivors working with recovering sex offenders and families and friends of abusers. To create lasting change we also count public opinion leaders, policymakers, the media, and professionals in the field among our constituents. STOP IT NOW! draws on a network of experts within the sex offender treatment and public health communities, within the media, and within the systems of child protection, family and intimate violence, and criminal justice.

STOP IT NOW! integrates these constituent perspectives throughout its work:

- Hosting public dialogues between survivors, recovering offenders, and family members in a variety of public community settings;

- Regularly corresponding with convicted sex offenders in prison to explore what would have made a difference to keep them from abusing and what they think they need to keep from abusing once they are released;

- Building coalitions and establishing advisory boards that link people who have never sat across the same table to promote a more integrated and effective response to prevent child sexual abuse in each community where a STOP IT NOW! program is established; and

- Networking with sexual abuse therapists, public health professionals, people who have been directly affected by this experience, the clergy, offender treatment providers, representatives from the criminal justice system and child protection systems.

STOP IT NOW! is changing how the sexual abuse of children is prevented through its three programs. They are:

1. *A public education program* that builds awareness, changes attitudes and motivates new behaviors in our target audiences: adult abusers, parents of youth with sexual behavior problems and family and friends of abusers;

2. *A research program* that compiles what we learn and brings new data to the professional community through journal articles and presentations; and

3. *A public policy program* that influences policymakers to make child sexual abuse a public health issue.

These three programs, working together, form the base from which has emerged a hopeful and innovative solution. Information about the programs is available at www.stopitnow.org.

Description of the Public Education Program

The purpose of the public education program is to reach individuals and motivate them to take appropriate actions to prevent or intervene when they suspect child sexual abuse. We have focused on three primary audiences:

- Adult male and female abusers;

- Family and friends of abusers; and

- Parents of sexually abusing youth.

Ads, public service announcements and public meetings related to each of these audiences except female abusers have been developed.

Although our success ultimately must be measured in behavior change in the primary audiences, a successful, stable program cannot be run without a thorough engagement with secondary audiences. These audiences, called stakeholders, consist of the following:

- The media;

- Community-based organizations;

- The legal and criminal justice systems;

- The child protection system;

- Victim and offender treatment providers; and

- Public health agencies.

In 1993, plans were started for the statewide campaign in Vermont, and the program was up and running by September 1995. In early 1998, planning started for the citywide campaign in Philadelphia and the program was launched in September 2000.

The public education program has reached its primary audiences through media and community action activities. For the media in Vermont, this has meant press conferences, release of monthly radio public service announcements, radio and TV talk shows, and work with reporters on special features for newspaper and TV. All media development and public service coverage has been donated to STOP IT NOW!

Given the limitations of one staff person, STOP IT NOW! VERMONT relies heavily on relationships with public officials, clinicians, and community-based organizations. STOP IT NOW! uses the tradition of the "town meeting" in community action activities. Public meetings are held with panels of people speaking as victim/survivors, family and friends, or parents of sexually abusing youth. These meetings have been well attended and covered successfully by the media.

STOP IT NOW! PHILADELPHIA focuses on three neighborhoods, one African-American, one Hispanic, and one Caucasian. The vast number of community-based organizations and the media "noise" in the city as a whole competes too heavily with our limited resources to permit an effective citywide media campaign at this time. Once this initial effort is evaluated, STOP IT NOW! will explore expansion to the entire city and surrounding areas.

STOP IT NOW! has developed and published three documents for our primary audiences. One is the guidebook for family and friends. Its special feature is the extensive listing of information such as warning signs in adults who may be sexual abusers. A second brochure is for parents of sexually abusing youth. A third brochure in Spanish has also been published. In addition, a helpline (1-888-PREVENT) serves as a source for our primary audiences to call for information and advice on how to take action.

Evaluation Has Validated the Concept

STOP IT NOW! VERMONT has had an extensive, self-financed evaluation from its inception. The evaluation reports focus on STOP IT NOW! VERMONT's efficiency and effectiveness at reaching the primary and secondary audiences.

For Philadelphia, the Centers for Disease Control and Prevention (CDC) have assumed the primary responsibility. The CDC has contracted with ORC/Macro International to conduct the evaluation. The initial results of public attitudes, one portion of the baseline evaluation of Philadelphia, was released in September 2001.

Following is a summary our evaluation of the first four years of the program in Vermont.

Finding No. 1: Abusers Will Call For Help. "Will an abuser call for help?" was the most common question asked of STOP IT NOW! VERMONT before we launched the pilot program. The answer is a resounding "yes." In the first four years of operation, STOP IT NOW! VERMONT received 657 calls to the helpline. The helpline provides unique information to adults who recognize that abuse may have occurred or is likely to occur, are willing to take some form of action (e.g., call the helpline), and do not know what to do in the situation.

- Who called?

  — 15% of callers were from abusers.

  — 50% of callers were from people who knew the abuser and/or victim.

  — 32% of callers were from men compared to an average of 10% male callers on other helplines.

Abusers calling for help contrasts sharply with the common view of the "typical" abuser. But calls were also received from others who know the abuser and typically the victim as well. The program views these as equally important calls since no one calls a child sexual abuse helpline without a valid reason. Many of these calls began with "I may be overreacting but . . ." and then described a behavior that is at least a warning sign that someone may have sexually abused a child.

- How did the caller hear of the helpline?

— 24.5% from traditional media (Radio 12.3%, newspapers 8.5%, and television 3.7%)

— 28.8% from the STOP IT NOW! VERMONT web site

— 25.2% from professionals in the field, other helplines and agencies

— 5.8% from friends, presentations, workshops, or not willing to share

Finding No. 2: Increase in Adults Who Can Talk About Sexual Abuse. "Breaking the silence" is a call to action endorsed by everyone working in the field of child sexual abuse prevention—from victim-based advocacy groups to sex offender treatment providers.

Most people would agree that if the way people talk could be changed, their response to an issue would change as well. Over the past four years, there has been a change in the way people talk about child sexual abuse. In fact, there has been a 40% increase in the number of Vermonters who could explain or define child sexual abuse.

Although four years is not adequate time to shift public attitudes on an issue, it is enough time to find indicators of awareness and change:

• *Talk about abuse.* The number of Vermonters who can explain child sexual abuse has increased dramatically (44.5% in 1995 to 84.8% in 1999).

• *Awareness.* Overall awareness is high in Vermont (78% think of child sexual abuse as a problem in Vermont).

• *ID sexual abuse.* Vermonters were able to correctly identify scenarios as "definitely sexual abuse" or "might be sexual abuse" (90.0% of the respondents answered correctly).

• *Abusers live in community.* Vermonters who recognize that abusers are likely to live in their communities increased (67.0% in 1995 to 73.7% in 1999).

Results of a survey of key decision makers in this field indicate that most people who were initially skeptical, suspicious, and confused about the program are far less so now. One person said about STOP IT NOW! VERMONT: "I see now how having programs to treat offenders can be as important as those that treat victims. If you get to the offenders and treat them, then maybe there won't be any more victims. It's attacking the problem at its source."

Finding No. 3: Adults Need Better Skills to Stop Abuse. "All of the signs were there, but no one bothered to ask me about them . . ." was said during a first interview with a sex offender in prison. Since that interview, STOP IT NOW! VERMONT has been trying to determine the following:

• What are these warning signs of people abusing and do people recognize them?

• Do people feel they have the knowledge and "permission" to say something and confront these behaviors?

• Why aren't more Vermonters taking advantage of the services now available?

STOP IT NOW! VERMONT commissioned Market Street Research of Northampton, Massachusetts, to conduct a random digit dial telephone survey of public opinions and attitudes toward child sexual abuse. The surveys were conducted in 1995, 1997, and 1999 of 200 Vermonters with a margin of error of 4.2% to 6.9%. We determined the following:

- *Warning signs.* In 1999. only one-third (38.0%) of Vermonters could name at least one warning sign in an adult or juvenile with sexual behavior problems. However, this represents a 10% increase from 27.5% in 1995 who could name a warning sign.

- *Skills.* In 1999, 87.8% of Vermonters told us they would take some direct action if they definitely knew about a case of child sexual abuse. However, if the sexual abuse was merely suspected, only 66.1% were willing to take some direct action. In most calls to the helpline, callers are unsure of what action to take and when advised, initially are unable to confront the situation in any way without significant coaching.

- *Disclosure.* Although Vermonters are significantly more likely to disclose sexual abuse than the rest of the country, two-thirds (66.2%) never disclosed their own sexual assault and therefore the abuse was unlikely to ever have been reported.

- *Resources.* Only 54.4% of Vermonters know where to refer someone with sexual behavior problems compared to 77.2% of Vermonters who know where to refer someone with a drinking problem.

- *Belief in treatment.* Many Vermonters doubt the abuser's willingness and ability to change (19.0% of Vermonters agree that abusers can stop if they want to) but believe significantly more in the effectiveness of treatment programs (68.8% of Vermonters agree abusers can stop with appropriate treatment).

- *Unsure of abuse.* When presented with four scenarios of sexual abuse, 42.5% of respondents either did not know whether the case was sexual abuse or thought it "might be abuse." This uncertainty when faced with a credible case of sexual abuse is echoed by many helpline calls which begin with the callers telling us "I may be overreacting, but . . ." and then going on to explain a situation of sexual abuse.

The data suggest that if an adult has direct evidence that sexual abuse has occurred, he or she will take direct action and report the sexual abuse. In fact, due in large part to a concurrent public awareness campaign conducted by the child protective services agency, Vermonters are significantly more likely to say that they will report or take direct action when presented with scenarios of sexual abuse. If the respondent was sure of abuse, he or she was 10% more likely to report in 1999 (80.2%) than in 1997 (70.2%).

However, experts would agree that in most realistic situations one can only suspect that there might be sexually abusive activities. In these cases, only 43.3% would report the abuse, a 6% increase since 1997. In these cases of suspecting abuse, adults still do not know what to look for or what to do when faced with these realistic cases of potential sexual abuse. Adults do not seem aware of their potential role in preventing child sexual abuse: identifying emerging problems, confronting difficult situations, reporting suspicions of sexual abuse, or referring someone to a qualified treatment provider.

Finding No. 4: Abusers Stopping the Abuse. Until quite recently society has responded primarily to one kind of child sexual abuse case—cases in which a child discloses sexual abuse by an adult or older child. Programs have been developed to teach the child to speak up. The legal protocols have been developed to respond to the child who reports abuse. Policies have been established to ensure that once an abuser is caught, he or she will remain visible for the rest of his or her life.

Many Vermonters believe that no one who sexually abuses will take responsibility for his or her sexually abusive acts. This belief may, in part, be due to the fact that no agency has any record of these individuals. Anecdotes from people who work with child protective services, clinicians, or district attorney's offices suggest that there are individuals who have taken responsibility for their actions, but no one formally recorded these data. Through a survey of clinicians and individual telephone interviews in each county prosecutor's office, STOP IT NOW! VERMONT was able to uncover some encouraging data:

- Through clinicians, STOP IT NOW! VERMONT has identified 118 people who have voluntarily sought out help for sexual behavior problems (twenty adults and ninety-eight adolescents to date).

- Through states' attorneys and victim advocates, STOP IT NOW! VERMONT has identified fifteen adults and ten adolescents who have turned themselves in to the legal system and noted that others have entered treatment without needing to enter the legal system.

These data demonstrate that some people who abuse are willing to reach out for help. Although the number of people stepping forward may seem small, they may in fact reflect a significantly larger number of victims saved from the trauma of sexual abuse.

Conclusion

The citizens of the United States have not yet begun a serious campaign to prevent the sexual abuse of children.

James Mercy, a scientist at the CDC, commented that child sexual abuse is the kind of disease that requires investing heavily in basic and applied research, devising systems to identify those affected, and requires implementing prevention campaigns to protect children. He comments that we need a "full court press" to eradicate this disease, as our society has eradicated other diseases in history (Mercy, 1999).

STOP IT NOW! advocates for a "full court press" to make the sexual abuse of children a national public health issue. STOP IT NOW!'s first-ever campaign to reach those who are abusing or who are at risk for abusing is demonstrating a promising solution to eliminate this age-old and often tragic problem.

References

Briere, J. N., & Elliott, D. M. (1994). Immediate and long-term impacts of child sexual abuse. *Sexual Abuse of Children: The Future of Children, 4*(2), 54–69.

Finkelhor, D. (1994). Current information on the scope and nature of child sexual abuse. *Sexual Abuse of Children: The Future of Children, 4*(2), 31–69.

Henry, F., & McMahon, P. (2000, May 16). *What survivors of child sexual abuse told us about the people who abuse them.* Poster presented at the National Sexual Violence Prevention Conference, Dallas, TX.

Kilpatrick, J. (1996, November). *From the mouths of victims: What victimization surveys tell us about sexual assault and sex offenders.* Paper presented at the 15th annual Research and Treatment Conference of the Association for the Treatment of Sexual Abusers, Chicago.

Mercy, J. (1999). Having new eyes: Viewing child sexual abuse as a public health problem. *Sexual Abuse: A Journal of Research and Treatment, 11*(4), 317–322.

Saunders, B. E., Kilpatrick, D. G., Hanson, R. F., Resnick, H. S., & Walker, M. E. (1999). Prevalence, case characteristics, and long-term psychological correlates of child rape among women: A national survey. *Child Maltreatment, 4*(3), 187–200.

Chapter 9

Characteristics of an Effective Sex Offender Therapist

Yolanda M. Fernandez, Ph.D. and Geris Serran, B.A.

Overview

Researchers and clinicians are concerned with the effectiveness of the current programs used to treat sexual offenders, and rightly so. Considering the devastating effects of sexual abuse on the victims (Conte, 1988; Koss & Burkhart, 1989), ensuring that treatment is maximally effective should be the goal of sexual offender therapists. Treatment programs in recent years have been based on a broad perspective of the problems experienced by sexual offenders, and these programs have been shown to reduce recidivism (Hanson, 2000); however, not every treatment program has been shown to be equally effective. Along with the method used, the therapist may be an important variable in the success of a program. This chapter reviews the research on what makes an effective therapist and whether these same characteristics are applicable in treating sex offenders.

Introduction

It is reasonable to assume that the way in which treatment is implemented will have an impact on the effectiveness of treatment. Despite a consensus among cognitive behaviorists that therapist characteristics influence treatment (Horvath, 2000), until recently little attention has been paid to the role of the therapeutic relationship in sexual offender treatment. This, no doubt, is due to the reliance in sexual offender treatment on a set of clearly specified procedures for effecting change (Marshall, Anderson, & Fernandez, 1999). In contrast to insight-oriented psychotherapists, cognitive-behavioral therapists have typically focused on therapeutic procedures to facilitate the acquisition of appropriate attitudes, perceptions, and skills necessary for these offenders to function prosocially. The client-therapist interaction in cognitive-behavioral therapy (CBT), has, to date, been given little, if any, weight (Horvath, 2000; Keijsers, Schapp, & Hoogduin, 2000; Sweet, 1984). Marshall, Anderson, and Fernandez (1999) suggest that whereas the early focus of behavior therapists on observable features of their clients may have led to significant advances in the development of effective treatments, ignoring the influence of the therapist may have been an error. In more contemporary research, interest in the entire context of the therapeutic session is evident across the many approaches to psychotherapy, including CBT (Saunders, 1999). This recent research suggests that the quality of the therapeutic relationship contributes significantly to the process of change even in purely behavioral treatments (Keijsers et al., 2000). The following review examines the literature on effective therapist styles across a variety of psychotherapeutic orientations, the clients' perceptions of the therapist, and the resulting therapeutic alliance. Finally, we offer suggestions concerning the characteristics that typify the most effective sexual offender therapists.

Therapist Style

The environment created by therapists through their interpersonal style, skills, and choice of techniques has been said to be the major effective element of therapy (Horvath, 2000). An overview of the research in this area suggests that effective therapists create an appropriate alliance with the client, believe the client can change, create opportunities for learning, expect the client to benefit from the therapy, and emotionally engage their clients. In addition, effective therapists display empathy, warmth, genuineness, respect, attentive listening, directiveness, and supportive challenging; they insist on between-session practice of skills, use humor, and demonstrate flexibility (Alexander, Barton, Schiavo, & Parsons, 1976; Beck, Rush, Shaw, & Emery, 1979; Egan, 1998; Frank, 1971; Kleinke, 1994; Kohut, 1990; Lambert, 1989; Luborsky, 1984; Rogers, 1975).

As mentioned previously, behavior-oriented therapists have traditionally stressed techniques over relationships in therapy. However, research has shown that CBT therapists employ relationship skills to the same extent as do therapists from other psychotherapy orientations (Keijsers et al., 2000). The behaviors and skills typically demonstrated by CBT therapists include presenting an active, directive stance, showing support and empathy, and displaying positive regard toward their clients (Keijsers et al., 2000). This description of CBT clearly encompasses the relationship conditions suggested by Rogers (1957) for promoting the healing process in clients.

Characteristics of Effective Therapists

The characteristics highlighted by Rogers as both necessary and sufficient for client change in therapy, namely, genuineness, empathy, and warmth, have been studied at length. Horvath (2000) notes the cumulative results of studies on Rogers's suggested conditions for therapy, which now number in the thousands, are generally supportive of the relationship between these conditions and positive outcomes in treatment. However, these three conditions, while viewed as necessary to establishing a positive therapeutic alliance, are no longer considered sufficient to effect client change. Other therapist features are now regarded as equally important, and some have been subjected to empirical analysis. The research literature on both Rogers's conditions and a number of additional features supports the contention that therapeutic outcome is to varying degrees dependent on the interpersonal skills of the therapist. To give the reader a flavor of this research, we briefly describe some of the data that provide evidence for the relationship between therapist characteristics and positive treatment outcome.

Warmth, Empathy, and Genuineness. The three features identified by Rogers (1957) as critical to therapy have repeatedly been shown to influence outcome in CBT across a variety of disorders (Keijsers et al., 2000). Therapist warmth, for example, consistently predicts positive treatment results (Orlinsky & Howard, 1986). As illustrations of this effect, studies have demonstrated that warm therapists, as compared to distant and cold therapists, produce greater reductions in smoking (Schmahl, Lichtenstein, & Harris 1972) and greater reductions in fear phobias (Morris & Suckerman, 1974).

Therapist empathy has also been found to have a consistent effect on treatment results in CBT (Keijsers et al., 2000). For example, a positive correlation has been observed between therapist empathy and problem solving in delinquent children (Kendall & Wilcox, 1980), reductions in depression (Burns & Auerbach, 1996), abstinence and controlled drinking in alcoholic-addicted clients (Miller, Taylor, & West, 1980), and coping in panic-disordered patients (Mathews, 1976). Most important, Burns and Nolen-Hoeksema (1992) found that with depressed patients, therapist empathy had direct effects in outcome and not just by facilitating treatment compliance. Interestingly, CBT therapists appear similar to their psychoanalytic counterparts when rated on their ability to communicate empathy during treatment sessions (Brunink & Schroeder, 1979).

Numerous authors (Frank, 1971; Kanfer & Goldstein, 1991; Kleinke, 1994; Schapp, Bennun, Schindler, & Hoogduin, 1993) have suggested that genuine therapists appear comfortable, honest, interested, and nondefensive, and Rogers (1980) declared treatment to be more effective when the therapist behaves in a sincere manner. In support of these claims, both therapist sincerity and respect have been linked to beneficial outcomes in therapy (Ford, 1978; Rabavilas, Boulougouris, & Perissaki, 1979).

Support, Encouragement, and Directiveness. CBT therapists appear to provide more supportive communications than do therapists from other psychotherapeutic orientations (Keijsers et al., 2000). There is evidence that therapist support increases clients' self-efficacy and their expectations that treatment will benefit them and reduces their sense of demoralization (Schapp et al., 1993). Improved expectations of outcome and efficacy encourage clients to believe in their newly acquired skills (Bandura, 1977). In addition, clients appear to be less resistant and aggressive with therapists who show high levels of support during therapeutic contact (Bandura, Lipsher, & Miller, 1960).

Once clients have adopted positive expectations about the outcome of therapy, therapists should then encourage them to actively participate in the therapeutic process. Active participation by clients is associated with an increased probability of completing treatment and experiencing positive outcomes (Garfield & Bergin, 1986). Participation can be encouraged through the use of homework assignments (Safran & Segal, 1990) and by focusing on increasing positive behaviors rather than reducing negative behaviors (Cullari, 1996).

Directiveness is often considered a fundamental feature of CBT. CBT therapists appear to take a more active and directive stance in treatment than do insight-oriented therapists (Keijsers et al., 2000). However, the authors note that in comparison to other responses (such as empathic statements) directive statements make up a small proportion of the communications of CBT therapists. Directive statements are used to encourage clients to practice skills and behaviors during and outside therapy sessions (Schapp et al., 1993), and research has shown that directiveness enhances problem-solving skills (Elliot, Barker, Caskey, & Pistrang, 1982), provides structure for clients, and enhances the likelihood of their active cooperation in treatment (Schapp et al., 1993). However, it has been shown that overly directive therapists engender resistance and negativity in their clients (Schapp et al., 1993). It appears that being overly directive may be countertherapeutic with certain clients. The evidence reveals that whereas a directive approach may be more effective with submissive or dependent clients (Beutler, Pollack, & Jobe, 1978), a reflective style appears to work best with aggressive or defensive clients (Ashby, Ford, Guerney, & Guerney, 1957).

Flexibility and Self-Disclosure. Ultimately a flexible approach to treatment, integrating both directiveness and reflectiveness when appropriate, seems to be the optimal method in therapy. Flexibility has been shown to be important for enhancing the therapeutic relationship (Schapp et al., 1993). Therapists who adjust their manner of interacting to accommodate different clients and tailor their choice of techniques to adapt to changes in the same client through the course of therapy appear to produce the most gains (Kottler, Sexton, & Whiston, 1994). Keijsers, Schapp, Hoogduin, and Lammers (1995) argue that it may not be the particular techniques therapists choose that create behavioral changes as much as the timing of delivery and under which circumstances they are accepted and complied with by the patients.

Self-disclosure has been regarded as an important therapeutic strategy to enhance patient self-disclosure. Interestingly, Keijsers et al. (2000) maintain that studies investigating the impact of therapist self-disclosure on treatment outcome do not lend support to the helpfulness of this technique or indicate an association with outcome. Similarly, Orlinsky and Howard (1986) suggest that therapist self-disclosure may be helpful but is not a particularly powerful intervention. In contrast, we suggest that sharing relevant personal experiences with clients can increase trust in therapy. Therapist self-disclosure, for example, has been shown to encourage clients to be more revealing about themselves (Hill et al., 1988; Jourard & Jaffe, 1970). However, therapists are cautioned that self-disclosure should be presented to illustrate a model for coping rather than serving the therapists' needs. In particular, therapists who present themselves as without problems in their life will likely, as a result, have clients who feel unable to identify with or live up to the standards of the therapist (Mahoney, 1974). Similarly, whereas moderate self-disclosure may be helpful in therapy, excessive self-disclosure may undermine the therapist's credibility and result in the client's questioning the therapist's competence (Curtis, 1982).

Client's Perceptions of the Therapist

In contrast to the research cited previously, it has been suggested that it is the client's subjective evaluation of the therapeutic relationship rather than the therapist's actual behavior that has the most impact on outcome (Horvath, 2000). That is, regardless of whether the therapist believes he or she is demonstrating positive therapeutic styles and techniques, there will be no relationship to outcome if the client does not perceive this to be so. Of course, it is unlikely that a poor therapeutic style will induce perception in the clients of a positive therapeutic relationship unless the therapist is overly protective and, as a consequence, not challenging. As it turns out, the client's perceptions are quite important.

It has been consistently reported that clients identify the relationship with the therapist as more important than the actual techniques employed (Llewelyn & Hume, 1979; Murphy, Cramer, & Lillie, 1984; Ryan & Gizynski, 1971; Sloane, Staples, Whipple, & Cristol, 1977). McLeod (1990) noted that clients' view of the process of therapy (i.e., being able to trust the therapist and having someone to talk to) was rated by clients as more important than technique. Although previous research has repeatedly demonstrated significant associations between Rogerian therapist conditions (empathy, warmth, positive regard, genuineness) and outcome, interestingly, such associations are more consistent when evaluated by the client rather than the therapist (Free, Green, Grace, Chernas, & Whitman, 1985). It appears that clients' perceptions of the therapist as warm, empathic, and supportive may be of more importance in terms of outcome than whether the therapist believes he or she is demonstrating these characteristics.

Clients' perceptions of the overall therapeutic experience have also been shown to be positively related to outcome. Client reports of positive emotional experiences during therapy are associated with successful treatment (Cooley & Lajoy, 1980). However, Saunders (1999) noted that clients' reports of their own emotional experience were related to their perception of the therapist's emotions. That is, positive client feelings were associated with perceived positive therapist feelings. Apparently clients feel particularly distressed when they feel inhibited or sense that the therapist is distracted (Saunders, 1999). In Saunders's (1999) study, clients rated session quality as greater and reported feeling relatively less distressed and inhibited when they perceived the therapist as confidently involved and not distracted and when they perceived mutual affection with the therapist.

In terms of clients' willingness to engage with a particular therapist, perceived expertise, more than attractiveness or even trustworthiness, predicts subjects' compliance with directives and treatment outcome (Corrigan, Dell, Lewis, & Schmidt, 1980; Heppner & Claiborn, 1989; Heppner & Dixon, 1981). Interestingly, however, perception of therapist expertise does not appear to be affected by the actual experience of therapy (Heppner & Heesacker, 1982, 1983). Clients appear to form their opinions of the therapist's expertise either before treatment is initiated or within the first session. Research has shown that improved patients versus nonimproved patients perceive their therapists to be competent and experienced (Bennun, Hahlweg, Schindler, & Langlotz, 1986), directive and active (Bennun et al., 1986), and confident and persuasive (Ryan & Gizynski, 1971). If the client perceives the therapist as lacking confidence and uninterested, it may bode poorly for client compliance, engagement in treatment, and treatment outcome (Saunders, 1999)

Research on client perceptions has regularly identified certain therapist features and strategies as critical to the success of therapy. McLeod (1990) found that clients identified therapists who understand, instill hope, encourage them, and seem interested as most helpful. Therapist sincerity has also been rated as a desirable quality by clients and positively related to beneficial outcomes (Ford, 1978). Llewelyn and Hume (1979) reported that clients felt a supportive stance on the part of the therapist was of considerable help. Support is experienced positively by clients and seen as rewarding (Elliot, 1986), and support is associated with a positive perception of the therapist and the session (Ford, 1978; Fuller & Hill, 1985). Unconditional regard and support seem important to clients, and they also report expecting some degree of directiveness from their therapist. In fact, clients describe feeling disappointed if direction is not provided during therapy (Proctor & Rosen, 1983). However, although clients may expect some direction from the therapist, they also report feeling more understood when asked open-ended questions which leaves them more freedom to respond. When asked closed questions, clients are more likely to simply describe problems rather than garner insight into their problems (Barkman & Shapiro, 1986; Hill, Carter, & O'Farrell, 1983). Consequently, as mentioned previously, a balance between reflectivenss and directiveness appears to be a preferable goal in therapy.

Although research on the use of therapist self-disclosure as a therapeutic technique may be considered somewhat inconclusive, clients' perceptions of such disclosures appear less ambiguous. Apparently, clients perceive personal sharing by the therapist as a positive addition to the therapeutic interaction. Doster and Nesbitt (1979) found that therapists who self-disclose were more positively viewed by their clients. In addition, clients report wanting to know at least some personal characteristics of their therapist (Braaten, Otto, & Handelsman, 1993).

Despite the emphasis by traditional cognitive-behaviorists on procedures over relationship characteristics, CBT therapists are perceived by their clients as being significantly more interpersonally skilled, displaying more accurate empathy, and having better therapist self-congruence than are psychodynamic therapists (Sloane, Staples, Cristol, Yorkston, & Whipple, 1975). Perhaps the explanation for this finding is that the techniques and procedures used by CBT therapists encourage the perception of these therapists as confident, helpful, and supportive. On the other hand, it may be that the focus on behavior rather than on the relationship in CBT allows the therapist to relax and act naturally, appearing more sincere, than a therapist who is more focused on influencing the relationship with the client in particular directions. Whatever the explanation, it is important for therapists of any orientation to note that how they perceive themselves and their own behavior is not necessarily how their clients perceive them. It may, in fact, be the clients' perception of the therapist that is related to positive outcome rather than the therapists' particular behaviors. Therapists should, therefore, rely less on their own interpretations of how to present a warm, empathic, and supportive stance and spend considerably more time considering what behaviors are perceived by their clients as demonstrative of such characteristics.

Therapist-Client Interaction

The therapist's characteristics and behaviors, the client's perception of the therapist, and the client's subsequent response all combine to create the therapeutic interaction. The therapeutic interaction or "therapeutic alliance" is defined as the collaborative and affective bond between therapist and patient (Martin, Garske, & Davis, 2000). It is believed that a positive therapeutic alliance creates an environment of safety and trust, and that such conditions are necessary for learning, implementing, and practicing the techniques that are ultimately responsible for therapeutic change (Horvath, 2000). Safran and Muran (1995) argue that the quality of the alliance may actually be more important than the type of treatment in predicting outcome. Certainly, research supports the importance of the alliance in effective therapy as numerous studies have demonstrated a relationship between the quality of the therapeutic alliance and therapeutic outcome (Frank, 1973; Frankl, 1978; Kanfer & Goldstcin, 1991); Luborsky, McLellan, Woody, O'Brien, & Auerbach, 1985; Rogers, 1961; Strupp, 1982; Yalom, 1980).

The quality of the alliance has been shown to emerge as early as the third session of treatment (Horvath, 2000). Alliance ratings by patients, therapists, and observers all have adequate reliability, but across sessions patients tend to rate the alliance more consistently. Apparently, patients view the alliance with their therapist as stable and are more likely to view it positively at termination if the initial assessment was positive (Horvath, 2000). This suggests that it is important for therapists to establish a positive alliance early on as that will affect the client's perceptions of the therapeutic relationship throughout the course of treatment. In addition, once a positive alliance is established, alliance disruptions may be used as opportunities for the client to practice new interpersonal behaviors to repair the relationship (Horvath, 2000).

As the relationship between therapist and client is one of interchange, it may be that some difficulties that arise in the therapeutic alliance are due to interaction problems rather than the particular behaviors of either the therapist or the client. Schindler, Hohenberger-Sieber, and Halweg (1989) studied a standardized treatment for chronic insomnia and found that nonimproved patients presented significantly fewer self-disclosures and fewer reports of change and emitted less cooperative statements following supportive statements from the therapist. In addition, the therapists of these non-improved clients used significantly fewer supportive statements in response to clients' self-disclosures, reports of change, and cooperative statements. As a result, Schindler proposed viewing therapy as an interactional context for supportive encouragement, positive feedback, and praise to promote desirable client behaviors. Consequently, therapists should examine their own behavior, how their clients respond to them, and how they in turn respond to the clients when attempting to create a more positive therapeutic alliance.

Other researchers have suggested that relationship difficulties in therapy may be due to timing problems. Keijsers et al. (1995) reported that directive statements and explanations in the first session of therapy were associated with negative outcome whereas such statements in the third session showed a trend toward positive outcome. A poor beginning to therapy may, therefore, be related to the timing of directiveness and advice given to the patient. That is, direction and advice giving may best be reserved for later sessions when trust has already been established.

Research Supports Therapeutic Alliance

It appears, then, that research supports the idea that the alliance between therapist and client may be therapeutic in and of itself. In fact, approximately 25% of variance in outcome measures of treatment effectiveness, across a variety of techniques, is accounted for by relationship factors (Morgan, Luborsky, Crits-Christoph, Curtis, & Solomon, 1982). Horvath and Symonds (1991) reported an average effect size of .26 between the quality of the alliance and outcome. Similarly, Martin et al. (2000) noted a moderate effect size of .22 between alliance and outcome using a meta-analysis of seventy-nine studies. This study further supported the alliance as a robust predictor of outcome by completing a "file drawer" analysis of the data. The authors estimated that it would take 331 studies averaging null results to reduce the correlation between alliance and outcome to .05. Consequently, it is unlikely that enough unpublished studies with null results exist to negate the relationship between alliance and outcome.

The research on therapist features and behaviors, clients' perceptions of the therapist, and the therapist-client interaction all provide evidence that how the therapist appears to the client (e.g., warm and sincere), the particular techniques chosen (e.g., support and reinforcement), and the interaction between the therapist and client all contribute to outcome. The evidence also suggests that CBT therapists demonstrate many of the features and strategies related to positive outcome in therapy.

Recently, CBT therapists have become more interested in understanding the process variables related to effective treatment. Unfortunately, however, this interest is not as widespread as it might have been, and, particularly, it is all but absent in the treatment of sexual offenders (Marshall, Anderson, & Fernandez, 1999). Kear-Colwell and Pollack (1997) and Marshall (1996) have all emphasized the importance of these factors for the treatment of sexual offenders. Consequently, the remainder of this chapter reviews process issues as they relate to the field of sexual offender treatment.

Approaches to Sexual Offender Treatment

The majority of current approaches to treating sexual offenders are CBT in nature, and most contain a relapse prevention component. The emphasis to date has primarily been on the development of treatment manuals and specific procedures to the neglect of therapeutic process (Marshall, Anderson, & Fernandez, 1999). Recently, however, as we noted, some sexual offender therapists have begun to recognize the importance of therapist qualities and behaviors. Considering the human cost of recidivism, therapists are concerned with facilitating change in sexual offender clients.

Three quite different approaches have been used in treating sexual offenders: (1)

the confrontational approach (Johnson, 1973), (2) the unchallenging approach, and (3) the motivational approach (Miller, 1983). Because these approaches differ extensively in their outlook on treatment, it follows that the characteristics of the therapist who uses either approach will differ as well.

Confrontational Approaches. The confrontational approach to motivating change involves challenging in an aggressive fashion the clients' minimizations, expressed perception and attitudes, denial, and behavior. The aim of confrontation, just as is true for more supportive challenges, is to achieve an admission of guilt and an acceptance of the significance of the problem of sexual offending. Often, the approach forces the offender to accept that he is powerless and unable to refrain from offending on his own. He is required to accept the label "sexual offender" and is led to understand that he requires extensive supervision and treatment. When clients are given this message, they may infer that they are incapable of making changes. In this respect it is surprising they succeed at all! Although, as Miller and Rollnick (1991) point out, this approach has been viewed by some as necessary to ensure behavior change, offenders often react to the labels and beliefs associated with the confrontational approach with resistance and disagreement, or simply passive acceptance.

Kear-Colwell and Pollack (1997) suggest that a therapist using the confrontational approach leads self-confident offenders to become resistant and argumentative, which is interpreted by the therapist as a problem within the client (i.e., hostility and lack of motivation). On the other hand, those clients with low self-esteem may simply agree with everything the therapist says in order to complete the treatment program with as little friction as possible. Either way, clients are not receiving the maximal benefits of treatment, which not only wastes resources but also puts victims at risk. Marshall (1996) suggests that therapists who adopt a confrontational approach view sexual offenders as "monsters" who are qualitatively different from other members of society. Garland and Dougher (1991) propose that confrontational therapists who adopt a confrontational approach feel anger and hostility toward their clients and are attempting to meet their own needs through their choice of response.

Advocates of a confrontational approach believe that to elicit behavior change, they must aggressively confront the client in order to ensure that he admits to every detail of every offense he has committed so he can make the necessary changes in his life. Marshall and Serran (2000) suggest that these assumptions are unfounded and that, in fact, a confrontational approach is counterproductive. The limited existing research supports this view. In work with both nonsexual offenders (Annis & Chan, 1983) and alcoholics (Miller & Sovereign, 1989), it has been shown that confrontational approaches generate little, if any, change whereas supportive challenges produce the greatest changes. Beech and Fordham (1997) examined the group atmosphere of twelve sexual offender treatment groups, using Moos's Group Environment Scale. In terms of change on a number of within-treatment measures (e.g., increases in self-esteem, empathy, assertiveness, cognitive distortions, understanding of high-risk factors, and the development of relapse avoidance plans), the most successful group had leaders who employed a helpful, supportive style. Overcontrolling leaders, who used confrontational challenges, had a detrimental effect on the group climate and generated little change. Overall the limited available data suggest that we need to adopt a supportive but firmly challenging approach when dealing with men who have sexually offended.

Unchallenging Approaches. On the opposite end of the spectrum, there are those who follow Rogers's (1957) dictum that therapists need to display unconditional positive regard for their clients. Two programs from the Netherlands appear to adopt this view (van Naerssen, 1991; van Zessen, 1991). This approach to treatment tends to be associated with the viewpoint that sexual offenders are victims and need to be treated as such. However, we suggest that this approach is neither helpful nor facilitative of change. These therapists risk being collusive and accepting of the offender's attempts to minimize his responsibility. They too often believe it is their responsibility to change their clients and to solve their clients' problems. Therapists adopting this style of treatment may inadvertently encourage the client to believe that his specific sexual desires are not of his own choosing; thus, he will be unable to make effective changes. The goal of the two Dutch programs mentioned previously is to assist child molesters in coming to terms with their pedophilic attraction. Although this may not be the goal of other overly supportive programs, nevertheless unconditional support may produce the same end result; that is, the clients may infer that the therapist does not regard sexual abuse as problematic.

Motivational Approaches. The motivational approach to treatment (Miller, 1983; Miller & Rollnick, 1991) aims at promoting change through understanding and acceptance. This approach highlights client, therapist, and environmental factors affecting motivation for change and provides various interventions to motivate clients. In adopting this positive approach to treatment, motivating our clients to make positive changes will most likely occur when we attempt to increase their self-esteem and empathy.

When clients view themselves as "sexual offenders," "rapists," or "child molesters," they are more likely to experience shame, which reduces their belief in their ability to change (Bumby, Marshall, & Langton, 1999). Instead, we suggest encouraging clients to view themselves as whole persons, who have a number of strengths but who have also engaged in abusive behavior. The goal is to engender guilt or remorse, which motivates change. This approach implies that the therapists treat clients in a respectful rather than degrading manner. Such therapists discourage the use of degrading labels for sexual offenders by the offenders themselves and by all staff who come in contact with them. Inappropriate jokes and the use of sarcasm are not effective responses and educating others becomes pertinent.

Within the session, therapists need to be encouraging and supportive in order to motivate clients and increase their self-efficacy. This is not to say that therapists should allow the clients to "get away with" inappropriate behavior. It is necessary for therapists to set limits, respond firmly, and challenge clients' behaviors. Challenging sexual offenders in a nonconfrontational but firm manner clearly implies to them that the therapist is not accepting their behavior but is accepting them as human beings. This positive approach to treatment (Marshall, 1996) results in an increase in the self-esteem of the offender, which not only instills a belief in the possibility of change but actually facilitates change (Marshall, Anderson, & Champagne, 1996). This approach places the responsibility for change in the hands of the client and assists him in finding ways of making change possible. Mann (1998) has made a sound argument that more effective therapists encourage their clients to build on their strengths by developing positive relapse plans rather than focusing only on negative issues. Relapse prevention strategies typically focus on ways of avoiding the various situations and factors that put sexual offenders at risk (Pithers, 1990). Though avoidance may be necessary on occasion, approach goals are more readily obtained and relapse plans should focus more on building a prosocial lifestyle (Fernandez & Marshall, 2000).

What Makes an Effective Sexual Offender Therapist?

The type of treatment approach adopted with men who have sexually offended indicates the overall belief system the therapist holds toward these clients. Beliefs about men who have sexually offended affect the way the therapist responds during treatment. As we have seen, therapists' behavior in treatment programs can range from a passive, disinterested style to a critical. hostile style. In either case, the therapist will reinforce beliefs the client already holds about the world and other people, and this will likely severely impede therapeutic progress. The foregoing review suggests that therapists who adopt a positive but firmly challenging approach to treatment possess certain qualities and characteristics that make this approach natural for them.

So what specific qualities should a therapist working with men who have sexually offended possess? This chapter has identified numerous positive therapeutic features were identified as critical for treatment to be effective. All schools of therapy have identified empathy, warmth, and genuineness as being therapist characteristics necessary to generate benefits from treatment. However, to be effective with sexual offender populations, therapists need to exhibit more than these personal characteristics. Sexual offenders are a challenging population to work with. Clients often feel apprehensive about entering treatment and may present as unmotivated or hostile. Therapists need to be prepared to work hard and be encouraging and energetic, especially within a group setting.

Therapists need to be able to understand their clients' perspective and use this understanding when interacting with their clients. For example, a man who has sexually assaulted a woman may have a fear of intimacy and may not trust women. However, he may express these fears in terms of hostility or through negative attitudes toward women. Having the ability to understand his reactions ensures that the therapist will respond appropriately and help the client work through these issues. Men who have sexually offended typically minimize aspects of their offenses or provide justifications. Although this behavior may be frustrating for a therapist, his or her ability to understand that these clients are simply trying to maintain self-esteem helps the therapist assist clients in accepting responsibility while recognizing that the clients have strengths.

Working within a group atmosphere, therapists need to be prepared for the challenges involved in providing treatment to ten or twelve different individuals with different treatment needs and different ways of responding. Thus, it is important for the therapist to be flexible and to be able to accept the stage of change the client is at. Therapists sometimes give up on clients who do not appear motivated; however, it is their job to motivate clients and to engage them in the treatment process. Because many clients, particularly in the early stages of treatment, present as defensive and may respond in an aggressive manner, therapists should respond in a reflective manner on these occasions. On other occasions, when the same client is in a more receptive mood, a more directive approach may be useful. Therapists need to understand their own limits and be able to accept that it is not their responsibility to change their clients, solve their clients' problems, or turn them into pleasant individuals. Rather, the therapist's job is to provide the opportunity, the information, the challenges, and the encouragement necessary to allow clients to choose their own path. In this way the therapist is able to give clients control over changing their lives and is there to help guide them.

Implications and Future Research

Research in the area of process variables in sexual offender therapy is a relatively recent undertaking. This is not to imply, however, that this area is not of significant importance. On the contrary, we would argue that examining the contextual features that promote the most effective treatment is the new wave of research for the future. In collaboration with Her Majesty's Prison Services in England, we have undertaken a research project aimed at examining the influence of therapist characteristics on within-treatment changes targeted in their program. As a first step in this process we (Marshall, Mulloy, & Serran, 1999) have reliably identified a number of therapist behaviors and have shown that some of these features were significantly related to changes in the targets of treatment with sexual offenders (Fernandez, Serran, & Marshall, 1999). We are now extending this research to a detailed examination of the therapist characteristics that distinguish successful from unsuccessful groups and that predict positive changes with treatment.

Further research needs to systematically examine different therapist styles to determine the most effective approach. In terms of group process, co-therapy teams should be evaluated to determine whether any particular combination of leaders (e.g., male and female leaders) is most effective. In our treatment groups, we typically tend to run "open-ended" groups, where each client progresses at his own pace and when one client finishes treatment, another enters the program. Open groups require a greater emphasis on process issues and discourage a more psychoeducational approach. Further research is necessary comparing open versus closed groups and process-oriented versus psychoeducational approaches. Attention to process issues will only further our knowledge in the area of treatment for men who have sexually offended. Only through systematic research will we be able to continue to improve treatment and to offer the best possible help to reduce the risk of recidivism.

Conclusion

It may appear from this chapter that to conduct effective treatment with a sexual offending population, the therapist needs to be "perfect." However, this is far from the truth. The overall goal is to present an appropriate coping model to the client. In therapy, we need to be human. We make mistakes as well, and sometimes we are not as effective as we would like to be during the session. Effective therapists continue to learn throughout their careers, and never "know it all." Clients learn from our modeling so that if we make a mistake, we can apologize, thereby demonstrating an appropriate way to deal with the errors we all make. We can also share our experiences with clients; appropriate self-disclosure can be a powerful tool to help clients learn better ways of approaching the stresses and difficulties they experience in their lives just as we do in our lives. Certainly, not everyone possesses the skills, qualities, or motivation to work with this often difficult population. However, those who do report this work as rewarding, even on the most difficult days.

References

Alexander, J. F., Barton, C., Schiavo, S., & Parsons, B. V. (1976). Systems behavioral intervention with families of delinquents: Therapist characteristics, family behavior and outcome. *Journal of Consulting and Clinical Psychology, 44*, 656–664.

Annis, H. M., & Chan, D. (1983). The differential treatment model: Empirical evidence from a personality typology of adult offenders. *Criminal Justice and Behavior, 10*, 159–173.

Ashby, J. D., Ford, D. H., Guerney, B. G., & Guerney, L. F. (1957). Effects on clients of a reflective and leading type of psychotherapy. *Psychological Monographs, 453*, 71.

Bandura, A. (1977). Self-efficacy: Toward a unified theory of behavioral change. *Psychological Review, 84*, 191–215.

Bandura, A., Lipsher, D. H., & Miller, P. E. (1960). Psychotherapists' approach-avoidance reactions to patients' expressions of hostility. *Journal of Consulting Psychology, 24*, 1–8.

Barkman, M., & Shapiro, D. A. (1986). Counselor verbal response modes and experienced empathy. *Journal of Counseling Psychology, 33*, 3–10.

Beck, A. T., Rush, P. J., Shaw, B. F., & Emery, G. (1979). *Cognitive therapy for depression.* New York: Guilford Press.

Beech, A., & Fordham, A. S. (1997). Therapeutic climate of sexual offender treatment programs. *Sexual Abuse: A Journal of Research and Treatment, 9*, 219–237.

Bennun, I., Hahlweg, K., Schindler, L., & Langlotz, M. (1986). Therapist's and client's perceptions in behavior therapy: The development and cross-cultural analysis of an assessment instrument. *British Journal of Clinical Psychology, 25*, 275–283.

Beutler, L. E., Pollack, S., & Jobe, A. M. (1978). "Acceptance," values and therapeutic change. *Journal of Consulting and Clinical Psychology, 46*, 198–199.

Braaten, E. B., Otto, S., & Handelsman, M. (1993). What do people want to know about psychotherapy? *Psychotherapy, 30*, 565–570.

Brunink, S., & Schroeder, H. E. (1979). Verbal therapeutic behavior of expert psychoanalytically oriented, Gestalt and behavior therapists. *Journal of Consulting and Clinical Psychology, 47*, 567–574.

Bumby, K. M., Marshall, W. L., & Langton, C. M. (1999). Shame and guilt, and their relevance for sexual offender treatment. In B. K. Schwartz (Ed.), *The sex offender: Theoretical advances, treating special populations, and legal developments* (pp. 5-1–5-12). Kingston, NJ: Civic Research Institute.

Burns, D. D., & Auerbach, A. (1996). Therapeutic empathy in cognitive-behavioral therapy: Does it really make a difference? In P. Salkovskis (Ed.), *Frontiers of cognitive therapy* (pp. 135–164). New York: Guilford Press.

Burns, D. D., & Nolen-Hocksema, S. (1992). Therapeutic empathy and recovery from depression in cognitive-behavioral therapy: A structural equation model. *Journal of Consulting and Clinical Psychology, 59*, 305–311.

Conte, J. R. (1988). The effects of sexual abuse on children: Results of a research project. *Annals of the New York Academy of Sciences*, 528, 310–326.

Cooley, E. J., & Lajoy, R. (1980). Therapeutic relationship and improvements as perceived by clients and therapists. *Journal of Clinical Psychology, 36*, 562–570.

Corrigan, J. D., Dell, D. M., Lewis, K. N., & Schmidt, L. D. (1980). Counseling as a social influence process: A review. *Journal of Counseling Psychology Monograph, 27*, 395–441.

Cullari, S. (1996). *Treatment resistance: A guide for practitioners.* Boston: Allyn & Bacon.

Curtis, J.M. (1982). The effect of therapist self-disclosure on patient's perceptions of empathy, competence, and trust in an analogue psychotherapeutic interaction. *Psychotherapy: Theory, Research, and Practice, 19*, 54–62.

Doster, J. A., & Nesbitt, J. E. (1979). Psychotherapy and self-disclosure. In G. J. Chelune (Ed.), *Self-disclosure* (pp. 177–224). San Francisco: Jossey-Bass.

Egan, G. (1998). *The skilled helper: A problem-management approach to helping.* Pacific Grove, CA: Brooks/Cole.

Elliot, R. (1986). Interpersonal process recall as a psychotherapeutic process research method. In L. L. Greenberg & W. M. Pinsof (Eds.), *The psychotherapeutic process: A research handbook* (pp. 503–507). New York: Guilford Press.

Elliot, R., Barker, C. B., Caskey, N., & Pistrang, N. (1982). Differential helpfulness of counselor verbal response modes. *Journal of Counseling Psychology, 29*, 354–361.

Fernandez, Y. M., & Marshall, W. L. (2000). Contextual issues in relapse prevention treatment. In D. R. Laws, S. M. Hudson, & T. Ward (Eds.), *Remaking relapse prevention with sex offenders* (pp. 225–235) New York: Guilford Press.

Fernandez, Y. M., Serran, G., & Marshall, W. L. (1999, September). *The reliable identification of therapist features in the treatment of sexual offenders.* Paper presented at the 18th annual Research and Treatment Conference of the Association for the Treatment of Sexual Abusers, Orlando, FL.

Ford, J. (1978). Therapeutic relationship in behavior therapy: An empirical analysis. *Journal of Consulting and Clinical Psychology, 46*, 1302–1314.

Frank, J. D. (1971). Therapeutic factors in psychotherapy. *American Journal of Psychotherapy, 25*, 350–361.

Frank, J. D. (1973). *Persuasion and healing* (2nd ed.). Baltimore: John Hopkins University Press.

Frankl, V .E. (1978). *The unheard cry for meaning: Psychotherapy and humanism.* New York: Simon & Schuster.

Free, N. K, Green, B. L., Grace, M. D., Chernas, L. A., & Whitman, R. M. (1985). Empathy and outcome in brief, focal dynamic therapy. *American Journal of Psychiatry, 142*, 917–921.

Fuller, F., & Hill, C. E. (1985). Counselor and helper perceptions of counselor intentions in relation to outcome in a single counseling session. *Journal of Counseling Psychology, 32*, 329–338.

Garfield, S., & Bergin, A. (Eds.). (1986). *Handbook of psychotherapy and behavior change.* New York: Wiley.

Garland, R. J., & Dougher, M. J. (1991). Motivational intervention in the treatment of sex offenders. In W. R. Miller & S. Rollnick, *Motivational interviewing: Preparing people to change addictive behavior* (pp. 303–313). New York: Guilford Press.

Hanson, R. K. (2000). *The effectiveness of treatment for sexual offenders: Report of the ATSA collaborative data research committee.* Paper presented at the 19th annual Research and Treatment Conference, San Diego.

Heppner, P. P., & Claiborn, C. D. (1989). Social influence research in counseling: A review and critique. *Journal of Counseling Psychology, 36*, 365–387.

Heppner, P. P., & Dixon, D. N. (1981). A review of the interpersonal influence process in counseling. *Personnel and Guidance Journal, 59*, 542–550.

Heppner, P. P., & Heesacker, M. (1982). Interpersonal influence process in real-life counseling: Investigating client perceptions, counselor experience level, and counselor power over time. *Journal of Counseling Psychology, 29*, 215–223.

Heppner, P. P., & Heesacker, M. (1983). Perceived counselor characteristics, client expectations, and client satisfaction with counseling. *Journal of Counseling Psychology, 30*, 31–39.

Hill, C. E., Carter, J. A., & O' Farrell, M. K. (1983). A case study of the process and outcome of time-limited counseling. *Journal of Counseling Psychology, 30*, 3–18.

Hill, C. E., Helms, J. E., Tichenor, V., Spiegal, S. B., O'Grady, K. E., & Perry, E. S. (1988). Effects of therapist response modes in brief psychotherapy. *Journal of Counseling Psychology, 35,* 222–233.

Horvath, A. O. (2000). The therapeutic relationship: From transference to alliance. *Journal of Clinical Psychology, 56,* 163–173.

Horvath, A. O., & Symonds, B. D. (1991). Relation between working alliance and outcome in psychotherapy: A meta-analysis. *Journal of Counseling Psychology, 38,* 139–149.

Johnson, V. E. (1973). *I'll quit tomorrow.* New York: Harper & Row.

Jourard, S. M., & Jaffe, P. E. (1970). Influence of an interviewer's self-disclosure on the self-disclosure behavior of interviewees. *Journal of Counseling Psychology, 17,* 252–257.

Kanfer, F. H., & Goldstein, A. P. (1991). *Helping people change.* New York: Pergamon Press.

Kear-Colwell, J., & Pollock, P. (1997). Motivation or confrontation: Which approach to the child sex offender? *Criminal Justice and Behavior, 24,* 20–33.

Keijsers, G. P. J., Schapp, C. P. D. R., & Hoogduin, C. A. L. (2000). The impact of interpersonal patient and therapist behavior on outcome in cognitive-behavior therapy. *Behavior Modification, 24,* 264–297.

Keijsers, G. P. J., Schapp, C. P. D. R., Hoogduin, C. A. L., & Lammers, M. W. (1995). Patient-therapist interaction in the behavioral treatment of panic disorder with agoraphobia. *Behavior Modification, 19,* 491–517.

Kendall, P. C., & Wilcox, L. E. (1980). Cognitive behavioral treatment for impulsivity: Concrete versus conceptual training in non-self-controlled problem children. *Journal of Consulting and Clinical Psychology, 48,* 80–91.

Kleinke, C. L. (1994). *Common principles of psychotherapy.* Pacific Grove, CA: Brooks/Cole.

Kohut, H. (1990). The role of empathy in psychoanalytic cure. In R. Langs (Ed.), *Classics in psychoanalytic techniques* (rev. ed., pp. 463–473). Northvale, NJ: Aronson.

Koss, M. P., & Burkhart, B. R. (1989). The long-term impact of rape: A conceptual model and implications for treatment. *Psychology of Women Quarterly, 13,* 133–147.

Kottler, J. A., Sexton, T. L., & Whiston, S. C. (1994). *The heart of healing: Relationship in therapy.* San Francisco: Jossey-Bass.

Lambert, M. J. (1989). The individual therapist's contribution to psychotherapy process and outcome. *Clinical Psychology Review, 9,* 469–485.

Llewelyn, S. P., & Hume, W. I. (1979). The patient's view of therapy. *British Journal of Medical Psychology, 52,* 29–35.

Luborsky, L. (1984). *Principles of psychoanalytic psychotherapy: A manual for supportive/expressive treatment.* New York: Basic Books.

Luborsky, L., McLellan, T., Woody, G. E., O'Brien, C. P., & Auerbach, A. (1985). Therapist success and its determinants. *Archives of General Psychiatry, 42,* 602–611.

Mahoney, M. J. (1974). *Cognition and behavior modification.* Cambridge, MA: Ballinger.

Mann, R. (1998, October). *Relapse prevention? Is that the bit where they told me all the things I couldn't do anymore?* Paper presented at the 17th annual Research and Treatment Conference of the Association for the Treatment of Sexual Abusers, Vancouver, British Columbia, Canada.

Marshall, W. L. (1996). The sexual offender: Monster, victim or everyman? *Sexual Abuse: A Journal of Research and Treatment, 8,* 317–335.

Marshall, W. L., Anderson, D., & Champagne, F. (1996). Self-esteem and its relationship to sexual offending. *Psychology, Crime and Law, 3,* 81–106.

Marshall, W. L., Anderson, D., & Fernandez, Y. M. (1999). *Cognitive behavioral treatment of sexual offenders.* London: Wiley.

Marshall, W. L., Mulloy, R., & Serran, G. A. (1999). T*he identification of treatment-facilitative behaviors enacted by sexual offender therapists.* Unpublished manuscript, Queen's University, Kingston, Ontario.

Marshall, W. L., & Serran, G. (2000). Improving the effectiveness of sexual offender treatment. *Trauma, Violence & Abuse: A Review Journal, 1,* 203–222.

Martin, D. J., Garske, J. P., & Davis, M. K. (2000). Relation of the therapeutic alliance with outcome and other variables: A meta-analytic review. *Journal of Consulting and Clinical Psychology, 68,* 438–450.

Mathews, A. M. (1976). Imaginal flooding and exposure to real phobic situations: Treatment outcome with agoraphobic patients. *British Journal of Psychiatry, 129,* 362–371.

McLeod, J. (1990). The client's experience of counseling and psychotherapy: A review of the research literature. In D. Mearns & W. Dryden (Eds.), *Experiences of counseling in action* (pp. 66–79). London: Sage.

Miller, W. R. (1983). Motivational interviewing with problem drinkers. *Behavioral Psychotherapy, 1,* 147–172.

Miller, W.R., & Rollnick, S. (1991). *Motivational interviewing: Preparing people to change addictive behavior.* New York: Guilford Press.

Miller, W. R., & Sovereign, R. G. (1989). The check-up: A model for early intervention in addictive behaviors. In T. Loberg, W. R. Miller, P. E. Nathan, & G. A. Marlatt (Eds.), *Addictive behaviors: Prevention and early intervention* (pp. 219–231). Amsterdam: Swets & Zeitlinger.

Miller, W. R., Taylor, C. A., & West, J. C. (1980). Focused versus broad-spectrum behavior therapy for problem drinkers. *Journal of Consulting and Clinical Psychology, 48,* 590–601.

Morgan, R., Luborsky, L., Crits-Christoph, P., Curtis, H., & Solomon, J. (1982). Predicting the outcome of psychotherapy by the Penn Helping Alliance Rating Method. *Archives of General Psychiatry, 39,* 397–402.

Morris, R. J., & Suckerman, K. R. (1974). Therapist warmth as a factor in automated systematic desensitization. *Journal of Consulting and Clinical Psychology, 42,* 244–250.

Murphy, P. M., Cramer, D., & Lillie, F. J. (1984). The relationship between curative factors perceived by patients in their psychotherapy and treatment outcome: An exploratory study. *British Journal of Medical Psychology, 57,* 187–192.

Orlinsky, D. E., & Howard, K. I. (1986). Process and outcome in psychotherapy. In S. L. Garfield & A. E. Bergin (Eds.), *Handbook of psychotherapy and behavior change* (3rd ed., pp. 311–384). New York: Wiley.

Pithers, W. D. (1990). Relapse prevention with sexual aggressors: A method for maintaining therapeutic change and enhancing external supervision. In W. L. Marshall, D. R. Laws, & H. E. Barbaree (Eds.), *Handbook of sexual assault: Issues, theories, and treatment of the offender* (pp. 363–385). New York: Plenum.

Proctor, E. K., & Rosen, A. (1983). Structure therapy: A conceptual analysis. *Psychotherapy, 20,* 202–207.

Rabavilas, A. D., Boulougouris, I. C., & Perissaki, C. (1979). Therapist qualities related to outcome with exposure in vivo in neurotic patients. *Journal of Behavior Therapy and Experimental Psychiatry, 10,* 293–294.

Rogers, C. R. (1957). The necessary and sufficient conditions of therapeutic personality change. *Journal of Consulting Psychology, 21,* 95–103.

Rogers, C. R. (1961). *On becoming a person.* Boston: Houghton-Mifflin.

Rogers, C. R. (1975). Empathic: An unappreciated way of being. *Counseling Psychologists, 5,* 2–10.

Rogers, C. R. (1980). *A way of being.* Boston: Houghton-Mifflin.

Ryan, V. L., & Gizynski, M. N. (1971). Behavior therapy in retrospect: Patient's feelings about their behavior therapies. *Journal of Consulting and Clinical Psychology, 37,* 1–9.

Safran, J. D., & Muran, J. C. (Eds.). (1995). The therapeutic alliance [Special issue]. *Session: Psychotherapy in Practice, 1*(1). (Reissued as millenial issue, February 2000)

Safran, J. D., & Segal. Z. V. (1990). *Interpersonal process in cognitive therapy.* New York: Basic Books.

Saunders, S. M. (1999). Clients' assessment of the affective environment of the psychotherapy session: Relationship to session quality and treatment effectiveness. *Journal of Clinical Psychology, 55,* 597–605.

Schapp, C., Bennun, I., Schindler, L., & Hoogduin, K. (1993). *The therapeutic relationship in behavioral psychotherapy.* Chichester, UK: Wiley.

Schindler, L., Hohenberger-Sieber, E., & Halweg, K. (1989). Observing client-therapist interaction in behavior therapy: Development and first application of an observational system. *British Journal of Clinical Psychology, 28,* 213–226.

Schmahl, D. P., Lichtenstein, E., & Harris, D. E. (1972). Successful treatment of habitual smokers with warm, smoky air and rapid smoking. *Journal of Consulting and Clinical Psychology, 38,* 105–111.

Sloane, R. B., Staples, F. R., Cristol, A. H., Yorkston, N. J., & Whipple, K. (1975). *Psychotherapy versus behavior therapy.* Cambridge, MA: Harvard University Press.

Sloane, R. B., Staples, F. R., Whipple, K., & Cristol, A. H. (1977). Patients' attitude toward behavior therapy and psychotherapy. *American Journal of Psychiatry, 134,* 134–137.

Strupp, H. H. (1982). The outcome problem in psychotherapy: Contemporary perspectives. In J. H. Harvey & M. M. Parks (Eds.), *The master lecture series: Psychotherapy research and behavior change* (Vol. 1, pp. 43–71). Washington, DC: American Psychological Association.

Sweet, A. A. (1984). The therapeutic relationship in behavior therapy. *Clinical Psychology Review, 4,* 253–272.

van Naerssen, A. (1991). Man-boy lovers: Assessment, counseling, and psychotherapy. *Journal of Homosexuality, 20,* 175–187.

van Zessen, G. (1991). A model for group counseling with male pedophiles. *Journal of Homosexuality, 20,* 189–198.

Yalom, I. D. (1980). *Existential psychotherapy.* New York: Basic Books.

Chapter 10

Community-Based Treatment Using the Therapist/Agent Model

by Michael J. Nilan, Ph.D., L.M.F.T. and Robin C. Hubbell, M.S.W., L.I.C.S.W.

Overview

The framework for this chapter came from five years of collaborative work in an urban community and a rural community in Minnesota. The collaborative model evolved from philosophical and operational discussions between a community-based treatment provider and court services/probation. The collaborative working arrangement gave birth to adult and adolescent community-based sexual offender treatment programs. The treatment models were delivered within the context of a co-therapist relationship involving the community-based therapist and county-based probation officers. The model described in this chapter varies within the context of urban versus rural environments while maintaining many areas of commonality.

Introduction

Depending on geography and available therapeutic resources, traditional treatment/therapy has been rendered via individual and/or group treatment models by either a single therapist or a co-therapist arrangement. Frequently the model provided by an individual therapist, when retrospectively analyzed, reveals a broader range of variable results. The individual therapist model requires the therapist to concentrate on both process and content without the benefit of another trained clinician to assist in identifying and recognizing the nuances involved in group therapy/treatment. Depending on the size of the group, some individual therapists have reported, in clinical supervision, that the responsibility can be overwhelming due to the intensity of the issues involved in treating this population. Conversely, cofacilitated therapy/treatment groups find therapists reporting, in clinical supervision, that the advantage of sharing the facilitator's responsibility provides a broader and deeper clinical breadth of group therapy/treatment.

This chapter discusses how the "therapist/agent model" provides adequate and consistent treatment/therapy to sexual offenders/abusers in community-based settings. The blending of therapy and community corrections deepens and broadens the scope of treatment provided. This broadening contributes to community safety.

Working in the Model

Community safety is enhanced by the exchange of information provided by this model. "Therapists have an obligation to the community at large to provide treatment and to assist the courts in monitoring sex offender behavior. Probation officers are sworn to protect the community and enforce the conditions of probation and supervision as stipulated by the courts" (Palmer & Childers, 1999, p. 1). Because probation officers have a wealth of information from the community via home visits, relationships with law enforcement, and contacts with social service agencies, the level of accountability is dramatically increased with the use of the model. This increased level of accountability is directly related to the treatment process in group settings, individual psychotherapy, family therapy, and psychoeducational programming. With experience as a guide and teacher, our conclusion to date has been that this represents the most important and significant advantage from the realm of single therapists providing community-based treatment. Substantiation regarding this advantage has been verified by interviews with judges, law enforcement, and community corrections/court services personnel throughout the state of Minnesota. The model further offers increased opportunities for immediate and extended family members/friends to become directly involved with the treatment of the offender/abuser. This model offers family/couples therapy as well as a specially designed curriculum to educate the friends and family supportive of the sexual-offending client. This curriculum decreases triangulation between offender and family member/friend and the professionals involved.

Various types of adjunctive services can be provided to include family therapy, relationship therapy, couple counseling, and topic specific informational/educational presentations (see Figures 10.1 and 10.2). Typically, the sexual offender/abuser who is involved in a community-based treatment program will have faced/confronted and overcome some of the initial hurdles involved with varying levels of denial directly related to his sexual offenses. The sobering effects of the presentence investigation and the firsthand experience of court proceedings cause the individual to begin the process of directly exploring his own sexual behaviors. The current reality of U.S. jurisprudence finds most sexual offender/abusers involved in a process of plea bar-

Figure 10.1
Community-Based Adult Sexual Offender Treatment Model

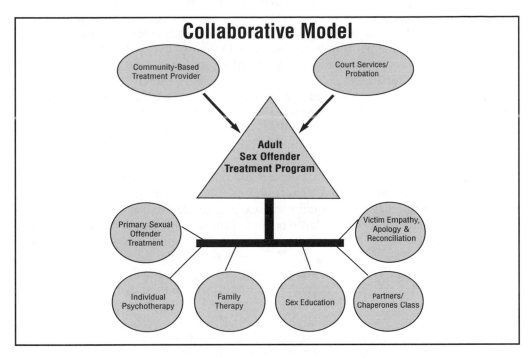

Figure 10.2
Community-Based Juvenile Sexual Offender Treatment Model

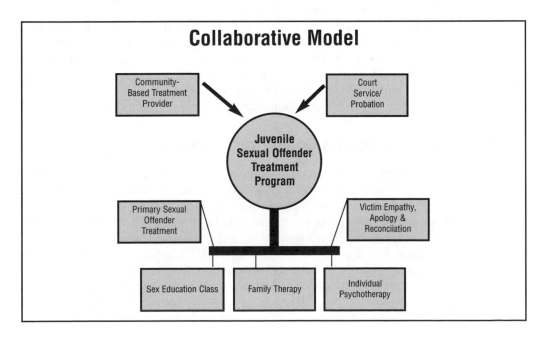

gaining. The reality of the plea-bargaining process generally results in the sexual offender/abuser having to consider his own behavior within the context of how it affects the victim(s) and also his immediate and extended family and relationships. This consideration begins the bridging between community corrections/court services, the sexual offender/abuser, and his or her family. The bridging provides the sexual offender/abuser an opportunity to discuss with his immediate and extended families the myriad secrets which accompany sexual offending. At the particular point at which the offender feels prepared to have family members/friends become involved in his treatment, one of the significant strengths of the collaborative model is that it provides a more well-rounded and comprehensive approach to the joining process (Ross, 1996). All those involved in the sexual offender/abuser's case, including court and social service personnel, therapists, and child protection and victim advocates are involved with the client on a weekly basis.

The joining process is the initial therapeutic relationship established between the treatment provider, the sexual offender/abuser, and his or her family. The very essence of the joining process requires the sexual offender/abuser to be able to sufficiently overcome his shame in order to begin to join with his family members/friends in a therapeutic manner. The therapist can assist in the cognitive and emotional components of the joining process. As an officer of the court, the agent has been entrusted with the responsibility of community safety and security (Smith, 1995). The challenge faced by the agent is to integrate principles of restorative justice into the community conscience.

Within the community in which the sexual offense was perpetrated, the collaborative model provides an increased scope and depth of treatment. The increased scope and depth of treatment are created by virtue of expanding the number of individuals associated with the sexual offender/abuser in the treatment process. These individuals, according to restorative justice principles, require the sexual offender/abuser to accept full and complete responsibility for his offense(s). In addition, community members are joined by the sexual offender/abuser and his family in establishing a new level of accountability by which the sexual offender/abuser will be judged throughout the course of histreatment. The community's needs are represented by the presence of the agent, and the clinical considerations involved in the treatment are represented by the presence of the therapist. Their successful interaction in joining with the sexual offender/abuser contributes to a more comprehensive treatment regiment.

Realities of Working in a Collaborative Model

The traditional mind-set of therapists frequently leads to gravitation to professional environments in which they feel a considerable amount of freedom to practice their art. Graduate training, internship/externships, practice experiences, and the reality of their work environments necessitate clinical collaboration. The traditional model of clinical collaboration, however, is among and between therapists themselves (Marshall & Barbaree, 1990a). Imagine, then, a therapist's reaction when told he or she will be expected to collaborate clinically with a nonclinically trained professional. This last statement captures the very essence of working in this collaborative type of model.

There may be a sense of a loss of freedom and a loss of power in the realm of case management and delivery of treatment programming. Frequently it masks itself as power struggles between therapist and agent when in reality it is an understanding of the change in the respective roles and the losses experienced by the therapist. Therapists who are successful in working in this model can only coexist when they confront and resolve their own issues of the perceived power struggle. It is helpful to remember that the goal is to work for change in thinking and behavior of the sexual offender/abusers and their family systems without becoming embroiled in a power struggle between therapist and agent. It requires therapists to rethink their traditional approach to treatment. The collaborative approach necessitates that a therapist work from a holistic and inclusive perspective as opposed to one of isolationism.

Therapists are required to shed their traditional role as the exclusive designer and director of treatment. This image is not always self-generated. It is often imposed upon the therapist by external systems such as community corrections, social services, law enforcement, the judiciary systems, and/or society at large. It is not uncommon for the therapist to experience a significant amount of professional turmoil early in his or her process of learning to work in this model, as the therapist may be threatened by the inherent power granted within the position of agent. The therapist frequently interprets the probation/parole agent's therapeutic interventions as challenging to the treatment process itself. Therapists who are successful in the model are successful in resolving this conflict in a collaborative manner.

Therapists who are successful in working with this model must be able to establish the same type of relationship with the probation/parole agent as they do with a traditional co-therapist. This requires the therapist to be open to the agent's opinions even if they are dramatically different from his or her own. It is not uncommon for these opinions to be perceived by the therapist as conflicting with the treatment process. It is at such times that the communication must focus on differences of opinion or approach without being detrimental to the treatment process. This can be done either between the therapist and agent in a posttreatment group conference or in a larger multidisciplinary team meeting. The larger multidisciplinary team consists of representatives from law enforcement, victim services, social services, consulting psychiatrists, and psychologists as well as the therapists and agents working within the model.

From the therapist's point of view, the agent's role is to bring to the model the following:

- Knowledge of details of offending behaviors;

- Knowledge of behaviors in the community;

- In-depth understanding of the sexual offender/abuser's history;

- Experiences of all court proceedings especially as they relate to the design of the specific probation conditions;

- The philosophy, values, and beliefs of community corrections; and

- The reality of functioning as a court appointed officer representing the community at large.

For agents to work collaboratively, the therapist needs to be assured that the agent has a through understanding of the treatment model and treatment dynamics and is willing to work in a clinical environment. The agent may also perceive pressure to yield some power and control to the therapist.

From the agent's point of view, the therapist's role is to bring to the model the following:

- A well-defined model of treatment;

- Through and complete knowledge and understanding of community based sexual offender treatment dynamics;

- Experience and clinical skills to deal effectively with resistance, denial and defensive mechanisms;

- Experience with issues of transference and countertransference;

- Willingness to be challenged/confronted and engaged in regular clinical supervision;

- Understand the concepts of catharsis, emotional expression and empathy; and

- Experience in providing relationship therapy and family therapy.

Concerns of Working Collaboratively

It has been our experience that therapists need to feel comfortable challenging probation agents, if and when they begin to usurp the role of therapist. Difficulties we have experienced with the collaborative model relate more directly to inconsistencies manifested by individual probation agents. These inconsistencies range from arriving late, leaving early, or not attending treatment groups consistently to tendencies to employ court services/probation leverage rather than allowing the therapeutic process to evolve. Also, treatment providers frequently employ structured behavioral rehearsals, a concept used in conjunction with the model of relapse prevention (Miner, Marques, Day, & Nelson, 1990). Probation agents frequently lack the clinical knowledge and understanding which underlie and substantiate this type of clinical intervention. They frequently react with fear and respond by rendering an opinion as structured behavioral rehearsals provide too much variability for a sexual offender/abuser in the community. In addition, our experience has found inconsistency in the probation agent's interpretation of the court's conditions of probation, individual differences in probation officers' challenges to clinical decisions, and a reluctance to consistently apply principles of restorative justice (Wolf, Conte, & Engel-Meinig, 1998) allowing individuals to successfully complete probation. One of the most difficult experiences with this model is in the size and structure of the multidisciplinary team. If the team is structured with a power differential between probation/parole agents and therapists, it may feel like a futile effort on the part of the therapist with little attention paid to the clinical impact on decisions by the team. If this power differential is allowed to enter the treatment milieu, a client may be able to perceive this and use it to challenge the effectiveness of the cofacilitative team. Therapists frequently are accused of employing too much leniency in working with clients and thus may have an inherent resistance to suspending or terminating clients from treatment and a tendency to allow too many opportunities for clients in community-based settings.

The job duties and responsibilities of probation officer/agents do not always lend themselves to their consistent attendance in areas of community-based sexual offender treatment where they have made a commitment to function in a cofacilitative and collaborative role. Individual differences of probation officers/agents may result in a style conflict with a therapist. The style conflict, if not quickly resolved, may affect individual clients as well as the overall flow and effectiveness of the group treatment component itself. Changes in county management and supervision may result in a change in philosophical and operational principles either directly or indirectly affecting the collaborative model. Probation officer/agent additions and departures can disrupt the group process and group synergy. Specific changes of probation officers/agents working in treatment groups result in changing the contextual nature of the group. This type of change frequently disrupts issues of trust, group communication, intimacy, and continuity.

Advantages of Working Collaboratively

There are many advantages to working within the collaborative model. Treatment costs to the client are reduced directly as they relate to charging for one therapist in group treatment rather than two, resulting in the county's decreasing its costs for treatment. Treatment funding and financing are made available by grants, creative loan arrangements, and insurance/third-party payment plans. The model provides for an increased frequency of contact between therapists and agents, creating a positive effect for clients through increased timeliness in response to their inquiries. This improvement in communication has a positive impact on community safety by decreasing the delays in response time between treatment providers and community corrections/court services. Thus if the client is struggling emotionally, probation/parole agents are alerted to a rise in the client's community risk level and can proceed accordingly. Another advantage of this model is that it increases the face-to-face contact between agents and their clients. It improves the communication between probation officers about respective clients as they are not necessarily in group with all those on their caseload. It allows for high-risk and crisis situations to be identified more quickly and cautions to be enacted with other agencies such as law enforcement and social services. This model decreases clients' tendency to minimize or overtly deny high-risk behaviors in the community, which often go unreported to the therapist and treatment group. Research on sexual offenders/abusers has shown high tendencies to deny, rationalize, and minimize accurate reporting of their behaviors within the community. The multiple layers of enhanced communication result in clients being therapeutically challenged not only by the treatment provider (Quinsey & Lalumiere, 1996) but also by court services/probation. These dual challenges increase client accountability as it relates to individual treatment work. This increase in accountability represents an overall reduction in the amount of time the client spends in community-based sexual offender programming.

Primary Treatment

Typically, cofacilitation takes place in the primary sexual offender treatment groups: the psychoeducational group/classes. The role of probation officers/agents varies based on the specific group modality. In the weekly treatment group, they assist in the treatment process itself. Their level of knowledge about the sexual offender assists in the confrontation and breakdown of denial and defense mechanisms about specific sexual offenses. Their role in sex education classes is to assist in facilitation of applying the specific content areas/concepts to the sexual offender's pattern of psychosexual development. In the supervisor/partner/parent class they teach specific content/topic areas relative to court services/community corrections information, rules, and regulations. For example, they teach concepts dealing with community registration/notification, DNA identification, requests for out-of-county/state travel permits, etc.

Aftercare Programming

In the area of aftercare programming, probation officer/agents generally cofacilitate in the weekly aftercare group check-in process, relapse prevention discussions, and the use of mentorship/sponsorship community members (see Figures 10.3 and 10.4). Their role in the weekly aftercare programming group is to assist in maintaining the necessary level of accountability to ensure continued community safety in a post-primary treatment milieu. As representatives of the court concerned with community safety, they are able to interpret and offer official opinions on probation conditions which have direct applicability to areas of behavioral rehearsal processing and relapse prevention review.

Advantages and Disadvantages of the Collaborative Model

Specific advantages and disadvantages of the collaborative model vary based on the philosophical beliefs of respective court services/county probation administration and management. In Minnesota specifically, the Department of Corrections is a state agency that has varying types of responsibility and accountability for public policy direction and interpretation of state law and mandates. Historically, state agency policy and mandate interpretations do not always coincide with individual county management. With continually increasing public pressure and community scrutiny, the Minnesota Department of Corrections has created a level of supervision for adult sexual offenders released from incarceration requiring supervision by state probation agents versus county probation officers. The level of supervision required by these state parole agents does not lend itself to any consistent involvement in a collaborative model. The state correctional system has a structured release and aftercare program separate from that found in the collaborative model.

The collaborative model offers county probation officers/agents an opportunity to have more frequent and regular contact with sexual offenders. It affords individual probation officers/agents the opportunity to meet and work with clients of other probation officers/agents within their county work areas. By design, the collaborative model should reduce the response time of specific questions posed by sexual offenders during various components of their community-based treatment. Ideally, probation officers/agents receive a significantly deeper and broader understanding of the depth and scope of community-based treatment programming. When the collaborative model is effectively managed and consistently applied, the length of time in treatment and the aggregate cost of sexual offender treatment programming should be reduced.

Figure 10.3
Community-Based Adult Sexual Offender Aftercare Model

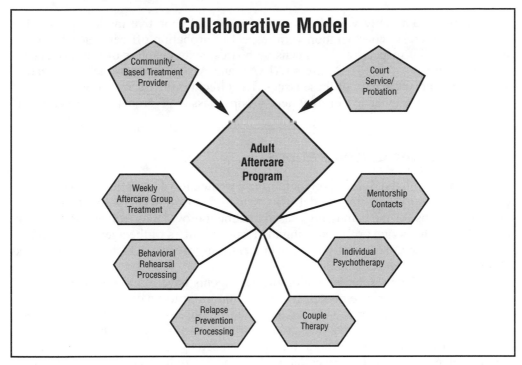

Figure 10.4
Community-Based Juvenile Sexual Offender Aftercare Model

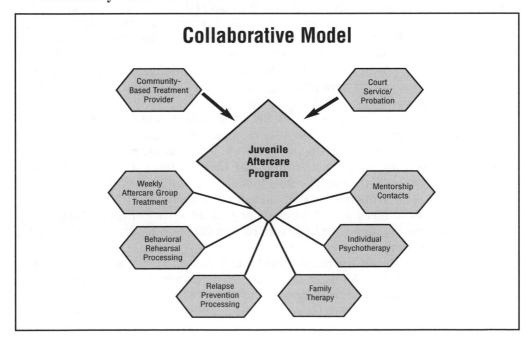

Considerations Necessitating Further Research and/or Interpretation

The most commonly voiced concern with the collaborative model involves the "conflict of interest" consideration with respect to probation officers/agents. Formal interpretations by respective state licensing boards, state chapters of the Association for the Treatment of Sexual Abusers (ATSA), and ATSA as a national organization could assist in clarification of these issues. The effect on the treatment process of the inconsistency in attendance in treatment groups/classes of probation officer/agents also needs to be researched.

Macrosystemic Considerations

We have found that it is important to have a written job description for both agents and therapists working in this model. This written description defines responsibilities and expectations for the community-based treatment provider as well as for court services. Within the context of identifying the responsibilities of the agent in the collaborative model, the job description assists in identifying areas in which agents will need additional training and education.

In our experience, some probation officers/agents have reservations about or no interest in the collaborative model. It is most important to involve both community-based treatment programs and court services in the discussion of respective agents' concerns. Frequently court services administration may need to consider adjusting caseloads to allow the required additional time needed by agents to work in the model. Ideally, cofacilitation within the collaborative model should attempt to pair both genders working together in the group process.

Clinical direction and individual treatment planning need to remain within the purview of the community-based treatment provider. This frequently can lead to disagreements, arguments, confrontations, or conflict within the cofacilitative team as they try to balance the clinical needs of the sexual offender abuser and the probation conditions. Ideally, a multidisciplinary team meeting should occur on a weekly basis at a minimum. These meetings allow for discussion of an individual client's treatment progress, discussion of treatment philosophies and techniques, and discussion of differences of opinion.

Funding options for treatment within the collaborative model need to be carefully explored and specifically identified prior to implementation of the model. Funding options may range from county-funded services or partial state funding to private insurance to out-of-pocket expenses paid by the sexual offenders/abuser themselves. As frequently happens with county or state funding, the dollars available for treatment may be used up prior to completion of treatment for those individuals being funded in this manner. In most areas in which community-based sexual offender/abuser treatment programming is offered, the trend is to require the sex offender/abuser to pay for his or her own treatment.

The community-based treatment provider and court services need to separately identify and specifically delineate their respective responsibilities. Often defense attorneys express concerns about the blurring of boundaries leading to a treatment provider becoming a mouthpiece for court services. In accord with the Association for the Treatment of Sexual Abusers (1997) and the "Standards of Practice for Adult Sexual Offender Treatment Providers," a significant clinical consideration is the need for unbiased clinical assessments, evaluations, and interpretations. This consideration extends from pretreatment assessments and evaluations to the treatment process itself, aftercare programming, and adjunct programming. Pretreatment assessments and evaluations can be randomly assigned to competent treatment providers within a geographic locale or a request for proposal can be tendered for consideration and choice of the most competent treatment providers. Clarity of role and responsibilities between therapists and agents dramatically reduces the blurring of boundaries, which frequently occurs within the context of treatment groups themselves. Aftercare programming concentrates on a client's consistent application of transitional issues (Marshall & Barbaree, 1990b) in mainstream issues. The major responsibility for community safety as it relates to overseeing these responsibilities rests with community corrections/court services and respective probation agents. The role of the treatment provider/therapist is specific to issues of relapse prevention as it applies to community reintegration.

Conclusion

Five years of experience in providing collaborative community-based sexual offender treatment programming does not represent a significant amount of data for a longitudinal study. It does, however, represent a significant amount of direct clinical experience in working collaboratively. There are no singular conclusions or advantages and disadvantages of the collaborative model. State licensing boards and national organizations vary with their opinions relative to the collaborative model. At this time in its evolution, the collaborative model warrants a comparative analysis with traditional models. Until this comparative analysis is accomplished, proponents of each model will continue to debate the advantages and disadvantages of their respective models. Theoretically, the basic tenets of the model can be effectively applied to community-based sexual offender/abuser treatment programming. Realistically, our experience has caused us to conclude that the success of this model lies in a team concept, mutual respect for the responsibilities and duties of both the therapist and the agent, and the need for a truly cooperative and collaborative working environment. This does little to resolve the ethical and clinical practice considerations that need to be addressed within the context of the collaborative model.

References

Association for the Treatment of Sexual Abusers. (1997). *Ethical standards and principles for the management of sexual abusers.* Beaverton, OR: Author.

Marshall, W. L., & Barbaree, H. E. (1990a). An integrated theory of the etiology of sexual offending. In W. L. Marshall, D. R. Laws, & H. E. Barbaree (Eds.), *Handbook of sexual assault: Issues, theories and treatment of the offender* (pp. 257–275). New York: Plenum.

Marshall, W. L., & Barbaree, H. E. (1990b). Outcome of comprehensive cognitive behavioral treatment program. In W. L. Marshall, D. R. Laws, & H. E. Barbaree (Eds.), *Handbook of sexual assault: Issues, theories and treatment of the offender* (pp. 257–275). New York: Plenum.

Miner, M. H., Marques, J. K., Day, D. M., & Nelson, C. (1990). Impact of relapse prevention in treating sex offenders: Preliminary findings. *Annals of Sex Research, 3,* 165–185.

Palmer, R., & Childers, T. (1999). The grand alliance—Probation officer and therapist. In B. K. Schwartz (Ed.), *The sex offender: Theoretical advances, treating a special population and legal developments* (pp. 12-1–12-7), Kingston, NJ: Civic Research Institute.

Quinsey, V., & Lalumiere, M. (1996). *Assessment of sexual offenders against children.* Thousand Oaks, CA: Sage.

Ross, R. (1996). *Return to the teaching.* Toronto: Penguin Books.

Smith, R. (1995). Sex offender treatment program planning and implementation. In B. K. Schwartz & H. R. Cellini (Eds.), *The sex offender: Corrections, treatment and legal practice* (pp. 7-1–7-13). Kingston, NJ: Civic Research Institute.

Wolf, S. C., Conte, J. R., Engel-Meinig, M. (1998). Assessment and treatment of sex offenders in a community setting. In L. E. A. Walker (Ed.), *Handbook on sexual abuse* (pp. 365–383). New York: Springer.

Part 3

Legal Issues

Mental health and criminal justice professionals (specifically prison personnel and probation and parole officers) who deal with both adult sex offenders and sexually inappropriate youth may find themselves increasingly involved with the courts. Public notification laws and involuntary commitment statues may require reports and testimony in determining risk before various boards or courtroom hearings. These professionals are rarely trained in how to give courtroom testimony, and this experience can prove highly stressful. For example, knowing whether one is being called on as an expert witness or a witness of fact can clarify many issues. However, it may be up to the witness to do the clarifying, as lawyers may attempt to elicit expert testimony from a witness of fact in order to save the expense of a fee. Every professional expecting to be called on to testify should acquaint him- or herself with the often subtle difference between these two types of judgments or even reviewing an old record may move a witness of fact into the expert witness category.

Other sensitive legal issues involve the confidentiality of treatment records, especially those subpoenaed in connection with public notification or involuntary commitment proceedings. Professionals may need to stand up to agencies that employ them to maintain their ethics.

If the mental health professional specializing in sex offender treatment resides in one of the fifteen states to have sexual predator laws enacted since 1990, he or she needs to be familiar with the specifics of these statues. In Chapter 11, Brian Holmgren discusses the wide variety of these laws. States vary according to their statutory schemes. They differ with respect to mental disorder requirements. Recent court challenges have questioned statutes that fail to include references to "total inability to control sexual impulses." States differ in qualifying offenses with some excluding incest convictions. The procedures differ widely, with some Departments of Corrections providing prescreening to district attorneys and others failing to do this. States also vary widely on burden and standard of proof.

Issues related more specifically to the testifying professionals include various standards for qualifying expert witnesses and the use of various risk assessment instruments. In addition, states vary widely on self-incrimination and confidentiality.

With what is at stake in these proceedings, professionals involved must be fully familiar with the statutory requirements as well as the most reliable and valid approaches for reaching a decision.

In Chapter 12, Charlene Steen, who is both a psychologist and a lawyer, offers valuable advice to mental health professionals dealing with the courts. She offers help in distinguishing between types and purposes of testifying including cases involving sentencing, the insanity defense, civil commitment, custody cases and damages. Dr. Steen also offers valuable suggestions for preparing assessments for the courts including interviewing, testing and risk assessment techniques.

Chapter 11

A Comparative Analysis of State Statutes Providing for the Involuntary Commitment of Sexually Violent Predators

by Brian Holmgren, J.D.

Overview

This chapter is designed to provide a comparative analysis of the statutory schemes of existing SVP statutes. There is a primary focus on elements of these statutes which will be most salient to nonlawyer[1] professionals dealing with their implementation, specifically those elements most likely to have an impact on their professional practice. A detailed comparison between the provisions of these varying statutes is beyond the scope of this chapter, both because of the number of jurisdictions which currently have these statutes[2] and because of the uniqueness of each state's laws.[3] Professionals who are involved with civil commitment laws will need to become intimately familiar with their state's statute and case law interpreting it.

Neither is this chapter intended to recommend one statutory scheme over another. The Kansas statute upheld in *Kansas v. Hendricks*[4] has a number of shortcomings but unfortunately may become a model on which other states pattern legislation simply because the statue has withstood initial constitutional challenges.[5]

Introduction

Since their inception a decade ago, civil commitment statutes for sexually violent predators have been controversial, generating a large amount of political debate, public policy consideration, and significant legal challenges. The landmark decision by the U.S. Supreme Court in *Hendricks* affirmed the constitutionality of statutes authorizing the involuntary commitment of sexually violent predators (hereinafter SVP statutes), at least in terms of double jeopardy and ex post facto challenges.[6] The *Hendricks* decision, however, did not end the legal and constitutional challenges to these laws[7] or the political and public policy debate over their utility.[8] These statutes will continue to face challenges, in large measure because of fundamental differences in the structure of these statutes, and perhaps more important, because of differences in how these statutes are implemented from one jurisdiction to another.

General Characteristics of SVP Statutes

Types of Statutory Schemes. There are a number of different statutory schemes characterizing SVP laws across the country. The vast majority of SVP statutes are designed to effect an involuntary civil commitment following completion of a convicted sex offender's criminal sentence to prison; that is, the commitment follows completion of the criminal sanctions for the underlying offense.[9] Some statutes also permit petitions to be filed against juvenile offenders.[10] At least one state provides that offenders who have been released on parole may be petitioned against if they engage in some conduct which subjects them to a petition, usually an overt act evidencing their likelihood of committing a new sexually violent offense.[11] A couple of states have contrasting statutory schemes, providing for commitment in lieu of or in addition to any criminal penalties, but occurring temporally at the beginning of the legal response to the offender's conduct rather than postincarceration.[12] Several states have statutes which apply to so-called sexually violent predators but do not involve involuntary civil commitment. Rather, these statutes focus on assessment of offenders for purposes of risk management and varying levels of community notification or supervision.[13] This chapter does not address the provisions of these statutes.

Qualifying Offenses. A common requirement for virtually all SVP statutes is that the offender must have been charged with or convicted of a sexually violent offense, often referred to as a predicate offense, before a petition may be filed. A detailed comparison of these predicate or qualifying offenses within the various SVP statutes is not possible because each state defines these predicate offenses according to its own unique set of criminal offenses. Generally, qualifying offenses include convictions[14] for adult rapes and sex offenses against children, as well as attempts to commit these crimes. Juvenile sex offenses[15] and sex offenses committed in another state[16] may also qualify. Crimes which are traditionally not considered sex offenses, but which may be sexually motivated (e.g., burglary and kidnapping), may also be included in the list of predicate offenses. However, not all sex offenses qualify as predicate offenses for subsequent SVP commitments. Notably, a large number of intrafamilial offenses[17] and computer Internet-related sex offenses, including child pornography and sexual exploitation, may not qualify under various statutory schemes. Other statutes provide that petitions may be filed if the offender is presently incarcerated for a nonpredicate offense as long as he has a past conviction for a qualifying predicate offense.

Initial Screening Procedures. Offenders are typically screened for possible SVP petitions during a specified period shortly before their anticipated release date from prison.[18] The initial screening procedures are designed to determine whether the offender meets the initial criteria for having a qualifying predicate offense and a qualifying mental disorder. This initial review may be done by institutional personnel or by a specially designated multidisciplinary team,[19] but it frequently is not done by mental health professionals. In several states, a petition cannot be referred without an extensive evaluation and the recommendation of a mental health professional.[20] Conversely, a substantial number of SVP statutes authorize an extensive mental health evaluation only after a petition is filed and a probable cause determination has been made.[21]

Screening procedures vary from state to state and usually include a detailed review of the offender's file history and his treatment and institutional records. They may also include an interview with the offender and the use of actuarial risk instruments and/or psychosocial evaluations. More than 90% of offenders screened for SVP petitions will not be referred for a formal petition.[22] Those satisfying preliminary screening criteria will frequently be evaluated more thoroughly before a petition is referred to a prosecutorial agency.[23]

Mental Disorder Requirements. In addition to the requirement of a predicate offense, the offender must also have a diagnosable mental abnormality or personality disorder which satisfies the filing criteria, and which makes the person likely to engage in acts of sexual violence in the future. Typically, these mental abnormalities or personality disorders are not specifically classified by the SVP statutes themselves but instead have been defined by practice in the different jurisdictions.[24] These mental disorders have commonly included various paraphilias such as sadism, pedophilia, and "paraphilias not otherwise specified." The latter category has in practice been used to classify rapists. Controversy has inured over the use of psycopathy,[25] conduct disorders, and antisocial personality disorders as qualifying mental disorders by experts.[26]

The U.S. Supreme Court specifically held in *Hendricks* that states are not confined to the terms or classifications generally used in the medical, psychiatric, or psychological fields in defining what types of mental disorders will satisfy legal and constitutional requirements.[27] Legally, the mental disorder criteria used by evaluators need not parallel criteria according to the *Diagnostic and Statistical Manual of Mental Disorders* (DSM-IV; American Psychiatric Association, 1994), but in practice, most evaluators and experts have attempted to follow such criteria. This will likely be a continuing area for litigation in terms of due process challenges to SVP statutes. In addition, evaluators and experts testifying in SVP cases may use varying professional standards and definitions for these criteria, which again may promote legal challenges to the implementation of the statutes.[28] In several states, the mental disorder determination may not be predicated exclusively on the offender's past record of convictions.[29]

More important, there must be a nexus between the diagnosed mental disorder and the predisposition to commit a sexually violent offense in the future. This issue involves an assessment of the likelihood of reoffense behavior, often predicated on the use of actuarial risk assessments, and is typically the crux of the legal and professional debate in any SVP case. However, there need not be a greater than 50% predicted recidivism rate using an actuarial assessment to satisfy either petitioning criteria or commitment. This is because the statutory criteria generally only require a "substantial likelihood" that the offender will commit further acts of sexual violence, not a requirement that they will "more likely than not" engage in such conduct. A precise cutoff rate on actuarial data (e.g., 30, 35, or 40%) has not been precisely defined either by practice, statute, or case law. This issue remains a continuing area of professional and legal controversy in SVP cases. Moreover, the risk of reoffense is not limited to a specific period (e.g., five or ten years) following release but, instead, is considered over the offender's entire lifetime, which suggests that actuarial and recidivism data based on longer, rather than shorter follow-up studies, should be considered when evaluating offenders in SVP cases. Unfortunately, most research in this area has used shorter follow-up periods.[30]

Another problem that frequently arises is the tendency of courts to liken the "mental disorder" or "mental abnormality" condition under SVP statutes with the "mental illness" criteria typically used in criminal cases to determine issues of legal insanity and nonresponsibility. Unfortunately, the U.S. Supreme Court contributed to this problem through some loose language in the *Hendricks* opinion. For example, the Court suggested that the Kansas statute's requirement of future dangerousness is linked to "the existence of a "mental abnormality" or "personality disorder" that makes it difficult, if not impossible, for the person to control their dangerousness."[31]

This equivalence was clearly not intended by the legislatures which enacted SVP statutes, and which used terms such as "mental abnormality" and "personality disorder" explicitly to avoid linkage with other statutes using the term "mental illness."[32] However, other courts considering the SVP criteria have also frequently suggested that the criteria for commitment are such that the offender cannot control his behavior because of his mental disorder.[33] This type of suggestion has made its way into professional articles discussing SVP statutes as well.[34]

The Kansas Supreme Court recently held that it was not constitutionally permissible to commit a sex offender as a sexual predator absent a showing that he was unable to control his dangerous behavior.[35] The Court relied heavily on the foregoing quoted language from the *Hendricks* decision. Conversely, the Washington, Illinois, and New Jersey Courts of Appeal have rejected arguments that *Hendricks* mandated "volitional impairment" as a separate due process requirement for SVP commitments.[36] A similar ruling was recently issued by the Arizona Supreme Court which overturned a lower court's holding relying on this dicta in *Hendricks*.[37] Fortunately, the U.S. Supreme Court has agreed to review the decision in *Crane* and will therefore have an opportunity to clarify the intent of its holding and language in the *Hendricks* case.[38]

Professionals involved with SVP cases must appreciate that SVP statutes require only a mental disorder which "predisposes" the offender to engage in acts of sexual violence, a requirement fundamentally distinct from a mental illness that prevents the offender from conforming his conduct to the requirements of the law (i.e., the ability to refrain from acting on his sexual impulses and desires). Volitional behavior is at the core of sexual offending, a fact well documented by research on offenders, and one central to the principal form of behavior modification and treatment for sex offenders.[39]

Few, if any, sex offenders have a complete or total lack of volitional control, even if they suffer from a serious mental illness or psychosis.[40] Sex offenders simply do not assault every person with whom they come into contact, a fact which demonstrates that offenders are capable of controlling their sexual behavior at least to some degree. However, if the rationale of the *Crane* decision was taken to its logical conclusions, the only sex offenders who could appropriately be subject to SVP commitment would be those few offenders who did offend against everyone with whom they came into contact or, like Mr. Hendricks, who were foolish enough to admit that they would reoffend if released.[41] The principle behind SVP statutes is precisely the opposite—to protect society from sexually violent predators who have chosen to act on their volition in the past and are likely to do so in the future. The presence of a diagnosable mental disorder indicates why these offenders are predisposed to act out sexually or violently and why they are at greater risk to do so in the future.

Filing of Petitions. Assuming the offender satisfies the initial screening criteria for a predicate offense and has a diagnosable mental disorder, he may then be referred for a petition. Statutes typically provide for various agencies to file SVP petitions. Usually these include the attorney general for the state or the district attorney in the jurisdiction in which the predicate offense was committed or in which the offender is scheduled to be released.

The filing of a petition will trigger a variety of procedural mechanisms with different time deadlines. Typically these include time limits on when hearings must be held, when evaluations and reports must be completed, and when documents must be turned over to the respective parties. These procedural mechanisms vary dramatically under the different SVP statutes and have a substantial impact on professionals who are involved with their implementation. Conflicts also frequently arise between the specific provisions of the SVP statute itself and other civil and criminal procedural rules which may be incorporated by reference.

All statutes provide a right of legal representation for the offender and the right to have an evaluation done by an independent expert. Statutes provide varying rights of discovery to offenders. These allow the attorney representing the offender access to information in the prosecutor's files as well as access to the reports, record information, and testing procedures used by the evaluators and access to the offender's institutional records. Some jurisdictions have reciprocal discovery procedures permitting the state to have access to materials within the control of the defense attorney or the defense expert. These matters are covered in more detail in the next section.

Statutes provide varying rights regarding procedural hearings, with some statutes providing rights to a jury trial and others only providing rights to a trial before a judge. All statutes provide a right of a preliminary hearing to determine probable cause on the petition. However, the standard of proof, the amount of evidence, and the number of witnesses needed at this stage vary considerably. For example, many states allow for a wide variety of hearsay evidence to be introduced at these preliminary hearings, thereby alleviating the necessity of calling multiple fact witnesses in addition to experts to satisfy probable cause standards. In other jurisdictions, the initial probable cause determination may be made ex parte by a judge upon a review of the petition and attachments, and without the necessity for an adversarial hearing with witnesses being questioned and cross-examined by attorneys.

The standards of proof required at trial also vary considerably with some SVP statutes providing that the state's burden of proof on the petition is the traditional civil burden of "clear and convincing evidence."[42] Most statutes, however, require the higher burden of proof typically reserved for criminal prosecutions of "beyond a reasonable doubt."[43] These varying burdens can raise interesting issues for experts offering opinions. For example, the expert is usually required to state his opinion to a reasonable degree of professional certainty. The expert will also be asked whether the offender is "likely"[44] to engage in sexually violent behavior in the future, which may be further defined by the statute or case law as "more probably than not" that the offender will reoffend. However, this opinion may not translate very well to a jury which must determine that "beyond a reasonable doubt" the offender should be committed.

If an offender is adjudicated to be a sexually violent predator under the respective statutory scheme, then a variety of dispositions may follow. Most statutes provide for an automatic commitment to a locked treatment facility. Texas is unique in requiring that all commitments are for outpatient treatment and supervision.[45] A few statutes require the court to consider alternative placements or less restrictive alternatives to housing a committed offender in a locked facility. The period of commitment may be indefinite, or limited to a specific period of time, usually one or two years.[46] With indefinite commitments the offender is provided an opportunity to petition for release after varying time periods. The state is thereafter required to establish that the commitment should continue. This may require the filing of a new petition and in some instances, a completely new trial. In other instances, the state is merely required to establish that the offender's mental disorder and dangerousness continue to such a degree that he cannot be safely released into the community, be afforded a less restrictive alternative placement, or be conditionally or unconditionally discharged. Under some statutory schemes the offender may be required to first establish that his circumstances have changed before a new hearing is required.

Offenders remain under the jurisdiction of the statute until they are unconditionally discharged. Realistically, unconditional discharge is unlikely to occur with most offenders because their mental disorder is not going to disappear. Accordingly, the goal for most committed offenders will generally be to seek the least restrictive conditions of confinement and supervision. Most statutes provide that violations of conditions of release and supervision are grounds for placement back in a confined treatment setting, while a few statutes make such violations a criminal offense.[47]

Access to and Consideration of Information

SVP statutes contain widely varying provisions for the dissemination of information to various parties involved with the proceedings. Professionals' access to information about the offender which will inform their decision-making process is critical regardless of the stage of the proceedings, (e.g., assessment and evaluation, trial, post-commitment). However, both SVP statutes themselves as well as other legal statutes and rules may circumscribe or hamper access to this information at different stages. Equally important is the need for professionals to document the information they considered and relied on in forming their opinions.

Certainly one of the most important sources of information is the offender's past offense history. Generally this information is contained in investigative reports (e.g., police and child protective services reports) or in the files of the prosecuting agency (e.g., district attorney and juvenile court). However, only two states, North Dakota and Washington, presently mandate retention of these records for an extended period of time.[48] Other information involving the offense history may be contained in presentence reports or prior psychosexual evaluation reports. However, access to these data may be restricted by specific statutes or by legal privileges and confidentiality strictures. Several states have incorporated specific provisions into their SVP laws dealing with issues of confidentiality and privilege[49] and access to and distribution of records and information. Others have defined this through case law.[50]

In some instances, it may be necessary for professionals to speak with the victim directly to obtain the types of specific information that may be necessary in a given case. Access to juvenile record information is also frequently necessary but frequently difficult or impossible to obtain. Records may be destroyed or otherwise protected by legal rules. However, at least one risk instrument (Psychopathy Checklist—Revised PCL-R; Hare, 1991) requires consideration of juvenile record information. Adequate use of this instrument may be negated if this information is not readily available.

SVP statutes differ significantly in the access they provide to information at different stages of the process. Arizona's statute provides one of the most comprehensive listings of data which are to be considered and made available to the parties.[51] By contrast, most of the other statutory schemes have failed to include this type of a listing, leaving practitioners to informally agree to or litigate issues of access to information. This may also leave practitioners with inadequate information to make informed decisions at critical stages of the process. For example, the initial screening and referral process will generally not contain file information of the type necessary to go to trial. Accordingly, a petition may be referred and filed which ultimately may prove to be unsupportable when additional information is gathered.

Other provisions of the SVP statute may proscribe additional access to information. For example, the SVP statute may define the type of discovery which will be available. Most SVP statutes follow the civil rules for discovery in one form or another. This may provide the right to depose witnesses, compel responses to interrogatories, and usually the right to subpoena documents. A professional's failure to honor these legal requirements can result in a finding of contempt by the court. This could involve a variety of sanctions including, for example, exclusion of the expert's ability to testify in the trial.[52]

Prosecutors handling SVP cases may also be required to disclose information that would otherwise be considered "exculpatory" or *Brady*[53] material in a criminal case. Although SVP statutes are technically considered civil rather than criminal proceedings, disclosure of exculpatory material may be encompassed by both an SVP statute's specific provisions affording respondents "all the rights possessed by defendants in criminal proceedings"[54] or by the prosecutor's higher ethical obligations as a minister of justice.[55]

Potentially more problematic is the fact that case law in some jurisdictions holds that prosecutors may be required to disclose exculpatory information contained in files of other state agencies even if the information is not in the prosecutor's own files and the prosecutor is not aware of the information.[56] Experts who conduct assessments and evaluations and who testify in SVP proceedings will generally be employed by state agencies, and this will also hold true for institutional and treatment records held by the prison system. As was discussed earlier, the prosecutor may also be indirectly affected by ethical guidelines governing other professionals. For example, psychologists involved in forensic work are ethically required to disclose contrary data or facts that would mitigate against their opinions. The prosecutor using that expert would be similarly obligated to identify and disclose that information.

Correspondingly, attorneys representing offenders on SVP petitions may be obligated to disclose adverse reports or turn over data that might support the petition, because of the civil nature of the proceedings. In the criminal setting, this same result would not follow.

Certainly one of the most important sources of information is the offender himself. SVP statutes vary significantly in the degree of access to information from the offender. Some statutes specifically provide the offender with rights against self-incrimination. These rights may include proscriptions on the use of the offender's silence at any stage of the proceeding. For example, the prosecutor may be prevented from asking jurors to draw a negative inference from the offender's refusal to cooperate in the evaluation process. Less clear is whether these Fifth Amendment privileges similarly prohibit the expert from drawing such a negative inference in his evaluation, conclusions, or testimony. Yet other statutes may provide for compelled examinations and permit the argument or drawing of a negative inference if the offender refuses to participate. A broader discussion of this issue is contained in a later section of this chapter.

Experts' Qualifications

An integral part of any SVP commitment scheme are the experts who evaluate offenders and testify in SVP proceedings, as well as those experts who treat committed offenders. In an effort to ensure appropriate expertise, several SVP statutes specifically define the qualifications for professionals involved with these roles.[57] Other statutes may only limit the qualifications for experts to psychologists or psychiatrists.[58] The highly specialized nature of SVP proceedings and the serious consequences which follow for offenders who are committed necessitate that experts involved in assessments and testimony possess the highest professional qualifications.

Issues involving expert qualifications arise in a variety of circumstances under SVP laws. First, the threshold for legal admissibility of expert opinions is often quite low,[59] arguably affording the opportunity for expert testimony by marginally qualified professionals in states which do not specify exacting qualifications under their SVP statute. Recently, the U.S. Supreme Court has articulated new requirements for the admissibility of expert testimony.[60] These requirements deal more with the subject matter of the expert's testimony rather than the expert's qualifications per se. Nevertheless, a marginal expert is probably less likely to be able to articulate the scientific underpinnings supporting his or her testimony than a truly qualified expert, which may result in the exclusion of the expert's testimony or reports. This is a good thing if it keeps out poorly qualified experts and unscientific testimony. However, it also has the potential to keep out well-accepted assessment tools if (1) the expert is not able to describe the research and principles supporting their use,[61] (2) the court is unable to understand the science well enough to make an informed decision on admissibility, or (3) an opposing expert is able to convince the court that the procedures or opinions are not generally accepted.[62]

Participation in professional organizations such as the American Psychological Association, the American Psychiatric Association, or the Association for the Treatment of Sexual Abusers (ATSA) is not a prerequisite to being qualified as an expert in SVP cases. Similarly, there is no required minimum period of professional practice, no requirement of subspecialization in the treatment or assessment of sex offenders, or any requirement that professionals be actively involved in practice in order to qualify as an expert in most SVP cases. Although these characteristics may be desirable from the standpoint of ensuring a higher level of expertise, historically, neither SVP statutes themselves nor the courts have made them a priority. A few states have enacted certification procedures for experts which take these factors into consideration. However, certification procedures have also served to entrench marginally competent experts within the SVP process, making it difficult to exclude experts who deviate from accepted standards of practice once they have achieved their certification status. Ultimately, a formalized review process for experts may need to be instituted to ensure a continuing high level of professional practice in this field. To date, no state has adopted such a practice.

Mental health professionals involved with providing treatment to offenders while incarcerated and those providing treatment to civilly committed offenders may also be called on to testify in SVP proceedings. Generally, it is not advisable to have these professionals qualified to offer expert opinions on commitment or continued detention of offenders because of the conflicts such testimony may pose to the ongoing treatment relationship. However, these professionals may be needed to provide information about the offender's progress in treatment in support of other expert's opinions.

Ethical considerations may also factor into the qualifications of experts and most certainly into the reports and opinions they offer. For example, the American Psychiatric Association has offered a detailed position statement opposing SVP statutes as a whole, strongly indicating that psychiatrists should not participate in this legal process.[63] Nevertheless, many SVP statutes mandate that SVP petitions be supported by the opinions of at least one psychiatrist, and most statutes specify that psychiatrists are one of the types of professionals who are able to do assessments and provide expert testimony. These conflicting positions between a major professional organization and a state's statutory scheme may pose significant dilemmas for some professionals. In addition, psychiatrists testifying in support of SVP petitions will frequently be cross-examined on the American Psychiatric Association's Task Force Report in an effort to undermine their opinions.

Psychologists will also be affected by ethical guidelines in terms of their qualifications and opinions. Both the American Psychological Association Code of Ethics[64] and the Specialty Guidelines for Forensic Evaluations[65] have a number of provisions which affect psychologists involved with SVP cases. Ethical rules involving the appropriate use of assessment tools, maintaining appropriate knowledge within the field, and the disclosure by experts of data which may weigh against the opinions they are offering all have an impact on the SVP process in a variety of ways. Although these ethical principles are not specifically referenced by SVP statutes themselves, they are nevertheless an important part of how those statutes are implemented. Professionals obligated by these considerations need to discuss these issues with other professionals, especially lawyers who use them, so that ethical conflicts can be avoided and professional standards can be maintained consistent with the objectives of the statutes. One of the quickest ways to undermine confidence in these statutes is for questions to be raised about the ethics of those participating in their implementation.

Risk Prediction and Actuarial Instruments

Risk assessment and risk prediction are essential components of every SVP commitment proceeding. Unfortunately, it is one of the most controversial and least settled areas of professional practice. Unquestionably, some of this controversy inures because of the manner in which the SVP statutes are drafted. Several factors contribute to this problem. First, as has already been discussed, SVP statutes vary in their provisions dealing with the qualifications of experts who testify. More important, these statutes have significant variance in terms of how they address the issue of risk assessment and the standards for risk prediction. Some statutes, such as Florida's, attempt to circumscribe the qualifications of both their experts and the types of risk instruments that may be employed by such experts. Most other SVP statutes contain no comparable provisions, leaving such standards to the individual expert who participates in the proceedings. As might be expected, such practice has sparked considerable professional debate and legal controversy.[66]

There are a number of legal issues which may be implicated by the use of various risk instruments. The first is whether the particular risk instrument satisfies legal standards for admissibility of scientific evidence. These legal standards also vary from state to state, with some states continuing to adhere to the old *Frye*[67] standard for admissibility of scientific evidence and other states adopting the more recently articulated standards of the *Daubert* and *Kumho* cases[68] interpreting the provisions of the Federal Rules of Evidence. The *Frye* test is an extremely conservative standard which historically has operated to exclude a wide range of expert testimony. Conversely, the *Daubert* and *Kumho* standards have expressly sought to broaden the admissibility of expert testimony consistent with the more liberal provisions for expert testimony under the Federal Rules of Evidence.[69] The importance of which standard is used in a particular state cannot be overstated. The differences between these two standards may be dispositive not only of whether a particular actuarial instrument may be used in a particular case but also within a given state. Exclusion of a specific risk instrument, or several risk instruments, may also have profound implications for the SVP statute as a whole as such exclusions may significantly hamper the ability of experts to offer convincing opinions regarding the offender's risk of reoffending and/or opinions supporting commitment.

The proponents of various risk instruments argue strenuously that actuarial data are the most scientifically reliable form of risk prediction, and their predictive value in comparison to the reliability of clinical judgment has been abundantly demonstrated.[70] Nevertheless, these proponents also concede that such instruments generally underpredict actual risk, arguably establishing that some if not all of the instruments have significant margins for error under the *Daubert* criteria. Does this mean that such instruments are not reliable for use in the courtroom?[71] Arguably not, because this error, specifically the problem of false negatives, weighs in favor of the offender in these circumstances.

Another potential difficulty comes, however, when experts attempt to account for some of this error through dynamic rather than static risk factors, or through expert testimony that includes clinical judgment and considerations of risk independent of the factors used within the actuarial instruments themselves.[72] There is considerable debate among experts on whether risk prediction should be exclusively based on actuarial data or whether it should include clinical judgment as well. This debate has significant legal implications for the admissibility of expert testimony. If one assumes that actuarial data have the most reliability in terms of its predictive value, then it should be the preferred basis for expert testimony, especially under the *Daubert* criteria. Ironically, many experts testifying in SVP cases suggest that such instruments are not reliable,[73] implicitly suggesting that either clinical judgment should be the governing basis for expert opinions or, alternatively, there is no reliable basis on which to make risk predictions. The second alternative would, of course, undermine the entire process of risk prediction in SVP cases, arguably necessitating dismissal of every petition. Here again, the qualifications and experience of the experts who testify on either side of this issue can play an enormous part in the potential outcome of the case, not to mention the integrity of SVP proceedings as a whole.

A number of additional issues involving actuarial instruments are implicated but not necessarily addressed by the specific provisions of various SVP statutes. In some states, the SVP statute may specifically provide for the admission of actuarial instruments,[74] while in other states such admission may be provided by case law interpreting the statutes.[75] Generally these statutory provisions or case law decisions have not sought to draw distinctions regarding the admissibility of individual instruments. Such distinctions may have some legal significance because certain instruments may have wider professional acceptance or a broader basis on which to establish scientific reliability than other instruments.

Nor is it clear whether a different standard for legal admissibility should result because SVP cases are civil rather than criminal. Although some precedent exists suggesting that higher standards of admissibility are required for criminal cases, other factors argue against such a result. First, the liberty and public safety interests at stake in SVP cases are as significant as serious criminal cases. Second, both the *Daubert* and *Kumho* decisions were civil cases and did not articulate a civil/criminal distinction in admissibility standards for expert testimony. Neither do the rules of evidence governing expert testimony draw distinctions between civil and criminal cases. Finally, the central admissibility criteria under *Daubert* is the reliability of the evidence and the scientific principles involved. These criteria are arguably not affected by whether the evidence is being offered in a criminal or a civil proceeding.

Another concern arises in determining the level of probability of reoffense necessary to support a recommendation in court. For example, must the risk instrument predict a greater than 50% probability of reoffense to warrant an admissible opinion by the expert? If not, what level of probability is required? These issues are largely undefined by the SVP statutes themselves. However some variation may result simply from whether the burden of proof under the statute is "beyond a reasonable doubt" or "clear and convincing" evidence.

The expert may still be able to rely on actuarial instruments in formulating an opinion even if the actual results of the instruments are not independently admissible at trial. However, the inability of the expert to discuss the specific facts informing his opinion may significantly undermine the expert's opinion in the eyes of the jury. In jurisdictions in which trials are before the court rather than a jury, a court may be more liberal in admitting actuarial instruments, reasoning that there is less likelihood of prejudice from admission of potentially less reliable data under these circumstances. However, if an actuarial instrument is deemed "unreliable" under *Daubert* criteria, then not only will the specific results from the instrument not be admissible but the expert should also be precluded from using any data from the instrument in formulating his opinions, regardless of whether the testimony is offered in a jury or court trial.

Other psychological instruments may not specifically predict risk but may still factor into assessments of offenders and assist in the prediction process. For example, plethysmograph results may assist in the diagnosis of the offender's mental disorder and may have some influence on clinical judgments in consideration with actuarial assessments. Similarly, the Minnesota Multiphasic Personality Inventory (MMPI) will not be useful for risk prediction or for classifying sex offenders according to a specific offender profile, but it may add input to certain mental diagnosis such as antisocial personality disorders and psychopathy that are correlated with risk, recidivism, and treatment prognosis.

There are also professional and ethical issues that are implicated by the use of various assessment tools and actuarial instruments. First, ethical guidelines require that professionals who use instruments be qualified to do so and use the instruments appropriately. This necessitates that in reports to the court and during testimony, any limitations associated with the use of a particular instrument, including limitations in terms of their predictive value, must be fully disclosed. The appropriateness of usage with specific offender populations, and conversely their lack of appropriateness with other offenders, must also be disclosed. Moreover, it may be unprofessional or unethical for experts not to use risk instruments irrespective of whether the data generated from the instruments may be admissible under legal precedent in the jurisdiction.[75] This usage may be professionally and ethically mandated if the expert believes that actuarial instruments represent an improvement over clinical judgment alone and provide more objective criteria on which to make predictions of risk. This professional judgment is not contingent upon legal determinations of admissibility or the specific provisions of a particular SVP statute.

Self-Incrimination and Confidentiality Issues

Do sex offenders have a right to remain silent during various stages of the SVP process? If so, at what stage of the process and to what extent? Can their silence be considered by professionals or fact finders in formulating opinions or judgments? The answers to these questions are as diverse as the differences between the respective SVP statutes themselves and reflect one of the most vexing issues confronting professionals dealing with these laws.

Given the classification of all SVP statutes as "civil" commitment statutes which do not impose criminal sanctions, one might reasonably argue that an offender does not have a Fifth Amendment privilege against self-incrimination. Indeed, this argument has been made successfully by the government under some SVP statutes.[77] In those states in which the privilege does not apply, the offender may be deposed or called as an adverse witness by the state and questioned about his past offense history. This testimony can be some of the most damaging evidence presented at the trial, often supplanting the evidence presented through the expert witnesses. If the offender refuses to answer these questions the state may seek to have the court instruct the jury that they are to draw negative inferences from the offender's refusal to answer the questions.[78]

Several SVP statutes, however, either explicitly or implicitly provide a privilege against self-incrimination. The Wisconsin and Illinois statutes provide that a respondent shall enjoy "all the constitutional rights available to a defendant in a criminal proceeding." This language has been interpreted to mean that the respondent has the right to remain silent, the right to refuse to participate in the evaluation process, and the right to refuse to testify. In addition, the government and/or its witnesses may not comment on that silence at trial.[79] Iowa's statute is similar, providing that an individual subject to civil commitment has all the rights provided to a criminal defendant. It is not clear yet whether this language implies the right to remain silent.

Does this privilege extend to aspects of the SVP process besides the trial, for example, to screening and assessment procedures prior to the formal referral of an SVP petition to the government and/or to such procedures after a formal referral has been made or a petition filed by the government? At least in Wisconsin and Illinois, the privilege probably extends to these prereferral procedures and most definitely to the postpetition process. That is, the offender can refuse to speak with professionals at these stages and both the professionals and the government will not be able to comment on this refusal at trial. The answer in Iowa is less clear and will ultimately be determined by judicial decisions interpreting the Iowa statute. In other states without these types of implicit or explicit self-incrimination provisions, it remains unclear what rights the offender has in terms of refusing to answer questions or participate in evaluation procedures, and what consequences may follow from such conduct.[80]

Can professionals consider the offender's silence or refusal to cooperate with interviews or assessments in formulating their judgments or offering their opinions? Are experts permitted to draw a negative inference about the offender's risk of reoffense based on this silence or lack of cooperation? May an expert conclude that an offender is concealing aspects of his dangerousness by refusing to discuss his offense history? Assuming the answer to these questions is yes, the expert may not be able to articulate this fact in courtroom testimony, at least in states providing a self-incrimination privilege, unless the defense opens the door to such testimony through cross-examination of the expert.[81] In states that do not have such a privilege, the expert will most likely be able to discuss how the offender's silence influences his judgments and opinions about the offender's dangerousness and his likelihood of reoffense.

Self-incrimination concerns may arise, however, even before an offender is evaluated for a possible SVP petition. In many jurisdictions, offenders will not be able to successfully complete treatment programs, within either an institutional or an outpatient setting, unless they provide a full disclosure of their offense behavior, involving the offense(s) of which they were convicted, to the treatment provider. In addition, many treatment programs require disclosure involving other sexual offense behavior for which the offender may not have been prosecuted or convicted. Although such disclosures may be viewed as necessary within the therapeutic setting, they also pose a risk that they may be later used against the offender in the context of SVP proceedings.

This can arise in a variety of contexts. For example, suppose the offender acknowledges in treatment that he committed several additional offenses against several other victims but was never prosecuted for these crimes. This disclosure might be mandated by the treatment provider as part of the offender's complete history or might be disclosed while discussing the cycle of conduct leading up to commission of the offense. Some programs may even mandate polygraph confirmation of this information. This information may assist the treatment provider in developing a relapse plan, but this same information could be used by an evaluator in the SVP process, or by the state at an SVP trial, to indicate that the offender is even more dangerous than the offense for which he was convicted might suggest. This information might also affect the actuarial risk assessments done on the offender, or at least modify the clinical judgments applied to the risk assessment. Conversely, the offender's refusal to discuss these issues in treatment may raise negative inferences in subsequent SVP proceedings as well, not to mention adversely affecting the likelihood that the offender will successfully complete the treatment program.

Unfortunately, the offender who is involved in a treatment program in a state that has an existing SVP statute, or in a state that is considering enacting one, may feel as though he is between the proverbial rock and a hard place. On the one hand, he may make disclosures that may assist in the completion of the treatment program but may later be used against him.[82] On the other hand, he may remain silent and risk being deemed noncompliant in treatment or have his silence potentially used against him by evaluators in subsequent SVP proceedings. Clearly these concerns can have a potential chilling effect on treatment or the willingness to participate in treatment.[83] Moreover, incarcerated offenders may legitimately complain that they are less likely to be released from prison on parole, or more likely to be petitioned against under the SVP laws, if they fail to participate in treatment while incarcerated, at the same time risking additional consequences by participating in those same treatment programs.

No simple solutions exist for these dilemmas, and the statutory provisions of existing SVP statutes have heretofore not contained specific provisions addressing these concerns. Similar issues have arisen within the context of probation and parole determinations in criminal cases resulting in a conflicting body of case law.[84] Ultimately, the courts and the legislatures will need to address these concerns and draft appropriate rules for both criminal cases and SVP procedures.

Victim Issues

The inception of SVP statutes has affected victims in a variety of ways. Professionals working with victims must be sensitive to the many ways these laws interact with victim rights and the manner in which victims are dealt with from the moment they enter the legal system. Most of these issues are not addressed by specific provisions within SVP statutes themselves. Instead, these issues are implicated indirectly, requiring professionals to reorient their traditional manner of handling victims to accommodate the changing demands placed on them by the advent of these new laws. This section is designed to identify some of these issues, and the limited manner in which SVP statutes may address them.

Clearly, the most significant impact SVP laws have had on victims has been the potential need for victims to once again become involved with the legal process many years after they thought they had achieved closure to the case. Prosecutors handling SVP cases have been compelled in many instances to contact victims ten, fifteen, or twenty years after their assault and ask them to participate once again as a witness in the SVP case. There are many who would debate the propriety of asking victims to participate in this process, and many who would suggest that prosecutors call victims to testify in SVP proceedings only to engender sympathy from jurors or to create a sense of outrage against the offender.[85] There are, however, a number of legal reasons for calling victims to testify in SVP cases.

First, to the extent that SVP statutes provide respondents "all the rights afforded to defendants in criminal trials," which include rights of confrontation and compulsory process, the prosecutor may be required to have the victim of an underlying sexual assault testify about that experience before an expert may comment on its significance at trial.[86] This may be even more true in states that require the prosecution to prove a recent overt act to establish the SVP commitment.

Second, the defendant may have entered a "no-contest" plea to the underlying sexual offense in the criminal case, thereby precluding the use of the plea, or the facts of the offense recited at the time of the plea, as an admission by the offender in the SVP case.[87] In addition, if there was no trial in the criminal case, and/or the victim did not testify, there would not be an admissible record of the victim's account of the offense. The offender's account of the incident at the time, or through later statements during treatment or evaluations, frequently differs significantly from the victim's version. Experts in the SVP cases often place significant weight on the offense accounts of victims, including the offender's behaviors leading up to the assault and his statements and conduct during the assault. This information may not be contained in the police or social service reports from victim interviews, or even in courtroom testimony, as the expert may be concerned with other issues on which victims may not be specifically questioned.

Moreover, an offender's pattern of behavior may become clear only through his later conduct with subsequent victims. Consequently, an earlier victim may not be questioned about such conduct or this information may not be set forth with sufficient detail within the investigative reports. Finally, in many instances victims are simply not questioned with as much attention to detail as is necessary to be presented in the SVP case, thereby preventing strict reliance on the victim's earlier statement as sufficient foundation for the later SVP case, even when the SVP statute may permit use of this type of "hearsay" evidence to be presented or considered by the expert.

The extent to which victims may or may not want to testify in SVP proceedings must also be considered, just as it must be in any criminal case. Victims may have a strong desire to participate in the SVP process, either through testifying or through discussions with the prosecutor involved in the case, because the SVP process directly involves the issue of whether their assailant will be released into the community.

Conversely, many victims express concern over the offender's renewed access to information about them personally which may need to be disclosed as part of the discovery process. Moreover, the civil nature of SVP proceedings may necessitate that victims be subject to depositions in addition to trial testimony, thereby mandating even greater involvement in the legal process and affording more opportunities for the victim to be harassed or retraumatized.

A few SVP statutes have specific provisions designed to address issues involving victim testimony. California, for example, provides that the details underlying a prior convicted-of offense may be shown by documentary evidence.[88] Other SVP statutes may implicitly provide that some types of documentary evidence are admissible, arguably permitting presentation or consideration of the victim's prior statements to police, social workers, or other professionals to be used without the need to call the victim personally. This issue is a complicated one from a legal-evidentiary standpoint. For example, some states' evidentiary codes permit the use of certain types of child hearsay in the criminal case (e.g., excited utterances and videotaped interviews of the victim).[89] The extent to which these provisions are incorporated or excluded by SVP statutes' adoption of civil or criminal procedural and evidentiary rules remains unclear. Certainly the rationale behind many of these types of rules (to facilitate testimony involving child witnesses) will not be applicable in SVP cases which proceed years later when the child victim has matured.

Although many states provide alternative means for victims to testify in criminal proceedings (e.g., use of closed-circuit television testimony and depositions in lieu of live testimony),[90] few SVP statutes specifically address this issue. Arguably, the civil nature of SVP proceedings should afford victims greater protections in this regard, as confrontation rights guaranteed by the Fourth Amendment are not strictly applicable under most SVP statutes, whereas they are in all criminal cases. Wisconsin's statute provides for testimony by telephone or by live audiovisual means (e.g., closed-circuit television).[91] In state's that do not include specific provisions within their respective SVP statue, consideration of alternatives to live victim testimony will necessitate interpretation of other statutory provisions for victim testimony in light of the SVP statute and/or appellate decisions providing case law authority.

Victim rights amendments which have been recently enacted in several states may also affect SVP statutes. Although most victim rights bills apply to criminal cases, their provisions may likely be interpreted to apply to SVP cases as well, given the close parity between many of the issues and interests of the parties involved. This may include the right to be consulted by the prosecutor on whether a SVP petition should be filed, whether the victim has a right to seek an independent petition if the prosecutor or other agency declines to recommend a petition, and so on. The provisions of these victim right's laws may be implicated in SVP cases even if the victim is not the same one named in the qualifying offense that forms the basis for the SVP petition. Not infrequently, criminal charges involving additional victims may be dismissed as part of the plea negotiation process in the underlying criminal case. However, these same victims may be called on to be witnesses in the subsequent SVP case, potentially implicating rights these victims may have under such amendments.

Although many SVP statutes contain some form of victim notification provision,[92] these provisions may represent only a small part of the rights provided to the victim under that state's victim's rights bill. Correspondingly, issues concerning victim compensation may also be implicated by the SVP proceedings. In many instances the SVP proceedings may create additional financial hardships on victims who are forced to attend additional hearings or participate in depositions. More critical may be the need for additional victim counseling or therapy when old traumas are revisited by the initiation of the SVP proceedings years later.

It is evident that professionals working with victims of sexual offenses will need to expand those services to victims currently involved with SVP proceedings. In addition, professionals currently working with victims in pending criminal cases would be well advised to include discussion of the potential for later SVP proceedings when discussing issues of closure with their clients. Even in states in which SVP laws are not presently enacted there is certainly the possibility that they may be at the time the offender is scheduled for release from custody. Victim compensation statutes and funding for such statutes will also need to consider that sexual assault victims may again become involved with the legal system years later and take appropriate steps to address these issues for the future.

Conclusion

Legislatures continue to enact laws that affect professionals who deal with the investigation, prosecution, treatment, and management of sex offenders. Few of these laws, with the possible exception of community notification and registration statutes, have had as broad an impact on professionals as those dealing with civil commitment of sexually violent predators. Undoubtedly, more states will draft SVP statutes and more and more professionals will be required to adjust their practices to the additional demands these laws entail. Differences within the statutory structure and specific provisions of these laws from state to state will continue to evolve, necessitating that professionals become intimately familiar with their own state's unique provisions.

The need to develop a consistent set of professional standards of practice in the implementation of these laws will potentially be frustrated by these differences. Although some states have been dealing with these laws for many years, they continue to refine their practice in accordance with new legal challenges and case law decisions, and, perhaps more important, in accordance with evolving professional knowledge in the field. It will take several years for other states with recently enacted laws to experience their own growing pains. It is hoped that they can learn from the lessons of other professionals in other states, and other states considering such laws can benefit from careful consideration of problems, challenges, and successful practices in those states that already have these laws. This chapter is but a small note in that evolving history but ideally one that will be of some assistance to professionals trying to gain an understanding of its complexity.

Acknowledgement

The author wishes to thank prosecutors David Hackett, Paul Stern, Margaret Graham, Lyn Kane, Therese Grantz, Karen Black, Richard Polin, and Lee Hettinger for their careful review and insightful suggestions to improve earlier versions of this manuscript and to ensure accuracy with the legal standards in their states. The author also wishes to acknowledge the efforts of prosecutor Erin O'Keefe, whose painstaking work summarizing many of these statutes formed the core body of research from which this chapter was developed. Finally, the detailed training materials of prosecutors Jean Mullen, Cindi Nannetti, and Tom Fallon were invaluable in identifying important issues with these laws.

Footnotes

[1] For a discussion of how SVP statutes affect prosecutors, see Holmgren, "Sexually Violent Predator Statutes—Implications for Prosecutors and Their Communities," *The Prosecutor*, pp. 20–41 (May/June 1998). See also Stern, "The Civil Commitment of Sexually Violent Predators—When We Know the Danger We Face, What Should Our Response Be?," 1(1) *Trauma, Violence & Abuse* 99–102 (2000).

[2] At present, sixteen states have SVP laws. See Ariz. Rev. Stat. Ann. §13-4601–13-4613 (1995); Cal. Welf. & Inst. Code §§6600–6608 (West 1996); Fla. Stat. Ann. §394.91o et seq. (1999); 725 Ill. Comp. Stat. Ann. §207/1 (1997); Iowa Code Ann. §229a (1998); Kan. Stat. Ann. §59–29a01 (1994); Mass. Gen. Laws ch. 123A (1999); Minn. Stat. Ann. §§253B.02, 253B.185 (1994); Mo. Rev. Stat. §589.400–589.425 (1998); N.D. Cent. Code §25–03.3–01 (1997); S.C. Code §44–48–30 (1998); Tex. Health & Safety Code §§841.001–841.147 (1999); Va. Code §§37.1-70.1–37.1-70.19 (effective July 1, 2001); Wash. Rev. Code §71.09.010 (1990); Wis. Stat. Ann. §§980.01–980.12 (1996). New Jersey had provided for commitment of sexually violent predators through its civil mental health commitment statute. See N.J. Stat. §30:4-82.4 (West 1994). However, they recently enacted a postincarceration commitment statute similar to those listed previously. See 1998 N.J. ALS 71 (1998).

[3] Exhibit 11.1, on pages 11-28 and 11-29, sets forth a partial comparison of various statutory provisions (see key to Exhibit 11.1 on page 11-30). A more detailed comparative analysis of SVP statutes is available from the American Prosecutor's Research Institute, National Center for Prosecution of Child Abuse. The Washington State Institute for Public Policy also has a variety of publications available. See, e.g., Lieb, *Washington's Sexually Violent Predator Law: Legislative History and Comparisons with Other States* (1996); Matson & Lieb, *Sexual Predator Commitment Laws in the United States: 1998 Update* (1998). Additional publications are available through the Institute's web site at www.wa.gov/wsipp.

[4] 521 U.S. 346, 117 S. Ct. 2072, 138 L. Ed. 2d 501, 1997 U.S. Lexis 3999 (1997).

[5] Some legal challenges to SVP statutes can be avoided by careful draftsmanship, inclusion of detailed provisions, and clear expressions of legislative intent. Arizona's statutory scheme reflects this type of process but has nevertheless undergone revision since it was first enacted. For a further discussion of this issue, see Holmgren, supra note 1.

[6] The Court in *Hendricks* ruled that SVP statutes were civil rather than criminal in nature. Accordingly, the continued involuntary detention of sexually violent predators following expiration of their criminal sentence of incarceration did not constitute a second criminal penalty, thereby violating the double jeopardy clause. In addition, the passage of such commitment laws subsequent to the offender's criminal adjudication did not violate ex post facto protections. The Court also concluded that the Kansas statute satisfied substantive due process requirements for involuntary civil commitment in that it required a finding of both a mental condition and future dangerousness. These and other legal challenges to SVP statutes are not discussed extensively in this chapter. For such a discussion, see Walsh and Flaherty, "Civil Commitment of Sexually Violent Predators," in B. K. Schwartz (Ed.), *The Sex Offender* (Vol. 3, pp. 34-1–34-12) (1999), and Walsh and Flaherty, "Non-*Hendricks*-Related Constitutional Challenges to Sexually Violent Predator Statutes," in B. K. Schwartz (Ed.), *The Sex Offender* (Vol. 3, pp. 36-1–36-8) (1999). See also Falk, "Sex Offenders, Mental Illness and Criminal Responsibility: The Constitutional Boundaries of Civil Commitment After *Kansas v. Hendricks*," 25 *Am. J.L. & Med.* 117–147 (1999); Daley, "Do Sexually Violent Predators Deserve Constitutional Protections?: An Analysis in Light of the Supreme Court's Ruling in *Kansas v. Hendricks*," 23 *S. Ill. U. L.J.* 715–734 (1999); Brakel & Cavanaugh, "Of Psychopaths and Pendulums: Legal and Psychiatric Treatment of Sex Offenders in the United States," 30 *N.M. L. Rev.* 69–94 (2000).

[7] Indeed, the U.S. Supreme Court recently decided Seling v. Young, 531 U.S. 250, 148 L. Ed. 2d 734 (2001), rejecting a habeas challenge to Washington's SVP statute based on the claim that the statute was unconstitutional and "punitive" as applied to *Young*. Washington's commitment center also

currently operates under an injunction including supervision by a court-appointed special master as a result of other legal challenges to the conditions of confinement and treatment implemented at the center. See Turay v. Seling, 108 F. Supp. 2d 1148 (W.D. Wash. 2000). Notably, Washington is the state with the oldest SVP statute so that one might expect that many of these legal challenges would have already been litigated. The Supreme Court's decision in *Young* also expressly stated that the Court's decision did not foreclose other legal challenges and potential redress through the state courts. For a discussion of some of those potential challenges, see Janus, "Foreshadowing the Future of *Kansas v. Hendricks*: Lessons Learned from Minnesota's Sex Offender Commitment Litigation," 92 *Nw. U. L. Rev.* 1279–1305 (1998); Jacquette, "Sexual Predator Law: A Pendulum Swung Too Far," 1(1) *Trauma, Violence & Abuse* 94–98 (2000); Brakel & Cavanaugh, supra note 6. The following cases represent some of the leading decisions in their respective jurisdictions dealing with constitutional and other legal challenges to SVP laws. Hubbart v. Superior Court, 969 P.2d 589 (Cal. 1999); In re Linehan, 557 N.W.2d 171 (Minn. 1996), *vacated and remanded for reconsideration,* 522 U.S. 1011 (1997), *reconsidered,* 594 N.W.2d 867 (Minn. 1999); In re Young, 857 P.2d 989 (Wash. 1993); State v. Post, 541 N.W.2d 115 (Wis. 1995); In re Hay, 953 P.2d 666 (Kan. 1998); Martin v. Reinstein, 987 P.2d 779 (Ariz. App. 1999); Grosinger v. M.D., 598 N.W.2d 799 (N.D. 1999); In re Detention of Samuelson, 727 N.E.2d 228 (Ill. 2000); Commonwealth v. Bruno, 735 N.E.2d 1222 (Mass. 2000); In re Crane, 7 P.3d 285 (Kan. 2000); In re Leon G., 218 P.2d 169 (Ariz. App. 2001); In re Detention of Garren, 2000 WL 1855129 (Iowa Dec. 20, 2000).

[8] For a discussion of the political and social policy debate over SVP statutes, and their predecessors, sexual psychopath laws, see Lieb, Quinsey, & Berliner, "Sexual Predators and Social Policy," in M. Tonrey (Ed.), *Crime and Justice: A Review of Research* (pp. 43–114) (1998); Brakel & Cavanaugh, supra note 6.

[9] All the states listed supra note 2, with the exception of Minnesota, have this type of SVP statutory scheme.

[10] California, Illinois, Massachusetts, New Jersey, South Carolina, Texas, Washington, and Wisconsin have such provisions.

[11] See Wash. Rev. Code §§71.09.020(3), 71.09.030(5) (1995). In Kansas if parole is revoked and the offender has a prior sex offense conviction, the state can file an SVP petition at the time of the offender's new release date.

[12] New Jersey and Minnesota are states that have such provisions. In addition, both Illinois and Minnesota have old "sexual psychopath" statutes which are still operational in addition to their SVP statutes. For a discussion of these laws, see Lieb, supra note 3; Matson & Lieb, supra note 3. The sexual psychopath statutes are not widely used in these states and similar laws have been repealed in most states. They are not discussed in this chapter and should not be confused with the SVP statutes cited in supra note 2.

[13] Ohio, North Carolina, and North Dakota recently enacted special procedures for the classification and registration of sexually violent predators, although the statutes do not provide for postincarceration civil commitments of these offenders. See N.C. Gen. Stat. §14–208.20 (1997); N.D. Cent. Code §12.1-32-15 (1997); Ohio Rev .Code §2950.09. For a further discussion of this distinction and a listing of states with these types of statutes, see Walsh and Flaherty chapters, supra note 6.

[14] Offenders who are found not guilty by reason of mental disease or defect, or offenders deemed incompetent to stand trial for a predicate offense, are also generally included. See Exhibit 11.1 for a comparison of states with these provisions. Several states also include convictions for "attempts" to commit the underlying sexual offense. Arizona, Florida, Iowa, Missouri, New Jersey, Kansas, Massachusetts, and South Carolina have statutes that contain such provisions. Washington also permits the state to prove at the SVP trial that a nonqualifying predicate offense meets the statutory requirements of being sexually motivated. For example, if an offender's prior conviction is for assault, a nonqualifying offense, prosecutors can nevertheless sustain a SVP petition if they can establish beyond a reasonable doubt through proof at the SVP trial that the assault was sexually motivated.

[15] Juvenile sex offenses may form the basis for commitment in several different ways. First, some states permit SVP petitions to be filed against offenders who are still juveniles. For a listing of states with such provisions, see Exhibit 11.1. Second, the juvenile offender may be detained in a correctional or treatment facility until after the age of majority, in which case the qualifying offense

will have occurred when the offender was a juvenile but the SVP petition will be filed when the offender is an adult. Third, some states provide that an adult offender may be the subject of an SVP petition if he was adjudicated delinquent for a qualifying sex offense as a juvenile, even if the present basis for confinement is not this sex offense. Finally, juvenile offenses (both sexual and non-sex-related) may influence various risk instruments used to assess the dangerousness of the offender.

[16] Some states also provide that a predicate offense may be from another state or under federal or military criminal codes. Arizona, Florida, Iowa, Kansas, New Jersey, Texas, and Washington have such provisions in their statutes.

[17] For example, Iowa, Missouri, and Washington qualify their list of predicate offenses with the additional requirement that the offense be "predatory" thereby eliminating intrafamilial offenses from consideration. Such offenses may, however, factor into other aspects of the SVP process (e.g. risk assessment), assuming there is another qualifying predatory sex offense on which a petition may be filed.

[18] See, e.g., Cal. Welf. & Inst. Code §§6601(b)–6601(c) (West Supp. 1999); Fla. Stat. Ann. §394.913 (1999); 725 Ill. Comp. Stat. Ann. §§207/30(c) & 207/10(c)(2) (West Supp. 1998); Tex. Health & Safety Code §841.021 (1999); Wash. Rev. Code §§71.09.025(1)(b)(v) & 71.09.040(4) (1999). Wisconsin's statute does not address this process; however, Department of Human Services procedures provide for a prepetition evaluation process. In Kansas, prosecutors are provided with prepetition clinical service report evaluations to assist in making the filing decision. Other statutes may provide for screening and referral of a petition well before completion of the prison term. In this circumstance, the timing of the referral and evaluation process may precede completion of the offender's treatment program in the institution. By contrast, Massachusetts has no prepetition screening procedures. The district attorney in Massachusetts is notified of the impending release of an offender and then determines whether to file a petition or not. Any evaluations of the offender are conducted after a petition is filed. See Mass. Gen. Laws ch. 123A, §§12(a) & 12(b) (1999).

[19] See, e.g., Fla. Stat. Ann. §394.913 (1999); Mo. Rev. Stat. §589.400–589.425 (1998); Tex. Health & Safety Code §841.022 (1999); Va. Code §37.1-70.3.

[20] See, e.g., Ariz. Rev. Stat. Ann. §§36-3702(B)(9)(a) and 36-3705(G) (West 1998); Cal. Welf. & Inst. Code §§6601(b)–6601(c) (West Supp. 1999); 725 Ill. Comp. Stat. Ann. §§207/30(c) & 207/10(c)(2) (West Supp. 1998); Tex. Health & Safety Code §841.023 (1999); Va. Code §37.1-70.5; Wash. Rev. Code §§71.09.025(1)(b)(v) & 71.09.040(4) (1999).

[21] Iowa Code Ann. §229A.5 (5) (1998); Kan. Stat. Ann. §59-29a05(D) (1998); Mass. Gen. Laws ch. 123A, §13 (1999); Mo. Rev. Stat. §632.489.4 (1998); N.D. Cent. Code §25-03.3-11(1998); S.C. Code §44-48-80(D) (1998). Under this type of scheme it is possible that the government may not meet its burden of establishing probable cause because it may not already have the opinion of a mental health professional who has diagnosed the offender and determined that the offender has a diagnosable mental disorder that will satisfy the requirements under the statute. In addition, filed petitions may need to be dismissed later if the subsequent evaluation suggests these deficiencies.

[22] See Doren, "Recidivism Base Rates, Predictions of Sex Offender Recidivism, and the 'Sexual Predator' Commitment Laws," 16(1) *Behav. Sci. & L.* 97–114 (1998); Schram & Darling Milloy, *Sexually Violent Predators and Civil Commitment: A Study of the Characteristics and Recidivism of Sex Offenders Considered for Civil Commitment But for Whom Proceedings Were Declined* (1998); Brakel & Cavanaugh, supra note 6, summarizing data from several states.

[23] In Washington prosecutors can file an SVP petition irrespective of whether the offender has been referred by the state's end-of-sentence review committee. By contrast, prosecutors in Florida and other states may not file a petition unless a referral has been made to the district attorney's office by the screening agency. In Massachusetts, the district attorney or attorney general files the petition without any input from a screening agency. See Mass. Gen. Laws ch. 123A, §12(b) (1999)

[24] Generally these mental disorders or mental abnormalities are broadly defined as a "congenital or acquired condition affecting the emotional or volitional capacity which predisposes the person to commit sexually violent offenses in a degree constituting such person a menace to the health and safety of others." See, e.g., Kan. Stat. Ann. §59–29a02(b) (1998). Virtually every state's definition parallels this language. Most states specifically include "personality disorders" and/or "conduct

disorders" within their statutory criteria. For a criticism of how SVP statutes classify mental disorders, see Schoop, "Sexual Predators and the Structure of the Mental Health System: Expanding the Normative Focus of Therapeutic Jurisprudence," 1(1) *Psychol., Pub. Pol'y & L.* 161–192 (1995).

[25] For a general discussion of the relationship between psychopathy and sexual offending, see Porter et al., "Profiles of Psychopathy in Incarcerated Sexual Offenders," 27(2) *Crim. Just. & Behav.* 216 (2000); Lieb, Quinsey & Berliner, supra note 8.

[26] See Schoop, supra note 24. See also Becker & Murphy, "What We Know and Do Not Know About Assessing and Treating Sex Offenders," 4 *Psychol., Pub. Pol'y & L.* 116–136 (1998), expressing the opinion that the qualifying mental health condition should be limited to the more serious sexual disorders—pedophilia, sexual sadism, and paraphilia not otherwise specified (NOS) (rape). Id. 118–119). However, several cases have specifically held that an antisocial personality disorder can satisfy the mental abnormality/personality disorder element. See State v. Adams, 588 N.W.2d 336 (Wis. Ct. App. 1998); In re Commitment of Taylor, 621 N.W.2d 386 (Wis. Ct. App. 2000).

[27] "[W]e have never required State legislatures to adopt any particular nomenclature in drafting civil commitment statutes. Rather we have traditionally left to legislators the task of defining terms of a medical nature that have legal significance. . . . Often those definitions do not fit precisely with the definitions employed by the medical community. . . . Legal definitions, however, which must 'take into account such issues as individual responsibility . . . and competency,' need not mirror those advanced by the medical profession." *Hendricks*, 117 S. Ct. at 2081.

[28] In Westerheide v. State, 767 So. 2d 637, 653–654 (Fla. Ct. App. 5th Dist. 2000), an equal protection claim asserted that the vagueness of the key terms of the act would lead to different standards and conclusions by the mental health professionals in different cases. This claim was rejected. The same claim was rejected in Commonwealth v. Bruno, 735 N.E.2d 1222 (Mass. 2000), where the Court emphasized that there were adequate procedural safeguards appointment of experts, cross-examination, etc.—such that any improper opinion can adequately be tested and challenged.

[29] See, e.g., Cal. Welf. & Inst. Code §§6600(a) (West Supp. 1999); 725 Ill. Comp. Stat. Ann. §§207/35(b), 207/35(e) (West Supp. 1998); Wis. Stat. Ann. §§980.05(1m), 980.05(4) (West Supp. 1998).

[30] For a thorough discussion of these issues, see Doren, supra note 22.

[31] *Hendricks*, 117 S. Ct. at 2080. Ironically, the *Hendricks* opinion elsewhere quotes from the preamble to the Kansas statute, which distinguishes between mental diseases or mental illnesses and mental disorders making them subject to commitment under the SVP law:

> [A] small but extremely dangerous group of sexually violent predators exist who do not have a mental disease or defect that renders them appropriate for involuntary treatment pursuant to the [general involuntary civil commitment statute]. . . . In contrast to persons appropriate for civil commitment under the [general involuntary civil commitment statute], sexually violent predators generally have anti-social personality features which are unamenable to existing mental illness treatment modalities. . . ."

Id. at 2077 (quoting from Kan. Stat. Ann. §59–29a01 (1994)). Washington's statute has a similar provision. See Wash. Rev. Code §71.09.010.

[32] See, e.g., In re Linehan, 557 N.W.2d 171 (Minn. 1996), noting that the sexual predator component of Minnesota's mental health commitment statute was specifically amended to avoid the necessity for establishing a "mental illness" that rendered the individual "utterly incapable" of controlling his sexual impulses). In addition, both the Minnesota and North Dakota statutes specifically provide that the finding of a mental condition pursuant to a SVP petition may not later be used to establish a defense to criminal charges based on a claim of nonresponsibility or incompetency. See Minn. Stat. Ann. §253B.185(3) (West 1996); N.D. Cent. Code §25-03.3-16 (1997). For an extended discussion of this issue and the problems associated with equating these terms, see Holmgren, supra note 1.

[33] For example, a judge's recent findings in a Washington SVP case contained the following passage:

> The second element, however, is one that distinguishes chapter 71.09 from the criminal statutes in our state. That is the requirement that there be some causal connection of a

person's future dangerousness to a specific mental illness. This second element incorporates a philosophy that if a person is committing dangerous or predatory acts because of a mental illness, it is, in a sense, an involuntary condition whereby he cannot control himself without treatment intervention. In that unique and unusual circumstance, the State of Washington has determined that in addition to penal sanctions, this sort of person should be civilly committed so that he can be treated for his mental illness before release.

See In re Detention of Mitchell Gaff, Transcript of Court's Decision, No. 94-2-07248-8 (Wash. Super., County of Snohomish, Dec.1, 2000).

[34] See Schoop, supra note 24.

[35] See In re Crane, 7 P.3d 285 (Kan. 2000). The court concluded that Kansas's SVP statute did not permit commitment unless it were proven that the offender cannot control his dangerous behavior, thereby removing future willful sexual predatory behavior as a basis for commitment. "To conclude otherwise would require that we ignore the plain language of the majority opinion in *Hendricks*." Unfortunately, the Kansas Supreme Court failed to appreciate that this so-called plain language in *Hendricks* was in fact dicta that was neither central to the Court's holding nor consistent with the volitional behavior of sex offenders. Compounding this problem is the fact that the Kansas Supreme Court ignored the plain language of the Kansas statute which defined the mental abnormality requirement as a "condition affecting the emotional or volitional capacity which predisposes the person to commit sexually violent offenses in a degree constituting such person a menace to the health and safety of others." See Kan. Stat. Ann. §59-29a02(a) (1999 supp.).

[36] See In re Detention of Gordon, 10 P.3d 500 (Wash. App. 2000); In re Commitment of W.Z., 2001 N.J. Super. Lexis 172; In re Varner, 734 N.E.2d 226 (Ill. App. 3d 2000). See also In re Linehan, 594 N.W.2d 867 (Minn. 1999), *cert. denied sub nom.,* Linehan v. Minnesota, 120 S. Ct. 587 (1999), where the majority of the Minnesota Supreme Court rejected a "total" lack of control standard and instead adopted a lack of "adequate" control standard as the standard necessitated by the *Hendricks* language.

[37] See In re Leon G., 26 P.3d 481 (Ariz. 2001). The lower court relied exclusively on the foregoing quoted language from *Hendricks*. See In re Leon G., 18 P.3d 169 (Ariz. App. 2001). The Arizona Supreme Court's decision in *Leon* is very well reasoned and potentially may be a preview of the decision the U.S. Supreme Court issues in *Crane*. As the Arizona Supreme Court noted in its opinion, the U.S. Supreme Court has repeatedly held that the Constitution permits the civil commitment of persons whose future dangerousness is causally linked to a mental disorder of some kind, but it has never required a separate showing of volitional impairment. See, e.g., Allen v. Illinois, 478 U.S. 364, 106 S. Ct. 2988, 92 L. Ed. 2d 296 (1986); Addington v. Texas, 441 U.S. 418, 99 S. Ct. 1804, 60 L. Ed. 2d 323 (1979); Foucha v. Louisiana, 504 U.S. 71, 112 S. Ct. 1780, 118 L. Ed. 2d 437 (1992); Jones v. United States, 463 U.S. 354, 103 S. Ct. 3043, 77 L. Ed. 2d 694 (1983); Seling v. Young, 531 U.S. 250, 121 S. Ct. 727, 148 L. Ed. 2d 734 (2001). The *Allen, Addington,* and *Foucha* cases were all cited extensively in the *Hendricks* opinion and *Seling* represents the Court's most recent decision on SVP statutes.

[38] See In re Crane, *cert. granted,* 121 S. Ct. 1483, 149 L. Ed. 2d 372 (2001). The Association for the Treatment of Sexual Abusers (ATSA) has written an amicus brief supporting reversal of the *Crane* decision. See Brief for the Association for the Treatment of Sexual Abusers as Amicus Curiae in Support of Petitioner, in Kansas v. Crane, No. 00–957, arguing that the "unable to control" standard of *Crane* is scientifically unsound and unworkable for professionals.

[39] See Pithers & Cummings "Relapse Prevention: A Method for Enhancing Behavioral Self Management and External Supervision of the Sexual Aggressor," in B. K. Schwartz & H. R. Cellini (Eds.), *The Sex Offender* (Vol. 1, pp. 20-1–20-32 (1995); Pithers "Relapse Prevention with Sexual Aggressors: A Method for Maintaining Therapeutic Gain and Enhancing External Supervision," in W. Marshall, D. Laws, & H. Barbaree (Eds.), *Handbook of Sexual Assault: Issues, Theories, and Treatment of the Offender* (1990).

[40] See, e.g., Brief for the Association for the Treatment of Sexual Abusers as Amicus Curiae in Support of Petitioner, in Kansas v. Crane, No. 00–957, at 3 (quoting Slobogin, "An End to Insanity: Recasting the Role of Mental Disability in Criminal Cases," 86 *Va. L. Rev.* 1199–1247 (2000) ("[A]s Morse and others have shown, even the most severely crazy people usually intend their acts and therefore have some control of them").

[41] The brief filed by ATSA and cited previously makes a compelling argument that the result of the

Crane decision would be to mandate release of a large number of dangerous sex offenders who might otherwise benefit from the types of prolonged residential inpatient treatment SVP commitments are designed to provide. Correspondingly, offenders who lack total volitional control (and thus might be committable under the *Crane* standard) are much less likely to respond to any treatment modalities that involve behavior modification. Effectively this would negate any legislative intent under SVP statutes to provide treatment to this class of dangerous offenders, as the only offenders likely to be committed are unlikely to be treatable.

[42] See Fla. Stat. Ann. §394.917(1) (1999); Minn. Stat. Ann. §253B.18(1) (West 1998); N.J. Rev. Stat. §30:4-27.32(a) (1998); N.D. Cent. Code §25-03.3-13 (1998). This is the minimum constitutional requirement for civil commitment according to the decision in Addington v. Texas, 99 S. Ct. 1804, 1813 (1979). The Court also held that the reasonable doubt standard was inappropriate for civil commitment proceedings given the difficulty of establishing this degree of certainty with psychiatric diagnosis.

[43] This was the standard under the Kansas statute upheld by the *Hendricks* decision, but the Court there was not specifically faced with the question whether the lesser standard of clear and convincing evidence would be adequate for SVP cases.

[44] Other statutes may require a different standard such as "more likely than not," "highly likely," or a "substantial probability." Despite the language of the SVP statute itself, case law interpreting the statute may impose a different standard for the expert. For example, Wisconsin's "substantially probable" requirement has been judicially construed to mean "much more likely than not" to reoffend. See State v. Curiel, 597 N.W.2d 697 (Wis. 1999). Similarly, Minnesota's "likely" future harm standard has been interpreted to require that the future harm be "highly likely." See In re Linehan, 557 N.W.2d 171 (Minn. 1996). Arizona's statutory language of "likely to engage in future acts of sexual violence" has been interpreted to mean "highly probable" for purposes of instructions provided to the jury. See In re Leon G., 26 P.3d 481 (Ariz. 2001). And Washington's standard of "more probably than not" has been construed to require a finding that the likelihood of reoffense is extremely high." See In re Young, 857 P.2d 989, 1008 (Wash. 1993). However, the jury instructions in Washington do not reflect this restrictive approach and this language has not been construed by practitioners in this fashion.

[45] See Tex. Health & Safety Code §§841.081 (1999). The Texas statute provides for a variety of stringent conditions of supervision akin to conditions of probation or parole release.

[46] California's statute is unique, requiring the state to recommit the offender every two years. Obviously, this requirement is extremely burdensome on professionals involved with the commitment laws in California. Other statutes require the state, at an annual hearing, to establish the offender's continued dangerousness. See Exhibit 11.1.

[47] See Tex. Health & Safety Code §§841.085 (1999).

[48] See, e.g., N.D. Cent. Code §25-03.3-04 (1997); Wash. Rev. Code §40.14.070.

[49] See, e.g., the Arizona, Florida, Iowa, Massachusetts, Missouri, New Jersey, North Dakota, South Carolina, and Wisconsin statutes cited supra note 2.

[50] See, e.g., King v. Riveland, 886 P.2d 160 (Wash. 1994).

[51] Ariz. Rev. Stat. Ann. §§36-3702(B), 36-3703(C), 36-3703(D) (West 1998).

[52] See, e.g., Ariz. Rev. Stat. Ann. §§36-3702(B), 36-3703(C), 36-3703(D) (West 1998), which provides that experts will not be allowed to testify unless they have shared information as required by statute.

[53] See Brady v. North Carolina, 373 U.S. 83, 83 S. Ct. 1194, 10 L. Ed. 2d 215 (1963). Exculpatory information is usually broadly defined as any material tending to negate against a finding of guilt or which might otherwise mitigate the severity of the offense or the degree of punishment that may follow from a conviction. In the context of SVP cases, this definition may be construed to require the prosecutor to disclose any information that might inure to the offender's benefit, including any information that might weigh against supporting a commitment petition or might support a placement other than in a confined treatment setting.

[54] See, e.g., 725 Ill. Comp. Stat. Ann. §§207/25(c), 207/25(e), 207/35(b) (West Supp. 1998); Wis. Stat. Ann. §980.05(1m) (West Supp. 1998).

[55] See, e.g., National District Attorney's Association, *National Prosecution Standards* (2d ed. 1991); American Bar Association, Model Rules of Professional Conduct; American Bar Association,

Criminal Justice Standards Committee, *ABA Standards for Criminal Justice: Prosecution Function and Defense Function* (3rd ed. 1993).

[56] See, e.g., State v. Brown, 552 S.W.2d 383 (Tenn. 1977), holding that the state was required to turn over exculpatory mental health records involving victim held within state mental health facility, noting "the duty to disclose is that of the state . . . not just that of the office of the prosecutor." Id. at 385. See also State v. Black, 745 S.W.2d 302, 307 (Tenn. Crim. App. 1987), district attorney required to provide defendant with discovery in the possession, custody, or control of state agencies which regularly report to the district attorney or have reported to him relative to the prosecution of the accused. See American Bar Association, Criminal Justice Standards Committee, *ABA Standards for Criminal Justice, Discovery and Procedure Before Trial* (2nd ed. 1980). But see State v. Lavallee, 765 A.2d 671 (N.H. 2001), holding that prosecutor's duty to produce exculpatory evidence extends only to evidence in the prosecutor's possession or in the possession of a law enforcement agency charged with the investigation and presentation of the case, but does not extend to evidence in the possession of other government agencies including social service agencies. Accord, Commonwealth v. Delp, 672 N.E.2d 114 (Mass. Ct. App. 1996).

[57] Arizona, for example, requires that their experts meet guidelines developed by the courts. See Ariz. Rev. Stat. Ann. §§36-3705(G), 36-3703(A) (West 1998). See also Exhibit 11.1.

[58] See, e.g., Cal. Welf. & Inst. Code §§6601(d), 6601(e), and 6601(g) (West Supp. 1999). See also Exhibit 11.1.

[59] See Rule 702 of the Federal Rules of Evidence which previously provided: "If scientific, technical or other specialized knowledge will assist the trier of fact to understand the evidence or determine a fact in issue a person qualified by knowledge, skill, experience, training or education, may testify thereto in the form of an opinion or otherwise." A number of legal commentators and courts have suggested that this rule permits weak experts to offer their opinions in court. See Stern, *The Preparation and Presentation of Expert Testimony in Child Abuse Litigation* (1997). See also Rocha v. Great Am. Ins. Co., 850 F.2d 1095 (6th Cir. 1988), commenting: "The problem that arises . . . in this age where the 'forensic expert' populates the judicial landscape in ever increasing numbers, is that there is a plethora of experts who look good on paper and do not reveal their shortcomings until they start testifying. Although we would hope the adversary system would be a safeguard against misinformation, such is not always the case." Rule 702 was recently revised to require the following additional criteria as a precondition to admissibility of expert testimony: (1) the testimony is based on sufficient facts or data, (2) the testimony is the product of reliable principles and methods, and (3) the witness has applied the principles and methods reliably to the facts of the case. These new criteria impose more stringent standards on experts and may help keep poorly qualified experts from testifying or from relying on poor scientific methodology. However, not all states have modified their own evidentiary codes in compliance with revised Fed. R. Evid. 702.

[60] See Daubert v. Merrell Dow Pharmaceuticals, Inc., 509 U.S. 579, 113 S. Ct. 2786, 125 L. Ed. 2d 469 (1993), and Kumho Tire Co. v. Carmichael, 526 U.S. 137, 119 S. Ct. 1167, 143 L. Ed. 2d 238 (1999).

[61] See Doren, supra note 22.

[62] A recent case in Florida involving several offenders excluded all expert testimony involving actuarial instruments. An expert testifying on behalf of the offenders was able to convince the three-judge circuit court panel that such instruments failed to satisfy legal standards for admissibility under Florida law, which follows a *Frye* standard for admissibility of expert testimony. See In re The Commitment of Roberto Valdez , Case No. 99–000045CI, slip op. (Fla., 6th Jud. Cir., Aug. 21, 2000). This decision is discussed further in the subsequent section on actuarial instruments.

[63] See American Psychiatric Association, *APA Task Force Report on Sexually Dangerous Offenders* (July 1998).

[64] See generally, American Psychological Association, *Ethical Principles of Psychologists and Code of Conduct* (1992).

[65] See generally Committee on Ethical Guidelines for Forensic Psychologists, Specialty Guidelines for Forensic Psychologists, 15(6) *L. & Hum. Behav.* 655–665 (1991).

[66] Compare, e.g., Janus & Meehl, "Assessing the Legal Standard for Predictions of Dangerousness in

Sex Offender Commitment Proceedings," 3(1) *Psychol., Pub. Pol'y & L.* 33–64 (1997), urging a very conservative approach to actuarial prediction, with Doren, supra note 22, suggesting actuarial methods underpredict dangerousness. See also Becker & Murphy, "What We Know and Don't Know About Assessing and Treating Sex Offenders," 4 *Psychol., Pub. Pol'y & L.* 116–137 (1998), "Whether the concern is false positives or false negatives also has social policy implications. Do we minimize false positives for protection of individual freedom, or do we try to minimize false negatives for protection of society? That question will not be answered by the data alone." By practice, evaluators in Texas and California may be required to use certain actuarial instruments. Arizona has been attempting to establish guidelines for both the qualifications of experts in these cases and the types of instruments that should be used to assess offenders.

[67] Frye v. United States, 293 F. 1013 (D.C. Cir. 1923). The *Frye* standard requires that "the thing from which the deduction is made must be sufficiently established to have gained general acceptance in the particular field in which it belongs." Id. at 1014.

[68] See supra note 60. Under the *Daubert* and *Kumho* decisions, there are five criteria to discern whether scientific evidence is sufficiently reliable to be admissible. These include (1) whether the theory or technique has been tested, (2) whether it has been subjected to peer review and publication, (3) what is the known or potential error rate of the theory or technique, (4) whether there are standards that control the technique's operation, and (5) does the theory or technique have widespread acceptance in the relevant scientific community.

[69] *Daubert* expressly held that the *Frye* standard had been done away with by adoption of the Federal Rules of Evidence. Nevertheless, one of the *Daubert* admissibility criteria includes the old *Frye* test of general acceptance within the relevant scientific community. It does not make that criteria dispositive, however, and arguably that criteria should be given less consideration than the other criteria in light of the discussion that this standard did not survive passage of the Federal Rules. Wisconsin follows neither a *Frye* nor a *Daubert* standard. Instead, Wisconsin has adopted a simple relevancy standard governing admissibility. Shortcomings in the expert's opinions or the data relied on are considered in terms of the weight to be given the expert's opinion, and the opposing party is afforded great latitude while cross-examining the expert to expose any shortcomings in his or her conclusions.

[70] See, e.g., Doren, supra note 22. See also Lieb, Quinsey, & Berliner, supra note 8.

[71] There are some defense experts who suggest that the actuarial instruments fail to meet legal and professional standards of reliability. See, e.g., Campbell, "Sexual Predator Evaluations and Phrenology: Considering Issues of Evidentiary Reliability," 18 *Behav. Sci. & L.* 111–130 (2000). More reasoned discussion of the problems associated with the use of actuarial instruments is provided by the authorities cited supra note 66. Notably, these authorities come from states that actually have existing SVP laws and these authors participate in the implementation of such laws. Still other defense experts concede that actuarial instruments are more reliable than clinical judgment but nevertheless argue that no method of risk prediction is sufficiently reliable.

[72] For a discussion of this problem see Hanson, *The Development of a Brief Actuarial Scale for Sexual Offense Recidivism, Public Works and Government Services of Canada* (1997); Hanson, "What Do We Know About Sex Offender Risk Assessment?" 4 *Psychol., Pub. Pol'y & L.* 50–72 (1998).

[73] See, e.g., Campbell, supra note 71. See also In re The Commitment of Roberto Valdez, supra note 62. In *Valdez*, the Court ruled that several actuarial instruments failed to satisfy *Frye* standards for general acceptance. These actuarial instruments included the Rapid Risk Assessment for Sexual Offense Recidivism (RRASOR), Minnesota Sex Offender Screening Tool—Revised (MnSOST-R), Minnesota Sex Offender Screening Tool (MnSOST), Violence Risk Appraisal Guide (VRAG), Hare Psychopathy Checklist—Revised (PCL-R), Sexual Violence Risk—20 (SVR-20), and the Static-99. Fred Berlin appeared on behalf of the defense and testified that the American Psychiatric Association had taken a position that predictions of the type required in SVP cases cannot be made accurately by any methods. He also testified that actuarial instruments have not been sufficiently tested, validated, or subjected to adequate peer review. A different result may have resulted if Florida followed a *Daubert* standard for admissibility of scientific evidence. Other trial courts in different Florida circuits have reached different results and this issue is presently before the Florida Court of Appeals. See Jackson v. State, Case No. 4D00-951 (Ct. App. 4th Dist). Conversely, several decisions have held that expert opinions predicting dangerousness or the use of actuarial instruments should not be subject to a *Frye* analysis. See People v. Ward, 71 Cal. App. 4th 368, 83

Cal. Rptr. 2d 828 (1999); State v. Strauss, 20 P.2d 1022 (Wash. Ct. App. 2001); Garcetti v. Superior Ct., 102 Cal. Rptr. 2d 214 (2001), *petition for review granted*, 20 P.2d 1084, 105 Cal. Rptr. 2d 788 (2001). These results may not have followed either in a state controlled by the *Daubert* or *Kumho* decisions or the revised Federal Rule of Evidence Rule 702.

[74] See, e.g., N.D. Cent. Code §§25-03.3-13 and 25-03.3-15 (1998).

[75] See, e.g., State v. Strauss, 20 P.2d 1022 (Wash. Ct. App. 2001); Garcetti v. Superior Ct., 102 Cal. Rptr. 2d 214 (2001), *petition for review granted*, 20 P.2d 1084, 105 Cal. Rptr. 2d 788 (2001) (RRASOR and Static-99); State v. Keinitz, 585 N.W.2d 609 (Wis. Ct. App. 1998) (VRAG); State v. Keinetz, 597 N.W.2d 712 (Wis. 1999) (VRAG); In re Detention of Thorell, 2000 WL 222815 (Wash. App. 2000) (unpublished) (RRASOR, VRAG, SORAG); In re Detention of Dean, 2000 WL 690142 (Wash. App. 2000) (VRAG, SORAG); State v. Bare, 2000 WL 1874113 (Wis. App. 2000) (RRASOR, VRAG); People v. Roberge, 2000 WL 1844791 (Cal. Ct. App. 2000) (RRASOR); In re Detention of Walker, 731 N.E.2d 994 (Ill. Ct. App. 2000) (RRASOR); People v. Otto, 95 Cal. Rptr. 2d 236 (2000) (RRASOR); People v. Turner, 93 Cal. Rptr. 2d 459 (2000) (RRASOR); State v. Wilson, 2000 WL 156908 (Wis. Ct. App. 2000) (RRASOR); People v. Poe, 88 Cal. Rptr. 2d 437 (1999) (RRASOR); In re Commitment of R.S., 2001 WL 438642 (N.J. Super. App. Div. April 20, 2001).

[76] The Public Policy Position Paper of ATSA recommends the following: "To most accurately evaluate the risk of future sexual violence, the evaluator should include the best available actuarial instruments that have been validated as risk predictors for the population to which they will be administered." Civil Commitment of Sexually Violent Offenders, adopted by the ATSA Executive Board of Directors on March 20, 2001, p. 2; Beaverton, OR, Association for the Treatment of Sexual Abusers, 2001 [On-line]. Available: www.atsa.com/ppcivilcommit.html.

[77] See In re Young, 857 P.2d 989 (Wash. 1993), holding that the Fifth Amendment was inapplicable under Washington's civil commitment statute.

[78] Even if the Fifth Amendment does not apply, efforts to question the defendant, whether at deposition or at trial, might result in the prosecutors conferring some form of immunity from prosecution, especially where responses to the questions posed may implicated the offender regarding previously uncharged offenses. See, e.g., In re Beverly, 342 So. 2d 481 (Fla. 1977) (applying that principle in general civil commitment cases); Griego v. Superior Court, 95 Cal. Rptr. 2d 351 (Cal. App. 2000).

[79] See State v. Zanelli (Wis. Ct. App. 1997). Compare In re Young, 857 P.2d 989 (Wash. 1993), holding that the Fifth Amendment privilege against self-incrimination does not apply to Washington's SVP statute and respondents do not have a right to remain silent.

[80] For example, Arizona's SVP statute does not contain a specific Fifth Amendment privilege, yet judicial decisions have provided respondents with some limited protections nevertheless. See, e.g., State *ex rel.* Romley v. Sheldon, 7 P.3d 118 (Ariz. App. Div. 1 2000), holding that SVP respondents do not have a general Fifth Amendment privilege that will allow them to refuse to participate in evaluation procedures or depositions, but the respondent does have limited rights to refuse to answer specific questions in such proceedings. Compare Holt v. Hotham *ex rel.* Super. Ct., 5 P.3d 948 (Ariz. App. Div. 1 2000), holding that contempt of court is an appropriate sanction for a respondent's general refusal to participate in the evaluation process.

[81] Under Rule 703 of the Federal Rules of Evidence, experts can rely on facts or data in forming their opinions which may not be admissible at trial, if the facts or data are of a type normally relied on by the experts in forming such opinions. There is little question that an offender's silence about his or her offense history (and account of his or her conduct) is the type of information professionals routinely rely on in formulating opinions about the individual offender.

[82] This problem may be compounded by rules under SVP statutes, or within treatment settings, that waive any confidentiality or privilege for an offender's disclosure of information during treatment.

[83] In McKune v. Lile, No. 00–1187, *cert. granted* (May 14, 2001), the U.S. Supreme Court will decide whether the revocation of correctional institution privileges violates the Fifth Amendment's privilege against self-incrimination where the revocation is based on the offender's failure to accept responsibility for his crimes as part of a mandated sex offender treatment program in the correctional system. This decision may also have profound implications for future SVP cases.

[84] For a further discussion of these issues, see Holmgren, "Forging New Alliances—Proposals for Change in Managing Sex Offenders in the Criminal Justice System," in B. K. Schwartz (Ed.), *The Sex Offender* (Vol. 3, pp. 7-1–7-20) (1999); Shevlin, "'Between the Devil and the Deep Blue Sea': A Look at the Fifth Amendment Implications of Probation Programs for Sex Offenders Requiring Mandatory Admissions of Guilt," 88 *Ky. L.J.* 485–504 (2000).

[85] This chapter is not the appropriate forum to respond to such challenges. However, as a prosecutor who has had to reach out to victims in such cases, this is one of the most difficult tasks prosecutors face. Other prosecutors from across the country have expressed similar concerns. Most prosecutors in local district attorney's offices who handle SVP cases, as well as many in the offices of the state attorney general, have extensive experience dealing with adult and child victims of sexual assaults, and are highly sensitive to victim considerations in both criminal and SVP cases.

[86] Massachusetts's statute provides for the admission of prior written statements by the victim so long as notice is provided to the opposing counsel. See Mass. Gen. Laws ch. 123A, §14(c) (1999).

[87] By contrast, a guilty plea in a criminal case can be used as an admission in later civil proceedings. Unfortunately, many prosecutors and judges permit no-contest pleas to be entered on sexual offenses. For a criticism of this practice, see Holmgren, supra note 84. At the time a plea is taken to a criminal charge, the court is required to assure itself that there is a factual basis for the plea (i.e., that there are sufficient facts supporting the offender's guilt for the charge). This is generally accomplished by the prosecutor reciting facts of the case and the court asking the offender if he admits to these facts, by the court asking the offender to say what happened or asking direct questions of the offender, or by the court reviewing the facts as set forth in the criminal complaint. A guilty plea will operate as an admission to these facts (as written or recited to or by the court) for later use in another legal proceeding, including a SVP proceeding, whereas a no-contest plea precludes such use.

[88] See Cal. Welf. & Inst. Code §6600(a) (West 1999). These include but are not limited to preliminary hearing and trial transcripts, probation and sentencing reports, and evaluations by the state department of mental health. This statute arguably helps to keep victims from testifying in order to establish the fact of a prior predatory offense and the conviction of same, but it may not provide the types of detailed specific information most helpful to expert witnesses regarding the offender's pattern of conduct, the nature of his mental disorder, and his likeliness to reoffend. This statute also would not preclude the necessity of having other victims testify when their victimization did not result in a criminal conviction (e.g., victims of other counts which may have been dismissed as part of a plea agreement or victims whose cases were never charged). Nevertheless, this information may be critically important to the experts, thereby necessitating testimony from these victims. Several SVP statutes either explicitly or through case law recognize the importance of admitting "other acts" evidence. See, e.g., Ariz. Rev. Stat. Ann. §13-4606E (1995); N.D. Cent. Code §§25-03.3-13, 25-03.3-15 (1998); In re Hay, 953 P.2d 666 (Kan. 1998); In re Young, 857 P.2d 989 (Wash. 1993).

[89] For an extensive discussion of these issues, see Myers, *Evidence in Child Abuse and Neglect Cases* (3d ed.) (1997). Some hearsay exceptions also apply to adult victims including excited utterances and statements made for purposes of medical diagnosis and treatment.

[90] See Myers, supra note 89. See also U.S. Department of Health and Human Services, National Clearinghouse on Child Abuse and Neglect, and National Center for Prosecution of Child Abuse, Child Abuse and Neglect State Statute Series 1998, Volume IV, Child Witnesses, No. 20, Use of Closed-Circuit Television Testimony; No. 21, Admissibility of Videotaped Depositions or Testimony; and No. 28, Special Procedures in Criminal Child Abuse Cases. Current versions of these publications are available at the National Center's website: www.ndaa-apri.org

[91] Wis. Stat. Ann. §§980.03(5), 980.11 (West Supp. 1998).

[92] See, e.g., Fla. Stat. Ann. §394.926 (1999); 725 Ill. Comp. Stat. Ann. §207/75(b) (West Supp. 1998). Iowa, Kansas, New Jersey, Washington, and Wisconsin have similar provisions. Missouri's statute mandates notification of the victim at various stages of the SVP proceeding and includes the right of the victim to be present at any proceeding. See Mo. Rev. Stat. §632.507 (1998). South Carolina's statute also mandates notification at various points of the proceedings and requires the prosecutor to confer with victims about the status and progress of the proceedings. See S.C. Code §§16-3-1110, 16-3-1560 (Supp. 1998).

Exhibit 11.1
Comparison of SVP Provisions

	AZ	CA	FL	IL	IA	KS	MA	MN
1. Timing of Petition	1	1	1	1	1, 3	1	1	1, 2
2. Mental Disorder Definition	4, 6, 7	4	5, 7	4	5	5, 7	5, 7	5, 6, 8
3. Predator Definition	9	9, 11	9	9	9, 10	9	***	9
4. Conviction Requirement	13, 14, 15	13, 14	13	13, 14	12, 13, 14, 15	13, 14, 15	13, 14, 15	
5. Juvenile Offenders	No	Yes		Yes			Yes	
6. Authority to File Petition	16, 17	16	16	16, 17	16, 17	17	16, 17	16
7. Venue	19, 20, 21	19	19	19	19	19†	19	18, 19
8. Prepetition Assess/ Preprobable Cause Assessment	Yes	Yes		Yes		Yes		Yes
9. Examiner Requirements	24	22, 23	25	24			24	22, 23
10. Discovery/Access to Information	28, 29, 30, 31	28, 30	26, 28, 30, 31	27, 28, 29	28, 30, 31	28, 30	28, 29, 30	28, 30
11. Procedural Rule	Civil	Civil	Civil	Civil		Both		
12. Jury Trial	Yes/C	Yes/B	Yes/B	Yes/B	Yes/C	Yes/C	Yes/A	No
13. Burden of Proof	BRD	BRD	CC	BRD	BRD	BRD	BRD	CC
14. Verdict Type		UN	UN*	UN	UN	UN	UN	
15. Fifth Amendment Privilege				Yes			No	
16. Commitment Period	Indef.	2 yrs.	Indef.	Indef.	Indef.	Indef.	Indef.	Indef.
17. Reexamination Period	Annual	Annual	Annual	6 mo. then annual	Annual	Annual	Annual	6 mos.
18. Availability of Conditional Release	Yes	Yes	No	Yes	No	Yes	No	Yes
19. Less Restrictive Alternative Placement	Yes	No	No	Yes	No	Yes	No	No

See key to Exhibit 11.1 on page 11-30.

Exhibit 11.1 (Continued)

	MO	NJ	ND	SC	TX	VA	WA	WI
1. Timing of Petition	1	1, 2	1	1	1	1	1, 3	1, 3
2. Mental Disorder Definition	5, 8	5, 7	4, 6, 7	5, 7	5, 8	5, 7	5, 7	4
3. Predator Definition	9, 10	9	9, 10	9	10, 11	9	9, 10	9
4. Conviction Requirement	13, 14	13, 14, 15		13, 14, 15	13, 14	13, 15	12, 13, 14, 15	13, 14
5. Juvenile Offenders		Yes		Yes	Yes		Yes	Yes
6. Authority to File Petition	17	16, 17		17	Special unit	17	16, 17	16, 17
7. Venue				19	Single county	19	19	19, 20
8. Prepetition Assess/ Preprobable Cause Assessment		Yes			Yes	Yes	Yes	Yes
9. Examiner Requirements	22, 23	22, 23	24			22, 23	24	22, 23
10. Discovery/Access to Information	28, 30, 31	28, 30, 31	28, 30, 31	28, 30, 31	28, 30, 31	28, 30	28, 30, 31	27, 30, 31
11. Procedural Rule Criminal					Civil	Civil		Criminal
12. Jury Trial	Yes/C	No	No	Yes/B	Yes/B	Yes/B	Yes/C	Yes/B
13. Burden of Proof	BRD	CC	CC	BRD	BRD	BRD	BRD	BRD
14. Verdict Type	UN			UN	UN	UN	UN	UN
15. Fifth Amendment Privilege						Yes	No	Yes
16. Commitment Period	Indef.	Indef.	Indef.	Indef.	Indef.	Indef.	Indef.	Indef.
17. Reexamination Period	Annual	Annual	Annual	Annual	Biennial	Annual	Not specified	6 mo. then annual
18. Availability of Conditional Release	No	Yes	Yes	Yes	Yes	Yes	Yes	Yes
19. Less Restrictive Alternative Placement	No	No	Yes	No	No**	Yes	Yes	Yes

See key to Exhibit 11.1 on page 11-30.

Key to Exhibit 11.1, on pages 11-28 and 11-29

1 = End of incarceration period, currently confined.

2 = Concurrent with criminal charge.

3 = Paroled offenders, discharged offenders (Iowa and Washington require an overt act).

4 = Mental disorder, mental disfunction, conduct disorder.

5 = Mental abnormality.

6 = Paraphilia, sexual disorder.

7 = Personality disorder.

8 = Psychopath, sexual psychopath.

9 = Sexually violent offense.

10 = Predatory behavior, nonincest offenses.

11 = Requirement of multiple victims, multiple offenses.

12 = Prior charged sexual offense.

13 = Prior conviction for sexually violent offense.

14 = Found not guilty by reason of mental disease, defect, or insanity for sexual offense.

15 = Found not competent for trial for sexual offense.

16 = District or County Attorney or State's Attorney.

17 = Attorney General.

18 = County where currently located.

19 = County where offense committed.

20 = County where offender expected to be released.

21 = Attorney General files if sexual offense in another state.

22 = Psychologist.

23 = Psychiatrist.

24 = Specially qualified expert.

25 = Mental health professional.

26 = Civil.

27 = Criminal.

28 = Specifically defined by statute.

29 = State has right to discovery.

30 = State afforded access to offender's records before petition filed.

31 = Mandatory waiver of offender's rights to confidentiality or privilege.

Note. BRD = beyond a reasonable doubt.

CC = clear and convincing evidence.

UN = unanimous.

[a] State has exclusive right to demand jury. [b] Both state and offender have right to demand jury. [c] Both state, offender or court have right to require jury.

* In Florida, if a majority of the jury find the person is an SVP but the verdict is not unanimous the state may refile the petition.

** In Texas, all commitments are for outpatient treatment and supervision.

*** In Massachusetts there is only a requirement of a prior sex offense or an attempt; there is no violence requirement.

[†] The Kansas SVP statute does not specify venue, but other civil statutes and case law dictate venue where the act occurred.

Chapter 12

The Expert Witness in the Sex Offender Case— A Practical Guide

by Charlene Steen, Ph.D., J.D.

Overview

Practitioners who assess and/or treat sex offenders are increasingly being called on by the legal system for their evaluations and testimony in court. It is important that these practitioners understand courtroom, assessment, and deposition fundamentals; the role of expert testimony in various types of cases; ethical behavior and issues; the elements of appropriate preparation; key issues in the particular sex offender case; accuracy in predicting future harm; professional and competent on-stand behavior; and self-care afterward. This chapter will assist professionals in this field in dealing with court-related issues.

Introduction

Although forensic psychologists are specially treained to interface with courts, few mental health workers are specifically trained to deal with the judiciary. This may present a particularly threatening and anxiety-provoking prospect to those dealing with sex offenders where decisions and recommendations are subjected to much short- and long-term public scrutiny

The Courts and Their Procedures

The U.S. court system can be very confusing. We have a federal system and fifty different state systems, with different laws and standards of proof required in each. A person conceivably could be charged with the same crime in each of these courts without double jeopardy attaching (in the unlikely case that the offender dragged the victim over each state line). In addition, within each court system, there are different types of court procedures: criminal prosecutions (criminal sanctions for delineated bad acts), civil court suits (monetary awards for delineated bad acts), family law litigation (divorce, custody, and visitation decisions), child welfare court suits (focusing on child protection due to parental unfitness, placement, visitation, and reunification decisions), and the now popular postsentence civil commitments of sex offenders with mental disorders (sexually violent predator and mentally disordered offender commitments and juvenile custodial facility extension commitments). Conceivably, an individual offender could be involved in court proceedings in all these courts on the same offending behavior as well. And, of course, juvenile offenders can also fall under similar multiple procedures, except that instead of being prosecuted in adult criminal court they can be prosecuted (have a petition as a juvenile delinquent sustained) in juvenile court.

Each type of court proceeding may require a different standard of proof. Criminal cases require the highest standard—beyond a reasonable doubt. Most states' family law and and child welfare court suits require just the preponderance of the evidence— the more-likely-than-not standard. Sexually violent predator (SVP) commitments require different standards in different states. In California, for example, there is a kind of double standard. The offender must be found "likely" to reoffend beyond a reasonable doubt. There is another standard applied in some states on these types of cases—and that is clear and convincing evidence, more than a preponderance but less than beyond a reasonable doubt. It is important the witness know the standard of proof required in the particular case.

Some court proceedings are heard by a jury which decides the issues; others either by waiver or by law use only a judge to make the decisions. Some jurisdictions require a jury of twelve persons; others require a lessor number of jurors. And if the jury cannot make a decision, there is a mistrial wherein the case usually can be heard again, and possibly again and again.

Because there are different issues at stake in each court—guilt; appropriate compensation for bad acts; fitness for parental custody; divorce custody and visitation; mental illness predisposing the commission of additional offenses; and concomitant risk prediction, treatment, and schooling recommendations, behavioral limitations, and so on, it is critical for the expert witness to understand the type of case and what is being asked of him or her. All too often, a so-called expert is called in on a sentencing decision to determine level of risk and appropriate treatment and control of the offender and mistakenly focuses on elements not at issue in the particular case, such as the meeting of SVP criteria. Although many of the issues may overlap, it is important to respond specifically to the question being asked of the expert in the particular type of case. If the expert is not clear on the focus of the trial and his or her evaluation, the appointing court or attorney should be asked.

There may also be different evidentiary rules in different courts, and some courts may require more specific formats to reports submitted to the court. For example, the federal courts have specific items which must be covered in reports by experts, and reports not following the court format are rejected.

Expert Witness vs. Witness of Fact

The mental health expert testifying in court will be called either as an expert witness or an ordinary (fact) witness. It should be noted that if one is merely called as an ordinary (fact) witness, not paid as or qualified as an expert, the ordinary witness can only state facts. "Mr. *X* was seen ten times in sex offender group, then did not come back," is an example of fact testimony. He or she cannot opine whether his risk was higher because Mr. *X* was a treatment dropout.

The role of the expert witness is to give an expert opinion. Experts should be aware of the standard of proof in the particular case and determine whether their opinions meet the degree of scientific certainty required in the particular case.

In criminal court, both pretrial and during trial, the expert may be called on for information about the general mental functioning of the alleged offender and risk factors regarding likelihood of reoffense—which may be used to help develop an appropriate plea bargain or information regarding the credibility of the alleged victim—such as accuracy of memory, signs of prevarication, and pressures on the alleged victim to change facts. (Relative to credibility issues, it is important for the expert to be an expert on memory research, research about signs of lying, child accommodation syndrome, and so on, before agreeing to testify on these issues.)

The expert witness is likely to be testifying in more than one hearing on a particular matter. For example, in SVP cases there is often a probable cause hearing, possibly a deposition, possibly a *Kelly-Frye* hearing (regarding the admissibility of the expert's evidence), then a trial. The expert witness should not skimp on preparation for the earlier testimonies. The prior statements, if different from the current ones, can be used to impeach testimony, showing that the expert either does not know something or was not telling the truth. It is important to be as accurate and truthful as possible. The expert should be prepared to explain the reasons for any differences in statements. The expert should not be afraid to say if he or she does not know the answer. He or she should not guess if not certain. It is critical for witnesses to tell the attorney if they do not fully understand the question.

Types of Testimony

Guilt vs. Innocence. Sometimes the expert is asked to determine whether the offender is or is not likely to have committed the offense(s). The expert should make it clearly known that there are no psychological tests or superior expert clinical knowledge that can determine guilt or innocence, and that he or she cannot make any such statements. Although there are personality clusters on various standardized instruments which can help categorize persons already found to have committed offenses, all persons with those personality clusters have not committed sex offenses. Similarly, there have been some claims that guilt or innocence can be determined by plethysmographic or Abel screen results, but there is inadequate proof that any of these methods are sufficiently accurate for guilt or innocence findings.

An example of an expert improperly determining the guilt issue was a sleep-sex case, where the alleged offender had a previously diagnosed sleep disorder. He was apparently unconscious of doing various things while sleeping, including bizarre sleepwalking activities and some sexual behaviors with his wife. His wife would awaken him, with great effort, during these sleep activities and he would have no memory of what had transpired. In the case before the court, the alleged offender reported sleeping on the living room sofa because his wife, who was eight months pregnant, was restless in bed. His 5-year-old daughter, some time during the night, crawled in with him. The next morning she told her mother that he had fondled her genitalia during the night. He claimed to remember nothing about the incident. A physician he had seen about his sleep behaviors wrote a report to the alleged offender's attorney saying that the man was unaware of what he was doing because of his sleep disorder. This was totally improper and unfounded. Nobody knows whether he was aware or was not aware of his molesting behavior. This is beyond the purview of the professional. The psychiatrist should only have verified that the man had been treated for a sleep disorder and related what was claimed to have happened in the past.

Sentencing Recommendations. After a person has been found guilty in criminal court, the expert is often called in for recommendations regarding sentencing or placement. General mental status and functioning, statistical likelihood of reoffense, and recommendation for specific programs and custody levels are typically at issue.

The expert is called on to make similar assessments in juvenile sexual delinquency actions, as when a juvenile has molested another sibling in the family. In the intrafamilial case, the expert is also often asked to make recommendations relative to the safety of the other children in the family—such as placement of the offending child, visitation, and family reunification.

Insanity. The expert may also be called on in determinations of sanity or insanity relative to both the guilt issue and ability or inability to stand trial. The alleged offenders not only have sanity/insanity issues but may also be sex offenders. At issue in these cases usually is severe cognitive impairment due to a psychosis or mental retardation, not paraphilias. The sex offender expert is more frequently called in after a person has been found not guilty by reason of insanity (or guilty but insane in some jurisdictions) of a sex offense and his counsel is trying to show that the offender has regained his sanity and should be released. Each state has different criteria for restoration to sanity.

An example of one such case is a man who had a brief but acute psychosis during which time he molested two children in a park. His mental state cleared shortly thereafter. He spent six years in a state mental hospital, never again manifesting any psychotic symptoms but admitting to other prior pedophilic behaviors in his treatment. Because California requires that the person no longer be a danger to others before sanity can be deemed restored, he was retained at the hospital due to his pedophilic history. He accomplished all the sex offender treatment goals set for him, but hospital staff were concerned about his risk of reoffense if he was returned to the community. The sex offender expert was called in by defense counsel to review his readiness for release and, in particular, to determine his level of dangerousness.

Postsentencing Recommendations. Postsentence in criminal court, the expert may also be called upon in sentencing modification procedures and for parole or probation recommendations.

Civil Commitment. Postincarceration, an increasingly popular use of the expert is in the civil commitment of SVPs. Mental illness of any kind plus risk of reoffense are the key issues, the latter as determined by diagnostic, behavioral, and statistical instruments and individual correlative factors. It should be noted that the expert cannot tell whether an individual offender will or will not reoffend, but can only make a determination via statistical and clinical factors of the offender's risk classification—the likelihood of a person with the same characteristics reoffending.

Some states have similar statutes relative to keeping juveniles in juvenile facilities for extended treatment due to dangerousness. For example, a young man at California Youth Authority, committed there at age 17 for molesting many children in his neighborhood, was scheduled to be released. Because he was diagnosed with pedophilia and had dropped out of and refused further recommended sex offender treatment while in custody, a petition was filed under California law to retain him for the purpose of treatment. A new petition for extension, should the youth still not have participated adequately in treatment, could be filed every two years, and the youth technically could be retained until he was an old man. The expert was called in by the prosecution in this case to evaluate the youth's mental disorder, risk of reoffense, and effect of treatment on persons with a similar profile. Also related to the SVP proceedings are mentally disordered offender (MDO) actions (variously named and with slightly different standards in different jurisdictions), which are extension actions after a prison sentence has been completed for the mental hospitalization of persons who are deemed acutely mentally ill and dangerous. Usually the foci relate to major mental illnesses, such as psychoses, rather than the paraphilias.

Child Welfare. Child welfare actions, often adjudicated in juvenile courts, related to unfitness of one or both parents to maintain custody of their child or children due to allegations of sexual abuse, use the expertise of the expert witness. Safety of the child is the focus of such actions, and experts are called on to evaluate the risk of harm from the offending and/or other parent, and later make recommendations relative to visitation, custody, and reunification when and if the perpetrator is removed from the home.

Sometimes allegations of sexual abuse are only made in the family courts, connected most commonly to divorce actions. Usually, recommendations regarding the safety and well-being of the child are the prime concerns, with the expert again not qualified to make determinations of guilt or innocence, but looking at the relationships between children and parents and emotional health of the parents and most likely making recommendations about visitation, custody, and/or reunification.

Damage Awards. Tort cases, where a victim is suing in civil court for monetary damages for sexual abuse, require experts of varying expertise—particularly on the harm sexual abuse can do to a person on the plaintiff's side and either the likelihood of prevarication or memory problems of the plaintiff on the defendant's side. As noted previously, the expert cannot make a determination of whether the defendant did or did not commit the alleged sex offense(s).

If the defendant was found guilty in criminal court of committing a sex offense, that finding is binding on the family and tort courts, however, relative to the offender's guilt or innocence. But if he is found not guilty, that does not mean he did not commit the offense, because the standard of proof is higher in the criminal litigation than in the civil court.

In all these types of cases, it is important to stay within the boundaries of one's expertise. It is often tempting to step outside of those boundaries when a high sum of money is being offered, but it is unethical and people can be severely damaged by an uninformed expert witness. Similarly, it is unethical to testify on behalf of a person paying the expert when the expert's findings do not substantiate the testimony.

Confidentiality Issues

Confidentiality can be a complex issue, again varying depending on the laws of the jurisdiction, the type of procedure, and the role of the expert. In criminal actions, where the expert is appointed by the court to evaluate an offender or alleged offender, there is no confidentiality as to the court and usually the parties. The psychologist (or other type of professional)-client privilege is not available. This is true of other court-ordered evaluations, such as custody, child welfare, juvenile, and so on. Nevertheless, it is always wise for the expert both to explain the lack and limits of confidentiality to the alleged offender or other person being evaluated and to have him or her sign a release of information to the parties to whom the court has requested any evaluation to go.

If the expert is hired by just one side—generally the defense attorney in a criminal action—the assessment is only released by the expert to that attorney and is not available to anyone else unless the attorney finds it in his or her client's best interests and presents it to the district attorney, court, or others. Again, this should be explained to the person being evaluated and he or she should sign a release of information just to his or her attorney, unless the attorney requests a release to other parties.

Attorneys may subpoena client records relative to assessment and treatment. Unless there is a release of information in place or the court has ordered such release, these documents are generally confidential. A release of information or court order is required. Subpoenaed documents in the SVP case are usually deemed nonconfidential relative to the SVP case, as the evaluator-expert has prepared the assessment for that purpose and both sides are entitled to all information. A release of information signed in advance makes this matter clean and clear. But the documents cannot be released in any other type of action unconnected with their purpose without either a release or court order.

For example, a young man was evaluated as a potential SVP and found not to fit the criteria. Later, in a custody action, the attorney for the children subpoenaed the SVP evaluation. This evaluation could not be surrendered without a release from the person who was evaluated or an order by the judge.

Similarly, a subpoena of the expert for deposition may or may not be allowed, depending on the type of action and role of the expert. It is always better to get releases of information so that the offender or other person being evaluated knows in advance what will be private and what will not before even the assessment is made.

Assessment Issues

It is important for experts to realize that their assessment findings and recommendations can have extremely severe consequences for an offender and his family. Loss of freedom, loss of contact with family members—all the most basic rights of an individual—are at stake. Consequently, it is critical that assessments be comprehensive and complete, using the latest and best data and instruments available.

Quality is often compromised in court-ordered evaluations when compensation is minimal. For example, one psychiatrist boasted that he could evaluate a sex offender for purposes of sentencing in less than an hour. He wrote one- to-two page reports, based only on a twenty- to thirty-minute interview with the offender. This is extreme negligence, but it often goes on when the expert is paid a minimal amount. In this case, the psychiatrist only earned $300 per evaluation and could not understand why other professionals on the evaluation panel were refusing to do these evaluations for that sum.

To perform an adequate assessment of a sex offender, it is necessary to do a mental status exam, an in-depth interview, standardized testing, a review of all police and probation reports—including those of prior cases—and a review the person's criminal history; to provide a diagnosis; to apply statistical risk assessment instruments and individual risk correlates; and to research alternative placement and treatment resources. As little as possible should be left to chance.

Data sources include primary, secondary, and tertiary data. With respect to primary data, usually the victims are not available for interview, but a full interview of the offender is extremely important. However, sometimes the offender will refuse to be interviewed, particularly in the SVP cases, on advice of counsel. In such cases, an evaluation must be made using secondary and tertiary data—all the records available. The evaluator's diagnoses should only use proven or reported behavioral facts which fit the criteria for a diagnostic category such as pedophilia, based on four convictions over a ten-year period for molesting children between ages 8 and 12, statements reported to a psychologist wherein the offender stated he sexually fantasized about children, and a disciplinary write-up for possession of kiddie porn, or antisocial personality disorder, based on a juvenile criminal history beginning when the offender was 13 years old, derived from the probation officer's report and the offender's adult criminal history of burglaries, robberies, and so on, immediately prior to incarceration.

More subjective diagnoses, such as a depressive disorder, should not be made by the noninterviewing expert because the expert does not know the offender's current functioning. Past diagnoses of this type, however, should be reported as diagnoses made by other professionals, giving date, reasons, and any medications prescribed.

The Personal Interview

The interview of an offender should include a basic mental status exam and a comprehensive developmental history covering the following:

1. Family history, including siblings, relationship with parents and siblings, divorce or abandonment issues, relationships with steprelatives or others living in the home, current support by family members, and so on.

2. Quality of life during different age periods (e.g., 0–12, 12–15, 15–19, adult), including enjoyable activities, trouble gotten into (fire setting, fighting, stealing, etc.).

3. Educational data, including extent of education, suspensions, expulsions, learning disabilities, attention-deficit/hyperactivity problems, special education placements, fighting or substances at school, and so on.

4. Work history, including length of jobs and why terminated.

5. Substance use and abuse history of the offender and his family, including alcohol as well as illegal substances.

6. Physical, sexual, and emotional abuse history of the offender.

7. Criminal history of the offender, including juvenile, and his family members.

8. Sex offending history, including offenses of all types: Ask about telephone scatalogia, exposing, frottage, and so on.

9. Offender's interpretation of the instant and prior sex offenses, including attitudes toward his/her and others' victims: empathy, entitlement, reasoning behind commission of the offenses, remorse, and so on. (This may not be pos-

sible if the offender is not yet adjudicated and is pleading not guilty. Hypotheticals can be used in such cases to partially elucidate such attitudes.)

10. Sexual and relationship history, including sexual development and behaviors, number of partners, length of relationships, live-in or not, children and the offender's responsibility for them, current relationships and their character, taking or offering money for sex, use of sexually explicit materials, and so on.

11. Lifestyle questions, including plans and goals for the future: anticipated sex offender treatment in the community, 12-Step program attendance, persons awaiting their release, financial situation, educational and work goals, and so on.

12. Psychological and medical histories, including prior hospitalizations, psychotherapy of all kinds (with releases signed to appropriate therapists), prior sex offender treatment in particular, medications prescribed, participation in self-help programs (e.g., Alcoholics Anonymous), and so on.

If the Hare Psychopathy Checklist—Revised (PCL-R; Hare, 1991) is to be used to evaluate the offender, it is suggested that the items on the rating sheet be integrated into the oral interview to avoid duplication and save time.

An outline of interview topics is advised, so that the expert does not accidentally omit any of the subjects needed to be covered. In addition, it is also recommended that an interview schedule completed by the offender (see Table 12.1, at the end of this chapter) used to make certain that nothing is overlooked or misstated.

Interviews with parents, spouse, and others who know the offender, usually by telephone due to location problems and time constraints, can often yield significant information about childhood problems and behaviors, historical events in the offender's life, recent changes the offender has made, and level of support the offender is likely to receive in the community. In addition, these persons can also sometimes give additional insight into the offense motivations of the offenders. However, the statements of support persons are often slanted in the offender's favor and should not be taken as gospel.

When interviewing an offender within a correctional or mental institution, it is necessary first to find out what is required for entry. This is not always logical. For example, Atascadero State Hospital, California's maximum security institution, only requires prearrangement of an interview room and presentation of credentials including picture ID, whereas Napa State Hospital, a minimum security institution in California, requires a court order as well as the foregoing. Some penal institutions require court orders, others require letter from the requesting attorney, and still others require no more than telephoned arrangements plus the universally required picture ID.

It is important to clear any electronic equipment to be brought into the facility in advance, as it may not be allowed to be brought in. Certain institutions have clothing color requirements, so an individual will not be mistaken for an inmate. Most have stringent rules prohibiting giving anything to an inmate or patient. Ask first, even before giving a card.

Above all, it is important to recognize that the institution's main function is to protect society and its inhabitants. As such, visitors may have to wait for an escort, or until a lock-down has been ended, or even reschedule at times, based on the availability of the inmate and staff.

Recommended Testing Instruments

Standardized testing of the offender can yield important information about his functioning. A short cognitive screener, such as the Neurobehavioral Cognitive Status Examination (COGNISTAT), is useful relative to the mental status exam and affords information about language skills, memory, abstraction abilities, reasoning, and judgment. This instrument also has a Spanish version for dominantly Spanish speakers.

The Shipley Institute of Living Scale (SILS) is a rapid IQ screener that covers both verbal and abstraction realms and offers a Wechsler Adult Intelligence Scale—Revised equivalent score. However, it should not be used for persons of other cultures or persons with known visual perception problems. The Test of Non-Verbal Intelligence—Third Edition (TONI-3). is a good intelligence screener for such persons. It also gives norms for several different cultures. Also recommended is the Wechsler Abbreviated Scale of Intelligence (WASI), a slightly more comprehensive instrument that takes a little more time to administer.

Following is a list of a few of the standardized personality tests that are useful in the evaluation of sex offenders:

1. *The Minnesota Multiphasic Personality Inventory—Second Edition* (MMPI-2) is the most comprehensive of the objective personality tests, giving a broad range of data. (However, if one has limited time with an inmate in jail or prison, it may not be logistically possible to use this instrument. Several shorter instruments can give an adequate range of information in a much shorter amount of time if time is a limiting factor.)

2. *The Millon Clinical Multiaxial Inventory—Third Edition* (MCMI-III) is particularly strong on personality disorders but much less comprehensive. It now has a Spanish edition. Its juvenile counterpart is the *Millon Adolescent Clinical Inventory* (MACI), even more complete and useful than the adult instrument.

3. *The Jesness Inventory* (JI), now normed on adults as well as minors, is particularly good for minors and younger adults, with scales predicting future criminal acts and providing information on problematic personality characteristics. It also classifies offenders into types with prognosis and recommendations for treatment.

4. *The Carlson Personality Survey (CPS)* is a short and simply written instrument to be used on incarcerated persons. Although designed as an adult instrument, it has also been normed on adolescent offenders. It gives profiles of offenders as well as just four scale scores, all relevant to reoffense and treatment recommendations. Its Spanish version, the *Psicologico Texto* (PT), has profiles specifically for Hispanics.

5. *The Personality Assessment Screener* (PAS) is a short screening version of the *Personality Assessment Inventory* (PAI). It is particularly good for offenders who are very defensive because it tends to overpathologize, bringing up prob-

lem areas that might be hidden. (The full PAI is too long and not as informative as the MMPI-2. In addition, its Spanish version has been too difficult for many offenders to read and comprehend.)

Depending on the characteristics and behaviors noted relative to the offender, a variety of specialized instruments should be used—instruments regarding substance abuse, such as the Substance Abuse Subtle Screening Inventory—Third Edition (SASSI-3) (with both adult and adolescent norms) and/or the Maryland Addictions Questionnaire (MAQ); measuring anger, like the State Trait Anger Expression Inventory—Second Edition (STAXI-2); measuring psychopathy, such as the PCL-R (requires intensive training for accuracy); measuring psychotic thinking, like the Whitaker Index of Schizophrenic Thinking (WIST); and so forth.

A number of instruments look specifically at sexual behavior and attitudes, none as comprehensive or well standardized as most of the general personality tests. Prentky and Edmunds (1997) have published a compilation of information on various psychometric instruments to assess sexual abusers: *Assessing Sexual Abuse: A Resource Guide for Practitioners.*

A few useful instruments include the following:

1. *The Hanson Sexual Attitudes Questionnaire* (SAQ) is a short instrument which gives normal to abnormal ranges of scores on the offender's perception of children as sexy and on attitudes of sexual entitlement—both topics on Hanson's Sex Offender Need Assessment Rating (discussed later), as well as including and scoring items from the Abel and Becker Cognitions Scale, which measures cognitive distortions of sex offenders.

2. *Miccio-Fonseca's Personal Sentence Completion Inventory* (PSCI) is a non-standardized informational instrument in sentence completion form which elicits sexual attitudes and history data.

3. *The Sex Role Egalitarianism Scale* (SRES) is an instrument that looks at male attitudes toward women in a variety of realms.

4. *The Blanchard Inventory of Dependent Sex* (BIDS) is a brief screener (easily faked, however) giving information about compulsive sexuality, empathy, etc.

5. *The Sex Offence Information Questionnaire—Revised* (SOIQ-R) is an experimental English instrument by T. E. Hogue, measuring various aspects of sex offense-related denial. Scores on the four categories of this test as well as the total score compare pretreatment versus posttreatment offenders.

The Multiphasic Sex Inventory (MSI), a much more comprehensive and better standardized instrument, is unfortunately very long (300 items) relative to the information it yields. It is also not valid for offenders who do not acknowledge culpability and may not be accurate for minor offenders or offenders without paraphilias (because they generally score high on the lie scale, which may not be accurate). There are also numerous other instruments, some specific to a particular type of offender.

Use of the plethysmograph or Abel screen to measure deviant arousal or the lack thereof can also be useful, as deviant arousal is correlated to sexual reoffense.

However, deviant arousal patterns can also be found independent of these instruments in the behavioral histories given relative to the offender. But arousal findings, again, cannot determine guilt or innocence and should not be given undue weight. They are just one type of finding, albeit an important one.

Similarly, polygraphs have been useful not only in determining the truth of what the offender says but in gaining all kinds of additional information offenders often offer when in fear of what the polygraph will show. In most proceedings this is not an available option, however. The Fifth Amendment privilege against self-incrimination generally prevents its use for trial purposes, and the results are also not admissible in many courts due to some concerns about accuracy.

Secondary and Tertiary Data

The more data there is on an offender, the more thorough the report. This also includes secondary and tertiary data, the data derived from police reports, prior and current probation reports, state and FBI criminal history records, prior psychological evaluations (including progress and treatment planning reports), all prison file data (including disciplinaries, positive accomplishments, psychological and classification reports, etc.), and court and parole records.

It may require some legwork and a release of information from the offender to obtain information from the penal institutions and psychiatric hospitals.

Statistical Assessment

Risk-of-sexual-reoffense predictions are usually a key part of any evaluation and expert testimony. An analysis of the accuracy of risk prediction relative to sex offenders by R. Karl Hanson (1998) found that actuarial methods of predicting risk were far superior to clinical methods. Consequently, the use of statistical instruments measuring reoffense likelihood and individual statistical correlates to sexual reoffense are critical elements of the expert's report and testimony.

Following are some of the better validated instruments, most with moderate predictive validity:

1. *The Rapid Risk Assessment for Sexual Reoffense Recidivism* (RRASOR; Karl Hanson, 1997), an instrument with only four variables, has been replaced by the Static-99, which correlates scores with the percentage likelihood of sexual reoffense for six different groups over five- and ten-year periods.

2. *The Static-99* (Hanson & Thornton, 1999) is a new, more accurate instrument. A combination of the RRASOR and the Structured Anchored Clinical Judgment (SACJ-Min), it uses more variables (10) to determine the likelihood of sexual reoffense, and is more accurate in prediction than either of the other two instruments individually. It also predicts over a longer period of time—fifteen years. Scores of a particular offender correlate with a specified percentage likelihood of sexual reoffense.

3. *The Minnesota Sex Offender Screening Tool—Revised* (MnSOST-R; Epperson et al., 1998), an actuarial risk assessment instrument developed by a team

headed by Epperson, of Iowa State University, with psychologists from the Minnesota Department of Corrections (where it is used), is also a strong predictor of sexual recidivism, with the highest reported statistical correlation to sexual reoffense of any instrument at this time, (although the cross-validation sample included the initial validation sample, raising the validity statistics somewhat). The instrument requires professional ratings on sixteen variables, including custody and treatment issues. Scores again correlate with a group likelihood percentage of sexual reoffense.

4. *The Violence Risk Appraisal Guide* (VRAG; Webster, Harris, Rice, Cormier, & Quinsey, 1994) and Sex Offender Risk Appraisal Guide (SORAG; Quinsey, Harris, Rice, & Cormier, 1998) are two actuarial instruments almost equally accurate for sex offender predictions, although only the latter is specific to sex offenders. They predict violent reoffense, which includes sex offending, but not just sexual recidivism. These instruments were developed after extended research. Like the former instruments, the VRAG and SORAG require professional rating on a number of variables, twelve on the VRAG and fourteen on the SORAG. The items on both emphasize criminal history, with additional questions on release failures, age, mental disorder, PCL-R score, and so on. The SORAG also has a 2-point item based on phallometry results. Risk categories range from a low of 1 to a high of 9 on both scales, with corresponding percentages, for a maximum period of ten years.

5. *The Registrant Risk Assessment Scale* (RRAS; Ferguson, Eidelson, & Witt (n.d.), a new risk instrument developed by psychologists for (and used in) the state of New Jersey, measures thirteen criteria in four weighted categories: seriousness of offenses, offense history, characteristics of offender, and community support. Numerical results place the offender in a high, medium, or low category for sexual reoffense

6. *The California Actuarial Risk Assessment Tables* (CARAT; Schiller & Marques, n.d.), still an experimental instrument, developed by researchers of the California Department of Mental Health, estimates recidivism risk based on known risk factors as they occur singly or in combination, based on data derived from the Sex Offender Treatment Evaluation Project (SOTEP) database. There are both rapist and child molester tables, predicting an offender's risk of recommitting a hands-on sex offense within five years. The instrument yields explicit probabilities of reoffense expressed in terms of the percent chance of reoffending (rather than correlations like the other instruments).

The Sexual Violence Risk—20 (SVR-20; Boer, Hart, Knopp, & Webster, 1997), developed by academics and forensic mental health professionals affiliated with the Mental Health, Law, and Policy Institute at Simon Fraser University, is not a statistical instrument. It is an assessment method attempting to systematize risk assessment of offenders, using researched risk factors. It does not yield norm-referenced or criterion-referenced scores but simply provides a rating scale for psychosocial adjustment, sex offenses, and future plans which are then clinically interpreted to place the offender in a high-, medium-, or low-risk category.

Although there are overlapping items on each of the instruments, using more than one can show a consistency in risk level (or inconsistency, as the case may be), which strengthens the predictive accuracy of the expert.

It should be noted, however, that most of these instruments load heavily on static factors—historical factors such as criminal history, prior family or school problems, or prior victim characteristics, which are unchanging. They do not evaluate change.

The only statistical instrument attempting to measure change as related to prediction of recidivism is the Sex Offender Need Assessment (SONAR; Hanson & Harris, 2000), developed specifically to evaluate change in risk among sexual offenders. It uses dynamic (changeable) risk factors, including five relatively stable factors (intimacy deficits, negative social influences, attitudes tolerant of sex offending, sexual self-regulation, and general self-regulation) and four acute factors (substance abuse, negative mood, anger, and victim access), which are rated by the expert, and which distinguish between between sex offense recidivists and non-recidivists. (Questions on the Hanson SAQ directly rate to a number of these items.)

This instrument is designed for use after the offender is out of prison and under community supervision, because some factors will change once the offender is in a less structured environment. Unfortunately, the majority of persons for whom change is a critical evaluative measure have never been out of prison or the mental hospital; thus the utility of the instrument for them is negligible.

David Thornton attempted to systematize a clinical method of determining risk after someone has been in treatment with his Structured Risk Assessment—Assessing Progress. Although the instrument gives some consistency to findings, it has not been statistically validated.

Likelihood of sexual reoffense can also be predicted using individual statistical risk correlates, in particular those derived from the meta-analytic research by Hanson and Bussière (1996) and Hanson and Harris (1998). The presence of individual static and dynamic correlates and their relative power show increased or decreased likelihoods of sexual reoffense. Although most of the correlation percentages are very low, because they are derived from meta-analyses of approximately 29,000 offenders they have much more power than such correlations derived from much smaller individual studies. Presence of a predominance of reoffense correlates indicates higher risk of sexual reoffense, although one cannot add the percentage correlations due to overlapping of the variables.

Findings on individual correlates not present in a specific instrument can also modify the findings on that instrument upward or downward to a modest degree. There is no way to tell how much they change findings on the basic instrument.

Alhough there are no near perfect instruments, most rely on dominantly unchanging historical factors, and individual correlates do not give us any real numerical data regarding likelihood of sexual reoffense, the use of this statistical information is critical to increased accuracy of prediction because it is the most accurate information we have.

Making the Report User-Friendly

When the expert writes a report, it is important that the report be user-friendly for nonprofessionals, psychologists, judges, and sometimes even the jury (although it is usually not given to them). The language should be kept simple and technical terms should be explained. Both sentences and paragraphs should be fairly short. Items such as the diagnoses, the test findings, risk data, and so on, should be set out clearly and defined. And the referral questions should be clearly answered.

Subtitles should be employed for ease of use. This helps the attorneys or judge flip to the subject of interest easily. One-line summaries at the end of a section are also helpful. (As noted previously, some courts—particularly the federal courts—have specific formats and/or topic headings that they require.)

General Guidelines for Testimony

The expert witness's function is to assist the trier of fact (judge or jury) by presenting scientific, technical, or other specialized knowledge. The rationale for this is that the judge or jury may not be able to adequately understand and make correct conclusions without the assistance of persons who are experts in the field, having the knowledge, experience, and information an ordinary person would not have.

To be effective in this function the expert witness must establish credentials, competency, knowledge, and integrity. The expert must be believable. Therefore, it is important to look like an expert. Someone who is dressed neatly, conservatively, and professionally is more likely to be perceived as an expert who is knowledgeable. Jurors respond emotionally to the expert testifying. For example, the expert is less likely to be believed if wearing baggy jeans and a sweatshirt to court. He or she just does not look like someone who knows a lot. In addition, some judges have thrown witnesses out of court who have not dressed appropriately. On the other hand, wearing excessively expensive watches and jewels is also likely to produce a negative reaction in the jury, whose members may connect these expensive items with bought testimony.

It is also important to talk as befits the role of the expert witness. This means one should speak professionally, not using slang or swear words, but using simple words the jury or judge will easily understand. Psychobabble or jargon should not be used. Psychobabble is just what it sounds like, terminology known only to the trade and incomprehensible to everyone else. The expert will basically be teaching the jury about sex offenders, their diagnoses, and what the diagnoses mean—particularly in relation to the specific statutes being dealt with, the effects of treatment on recidivism, the levels of reoffense for specific types of offenders, and so forth. The expert must do this in a way the jury and judge will understand and make it interesting for them if he or she can. The expert should neither talk over the jury or judge's heads in such a scientific way that they will be lost nor talk down to them as if they were stupid. It is important not to alienate them. The expert wants them to respect him or her and understand what they are being told, and the expert must, in turn, have respect for them. Jurors are usually extremely sensitive to how the expert witness presents him- or herself and will be offended if the expert appears biased, dishonest, argumentative, or pompous. The expert must remember that these negative jury impressions can affect the outcome of the case.

It also helps to look at the jurors when explaining things to them. They are more likely to be attentive when the answer is addressed to them. Similarly, the expert witness should be careful not to fidget or do things that will distract the jury's attention away from the responses to the questions. Gum chewing is definitely forbidden. If nervous, the expert can practice being on the stand beforehand with a friend or colleague asking questions. Reminding him- or herself that opinions are being presented based on the known and available information, that the expert cannot know everything, and that it is the trier of fact (judge or jury) who makes the decisions are important realizations. In addition, the expert witness should not be emotionally tied in with the particular attorney's desires for case outcome. The expert is a neutral examiner who presents objective findings which may fall dominantly on one side or another.

Demeanor should be appropriate. The expert witness should be him- or herself as much as possible, but should not make jokes about serious matters. Being properly serious and considered in statements will be better accepted by the trier of fact. The expert witness should display confidence but not arrogance.

The attorneys should have copies of the expert's curriculum vitae, because he or she will have to be qualified on the stand as someone with expert knowledge in this particular field. It is important to make certain that the curriculum vitae is accurate, complete, and scrupulously honest.

The expert witness will probably be questioned on some of the items in this document as well as the number of times he or she has testified in this type of case and/or the number of offenders in this type of case he or she has previously assessed. It is critical not to lie or exaggerate, because the expert can be challenged at a later time and lose credibility. Some attorneys have gone to great lengths to check up on the credentials of expert witnesses in order to discredit them. On the opposite end of the spectrum, if one's curriculum vitae reflects vast experience and training, the professional qualifications, if properly presented by the attorney, can enhance veracity and presumed knowledge.

Preparation

Before appearing on the stand or at a deposition, the expert witness needs to adequately prepare. This means that he or she should study all the technical data being used, such as statistical data relative to instruments and sex offenders in general, and review the report and underlying facts. Because the expert witness's file will be brought to the stand, it is good to make an outline of the key items that will probably be asked and to organize the file, tabbing it with the topic sections, such as probation reports or prison disciplinaries or prior psychological evaluations, so that he or she can flip easily to the section if asked a question that cannot be answered without referring to the particular report.

It is best to meet and talk with the retaining attorney (if there is one) prior to appearing to clarify what he or she will be asking and what types of questions can be expected from the opposing counsel. It is also important to inform the retaining attorney what some of the more important findings were, so the attorney will make sure to ask about them.

Depositions

Depositions are relatively informal civil pretrial hearings with a court reporter present wherein opposing counsel asks questions in order to discover information about the expert's background and professional history, what he or she knows and might say, and possible relevant information not in the written report. The attorney wants to find areas of bias, inadequate knowledge, and discrepancies.

Depositions are taken under oath. Although depositions are not allowed in criminal trials, the sex offender expert is likely to be deposed in SVP cases—which are a kind of civil action—as well as in family law and tort actions. Information recorded in the deposition transcript can be used to discredit the expert witness in subsequent hearings.

In a deposition, the expert witness can be asked all kinds of questions often not allowable in the actual court proceedings. Some will be of questionable relevance to the case. The retaining attorney will probably set some limits if the questions go too far afield. But the expert too will have to be on guard for questions that might violate another person's privacy, such as the names and locations of all the defendants for whom the expert has testified on the defense side of a case. If the expert refuses to answer the questions, the attorney can go back to the judge and get an order for response to certain questions, and possibly even sanctions against the expert if the questions were reasonable ones, or if the questions were unreasonable, the judge can refuse to require responses.

The opposing counsel may attempt to intimidate or lead the expert witness astray with questions that misquote what was said. It is important to clarify statements made in such cases.Sometimes the opposing counsel may get abusive. If the retaining attorney does not protect the expert from hostile personal attacks, or does not insist on adequate breaks, for example, the expert witness may comment on the abuse, request less hostility, and request breaks. If these do not occur, the expert has the power to terminate the deposition (although the opposing attorney can go back into court, once again, for an order for compliance which may or may not be granted).

Testimony in Court

On the stand in court it is important to be as unbiased as possible. Even though the expert witness may be hired by one side, it is important that he or she present as an independent evaluator who has taken all known factors into consideration. The expert witness does not belong to the side that hires him or her. Factors present on both sides must be acknowledged. Opinions must be based on independent consideration of all the elements present as related to the most accurate and current research.

If the expert witness discovers that he or she has made a mistake as to fact or opinion (e.g., attributed too many priors to an offender or misgraded a statistical risk instrument), it is important to bring that to the attention of the attorneys and the court. Everyone occasionally makes a mistake. It is when the expert attempts to cover it up, lies, or denies the mistake that the jurors become upset and disregard all that the expert has to say.

Opinions must be supported by thorough and reliable methodology, as evidenced by the evaluation that was completed. Tests and research used should be supported by peer reviewed literature.

The standards for sufficiency and acceptability of the bases of opinions are found in the *Daubert* case (1993). The findings in that case are the basis for challenging opinions. Under *Daubert*, opinions must be based on empirically tested scientific methodology and scrutinized by the relevant scientific community, the error rate of all instruments must be shown, the conclusions of the methodology must be accepted generally within the relevant scientific community, and the expert's theory must have existed before the litigation began.

The opposing counsel may demand what is commonly called a *Kelly-Frye* hearing. This is a hearing preliminary to trial to determine whether the evidence to be presented meets the foregoing standards. The expert witness is usually called on to testify about the sources of information used in coming to an opinion.

Direct and Cross-Examination

At both the preliminary hearings and at the trial (but not at a deposition), the retaining attorney will do what is called a "direct examination" of the expert witness, establishing qualifications and providing the facts and opinions needed for his or her side of the case. The expert witness will be given time to explain fully all opinions and the bases for them. Occasionally, in the direct examination the attorney will ask questions he or she knows opposing counsel would ask in an attempt to show that the expert is biased (e.g., how much the expert is being paid). This is to diffuse the opposing counsel's potential attacks on credibility.

The opposing attorney will "cross-examine" the expert witness, asking much more difficult questions in an attempt to discredit the expert and his or her testimony. Questions can be expected about sources of information, the assumptions on which the opinions have been based, the degree of certainty of the opinion, what sources were used to come to the opinion, the validity and deficits of each of the sources, if testing instruments were administered personally and correctly, and why the opinions of opposing experts may be different. The opposing attorney will attempt to show inadequacies in the expert's training or evaluation and will attempt to show a lack of knowledge on the expert's part, sometimes asking about data in journals or books the expert may or may not have read. Prior testimony discrepancies will also be questioned.

The general rule for the expert witness in the cross- or recross-examinations is to "keep cool." If an answer is not known, the expert should say so. He or she should stay within the area of expertise, acknowledging when a question goes beyond that expertise. For example, if the expert witness is asked about technical statistical methodology which is unknown to him, the expert should acknowledge not knowing that information but can qualify his expertise by noting that he knows the data relative to sex offenders. One expert explained this to the jury relative to this situation, "I know how to drive a car, but I can't build one."

The expert witness should be careful not to get defensive. He or she should not exaggerate to make a point or guess in an attempt to avoid looking stupid. If asked about a document or prior quotation, asking to read it over before responding is recommended. It is useful to pause and collect thoughts before answering. Information not asked should not be volunteered—ideally the retaining attorney will bring that information out in redirect examination. (Usually the expert can talk to the retaining attorney at break about what he or she thinks may be important to ask to rehabilitate testimony or explain some issue that was raised. The attorney will judge whether such issues are important and should be asked about.)

After the direct and cross-examinations, both attorneys will be given a second chance, known as redirect examination and recross-examination. The only limitation is that both the redirect and recross must stay within the scope of the prior information presented.

Sometimes the judge will also ask some questions, trying to clarify matters either for him- or herself or the jury. Again, the questions should be answered honestly, directly, simply, and to the best of the expert's ability.

During court recesses, it is advisable not to speak about the case in a public area. It cannot be known if a stray juror or two might be within hearing distance. If retaining counsel wants to talk to the expert about some issue in the case, he or she should go to a private office to discuss it. The jury should not be influenced in any way via an overheard comment outside of the courtroom, or the trial will be invalid and a mistrial declared. Likewise, it is important not to laugh about what went on in court in a public area. Dignity should be maintained even during the recess. Outside influences, either positive or negative, on the jury are contrary to court rules and bad form.

Afterward

The expert witness may feel like he or she "blew it" after testifying, because of mistakes made, some critical information not known, and/or disregarding of the expert's opinion in the verdict. It is important to reframe this as a learning experience. It teaches the expert what must be done to be a more effective expert witness in the future.

Remember, too, that as an expert witness, one is educating the public and the court about sex offenders in general, influencing future decisions, and even improving future legislation. It is not just this particular case that is important.

Occasionally, the expert witness may have predicted that a person was at low risk of reoffense and the jury decided the case based on that opinion, yet a few months later the offender did in fact reoffend, hurting someone badly. It is natural to feel terrible about this. But the expert witness is not responsible. If the offender fell within the low-risk category, the testimony was correct. There is no way of knowing absolutely if a specific person will reoffend. And to lock everyone up because of a few false negatives is also to ruin many lives. Opinions can never be perfect, nor can the instruments be. The expert must only keep up with the most current information and testify the best that is possible.

Adequate self-care is important in this field due to the multiple stresses of testimony and error. Having a formal or informal support group where the court experiences can be processed is helpful. And recreation, friends, family, and activities will keep the expert from burning out.

Conclusion

The effective expert witness in the sex offender case is one who knows the basics of the legal system and the needs of the specific case, is familiar with standard testing instruments and statistical instruments and data, is aware of and sensitive to confidentiality issues, has made a comprehensive analysis of the significant factors in the case, has prepared a thorough evaluation of the defendant, is adequately prepared for hearings and court testimony, and testifies in an honest, nonbiased, direct fashion. In addition, keeping up with the latest data regarding sex offenders is critical, particularly as research in this field is burgeoning and new and more accurate information is being constantly added to what is already known.

References

Alexander, M. A. (1999). Sexual offender treatment efficacy revisited. *Sexual Abuse: A Journal of Research and Treatment, 11*(2), 101–116.

Babitsky, S., Mangraviti, J. J., & Todd, C. J. (2000). *The comprehensive forensic services manual: The essential resources for all experts.* Falmouth, MA: SEAK.

Boer, D. P., Hart, S. D., Kropp, P. R., & Webster, C. D. (1997). *Manual for the Sexual Violence Risk— 20: Professional guidelines for assessing risk of sexual violence.* Burnaby, British Columbia: The Mental Health, Law, & Policy Institute, Simon Fraser University.

Cantor, B. J. (1997). *The role of the expert witness in a court trial (a guide for the expert witness).* Belmont, MA: Civil Evidence Photography Seminars.

Daubert et al. v. Merrill-Dow Pharmaceutical, 509 U.S. 113 (1993).

Doren, D. (1999). *Using and testifying about sex offender risk instrumentation.* Paper presented at 1999 annual conference of the Association for the Treatment of Sex Offenders.

Epperson, D. L., Kaul, J. D., Huot, S. J., Hesselton, D., Alexander, W., & Goldman, R. (1998). *Minnesota Sex Offender Screening Tool—Revised (MnSOST-R): Development, performance, and recommended risk level cut scores* [On-line]. Available: http://psych-server.iastate.edu/faculty/ epperson/MnSOST-R.htm.

Ferguson, G. E., Eidelson, R. J., & Witt, P. H. (n.d.). *RRAS validity study* [On-line]. Available: http://inpsyte.asarian-host.org/njrras.htm.

Frye v. United States, 293 F. 1013, 1014 (D.C. Cir. 1923).

Hanson, R. K. (1997). *The development of a brief Actuarial Risk Scale for Sexual Offense Recidivism* (User Report 97–04). Ottawa: Solicitor General of Canada.

Hanson, R. K. (1998). What do we know about sex offender risk assessment? *Psychology, Public Policy, and the Law, 4*(1/2) 50–72.

Hanson, R. K., & Bussière, M. T. (1998). Predicting relapse: A meta-analysis of sexual offender recidivism studies. *Journal of Consulting and Clinical Psychology, 66*(2), 348–362.

Hanson, R. K., & Harris, A. (1999). *Where should we intervene? Dynamic predictors of sex offense recidivism.* Ottawa, Ontario: Corrections Research, Solicitor General of Canada.

Hanson, R. K., & Harris, A. (2000). *The Sex Offender Needs Assessment Rating (SONAR): A method for measuring change in risk levels* (User Report 2000-1). Ottawa: Solicitor General of Canada.

Hanson, R. K., & Thornton, D. (1999a). Improving risk assessments for sex offenders: A comparison of three actuarial scales. *Law and Human Behavior, 24*(1), 119–136.

Hanson, R. K., & Thornton, D. (1999b). *Static-99: Improving actuarial risk assessments for sex offenders* (User Report No. 99-02). Ottawa: Solicitor General of Canada.

Hare, R. D. (1991). *The Hare Psychopathy Checklist—Revised.* North Tonowanda, NY: Multi-Health Systems.

Melton, G. B., Petrila, J., Poythress, N. G., & Slobogin, C. (1987). *Psychological evaluations for the courts.* New York: Guilford Press.

Prentky, R. A., & Burgess, A. W. (2000). *Forensic management of sexual offenders.* New York: Kluwer Academic/Plenum .

Prentky, R., & Edmunds, S.B. (1997). *Assessing sexual abuse: A resource guide for practitioners.* Brandon, VT: Safer Society Press.

Prentky, R.A., Harris, B., Frizzell, K., & Righthand, S. (2000). An actuarial procedure for assessing risk with juvenile sex offenders. *Sexual Abuse: A Journal of Research and Treatment, 12*(2), 71–87.

Prentky, R. A., Lee, A. E. S., Knight, R. A., & Cerce, D. (1997). Recidivism rates among child molesters and rapists: A methodological analysis. *Law and Human Behavior, 21*(6), 635–659.

Quinsey, V. L., Harris, G. T., Rice, M. E., & Cormier, C. A. (1998). *Violent offenders: Appraising and managing risk.* Washington, DC: American Psychological Association.

Schiller, G., & Marques, J. (n.d.). *The California Actuarial Risk Assessment Tables (CARAT) for rapists and child molesters.* Unpublished manuscript, California Department of Mental Health.

Schram, D. D., Milloy, C. D., & Rowe, W. E. (1991). *Juvenile sex offenders: A follow-up study of reoffense behavior.* Research funded by the Washington State Institute for Public Policy.

Webster, C. D., Harris, G. T., Rice, M. E., Cormier, C., & Quinsey, V. L. (1994). *The Violence Prediction Scheme: Assessing dangerousness in high risk men.* Toronto: Centre of Criminology, University of Toronto.

Witt, P. H., DelRusso, J., Oppenheim, J., & Ferguson, G. (1996). Sex offender risk assessment and the law. *Journal of Psychiatry and Law, 24,* 343-377.

Worling, J. R. (2000). *Personality-based typology of adolescent male sexual offenders: Differences in recidivism rates, victim-selection characteristics, and personal victimization histories.* Unpublished manuscript.

Worling, J. R., & Curwen, T. (1998). *Adolescent sexual offender project: A 10-year follow-up study.* Toronto: SAFE-T Program and Ontario Ministry of Community and Social Services.

Worling, J. R., & Curwen, T. (2000). *The "ERASOR": Estimate of Risk of Adolescent Sexual Offense Recidivism (version 1.2).* Toronto: SAFE-T Program.

Table 12.1
Offender Questionnaire

Name_____ Date_____

I. SEXUALITY INFORMATION

1. From where did you learn most about sex? Parents _____ Brother(s) and/or sister(s) _____ Friends _____ Books _____ School _____ Other _____

   Is it easy to talk about sex at home? _____ Do you often? _____ With whom _____

   Did you ever play sex games as a young child? _____
   What kinds of games? _____

   Were you ever punished for sexual activities as a child? Many times _____ A few times _____
   One time _____ Never _____
   If so, what were you punished for doing? _____

2. How old were you when you first kissed a girl romantically? _____
   Can you remember the incident? _____
   Was it a pleasant experience? _____ Were you afraid? _____
   Did it go any further than kissing? _____ How far?_____

   At what ages did you have your first other types of sexual experiences with girls:
   Petting or fondling above the waist _____
   Petting or fondling below the waist _____ Masturbation _____ Gave oral sex _____ Received oral sex _____
   Sexual intercourse _____
   Anal sex _____ Other _____

   Did you care about the girls/women with whom you have had sexual relationships? _____
   Have you just had sex with any female who would for the sake of having sex? _____
   Which way has happened most frequently? _____

   What is the usual age difference between you and the females you are attracted to? _____

3. Have you had any sexual relationships with males? _____ What ages? _____

   Are you more attracted to males or females? _____ Equally attracted to both? _____

   What age males are you most attracted to? _____

   If you consider yourself homosexual or bisexual, have you felt comfortable enough about it to tell anyone? _____
   Who?_____

   What types of sexual experiences have you had with males? Kissing _____ Petting or fondling _____
   Masturbation _____ Gave oral sex _____ Received oral sex _____ Gave anal sex _____
   Received anal sex _____
   Other_____ What? _____

   Have you cared about the males you have had sexual experiences with? _____

   Have you just had sex with any male who would for the sake of having sex? _____

   Which way has happened most frequently?_____

   What is the usual age difference between you and the males you are attracted to? _____

   Have you ever had any group sex experiences? _____ What combinations? _____

4. Have you ever received money for sex (hustled)? _____ If so, how old were you when you first did this? _____
How long did you do it? _____ Are you still doing it? _____ How did you first get into it?_____
Why?_____

Were you on the run when you first started? _____

What kinds of sex did you trade for money? Fondling _____ Masturbation _____ Giving oral sex _____
Receiving oral sex _____ Giving anal sex _____ Receiving anal sex _____ Other _____

Have you ever purchased sex? With males? _____ Approximate ages? _____ With females? _____
Approximate ages? _____

5. How old were you when you started masturbating? _____
How often do you usually masturbate? More than once a day _____ Once a day _____
A few times a week _____
Once a week _____ A few times a month _____ Once a month _____ Rarely _____ Never _____

Around the time you committed your offense(s), how often were you masturbating?
More than once a day _____ Once a day _____ A few times a week _____ Once a week _____
A few times a month _____ Once a month _____ Rarely _____ Never_____ Don't know _____

6. How often do you look at sexy magazines or books (Playboy, etc.)? Often _____ Rarely _____ Never _____

Around the time you committed your offense(s), had you been looking at sexy magazines or books? _____
If yes, which?_____

7. How often do you see X-rated films or videos? Often _____ Rarely _____ Never _____

Around the time you committed your offense, had you been looking at any X-rated films or videos? _____
If yes, which?_____

8. When you daydream, how often do you have the following fantasies?
Sex with someone you know your age: Often _____ Sometimes _____ Rarely _____ Never _____
Sex with someone famous: Often _____ Sometimes _____ Rarely _____ Never _____
Sex with a stranger: Often _____ Sometimes _____ Rarely _____ Never _____
Sex with more than one person: Often _____ Sometimes _____ Rarely _____ Never _____
Sex with minor (12–17): Often _____ Sometimes _____ Rarely _____ Never _____
Sex with a child (8–11): Often _____ Sometimes _____ Rarely _____ Never _____
Sex with child (4–7): Often _____ Sometimes _____ Rarely _____ Never _____
Sex with a baby or toddler: Often _____ Sometimes _____ Rarely _____ Never _____
Being forced to have sex: Often _____ Sometimes _____ Rarely _____ Never _____
Forcing someone to have sex: Often _____ Sometimes _____ Rarely _____ Never _____
Causing pain during sex: Often _____ Sometimes _____ Rarely _____ Never _____
Receiving pain during sex: Often _____ Sometimes _____ Rarely _____ Never _____
Tying someone up during sex: Often _____ Sometimes _____ Rarely _____ Never _____
Sex involving an animal: Often _____ Sometimes _____ Rarely _____ Never _____

Do you have other fantasies while daydreaming? _____ What kinds?_____

9. When you are masturbating, how often do you have the following fantasies?
Sex with someone you know your age: Often _____ Sometimes _____ Rarely _____ Never _____
Sex with someone famous: Often _____ Sometimes _____ Rarely _____ Never _____
Sex with a stranger: Often _____ Sometimes _____ Rarely _____ Never _____
Sex with more than one person: Often _____ Sometimes _____ Rarely _____ Never _____
Sex with minor (12–17): Often _____ Sometimes _____ Rarely _____ Never _____
Sex with a child (8–11): Often _____ Sometimes _____ Rarely _____ Never _____
Sex with child (4–7): Often _____ Sometimes _____ Rarely _____ Never _____
Sex with a baby or toddler: Often _____ Sometimes _____ Rarely _____ Never _____
Being forced to have sex: Often _____ Sometimes _____ Rarely _____ Never _____
Forcing someone to have sex: Often _____ Sometimes _____ Rarely _____ Never _____
Causing pain during sex: Often _____ Sometimes _____ Rarely _____ Never _____

Receiving pain during sex: Often _____ Sometimes _____ Rarely _____ Never _____
Tying someone up during sex: Often _____ Sometimes _____ Rarely _____ Never _____
Sex involving an animal: Often _____ Sometimes _____ Rarely _____ Never _____

Do you have other fantasies while daydreaming? _____ What kinds?_____

10. How many times have you done the following things? Bare-assed someone _____ Peed in public _____
    Made obscene phone calls without identifying yourself _____
    Peeped at someone without their knowing it _____
    Peeped at someone in the nude without their knowing it _____ Masturbated in public _____
    Sexually rubbed against someone in a public place _____ Stolen women's underwear _____
    Put on women's underwear _____ Masturbated while stroking women's underwear _____
    Dressed up in women's clothes _____ Masturbated while wearing women's clothes _____
    Shown someone your genitals from a distance _____ Had sexual contact with animals _____
    What animals?_____

II. MISCELLANEOUS INFORMATION

1. How frequently did you drink alcoholic beverages? More than once a day _____ Once a day _____
   A few times a week _____ Once a week _____ A few times a month _____ Once a month _____
   Rarely _____ Never _____ Not any more _____

   What did you usually drink? Beer _____ Wine _____ Whiskey _____ Vodka _____ Other _____

   Had you been drinking around the time you committed your offense? _____ About how much? _____
   What? _____

   Do you think you have a drinking problem? _____

   Has anyone ever said you have a drinking problem? _____ Who? _____

   Have you ever had counseling or gone to AA for your drinking? _____

2. Which of the following drugs have you tried? Marijuana _____ Hash _____ Glue _____ Crank _____
   Crystal _____ Mushrooms _____ Cocaine _____ Quaaludes _____ Acid _____ Bennies _____
   Sentynal _____ Amphetamines _____ PCP (Angel Dust) _____ Peyote _____ Ecstacy _____
   Psylosibin _____ Crack or rocks _____ Heroin _____ Other _____

   How have you used them? Smoking _____ By mouth _____ By nose _____ By injection _____

   Which do you use most frequently? _____
   How often? More than once a day _____ Once a day _____ A few times a week _____ Once a week _____
   A few times a month _____ Once a month _____ Rarely _____ Not any more _____ Never _____

   Had you been using any drugs around the time you committed your offense? _____ Which? _____
   How much?_____

   Do you think you have a drug problem? _____ Has anyone ever said you have a drug problem? _____
   Who?_____ Have you ever had counseling or gone to a drug program for this? _____ Which? _____

3. What are some of things you that got you in trouble when you were younger? Lying _____
   Cheating on tests _____ Swearing _____ Cutting school _____ Fighting _____
   Talking back to your parents _____ Talking back to teachers _____ Drinking _____ Smoking _____
   Using drugs _____ Sexual activities _____ Coming home late _____ Staying out all night _____
   Not doing chores _____ Stealing _____ Using the family car without permission _____
   Driving without a license _____ Setting fires _____ Vandalism (defacing property _____
   Sex offenses? _____ Which? _____ Other (please list)_____

III. SEXUAL OFFENSE(S)

1. Names of your most recent sex offense(s) _____

2. Victims' names _____
   Victims' ages _____ Victims' sex(es) _____

3. Location of offense(s) (be very specific)_____

4. How did you pick the victims? I didn't think anyone would know if I picked her/him _____
   I liked her/him _____ I was sexually attracted to her/him _____ She/he wanted sex _____
   She/he was around and easy to get at _____ I hated her/him and wanted to get even _____
   She/he started it _____ I was angry at my parents because she/he was the favorite
   I was angry at someone else _____ Who? _____
   Other _____

   If she/he wasn't around, who else would you have picked? _____

5. What did you do to the victims? Stand nude in front of her/him _____ Mouth kiss _____
   Tongue kiss _____ Touch the victims over her/his clothes _____ Under her/his clothes _____
   Touch what parts of the body? Breasts _____ Nipples _____ Penis _____ Crotch _____
   Balls _____ Pussy _____ Rear end (ass) _____ Stick your fingers in her/his ass _____
   Stick your fingers up her vagina _____ Other _____
   Put your mouth on what part of the body? Breasts _____ Nipples _____ Crotch _____
   Make her/him touch you where? Breasts _____ Nipples _____ Crotch _____ Penis _____
   Balls _____ Pussy _____ Rear end (ass) _____ Stick her/his fingers up your ass _____
   Other _____

   Did you dry hump her/him(simulate intercourse)? _____

   Put your penis where? On her/his chest _____ On her/his crotch area (not in) _____
   In her vagina _____ On her/his rear end (not in)_____ In her/his rear end _____
   In her/his mouth _____ Other _____

   Insert any objects in her/his vagina or anus _____ What? _____

6. Did you think the victims wanted to do it? _____ If so, why did you think so? _____

7. Did any victims ask you to stop? _____ Whimper or cry? _____

   Did it surprise you? _____

   Why did you stop? _____

   Why didn't you do more?_____

8. Did you have an erection (penis get hard)? _____ Did you ejaculate (come)? _____

9. What did you say to your victims so they wouldn't tell? Threaten to hurt victim _____
   Threaten to kill victim _____ Threaten to hurt or kill victim's parent _____
   Threaten to hurt or kill a brother or sister of the victim _____ Show victim a weapon _____
   Threaten to tell the victim's mother or father _____ Tell victim she/he was bad _____
   Other _____

10. If you were alone with any victim, would you be tempted to repeat the offense?_____

    Do you know anyone similar to the victims who would tempt you to do the same? _____

    Are you ever alone around that person? _____ Who is the person? _____

    What would you do if you were left alone with that person? _____

Part 4

Adult Treatment Issues

The heterogeneity of the sex offender population has been discussed earlier in this volume. Even excluding children, adolescents, females, and individuals with disabilities or cultural differences, we are still left with a widely diverse group. These adult sex offenders vary, for example, in the degree of violence they demonstrate, the deviance that motivates them, their degree of criminality or psychopathy, and their motivation for treatment. They are in the criminal justice system—pretrial, presentence, incarcerated, on probation or parole, or involuntarily committed. Placement may determine how motivated they will be for treatment and the time they can devote to it. Sex offenders living in different locations may or may not be subjected to voluntary commitment, intrusive public notification, disproportionately long sentences, inadequate supervision, and opportunities for treatment.

It is unfortunate that when the U.S. Congress hands down a mandate for all states, it deals with an untried and uninterested approach to management: public notification. It could have made federal block grants contingent upon establishing the containment approach for managing this population, thereby ensuring treatment, specialized supervision, and the use of polygraphy.

In determining how to respond to the numerous needs of adult sex offenders in the myriad environments in which we find them, we need all the tools and techniques we can muster. We also need research to show which models are most effective.

The current thinking is that cognitive-behavioral techniques work best. However, how many systems have actually used only cognitive-behavioral techniques? And which cognitive techniques did they use: that of Yochelson and Samenow? relapse prevention? dialectical behavioral treatment? reasoning and rehabilitation? Did these programs use a variety of other techniques at the same time and how much of their success is attributable to these other modalities. Personally knowing many of the most studied programs, this author can attest that issues are not as clearly defined as we may think.

In addition, there is a dearth of research on community-based programs. These programs may be situated in private practices with one or two therapists who may not have the inclination, time, resources, or access to criminal databases that would facilitate long-term follow-up. Moreover, they may not have the numbers needed for an adequate research sample. It will probably take a carefully planned federal research project that could compare and contrast different dynamics to give us some meaningful answers as to "what works" and "with whom"?

The vast majority of treatment with sex offenders is still conducted with adult males in either institutional or outpatient settings. Programs responding to the 2000 Safer Society survey identify themselves as being almost exclusively cognitive-behavioral in approach. Actually, this number has been influenced by the format of the questionnaire, which presents modalities in an either/or format. Therefore, one either does cognitive-behavioral treatment or relapse prevention or psychodynamic but not an integrated combination of all of the above. There is a whole other school of treating sexually inappropriate behavior that includes an addictions approach. It is unfortunate that these two schools of treatment are antagonistic toward each other because they can be quite complementary, as is demonstrated in the substance abuse field.

Although programs are consistently showing respectable treatment effects, therapists in this area should not be content to rest on their laurels but should be actively searching to improve their approaches. One area in which there does seem to be significant transformation is in the approach to confrontation. Most treatment programs are moving away from the heavy-duty confrontation that evolved from such substance abuse programs as Synanon or Delancey Street. Approaches such as motivational interviewing are being used as a positive approach to convincing a sex offender that it is in his best interest to change rather than scaring individuals into appearing to change. Techniques such as eye movement rapid desensitization (EMDR) and dialectical behavioral treatment are also being adapted for use with sex offenders. It is hoped that such adaptation and innovation will continue with this population.

Medical interventions are one of the oldest approaches to treating sex offenders ranging from physical castration to the use of a variety of medications. Erik B. Nelson, Cesar A. Soutello, Melissa P. DelBello, and Susan L. McElroy (Chapter 13) give a complete review of the research and use of cyproterone, medroxyprogesterone, LHRH agonists, and serotonergic antidepressants. Studying the efficacy of these pharmocological agents may eventually lead us to a better understanding of the etiology of sexually deviant behavior.

Steven Sawyer (Chapter 14) outlines how to do group therapy with adult sex offenders. After discussing a history of doing group therapy with forensic populations, he delineates the basic goals of this therapeutic modality. Among these goals are instilling hope, imparting information, helping the participant feel that he is not alone, developing empathy and altruism, and correctively recapitulating a functional family group, to name a few. This author has developed a way of assessing group functioning through the use of the Group Climate Questionnaire, which measures engagement, conflict, and avoidance. In addition, he discusses a variety of ethical considerations which can present very sticky issues with this population.

There has been an ongoing controversy between sex offender professionals as to whether sex offenders should be treated for their own victimization. In one camp are those therapists who believe that allowing sex offenders to discuss how they themselves were abused fosters a "poor me" attitude and interferes with the assumption of responsibility. In the other camp are therapists who point out that offenders who have been sexually abused may either deny the impact the abuse had on them, and therefore can deny the impact it has had on their victims, or may remain emotionally closed off from their own abuse and thus unable to experience the emotions of empathy or legitimate shame. Laurie Guidry (Chapter 15) presents a lengthy discussion of this controversy as well as a twelve-session modular approach to integrating sex offender treatment with treatment for the offender's own victimization. This is a tripartate model that focuses on (1) the revisioning, recontextualization, and renarration of the offender's own abuse; (2) understanding how abuse developed into abusing based on an understanding of sexualization, stigmatization, betrayal, and powerlessness; and (3) enhancing self-building techniques designed to improve self-regulation.

Sex offender treatment has adapted much from substance abuse treatment. Denise Hughes-Conlon (Chapter 16) presents a variety of techniques used with domestic abusers that can be used with sex offenders. These two problems have much more overlap than has previously been discussed. Often, because incest offenders appear to be relatively passive and even law abiding compared to the antisocial rapist, it has been assumed that the way they present in prison or outpatient therapy is the way they present in their personal life. However, this very social passivity may translate into tyranny in their homes, where family members are treated as chattel. Using some of the cycles that have been developed for batterers may be quite helpful to the sex offender therapist.

Chapter 13

The Psychopharmacological Treatment of Sex Offenders

by Erik B. Nelson, M.D., Cesar A. Soutullo, M.D., Melissa P. DelBello, M.D., and Susan L. McElroy, M.D.

Overview

The majority of treatment studies of sex offenders and patients with paraphilias has focused on the antiandrogens, and more recently selective serotonin reuptake inhibitors (SSRIs). Although preliminary, open data suggest that cyproterone acetate (CPA), medroxyprogesterone (MPA), gonadotropin-releasing hormone (GnRH) agonists, and SSRIs all may reduce the frequency and intensity of paraphilic urges and behaviors. Double-blind placebo-controlled studies have been performed with CPA and MPA with mixed results. Additional double-blind placebo-controlled studies are needed to evaluate the possible role of antiandrogens, GnRH agonists, SSRIs, and other psychotropic medications in patients with paraphilias.

Introduction

Sexual violence is an enormous public health problem. In 1993, 485,290 Americans were victims of rape or other sexual assaults (U.S. Bureau of Justice Statistics, 1996). That year there were 1,238 federal prisoners and 81,400 state prisoners sentenced for rape and other forms of sexual assault (U.S. Bureau of Justice Statistics, 1996). Moreover, each year, between 100,000 and 500,000 children are sexually molested by males, and it is estimated that 10–20% of children in the United States have been sexually molested by the age of 18 (U.S. Bureau of Justice Statistics, 1996). High rates of child molestation have also been reported in Canada, Australia, and Western Europe (Rösler & Witztum, 1998). For example, a general population survey of a random sample of 9,953 adults in Ontario, Canada found that 12.8% of females and 4.3% of males reported a history of childhood sexual abuse (MacMillan, Fleming, & Trocme, 1997).

Differential Diagnosis of Sexual Offending Behavior

Extensive research has documented a relationship between violent crime and mental illness (Hodgins, 1992, 1998; Hodgins, Mednick, Brennan, Schulsinger, & Engberg, 1996; Marzuk, 1996; Monahan & Steadman, 1994; Swanson, 1993; Swanson, Holzer, Ganju, & Jono, 1990; Tiihonen, Isohanni, Rasanen, Koiranen, & Moring, 1997; Volavka, 1999). Specifically, studies have demonstrated elevated rates of violent behavior and violent crime among persons in the community with psychotic disorders, mood disorders (especially bipolar disorder), substance use disorders, and antisocial personality disorder. Conversely, elevated rates of psychotic, mood, substance use, and personality disorders have been found among persons who commit violent crimes. However, very little systematic research has examined the relationship between sexual violence and mental illness, including few systematic studies of the psychiatric diagnoses of persons who commit sexual crimes. Nonetheless, available studies suggest (discussed later) that a substantial proportion of sex offenders may have a wide range of psychiatric disorders. These disorders include paraphilias, substance use disorders, mood disorders, psychotic disorders, and personality/conduct disorders (Becker, Kaplan, Tenke, & Tartaglini, 1991; Bradford & McLean, 1984; Dietz, Hazelwood, & Warren, 1990; Galli et al., 1999; Grossman & Cavanaugh, 1990; Henn, Herjanic, & Vanderpearl, 1976; Kavoussi, Kaplan, & Becker, 1988; Langevin et al., 1988; Lewis, Shankok, & Pincus, 1979; McElroy et al., 1999; Packard & Rosner, 1985). Sexual aggression and/or paraphilias may also be related to mental retardation or brain trauma in some cases (Goldberg & Buongiorno, 1982).

Growing research suggests that many persons who commit sexual crimes in particular have paraphilias and mood disorders (Abel, 1989; Abel & Osborn, 1992; Black, Kehrberg, Flumerfelt, & Schlosser, 1997; Bradford & Wiseman, 1995; McElroy et al., 1998). For instance, Raymond, Coleman, Ohlerking, Christenson, and

Miner (1999) interviewed forty-five pedophiles using the Structured Clinical Interview for DSM-IV (SCID) and found that 67% had met criteria for a mood disorder in their lifetime. Similarly, in our ongoing study of psychiatric disorders in convicted sex offenders, we found that 75 of 104 (72%) patients met criteria according to the fourth edition of *Diagnostic and Statistical Manual for Mental Disorders* (DSM-IV; American Psychiatric Association, 1994) for a paraphilia, and 61 (59%) met DSM-IV lifetime criteria for a mood disorder; 36% of the patients met lifetime criteria for a DSM-IV bipolar disorder. Moreover, the presence of a paraphilia was associated with the presence of a mood disorder: 68% of sex offenders with a paraphilia had a comorbid mood disorder, compared with only 23% of sex offenders without a paraphilia. The rate of bipolar disorder was quite high among the paraphilic sex offenders compared with the nonparaphilic offenders: 41% versus 14% ($p < .05$ by Fisher's exact test).

Available studies also suggest that alcohol and substance use disorders are particularly common among sex offenders. In their study of forty-five pedophilic sex offenders, Raymond et al. (1999) found that 60% had a lifetime diagnosis of a substance use disorder. In our study of 104 sex offenders, 85 (82%) had a lifetime alcohol or drug use disorder (McElroy, 2000). Indeed, some authorities have argued that paraphilias should be viewed as sexual addictions.

Another group of disorders reported to be common in sex offenders are the cluster B and C personality disorders in adults and conduct disorder in adolescents. Raymond et al. (1999) diagnosed a cluster B personality disorder in 33% of their population of forty-five pedophilic sex offenders. In our study of 104 sex offenders, we found that 80 (77%) had a cluster B personality disorder and 29 (28%) had a cluster C disorder. Conversely, data suggest that persons with borderline and antisocial personality disorders may have elevated rates of paraphilias and other disturbances of sexual behavior (Virkkunen, 1976). In a study of the sexual histories of eighty patients who met DSM-III criteria (American Psychiatric Association, 1980) for borderline personality disorder, Zubenko, George, Soloff, and Schulz (1987) reported that nine (11%) had paraphilias.

Finally, sexual aggression and/or paraphilias may also be related to mental retardation, brain trauma, dementia, temporal lobe seizures and medical treatments in some cases (Blumer & Migeon, 1975; Bradford & Pawlak, 1987; Cooper, 1987; Fernandez & Durso, 1998; Goldberg & Buongiorno, 1982; Hodgins, 1992; Leo & Kim, 1995; MacKnight & Rojas-Fernandez, 2000; Myers, 1991; Wiseman, McAuley, Freidenberg, & Freidenberg, 2000).

Understanding the relationships among sexual offending behavior, paraphilias, mood disorders, addictions, personality, and brain function may have important implications for the medical as well as psychological treatment of persons who commit sexual crimes. The psychopharmacological treatment of sex offenders must therefore address the treatment of paraphilias and other potential comorbid psychiatric, neurological, and medical conditions.

Paraphilias

Definition of Paraphilias. Paraphilias are defined in DSM-IV as "sexual disorders with recurrent, intense, sexually arousing fantasies, sexual urges, or behaviors generally involving 1) non-human objects, 2) the suffering or humiliation of oneself or one's partner, or 3) children, or non-consenting persons" (American Psychiatric Association, 1994, p. 522–523). These include exhibitionism, fetishism, frotteurism, pedophilia, sexual masochism, sexual sadism, transvestic fetishism, voyeurism, and paraphilia not otherwise specified (NOS) (i.e., telephone scatologia, necrophilia, partialism, zoophilia, coprophilia, klismaphilia, urophilia, biastophilia, and ephebophilia). There is considerable controversy over whether rape is a paraphilia. We would classify compulsive or serial rapists as having the DSM-IV diagnosis of paraphilia NOS as they have recurrent, intense, sexually arousing fantasies, sexual urges and/or sexual behaviors that involved nonconsenting persons. Many rapists would meet the criteria of sexual sadism as well, as they are frequently aroused by the suffering or humiliation of their victim.

The onset of paraphilic behaviors is usually during adolescence, and individuals usually suffer from multiple paraphilias (Abel & Osborn, 1992). Nonparaphilic sexual addictions (NPSAs), also called compulsive sexual behaviors, sexual compulsions, or paraphilia-related disorders, are not included in DSM-IV as formal mental disorders, but are examples of sexual disorder NOS (Black et al., 1997; Kafka, 1995). They include compulsive masturbation, compulsive sexual promiscuity, telephone scatologia, dependence on pornography/sexual accessories to achieve or maintain sexual arousal, or severe partner incompatibility due to increased sexual desire. Although paraphilias and NPSAs differ in the degree of deviance of the associated sexual fantasies or behaviors, there is considerable overlap between these two conditions, as many persons with paraphilias also have NPSAs (Kafka, 1994a).

Relationship of Paraphilias to Other Mental Disorders. Preliminary data on comorbidity, phenomenology, and treatment response suggest that paraphilias may be related to other major psychiatric disorders, including mood, obsessive-compulsive, impulse control, and substance use disorders. The overlap of paraphilias and mood disorders has been discussed. Patients with paraphilias have also been reported to have apparently high rates of anxiety, impulse control, and substance use disorders. Regarding phenomenological similarities, the sexual fantasies and behaviors associated with paraphilias and NPSA are often experienced as compulsive, uncontrollable, or irresistible, as are the obsessions and compulsions in obsessive-compulsive disorder (OCD), the impulses and behaviors in impulse control disorders (ICDs), and the cravings and substance use behaviors in substance use disorders (Pearson, 1990; Perilstein, Lipper, & Friedman, 1991; Zohar, Kaplan, & Benjamin, 1994). Moreover, paraphilic impulses are often associated with anxiety, tension, or depressed mood similar to major depression, and paraphilic behaviors may be associated with euphoria that resembles hypomania (Croughan, Saghir, Cohne, & Robins, 1981).

Goal of Treatment of Paraphilias. The goal of pharmacotherapy of paraphilias according to various authorities, including the American Psychiatric Association Task Force on Sexually Dangerous Offenders (1999), is to reduce and/or eliminate the intensity and frequency of deviant sexual fantasies and behaviors without significantly reducing normal sexual thoughts and behavior. For patients with NPSA, the aim would be similar with the distinction that psychopharmacological treatment would decrease the severity of excessive, nondeviant sexual fantasies and behaviors.

Psychopharmacological Treatment of Paraphilias and NPSA

Specific guidelines for the pharmacotherapy of sex offenders and patients with paraphilias do not presently exist due to the lack of controlled clinical trials in these populations. There are no medications currently approved by the U.S. Food and Drug Administration (FDA) for the treatment of paraphilias, sexual aggression, or NPSAs. The majority of clinical trials performed to date have evaluated various antiandrogens in persons (primarily men) who have committed sexual crimes, many of whom also have paraphilias (Bradford & Pawlak, 1993a; Cooper, 1981; Wincze, Bansal, & Malamud, 1986). Many of these trials suggest antiandrogens reduce the deviant fantasies and behaviors of paraphilias. Open-label studies suggest that patients seeking treatment for these disorders may respond to agents effective in mood disorders, OCDs, and ICDs, such as antidepressants (particularly SSRIs) (Federoff, 1993; Greenberg, Bradford, Curry, & O'Rourke, 1996a, 1996b; Kafka, 1991a, 1991b, 1994b; Kafka & Prentky, 1992), but also to antipsychotic agents and mood stabilizers (Cesnik & Coleman, 1989; Kafka, 1991b; Ward, 1975). However, most of the studies in this population are limited due to being uncontrolled and small sample sizes.

Antiandrogen Therapy

Androgens. Androgens are male sex hormones, with testosterone being the principal androgen (Griffin & Wilson, 1998). It is produced mostly by the testicles but also in smaller amounts by the adrenal glands. Its behavioral effects include the promotion of sex drive, assertiveness, and aggression in men and women (Berlin & Meinecke, 1981), and, in men, sexual arousal, orgasm, and ejaculation (Rubinow & Schmidt, 1996). Secondary physical sex characteristics are maintained by its metabolite dihydrotestosterone (DHT). Other effects of testosterone include promoting growth hormone secretion, enhancing dopaminergic and noradrenergic neurotransmission, and reducing serotonergic and opioid neurotransmission (Rubinow & Schmidt, 1996).

Substantial evidence suggests that androgens are an essential biological determinant of sexual desire in humans (Berlin & Meinecke, 1981; Segraves, 1988). Men with low testosterone levels due to gonadal hypofunction or castration show reduced sexual interest and activity, which are normalized with exogenous testosterone and restoration of testosterone levels. Withdrawal of exogenous testosterone in such men results in a rapid decrease in sexual interest and activity. Sexual desire is reestablished within a few weeks of restarting replacement therapy (Davidson, Kwan, & Greenleaf, 1982; Kwan, Greenleaf, Mann, Crapo, & Davidson, 1983; Skakkebaek, Bancroft, Davidson, & Warner, 1981).

The role of androgens in human sexual aggression is presently unclear. Some reports (Raboch, Cerna, & Zemek, 1984), but not all (Bradford & McLean, 1984), describe elevated serum testosterone in some sexually aggressive men, and altered testosterone levels are often associated with changes in libido (Berlin & Meinecke, 1981). Indeed, some investigators have argued against the importance of testosterone in the etiology of sexual aggression, noting that the broad individual differences in testosterone levels seen in samples of normal adult men are unrelated to individual variations in sexual drive or behavior (Schiavi & Segraves, 1995).

Castration has been used to treat sex offenders with and without paraphilias. The rationale for this procedure is that deviant sexual behavior may be caused or facilitated by testosterone, as variations in testosterone may be associated with alterations in libido and sexual behavior (Berlin & Meinecke, 1981). Follow-up studies evaluating recidivism rates for castrated sex offenders, in whom testosterone is nearly completely and irreversibly abolished, have found a range between 2.3% and 4.1% over six weeks to twenty years, compared with 75% to 80% over this time frame in untreated sex offenders (Greenberg & Bradford, 1997). However, important questions about the methodology of these studies, as well as the ethics of this procedure, have been raised by other authors (Heim & Hursch, 1979).

Antiandrogens are medications that block the synthesis or action of androgens (Griffin & Wilson, 1998) and, thus, are alternatives to surgical castration for reducing sexual drive and sexual deviant behaviors (Richer & Crismon, 1993). Treatment studies of antiandrogens for paraphilias and sexual offending behavior are reviewed later.

Cyproterone Acetate. CPA, a synthetic steroid that is structurally similar to progesterone, has been shown to possess antiandrogenic, antigonadotropic, and progestational effects. Specifically, CPA inhibits intracellular uptake of testosterone by blocking the androgen receptor. It also inhibits the secretion of GnRH from the hypothalamus, and secretion of gonadotropins from the pituitary gland, thereby reducing serum levels of testosterone. Through these actions, CPA reversibly inhibits spermatogenesis and decreases ejaculate volume (Rösler & Witztum, 2000).

Studies of CPA in patients with deviant sexual behavior have included four case reports (Bradford & Pawlak, 1987; Cooper, Cernovsky, & Magnus, 1992; Cooper, Ismail, Phanjoo, & Love, 1972; Van Moffaert, 1976) ($N = 5$); eight case series (Baron & Unger, 1977; Bártová, Buresová, Hajnová, Náhunek, & Svestka, 1984; Berner, Brownstone, & Sluga, 1983; Bradford & Pawlak, 1993b; Davies, 1974; Laschet & Laschet, 1971; Ortmann, 1980) ($N = 252$, range 10–110); one double-blind comparison to ethinyl estradiol (Bancroft, Tennent, Loucas, & Cass, 1974) and three double-blind, placebo-controlled studies (Bradford & Pawlak, 1993a; Cooper, 1981; Cooper, Sandhu, Losztyn, & Cernovsky, 1992). Table 13.1 summarizes all the open-label trials with ten or more subjects and all of the controlled trials that were available for our review. These reports describe the treatment of persons with paraphilias, NPSA, and/or sexual offending behaviors (Baron & Unger, 1977; Bártová et al., 1984; Berner et al., 1983; Bradford & Pawlak, 1993b; Cooper et al., 1972; Cooper et al., 1992; Davies, 1974; Laschet & Laschet, 1971; Ortmann, 1980). Various measures were used to assess response, including intensity and frequency of paraphilic fantasies and behaviors (Davies, 1974), testosterone levels (Bradford & Pawlak, 1993b), sexual drive (Baron & Unger, 1977; Laschet & Laschet, 1971), and changes in penile tumescence in response to evocative stimuli (Bártová et al., 1984; Bradford & Pawlak, 1993b). Response rates in the case series ranged from 60% (Baron & Unger, 1977) to 100% (Laschet & Laschet, 1971) using CPA doses from 50–200 mg/day. Durations of treatment in these studies ranged from two months (Bradford & Pawlak, 1993) to four years (Laschet & Laschet, 1971) with relapse rates ranging from zero (Ortmann, 1980) to 28% (Berner et al., 1983). One double-blind study compared CPA to ethinyl estradiol in a crossover design (Bancroft et al., 1974). In this study, twelve sex offenders were treated with either 100 mg of CPA or ethinyl estradiol for a period of six weeks and then crossed

**Table 13.1
CPA Studies (Trials With $N \geq 10$ and Controlled Trials)**

Author	Drug/Dose	Population	N	Design	Duration	Variables	Results
Laschet, 1971	CPA 50–200 mg/day	50% were sex offenders; most with paraphilias or NPSA	110	Open-label	6–48 mos.	Not stated	All cases reported to have "reduced sexuality" which led to interruption of the "perverse cycle"
Baron, 1977	CPA 200 mg/day	Sex offenders	10	Open-label	12 mos.	Self-report of sexual behavior	All 6 completers reported decreased sexual interest and behavior during the trial
Davies, 1974	CPA 50–200 mg/day	"Sexually deviant" pts. (16 sex offenders)	50	Open-label	6 mos. to 3 yrs.	Self-report of deviant sexual behavior and fantasies	No sexual offenses committed by the sex offender group during treatment; decrease in sexual fantasy in pts. with paraphilia and NPSA; decreased deviant sexual behavior in pts. with SCZ and dementia
Berner, 1983	CPA 100 mg/day	Sex offenders	21	Open-label	1–2 yrs	Rearrest rate	28% rearrested (not stated if this was during or after CPA treatment)
Bradford & Pawlak, 1993b	CPA 50–200 mg/day	Sex offenders with pedophilia	20	Open-label	2–3 mos.	Penile tumescence testing in response to evocative stimuli	CPA significantly decreased penile response to evocative stimuli; response to deviant > than nondeviant stimuli
Bancroft, 1974	CPA 100 mg/day and ethinyl estradiol	Inpatient sex offenders	12	Double-blind crossover comparison to ethinyl estradiol	36 wks.	Self-report of sexual interest and frequency of sexual acts; phallometric and self report measures of response to evocative stimuli	Significant decrease in sexual interest and frequency with drug treatment compared to no treatment phase, phallometric eval. showed significant decrease with CPA only
Cooper, 1981	CPA 100 mg/day	Outpts., most with paraphilias, some sex offenders	9	Double-blind, placebo-controlled crossover	4 wks. of both CPA and PLC	Rating of pts.' self-report of intensity of sexual thoughts and excitement during masturbation; frequency of sexual behavior	CPA > PLC on all parameters
Cooper, 1992	CPA 100–200 mg/day and MPA 100–200 mg/day	Sex offenders with pedophilia	7	Double-blind, placebo-controlled crossover comparison to MPA	28 wks.	Self-report of sexual behavior and fantasies; record of sexual behavior observed by nursing staff; phallometric measures of response to evocative stimuli	Trend toward decrease in sexual arousal on all measures with both MPA and CPA compared to placebo
Bradford & Pawlak, 1993a	CPA 50–200 mg	Outpts. with paraphilias, mostly sex offenders	19	Double-blind, placebo-controlled crossover	12 mos.	Self-report of sexual behavior and fantasies; phallometric and self report measures of response to evocative stimuli	CPA decreased deviant sexual fantasies and measures of penile response to evocative stimuli compared to baseline, but change not significant compared to PLC

CPA = cyproterone acetate; PLC = placebo; MPA = medroxyprogesterone acetate.

over to the other treatment. Patients were also evaluated during a six-week no-treatment phase. Patients reported a significant decrease in overall sexual interest and frequency of sexual acts with both drugs compared to no treatment but improved on phallometric measures of response to evocative stimuli with CPA treatment only.

In the first controlled study, nineteen sex offenders who met DSM-III-R (American Psychiatric Association, 1987) criteria for a paraphilia (twelve with pedophilia) were treated with 50–200 mg/day of CPA in a double-blind, placebo-controlled, crossover design (four alternating three-month periods on placebo or CPA). Compared to baseline, CPA decreased sexual arousal to evocative stimuli as measured by self-report, but did not decrease arousal compared to the placebo phase (Bradford & Pawlak, 1993a). Moreover, no significant difference was seen between CPA and placebo on penile tumescence measures. CPA treatment was, however, associated with significantly reduced overall sexual activity, total Brief Psychiatric Rating Scales (BPRS) scores, and testosterone and follicular stimulating hormone (FSH) levels compared with placebo treatment. In the second study, nine outpatients with hypersexuality and/or "sexual-acting-out" behaviors with social and/or legal implications were treated in a twenty-week double-blind, placebo-controlled crossover trial with CPA 100 mg/day or placebo (four-week periods of CPA or placebo separated by four-week periods of no treatment) (Cooper, 1981). Outcome measures were frequency of sexual activity, overall sexual interest, number of spontaneous daytime erections, and level of excitement during masturbation. CPA significantly reduced sexual interest and patients' rating of their level of physiological arousal during masturbation compared with placebo and no treatment. However, CPA affected sexual arousal more than the intensity of interest in deviant sexual objects. The third study was a double-blind, placebo-controlled, crossover trial of CPA (100 mg and 200 mg), MPA (100 mg and 200 mg), and placebo in seven patients with DSM-III-R pedophilia (Cooper, Cernovsky, & Magnus, 1992). Although the sample size was too small to evaluate statistically, trends were seen toward both agents reducing overall sexual fantasies, frequency of morning erections, frequency and pleasure of masturbation, and intensity of sexual frustration compared with placebo. Deviant and nondeviant sexual fantasies were not evaluated separately in this study. Penile response to evocative stimuli was reduced as well, although somewhat less consistently. Also, sexual arousal appeared to be affected equally by CPA and MPA. Side effects seen with CPA include gynecomastia, weight gain, thromboembolism, depression, and, rarely, hepatic toxicity (Rösler & Witztum, 2000).

Summary of CPA Studies. In summary, four case reports and eight case series all suggest that CPA is effective in decreasing testosterone levels, sexual desire, sexual arousal, and sexual behavior in a dose range of 50–200 mg in sex offenders, most with various paraphilias. The results of three double-blind, placebo-controlled studies and one double-blind comparison study of CPA for the deviant sexual fantasies and behaviors of paraphilias, however, are mixed with only one study (Cooper, 1981) clearly showing statistically significant improvement on all measures used. Limitations of many of these studies include small sample sizes, the inclusion of heterogeneous diagnostic groups, lack of structured clinical interviews and assessment measures, variable durations of treatment (range: five weeks to three years), confounding effect of concomitant psychotherapy, and the questionable validity of patients' self-reports of sexual symptoms (e.g., no study used polygraphy to validate patients' responses).

Medroxyprogesterone Acetate. MPA is a progestogenic agent that possesses strong antigonadotropic activity. It has been shown to suppress FSH and luteinizing hormone (LH) release from the pituitary gland, thus reducing the secretion of testosterone from the testes (Rösler & Witztum, 2000). Reduction of testosterone to castration levels occurs within weeks of initiating high-dose therapy (Rösler & Witztum, 2000). Erectile and ejaculatory capacity, along with sexual drive, generally return to baseline within seven to ten days of discontinuation of MPA (Money, 1987).

Numerous case reports describe the successful use of MPA in the treatment of sex offenders and patients with paraphilias (Cordoba & Chapel, 1983; Lehne, 1984–1986; Myers, 1991; Pinta, 1978; Spodak, Falck, & Rappeport, 1978). Case reports also describe successful MPA treatment of patients with aberrant sexual activity associated with mental retardation (Ross, Bland, Ruskin, & Bacher, 1987) and hypersexuality associated with dementia (Cooper, 1987). Four small case series (total $N = 33$) with small number ($N < 17$) ($N = 78$, range 8–17) describe MPA treatment of patients with paraphilias (Blumer & Migeon, 1975; Gottesman & Schubert, 1993; Kravitz, Haywood, Kelly, Liles, & Cavanaugh, 1996; Money, Wiedeking, Walker, & Gain, 1976). In these studies, patients received MPA in a dosage range of 60 mg/day (oral dose) to 900 mg/week (injectable dose) for a duration of two to fifty-five months. Between 85% (Kravitz et al., 1996) and 100% (Blumer & Migeon, 1975; Gottesman & Schubert, 1993; Money et al., 1976) of the patients reported a positive response to MPA variously described by reduced frequency of paraphilic fantasies and behaviors, decreased frequency of erections and ejaculations, and reduced level of sexual arousal.

Seven open case series have evaluated larger numbers of patients with paraphilias ($N > 20$ each; total $N = 217$), patients with sexually deviant behaviors, or sex offenders, many with paraphilias (Berlin & Coyle, 1981; Fedoroff, Winser-Carlson, Dean, & Berlin, 1992; Gagne, 1981; Kravitz et al., 1995; McConaghy, Blaszczynski, & Kidson, 1988; Meyer, Cole, & Emory, 1992; Money & Bennett, 1981), treated with MPA. Table 13.2 (on pages 13-10 and 13-11) summarizes all the open-label trials with ten or more subjects and all the controlled trials that were available for our review. MPA dosages in these reports ranged from 100 to 1,000 mg/week and treatment durations from three months to twelve years. Three of these open studies included a non-randomly assigned control group of sex offenders who did not receive MPA during their treatment (Fedoroff et al., 1992; McConaghy et al., 1988; Meyer et al., 1992). Taken together, these studies reported decreases in paraphilic urges and/or behaviors sexual arousal, and testosterone levels, as well as improvement in psychosocial functioning with MPA treatment. Rates of relapse of offending behavior ranged from 3 to 50% for MPA-treated subjects compared with 58 to 68% for control subjects (Fedoroff et al., 1992; Kravitz et al., 1995; Meyer et al., 1992; Money & Bennett, 1981). However, one study found no significant difference in response among three groups of sex offenders treated with MPA alone, MPA plus imaginal desensitization therapy (ID), or ID alone (McConaghy et al., 1988). In another study, risk factors for reoffending in MPA-treated patients included high baseline plasma testosterone levels, exhibitionism, active substance abuse, and history of head injury (Meyer et al., 1992).

It is important to note, however, that the results of the five double-blind, placebo-controlled studies on the treatment of sex offenders with MPA are mixed as compared to the largely positive findings in these open studies. In the first double-blind, placebo-controlled trial, Langevin, Paitch, Hucker, Newman, and Ramsay (1979) random-

Table 13.2
MPA Studies (Trials With $N \geq 10$ and Controlled Trials)

Author	Drug/Dose	Population	N	Design	Duration	Variables	Results
Money, 1976	MPA 100–400 mg/wk i.m.	Sex offenders with paraphilia	10	Open-label	6–35 mos.	Self-report of sexual behavior and fantasies	All pts. reported at least 50% decrease in erections and sexual behavior
Gagné, 1981	MPA 200–600 mg/wk i.m.	Sex offenders, some with paraphilias	48	Open-label	12 mos.	Self-report of sexual behavior and fantasies	40 pts. reported a decrease in deviant sexual fantasies and behaviors
Money, 1981 Berlin, 1981	MPA 75–600 mg/wk i.m.	Sex offenders with paraphilias, mostly pedophilia	20	Open-label follow-up to Money, 1976	3–69 mos.	Relapse rate of offending behavior based on patient interview and collateral data	3 out of 6 pts. relapsed while on MPA; 6 out of 9 relapsed within 1 yr. off MPA, 4 out of 5 relapsed after more than 1 yr.
McConaghy, 1988	MPA 150 mg per 2–4 wks. i.m.	Sex offenders, 22 with paraphilias	30	Open-label comparison of MPA, imaginal desensitiza- tion (ID) and MPA + ID	6 mos.	Self-report of sexual behavior and fantasies	No significant difference between the 3 groups; 16 out of 20 pts. who received MPA responded
Fedoroff, 1992	MPA 300–500 mg/wk i.m.	Outpatient sex offend- ers with paraphilias	46	Open-label chart review	> 5 yrs.	Relapse of sexual offending during outpt. treatment program	4 out of 27 (15%) pts. relapsed on MPA; 13 out of 19 (68%) not treated with MPA relapsed (p < .01)
Meyer, 1992	MPA 300-800 mg/wk i.m.	Outpatient sex offend- ers with paraphilias	40	Open-label chart review, pts. treated with MPA vs. non-ran- dom con- trol group	6 mos. to 12 yrs.	Self-report of sexual behavior and fantasies; reoffense rate	39 out of 40 (98%) pts. reported decrease in sex drive with most reporting increased control over deviant urges; 7 out of 40 (18%) reoffended while on MPA; 12 out of 21 controls (58%) reoffended
Kravitz, 1995	MPA 150–1000 mg/wk i.m.	Sex offenders with paraphilias	29	Open-label	6 mos.	Self-report of sexual behavior and fantasies; reoffense rate	All pts. reported complete remission of deviant fantasies during treatment; one pt. relapsed during the 6-month trial
Kravitz, 1996	MPA 158–900 mg/wk i.m.	Outpatient sex offend- ers with paraphilias	13	Open-label	1–55 mos.	Self-report of deviant sexual behavior	85% of pts. reported no deviant fantasies or behavior while on MPA treatment; 62% continued to have non- deviant fantasies

ly treated eight exhibitionists with 100 mg of MPA or placebo for fourteen days and then crossed them over to the other treatment condition. A significant difference between placebo and MPA was seen for patients' self report of level of sexual arousal only. No difference between the two treatment arms was found when patients were

**Table 13.2
(Continued)**

Author	Drug/Dose	Population	N	Design	Duration	Variables	Results
Buresová, 1990	MPA 200–400 mg per 2 wks, diethyl-stilbestrol 6.25–27.5 mg	Pts., mostly with paraphilia	11	Double-blind crossover comparison to diethyl-stilbestrol	12 mos.	Sexual activity; penile response on plethys-mography	Significant decrease in sexu-al activity with MPA and DES; no change in plethys-mography
Langevin, 1979	MPA 100 mg/day	Sex offenders with exhibitionism	8	Double-blind, placebo-controlled crossover	14 days	Objective penile response to evocative stimuli measured with plethysmography; 5 point self-report arousal scale	No difference MPA vs. PLC with pleth.; Signif. improve-ment (MPA > PLC) on verbal report (p < .05)
Wincze, 1986	MPA 160 mg/day	Sex offenders with pedophilia	3	Double-blind, placebo-controlled crossover	79–119 days	Self-report of sexual behavior and deviant urges; subjective arousal to evocative stimuli; penile response to evocative stimuli measured with plethys-mography	2 pts. reported decreased urges on PLC, while only 1 pt. on MPA; all reported decreased arousal to stimuli (MPA > PLC); but none showed response to MPA with plethysmography
Hucker, 1988	MPA 200 mg/day	Sex offenders with pedophilia	18	Double-blind, placebo-controlled trial	3 mos.	Sexual fantasies; frequency of masturbation; measure of arousal by plethys-mography; frequency of erections and orgasm	Only significant change was decrease in fantasies with MPA; 7 pts. dropped out of trial
Kiersch, 1990	MPA 100-400 mg/wk i.m.	Sex offenders, most with pedophilia	8	Double-blind, placebo-controlled crossover	22–64 wks.	Patient self-report of deviant fantasies and masturbation; objective penile response to evocative stimuli mea-sured with plethysmog-raphy	Only 1 out of 5 pts. respond-ed to MPA and not PLC; deception suspected
Cooper, 1992	MPA 100-200 mg/day, CPA 100-200 mg/day	Inpatient sex offend-ers with pedophilia	7	Double-blind, placebo-controlled crossover comparison to CPA	28 wks.	Self-report of sexual behavior and fantasies; record of sexual behav-ior observed by nursing staff; phallometric mea-sures of response to evocative stimuli	Trend toward decreased sex-ual arousal on all measures on both MPA and CPA com-pared to placebo
CPA = cyproterone acetate		MPA = medroxyprogesterone acetate			PLC = placebo		

tested using plethysmography. In the second controlled study, Wincze et al. (1986) treated three men with pedophilia with oral MPA 160 mg/day (thirty to fifty-six days total) and placebo (thirty-five to fifty-six days total) in a crossover design. Two of three subjects on placebo and only one of three on MPA reported significant reduc-tion in deviant urges, and no subject had increased urges during the final placebo phase during which MPA was discontinued. During the MPA treatment phase, all three subjects had decreased subjective arousal to target stimuli. However, only one patient had decreased erections in response to stimuli in the laboratory setting. This study suggests that the validity of self-report scales is questionable in this population, as there was less evidence of decreased arousal in laboratory settings than was reported on subjective measures, and because patients were just as likely to report decreased arousal on placebo as when they were on MPA

In the third controlled trial, eighteen sex offenders with pedophilia were randomly assigned to treatment with MPA 200 mg/day or placebo for three months (Hucker, Langevin, & Bain, 1988). The only significant change observed was a decrease in sexual fantasies with MPA compared to placebo. Deviant and nondeviant sexual fantasies, however, were not evaluated separately in this study. There was no significant difference in the frequency of sexual activity or in the frequency or intensity of erections between drug and placebo.

In the fourth controlled trial, eight "hard core" sex offenders (pedophiles, $N = 6$; rapists, $N = 2$) were treated with MPA 100–400 mg intramuscularly per week and placebo (saline injections) in alternating sixteen-week periods (Kiersch, 1990). Four subjects completed the sixty-four-week study, whereas the remaining four completed only twenty-two to thirty-four weeks. Five patients in this study reported a decrease in deviant fantasies from baseline while on MPA. However, this was not substantiated by the measurements of these patients' responses to evocative stimuli using plethysmography. Moreover, all but one of the five patients who reported a response to MPA also reported responding to the saline injections. Pedophiles reported decreased sexual drive and reduction in deviant fantasies, but children continued to be their primary sexual object. The authors concluded that subjects reported "what they felt were desirable responses," and that self-report measures were inaccurate and misleading in this group. A limitation of this study is that the long half-life of MPA in the depot injectable form may also have contributed to the high response to placebo, as any therapeutic effect of MPA may have continued into the placebo phases.

As discussed earlier, in the fifth controlled study, MPA and CPA were found to be equally effective in reducing overall sexual fantasies, morning erections, and masturbation in seven patients with DSM-III-R paraphilias with a trend toward superiority over placebo for both drugs (Cooper, Sandhu, et al., 1992). Penile responses to evocative stimuli were also decreased with active drug treatment, but not as consistently as the subjective measures of sexual arousal. The authors concluded that the effects of both MPA and CPA in lowering sexual drive could be overridden by "powerful evocative stimuli." They hypothesized that this effect might not be particularly important in clinical practice, as only a moderate reduction of sexual interest may be needed to help patients resist committing sexual offenses. Finally, a double-blind, crossover comparison of MPA 200–400 mg/week and diethylstilbestrol showed a decrease in sexual activity from baseline with both drugs, but no changes on measures performed with plethysmography (Buresová, Bártová, & Svestka, 1990).

Summary of MPA Studies. In summary, we found at least thirteen case reports, twelve case series, and five placebo-controlled studies that evaluated sex offenders treated with MPA. The results from open reports, some with large numbers of patients treated over long periods, appear promising, with reduction in paraphilic behaviors, recidivism, and relapse rates with MPA doses up to 160mg/day orally or 100–400 mg/week intramuscularly. However, these results have only been partially replicated in the limited number of controlled studies available to date. Four out of five placebo-controlled studies showed decreases in verbal reports of sexual symptoms (three with statistically significant difference from placebo), but only one of these studies reported efficacy on more objective measures (i.e., plethysmography). Moreover, as with the data on CPA, significant limitations decrease the power of many of these studies' findings. These limitations include small sample sizes, inclusion of heterogeneous diagnostic groups, lack of structured clinical interviews, variable length of treatment, possible confounding effect of concomitant psychotherapy, and heterogeneous outcome measures.

Careful consideration should be given to the use of this drug given its side effect and compliance profile. Common side effects with MPA include weight gain, lethargy, depression, cold sweats, nightmares, dyspnea, hyperglycemia, hypoglycemia, and leg cramps. MPA lacks many of the feminizing effects of the estrogenic agents, although some of these may still occur. Rare but potentially fatal side effects of this drug include thrombosis and pulmonary embolism.

Gonadotropin-Releasing Hormone Agonists. Gonadotropin-releasing hormone (GnRH), also known as luteinizing hormone releasing hormone (LHRH), is a peptide released from the hypothalamus that triggers the release of LH, a gonadotropin, from the pituitary gland, as well as the release of FSH in women. LH stimulates gonadal testosterone production in men and regulates the menstrual cycle and other estrogen-related activities in women. GnRH also appears to act as a neurotransmitter in the central nervous system (Crenshaw & Goldberg, 1996). Chronic administration of GnRH agonists causes downregulation of receptors on gonadotropin-releasing cells in the pituitary, which causes a decrease in LH secretion. This, in turn, decreases the testicular secretion of testosterone, reaching castration levels with continuous dosing (Rösler & Witztum, 2000).

To date, there are no controlled studies of a GnRH agonist in sex offenders or patients with paraphilias. However, we found four case reports (Cooper & Cernovsky, 1994; Dickey, 1992; Rich & Ovsiew, 1994; Rousseau, Couture, Dupont, Labrie, & Couture, 1990) and two case series (Rösler & Witztum, 1998; Thibaut, Cordier, & Kuhn, 1993) reporting successful treatment of paraphilias and deviant sexual behaviors with GnRH agonists. In the single-case reports, patients with exhibitionism and pedophilia were reported to respond to the GnRH agonists ethylamide (Rousseau et al., 1990) and leuprolide (Cooper & Cernovsky, 1994; Dickey, 1992; Rich & Ovsiew, 1994) with significant decreases in sexually deviant behaviors (Dickey, 1992; Rich & Ovsiew, 1994; Rousseau et al., 1990) or fantasies (Cooper & Cernovsky, 1994) for twenty-four to twenty-six weeks. One of these reports was a controlled, crossover case study that showed a greater response to leuprolide than to both CPA and placebo (Cooper & Cernovsky, 1994). Yet another report included a patient who was treated with leuprolide in combination with flutamide, an androgen receptor antagonist (Rousseau et al., 1990). Another report described the successful treatment of a patient who had been refractory to CPA and MPA (Dickey, 1992).

Two case series describe the use of triptorelin 3.75 mg/month (Rösler & Witztum, 1998; Thibaut et al., 1993) in a total of 36 men with paraphilias for a range of six to

Table 13.3
GnRH Agonist Studies (Trials With $N \geq 5$)

Author	Drug/Dose	Population	N	Design	Duration	Variables	Results
Thibaut, 1996	Triptorelin 3.75 mg/mo i.m.	Inpts. with paraphilias; 4 sex offenders	6	Open-label	1–7 yrs	Self-report of sexual behavior and fantasies	5 out of 6 pts. reported decreased sexual activity and behavior and no deviant sexual behavior during treatment
Rösler, 1998	Triptorelin 3.75 mg/mo i.m.	Outpts. with paraphilia (mostly pedophilia); 16 were sex offenders	30	Open-label	8–42 mos.	Pts. self-report on Intensity of Sexual Desire and Symptoms Scale which measures sexual interest, activity, and fantasies	Complete resolution of paraphilic acts; significant decrease in score on Intensity of Sexual Desire and Symptoms Scale

42 months (see Table 13.3). The combined response rate in these studies was 97% for significantly reducing paraphilic urges and/or behaviors. In one study, thirty of thirty patients responded to triptorelin alone (Rösler & Witztum, 1998). All five patients who discontinued treatment during the study reported a return of deviant fantasies and/or behaviors. In the other study, five out of six patients responded to treatment with triptorelin (Thibaut et al., 1993). Triptorelin was given in combination with CPA for a portion of the trial in all six patients and for the entire duration of the trial in two patients. One of the two patients who discontinued treatment during the trial reported a return of deviant fantasies and behaviors. A significant reduction in testosterone levels was also reported in these studies.

Summary of GnRH Agonist Studies. Regarding GnRH agonists, four case reports and two case series have reported a total of forty patients with paraphilias, some of whom were sex offenders, successfully treated with triptorelin or leuprolide. However, these studies are limited by small sample sizes, combined use of LHRH agonists with other antiandrogens in some cases, and lack of controlled designs and objective physiological measures.

Summary of Antiandrogen Studies. Studies suggest that antiandrogens decrease both normal and deviant sexual arousal and sexual interest. This decrease appears to correlate with a decrease in paraphilic fantasies and behaviors. However, decreased sexual arousal in response to evocative stimuli has not been demonstrated in most controlled trials with antiandrogens, often contradicting the results based on patients' verbal reports from these same studies. Deceptiveness in this patient population is one explanation for this discrepancy. Other possible explanations are that evocative erotic stimuli override the effects of antiandrogens, or, as some data suggest, erections in response to these stimuli are not androgen-dependent (Rubinow & Schmidt, 1996). Moreover, it has not yet been shown that that these agents specifically decrease deviant more than nondeviant fantasies and behaviors. Some evidence suggests that these agents do not change the object of the patient's sexual interest and, thus, do not have the effect of "normalizing" the deviant sexual focus of patients with paraphilias.

Antidepressant Therapy

The rationale for treatment of paraphilias with antidepressants is severalfold. First, as discussed earlier, paraphilias are associated with affective symptoms and mood disorders (McElroy, Keck, Hudson, Phillips, & Strakowski, 1996; Raymond et al., 1999). Second, paraphilias resemble OCD and other obsessive-compulsive spectrum disorders—conditions which respond to SSRIs (Berlin, Malin, & Thomas, 1995). Third, preliminary evidence suggests a high level of comorbidity between paraphilias and other psychiatric disorders that respond to antidepressants, such as anxiety disorders other than OCD, ICDs, and substance use disorders (Galli et al., 1999; Galli, Raute, McConville, & McElroy, 1998; Kafka, 1991a; McElroy et al., 1999).

Since 1990, at least twenty case reports or series have been published describing a positive response of paraphilias, NPSAs, or sexual compulsions to treatment with antidepressants. Most of these reports describe treatment with an SSRI or the highly serotonergic tricyclic antidepressant clomipramine. All but one study (Stein et al., 1992) reported a clinically significant reduction of paraphilic symptoms with antidepressant treatment. However, all but two of these studies (Kruesi, Fine, Vallrdares, Phillips, & Rapoport, 1992; Zohar et al., 1994) are open reports (eleven single cases) or retrospective reviews.

Specifically, five case reports describe the use of fluoxetine (20–80 mg/day for two to six months) in seven men with paraphilias, with responses ranging from moderate to marked (for a list of trade names of drugs discussed in this chapter, see Exhibit 13.1, on page 13-30). One report describes the resolution of paraphilic behaviors in a man with schizophrenia and compulsive masturbation using fluoxetine (20–80 mg/day) and haloperidol (15 mg/day) (Kornreich, Den Dulk, Verbanck, & Pelc, 1995), and another describes the response of a man with OCD, dysthymia, pedophilia, and sexual sadism to fluoxetine and risperidone (Bourgeois & Klein, 1996). Clomipramine 50–250 mg/day succesfully reduced paraphilic symptoms in five cases of men with exhibitionism (Casals-Ariet & Cullen, 1993; Torres & Cerqueira, 1993; Wawrose & Sisto, 1992), one of whom had failed an eight-month fluoxetine trial (80 mg/day) (Casals-Ariet & Cullen, 1993).

There are six case series (sample sizes ranging from ten to ninety-five) describing the use of antidepressants in paraphilias and NPSAs (Table 13.4, on page 13-16, summarizes all the trials with ten or more subjects). Of twenty-four men with paraphilia ($N = 13$) or "paraphilia-related disorders" ($N = 11$) treated with open-label sertraline for at least four weeks (dose range 25–250 mg/day; mean dose 100 mg), eleven (45%) showed at least a 50% reduction in the total number of orgasms due to paraphilic behavior and the average time involved in paraphilic or paraphilia-related activities (Kafka, 1994b). Six (67%) of nine men who did not respond to sertraline in this study responded during an extension trial using fluoxetine (duration twelve to sixty weeks; dose range 10–80 mg/day; mean dose 50 mg). Overall, seventeen (71%) of twenty-four men who received at least four weeks of sertraline and/or fluoxetine sustained a clinically significant response, in some cases lasting more than one year. However, four men on sertraline required augmentation with methylphenidate 10–20 mg/day, trazodone 200 mg/day, or lithium 600 mg/day, and three men on fluoxetine required adjunctive methylphenidate (20–30 mg/day). A recent open-label trial in twenty-six patients with paraphilia or paraphilia-related disorders showed a signifi-

Table 13.4
Antidepressant Studies (Trials With $N \geq 10$)

Author	Drug/Dose	Population	N	Design	Duration	Variables	Results
Kruesi, 1992	CMI 75–250 mg vs. DMI 100-250 mg	Outpts. with paraphilias	15	Double-blind, crossover comparison	7 wks. (2 wks. PLC run-in)	Self-report of paraphilic behavior; "Obsessional features" of paraphilia rated on Leyton Obsessional Inventory	Significant improvement from baseline with both drugs; no statistically significant difference between the two
Stein, 1992	FLX 20–80 mg, FLV 200–300 mg, CMI 200–400 mg	Outpts. with paraphilias, NPSA, or sexual obsessions	13	Open-label, retrospective chart review	4 wks. to 12 mos.	Clinical Global Impressions change score for sexual symptoms	No improvement in all 5 pts. treated for paraphilia; moderate improvement in 2 out of 5 pts. with sexual addictions; moderate-marked improvement in 2 out of 3 pts. with sexual obsessions.
Kafka, 1994	SER 25–250 mg, FLU 10–80 mg/day	Outpts. with paraphilias and NPSA	24	Open-label	SER = 4–24 wks. FLX = 12–60 wks.	Self-report of number of orgasms related to deviant sexual activities and average time/day involved in deviant sexual activity	11 out of 24 pts. at least 50% improved with SER; 6 out of 9 pts. with FLX.
Bradford, 1995	SER 50–200 mg/day	Outpts. with pedophilia	19	Open-label	12 wks.	Rating of pts.' self-report of frequency and intensity of fantasies; penile response to evocative stimuli measured with plethysmography, change in obsessions on the YBOCS	Significant decrease in fantasies, penile response to evocative stimuli and obsessions.
Greenberg, 1996	FLX, FLV, SER; doses not stated	Outpts. with paraphilias	95	Retrospective, open-label comparison of therapy to SSRIs + therapy	12 wks.	Pts.' report of paraphilic behaviors	Both groups showed a clinically significant decrease in paraphilic behaviors; the group treated with SSRIs + therapy had a significantly better response than the nonmedication group
Greenberg, 1996	FLV, FLX, SER; Doses not stated	Pts. with paraphilias	58	Open-label, retrospective chart review	12 wks.	Clinical Global Impression Scale—rating of pts.' self-report of frequency and intensity of fantasies	Significant decrease in fantasies from baseline when all SSRIs combined; no significant difference between the 3 agents
Kafka, 2000	SSRI + methylphenidate 20–100 mg/day	Outpts. with paraphilias or NPSA; 17 with comorbid ADHD	26	Open-label	2–30 mos. on the combination	Pts.' report of total number of sexual behaviors related to sexual disorder resulting in orgasm and total time spent in behaviors related to sexual disorder	Significant decrease in the number of orgasms due to and total time spent in behaviors related to sexual disorder with initial SSRI. Further significant improvement seen with addition of methylphenidate
Coleman, 2000	Nefazodone 50–400 mg/day	Outpts. with NPSA ("sexual disorder NOS")	14	Open label, retrospective chart review	Mean = 13.4 mos.	Clinician rating of pts.' reports of level of intrusive sexual thoughts	6 pts. reported a decrease in recurrent sexual thoughts; 5 reported these thoughts completely resolved.

CMI = clomipramine; DMI = desipramine; FLV = fluvoxamine; FLX = fluoxetine; SER = sertraline.

cant decrease in the number of orgasms due to paraphilic behavior and total time spent involved in paraphilia-related behaviors after treatment with an SSRI (Kafka & Hennen, 2000). Further improvement was obtained after the addition of methylphenidate in this study.

In a retrospective review of fifty-eight men with paraphilias treated for twelve weeks, Greenberg et al. (1996a) reported that fluoxetine, fluvoxamine, and sertraline were equally effective in reducing paraphilic fantasies. This group also reported a 12-week retrospective open-label comparison of 95 subjects with paraphilias treated with SSRIs plus psychosocial intervention versus 104 subjects treated with psychosocial intervention alone (Greenberg et al., 1996b). Both groups showed a clinically significant decrease in paraphilic behaviors over twelve weeks, but the group treated with SSRIs had a significantly greater response than did the nonmedication group. Moreover, a twelve-week, open-label trial of sertraline (50–200 mg/day) in sixteen males with pedophilia showed a significant decrease from baseline to last visit in pedophilic fantasies, overall sexual activity, penile response to descriptions of pedophilic acts, ratings of obsessions, and frequency of masturbation (Bradford & Wiseman, 1995).

To our knowledge, the only study of SSRIs in paraphilias reporting a lack of effectiveness is a retrospective review of SSRI treatment of thirteen men with paraphilias ($N = 5$), NPSA ($N = 5$), or sexual obsessions/compulsions ($N = 3$) (Stein et al., 1992). Patients' comorbidity included OCD ($N = 9$), major depression ($N = 3$), substance abuse ($N = 2$), and social phobia ($N = 1$). Only four of the thirteen patients in this study who were diagnosed with sexual obsessions, sexual addictions, or NPSA and none of the five patients with paraphilias responded to therapeutic trials of fluoxetine (60–80 mg/day), clomipramine (400 mg/day), or fluvoxamine (200–300 mg/day).

Finally, a recent study reported significant benefit with the serotonin antagonist nefazodone in a sample of fourteen patients with hypersexuality (Coleman, Gratzer, Nesvacil, & Raymond, 2000). This retrospective, open-label chart review reported that nefazodone 50-400 mg/day effectively eliminated intrusive sexual thoughts in five patients and significantly decreased them in six additional patients.

We found only two blinded controlled studies of antidepressants in the treatment of paraphilias (Kruesi et al., 1992; Zohar et al., 1994). In the larger study, fifteen men with paraphilias referred from the general community (i.e., outpatients not participating in a sex offender program) were treated in a double-blind, crossover comparison of clomipramine and desipramine (five weeks on each drug) (Kruesi et al., 1992). After a single-blind, two-week placebo period, four placebo responders were dropped from the study. Four of eight subjects who completed the study were clinically depressed. The dose range used for clomipramine was 75–250 mg/day (mean = 162.5 mg) and 100–250 mg (mean = 212.5 mg) for desipramine. Both drugs reduced paraphilic urges and behaviors compared to baseline with no significant difference noted between them. Three men remained on tricyclic antidepressants for up to nine months after the study was completed. By contrast, the other study, a controlled case report, described successful SSRI, but not desipramine, therapy in a man who sought treatment for ego-dystonic exhibitionism. Fluvoxamine 300 mg/day effectively eliminated this patient's exhibitionistic impulses and behaviors after two weeks. These symptoms returned after the patient was switched to open-label desipramine 300 mg/day and later during a single-blind placebo phase (Zohar et al., 1994). Although both of these studies support the efficacy of antidepressants in the treatment of paraphilias, they contradict one another regarding the question of whether serotonergic agents have greater efficacy than do tricyclic antidepressants for these disorders.

There are a number of methodological limitations to the studies of antidepressants in paraphilias. First, the majority are open, single case reports, case series, or retrospective reviews. In addition, the sexual disorders studied are heterogeneous, including paraphilias, NPSA, and OCD with sexual compulsions. Moreover, some studies use combined treatments, including augmentation of SSRIs with lithium, trazodone, methylphenidate, or antipsychotics. In many of these reports, pharmacotherapy was combined with psychotherapy or psychosocial interventions, and only one study (Greenberg et al., 1996b) attempts to control for this variable. Finally, only one of these studies used any type of objective measure to assess response (arousal to paraphilic images measured by penile plethysmography), while the others relied only on self-reported frequency of masturbation, paraphilic fantasies and/or behaviors. Our group (Nelson et al., 2000) and others (Kiersch, 1990; Kravitz et al., 1995) have begun to question the validity of self-report measures in this population, as many patients, especially those involved in the criminal justice system, are dishonest about their symptoms during treatment.

Antipsychotics

Dopamine appears to be an important neurotransmitter involved in the experience of pleasure, including sexual feelings. Dopamine also appears to be integral to the physiological mechanisms underlying reinforcement, reward, and other processes intrinsic to sexual attraction, desire, arousal, response, orgasm, and satisfaction (Crenshaw & Goldberg, 1996). As one would expect, studies document decreased libido and erectile dysfunction (23–54 % incidence) in patients treated with dopamine antagonists such as chlorpromazine, pimozide, thiothixine, sulpiride, haloperidol, and fluphenazine (Kotin, Wilbert, Verburg, & Soldinger, 1976; Meco, Falachi, & Casacchia, 1985).

Since the 1960s, antipsychotics have been used to treat sexually deviant behaviors (Bartholomew, 1968). One case report, six case series, and one double-blind, placebo-controlled study report the successful use of typical antipsychotic agents in the treatment of sex offenders and patients with hypersexuality and sexually deviant behavior (Bartholomew, 1968; Deberdt, 1971; Field, 1973; Kamm, 1965; Tanghe & Vereecken, 1970; Tennent, Bancroft, & Cass, 1974; Zbytovsky, 1993). (Table 13.5 summarizes all the open-label trials with ten or more subjects and all the controlled trials that were available for our review.) Specifically, these studies evaluated fluphenazine (50 mg/month), haloperidol (5 mg/day and 37.5 mg/month), thioridazine (300 mg/day), and benperidol (0.2–1.25 mg/day). They report decreased sexual interest, decreased frequency of orgasms and intercourse, and decreased paraphilic urges and behaviors in subjects treated for up to four years with these agents. Side effects included sedation, extrapyramidal symptoms, and gynecomastia (Bartholomew, 1968; Tennent et al., 1974). The one controlled study (Tennent et al., 1974) showed a decrease in sexual interest with benperidol compared to chlorpromazine and placebo but no significant change in sexual activity or penile response to erotic stimuli.

Table 13.5
Antipsychotic Studies (Trials With $N \geq 10$)

Author	Drug/Dose	Population	N	Design	Duration	Variables	Results
Bartholo-mew, 1968	Fluphenazine 25 mg per 2 wks. i.m.	Outpts., mostly sex offenders with para-philias)	26	Open-label	24 wks.	Self-report of sexual drive and activity	17 out of 26 pts. reported decreased sex drive.
Field, 1973	Benperidol 0.5–1.0 mg/day	Sex offenders; 50% in prison, 50% on parole	28	Open-label	Not stated	Self-report of sexual interest and behavior	All pts. reported diminished sexual drive and decreased ability to obtain erections and that abnormal sex drive was controlled. However, 2 pts. noted no decrease in fantasies
Zbytovsky, 1993	Haloperidol-D 37.5–75 mg per 6 wks. i.m.	Sex offenders, most with paraphilias	30	Open-label	8-50 mos.	Changes in sexual behavior; changes in penile tumescence plethysmography (? evocative stimuli used)	Decrease in sexual interest and frequency of sexual activity; decrease in penile "reactions" on plethysmography.
Tennant, 1974	Benperidol 1.25 mg/day, chlor-prom-azine 125 mg/day	Inpatient sex offend-ers with pedophilia	12	Double-blind, placebo-controlled crossover	18 wks.	Self-report of sexual interest and behavior; penile response to plethysmography	Significant decrease in sexu-al interest with benperidol compared with chlorpro-mazine and PLC; no differ-ence on the other variables.

PLC = placebo.

As reviewed previously, haloperidol (Kornreich et al., 1995) and risperidone (Bourgeois & Klein, 1996) were reported to be effective in combination with fluoxetine in two men with compulsive masturbation and sadistic pedophilia, respectively. There are also two recent reports of sexual disorders responding to atypical antipsychotics alone. One of these describes a man with dementia, Parkinsonism, and hypersexuality refractory to CPA (MacKnight & Rojas-Fernandez, 2000) who responded to 25 mg of quetiapine. In the second case, a man with zoophilia associated with carbidopa/levodopa and pergolide treatment for Parkinsonism responded to 50 mg of clozapine (Fernandez & Durso, 1998).

Mood Stabilizers and Anticonvulsants

Anticonvulsant agents and mood stabilizers have been used to treat excessive and aberrant sexual behavior in a few cases. One rationale for treatment with these agents is that they have been shown to be helpful in a number of disorders involving poor impulse control, including bipolar disorder, intermittent explosive disorder, and trichotillomania (Christenson, Popkin, Mackenzie, & Realmuto, 1991; Siassi, 1982). Another is that lithium may interfere with libido and erection in some patients (Blay, Ferraz, & Calil, 1982; Vinarova, Uhlir, Stika, & Vinar, 1972).

We found four case reports and two case series describing the use of lithium as monotherapy or in combination with antidepressants in the treatment of sex offenders and patients with paraphilias and/or NPSAs (Bártová, Hajnová, Náhunek, & Svestka, 1979; Bártová et al., 1984; Cesnik & Coleman, 1989; Kafka, 1991a; Rubenstein & Engel, 1996; Veenhuizen, Van Strien, & Cohen-Kettenis, 1992). Lithium dosages ranged from 600–1,500 mg/day, and responses included decreased paraphilic urges/behaviors, reduced reactivity on plethysmography, and decreased recidivism. In one study, improvement in paraphilic symptoms with lithium and sertraline was sustained for one year (Rubenstein & Engel, 1996).

Few reports of other mood stabilizers in sex offenders or patients with paraphilia have been published to date. Carbamazepine 1,200 mg/day succesfully ameliorated paraphilic symptoms in a man with organic personality disorder, partial complex seizures, and several paraphilias who had not responded to phenytoin and phenobarbital (Goldberg & Buongiorno, 1982). In contrast, in a retrospective study of valproate in patients with paraphilia and bipolar disorder, our group observed significant improvement of paraphilic symptoms in only two out of nine patients (22%) despite a significant reduction in mood symptoms (Nelson et al., 2000). Due to the evidence of a high co-occurrence of paraphilias and bipolar disorder, the use of mood stabilizers in sex offenders with paraphilias and bipolar disorder requires further study.

Two anticonvulsant drugs not typically used as mood stabilizers, phenytoin and primidone, were reported to be beneficial in the case of a man with transvestism, a history of head trauma, and electroencephalograph abnormalities (Wålinder, 1965). Paraphilic symptoms returned in this patient after these anticonvulsant drugs were discontinued.

In summary, two case reports and two case series describing lithium monotherapy, two case series and three reports of lithium added to antidepressant therapy, and one report of carbamazepine monotherapy make up the existing evidence supporting the use of mood stabilizers in paraphilias. However, given the preliminary evidence suggesting a high comorbidity of paraphilias and mood disorders, the use of mood stabilizers in sex offenders with paraphilias and bipolar disorder warrants further investigation.

Buspirone

Buspirone, an anxiolytic agent with serotonin-1a receptor agonist properties, has been reported to augment SSRI treatment of OCD (Goodman, McDougle, & Price, 1992). The evidence supporting the use of buspirone (range dose 20–35 mg/day) in the treatment of paraphilias is currently limited to three case reports (total $N = 4$) that describe marked responses in men with transvestic fetishism (Fedoroff, 1988), sexual sadism (Fedoroff, 1992), exhibitionism, and telephone scatologia (Pearson, Marshall, Barbaree, & Southmayd, 1992). Buspirone was given as monotherapy in all cases but one, in which it was given concomitantly with doxepin and alprazolam (Fedoroff, 1992).

Reports of Miscellaneous Drugs in Paraphilias

Additional reports have described the treatment of pathological sexual behavior using medications from drug classes other than those discussed previously. For instance the treatment of hypersexuality in dementia with the "nonhormonal antiandrogens" cimetidine, spironolactone, and ketoconazole has been retrospectively reported (Wiseman et al., 2000). Fourteen of twenty patients responded to cimetidine alone, whereas the remaining six patients responded to the addition of ketoconazole and/or spironolactone. One case report has described two children with Tourette syndrome and exhibitionistic and/or frotteuristic behaviors that responded dramatically to naltrexone 37.5 mg/day (Sandyk, 1988). In addition, as discussed earlier, the stimulant methylphenidate has been reported to be beneficial in augmenting SSRI treatment of patients with paraphilias and paraphilia-related disorders (Kafka & Hennen, 2000).

Strategies for Selecting Initial Pharmacotherapy

Currently, due to the paucity of double-blind, controlled studies and the methodological limitations and contradictory results of those that have been conducted, the existing evidence provides no firm guidelines for the pharmacotherapy of sex offenders. Indeed, despite laws in some states mandating medical treatment of sex offenders, no drug is approved by the FDA for the treatment of sexual aggression, sexual deviancy, or paraphilias.

One potential approach to conceptualizing the management of these patients' psychopharmacological treatment, therefore, emphasizes the high incidence of mental illness in this population and the importance of carefully assessing the patient for psychiatric disorders such as paraphilias, mood disorders, ICDs, anxiety disorders, psychotic disorders, substance use disorders, and Axis II disorders. In this model, the initial treatment of the sex offender would vary according to the psychiatric diagnoses that were detected. For example, a patient with a paraphilia and comorbid unipolar depression would be started on an SSRI as these agents may be effective in reducing paraphilic urges and behavior and would also likely benefit the patient's depressive disorder (Fedoroff, 1995; Gijs & Gooren, 1996). A similar strategy would be used if the patient had comorbid ICD, OCD, or other anxiety disorder as these conditions may improve with SSRI therapy as well. If initial SSRI treatment did not adequately reduce the patient's deviant or excessive sexual urges, augmentation with, or switching to, an antiandrogen could be considered. Conversely, if comorbid bipolar disorder was suspected, the patient would be started on a mood stabilizer, as an antidepressant might worsen or precipitate hypomania, mania, or cycling and thereby secondarily increase paraphilic symptoms (McElroy et al., 1999). Although evidence for a direct benefit with mood stabilizers in paraphilias is, at this point, purely anecdotal, these treatments could relieve paraphilic symptoms indirectly by decreasing impulsivity due to mania and facilitating the patient's ability to participate in psychosocial treatments by reducing mood symptoms. Similarly, comorbid psychosis would necessitate the initiation of antipsychotic therapy, which might also help to control paraphilic urges and behaviors. If mood stabilizer treatment or antipsychotic treatment were helpful for mood symptoms and/or psychosis but did not adequately reduce the patient's paraphilic symptoms, the mood stabilizer or antipsychotic could be augmented with an antiandrogen and/or an SSRI. Indeed, future research may show that a substantial proportion of sex offenders may respond best to combination or multimodal therapy, particularly those with paraphilias and other Axis I disorders.

Significant controversy exists about which treatment should be used in patients who have a paraphilia and no significant Axis I comorbidity. There is general agreement that antiandrogens and SSRIs are the two classes of drugs with the most evidence of direct effectiveness in these disorders. However, no drug from either class has been proven efficacious in an adequate study of any paraphilia. Thus, some experts argue that sex offenders with paraphilias should first be treated with antiandrogens (Gijs & Gooren, 1996; Rösler & Witztum, 2000) based on the fact that existing placebo-controlled studies with these agents have shown a reduction in at least some aspects of paraphilias (CPA: one out of three studies > placebo; MPA: three out of five studies > placebo on at least one measure) and there are no comparable placebo-controlled data for SSRIs. However, it is important to note that these findings are somewhat mixed. In some of these studies, patients improved on self-report measures of paraphilic urges and behavior but showed no difference from placebo in response to evocative stimuli as measured by plethysmography. Other experts have cited this as lack of conclusive evidence of the efficacy of antiandrogens and argued that one should start with an SSRI, given the lower risk associated with these agents (Fedoroff, 1995; Greenberg & Bradford, 1997). Presumably, with either of these strategies if a patient did not respond to the initial therapy, one could switch to, or augment with, the other agent.

Our group believes that based on the current evidence, one cannot ascribe to a specific algorithm for treating paraphilias in sex offenders. For instance, it appears important to look at the nature of the patient's paraphilia to determine the degree of deviance and the potential dangerousness of past behaviors and offenses. One should also assess the degree of psychopathy exhibited by the patient as it may have a bearing on the risk of recidivism. Thus, a patient with a history of more violent sexual offenses and a high level of psychopathy would be offered an antiandrogen first, despite the potential for more serious side effects and decreased tolerability, based on the presence of evidence from controlled studies that these agents are effective. In the patient with lower risk of reoffending and a less dangerous offending history one would want to initiate therapy with an SSRI due to the greater risk of serious side effects with the antiandrogens.

One way to approach this controversy is from the standpoint of whether pharmacotherapy is designed to decrease sex drive in general, and thus secondarily decrease paraphilic urges and behavior, or to preferentially treat deviant sexual urges based on the theory that paraphilic symptoms are related to an obsessive-compulsive spectrum disorder (American Psychiatric Association Task Force, 1999). Presumably, antiandrogen therapy would attempt to accomplish the first aim, whereas SSRIs would aim for the latter goal. Although it has not yet been established that SSRIs work by decreasing deviant urges preferentially, or that antiandrogens work only by lowering overall sexual drive, some data suggest that this difference exists. This finding has implications for drug choice in sex offenders as some individuals may be more appropriate for one or the other treatment based on certain features of their paraphilia and offending history. For instance, antiandrogens may be preferable in patients who are more impulsive and have ego-syntonic symptoms, and are therefore more likely to be deceptive about their symptoms, as suppression of the patient's overall sex drive may provide a more reliable reduction in paraphilic symptoms and behavior. Conversely, patients whose fantasies and deviant behaviors are more ego-dystonic and ritualistic may be more likely to respond to SSRI therapy, as these patients' symptoms may more closely resemble the obsessive-compulsive symptoms.

In short, in the absence of controlled treatment data, the pharmacotherapy of sex offenders remains an empirical process. Nonetheless, medical treatment of primary psychiatric morbidity and suppression of abnormal sexual drives and behavior are crucial elements in the comprehensive treatment of sex offenders.

Conclusion

Sexual violence is an enormous public health problem associated with significant costs to society and human suffering. Sex offenders have been shown to have high rates of psychiatric disorders, particularly paraphilias. Paraphilias are prevalent in sex offenders and seem to have high rates of comorbidity with mood, substance use, and OCDs.

Available preliminary evidence suggests the possible efficacy of hormonal treatments (CPA, MPA, and GnRH agonists) in the treatment of paraphilias. However, the results of open trials appear to be more positive than the few available controlled studies. Open reports show a reduction in sexual behaviors, fantasies, and urges and a reduction in recidivism.

Although preliminary, studies of SSRIs in the treatment of paraphilias are encouraging. Double-blind placebo-controlled studies are needed to evaluate the acute and long-term efficacy of SSRIs in the treatment of paraphilias. The results of studies using other psychotropic medications such as antipsychotics and buspirone in paraphilias are promising. Further studies of the treatment, and underlying biology of paraphilias and NPSA are needed to better understand these disorders, which have important medical, societal, and public health implications.

References

Abel, G. (1989). Paraphilias. In H. Kaplan & B. Sadock (Eds.), *Comprehensive textbook of psychiatry* (5th ed., pp. 1069–1085). Philadelphia: Williams & Wilkins.

Abel, G., & Osborn, C. (1992). The paraphilias: The extent and nature of sexually deviant and criminal behavior. *Psychiatric Clinics of North America, 15*, 675–687.

American Psychiatric Association. (1980). *Diagnostic and statistical manual of mental disorders* (3rd ed.). Washington, DC: Author.

American Psychiatric Association. (1987). *Diagnostic and statistical manual of mental disorders* (3rd ed., rev.). Washington, DC: Author.

American Psychiatric Association. (1994). *Diagnostic and statistical manual of mental disorders* (4th ed.). Washington, DC: Author.

American Psychiatric Association Task Force on Sexually Dangerous Offenders. (1999). *Dangerous sex offenders: A task force report of the American Psychiatric Association.* Washington, DC: Author.

Bancroft, J., Tennent, G., Loucas, K., & Cass, J. (1974). The control of deviant sexual behaviour by drugs. I. Behavioural changes following oestrogens and anti-androgens. *British Journal of Psychiatry, 125*, 310–315.

Baron, D. P., & Unger, H. R. (1977). A clinical trial of cyproterone acetate for sexual deviancy. *New Zealand Medical Journal, 85*, 366–369.

Bartholomew, A. A. (1968). A long-acting phenothiazine as a possible agent to control deviant sexual behavior. *American Journal of Psychiatry, 124*, 917–923.

Bártová, D., Hajnová, R., Náhunek, K., & Svestka, J. (1979). Comparative study of prophylactic lithium and diethylstilbestrol in sexual deviants. *Activitas Nervosa Superior (Praha), 21*, 163–164.

Bártová, D., Buresová, A., Hajnová, R., Náhunek, K., & Svestka, J. (1984). Comparison of oxyprothepine deconoate, lithium and cyproteron acetate in deviant sexual behaviour. *Activitas Nervosa Superior, 26*, 278.

Becker, J. V., Kaplan, M. S., Tenke, C. E., & Tartaglini, A. (1991). The incidence of depressive symptomatology in juvenile sex offenders with a history of abuse. *Child Abuse and Neglect, 15*, 531–536.

Berlin, F., Malin, H., & Thomas, K. (1995). Nonpedophiliac and nontransvestic paraphilias. In G. Gabbard (Ed.), *Treatment of psychiatric disorders* (pp. 1941–1958). Washington, DC: American Psychiatric Press.

Berlin, F. S., & Coyle, G. S. (1981). Sexual deviation syndromes [clinical conference]. *Johns Hopkins Medical Journal, 149*, 119–125.

Berlin, F. S., & Meinecke, C. F. (1981). Treatment of sex offenders with antiandrogenic medication: Conceptualization, review of treatment modalities, and preliminary findings. *American Journal of Psychiatry, 138*, 601–607.

Berner, W., Brownstone, G., & Sluga, W. (1983). The cyproteronacetat treatment of sexual offenders. *Neuroscience and Biobehavioral Review, 7*, 441–443.

Black, D., Kehrberg, L., Flumerfelt, D., & Schlosser, S. (1997). Characteristics of 36 subjects reporting compulsive sexual behavior. *American Journal of Psychiatry, 154*, 243–249.

Blay, S. L., Ferraz, M. P., & Calil, H. M. (1982). Lithium-induced male sexual impairment: Two case reports. *Journal of Clinical Psychiatry, 43*, 497–8.

Blumer, D., & Migeon, C. (1975). Hormone and hormonal agents in the treatment of aggression. *Journal of Nervous and Mental Disorders, 160*, 127–137.

Bourgeois, J. A., & Klein, M. (1996). Risperidone and fluoxetine in the treatment of pedophilia with comorbid dysthymia [letter]. *Journal of Clinical Psychopharmacology, 16*, 257–258.

Bradford, J. M., & McLean, D. (1984). Sexual offenders, violence and testosterone: A clinical study. *Canadian Journal of Psychiatry, 29*, 335–343.

Bradford, J. M., & Pawlak, A. (1987). Sadistic homosexual pedophilia: Treatment with cyproterone acetate—A single case study. *Canadian Journal of Psychiatry, 32*, 22–30.

Bradford, J. M., & Pawlak, A. (1993a). Double-blind placebo crossover study of cyproterone acetate in the treatment of the paraphilias. *Archives of Sexual Behavior, 22*, 383–402.

Bradford, J. M., & Pawlak, A. (1993b). Effects of cyproterone acetate on sexual arousal patterns of pedophiles. *Archives of Sexual Behavior, 22*, 629–41.

Bradford, J., & Wiseman, R. (1995). *An open pilot study of sertraline in the treatment of outpatients with pedophilia.* Paper presented at the annual meeting of the American Psychiatric Association, Miami, FL.

Buresová, A., Bártová, D., & Svestka, J. (1990). Comparison of pharmacotherapeutic procedures in the treatment of sexual deviant behaviour. *Activitas Nervosa Superior (Praha), 32*, 299–301.

Casals-Ariet, C., & Cullen, K. (1993). Exhibitionism treated with clomipramine [letter; comment]. *American Journal of Psychiatry, 150*, 1273–1274.

Cesnik, J., & Coleman, E. (1989). Use of lithium carbonate in the treatment of autoerotic asphyxia. *American Journal of Psychotherapy, 43*, 277–286.

Christenson, G. A., Popkin, M. K., Mackenzie, T. B., & Realmuto, G. M. (1991). Lithium treatment of chronic hair pulling. *Journal of Clinical Psychiatry, 52*, 116–120.

Coleman, E., Gratzer, T., Nesvacil, L., & Raymond, N. C. (2000). Nefazodone and the treatment of nonparaphilic compulsive sexual behavior: a retrospective study. *Journal of Clinical Psychiatry, 61*, 282–284.

Cooper, A. J. (1981). A placebo-controlled trial of the antiandrogen cyproterone acetate in deviant hypersexuality. *Comprehensive Psychiatry, 22*, 458–465.

Cooper, A. J. (1987). Medroxyprogesterone acetate (MPA) treatment of sexual acting out in men suffering from dementia. *Journal of Clinical Psychiatry, 48*, 368–370.

Cooper, A. J., & Cernovsky, Z. Z. (1994). Comparison of cyproterone acetate (CPA) and leuprolide acetate (LHRH agonist) in a chronic pedophile: A clinical case study. *Biological Psychiatry, 36*, 269–271.

Cooper, A. J., Cernovsky, Z., & Magnus, R. V. (1992). The long-term use of cyproterone acetate in pedophilia: A case study. *Journal of Sex and Marital Therapy, 18*, 292–302.

Cooper, A. J., Ismail, A. A., Phanjoo, A. L., & Love, D. L. (1972). Antiandrogen (cyproterone acetate) therapy in deviant hypersexuality. *British Journal of Psychiatry, 120*, 59–63.

Cooper, A. J., Sandhu, S., Losztyn, S., & Cernovsky, Z. (1992). A double-blind placebo controlled trial of medroxyprogesterone acetate and cyproterone acetate with seven pedophiles. *Canadian Journal of Psychiatry, 37*, 687–93.

Cordoba, O. A., & Chapel, J. L. (1983). Medroxyprogesterone acetate antiandrogen treatment of hypersexuality in a pedophiliac sex offender. *American Journal of Psychiatry, 140*, 1036–1039.

Crenshaw, T., & Goldberg, J. (1996). *Sexual pharmacology.* New York: Norton.

Croughan, J., Saghir, M., Cohne, R., & Robins, E. (1981). A comparison of treated and untreated male cross-dressers. *Archives of Sexual Behavior, 10*, 515–528.

Davidson, J., Kwan, M., & Greenleaf, W. (1982). Hormonal replacement and sexuality. *Clinical Endocrinology and Metabolism, 11*, 599.

Davies, T. S. (1974). Cyproterone acetate for male hypersexuality. *Journal of Internal Medicine Research, 2*, 159–163.

Deberdt, R. (1971). [Benperidol (R4584) in the treatment of sexual offenders]. *Acta Psychiatrica Belgique, 11*, 396–413.

Dickey, R. (1992). The management of a case of treatment-resistant paraphilia with a long-acting LHRH agonist. *Canadian Journal of Psychiatry, 37*, 567–569.

Dietz, P. E., Hazelwood, R. R., & Warren, J. (1990). The sexually sadistic criminal and his offenses. *Bulletin of the American Academy of Psychiatry and Law, 18*, 163–178.

Fedoroff, J. P. (1988). Buspirone hydrochloride in the treatment of transvestic fetishism [see comments]. *Journal of Clinical Psychiatry, 49*, 408–409.

Fedoroff, J. P. (1992). Buspirone hydrochloride in the treatment of an atypical paraphilia. *Archives of Sexual Behavior, 21*, 401–406.

Fedoroff, J. (1993). Serotonergic drug treatment of deviant sexual interests. *Annals of Sex Research, 6*, 105–121.

Fedoroff, J. (1995). Antiandrogens vs. serotoninergic medications in the treatment of sex offenders: A preliminary compliance study. *Canadian Journal of Human Sexuality, 4*, 111–122.

Fedoroff, J., Winser-Carlson, R., Dean, S., & Berlin, F. (1992). Medroxy-progesterone acetate in treatment of paraphilic sexual disorders. *Journal of Offender Rehabilitation, 18*, 109–123.

Fernandez, H. H., & Durso, R. (1998). Clozapine for dopaminergic-induced paraphilias in Parkinson's disease. *Movement Disorders, 13*, 597–598.

Field, L. H. (1973). Benperidol in the treatment of sexual offenders. *Medical Science and Law, 13*, 195–196.

Gagne, P. (1981). Treatment of sex offenders with medroxyprogesterone acetate. *American Journal of Psychiatry, 138*, 644–646.

Galli, V., McElroy, S., Soutullo, C., Kizer, D., Raute, N., Keck, P., & McConville, B. (1999). The psychiatric diagnoses of twenty-two adolescents who have sexually molested other children. *Comprehensive Psychiatry, 40*, 85–88.

Galli, V. B., Raute, N. J., McConville, B. J., & McElroy, S. L. (1998). An adolescent male with multiple paraphilias successfully treated with fluoxetine. *Journal of Child and Adolescent Psychopharmacology, 8*, 195–197.

Gijs, L., & Gooren, L. (1996). Hormonal and psychopharmacological interventions in the treatment of paraphilias: An update. *Journal of Sex Research, 33*, 273–290.

Goldberg, R. L., & Buongiorno, P. A. (1982). The use of carbamazepine for the treatment of paraphilias in a brain damaged patient. *International Journal of Psychiatry and Medicine, 12*, 275–279.

Goodman, W. K., McDougle, C. J., & Price, L. H. (1992). Pharmacotherapy of obsessive compulsive disorder. *Journal of Clinical Psychiatry, 53*(Suppl.), 29–37.

Gottesman, H. G., & Schubert, D. S. (1993). Low-dose oral medroxyprogesterone acetate in the management of the paraphilias. *Journal of Clinical Psychiatry, 54*, 182–188.

Greenberg, D., & Bradford, J. (1997). Treatment of paraphilic disorders: A review of the role of selective serotonin reuptake inhibitors. *Sexual Abuse: A Journal of Research and Treatment, 9*, 349–360.

Greenberg, D. M., Bradford, J. M., Curry, S., & O'Rourke, A. (1996a). A comparison of treatment of paraphilias with three serotonin reuptake inhibitors: A retrospective study. *Bulletin of the American Academy of Psychiatry and Law, 24*, 525–532.

Greenberg, D., Bradford, J., Curry, S., & O'Rourke, A. (1996b). *A controlled study of the treatment of paraphilia disorders with selective serotonin reuptake inhibitors.* Paper presented at the annual meeting of the Canadian Academy of Psychiatry and the Law, Tremblay, Quebec.

Griffin, J. E., & Wilson, J. D. (1998). Disorders of the testes and male reproductive tract. In J. D. Wilson, D. W. Foster, H. M. Kronenberg, & P. R. Larsen (Eds.), *Williams textbook of endocrinology* (9th ed., pp. 819–875). Philadelphia: Saunders.

Grossman, L. S., & Cavanaugh, J. L., Jr. (1990). Psychopathology and denial in alleged sex offenders. *Journal of Nervous and Mental Disorders, 178*, 739–744.

Heim, N., & Hursch, C. J. (1979). Castration for sex offenders: Treatment or punishment? A review and critique of recent European literature. *Archives of Sexual Behavior, 8*, 281–304.

Henn, F., Herjanic, M., & Vanderpearl, R. (1976). Forensic psychiatry: Profiles of two types of sex offenders. *American Journal of Psychiatry, 133*, 694–696.

Hodgins, S. (1992). Mental disorder, intellectual deficiency, and crime. Evidence from a birth cohort. *Archives of General Psychiatry, 49*, 476–483.

Hodgins, S. (1998). Epidemiological investigations of the associations between major mental disorders and crime: Methodological limitations and validity of the conclusions. *Social Psychiatry and Psychiatric Epidemiology, 33*(Suppl. 1), S29–S37.

Hodgins, S., Mednick, S. A., Brennan, P. A., Schulsinger, F., & Engberg, M. (1996). Mental disorder and crime. Evidence from a Danish birth cohort. *Archives of General Psychiatry, 53*, 489–496.

Hucker, S., Langevin, R., & Bain, J. (1988). A double blind trial of sex drive reducing medication in pedophiles. *Annals of Sex Research, 1*, 227–242.

Kafka, M. (1991a). Successful antidepressant treatment of nonparaphilic sexual additions and paraphilias in men. *Journal of Clinical Psychiatry, 52*, 60–65.

Kafka, M. P. (1991b). Successful treatment of paraphilic coercive disorder (a rapist) with fluoxetine hydrochloride. *British Journal of Psychiatry, 158*, 844–847.

Kafka, M. P. (1994a). Paraphilia-related disorders—Common, neglected, and misunderstood. *Harvard Review of Psychiatry, 2*, 39–42.

Kafka, M. (1994b). Sertraline pharmacotherapy for paraphilias and paraphilia-related disorders: An open trial. *Annals of Clinical Psychiatry, 6*, 189–195.

Kafka, M. (1995). Sexual impulsivity. In E. Hollander & D. Stein (Eds.), *Impulsivity and aggression* (pp. 201–228). New York: Wiley.

Kafka, M. P., & Prentky, R. (1992). Fluoxetine treatment of nonparaphilic sexual addictions and paraphilias in men. *Journal of Clinical Psychiatry, 53*, 351–358.

Kafka, M. P., & Hennen, J. (2000). Psychostimulant augmentation during treatment with selective serotonin reuptake inhibitors in men with paraphilias and paraphilia-related disorders: A case series. *Journal of Clinical Psychiatry, 61*, 664–70.

Kamm, I. (1965). Control of sexual hyperactivity with thioridazine. *American Journal of Psychiatry, 121*, 922–923.

Kavoussi, R. J., Kaplan, M., & Becker, J. V. (1988). Psychiatric diagnoses in adolescent sex offenders. *Journal of the American Academy of Child and Adolescent Psychiatry, 27*, 241–243.

Kiersch, T. A. (1990). Treatment of sex offenders with Depo-Provera. *Bulletin of the American Academy of Psychiatry and Law, 18*, 179–187.

Kornreich, C., Den Dulk, A., Verbanck, P., & Pelc, I. (1995). Fluoxetine treatment of compulsive masturbation in a schizophrenic patient [letter]. *Journal of Clinical Psychiatry, 56,* 334.

Kotin, J., Wilbert, D. E., Verburg, D., & Soldinger, S. M. (1976). Thioridazine and sexual dysfunction. *American Journal of Psychiatry, 133,* 82–85.

Kravitz, H. M., Haywood, T. W., Kelly, J., Wahlstrom, C., Liles, S., & Cavanaugh, J. L., Jr. (1995). Medroxyprogesterone treatment for paraphiliacs. *Bulletin of the American Academy of Psychiatry and Law, 23,* 19–33.

Kravitz, H. M., Haywood, T. W., Kelly, J., Liles, S., & Cavanaugh, J. L., Jr. (1996). Medroxyprogesterone and paraphiles: Do testosterone levels matter? *Bulletin of the American Academy of Psychiatry and Law, 24,* 73–83.

Kruesi, M., Fine, S., Vallrdares, L., Phillips, R., & Rapoport, J. (1992). Paraphilias: A double-blind crossover comparison of clomipramine versus desipramine. *Archives of Sexual Behavior, 21,* 587–593.

Kwan, M., Greenleaf, W. J., Mann, J., Crapo, L., & Davidson, J. M. (1983). The nature of androgen action on male sexuality: A combined laboratory–self-report study on hypogonadal men. *Journal of Clinical Endocrinology and Metabolism, 57,* 557–562.

Langevin, R., Bain, J., Wortzman, S., Hucker, S., Dickey, R., & Wright, P. (1988). Sexual sadism: brain, blood and behavior. *Annals of New York Academy of Science, 528,* 163–171.

Langevin, R., Paitch, D., Hucker, S., Newman, S., & Ramsay, G. (1979). The effects of assertiveness training, provera, and sex of therapist in the treatment of genital exhibitionism. *Journal of Behavior Therapy and Experimental Psychiatry, 10,* 275–282.

Laschet, U., & Laschet, L. (1971). Psychopharmacotherapy of sexual offenders with cyproterone acetate. *Pharmakopsychiatrie Neuropsychopharmakolgic, 4,* 99–104.

Lehne, G. (1984–1986). Brain damage and paraphilia: Treated with medroxyprogesterone acetate. *Sexuality and Disability, 7,* 145–158.

Leo, R. J., & Kim, K. Y. (1995). Clomipramine treatment of paraphilias in elderly demented patients. *Journal of Geriatric Psychiatry and Neurolology, 8,* 123–124.

Lewis, D. O., Shankok, S. S., & Pincus, J. H. (1979). Juvenile male sexual assaulters. *American Journal of Psychiatry, 136,* 1194–1196.

MacKnight, C., & Rojas-Fernandez, C. (2000). Quetiapine for sexually inappropriate behavior in dementia [letter]. *Journal of the American Geriatric Society, 48,* 707.

MacMillan, H., Fleming, J., & Trocme, N. (1997). Prevalence of child physical and sexual abuse in the community. Results from the Ontario Health Supplement. *Journal of the American Medical Association, 278,* 131–135.

Marzuk, P. M. (1996). Violence, crime, and mental illness. How strong a link? [editorial]. *Archives of General Psychiatry, 53,* 481–486.

McConaghy, N., Blaszczynski, A., & Kidson, W. (1988). Treatment of sex offenders with imaginal desensitization and/or medroxyprogesterone. *Acta Psychiatrica Scandinavica, 77,* 199–206.

McElroy, S. (2000). *Psychopathology and pharmacotherapy of sexually aggressive offenders.* Paper presented at the annual meeting of the American Psychiatric Association, Chicago.

McElroy, S., Keck, P., Hudson, J., Phillips, K., & Strakowski, S. (1996). Are impulse control disorders related to bipolar disorder? *Comprehensive Psychiatry, 37,* 229–240.

McElroy, S., Soutullo, C., Taylor, P., Nelson, E., Beckman, D., & Keck, P. (1998). *Psychiatric features of 30 sex offenders.* Paper presented at the annual meeting of the American Psychiatric Association, Toronto.

McElroy, S., Soutullo, C., Taylor, P., Nelson, E., Beckman, D., Strakowski, S., & Keck, P. (1999). Psychiatric features of 36 persons convicted of sexual offenses. *Journal of Clinical Psychiatry, 60,* 414–420.

Meco, G., Falachi, P., & Casacchia, M. (1985). Neuroendocrine effects of haloperidol decanoate in patients with chronic schizophrenia. In D. Kemali & G. Ragagni (Eds.), *Chronic treatments in neuropsychiatry* (pp. 89–93). New York: Raven Press.

Meyer, W. J. D., Cole, C., & Emory, E. (1992). Depo provera treatment for sex offending behavior: An evaluation of outcome. *Bulletin of the American Academy of Psychiatry and Law, 20,* 249–259.

Monahan, J., & Steadman, H. (1994). *Violence and mental disorder: Developments in risk assessment.* Chicago: University of Chicago Press.

Money, J. (1987). Treatment guidelines: Antiandrogen and counseling of paraphilic sex offenders. *Journal of Sex and Marital Therapy, 13,* 219–223.

Money, J., & Bennett, R. (1981). Post adolescent paraphilic sex offenders: Antiandrogenic and counseling therapy follow up. *International Journal of Mental Health, 10,* 122–133.

Money, J., Wiedeking, C., Walker, P. A., & Gain, D. (1976). Combined antiandrogenic and counseling program for treatment of 46, XY and 47, XYY sex offenders. In E. J. Sachar (Ed.), *Hormones, behavior, and psychopathology* (pp. 105–20). New York: Raven Press.

Myers, B. A. (1991). Treatment of sexual offenses by persons with developmental disabilities. *American Journal of Mental Retardation, 95,* 563–569.

Nelson, E., Brusman, L., Holcomb, J., Soutullo, C., Beckman, D., Welge, J., Kuppili, N., & McElroy, S. (2000). Divalproex sodium in sex offenders with bipolar disorder and comorbid paraphilias. *Journal of Affective Disorders, 64,* 249–255.

Ortmann, J. (1980). The treatment of sexual offenders: Castration and antihormone therapy. *International Journal of Law and Psychiatry, 3,* 443–451.

Packard, W. S., & Rosner, R. (1985). Psychiatric evaluations of sexual offenders. *Journal of Forensic Science, 30,* 715–720.

Pearson, H., Marshall, W., Barbaree, H., & Southmayd, S. (1992). Treatment of a compulsive paraphiliac with buspirone. *Annals of Sex Research, 5,* 239–246.

Pearson, H. J. (1990). Paraphilias, impulse control, and serotonin [letter; comment]. *Journal of Clinical Psychopharmacology, 10,* 233.

Perilstein, R. D., Lipper, S., & Friedman, L. J. (1991). Three cases of paraphilias responsive to fluoxetine treatment. *Journal of Clinical Psychiatry, 52,* 169–170.

Pinta, E. R. (1978). Treatment of obsessive homosexual pedophilic fantasies with medroxyprogesterone acetate. *Biological Psychiatry, 13,* 369–373.

Raboch, J., Cerna, H., & Zemek, P. (1984). Sexual aggressivity and androgens. *British Journal of Psychiatry, 151,* 398–400.

Raymond, N. C., Coleman, E., Ohlerking, F., Christenson, G. A., & Miner, M. (1999). Psychiatric comorbidity in pedophilic sex offenders. *American Journal of Psychiatry, 156,* 786–788.

Rich, S. S., & Ovsiew, F. (1994). Leuprolide acetate for exhibitionism in Huntington's disease. *Movement Disorders, 9,* 353–357.

Richer, M., & Crismon, M. L. (1993). Pharmacotherapy of sexual offenders. *Annals of Pharmacotherapy, 27,* 316–320.

Rösler, A., & Witztum, E. (1998). Treatment of men with paraphilia with a long-acting analogue of gonadotropin-releasing hormone *New England Journal of Medicine, 338,* 416–422.

Rösler, A., & Witztum, E. (2000). Pharmacotherapy of paraphilias in the next millennium. *Behavioral Science and Law, 18,* 43–56.

Ross, L. A., Bland, W. P., Ruskin, P., & Bacher, N. (1987). Antiandrogen treatment of aberrant sexual activity [letter]. *American Journal of Psychiatry, 144,* 1511.

Rousseau, L., Couture, M., Dupont, A., Labrie, F., & Couture, N. (1990). Effect of combined androgen blockade with an LHRH agonist and flutamide in one severe case of male exhibitionism. *Canadian Journal of Psychiatry, 35,* 338–341.

Rubenstein, E. B., & Engel, N. L. (1996). Successful treatment of transvestic fetishism with sertraline and lithium [letter]. *Journal of Clinical Psychiatry, 57,* 92.

Rubinow, D. R., & Schmidt, P. J. (1996). Androgens, brain, and behavior. *American Journal of Psychiatry, 153,* 974–984.

Sandyk, R. (1988). Naltrexone suppresses abnormal sexual behavior in Tourette's syndrome. *International Journal of Neuroscience, 43,* 107–110.

Schiavi, R. C., & Segraves, R. T. (1995). The biology of sexual function. *Psychiatric Clinics of North America, 18*, 7–23.

Segraves, R. (1988). Hormones and libido. In S. Leblum & R. Rosen (Eds.), *Sexual desire disorders* (pp. 271–312). New York: Guilford Press.

Siassi, I. (1982). Lithium treatment of impulsive behavior in children. *Journal of Clinical Psychiatry, 43*, 482–484.

Skakkebaek, N. E., Bancroft, J., Davidson, D. W., & Warner, P. (1981). Androgen replacement with oral testosterone undecanoate in hypogonadal men: A double-blind controlled study. *Clinical Endocrinology (Oxford), 14*, 49–61.

Spodak, M., Falck, Z., & Rappeport, J. (1978). The hormonal treatment of paraphilias with depo provera. *Criminal Justice and Behavior, 5*, 304–313.

Stein, D. J., Hollander, E., Anthony, D. T., Schneier, F. R., Fallon, B. A., Liebowitz, M. R., & Klein, D. F. (1992). Serotonergic medications for sexual obsessions, sexual addictions, and paraphilias. *Journal of Clinical Psychiatry, 53*, 267–271.

Swanson, J. (1993). Alcohol abuse, mental disorder, and violent behavior. An epidemiologic inquiry. *Alcohol Health Research World, 17*, 123–132.

Swanson, J. W., Holzer, C. E. D., Ganju, V. K., & Jono, R. T. (1990). Violence and psychiatric disorder in the community: Evidence from the Epidemiologic Catchment Area surveys. *Hospital and Community Psychiatry, 41*, 761–770.

Tanghe, A., & Vereecken, J. (1970). Some experiences with a new neuroleptic: Benperidol. *Encephale, 59*, 479–485.

Tennent, G., Bancroft, J., & Cass, J. (1974). The control of deviant sexual behavior by drugs: A double-blind controlled study of benperidol, chlorpromazine, and placebo. *Archives of Sexual Behavior, 3*, 261–271.

Thibaut, F., Cordier, B., & Kuhn, J. M. (1993). Effect of a long-lasting gonadotrophin hormone-releasing hormone agonist in six cases of severe male paraphilia. *Acta Psychiatrica Scandinavica, 87*, 445–450.

Tiihonen, J., Isohanni, M., Rasanen, P., Koiranen, M., & Moring, J. (1997). Specific major mental disorders and criminality: A 26-year prospective study of the 1966 northern Finland birth cohort. *American Journal of Psychiatry, 154*, 840–845.

Torres, A. R., & Cerqueira, A. T. (1993). Exhibitionism treated with clomipramine [letter; comment]. *American Journal of Psychiatry, 150*, 1274.

U.S. Bureau of Justice Statistics. (1996). *Criminal victimization in the United States: A National Crime Victimization Survey Report, 1993.* Washington, DC: Author.

Van Moffaert, M. (1976). Social reintegration of sexual delinquents by a combination of psychotherapy and anti-androgen treatment. *Acta Psychiatrica Scandinavica, 53*, 29–34.

Veenhuizen, A., Van Strien, D., & Cohen-Kettenis, P. (1992). The combined psychotherapeutic and lithium carbonate treatment of an adolescent with exhibitionism and indecent assault. *Journal of Psychology and Human Sexuality, 5*, 53–64.

Vinarova, E., Uhlir, O., Stika, L., & Vinar, O. (1972). Side effects of lithium administration. *Activitas Nervosa Superior, 14*, 105–107.

Virkkunen, M. (1976). The pedophilic offender with antisocial character. *Acta Psychiatrica Scandinavica, 53*, 401–405.

Volavka, J. (1999). The neurobiology of violence: An update. *Journal of Neuropsychiatry and Clinical Neuroscience, 11*, 307–314.

Wålinder, J. (1965). Transvestism, definition and evidence in favor of occasional derivation from cerebral dysfunction. *International Journal of Neuropsychiatry, 1*, 567–573.

Ward, N. (1975). Successful lithium treatment of transvestism associated with manic-depression. *Journal of Nervous and Mental Disorders, 161*, 204–206.

Wawrose, F. E., & Sisto, T. M. (1992). Clomipramine and a case of exhibitionism [letter]. *American Journal of Psychiatry, 149*, 843.

Wincze, J. P., Bansal, S., & Malamud, M. (1986). Effects of medroxyprogesterone acetate on subjective arousal, arousal to erotic stimulation, and nocturnal penile tumescence in male sex offenders. *Archives of Sexual Behavior, 15*, 293–305.

Wiseman, S. V., McAuley, J. W., Freidenberg, G. R., & Freidenberg, D. L. (2000). Hypersexuality in patients with dementia; possible response to cimetidine. *Neurology, 54*, 2024.

Zbytovsky, J. (1993). Haloperidol decanoate (Janssen) in the treatment of sexual deviations. *Cesko-Slovenská Psychiàtre, 89*, 15–17.

Zohar, J., Kaplan, Z., & Benjamin, J. (1994). Compulsive exhibitionism successfully treated with fluvoxamine: A controlled case study. *Journal of Clinical Psychiatry, 55*, 86–88.

Zubenko, G. S., George, A. W., Soloff, P. H., & Schulz, P. (1987). Sexual practices among patients with borderline personality disorder. *American Journal of Psychiatry, 144*, 748–752.

Exhibit 13.1
List of Medication Trade Names

Benperidol—Anquil	Lithium—Lithonate, Lithobid, Eskalith
Buspirone—Buspar	Medroxyprogesterone acetate—Provera; DepoProvera
Carbamazepine—Tegretol	Methylphenidate—Ritalin
Chlorpromazine—Thorazine	Naltrexone—Revia
Cimetidine—Tagamet	Nefazodone—Serzone
Clomipramine—Anafranil	Phenytoin—Dilantin
Clozapine—Clozaril	Pimozide—Orap
Cyproterone acetate—Androcur	Primidone—Mysoline
Desipramine—Norpramin	Quetiapine—Seroquel
Ethinyl estradiol—Estinyl	Risperidone—Risperdal
Ethylamide—Deslorelin	Sertraline—Zoloft
Fluoxetine—Prozac	Spironolactone—Aldactone
Fluphenazine—Prolixin	Sulpiride—Dolmatil, Sulpitil
Flutamide—Eulexin	Thioridazine—Mellaril
Fluvoxamine—Luvox	Thiothixine—Navane
Haloperidol—Haldol	Triptorelin—Decapeptyl
Ketoconazole—Nizoral	Valproate—Depakote
Leuprolide—Viadur	

Chapter 14

Group Therapy With Adult Sex Offenders

by Steven Sawyer, L.I.C.S.W., C.G.P.

Overview

Group therapy is widely used as a primary treatment modality for treating adult sex offenders. There is a rich history of group therapy research and literature on the therapeutic effects of treatment in a group yet there has been little research on the therapeutic benefits of group based interventions for sex offenders. This chapter presents a brief history of group therapy, summarizes the literature, and discusses effective group characteristics. Assessment, ethics, and therapist issues are also discussed. The chapter argues that sex offender treatment can be made more effective when the group is used to its full potential.

Introduction

"What happens in this group should have happened in our family. . . . This group is like an organism, it can change and adapt but it is not the same when someone leaves."

—former group member

The power of a group to influence its members and its provision of a forum of safety and support where all members make a contribution are some of the reasons people join groups. These same factors are at work in treatment groups and are essential to the effectiveness of a group intervention. When a group process illuminates the emotional and relational strengths and foibles of its members, the opportunity is created to experience acceptance, belonging, support, and a sense of giving. These affective experiences in the context of a structured treatment program become unique opportunities for group members to experience trust, emotional attachment, confrontation, fear and safety in the midst of some of the most painful and shameful disclosures they could possibly make. When sex offender treatment occurs in a group, it behooves the treating clinician to maximize the effect of the group milieu by capitalizing on opportunities for members to benefit from the group experience. This chapter will explore group therapy theory and history and its application to the treatment of sex offenders.

Groups Are the Most Common Approach

The literature describing the treatment of adult sex offenders consistently references the use of groups as the preferred treatment modality. Marshall & Barbaree (1990) observed, however, that group treatment may be employed for reasons of expediency such as group work being more time or cost efficient. These same authors also observed some of the possible benefits of treatment in a group such as members providing insight into each other's problems or acquiring new modes of thinking, but no comment was offered as to the efficacy of the group mode of treatment. As reported in the Safer Society National Survey of Treatment Programs and Models (1994), 86% of treatment programs treating adult male sex offenders (89% of adolescent programs) used group as a primary treatment modality. The published outcome research related to sex offenders focuses on cognitive-behavioral theory and suggests that group treatments with this approach appear to be effective (Marshall, 1996). However, interestingly enough, few articles have been written about the specific therapeutic processes and impact of group treatment with sex offenders (Beech & Fordham, 1997).

This raises several interesting questions: Are group process phenomena ignored in the service of maintaining control, managing structure, and changing cognitions? Are clinicians who treat sex offenders essentially conducting individual treatment in a group? Are clinicians utilizing group processes and simply not measuring the effect and influence of those processes? No treatment survey to date has answered these questions, but according to group theory, it is likely that most clinicians are utilizing group dynamics without particular attention to those processes. If this is accurate, then more traditional group therapy theory offers much guidance and is not antithetical to current sex offender treatment theory. In fact, it offers a valuable contribution to the structured cognitive behavioral approach commonly described in sex offender treatment. As Rutan and Alonso stated: "Group therapy, by its very format, offers unique opportunities to experience and work on issues of intimacy and individuation. In such groups the community is represented in the therapy room. It is usually impossible for individuals to view themselves as existing alone and affecting no one while in a group therapy situation over any significant period of time" (cited in Rutan & Stone, 1993, p. 8).

Intimacy and individuation are common issues for sex offenders. In this author's view, however, one of the most significant issues for sex offenders to address is their self centered perspective in which they lack empathy and act solely in service of their own needs.

History of Group Therapy

Group therapy has its roots in the early 1900s. Scheidlinger (2000) wrote, "Although groups devoted to healing are as old as mankind, the professionally guided helping group is an American invention. In 1905, Joseph Pratt, a Boston internist, first organized 'classes' for his indigent tubercular patients. Designed initially to impart proper home care measures, Pratt's approach soon revealed broader therapeutic potentials" (p. 316).

Early group work drew on analytic concepts popular at the time, but Rutan and Stone (1993) summarized two authors, LeBon and McDougal, who offered opposing appraisals of the group impact, the latter offering an optimistic and important view that shifted group thinking. LeBon (1920) observed a negative effect of groups on individuals, concluding that the group contributed to "a diminishing of human functioning." He observed that individuals experienced increased strength—even invincibility—suggestibility, and contagion when in groups. The result of this negative effect is a loss of self and the individuals' ability to act on their own will. In contrast, McDougal (1920), while also observing the potential negative effect, noted an important additive when individuals are in groups. He observed that when groups were organized around a clearly defined common purpose the group had the potential to enhance individual behavior.

About these early developments, Rutan and Stone (1993) noted, "Thus two of the earliest authors on the impact of groups upon individuals identified several important phenomena: the power of groups to affect the behaviors of individuals; the presence of contagion or the capacity of groups to fill each of the members with affects; and the importance of organization, group agreements and goals" (p. 11)

A slight digression might add to our discussion of the origin of the meaning of "group." The definition of group includes "an assemblage of persons, animals, or material standing near together so as to form a collective unity; a knot (of people), a cluster (of things)." The *Oxford English Dictionary* (1989) traces the early origins of the word "group"—originating from French "groupe," Italian "gruppo" or knot, and Spanish "grupo," "gorupo," and "grupa," meaning knot, cluster, and group (p. 620). First used in the 1600s to describe artistic elements of fine art, the term "group" was used in the 1700s to describe people with some common traits. These early definitions and uses juxtaposed the individual against the group with the group representing a source of commonality or common bond. As early group therapy authors identified, a group offers not only strength and solace but also a presence against which the individual may push to craft his own sense of confidence and self concept.

Literature on Group Therapy Is Extensive

The literature on group therapy is rich with theory and practice relevant to anyone working with groups and offers considerable insight into the limits of group therapy, group processes, benefits, and curative factors. Theories of group therapy posit that group dynamics are in operation in all groups, implying that a key ingredient of the therapeutic process is missed unless the clinician uses those group processes. That said, there is evidence that some clinical populations lack the capacity to develop therapeutic group dynamics. The literature suggests that a group format is useful for most sex offenders and other forensic populations but also cautions that the specific clinical population and group approach are variables that must be addressed in designing and implementing a group-based intervention.

Some studies have documented the benefit of group therapy approaches with forensic populations. Stein and Brown (1991) described a study that found clients with mental illness and antisocial personality disorder were unable to form the therapeutic group dynamics described by Yalom (1995), but there are published studies that document the successful use of groups. MacDevitt and Stanislow (1987) compared curative factors across forensic groups in differing levels of incarceration. They found differences between the study groups, previous forensic groups studied by Long and Cope (1980) and outpatient groups studied by Yalom. Catharsis was among the top four factors in all groups studied whereas family reenactment and identification were among the lowest two for each offender classification. There were numerous differences between these groups and previous research. Pithers (1994) described a group-based intervention designed to enhance sex offender empathy skills. Schwartz (1995) described the early history of treating sex offenders in groups, including a recidivism study of offenders treated in groups that showed a lower reoffense rate for those treated in group therapy. Burtenshaw (1997) described a study asking incarcerated chemically dependent inmates to rank the importance of therapeutic factors. He found the least variation between ethnic groups. He also found an overall trend for all subjects to place a high value on the factors of self-understanding and catharsis. Marshall, Bryce, Hudson, and Ward (1997) described a group-based treatment component designed to increase intimacy skills for nonfamilial male child molesters. These studies outlined the specific group theory (relapse prevention or cognitive/behavioral) or treatment targets (intimacy skills) but did not address the interactional processes within the group. Schwartz (1988) discussed interpersonal techniques for treating sex offenders and described a history of the use of group therapy with sex offenders in prison settings and outpatient therapy. Such work provided some techniques for group formation and some theoretical perspectives about the inner workings of the sex offender treatment group. Other articles documented the use of group therapy with sex offenders without detailing the specific group processes.

Two articles defined the specific theoretical orientation of the group process. Ganzarain and Buchele (1990) described a psychodynamic approach with incest perpetrators and Frey (1987) described a mini-marathon approach with incest offenders. Another study discussed the role of the therapist in group therapy with drug abusers (Page, Campbell, & Wilder, 1994), and Fowler, Burns, and Roehl (1983) discussed the importance of group therapy in incest counseling. Marshall and Barbaree (1990) discussed the difficulty in program evaluation when programs vary in content and do not provide detailed program descriptions when reporting outcome results. These studies contributed to the belief that group therapy was a helpful modality but left the question of the specific therapeutic action unanswered.

Group Effectiveness and Therapeutic Contribution

Most clinicians who had college courses related to group work were introduced to the works of Yalom (1995), Rutan and Stone (1993), or MacKenzie (1983), although none of these authors specialized in sex offender treatment. Although much of the group therapy literature has a psychodynamic theoretical basis, many articles also focus on cognitive, time-limited, or issue-focused approaches. The literature on group psychotherapy documents the efficacy of group work from many venues and theoretical perspectives (Dies, 1986; Tillitsky, 1990; Yalom, 1995). Yalom (1995) goes even further by saying "The research evidence for the overall effectiveness of group psychotherapy is so compelling that it is time to direct our efforts toward a fuller understanding of the necessary conditions for effective psychotherapy" (p. 47). Many authors write about specific techniques and perspectives to apply to the group to increase effectiveness. Several examples illuminate the possibilities.

Shields (2000) described the treatment of character disorder in group therapy. He offered valuable lessons for the group therapist that redefine and interpret the antisocial group member. For example, "Cherish the troublesome as one road to the core of the self" is based on the need for engagement that feels real and not merely compliant. Although the pure psychodynamic perspective lacks the cognitive and behavioral elements used today in sex offender treatment, it offers a unique perspective that is useful in group therapy for addressing long-standing behavioral and relational patterns that are contributors to an offense cycle, dysfunctional relationships, and low self-esteem. Certainly, lack of interpersonal engagement is a feature shared by many sex offenders and is at the root of some sex offenses.

Councileman and Gans (1999), writing about the meaning of a missed session, observed, "Most group therapists have noticed that a group feels different if a particular member is not present. Just as in cooking where omission of a single ingredient can significantly alter the flavor of a dish, every member contributes to the chemistry of the group. Much can be learned about a member's role by how the group changes (or does not change) in his or her absence" (p. 7).

Hence, using the group in its entirety and the relationships therein allows the members to experience the meaning and impact of the group relationships. This perspective shifts the focus from the individual to the group and is an opportunity to focus on cohesion, a key ingredient in effective groups.

Why Is Group Effective?

There is no specific empirical evidence of the efficacy of sex offender treatment in a group format. In fact, there is professional debate as to whether group treatment is always the most appropriate approach (Maletsky, 1999). The debate about efficacy is complicated by the many variants of treatment (Marshall & Barbaree, 1990). This raises some interesting questions. If group is the primary modality, is individual treatment also offered? Is there a behavioral component? Is family or relationship therapy also offered? What role does the therapist assume in group facilitation: the role of ultimate power? or the role of facilitation of the group process and deferring to group decisions? These variations affect the group action and have an impact on the individual client. Hence, we are left to surmise and hypothesize in an attempt to explain why we believe group is the most efficacious mode of treatment. The literature on group therapy offers some clues about effective group processes that apply to treatment of sex offenders.

Let me begin with what I believe is the single most important curative factor in the group treatment of sex offenders: cohesion. Yalom (1995) defined cohesion as "the resultant of all forces acting on all the members to remain in the group . . . or . . . the attractiveness of a group for its members" (p. 48). Another way to think about cohesiveness is that it is the glue that holds the group together, the degree of "groupness" or attachment members feel for the group. One result of cohesion is that group members feel ownership for the success of its members.

Yalom (1995) proposed that the curative factors he outlined were in operation in most types of groups:

- Instillation of hope;
- Universality;
- Imparting information;
- Altruism;
- Corrective recapitulation of family group;
- Development of socialization techniques;
- Imitative behavior;
- Interpersonal learning;
- Group cohesiveness;
- Catharsis; and
- Existential factors.

These factors have become standards in the field and have been studied in forensic settings (Morgan, Winterowd, & Ferrell, 1999; Stein & Brown, 1991) and specifically with sex offenders (Beech & Fordham, 1997). Yalom (1995) argued;

> One of the most important underlying assumptions . . . is that interpersonal interaction is crucial in group therapy. The truly potent therapy group first provides an arena for patients to interact freely with others, then helps them to identify and understand what goes wrong in their interactions, and ultimately enables them to change those maladaptive patterns. I believe that groups resting solely on other assumptions, such as psychoeducational or cognitive behavioral principles, fail to reap the full therapeutic harvest of group therapy. Each of these forms of group therapy can, in my view, be made even more effective by incorporating a focus on interpersonal process." (p. xiv)

Applying Factors to Sex Offender Treatment

Assume for a moment that the therapeutic factors Yalom describes are potential contributing factors in the success of group-oriented programs. How are these factors relevant to the goals of structured sex offender treatment? The goals of structured treatment include, among others, changing cognitions, increasing awareness of cognitive and behavioral chains, improving communication and social skills and increasing empathy. Educating a group about cognitive distortions and requiring the members to publicly describe their pattern of dysfunctional cognitions exposes their erroneous thought processes and allows for the group to correct misconceptions and beliefs. When this exercise is followed with group interaction about how other members share the same faulty cognitions and their collective sharing of how unreasonable the cognitions are, then the man "in focus" gains the opportunity to feel less shameful in front of his peers. He learns that some of his thoughts are not unique (Universality) and that other group members have the opportunity to offer aid and assistance to a fellow group member (Altruism). If these interactions occur in a context in which trust has been established, group cohesion can be increased or reinforced. This cohesion strengthens the group bond, which enhances capacity for empathy and commitment to treatment.

If cohesion contributes to treatment success and treatment success is correlated with reduced risk for reoffense, the group and its members reap additional benefits from the interactive element of the group process. If the group members are allowed to interact freely outside the goal structure, they are able to experience each other's unique views about their offenses, relationships, quirks of personality, and fears and concerns. In this free exchange the group experiences each other as equals, as fellow group members, without the therapeutic demands of the treatment structure. This then becomes an opportunity for the therapist to observe leadership within the group, passivity of particular individuals, and interactional patterns within the group.

If the curative factors Yalom identifies are at work in pure cognitive-behavioral formats and in groups that include an interpersonal element, then discussion among those working with sex offenders about the effect of group processes would both enhance understanding of the factors of effective treatment and inform practitioners about treatment efficacy. The factors described as "curative" by Yalom apply to any group process in any venue. Further exploration and elucidation of the factors that make a group experience effective and efficient would contribute to our understanding of how and why group is an effective intervention modality with sex offenders.

Group Characteristics

Following is a list of characteristics that make group work a rich therapeutic experience and enhance the effect of treatment.

- The group represents the larger outside community; therefore, while in the group, the client demonstrates his style or pattern of interacting in the community, thus providing access to that pattern within the group. When natural interaction is allowed to occur, group members have an *in vivo* experience of each other's interactional style.

- Group therapy brings to bear the strength and reparative power of relationship when relationships are allowed to form in the group. For example, much of the work in sex offender treatment has the potential to be shame inducing. When shame is experienced, relationship is one of the most powerful and effective mediums for reparation (Kaufman, 1980). If a group member experiences shameful feelings in the trusting atmosphere of a group, he can also experience the support and shared experience of other members and avoid the alienation often experienced as a result of a shameful experience.

• Treatment in a group accomplishes the goal of engaging a person in relationships, which allows access to the characterological and relational traits capable of harm. Allowing personality traits such as narcissism, relational distance, callousness or deceit to be exposed in group relationships creates the opportunity for group members to confront and work through interpersonal hostility. The interpersonal approach occurs in the present rather than, for example, a therapist lecturing about some abstract past behavior which is easy to intellectualize or refute.

• Treatment seeks interpersonal change. Interpersonal change occurs when behavioral, attitudinal, or affective changes occur in the context of relationships, not simply in the context of one's own thought processes. This is the opportunity to witness change and not just "talk the talk."

• Treatment in a group allows for the transference relationship to develop across multiple relationships and allows for multiple sources of feedback and support. One of the most powerful aspects of a group is the various sources of feedback, support, and challenge that are available, thus freeing the therapist from the center of attention. It is this group interaction that fosters cohesion, empowers group members, and increases trust and empathy.

• Treatment in a group with a culture of honest and supportive confrontation creates norms that encourage both disclosure and challenge from multiple perspectives. This group culture offers support while demanding that members reveal the behaviors, thoughts, and affective states related to their offense. The group norm becomes one that expects individual risk taking that exposes painful or shameful material in the arms of group support or confrontation when appropriate.

Most authors and practitioners seem to agree that treatment of sex offenders should occur in a group. Most also seem to agree that treatment of sex offenders should address relationship issues (how else can we treat empathy deficits, communication skills, or intimacy deficits?). That said, if change is the goal, ideally the client will demonstrate his dysfunctional and harmful relationship patterns and then demonstrate change in those patterns. Assuming we want the change integrated (in other words, not just a cognitive concept but a change integrated with behavior and affect in relationships), this type of change is easily demonstrated and observable in the group.

Example: "Tom" was sexually abused as a child. He had sexually abused several boys over many years. He had poor communication skills with adult peers and he lacked confidence to be assertive and was reluctant to express any strong emotions. When preparing his aftercare plan he identified anger as a precursor that triggered fantasies of young boys. He described his intent to express anger toward his wife when it occurred and to go to her whenever he was angry. However, he never openly expressed anger in the group, even when he was visibly distressed. When he disagreed with a group member he was unable to be assertive and speak his mind. The group challenged him on the disconnect between his intent and his actions. The result was an illumination of the inconsistency between his thoughts and actions as his behavior was exposed in the group. This challenge left him in a quandary for some time, as he was not initially aware of this pattern. During this group interaction he was able to experience the same phenomenon he displayed with his wife, allowing the opportunity to rework the pattern with supportive peers. The group challenged him in a supportive manner and held him accountable without shaming him. He was able to see how inconsistent he was while also feeling the support of the group members.

In a group that is functioning optimally, the feedback from the group is offered in a supportive and empathic atmosphere where it is experienced as heartfelt and genuine, not critical and demeaning. One of the essential ingredients to effective group functioning is the progression of natural developmental processes.

Group Development

There are numerous theories of group developmental process. Regardless of the preferred theory, there is general agreement that group relationships progress through somewhat predictable stages over time. Understanding the concept of development and observing the movement of the group over time allows the group therapist additional data to help the group develop more constructive and helpful relations. Theories and models of group development have been described in the past twenty years. Yalom (1995) proposed a three-stage model: (1) orientation, hesitant participation, search for meaning, and dependency; (2) conflict, dominance, and rebellion; and (3) development of cohesion. Tuckman (1965) proposed a four-stage model: (1) forming, (2) storming, (3) norming, and (4) performing. Beck (1981) proposed a nine-stage model: (1) making a contract, (2) establishing a group identity, (3) exploring a group identity and direction, (4) establishing intimacy, (5) exploring mutuality, (6) achieving autonomy through reorganization of the group's structure, (7) self-confronting and achieving interdependence, (8) achieving independence and the transfer of learning, and (9) terminating.

These models suggest a progression in the group relationships that begins with initial relationship formation; progresses to more complex issues of trust, conflict, and intimacy; and concludes with a deeper level of interpersonal interaction. Developmental theory suggests that each group moves through these stages at a unique pace and that when new members are added, the group must return to early stage developmental issues.

Any ongoing group experiences some developmental process, and the therapeutic benefits are ultimately tied to the group's ability to successfully navigate these stages. Ultimately, as observed by MacKenzie (1993), future success is correlated to relatedness, which is a function of developmental progress. Consequently, attending to stages of developmental growth and assisting the group to move beyond initial reluctance toward trust and cohesion maximizes the group opportunity.

Assessment of Group Functioning

Assessing group processes allows the therapist to test his or her perceptions of the group while gaining some "distance" from biases and preconceived notions about how well or poorly the group is operating. This can be accomplished through supervisor observation, by having one of the therapists "sit out" of the group circle and observe the group process without interacting or by using a group assessment measure. Various studies have measured group processes and functioning (Beech & Fordham, 1997; MacKenzie & Tschuschke, 1993). Two instruments that assess common group factors known to be aspects of effective group functioning have been used extensively and can easily be applied to sex offender groups

One instrument is the Group Climate Scale (Moos, 1994). Of the scale, Moos wrote, "The Group Climate Scale can be used to describe group environments and how well they are implemented, to compare members' and leaders' views of their group, and to compare actual and preferred group environments. Individual members' views can be compared with one another" (p. 5). This type of instrument provides the therapist with a comparison of members' perceptions and experiences compared to each other and to the therapist. The scale measures three dimensions: Relationship, Personal Growth, and System Change. Relationship scales are Cohesion, Leader Support, and Expressiveness; personal growth scales are Independence, Task Orientation, Self-Discovery, and Anger and Aggression. System Change scales are Order and Organization, Leader Control and Innovation. In a study of sex offender treatment groups, Beech and Fordham (1997) used this instrument to assess group functioning across multiple groups and sites. The findings are significant for the field as they found differences across groups and between leadership styles resulting in a different "profile" of a successful group. Also of interest was their finding of differences between leaders and members scores, suggesting that leaders may perceive their role, relationship to the group, and contribution differently from group members.

The Group Climate Questionnaire—Revised (MacKenzie, 1983) measures three dimensions: Engagement, Conflict, and Avoidance. The results provide an indication of the group interaction. Engagement is a measure of the extent to which the group members are connected to and actively participating in the group process. Engagement is measured by statements such as "The members liked and cared about each other" and "The members revealed sensitive and personal information and feelings." Conflict is measured by the degree of actual conflict in the group such as "The members rejected and distrusted each other" or "The members were distant and withdrawn from each other." Avoiding is measured by such statements as "The members avoided looking at important issues going on between themselves." The actions of these constructs within the group are interwoven. A group that is engaged and cohesive would tend to identify interpersonal conflicts, and these conflicts would be significant enough to have the group attempt to work them out. By contrast, a group that is not engaged might avoid conflict, not reveal personal information and care less about other members. A group that is engaged, interacts with each other, and does not avoid relationship conflict is correlated with higher levels of member satisfaction and change. This measure provides a snapshot of the group functions at a point in time. It can be used as frequently as weekly to assess group functioning. In a study using the scale concepts, MacKenzie and Tschuschke (1993) found that "relatedness," as measured by Engagement items on this scale, was correlated with positive outcome in inpatient psychotherapy groups where relatedness was closely associated with the concept of cohesion.

In a brief unpublished study using both scales on nineteen existing adult outpatient treatment groups with a total of twelve therapists, this author found surprising consistency across groups and across time as well as some significant differences between some groups and both similarities and differences between group member and leader perceptions. The results led to helpful discussions about therapist style, group composition, facilitation philosophy, and group functioning. There are multiple applications to sex offender treatment. Measuring the various constructs known to contribute to effective group outcome provides clinicians and program supervisors with more objective measures of group functioning. This information can contribute to treatment planning and supervision and serve to improve the overall treatment effect.

Group Therapy and Sex Offender-Specific Issues

How is group work helpful with the particular goals of sex offender treatment? To begin with, prior to treatment few sex offenders have ever talked about their offenses with anyone, with the exception of a spouse (when the initial disclosure was made) or the police. To come to the realization in the group that the offense was planned, that there was intent and prior fantasy that supported the behavior, and that he is not alone allows the offender to be able to admit the offense, experience congruent affect, feel shame, and experience the support of the group. Through this experience he learns he can tolerate the overwhelming emotional pain of coming full face with the reality of his actions.

In a group atmosphere that facilitates give-and-take and interpersonal relationships, communication skills are practiced constantly. Each member must learn to express himself accurately and also learn to listen and understand the other members. Effective communication skills are essential to meet emotional and relational needs as an adult, skills many offenders are lacking. As part of learning socialization skills, pedophiles (who are often passive in adult peer relationships) are forced to interact with adult males and face their fears of intimacy, intimidation, and relational incompetence. Power and control issues, common for rapists, are revealed in a group where one member is dominant. If the focus of the group is on the interpersonal interactions, each member must face his reaction to the dominant member. Some may confront, others may "fight power with power," others may retreat to their typical passive mode. All these patterns are revealed and available to the group therapist for therapeutic intervention. Perhaps most important, attachment to or detachment from the group, is an important factor that is easily accessible in a group interaction. Trust issues must first be addressed and cohesion must be established and strengthened to allow exposure of the inner workings of relationships. When the group relationships matter to each group member, interpersonal caring is revealed, disclosure increases, and "the health of the whole" becomes the focus of the group interactions. This focus transcends each offense and provides the platform for each member to reveal and work through his unique underlying issues and offense precursors.

> Example: A 40-year-old man who had a long history of attraction to boys and several early-adolescent male victims presented his escape strategies that included using his support system if he found himself in his reoffense cycle. As he described his progression to another offense, he believed his support group would "see through" his defenses and intervene on his cycle. His belief was based on his past ability to deceive others and the fact that he had changed and was no longer as guarded and manipulative. The group was challenged to explain how they could see though defenses and whether they would pursue him if they suspected he was being deceitful. The ensuing discussion revealed a deep caring about his success and, to the surprise of some members, a depth of caring about their own contribution to each other's success. The result was a new revelation that they would do all they could to help another group member and that they had a commitment to "do all they could" which showed an ownership of the group's success that the members had not previously experienced.

This discussion went far beyond the "task" of presenting an escape plan. Group cohesion was strengthened and members felt attachment, empathy, and renewed trust of each other and the group process.

Therapist Issues

In all therapeutic endeavors, the therapist is in a position of authority and, accurately or not, is often viewed by the client as powerful and knowledgeable. Hence, the client ascribes to the therapist trust and dependence. It is this unequal relationship that makes clients vulnerable and also opens the client to change in a trusting environment. This dynamic is no different in a group setting. Group leaders have the same ethical obligations as do individual therapists. Establishing clear group rules about group functioning, boundaries, relationships, attendance, and payment is essential for effective group operation (American Group Psychotherapy Association, 1991). Likewise, the group therapist must monitor his or her countertransference. There is nothing more tempting when running a group than to jump to challenge, correct, or confront a member when he utters a particularly profound distortion, when what is most beneficial to the group is to work with the group to identify and challenge their fellow member. The group therapist's perceived omnipotence, superior observation skills, or own outrage may be the trigger to jump in to intervene. When the therapist succumbs to this temptation, he or she robs the group members of an opportunity to contribute to the group success. Also, an opportunity is missed to observe the group in action; to see if members hear the same horrendous distortion, to see if members are assertive enough to confront or to observe collusion when members allow such obvious inappropriate thinking. Allowing or expecting the group to accurately challenge each other reinforces their ability to successfully change, to try out new social skills, to experience the benefit of newly learned communication skills and the trust and safety of increasing cohesion as they negotiate conflict and observe each others' struggles. These circumstances can be monitored through cofacilitation whenever possible or through regular supervision that focuses on the group interactional processes.

Professional Issues

Most licensing boards and professional organizations have ethics statements and some have standards of practice. The American Group Psychotherapy Association (AGPA; 1991) published *Guidelines for Professional Practice*, which includes sections on Responsibilities to Patients/Clients and Professional Standards. The section Responsibilities to Patients/Clients is organized around three basic tenets: respect for each client and client rights, privacy/confidentiality, and public protection/professional incompetence. The section on professional standards focuses on the integrity of the practice of group psychotherapy, specifically, to maintain competence, to contribute to professional knowledge, and to report incompetent professionals. The Association for the Treatment of Sexual Abusers (1997) published *Ethical Standards and Principles for the Management of Sexual Abusers*. This document addresses ethical standards in categories that include professional conduct, client relationships, confidentiality, professional relationships, research and publications, public information, and advertising and compliance procedures. The section titled "Principles for the Management of Sexual Abusers" includes sections on educational and professional experience of service providers, underlying principles, evaluation, treatment, arousal control, cognitive therapy, relapse prevention, victim awareness and empathy, social competence, healthy relationships, couple and parent therapy, reunification, pharmacological agents, follow-up treatment, use of physiological agents, special populations, and dual diagnosis. The International Association for the Treatment of Sex Offenders recently adopted standards of care that also address client protection and professional standards. These standards—*Treatment of Adult Sex Offenders: Standards of Care* (Coleman et al., 1995)—originally published in 1995, outline types of treatment, professional competence, antecedents to sex offender treatment, and fourteen principles of standards of care. Although this document does not specifically call for group therapy, it does obligate the professional to attain the minimal level of competence for the treatment modality he or she employs and offers group therapy as a possible treatment modality. These organizations provide varying degrees of standards that protect the client and the integrity of the clinical practice. As with any professional practice, there are limits within which professionals must operate. The group therapist has the same obligations and demands on his or her practice. Though many of the standards overlap with licensing bodies, the fact that AGPA states that a group therapist must not practice outside his or her competence reinforces the expectation of competence in providing group therapy. Just as not every psychologist can interpret psychological testing, not every mental health practitioner is a competent group therapist. Anyone providing group therapy has the obligation to attain a level of competence adequate for the setting and clients they serve. Likewise, the organization has an obligation to support group therapy and adequate supervision for group therapists (Cox, Ilfield, Ilfield, & Brennan, 2000).

Conclusion

There is a long history of group therapy in the United States and a growing body of literature about effective treatment of sex offenders. Although research on the evidence of effective sex offender treatment has reviewed many group-based programs, few studies have focused on the group processes that contribute to effective treatment. The few studies that have examined group processes were based on group theory postulated by Yalom or Moos and support the notion that therapeutic factors attained through relationships within the group are key to getting maximum benefit from the group mode of treatment. Drawing on relationship interactions, cohesion, individual contribution, and other factors identified by numerous authors is the most strongly supported approach to maximize the benefit of treating in a group.

Though many programs treat sex offenders in a group, not all programs treat the group processes and relationships. The potential exists to strengthen relationship skills, communication skills, and empathy through the curative power of cohesion within the group. Cohesion can be strengthened through working with the group relationships within the goal-oriented structure of most sex offender treatment programs. The difference between group therapy and a group-based intervention rests primarily on this point. A group-based intervention can be enhanced by facilitating the attainment of the curative or therapeutic factors identified in the group therapy literature. An examination of what constitutes group therapy, how groups are facilitated, and how and why the group venue is effective would deepen our understanding of effective treatment.

References

American Group Psychotherapy Association. (1991). *Guidelines for group psychotherapy practice.* New York: Author.

Association for the Treatment of Sexual Abusers. (1997). *Ethical standards and principles for the management of sexual abusers.* Beaverton, OR: Author.

Beck, A. (1981). Developmental characteristics of the system forming process. In J. E. Durkin (Ed.), *Living groups: Group psychology and general systems theory* (pp. 316–322). New York: Brunner/Mazel.

Beech A., & Fordham, A. S. (1997). Therapeutic climate of sexual offender treatment programs. *Sexual Abuse: A Journal of Research and Treatment, 8*, 219–237.

Burtenshaw, R. P. (1997, August). An ethnic comparison of the ranked value of Yalom's therapeutic factors among chemically dependent incarcerated adult males in group psychotherapy. *Dissertation Abstracts International, 58*(2-A).

Coleman, E., Dwyer, S. M., Abel, G., Berner, W., Breiling, J., Hindman, J., Honey-Knopp, F., Langevin, R., & Pfafflin, F. (1995). The treatment of adult sex offenders: Standards of care. *Journal of Offender Rehabilitation, 23*(3–4), 5–11.

Councilman, E. F., & Gans, J. S. (1999). The missed session in psychodynamic group psychotherapy. *International Journal of Group Psychotherapy, 49*(1), 71–86.

Cox, P. D., Ilfield, Jr., F., Ilfield, B. S., & Brennan, C. (2000). Group therapy program development: Administrator collaboration in new practice settings. *International Journal of Group Psychotherapy, 50*(1), 3–24.

Dies, R. (1986). Practical theoretical, and empirical foundations for group psychotherapy. In A. Francis & R. Hales (Eds.), *The American Psychiatric Association annual review* (Vol. 5; pp. 659–677). Washington, DC: American Psychiatric Press.

Fowler, C., Burns, S. R., & Roehl, J. E. (1983). The role of group therapy in incest counseling. *International Journal of Family Therapy, 5*(2), 127–135.

Frey, C. (1987). Mini-marathon group sessions with incest offenders. *Social Work, 32*(4), 534–535.

Ganzarain, R., & Buchele, B.J. (1990). Incest perpetrators in group therapy: A psychodynamic perspective. *Bulletin of the Menninger Clinic, 54*(3), 295–310.

Kaufman, G. (1980). *Shame: The power of caring.* Cambridge, MA: Schenkman.

LeBon, G. (1920). *The crowd: A study of the popular mind.* New York: Fisher Unwin.

Long, L., & Cope, C. (1980). Curative factors in a male felony offender group. *Small Group Behavior, 11*, 389–398.

MacDevitt, J. W., & Stanislaw, C. (1987). Curative factors in male felony offender groups. *Small Group Behavior, 18*(1), 72–81.

MacKenzie, K. R. (1983) The clinical application of a group climate measure. In R. R. Dies & K. R. MacKenzie (Eds.), *Advances in group pychotherapy: Integrating research and practice* (pp. 159–170). New York: International Universities Press.

MacKenzie, K. R., & Tschuschke, V. (1993). Relatedness, group work, and outcome in long-term inpatient psychotherapy groups. *Journal of Psychotherapy Practice and Research, 2,* 147–156.

Maletzky, B. M. (1999). Groups of one. *Sexual Abuse: A Journal of Research and Treatment, 11*(3), 179–181.

Marshall, W. L. (1996). Assessment, treatment, and theorizing about sex offenders: Developments during the past twenty years and future directions. *Criminal Justice and Behavior, 23*, 162–199.

Marshall W. L., & Barbaree, H. E. (1990). Outcome of comprehensive cognitive behavioral treatment program. In W. Marshall & H. Barbaree (Eds.), *Handbook of sexual assault: Issues, theories and treatment of offenders* (pp. 363–385). New York: Plenum.

McDougall, W. (1920). *The group mind.* New York: Putnam.

Moos, R. (1994). *Group Environment Scale: A social climate scale.* Palo Alto, CA: Consulting Psychologists Press.

Morgan, R. D., Winterowd, C. L., & Ferrell, S. W. (1999). A national survey of group psychotherapy services in correctional facilities. *Professional Psychology: Research and Practice, 30*(6), 600–606.

National Survey of Treatment Programs and Models. (1994). Brandon, VT: Safer Society Program and Press.

Oxford English Dictionary (2nd ed.). (1989). Oxford, UK: Clarendon Press.

Pithers, W. D. (1994). Process evaluation of group therapy component designed to enhance sex offender empathy for sexual abuse survivors. *Behavior Research and Therapy, 32*(5), 565–570.

Rutan, J. S., & Stone, W. N. (1993). *Psychodynamic group psychotherapy* (2nd ed.). New York: Guilford Press.

Scheidlinger, S. (2000). The group psychotherapy movement at the millennium: some historical perspectives. *International Journal of Group Psychotherapy, 50*(3), 315–339.

Schwartz, B. K. (1988). Interpersonal techniques in treating adult sex offenders. In *A practitioners guide to treating the incarcerated male sex offender.* Washington, DC: U.S. Department of Justice, National Institute of Corrections.

Schwartz, B. K. (1995). Group therapy. In B. K. Schwartz & H. R. Cellini (Eds.), *The sex offender: Corrections, treatment and legal practice* (pp. 14-1–14-16). Kingston, NJ: Civic Research Institute.

Shields, W. (2000). Hope and the inclination to be troublesome: Winnicott and the treatment of character disorder in group therapy. *International Journal of Group Psychotherapy, 50*(1), 87–103.

Stein, E., & Brown, J. D. (1991). Group therapy in a forensic setting. *Canadian Journal of Psychiatry, 36*(10), 718–722.

Tillitski, C. (1990). A meta-analysis of estimated effect sizes for group vs., individual vs. control treatments. *International Journal of Group Psychotherapy, 40*, 215–224.

Tuckman, B. W. (1965). Developmental sequence in small groups. *Psychological Bulletin, 63*, 384–399.

Yalom, I. (1995). *The theory and practice of group psychotherapy* (4th ed.). New York: Basic Books.

Chapter 15

Addressing the Victim/Perpetrator Dialectic—Treatment for the Effects of Sexual Victimization on Sex Offenders

by Laurie Guidry, Psy.D.

Overview

In the following chapter, some of the central and somewhat contentious issues surrounding the treatment of the sequelae of early sexual abuse within the population of sexual perpetrators are identified. In spite of the conflicting professional stances found and the influence of misinformed and/or misdirected social opinions, a clear and grounded argument is made here for addressing the clinical concerns related to sexual abuse in the treatment of sex offenders. Following a review of the impact of sexual abuse on males, this chapter offers historical and contemporary support for the concept of the victim/perpetrator dialectic (VPD). Finally, this chapter presents the central tenets and goals of the VPD treatment module, designed to enhance the effect of SOST and informed by the research on both sex offenders and male survivors of sexual abuse. The VPD model attempts to address the gap in the integrated treatment of adult male sex offenders who have also been sexually victimized in childhood. As such, this "offender-informed/trauma-based" model can (1) augment and complement cognitive-behavioral forms of sex offender-specific treatment (SOST), (2) facilitate recovery from the negative psychological effects of childhood sexual abuse, and (3) promote the reconciliation of the conflicted victim/perpetrator dialectic in an effort to decrease the incidence of sexually abusing behavior.

Introduction

The relationship between early sexual victimization and the development of later sexually aberrant behavior has been an extensively examined and hotly debated topic. Ambivalence in the sex offender treatment field regarding the strength and relevance of this relationship, and the subsequent need for intervention, appears to be rooted, among other things, in the fear of fostering the socially undesirable "abuse excuse" mentality in the treatment of sex offenders. Linear causal connections have been hypothesized and subsequently deconstructed, secondary to the argument that not everyone who was sexually abused in childhood goes on to perpetrate sexual abuse in adulthood. However, these types of simplistic counterarguments fail to address the underlying nature of the clinically important relationship between early sexual abuse and later aberrant sexual behavior—a relationship that appears to be relevant for a sizable number of sexual perpetrators. Although the link between early sexual abuse and later sex offending behavior may clinically range from being a replicative and transparent cycle to a complex and nonlinear process, it seems incumbent upon sex offender-specific treatment (SOST) providers to make an informed effort at addressing this dialectical dimension of a perpetrator's clinical presentation.

Barriers to Treating Sexual Abuse Among Sex Offenders

"To Treat or Not to Treat . . .": The Historical Context. What is the original source of divisive controversy over addressing sexual victimization issues among sexual offenders? The roots of this contention are linked to the early forms of sex offender treatment that emerged simultaneously but separately on the East and West Coasts of the United States during the 1950s and 1960s (B. Schwartz, personal communication, 2001). During this period in the East, in states such as New Jersey and Massachusetts, psychoanalysis was the treatment of choice for just about everything, including (and perhaps especially) sexual deviance. Treatment programs for sex offenders, like the one established at the Massachusetts Treatment Center centered around addressing an individual's personal history of victimization and, of course, his relationship with his mother. In contrast, on the West Coast the void in treatment for sex offenders was filled when incarcerated perpetrators themselves designed their own intervention. With an understandably confrontive, no-holds-barred, hot-seat format, this approach had no tolerance for the perceived coddling found in the psychodynamic approach, and no room for the vulnerability inherent in exploring one's own victimization. This fractioned evolution reflects the larger contextual split in psychology at the time between psychodynamic and cognitive-behavioral treatment. SOST in this country, therefore, initially evolved from two philosophically distinct and conflicting paradigms.

In the late 1980s, Washington State itself, while proving to be the most progressive state in treating sex offenders, literally split into two factions with two separate professional organizations for sex offender treatment identified. On the west side of Lake Washington, the confrontive model gave way to an increasingly cognitive-behavioral approach, whereas on the east side cognitive-behavioral treatment was supplemented by a willingness to deal with with early childhood abuse. The western cognitive behavioral approach gained popularity as key pioneers gained positions of power in professional organizations such as the Association for the Treatment of Sexual Abusers. This approach eventually made its way across the country.

At the present time, when one refers to "standard" sex offender treatment, there is an assumption that one is referencing the cognitive-behavioral approach that has been empirically grounded in the most current research literature but pays little heed to victim issues. What seems to be true, however, though not articulated clearly in the contemporary literature in the sex offender treatment field, is that major inpatient treatment centers, such as those found in Minnesota, Wisconsin, Ohio, Montana, New Jersey, Vermont, Massachusetts, and Oklahoma, continue to address victim issues extensively among the sex offenders they treat. Different facilities have developed different models, but it is our misfortune that none have been widely published. In the meantime, outpatient providers of sex offender treatment appear to have inherited the divisive debate, with some camps focusing on victim issues to the exclusion of cognitive-behavioral issues, others emphasizing cognition and behavior to the exclusion of addressing the effects of early abuse on the perpetrator, and few programs seeking integration. This nearly polarized "all or nothing" position can foster either an over- or underresponse to the significant issues of sexual victimization among sexual perpetrators. This professional ambivalence only works to limit the application of potentially effective, integrated treatment approaches for sex offenders.

Ambivalence in the SOST Field. It is becoming clearer that there are significant numbers of male survivors of childhood sexual abuse, and that many have demonstrated subsequent negative effects that respond positively to therapeutic intervention. Rooted in the evolutionary history of the sex offender treatment field just noted, however, there appears to be an ongoing lack of consensus regarding the relevance of addressing early sexual victimization issues within adult SOST. Many researchers deny the link between early victimization and later offending (Bauserman & Rind, 1997; Fischer, 1992). Hindman's (1988) research indicated that a majority of the offenders in her study lied about their own histories of abuse. These observations, however, may be unduly influenced by the research sample population characteristics (i.e., samples of college students or outpatient offenders located in a demographically sophisticated and wealthy area). Others adhere to the claim that acknowledging and working with offender victim issues only reinforces cognitive distortions and limits offender responsibility for their deviant sexual behavior (Graham, 1996; Marshall, 1996b). This would seem to occur only in modalities that were essentially uninformed by the clinical research available and would possibly be considered unethical practice. In either case, these articulated positions have added fuel to the controversy and have worked to promote ongoing professional ambivalence.

Even while a certain degree of "lip service" seems to get paid to early child abuse issues in the course of adult SOST (E. Coleman, personal communication, 1997; J. Becker, personal communication, 1998), in large measure outpatient treatment programs do not appear to be aggressively treating this often critical mental health issue in the adult sex offender population. Many seem to imply that they work on offender victim issues during the victim empathy component of standard SOST. How this is done, however, appears to be rather vague, and no clear guidelines for treating sexual abuse sequelae among adult sex offenders have been articulated in the treatment literature.

Some treatment providers do report addressing sexual abuse issues within the context of SOST. A recent survey of SOST treatment programs, however, indicates that there is a trend away from the treatment of early victimization issues in standard adult sex offender programs (Freeman-Longo, Bird, Stevenson, & Fiske, 1994). These

SOST program survey results may be confounded by the limited capacity of the respondent to indicate the presence of an integrated treatment approach and may reflect only minor changes in treatment trends. However, if present, the indicated trend away from victim issues is troubling as the exclusion or cursory examination of these issues within the context of SOST could be a contributing factor to poorer overall treatment outcomes and subsequent relapses in offending behavior (Schwartz & Bergman, 1995).

In contrast with the limited and diminishing opportunities to address clinical concerns related to early childhood sexual abuse in standard adult SOST are those treatment programs and approaches that focus solely, or even primarily, on addressing the adult sex offender's early victim issues. These treatment paradigms frequently do not require that perpetrators take responsibility for their offending behavior, alter cognitive distortions, learn to manage their deviant sexual arousal, proactively engage in relapse prevention, or participate in other components of ethical SOST. These kinds of approaches can, perhaps inadvertently, perpetuate an "abuse excuse" cognitive frame wherein adult sexual offending behavior is "explained away" and "excused" by early childhood sexual trauma. This limited, unidimensional construction of sex offender treatment may inadvertently impede the effective treatment of sexual abusers.

First, the linear simplicity of this concept belies the complexity of the many factors that influence offending behavior and can obstruct efforts at effective intervention and understanding. Effective treatment, as indicated in the research literature, has been identified as cognitive-behavioral-based approaches that target many variables associated with sexually deviant behavior. There is no current empirical research data available that support the superior efficacy of treating victim issues alone and to the exclusion of other elements identified in more standard forms of SOST.

Second, this narrow treatment frame fosters a view of sex offenders that fails to encompass the criminal nature of offending behavior, undermining efforts to encourage individual accountability, responsibility, and self-agency. Childhood abuse should never be understood as an excuse for any behavior. It is a reality in the lives of too many whose traumatically informed efforts at adaptation can develop into primary sources of distress and destruction in adulthood. But though the occurrence of childhood sexual abuse is no "excuse" for later sexual offending, neither is sexual offending an excuse not to treat perpetrators for the effects of childhood sexual abuse on their lives.

Focus of Treatment in SOST

The central aim of traditional adult sex offender-specific treatment is to teach sex offenders methods to help decrease the incidence of their sexually abusive behavior. Using cognitive-behavioral, psychopharmocological, and relapse prevention techniques, treatment interventions have been designed to decrease deviant sexual arousal, foster the development of victim empathy, improve deficits in social skills, provide appropriate sex education training, facilitate relapse prevention efforts, and challenge cognitive distortions that operate to maintain the offending behavior (Abel & Becker, 1984; Marshall, 1996b; Pithers & Cummings, 1995). The factors targeted by these treatment modules are understood in some ways, and to varying degrees, as contributory variables in sexual perpetrating behavior. With the principal focus on controlling offending behavior, however, mental health issues related to sexual victimization that may compromise this effort often receive little or no attention in sex offender treatment programs.

Although currently expanding, there is limited research on childhood sexual abuse (CSA) among males in general. The dearth of male CSA literature paired with the restricted focus of the SOST approach limits the treatment provider's capacity to respond effectively to the potential co-occurring manifestation of both a paraphilia and a complex trauma response to early sexual victimization. The presence of a history of sexual victimization, with all the potential symptomatology that is implied, could, if left unattended, seriously compromise the efficacy of adult SOST. The presence of unaddressed sequelae derived from sexual abuse could lead to increased risk of recidivism for a sexual offense in the presence of acute distress related to an individual's history of sexual abuse and could potentially lead to iatrogenic effects in the offender/victim client.

A principal concern in addressing an individual's sexual abuse issues in clinical work with sex offenders lies in the disorienting identification of a sexual perpetrator as a "victim." Many feel that doing so communicates a level of tolerance for the offender's sexually deviant behavior because the construct of "victim" necessarily precludes the possibility of "perpetrator." There is also concern that acknowledging earlier victim issues may also be countertherapeutic to the primary goals of SOST by allowing the offender to be held not accountable for his deviant behavior. However, treatment for those who find themselves in the overlap between victim and perpetrator, as we shall see, can be designed in such a way as to reinforce and augment the goals of SOST rather than work in opposition to them.

Adult Male Survivors of Sexual Abuse. Issues related to male childhood sexual victimization and its prevalence and effects have become a growing clinical concern. Empirical research on gender-specific effects of early sexual abuse has been increasingly generated over the past ten years (Dhaliwal, Gauzas, Antonowicz, & Ross, 1996; Gordon, 1990; Hunter, 1991; Watkins & Bentovim, 1992; Young, Bergandi, & Titus, 1994). The impact of sexual victimization on males is reviewed in detail later. It is important to note here, however, that early treatment models for male survivors were based on female treatment paradigms and failed to address issues related to the unique experience of male sexual victimization. Later models seek to capture and target the gender-specific effects of CSA unique to male survivors as they move through the context of contemporary patriarchal society.

However, many current treatment paradigms for male victims of sexual abuse back away from acknowledging issues or treating symptoms related to the manifestation of sexual perpetrating behavior. Adult engagement in sexually deviant behavior, often (mis)understood as an exclusively "male issue," has not been readily recognized in the traditional sexual abuse treatment literature, which, as noted earlier, has been primarily focused on females. As a result, there are a limited number of well-established therapeutic responses identified to address the clinical needs of adult survivors of sexual abuse (male or female) who present with sexually deviant behavior.

In addition, researchers and clinicians in the arena of male sexual abuse often steer away from examining and addressing the link between earlier sexual victimization and later sexual offending. This expression of professional reluctance may have two sources. Researchers may fear that their efforts to identify the manifestation of trauma-based sequelae in males will be negatively associated with creating a psychologically based, rational, but publicly unacceptable, justification for criminal sexual behavior. Also, clinicians working with male victims of childhood sexual abuse may be concerned that clients could suffer further stigmatization and psychological distress if an increased risk for sexual perpetration is acknowledged as a relevant clinical concern. This further stigmatization may drive sexually abused males even further away from accessing appropriate and needed treatment. The presence of sexually aberrant behavior in an adult survivor of sexual abuse, therefore, can discourage the pursuit of treatment and/or significantly complicate standard adult trauma treatment approaches that have limited means of responding to the sexually deviant aspect of a patient's clinical presentation.

Socially Driven Concerns. The public and professional debate regarding the nature of the relationship between sexual victimization and later sex offending is a heated and politically loaded one. One source of influence in the all-or-nothing position regarding treating sexual victimization issues in the sex offender treatment field may be rooted in the emotionally amplified sociocultural response to sexual deviants. However valid, knee-jerk, emotionally charged societal reactions can fuel inflammatory media headlines which promote the public demand for a "quick fix" to complicated sociopolitical and human rights issues. Issues related to sexual perpetration certainly warrant a strong response from our society. A sound course of action regarding treatment and management of sex offenders, however, ought not to be determined by an emotional riptide in the wave of social opinion. Rather, such a course of action should be grounded in research and distilled from the commitment to exploring viable options directed toward decreasing the incidence of sexual abuse.

Uninformed and unexamined public outcries against "the abuse excuse" for horrific sex crimes may underlie the ambivalence among some sex offender treatment providers to address a sexual perpetrator's own victim issues. Clinical work with this population is often held in negative esteem by the public as well as by other health professionals. It is often difficult enough to justify the clinical treatment of sexual perpetrators without appearing to be a "sex offender apologist" much less function as an advocate for attending to their needs for healing from sexual abuse. Perhaps the trend away from addressing personal victimization issues in SOST represents a publicly shaped professional attitude—one that is more reflective of our society's strong feelings toward sexual perpetrators and less a reflection of an informed clinical response to the needs of sex offenders with histories of sexual victimization.

Reactionary rhetoric can sometimes promote public policy that is not always in the best interest of the community or in the best interest of effective sex offender treatment. Emotionally charged societal pressures, lacking the balance of a measure of objective and informed rationale, can either force the restriction of effective treatment or prompt the misguided application of the "therapy du jour" to high-risk client populations such as sexual perpetrators with specialized needs. Neither serves well the victim, the offender, or the social community as a whole. In addition, powerful sociopolitical forces shape the dichotomous construction that offenders should be punished and victims should be treated. There is little or no sociocultural framework (and even less patience) to understand the overlap between the two.

Rationale for VPD Treatment Component

The presence of psychological distress related to sexual victimization can be exponentially compounded by the presence of sexual deviance in adult male survivors of childhood sexual abuse. As a result, sex offenders who have been sexually victimized in childhood may often carry a complex, clinically difficult, and unidentified "dual diagnosis" that presents as a paraphilic disorder in a complementary and conflicted relationship with other diagnostic expressions of sexual victimization. Clearly, not all male survivors of childhood sexual abuse develop a paraphilia in response to their abuse. Nor does every individual demonstrate clinical sequlae as a result of being sexually abused. For instance, not all females sexually victimized in childhood go on to develop posttraumatic stress disorder (PTSD), borderline personality disorder, complex PTSD symptoms, or the trauma reenactment syndrome identified by Miller (1994). However, in light of the interactional relationship between the biologically mediated responses to sexual abuse and the socioculturally circumscribed response demanded of males (i.e. "I cannot a victim be!"), one may consider the appearance of "sexual deviance" a more likely response to childhood sexual abuse and wonder at the aberration of not becoming sexually deviant as a result of early sexual victimization.

As treatment methodology for sexual abusers has advanced, there has been a two-fold movement toward (1) addressing the special needs of subpopulations of offenders and (2) integrating and tailoring treatment so that efficacy is maximized. Attention to the clinical needs of subpopulations of sex offenders can be seen in the development and research of treatment for sex offenders who are mentally challenged (Coleman & Haaven, 2001); adolescent sex offenders, both male and female (Bumby & Bumby, 1995; Cellini, 1995; Miner, & Crimmins, 1995; Ryan & Lane, 1997); female sex offenders (Schwartz & Cellini, 1995); geriatric sex offenders (Johnson, 1995); Hispanic sex offenders (Carrasco & Garza-Louis, 1995); and American Indian sex offenders (Ertz, 1995).

In addition, Marshall and Eccles (1991) argue that ongoing research is needed to develop the most effective treatment approach for each subgroup of offender type. Because cognitive-behavioral treatment is not universally effective across all subtypes of sexual offenders (i.e., rapists, pedophiles, exhibitionists, etc., exhibit different efficacy rates in response to cognitive-behavioral treatment), evolving treatment models increasingly need to address the special needs of each sexual perpetrator subtype (Abel, Osborn, Anthony, & Gardos, 1992; Allam, Middleton, & Browne, 1997; Marshall, Jones, Ward, Johnston, & Barbaree, 1991). Pedophiles, for example, with prior histories of sexual abuse could be considered an offender subtype. Research indicates that more pedophiles report histories of CSA than do other offender subgroups (Freund & Kuban, 1994; Groth, 1979; Seghorn, Prentky, & Boucher, 1987). As such, they may demonstrate increased treatment response to the integration of an intervention component that augments SOST by addressing early victim issues.

There is growing momentum in the field toward "technical eclecticism," theoretical integration, and flexibility in order to tailor interventions to the specific and differentiated clinical needs of offender subgroups in an effort to increase treatment efficacy. In this manner, the multiple and complex dimensions that inform the offender's behavior can be more effectively and economically addressed. Such a treatment approach reflects the development of the contemporary multifactorial etiological models and the necessity of attending to specific clinical needs of different offender populations (Allam et al., 1997). Typologies and key variables such as history of sexual abuse, repeat offending, victim gender, and relationship to the victim, which help delineate heterogeneous groups of offenders (Craissati & McClurg, 1996), can serve as guidelines for the identification of relevant clinical treatment subgroups.

In spite of the ambivalence in the field regarding the nature of the relationship between early sexual abuse and later offending behavior, it seems as though a rather large number of sexual perpetrators have in fact been victims of early childhood abuse (Dhawan & Marshall, 1996; Dutton & Hart, 1992; Graham, 1996; Groth, 1979; Hanson & Slater, 1988; Hunter, 1990; Langevin, Wright, & Hardy, 1989; Longo & Groth, 1983; Prentky & Knight, 1993; Seghorn, Prentky, & Boucher, 1987). The correlational nature of the victim-to-offender relationship fails to negate or diminish the reality of the negative effects of childhood sexual abuse observed in adult survivors, be they sexual offenders or not. The overt manifestation of the VPD in sex offenders further reinforces the need for a treatment intervention designed specifically to address and deconstruct this complex trauma response in male sex offenders in such a way as to both facilitate the clinical objectives of SOST and foster recovery from the negative impact of childhood sexual abuse.

As such, sexual perpetrators who were abused in childhood require an integrated treatment approach that can address their offending behavior, the psychological sequelae of their early victimization experience, and the complex relationship between the two. As Marshall (1996a) notes:

> Sexual offenders must take responsibility for their behavior and one of the difficulties in treating these men is to have those who were abused understand the role their victimization (and their enduring distress over it) may have played in the etiology and maintenance of their offending, while at the same time having them understand that they still made the choice to offend. (p. 321)

Recently, the field of treatment for sexual abusers has shown a strong trend toward addressing the offender as a whole and complex person with issues and concerns across multiple domains including the physiological, the cognitive-behavioral, the affective, the interpersonal, the familial, the societal, and the spiritual (Schwartz, 1995). Furthermore, there is a strong working hypothesis that addressing personal victimization issues can only support efforts at relapse prevention and contribute to decreased recidivism among offenders for whom early abuse is a salient issue.

Dhawan & Marshall (1996) suggest that "a history of sexual abuse appears to be an important factor in the backgrounds of sexual offenders" (p. 7); they recommend that CSA in sex offenders be addressed in treatment. CSA in the lives of many offenders can present as such a central treatment concern that it cannot be ignored. Fostering the integration of the two identities of victim and perpetrator could promote significant treatment outcomes that may serve to (1) increase victim empathy on the part of the offender (a treatment goal in SOST), (2) reinforce efforts at relapse prevention by increasing awareness of potential triggers, (3) assist offenders in more clearly understanding one of many of the factors that may have contributed to their offending behavior, (4) promote treatment for clinical concerns related to CSA that may actively contribute to offending behavior (physiological hyperarousal, masked depression, anger, flashbacks, compulsive behavior patterns, etc.), and (5) increase accountability for sexually abusive acts as the offender comes to understand that, as a victim himself, he was not responsibile for his sexual abuse. Supporting the cognitive reframe of the perpetrator's role as victim in his own abuse can actually reinforce the fact that as the offender, he was completely responsible for his abusive act(s).

It is clear that sexual deviance, like many other forms of aberrant behavior, is a multidetermined phenomenon. Also true is the fact that the sequelae of childhood sexual abuse can be complex, manifesting along multiple dimensions. In spite of the professional and social discomfort that the notion engenders, it can no longer be denied that a significant interactional relationship can, and often does, exist between these two differentially disturbing phenomenon. For many adult sex offenders, the link between a traumatic and/or distorted sexualization process in childhood and the subsequent development of sexual deviance has important clinical treatment implications. The treatment population that emerges secondary to the overlap between CSA males and adult sex offenders forms a significant subgroup that clinically requires, and ethically demands, effective treatment interventions. A thorough review of the impact of sexual victimization on males will aid in understanding the complex treatment needs that emerge from the VPD population.

The Impact of Sexual Abuse on Males: A Review of the Literature

Introduction. The sociocultural denial of the prevalence and impact of early sexual victimization on the developing male is in the early stages of deconstruction. Thus, knowledge of the incidence and effects of CSA on males is starting to emerge and the burgeoning evidence reveals several key points. First, underreporting, secondary to the traditional patriarchal paradigms that eliminate the social role of "victim" for men, has led to a severe underestimation of the number of males sexually victimized in childhood. Second, these same sociocultural forces have contributed to the "invisible" nature of many of the negative effects of CSA on males as hypermasculinity is touted as a prominent social value. The tendency toward sexual aggression and antisocial behavior is often seen as a "given" among men and boys, and distortions in intimate relationships are relegated to the undervalued arena of "women's issues." Third, the pervasive and negative effects of CSA, in spite of the normative male responses of denial and minimization, are frequently carried into adulthood, presenting significant barriers to psychological and emotional well-being and resulting in complicated mental health concerns for the adult male victim.

General Effects of Childhood Sexual Abuse. Since the early 1980s, research on the effects of child sexual abuse has grown increasingly sophisticated in both methodology and scope, with the focus shifting from early adult retrospective studies to more recent studies on child victims (Beitchman et al., 1992; Briere & Runtz, 1993; Brown & Finkelhor, 1986; Finkelhor, 1990; Kendall-Tackett, Williams, & Finkelhor, 1993). Brown & Finkelhor's (1986) seminal and oft-cited research review was limited in breadth to the effects of childhood sexual trauma on females but provided an aggregated, empirically based response to those who argued against the existence of early sexual victimization of females and denied its subsequent negative impact. They identified both initial and long-term effects of sexual trauma on women. Based primarily on a review of adult retrospective studies, initial negative effects gleaned from the research literature included "reactions of fear, anxiety, depression, anger and hostility, and inappropriate sexual behavior" (Brown & Finkelhor, 1986, p. 69). Long-term effects were identified by the manifestations of "depression, self-destructive behavior, anxiety, feelings of isolation and stigma, poor self-esteem, a tendency toward revictimization, and substance abuse" (Brown & Finkelhor, 1986, p. 72).

Beitchman et al. (1992) expanded their review and surveyed interim research on the long-term effects of CSA and the impact of abuse-specific variables. Their findings identified adult clinical symptomatology associated with CSA and highlighted the relationship between abuse-specific variables and long-term outcomes. Adult symptomatology supported in the literature included sexual disturbances, anxiety and fear, depression, revictimization, and suicidality (when physical and sexual abuse occur concurrently). With regard to abuse-specific variables, Beitchman et al. (1992) concluded the following: (1) the relationship between age of onset of abuse and later negative outcomes remains unclear, (2) abuse of long duration is positively associated with increased negative effects, (3) the presence of force and/or threat contributes to greater impact, (4) abuse involving penetration is related to increased long-term harm, (5) sexual abuse perpetrated by a father or stepfather is associated with increased long-term negative outcomes, and (6) male victims demonstrate sexual dysfunction in adulthood.

A review by Kendall-Tackett et al. (1993) offers a comprehensive survey of the research literature on the effects of sexual abuse on child victims for the purpose of bringing to light treatment-relevant implications and providing the basis for theory building. Although the reviewers made no distinctions between studies that may have differentially involved female and/or male children, research on comparisons between sexually abused and non-sexually abused children in both clinical and nonclinical samples revealed common symptoms that were calculated from effect sizes of between-group comparisons. Seven childhood symptoms of sexual abuse were identified: anxiety, sexualized behavior, depression, withdrawal, aggression, and both internalizing and externalizing behavior (the former includes inhibition and overcontrolled behavior; the latter includes antisocial and undercontrolled behavior). Reviewers also noted that clinical samples of sexually abused children, when compared with their nonabused clinical counterparts, demonstrated significant similarities but differed on two dimensions: PTSD and sexualized behavior. Attempts to account for this type of variance in childhood symptomatology led to research on the central characteristics of the abuse experience.

Kendall-Tackett et al.'s (1993) summary of review findings revealed "that molestation that included a close perpetrator; a high frequency of sexual contact; a long duration; the use of force; and sexual acts that included oral, anal, or vaginal penetration lead to a greater number of symptoms for victims" (p. 171). By expanding the dimensions considered in CSA and demonstrating the lack of evidence for a single traumatizing process, they affirmed the theoretical leaning toward a more sophisticated conceptualization of CSA and provided support for the ongoing development of multifaceted models of traumatization that guide evolving treatment designs.

However, early groundbreaking, theory-building research in the field of sexual abuse failed significantly to recognize that a masked portion of the population they were examining included male victims of sexual abuse.

Exploring Male Sexual Victimization. Though the existence and indeed the pervasiveness of CSA have been substantiated by the research literature, the fact that a portion of children identified as victims are young boys has often been neglected. That these young boys frequently grow into psychologically distressed adult males has also frequently been ignored, denied, and overlooked. The women's movement carried firward early struggles for the recognition of child abuse (Herman, 1992). This momentum fueled research that fostered theories of sexual abuse and treatment interventions based primarily on females. It is only in recent years, in the wake of earlier and fervent research on child abuse coupled with the wave of increased sex crimes, that the unseen and unheard population of male victims of childhood sexual trauma is beginning to be recognized (Seplar, 1990; Young et al., 1994). As we shall see, a large part of this extant marginalization and invisibility is paradoxically rooted in the same patriarchal soil that kept the sexual abuse of female children underground.

Prevalence. Although it is a complex task to estimate the true incidence and prevalence of CSA, prevalence rates among males have been determined to fall within the range of 3% to 31% in a review of mixed-population samples (Peters, Wyatt, & Finklehor, 1986). This compares with the 6–62% determined prevalence range of CSA for females. Mendel (1995) reviewed the studies of prevalence of sexual abuse among males and clustered the findings within three sample groupings: general population, 3–16%; student population, 4.8–33%; and other specific populations (homosexuals, offenders, juvenile runaways, clinical population, etc.), 2.5–90%. Dhaliwal et al.'s (1996) review of the prevalence literature indicates a range of CSA of 4.8–30% among college students, 2.8–30.6% among general households, and 3–36.9% among clinical samples. The ratio of girls to boys abused has narrowed in recent years. Currently, the general consensus that between one in five and one in eight males have been sexually abused in childhood is considered a reasonable approximation (Mendel, 1995).

Methodological Considerations. There are several important factors to consider when trying to understand the variance among these prevalence figures and when attempting to reconcile contradictory findings among studies on male CSA. First, research on male child sexual abuse is in its infancy when compared with the research on female victims (Dhaliwal et al., 1996; Violato & Genuis, 1993a). Thus, many early studies are exploratory, definitions of what constitutes sexual abuse vary from study to study, and diverse sample populations are examined utilizing different methodological and data-gathering approaches and a variety of statistical analyses. Within these early research efforts there may be an absence of matched controls or the lack of objectively rated dependent measures. In addition, emphasis on clinical population samples elicits questions regarding the generalizability of the research outcomes. As a result, research findings are frequently contradictory and/or comparisons between studies can seldom be made. These methodological confounds complicate efforts to establish stable prevalence patterns and validate the nature and extent of CSA among males.

Underreporting. Underreporting of male CSA has also been identified by many as a significant complicating factor in the research of the childhood sexual victimization of males (Cermak & Molidar, 1996; Dhaliwal et al., 1996; Dimock, 1988; Etherington, 1995; Hunter, 1991; Lew, 1990; Mendel, 1995; Reinhart, 1987; Schwartz, 1994; Seplar, 1990; Urquiza & Keating, 1990; Violato & Genuis, 1993a; Watkins & Bentovim, 1992; Young et al., 1994) Evidence substantiating the claim of underreporting can be found in the retrospective self-reports of adult males, which reveal a higher incidence of CSA than indicated by official reports on children through human service agencies (Cermak & Molidar, 1996). It is estimated that three to four times more incidents of male sexual abuse occur than are disclosed (Violato & Genuis, 1993a), and that underreporting in this population is a "consistent and universal phenomenon" (Watkins & Bentovim, 1992). Initially, the field of sexual abuse emerged from the rape crisis movement which, among other good things such as victim advocacy, crisis response, treatment, etc., resulted in the "feminization of victimization" (Seplar, 1990, p. 74; Young et al., 1994). The simultaneous and dichotomous development of the "masculinization of oppression" (Mendel, 1995, p. 21), however, has led to a male offender-female victim paradigm, embedded in a patriarchal culture, that goes far to facilitate the underreporting of the incidence of male CSA (Cermak & Molidar, 1996; Young et al., 1994). The male socialization process within this context precludes males reporting sexual abuse for many reasons. First, males are seen through this sociocultural lens as strong, dominant, powerful (Mendel, 1995) aggressors (Dhaliwal et al., 1996; Schwartz, 1994). For a male to be identified as a victim of sexual abuse would name/identify a vulnerability to victimization that is unacceptable by the standards imposed on men by men (Cermak & Molidar, 1996; Etherington, 1995; Schwartz, 1994; Young et al., 1994).

Second, whereas the role of "victim" is compatible with a woman's social experience, it is completely contradictory to a man's (Brownmiller, 1975) and conflicts with the socially accepted definition of masculinity (Schwartz, 1994). For males, then, being labeled a "victim" would result in social stigmatization that would identify them as "inadequate," "female-like," or "homosexual" (Dhaliwal et al., 1996). The extant and irrational fear of a homosexual label, fostered by both a homophobic society and the perception that only homosexual men perpetrate sexual abuse against male children, is noted as a primary cause for underreporting by many investigators (Becker, 1988; Cermak & Molidar, 1996; Dahliwal et al., 1996; Etherington, 1995; Hunter, 1991; Mendel, 1995; Schwartz, 1994; Urquiza & Keating, 1990; Violato & Genuis, 1993a; Watkins & Bentovim, 1992; Young et al., 1994).

Third, men are conditioned to hide their emotional and physical vulnerability (Cermak & Molidar, 1996; Dimock, 1988; Schwartz, 1994). When faced with the dissonant experience of being both a male and a victim, male victims can engage defense mechanisms such as minimization, denial, dissociation, repression, identification with the aggressor, and other forms of assimilation and accommodation that would preclude reporting the abuse incident (Brown & Finkelhor, 1986; Cermak & Molidar, 1996; Etherington, 1995; Schwartz, 1994; Urquiza & Capra, 1990). Hunter (1991) asserts that males have limited access to nonverbal memories secondary to their primarily cognitive, rather than affective, orientation. As a result, males are not likely to be aware of the subtle sensations that may facilitate the retrieval of traumatically induced memories that could lead to a report of the incident.

Other sources for the underreporting of the sexual victimization of male children identified in the literature include shame and the fear of being considered mentally ill (Violato & Genuis, 1993a); the idea that males should be able and strong enough to protect themselves from abuse and the fear that the victim will be blamed for the abuser's transgressions (Schwartz, 1994); concern that the traditional male ethic of self-reliance, having been violated, will be circumscribed, resulting in loss or limits of freedom and independence (Cermak & Molidar, 1996; Finklehor, 1979; Urquiza & Keating, 1990); confusion over what may have been pleasurable and/or sexually arousing aspects of the abuse episode(s) (Watkins & Bentovim, 1992); the denial of both father-son incest and child-child abuse (Watkins & Bentovim, 1992); and the failure of human services professionals, denying the existence of male CSA and/or minimizing its effects, to ask the appropriate questions that would bring the occurrence of male sexual abuse to light (Dahliwal et al., 1996; Reinhart, 1987; Urquiza & Keating, 1990).

A final barrier to accurate reporting of the incidence of CSA in males emerges from the covert social bias that "[j]ust as we see males as abusers rather than the abused, we see females as the victims rather than the victimizers" (Mendel, 1995, p. 21). Once again, the male socialization process functions to encourage males to seek multiple female sexual experiences. Sex with an older woman is more often viewed as "a lucky break" or part of a normative sexualization process rather than sexual abuse (Cermak & Molidar, 1996; Dahliwal et al., 1996; Dimock, 1988; Fromuth & Burhart, 1989; Watkins & Bentovim, 1992). However, both the element of coercion and a child's inability to give appropriate consent, informed by the potential negative consequences of such behavior, is present in this often socially sanctioned yet sexually abusive interaction (Urquiza & Keating, 1990).

The very notion (much less the occurrence) of female sexual perpetration is currently as difficult for society to accept, as was the initial existence of child abuse. Even more difficult to entertain is that women have the capacity for sexual aggression as "[a]buse—particularly sexual abuse—does not fit the cultural construction of femininity" (Mendel, 1995, p. 27). However, recent research demonstrates an increase in reports of female sexual perpetration with prevalence rates ranging from 3–78% among abused populations (see Mendel, 1995, for complete review). Because male victims often have trouble defining such encounters as sexual abuse, these incidents remain unreported (Etherington, 1995). Moreover, if a male experiences this event as unwelcome, frightening, or negative in any manner, he would be silenced even further for fear of being labeled "unmanly" or homosexual (Dimock, 1988).

Because of the difficulty of males to identify this type of behavior as abusive, researchers are beginning to ask about "sexual activity with adults" rather than simply "experiences of sexual abuse" (Mendel, 1995). Fromuth and Burkhart (1989) reveal that among a college student population, 78% of perpetrators identified were female. Although the subjects did not consider these experiences "abusive," they did note significant negative consequences as a result of these episodes. This is not to say that the prevalence of female perpetrators approaches the rates of male sexual offenders or to diminish in any way the sexual abuse of females by males perpetrators. It is to point sharply to the social constructions that blind us to the sexually abusive experiences of males and to shed light on the fact that the prevalence rates of the childhood sexual abuse of males are largely underestimated. It should also be noted that evidence suggests that whether or not an individual consciously acknowledges, recognizes, or reports an event as sexually abusive, the negative effects of sexual abuse remain evident, have repercussions in an individual's adult life, and do not preclude the need for appropriate treatment intervention (Cermak & Molidar, 1996; Urquiza & Keating, 1990).

The factors that contribute to the underreporting of the incidence of male sexual abuse also have important treatment implications. The very process by which many males are socialized can impede effective treatment due to oppressive, maladaptive socially constructed beliefs and attitudes. Reinforcing the notion that men are invulnerable, cultivating identification with the aggressor, and reifying the sexist concept of male dominance compromise treatment efforts aimed at self-acceptance, exploration of one's vulnerabilities, and the examination of inequitable gender practices. Distorted notions of what constitutes sexual abuse and confusing experiences of sexual arousal secondary to CSA also present significant treatment concerns that demand attention. It is therefore essential that effective treatment approaches with adult male victims of early sexual abuse include therapeutic means to address and deconstruct the socially reinforced, countertherapeutic, and misinformed beliefs that often surround the experience of CSA in males.

Childhood Sexual Abuse of Males. In spite of the methodological confounds and barriers to accurate prevalence and incidence rates, sound research on CSA of males has increased in recent years. As a result, more knowledge is being gained regarding the impact of these experiences on males, and important trends, relevant to treatment implications, are beginning to emerge (Violato & Genuis, 1993a). A review of the growing literature on the negative effects of CSA on males is explored here and provides evidence to soundly disconfirm the unfounded and oppressive hypothesis that the sexual victimization of male children is a benign event. In direct contrast, in fact, the literature demonstrates that the effects of CSA on males is pervasive and can be the source of extreme psychological and emotional distress for many adult males. Thus, this chapter offers evidence that the symptomatic expression of CSA demands treatment (whether in a nonoffender or an offender population).

Similarities and Distinctions Between Male and Female Children—Initial Effects of CSA. The methodological issues noted earlier often plague early research efforts. Secondary to these types of developmental issues, the emerging research on male victims of sexual abuse understandably shows contradictory findings regarding gender distinctions in response to childhood sexual victimization. Some research comparing the initial effects of sexual abuse between boys and girls indicates that there are no significant differences in their responses (Finkelhor, 1990; Young et al., 1994). In an update of his work with A. Brown in 1985, Finkelhor (1990) reviews the literature on both the initial and long-term effects of sexual abuse, this time including research that addresses the impact of sexual victimization on males. Finkelhor (1990) notes that the empirical research to date had demonstrated "that there are far more similarities than differences" in the responses to sexual abuse demonstrated by male and female children (p. 325). For instance, both boys and girls exhibit common symptoms such as fears, sleep disturbances, and distraction. However, Finkelhor also noted that there is evidence to support the observation that boys tend to externalize their response to sexual abuse by acting out in aggressive ways, as compared with girls who internalize their response which manifests in depressive symptoms.

In a clinical sample of twenty males and twenty females with matched controls, Young et al. (1994) found no significant differences between male and female latency-age children on measures of self-concept, depression, problems with peers, levels of assertiveness and degree of submission, and range of expressed anti- and prosocial behavior. However, a main gender effect that was found indicated that sexually abused boys perceived themselves to be more aggressive than their female counterparts, who saw themselves as more submissive (Young et al., 1994). These findings point to a number of potential conclusions. First, it is possible that early responses to sexual abuse are not gender-specific and present similarly in male and female children. Second, it is possible that the dependent measures used, secondary to limited sensitivity, failed to capture the specific, and perhaps gender-differentiated, response to sexual abuse in children. There were no measures, for example, that acknowledged or adequately accounted for gender-based differences in response to stress, coping, adaptation, social values, and family relationships (Urquiza & Capra, 1990). It is possible that the distinctions being sought could be discovered along these dimensions. And third, early common manifestations of psychological distress as a result of sexual abuse among children do not preclude a differentiation in response later in life.

In contrast, in an early review of the research literature, Vander Mey (1988) (citing R. L. Geiser) notes that "the sexual abuse of male children is a poorly understood area of child abuse, replete with much misinformation and many myths . . . the dynamics of the sexual abuse of males have little in common with those involving females" (p. 61). Following a review of the twenty-three empirical studies to date on male sexual victimization, Vander Mey (1988) concluded that gender-specific responses to sexual abuse in male children included an increased sense of shame and self-blame, fear of homosexuality, tendency toward drug and alcohol abuse, engagement in pornographic enterprises, self-destructive behavior, and the propensity to sexually victimize others.

In a more recent review of the literature, which includes quantitative and qualitative research findings, Urquiza and Capra (1990) highlight both gender-specific and gender-different responses to childhood sexual abuse. Structured as a male version of Brown and Finkelhor (1986), Urquiza and Capra (1990) suggest that "the sexual victimization of boys has a detrimental effect on behavior, self-concept, psychophysiological sympotmatology and psychosexual behaviors and functioning" (p. 113). Both behavior disturbances, such as aggressiveness, delinquency, and acting out, and aberrant sexual behavior, such as sexual compulsivity, sexual acting out, and confusion regarding sexual issues, distinguish the initial effects of sexual abuse on males from that of females (Urquiza & Capra, 1990).

Cermak and Molidar (1996) summarize and identify a range of behaviors, specific to adolescent males, that serve as both indicators and effects of sexual victimization. These gender-specific, behavioral expressions of sexual abuse include infantile play and speech patterns; pursuing relationships with younger children; socializing with age-appropriate peers only when directed to; anxiety and avoidance behaviors; paranoid and phobic behaviors; dreams with themes of being chased, punished, or isolated; and change in body image and tendency to either be compulsively clean or demonstrate no regard for appearance (Cermak & Molidar, 1996). These, and the other noted findings, lend support to the premise that there are differences between the initial effects of sexual abuse on boys and girls.

Distinctions Between Adult Male and Female Response to CSA. Research comparing the effects of childhood sexual abuse between women and men demonstrates some significant differences as well as essential similarities (Briere, Evans, Runtz, & Wall, 1988; Gordon, 1990; Hunter, 1991; Young et al., 1994). Of note, however, is the finding by Briere et al. (1988) indicating that less severe sexual abuse against males resulted in symptomatology equivalent to that of more severely abused women. Hunter (1991) indicates that comparisons of the Minnesota Multiphasic Personality Inventory (MMPI) scores between abused men and women reveal that sexually abused males demonstrate higher levels of anxiety than do their female counterparts. Male victims also appear to worry and perseverate to a greater degree than do women over issues and conflicts regarding identity in response to early sexual victimization. Hunter (1991) goes on to note that these results reflect the observations made in a clinical context that abused males struggle with a gender-specific response to trauma that fosters insecurity regarding their masculine identity.

These research results, coupled with Dhaliwal et al.'s (1996) findings that sexually abused males overuse avoidant coping skills and underuse confrontive coping skills in comparison to the more adaptive and positive coping strategies employed by sexually abused women, "may imply that the trauma of sexual abuse is more distressful for males than females" (p. 627). Further research efforts may substantiate that secondary to differences in temperament, coping styles, and socialization processes, comparisons of the effects of sexual abuse on male and female children is an "apples and oranges" exercise. Treatment, therefore, should be designed to address the needs unique to male and female survivors of early sexual victimization

Long-Term General Effects on Males. The subsequent filtering of the sexual abuse event through coping and meaning-making processes unique to males socialized in a patriarchal, male-dominant society leads to further distinctions in effects that are only now being identified in the literature. A review of the research does indicate that the long-term negative effects of CSA on adult males are pervasive and impact multiple domains of functioning.

Dhaliwal et al. (1996) offer one of the most thorough reviews of the literature on the long-term effects on adult male victims of CSA. A broad sweep of the findings reveals that the externalized response and coping style present and noted in childhood continue into adulthood in the form of aggressiveness, antisocial behavior, and disinhibited control over behavior. Though findings regarding emotional stability, depression and suicidal tendencies, and self-esteem, proved contradictory and, therefore, largely inconclusive, support was found for difficulties with intimate relationships and problems with sexuality and sexual functioning. An association between CSA and later substance dependence received equivocal support in the literature (Dhaliwal et al., 1996; Dimock,1988; Finkelhor, 1990; Gordon, 1990; Urquiza & Capra, 1990; Watkins & Bentovim, 1992).

The presence of psychiatric difficulties in adult males sexually abused as children has been noted by many researchers. Briere et al. (1988) noted increased scores on the Trauma Symptom Checklist (TSC-33) when abused males were compared with nonabused males in a clinical population. Scores on the TSC-33 for abused males indicated the heightened presence of dissociation, anxiety, depression, anger, and sleep disturbance. Collings (1995), studying a sample of university males, found increased indices of psychological maladjustment on measures of the Brief Symptom Inventory (BSI) for adult subjects who had experienced contact forms of sexual abuse in childhood ("hands-on" abuse where physical contact is made with the victim). On all scales, which included somatization, obsessive-compulsive, interpersonal sensitivity, depression, anxiety, hostility, phobic anxiety, paranoid ideation, and psychoticism, contact-abuse subjects scored higher than did their control or noncontact-abuse counterparts. Collings (1995) concluded that sexually abused male children grow into psychologically distressed adult men and carry the legacy of their trauma with them into adulthood.

Roesler and McKenzie (1994) reported scores well above the population mean in a sample of sexually abused males. Scores on depression, self-esteem, trauma symptoms, dissociation, and PTSD were all elevated in adult male subjects from a mixed sample population. Watkins and Bentovim (1992) indicated support for increased depression and anxiety among males sexually abused as children and Schulte, Dinwiddie, Pribor, and Yutzy (1995), examining a clinical population, provided further support for this finding. Lew (1990) indicated from clinical observations, increased incidence of anxiety, confusion, and PTSD among CSA males. Hunter (1991) noted increased dysfunction as indicated by the scores of CSA males on the MMPI when compared with non-CSS males. Finkelhor (1990) noted research that indicates that males are twice as likely to have a psychiatric disorder if they have been sexually abused as a child. And Fromuth and Burkhart (1989) reported poorer overall psychological adjustment in CSA males.

Lisak and Luster (1994), in a study of ninety university males, examined the relationship between CSA in males and the broader, nonpsychiatric domains of occupational, educational, and relational functioning. Men with histories of childhood sexual abuse scored significantly higher on measures of Negative Grade School, High School and College Experiences, Total Number of Jobs, Negative Reasons for Leaving Jobs, and Negative Reasons for Ending Relationships than did nonabused males. The school experiences of sexually abused males included getting into trouble at school, rejection by peers, and difficulty with academics. In college, their difficulty reflected issues of low self-confidence, low academic goals, withdrawing, changing majors, and dropping out. Occupationally these men struggled to get along with supervisors and coworkers and changed jobs for a number of reasons ranging from boredom to financial reasons to illness and injury. Their intimate relationships came to an end more often due to affairs, repetitive conflicts, or abuse by one or the other partner. Lisak and Luster (1994) concluded that the negative effects of CSA manifest in "a broad range of indices of impaired adjustment among sexually abused men, with interpersonal troubles running through their histories as a common thread" (p. 519). Finkelhor (1990) cited research to support dysfunction in broader domains, noting that victims of CSA have greater marital discord, less sexual satisfaction, and lower levels of religious beliefs. Violato and Genuis (1993b), in a sample of university males, found abused males more likely to enroll in nonprofessional education training than nonabused males.

The dysfunctional family environment of men sexually abused as children is often cited as a confound of the effects of sexual trauma (Violato & Genuis, 1993b). Collings (1995), aware that a dysfunctional family background can serve as a risk factor for subsequent forms of child abuse, controlled for the influence of family background when studying the association between CSA and later adult adjustment. After eliminating the effects of parental rejection and abusiveness, the significant relationship between contact sexual abuse and later psychological adjustment remained. These findings "suggest that the long-term effects of sexual abuse observed in the present study are not merely artifacts of dysfunctional parenting behavior" (Collings, 1995, p. 4). These results are supported by the early findings of Fromuth and Burkhart (1989) and of Inderbitzen-Pisaruk, Shawchuk, and Hoier (1992). Both research endeavors sought to control for the possible effects of family and environmental background factors such as parental adequacy in the case of the former and specific living situations and socioeconomic environment in the case of the latter. These factors are intuitively considered to be confounding variables in the effects of CSA. However, in spite of controlling for these factors, the negative effects on functioning secondary to CSA observed in each study remained. These types of research findings can help lead to the development of more responsive and effective treatment interventions as the victims' needs become more clearly disentangled from general dysfunction factors.

Effects on Sexuality: Development, Functioning, Behavior, and Identity. Numerous research studies, both quantitative and qualitative, point to the negative consequences of sexual abuse on the developing sexuality, sexual behavior, and functioning of the abused male child. Tharinger (1990) noted that in the process of getting their own needs met, sexual abusers can distort a child's evolving sexual development and negatively influence the child's sexual socialization or "acculturation" process (p. 332). Finkelhor and Brown (1985) proposed that childhood sexual abuse entailed a process of traumatic sexualization of the victim "in which a child's sexuality is shaped in developmentally inappropriate and interpersonally dysfunctional ways" (p. 531).

The impact of CSA on developing sexuality, functioning, and behavior is one of the most widely researched issues in the area of male CSA. Urquiza and Capra (1990) point to research which indicates that sex-related issues can be found within preschool, school-age, and adolescent populations of sexually abused children. Several behaviors observed in young boys that have been linked to a history of CSA include: inappropriate sexualized behavior, including sexualized and aggressive behaviors (Cermak & Molidar, 1996; Inderbitzen-Pisaruk et al., 1992; Kendall-Tackett et al., 1993; Roane, 1992; Violato & Genuis, 1993b), open masturbation, excessive sexual curiosity, and frequent exposure of the genitals (Brown & Finkelhor, 1986). Kendall-Tackett et al. (1993) noted that sexualized behaviors appear to be a constant in presentations of sexually abused children across a variety of population samples. Watkins and Bentovim (1992) indicated that there are three primary expressions of distress related to developing sexuality in young boys: (1) confusion over one's sexual identity, (2) inappropriate attempts to reassert one's masculinity, and (3) recapitulation of the abuse experience.

In adolescent males, recapitulation of the abuse (Freeman-Longo, 1986; Urquiza & Capra, 1990; Violato & Genuis, 1993a, 1993b; Watkins & Bentovim, 1992); sexual dysfunction in the form of inhibited libido, premature ejaculation, erectile difficulties, and failure to ejaculate (Watkins & Bentovim, 1992); and deviant sexual arousal patterns (Becker, 1988) are identified as negative effects secondary to early sexual abuse.

In adult males, research indicates that the manifestations of the effects of CSA in the domain of adult sexuality include the following: sexual adjustment (Brown & Finkelhor, 1986), sexual promiscuity (Briere & Runtz, 1993), lower sexual self-esteem (Reinhart 1987; Urquiza & Capra, 1990; Watkins & Bentovim, 1992), sexual dysfunction (Beitchman et al., 1992; Dhaliwal et al., 1996; Dimock, 1988; Etherington, 1995; Fromuth & Burkhart, 1989; Hunter, 1991; Lisak, 1994; Myers, 1989; Lew, 1990; Roesler & McKenzie, 1994; Watkins & Bentovim, 1992), sexual identity crisis/confusion (Dahliwal et al., 1996; Dimock, 1988; Gilgun & Reiser, 1990; Hunter, 1990; Lew, 1990; Myers, 1989; Urquiza & Capra, 1990), sexual problems, such as erectile dysfunction, premature or retarded ejaculation (Dimock, 1988; Fromuth & Burkhart, 1989; Hunter, 1990; Lew, 1988; Myers, 1989), promiscuity (Dahliwal et al., 1996; Schwartz, 1994), problems with intimacy (Dimock, 1988; Hunter, 1990; Lew, 1990), sexual compulsivity (Dimock, 1988; Gilgun & Reiser, 1990; Lew, 1990; Myers, 1989; Schwartz, 1994), gender identity confusion (Dimock, 1988; Gilgun & Reiser, 1990), sexual dissatisfaction (Etherington, 1995; Finkelhor, 1990), homophobia (Gilgun & Reiser, 1990; Lew, 1990; Myers, 1989; Schwartz, 1994), and increased risk of perpetrating sexual abuse (Etherington, 1995; Genuis, Thomlison, & Bagley, 1991; Gilgun & Reiser, 1990; Gordon, 1990; Vander Mey, 1988; Violato & Genuis 1993b; Watkins & Bentovim, 1992).

Violato and Genuis (1993b), in an exploratory study of 200 university men, determined that significantly more abused males indicated interest in having sex with male children ($x = 7.16$, $p < .05$) than did nonabused males. This lends support for earlier research presented by Urquiza and Crowly in a paper presented at the fourth conference on the sexual victimization of children (cited in Finklelhor, 1990). In a college sample, males sexually abused in childhood were more likely to express a desire to hurt others and a sexual interest in children.

When asked regarding their sexual interest in children, 25% of sexually abused males reported that they had sexual fantasies involving children compared with only 9% of their nonabused counterparts. And 13% of male victims indicated a desire to fondle or engage in sexual activities with a child compared with only 6% of nonabused males. These findings lend support for the argument that males who have been sexually abused in childhood may be at higher risk for becoming sexual perpetrators.

Methodological issues plague these studies and others noted in the research. However, there are several important and indisputable conclusions that can be drawn from these findings: (1) many males have been sexually abused in childhood, a fact that can no longer be dismissed; (2) many of these men suffer significant adverse effects as a result of their abuse; (3) there are "a multitude" of negative effects secondary to this abuse that are unique to the experience of men; and (4) appropriate treatment must be designed that can effectively address the sequelae of CSA in adult males (Dhaliwal et al., 1996).

Effective treatment for the long-term effects of CSA in adult males must be responsive to the heterogeneous manifestation of symptoms indicated by these emerging research findings. Male survivors of CSA may develop unique constellations of interactive symptomatology that require an informed and integrated treatment approach. The effects on psychological, social, and sexual functioning, as well as the complex interplay of these elements, should be included in any effective treatment regime for adult male victims of CSA.

Addressing the Victim/Perpetrator Dialectic

Early studies began the exploration of the importance of the role that childhood sexual victimization may play in the development of sexually aberrant behavior. Groth (1979) reported that 31% of the sexual offenders he investigated had histories of childhood sexual abuse. In a review of the literature, Hanson and Slater (1988) revealed that studies indicated a range between 0 and 67% (average of 28%) of sexual offenders with prior histories of sexual abuse. Langevin et al. (1989), in an archival data review of 479 sex offenders, reported a 42% prevalence rate of childhood sexual abuse among offenders. These rates compare with a range of 7% to 17% prevalence rates noted among the general population (Hunter, 1990; Peters et al., 1986).

Methodological problems such as differences in or informal definitions of sexual abuse, motivation of the sample population to fabricate or inflate histories of early sexual trauma, lack of appropriate control groups, and lack of representative samples were apparent in these early research efforts. However, more recent studies, attempting to address these methodological issues, provide support for and expand on earlier reports of a high prevalence rate of childhood sexual abuse among sexual offenders. Dhawan and Marshall (1996), for instance, report a prevalence rate of 58% (62% of rapists and 50% of pedophiles) among incarcerated offenders compared with 20% rate among nonsexual offender inmates. Romano and De Luca (1996), in a study of the characteristics of perpetrators with sexual abuse histories, found a 59% prevalence rate among imprisoned sex offenders compared with a 29% rate among nonsexual offenders and 17% among university males. Graham (1996) notes a 70% prevalence rate of early sexual abuse among sexual offenders on a treatment milieu.

In a survey of a nonoffending population, Bagley, Wood, and Young (1994) found a statistically significant link between a history of CSA and current sexual activity or interest involving minors. The prevalence rate of CSA within this sample was 15.6 %. As high as 26.2% of the sample reported sexual interest in male minors, whereas 22.3% anonymously reported sexual activity with adolescent males. Discriminate analysis of these findings revealed few false positives and CSA history successfully predicted sexual interest in or activity with minors. Further, current research reveals that sex offenders who had been sexually molested in childhood report three times as many victims as offenders with no sexual abuse history (Renshaw, 1994). Incarcerated offenders with a history of childhood sexual victimization were five times more likely to commit sexual abuse against a stranger and eight times more likely to sexually assault a family member than were their nonabused counterparts (Dutton & Hart, 1992). These findings support the contention that, for at least a subpopulation of sexual perpetrators, there is a significant relationship between CSA and later sexual deviance. These results not only point to the prevalence of CSA among sex offenders but also illuminate the emergent and complex relationship between early sexual victimization and later sexual deviance.

Traumatic Reenactment? The hypothesis that childhood sexual victimization leads to adult sexual offending secondary to the offender/victim reenacting the early experience of abuse has received much attention (Briere & Smiljanich, 1993; Dhawan & Marshall, 1996; Dutton & Hart, 1992; Freeman-Longo,1986; Greenberg, Bradford, & Curry, 1993; Groth, 1979; Hanson & Slater, 1988; Langevin et al., 1989; Longo & Groth, 1983; Prentky & Burgess, 1991; Prentky & Knight, 1993; Romano & De Luca, 1996, 1997; Seghorn et al., 1987). Identified and researched under numerous terms such as the "dracula syndrome" (Schwartz & Cellini, 1995), the victim-to-victimizer cycle (Burgess, Hartman, McCormack, & Grant, 1988), the abused-abuser theory (Freund, 1994; Garland & Dougher, 1990), and the victim-to-abuser cycle (Bagley et al., 1994; Ryan, 1989), a transformational association between these two experiences has been implied in the past.

Researchers have worked to understand both the importance and the nature of the link between CSA and sexual offending. Groth (1979) and Freeman-Longo (1986) are important early researchers who identified the theoretical gap between male sexual victimization and subsequent sexual deviance. They found that incarcerated sexual offenders who were sexually abused in childhood often replicated their victimization experiences as adults. Both age and type(s) of sexual offense perpetrated against the offenders as children corresponded to the age of their own victim(s) and the type(s) of offense(s) they perpetrated against them.

More recent research has lent some support to these findings by identifying the isomorphic nature of offending behavior patterns when compared with earlier experiences of abuse within a prison population. Among incarcerated offenders, Dutton and Hart (1992) demonstrated that those who were sexually abused in childhood were more likely to sexually abuse others in adulthood when compared with offenders who were physically abused in childhood and subsequently physically abused others in adulthood. Briere and Smiljanich (1993) report that 80% of incarcerated sex offenders with histories of sexual abuse by a female perpetrator had committed sexual assaults against women. In a comparison study between pedophiles (those sexually aroused by prepubertal children) and hebephiles (those sexually aroused by pubertal children) who were sexually abused in childhood, it was found that "both groups appear to chose their age specific victims in accordance with the age of their own experience of sexual victimization" (Greenberg et al., 1993, p. 432). Prentky and Knight (1993) also found partial empirical support for this corresponding age component of the recapitulation hypothesis among child molesters. Perpetrators who reported onset of deviant sexual behavior prior to age 15 also report that they were sexually abused at a younger age when compared with adult-onset offenders who also had experienced sexual abuse.

In a recent exploratory study, Romano and De Luca (1997) noted significant trends in the hypothesized direction toward patterns of reenactment along several dimensions. Offenders reported correspondences between their age at the time of their abuse and the age(s) of their own victim(s), as well as a correspondence between their age at the time of onset of offending behavior and the age of their own perpetrator. Other variables researched such as duration and frequency of abuse, sexually abusive acts (specifically, fondling, and oral acts), and relationship to offender (familial or stranger) also demonstrated trends in the hypothesized direction. The small sample size under investigation ($n = 24$) limited the achievement of statistical significance.

The trends indicated, however, are important and these preliminary empirical findings, the first to examine this range of variables, provide support for the essential role early trauma plays in shaping later sexual offending behavior.

These empirical findings are not meant to point to a reductionistic understanding of the relationship between adult sexually deviant behavior and CSA. It is also important to note that research reveals additional important relationships between, and risk factors associated with, later sexual offending and early negative experiences such as dysfunction and violence within the family of origin of an offender, alcoholism, and negative relationship between father and son (Bagley et al., 1994; Haapasalo & Kankkonene, 1997; Hanson & Slater, 1988; Langevin et al., 1989; Prentky et al., 1989; Seghorn et al., 1987). Rather, the research that seeks to distill the victim-to-perpetrator connection provides support for informed consideration of the relevance of trauma to the origins of sexually deviant behavior within the noted constellation of factors that influence such behavior.

VPD and Distortions in Sexualization. Research indicates that children can suffer profound disturbances in their process of becoming sexual beings as a result of childhood sexual victimization. Healthy sexualization occurs secondary to a balance between "safeguards and freedom" (Tharinger, 1990) whereas distorted sexual development is often characterized by rigid sexual beliefs or inappropriate interpersonal boundary violations. Both processes are significantly influenced and shaped by both family and sociocultural context. Developmental theories postulate that experiences of CSA force children prematurely into stages of the sexualization process for which they are unprepared. This early negative erotization process can have a devastating impact on their subsequent psychosexual development (Gilgun & Reiser, 1990; Ryan, 1997; Yates, 1982).

Tharinger (1990) points to several theories hypothesized to account for the development of sexually deviant behavior subsequent to sexual victimization in childhood. Sexual deviance, with childhood abuse at its roots, is viewed by some to be (1) a maladaptive effort to adapt to distortions in sexual development created by the abuse, (2) representative of a pathological process wherein the means by which ordinary needs of affection become sexualized, (3) due to a deficit of inhibitory control of sexual impulses secondary to premature sexualization, (4) an expression of the repetition compulsion as a way to master early sexual trauma, (5) a result of social learning processes, or (6) a method used by the victim, who has internalized a self-view of being bad and worthless, secondary to the abuse, to gain power and attention (Tharinger, 1990).

Young children sexually abused in childhood demonstrate a range of inappropriate sexual behaviors. Currently referred to as abuse reactive, these sexualized behaviors are understood to be derived from early sexual trauma. These behaviors also appear to be preliminary to later offending behavior. Ryan (1989) makes the observation that young (ages 6–11) male sexual abuse victims often begin demonstrating offending behavior patterns that extend beyond "sexually reactive" to include the grooming, planning, calculating and rationalizing behavior demonstrated by their perpetrators.

Finkelhor and Brown (1985) offer an empirical, multidimensional model of the traumatic impact of CSA that serves well to illuminate the victim-to-perpetrator process. Finkelhor and Brown identify the effects of early sexual abuse in terms of four general traumagenic dynamics (or trauma-causing factors): (1) traumatic sexualization, or "the process in which a child's sexuality (including both sexual feelings and sexual attitudes) is shaped in a developmentally inappropriate and interpersonally dysfunctional fashion as a result of sexual abuse"; (2) betrayal, or the discovery by the victim that one has been harmed by a person who was trusted and/or depended on; (3) powerlessness, or disempowerment of the victim; and (4) stigmatization, which occurs secondary to the negative communications (such as shame or guilt) to the victim regarding the abuse experience that can subsequently become internalized (p. 531). It is the convergence of all four of these factors in an experience of sexual abuse that makes the impact of sexual victimization in childhood distinct from other forms of early abuse.

With regard to the sexual abuse victim-to-perpetrator process, one can see how the interaction of these four traumagenic factors could influence sexually aberrant behavior. Although each factor may carry a differentially weighted salience for each victim, it may be that male victims who later perpetrate sexual crimes are more heavily influenced by such factors as traumatic sexualization and powerlessness.

Many male victim/perpetrators have noted that some or all parts of their early sexual abuse experience were enjoyable secondary to the pleasure of sexual arousal and/or the much-needed affection and attention they received from adult pedophiles (Briggs & Hawkins, 1996). In fact, many offenders have clearly indicated that they find memories or fantasies of their own abuse sexually arousing, and others have demonstrated sexual arousal to their own sexual abuse when assessed by the penile plethysmograph (Freeman-Longo, 1986; Ryan, 1989). In spite of these "positive" experiences, and often the denial of CSA and/or its impact, there is clear evidence that males sexually abused in childhood demonstrate significant deficits in self-esteem and psychological well-being (Briggs & Hawkins, 1996; Cermak & Molidar, 1996; Dube & Herbert, 1988; Fromuth & Burkhart, 1989; Urquiza & Keating, 1990).

In addition, the pairing of this sexual abuse fantasy with affection and/or such a potent and powerful reinforcer as sexual arousal and orgasm can lead to trauma-bonded behavior which can include reenacting the abuse. This trauma-bonded behavior that can lead to sexual offending behavior patterns is frequently not addressed in sex offender treatment. In developing an effective intervention for sexual perpetrators abused in childhood, examination of an individual's distorted and/or traumatic sexualization process is essential. In the VPD treatment model, exploration and understanding of the idiosyncratic VPD are central treatment goals.

Burgess et al. (1988) identified a four-phase process that contextualizes the experience of CSA and seeks to illuminate a cognitive processing link from victim to perpetrator. It is Phase 2 of the model, which includes actions related to the abuse, the child's coping and defensive response pattern, and possible encapsulation of the trauma if it remains undisclosed, that provides a hypothesis regarding how sexual abuse can result in potential recapitulation. Burgess et al. (1988) indicated that information processing of traumatic material during this phase results in "trauma learning" as the child attempts to reconcile dissonant sensory, perceptual, and cognitive experiences that occur during the sexual trauma. "[B]ehavioral adaptations at three levels emerge in overt behavioral patterns specifically reflecting the abuse itself" (p. 406). Vacillations between victim and perpetrator behavior provide the child with a two-dimensional perspective of the abuse experience; a view through the eyes of the victim as well as those of the offender. Undisrupted repetition leads to an intractable behavior pattern that blurs and eventually erases the line between victim and offender, with the child ultimately identifying with the aggressor. The results of this "hardwiring" process manifest in aberrant sexual behavior and represent a critical pathological component that should be addressed in treatment.

CSA in Juvenile Offenders. Recognition of the emergent manifestations of maladaptive behavior secondary to the premature sexualization of children is reflected in the growing concern for the high prevalence rate of adolescent sex offenders as well as the interest in their histories of prior victimization. These concerns have been articulated extensively in the literature and are plagued by similar methodological issues and considerations noted earlier. Nonetheless, many chronic sexual-offending behavior patterns are said to begin in early adolescence (Aljazireh, 1993; Becker, 1988; Ryan, 1997, Longo, 1982; Longo & Groth, 1983). Abel, Mittleman, and Becker (1985) reported that more than 50% of adult sex offenders admit that they began offending during early adolescence. Worling (1995) reported a 31% prevalence rate of early sexual trauma among juvenile sex offenders. And current treatment programs for adolescent sex offenders heavily emphasize the importance of addressing early victimization and consider childhood sexual trauma to be a central treatment issue (Freeman-Longo et al., 1994). These findings have important implications for understanding, at least in part, the link between adult offending and early CSA, providing a developmental perspective on the etiological pathway from CSA to adult sex offending behavior.

The Victim/Perpetrator Dialectic. There is evidence to support the idea that the victim and offender populations are "not distinct and mutually exclusive" but that there can be significant overlap between the two (Briggs & Hawkins, 1996, p. 222). Others state that early CSA is neither a necessary nor a sufficient condition to account for future sexual offending behavior (Hanson & Slater, 1988). Early sexual trauma is viewed in this manner as a nonspecific variable that disallows a causal relationship to be established between early childhood abuse and later sexual deviance. There are certainly important contextual and mediating factors (family-of-origin issues and abuse-related factors, age at time of abuse, relationship to the abuser, degree of force, gender, etc.) that need to be considered in the evolution of the dynamic victim-to-perpetrator relationship. However, Greenberg et al. (1993), acknowledging that multiple factors in a child's development can moderate or amplify the response to sexual trauma, noted the following: "A variable may be nonspecific but still causal. Nonspecificity rules out a simple univariate causal model, but does not preclude factors such as sexual abuse in the child molester's own childhood as a cause of this disorder. In a complex multivariate causal model nonspecific relationships cannot be ruled out as potential causes" (p. 435).

It seems that a unidimensional, linear causal link would be an oversimplification of such a complex relationship as the victim/perpetrator dichotomy. The abused offender dialectic must then be understood as an interactive and conflicting relationship between two paradoxically dichotomous yet merged self-experiences. This dichotomy, generated from early developmental distortions, exists dynamically within an evolving, multidetermined but individually understood context. Once again, it should be noted that such a complex clinical picture demands a multivariate understanding and multi-dimensional treatment approach to adequately address the complex clinical concerns presented by sexual perpetrators who have been sexually victimized as children.

Developing VPD Treatment for Sexual Perpetrators. Current approaches to treating the effects of CSA are rooted in early studies of hysteria by Jean-Martin Charcot, Pierre Janet, and Sigmund Freud and Joseph Breuer in the late 19th century. Working with women who exhibited such contemporary manifestations of psychopathology as dissociative disorders, somatoform disorders, mood and anxiety disorders, and PTSD and character disorders such as histrionic and borderline personality disorder in response to early sexual trauma, these men of science unearthed the dark secret and the pervasive effects of the childhood sexual victimization of women. However, the discovery of this aspect of the underbelly of human behavior (specifically abusive human male behavior) was far from celebrated. Instead, awareness of the sexual abuse of female children was suppressed by the societal ego of Victorian times that could not tolerate this internal cultural conflict. Freud's denial in the form of recantation and reformulation of his seduction theory (which had argued brilliantly for the link between reality-based experiences of childhood sexual trauma and the symptoms of hysteria) closed the lid on this Pandora's box. With no political context to support or demand the examination of such a difficult area of social pathology, these ideas remained unearthed until the women's movement of the 1970s brought the issue back into the light with a vengeance (Herman, 1992).

Research of and treatment for female sexual assault, childhood abuse, and battered women became legitimate areas of concern within the field of psychology as a result of the women's movement. It seems that the reality of abuse and its effects could only move into the light of social consciousness on the wave of a significant political movement. A series of wars spawned groundbreaking research on male vulnerability to traumatic stress and contributed to the early formulations of the sexual assault of women in terms of PTSD. However, as research and treatment in the area of childhood trauma and CSA expanded, an important element appears to have been lost in the din of the outcries against such abuse. What had been lost is that an unspecified portion of sexually abused children are boys; boys who grow up to be men who suffer significant and distressing sequelae secondary to their abuse. In recent years there has been a small uprising in the form of the "men's movement" that calls for the recognition of males as potential victims of CSA. Secondary to underreporting, and the minimization of both prevalence rates and the negative effects of CSA on males, research and treatment development are only now beginning to accurately capture the breadth and full implications of this clinical concern for males. This slow growth in clinical research and treatment points to the ongoing societal denial of male sexual victimization. As has been noted, research indicates that males, like their female counterparts, are affected by CSA on multiple levels. There are differences, however, between the female and male context for and response to CSA that need to be understood in order to develop effective treatment interventions.

CSA Treatment With Females. As just noted, the fundamental tenets of mainstream treatment for adults sexually abused in childhood are derived primarily from research on the sexual victimization experiences of women. The focus of treatment, therefore, has been on addressing symptomatology identified in the research on female victims of sexual abuse. Identified treatment goals include decreasing self-destructive and self-harming behavior (Miller, 1994), decreasing symptoms of physiological hyper-arousal (van der Kolk, McFarlane, & Weiseth, 1994), alleviating intrusive memories and flashbacks (van der Kolk et al., 1994: Shapiro, 1995), and reconstructing one's trauma history from a place of resilience and hope (Miller, 1994). Application of treatment models for sexually victimized sex offenders based on women's response to sexual trauma may provide some useful general guidelines.

Complex PTSD. Herman (1992), in an effort to distinguish the effects of chronic trauma from the circumscribed symptoms of PTSD (i.e., reexperiencing the trauma, increased physiological arousal, and avoidance of stimuli related to the trauma) (American Psychiatric Association, 1994), and to capture not only an acute reaction to a single traumatic event but rather the spectrum of potential responses to traumatic stress, identifies the "complex post-traumatic stress disorder" (p. 119). Herman (1992) identified seven diagnostic criteria, including the following: (1) a history of being subjected to totalitarian control over a lengthy period (includes hostages, prisoner of war, battering, CSA, etc.) and (2) alterations in affect regulation, consciousness, self-perception, perception of perpetrator, relations with others, and systems of meanings. Herman's treatment model encompasses three stages of recovery from the negative effects of trauma such as chronic CSA. The aim of the first stage is to create a sense of safety, the second is to foster remembrance and mourning, and the third is to cultivate reconnection with ordinary life. Herman goes on to note that this simplistic guideline belies the complexity of comprehensively addressing the multiply-manifested effects of trauma.

Herman's (1992) remembrance and mourning stage of treatment parallels reexperiencing the trauma and integration of memories in other treatment models of trauma. This process allows the victim to restructure the story of trauma in an effort to transform the trauma memory in a way "that affirms the dignity and value of the survivor" (p. 179). The goal of this stage is not catharsis to purge trauma memories but integration to incorporate them. She refers to two techniques: (1) flooding, which entails intense exposure to trauma stimuli, and (2) testimony, which creates a detailed and extensive record of the abuse experience that helps to facilitate the renarrating process of the trauma. Herman notes the limits of their success, however, in being effective for hyperarousal and intrusive memories but less effective with psychosocial problems, social withdrawal, and constrictive symptoms such as numbing.

In the final stage of reconnection, Herman (1992) notes that the survivor must learn to defend herself, reconcile with herself, and connect with others. For male survivors, however, a useful emphasis may not be on defending oneself but rather on learning to accept one's vulnerability while maintaining a sense of oneself as strong and competent. Reconciling with oneself by creating a life with meaning and perhaps connecting with others for the first time are valuable treatment goals for both male and female survivors of CSA. For males, however, self-reconciliation may often be linked with gender acceptance issues (Mendel, 1995). Discovery of one's membership in an oppressive group secondary to insights gained through therapy could initially lead to shame. However, this discovery could also provide fuel for the "survivor mission" Herman (1992) speaks of that mobilizes survivors of CSA to social action that can foster change on a dimension beyond the personal.

Herman (1992) closes by stating that trauma resolution is never complete and involves an ongoing process in one's personal evolution throughout his or her lifetime. This is a useful frame for male victims of CSA to work toward integrating and accepting as they battle against the desire for quick-fix, action-based solutions to the complex and pervasive effects of CSA. It is also a familiar goal with sex offenders who, through treatment, come to understand that their struggle with sexual deviance is lifelong and requires on going attention.

Trauma Reenactment Syndrome. Recognizing that "there are more complex ways to work with trauma survivors than the oversimplified 'remembering/catharsis/confronting/rebuilding' formula" for PTSD treatment, Miller (1994) offered a cogent model to address "the physical and psychological reenactments of childhood trauma expressed in self-harmful ways" (p. 7). Trauma reenactment syndrome (TRS) captures a more specific range of behaviors that arise secondary to childhood abuse. These destructive behaviors manifest in women in such ways as bulimia/anorexia, substance abuse and addiction, and acts of self-mutilation such as cutting and burning. Miller made a distinction between female victims' self-directed destructive behavior and male victims' other-directed destructive behavior. However, her theory could be extended to include male CSA victims and CSA offenders rather easily. For example, it could be hypothesized that CSA offenders exhibit TRS symptoms in the form of physical violence against others, engaging in thrill-seeking behavior such as criminal activity, enacting interpersonal violence against others, and reenactments of sexual abuse in the form of rape and child sexual assault. Miller postulated that these types of behaviors, often direct replications though sometimes not, symbolically capture the childhood trauma. She went on to explain the meaning of this behavior. In the following, male pronouns and applications have been inserted in parenthesis:

> The pattern of symptoms tells a story of how the child learned to be in relationships and learned to be with (him)self. The symptom is (his) survival skill, no matter how dangerous and hurtful it is. The (other)-injurious behavior serves many functions: in a strange way, it serves both to keep others at a distance and to keep (him) from feeling alone. (He) experiences the behavior itself as a relationship. It may help (him) feel alive when (he) is overwhelmed with feelings of numbness. Paradoxically, it can serve as a well to keep (him) from feeling unbearable (sadness, shame), or grief. (His) behavior is also a cry for help, a request for the protection (he) did not receive as a child. (Miller, 1994, p. 9)

Miller (1994) based her model on four essential assumptions: (1) understanding context, or the personal, social, intellectual, phenomenological, interactive, emotional environment of the individual is essential to understanding and treatment; (2) manifest symptoms must be viewed in a historical context as adaptive, coping response that communicates internalization of past abuse; (3) symptoms serve important functions such as distraction, punishment, soothing; and (4) a safe relational environment is needed to support the trauma work.

Miller (1994) identified the internalized roles that the survivor vacillates between as the "triadic self" and included not only the internalized child victim and the adult perpetrator, but the nonprotecting bystander as well. This three-dimensional self-concept of the CSA survivor can allow males to move beyond their generally rigid two-dimensional internalization of victim and perpetrator that fosters self-blame and responsibility for the abuse. Cultivating a "protective presence" (Miller, 1994), then, becomes a central and useful treatment goal which allows victims of CSA to begin to learn nurturing self-care skills they were unable to access and master in childhood.

This treatment approach seems quite adaptable to both CSA offenders and CSA nonoffending males as well. Pragmatic, contextually informed and systematically building on strengths and developing skills, this model has the flexibility to incorporate the gender-specific effects of the sociocultural processes that affect and distinguish CSA males' interpretation of the meaning of their trauma. Miller (1994) also addressed physiological arousal that can lead to reenactment behavior for women. She has recently added a body-based component to her evolving treatment model that helps CSA women develop skills to mediate physiological arousal that triggers destructive behavior (Miller & Guidry, 2001). These body/mind techniques are clearly relevant to the clinical needs of both sex offending and nonoffending male survivors of CSA and can be easily transplanted and included in developing models of treatment.

Other Contemporary Models. Two additional models should be noted, components of which may prove effective in application to the impact of CSA in sex offenders. Linehan's (1993) dialectical behavior therapy (DBT), for instance, offers a cognitive-behavioral treatment approach designed to help females diagnosed with borderline personality disorder (BPD) to extinguish self-harming behavior. Employing dialectical philosophy with a blend of Zen Buddhism and empirically validated cognitive-behavioral treatment methods, DBT has been successful in decreasing self-destructive behaviors in BPD females. Through such skill-building techniques as emotion regulation and distress tolerance, clients learn how to manage intense affect that triggers maladaptive behaviors. The implications for CSA offenders are clear and, in fact, many aspects of offender-specific treatment are based on similar techniques to control deviant behavior. Aspects of mindfulness, such as seeking balance between rational mind, irrational mind, and wise mind, as well as dialectical understanding of the simultaneous movement toward acceptance and change, could broaden an offender's frame of reference when dealing with contradictory and emotionally conflicted issues that may trigger relapse. One problem with Linehan's (1993) model is that, at the present time, it fails to address the trauma that underlies the behavior. In this sense, DBT parallels much of the work in SOST. Skills are often successfully developed to help diminish deviant behavior, but underlying issues, such as sexual, physical, or emotional trauma and their connection to offending behavior, often fail to receive the adequate attention they require.

Eye movement desensitization and reprocessing (EMDR) is a relatively new technique developed by Shapiro (1989, 1995, 1997) for addressing the sequelae of trauma, particularly the intrusive symptoms that appear to be so central to the development of PTSD and have so long been resistant to treatment. The technique involves directing the client to engage in saccadic eye movements while simultaneously evoking images and feelings associated with the traumatic event. Though not well understood, EMDR is demonstrating clinical efficacy in diminishing and/or alleviating intrusive symptoms of PTSD and empirical validation is being gathered (Rothbaum, 1997; Shapiro, 1989). Although application of this method would fall short in addressing the significant psychosocial aspects that demand attention and the sociocultural context that demands understanding in addressing CSA in sex offenders, an intriguing possibility is revealed in considering the application of EMDR to abused offenders. If an offender's deviant arousal is paired with a memory of CSA, there is the potential that the application of EMDR could diminish or eliminate physiological arousal to this memory, subsequently decreasing the risk of reoffending behavior and perhaps eliminating unwanted, intrusive deviant fantasies. As noted earlier, little attention has been paid to "unpairing" deviant arousal to specific memories of sexual abuse. EMDR or other cognitive-behavioral techniques have the potential to begin to address this treatment gap.

Adapting Contemporary Models to Address CSA Offender Needs. Direct transpositions of these models with sexually victimized sex offenders would likely fall short on several fronts. First, these models would fail to address the significant role that male socialization processes seem to play in many men's gender-specific response to trauma. Based on the dichotomous and patriarchally cultivated notion that women are the oppressed and men are the oppressors, there may be little room to recognize or accept the actual vulnerability of males to sexual victimization. Second, the relational nature of many of these treatment paradigms assumes an interpersonal capacity that is limited in some men as a result of sociocultural influences, impaired in many male CSA survivors, and almost completely nonexistent in many CSA offenders (Marshall & Christie, 1982). Third, the initial focus of many of these models on acknowledging one's victimization and addressing feelings of powerlessness (constructs laden with female overtones, and implications of weakness and vulnerability in the cognitive schemas of most men) may force CSA offenders to prematurely access the very aspect of the abuse that most centrally distresses them.

The hypermasculine response often seen in CSA males arises from the experience of "demasculinization" secondary to their sexual victimization. These issues of power and control and the "rape" of their masculinity may prove to be even more affectively loaded for males who recapitulate their sexual trauma. Demanding CSA offenders to access these feelings related to their victimization early in treatment is tantamount to prematurely asking female CSA victims to "get tough," "be strong," or "get in touch with their anger" before other relevant feelings have been adequately explored and validated. The results would likely be as countertherapeutic as well.

Finally, most of the female-based treatment models would fail to recognize the central and complex VPD that demands attention in the treatment of CSA in sex offenders. Miller (1994, 1996) is the exception in her articulation of the TRS. In this model, Miller offered a useful therapeutic paradigm that could effectively be applied to CSA offenders, providing them with a heuristic framework to foster understanding of their sexually deviant behavior without relinquishing their responsibility for it.

CSA Treatment With Males. The growing but still sparse literature on male victims of CSA points to a significant treatment gap and the need for effective, research-informed interventions specifically designed to address the clinical needs of sexually victimized males. Initial erroneous assumptions that (1) not many males would require treatment because not many males were sexually abused, (2) males did not suffer significant negative effects from CSA, and (3) those who did would fit neatly into the prevailing female treatment paradigms, may have slowed treatment development. Many evolving models of treatment for male survivors of CSA are, however, attentive to problematic male socialization processes. Several interventions articulated in the literature have room for a critique of traditional gender socialization and an active exploration of the impact of this process on sexually victimized males (Lisak, 1995). Treatment interventions designed specifically for male survivors of CSA attempt to be responsive to many of the gendered idiosyncrasies of the male response to sexual victimization.

Struve (1990), for example, noted nine factors that "distinguish recovery efforts of male survivors from those of their female counterparts" (p. 36) and highlighted the impact of patriarchal social systems on the recovery of male victims: (1) reluctance to seek treatment; (2) tendency to minimize the experience of victimization; (3) difficulty accepting shame and guilt; (4) propensity toward exaggerated efforts to reassert masculine identity; (5) difficulties with male intimacy; (6) confusion about sexual identity; (7) behavior patterns with power/control dynamics; (8) a tendency to externalize feelings; and (9) vulnerability to compulsive behaviors. Although the empirical research indicates that the differences between younger male and female response to CSA are minimal, it appears that the measures used are insensitive to, and therefore fail to capture, the significant variations in the subsequent processing of CSA in men and women. Seplar (1990) offers the following:

> While the youngest male victims may not be gender-specific in their response to the victimization, early socialization and the cultural rites of passage that accelerate as young males near puberty clearly create different means of cognition, perception, behavior, and sexuality. Issues of violence and control may be central, but the core of the crisis precipitated by the victimization most likely is distinct from a similar victimization experienced by a female. As such it may be unresponsive to, or further precipitated by, a program model that assumes universality when it comes to sexual victimization. (p. 76)

Mendel (1995) identified three issues of particular salience for male CSA survivors that include (1) concern over one's masculinity and the distorted interface of his masculinity with his experience of sexual victimization, (2) pervasive shame and gender-based shame secondary to recognizing one's membership in an oppressive group, and (3) identification with the role of victim, perpetrator, or rescuer and fear of recapitulating his experience of sexual victimization.

Although some of the treatment models developed for male survivors of CSA offer the means to address identified gender-specific needs, most fall short in offering effective intervention with the dual diagnosis of victim/perpetrator. In addition, many of these models currently lack theoretical sophistication and empirical validation. Also, many fail to address, or choose to separate rather than integrate into treatment, the unacknowledged "elephant in the room" in the form of the potential risk of sexual perpetration for many CSA males. It remains obvious however, that CSA offender treatment should be comprehensive and integrative in its application, and the development of effective treatment should consider the multiple and complex clinical needs which CSA offenders present. Gender-specific effects identified in both the treatment and research literature on male survivors of CSA should be taken into account in developing an effective response to CSA in sex offenders.

Adult SOST. The treatment gap for male survivors of CSA who are also sexual perpetrators is wide at present. Many aspects of SOST have been clearly articulated in the literature and empirically researched, but treatment guidelines to address personal victimization issues of sex offenders have not been delineated.

Prendergast (1991) identified a highly confrontive technique, using marathon therapy sessions and specific badgering techniques with incarcerated sex offenders, that fosters regression and subsequent reliving of the initial trauma. Prendergast's ROARE technique was featured in the 1980 television film *Rage*. Schwartz and Bergman (1995) identified drama therapy as a powerful means of working with the personal victimization issues of sex offenders. Through extensive role play, the original trauma is reenacted with abreaction and/or catharsis as the goal.

The importance of abreaction in trauma work cannot be minimized, but it may have limitations in application to an outpatient sex offender treatment population as such intense therapy experiences, if mismanaged, could leave a patient vulnerable to dysregulated emotions with minimal external supports in place. Recent approaches to addressing issues of trauma reenactment have moved away from abreaction as an outcome and focus more on recognizing and reinforcing resilience; the development of skills to address emotional, physiological, and spiritual distress; and the transformation of the trauma story (Miller, 1996).

As noted earlier, the ambivalent attitude in the field of SOST seems to span the range of "all, none, or unexamined" regarding treatment applications for CSA issues in adult sex offenders. The movement away from addressing CSA in adult offenders is contradictory to the increasing trend toward the development of treatment programs designed to meet the emerging specialized and differential clinical needs of subpopulations of offenders. There is a constant demand to explore and discover increasingly effective and economical treatment interventions for sex offenders. Clearly this points to the need for an effective treatment model to address CSA issues in adult offenders that would be designed to augment standard SOST programs and foster the integration of accountability and acceptance.

VPD Treatment Module. The VPD treatment module was designed in response to the clinical dilemma represented by the population found in the overlap between perpetrators of sexual abuse and victims of sexual abuse. Designed to augment and reinforce standard forms of adult cognitive-behavioral SOST, the focus of the VPD module is on addressing the negative effects of childhood sexual abuse as manifested in the adult male sex offender population. This treatment model, implemented following the completion of standard SOST, would be employed with offenders whose sexually deviant behaviors are determined to be salient to their offending behavior patterns. The module, which runs for twelve weeks in a group therapy format, addresses both general and gender-specific sexual abuse effects in an effort to improve functioning across the multiple domains negatively affected by early sexual trauma.

While the VPD model works to diminish the sequelae of early sexual victimization, both independent of and in relationship to sexually deviant behavior, a central goal of the model will be to work toward the reconciliation of the discordant VPD unique to the population of sexual perpetrators who were also sexually victimized in childhood. The resolution of the conflict reflected in the VPD will further enhance the efficacy of sex offender-specific treatment by contributing to the decrease of deviant sexual arousal, facilitating relapse prevention efforts on the part of the offender and fostering recovery from the often debilitating sequelae of CSA.

VPD Goals. The VPD model represents an effort toward an integrated treatment paradigm. This treatment model (1) augments SOST treatment, (2) facilitates recovery from the negative psychological effects of CSA, and (3) promotes the reconciliation of the conflicted VPD. It is hypothesized that treatment designed to foster the resolution of the discordant victim/perpetrator dichotomy will enhance the efficacy of SOST by contributing to the decrease of deviant sexual arousal and facilitating relapse prevention efforts on the part of the offender.

The VPD treatment model is presented as an augmentation of SOST in an effort not only to support and reinforce the acquisition of techniques to control deviant behavior but also to use client gains from SOST to foster recovery from CSA. Thus, it is important that, in general, an offender with a history of sexual victimization take responsibility for both his offending behavior and his treatment before addressing his own victim issues in order to circumvent the potential reinforcement of a "victim" stance. For some, the psychological sequelae of earlier sexual trauma (depression, suicidality, self-destructive behavior, etc.) may be so active that addressing and managing primary CSA-related symptomatology as a first course of treatment may be clinically appropriate. This should be determined during the initial assessment process for SOST.

For others, however, augmenting SOST with CSA treatment serves several purposes. First, applying CSA treatment as an adjunct to SOST can minimize the degree to which the "abuse excuse" will be misused by offenders and misunderstood by the public as the only factor that contributes to sexual offending behavior. Second, addressing CSA issues can reinforce accountability for sexual offending behavior by further deconstructing cognitive distortions about, and actively reinforcing accurate understanding of, the role of both the victim and the perpetrator. Third, this treatment sequence can enhance the offender's efforts at maintaining SOST treatment gains. Postintensive phase SOST offenders will have acquired skills that will allow them to: (1) control deviant arousal, (2) identify and challenge cognitive distortions, (3) manage stress more effectively, and (4) activate relapse prevention strategies. These fundamental SOST treatment gains will be put into action and their application reinforced as the group members begin to address their own personal victimization.

It is important to understand that some of the techniques and underlying principles used in the VPD treatment model are derived from SOST treatment. As such, these two treatments are not separate and distinct but complementary. Ideas and concepts discussed in SOST will be a relevant part of the underpinnings and dialogue within the VPD treatment group. By working from already cultivated treatment motivation, the complex task of addressing early sexual victimization in the lives of sexual perpetrators can be enhanced and treatment efficacy promoted. The complementary nature of the CSA treatment model itself is designed to both reflect and support the integration of the VPD. The treatment structure itself provides an exemplar for the dynamic effort at synthesizing the internal split between the client's offending- and victimized-self states that will be fostered in treatment.

The second goal—alleviating the psychological distress associated with CSA— also complements SOST goals. To the degree that an individual's early victimization and subsequent symptomatic presentation contribute to his offending behavior, this goal also represents an effort to decrease the incidence of sexual offending behavior. Identifying and addressing CSA-related sequelae, as identified in the literature on the effects of CSA on males, is central to this model. It is important to note that because the targeted population is so broad and heterogeneous by nature, the constellation of interacting factors and symptoms represented within the group may be quite diverse. Within the design of the treatment model, therefore, is an attempt to address both the nomothetic and idiographic expression of CSA-related issues within the group. In this way, once again, the structure of the treatment model reflects the third goal of creating balance and integration by accessing and understanding both the general and the specific domains of relevance.

The unresolved, and at times unacknowledged, tension held within the VPD is hypothesized to contribute to the increased risk for reoffending. The third goal— empowering the reconciliation and synthesis of this tension—therefore, could further decrease risk of relapse. Providing clients with the tools to develop an adaptive cognitive schema regarding the dialectical relationship between themselves as a victim and themselves as a perpetrator may also decrease CSA-related symptoms. Cognitive distortions are created to assuage the experience of negative affect that can be associated with both deviant behavior and experiences of abuse. With CSA offenders, often the initial, and at the time adaptive, meaning-making distortions that arose in response to their own victimization are isomorphic with the distortions that facilitate and maintain sexually deviant behavior. For example, an adjudicated sexual offender, whose offending behavior included urinating in the mouths of his child victims, recounts his own experience of victimization. At age 6, he was forced to perform oral sex with an older male. Mistaking his perpetrator's ejaculate for urine, the client went on to re-create his interpretation of his own victimization. He reports that it was not until he went into treatment that he realized that he had mistaken semen for urine. In SOST treatment with CSA offenders, although the cognitive distortions related to their offense are addressed, the primary ones related to their own victimization remain untouched. The VPD treatment model addresses these significant distortions. As a result, the relationship between the client as victim and the client as perpetrator is further illuminated and can begin to be integrated into the individual's sense of himself as a dynamic and evolving whole person. This integration has the potential to begin to foster the resolution of some of the CSA-related sequelae that cause psychological distress by actively increasing awareness and understanding. This effort may also help to decrease the client's risk of re-offending by further deconstructing the cognitive distortions that can promote and provoke offending behavior and reinforcing a self-reflexive stance.

Central Tenets of the VPD Treatment Module. The dynamic constellation of abuse-related symptomatology and the co-occurring expression of paraphilia presents a biopsychosocially complicated set of clinical challenges unique to sex offenders with a history of CSA. The complex and multifactorial nature of this clinical phenomenon in sexually abused sex offenders, demands an integrated treatment approach. The VPD model of addressing the sequelae of sexual victimization among sexual abusers includes the following central tenets:

1. A treatment process whereby the pairing between CSA and offending behavior at sensory, perceptual, and cognitive levels is unlinked. Derived from Burgess et al.'s (1987) information-processing model of the victim to perpetrator process, treatment mechanisms to facilitate the multileveled dismantling of the distorted associations between early sexual victimization and later sexual deviance are critical to effective VPD intervention. Visual, experiential and written exercises allow group members to re-vision, recontextualize, and renarrate their early experiences of sexual trauma. These interventions are designed to facilitate integration of the abusive episode(s) in a more complete, comprehensible, and acceptable form.

2. A treatment structure wherein the full scope of the individual's traumatic sexualization process can be examined in light of the multiple biopsychosocial factors influencing both his idiographic response to CSA and its relationship to his offending behavior patterns. The group process itself is structured as a journey toward increasing awareness of the hidden issues that can potentially affect a group member's early response to sexual trauma. Through psychoeducation, group discussion, dyad sharing, and journaling, participants can discover for themselves the factors that shaped their reaction to their own sexual abuse. The distinction of this treatment component arises from Finkelhor and Brown's (1985) four-factor theory of CSA that identifies the concurrent experience of traumatic sexualization, stigmatization, betrayal, and powerlessness as a unique outcome to CSA. An integrated VPD intervention will clinically attend to the interactive expression of these elements and their connection to sexually deviant behavior. In addition, treatment methods should be sensitive to and contextualized by knowledge of the powerful influence of patriarchal socioculturalization practices (Lisak, 1995; Struve, 1990) and the gender-specific, psychophysiological effects of traumatic and/or distorted sexualization processes (Dhaliwal et al., 1996; Tharinger, 1990; van der Kolk et al., 1996).

3. A skills-building component to foster self-care/self-management/self-empathy techniques (i.e., stress management, emotion regulation, and alternative self-soothing practices), enhance interpersonal relationship capacities, and establish mindfulness meditation practices (Linehan, 1993; Miller, 1994, 1996; Pithers & Cummings, 1995). The development of improved, effective, and adaptive self-regulatory capacities can enhance relapse prevention goals, promote self-efficacy and agentic capacities, and negate the evocative pull of the "abuse excuse." In cultivating a "protective presence" (Miller, 1994, 1996) within both the internal and external environment by identifying, developing, and accessing positive sources of support and comfort, CSA offenders can begin to "unlearn" negative coping and learn effective and appropriate self-soothing responses to stress and negative affect. The discipline of mindfulness practice can foster a sense of mind/body mastery and serenity that can circumvent distressful compulsive sexual urges and diminish impulsive behavior.

4. A cognitive restructuring process to facilitate the organization of cognitive schema that would integrate disparate and conflicting aspects of the self and provide a frame for the synthesis of the victim/perpetrator dialectic. CSA offenders' cognitive distortions surrounding their own CSA experience (denial, minimization, etc.), often parallel those that reinforce and maintain their own sexually deviant behavior patterns and function to defend against negative and distressing affect (Dudek, Nezu, & Nezu, 1997). Identification of these thinking errors and challenges to and disconfirmation of these isomorphic cognitive distortions (Abel et al., 1984), similar to the process employed in standard sex offender treatment, will help alleviate faulty cognitions that are both harmful and dangerous to the victim/perpetrator.

In addition, Miller's (1994, 1996) model of trauma reenactment offers a unique perspective on the idea of recapitulation of early trauma experiences. First, in this structure, it can be understood that it is not the role of the perpetrator or the victim that is being reenacted in current sexual offending but the relationship between the victim, the perpetrator, and the nonprotecting bystander (or the one who did not stop the abuse). Second, this model offers an exploration of the protective presence, a source of strength, comfort, and resilience that is cultivated within each participant. An exploration and integration of Miller's formulation of the triadic self, would (a) promote the reorganization of maladaptive schema, (b) provide a psychological structure within which the function of VPD can be understood without minimizing offender responsibility for his or her own sexually deviant behavior action, and (c) foster the capacity for self-acceptance, insight, and positive action.

5. A treatment structure that models and fosters a dialectical balance between acceptance and change (Linehan, 1993), between intimacy and independence (Lisak, 1995), between accountability and compassion (E. Coleman, personal communication, 1997), and between the dichotomous experiences of self-as-victim and self-as-perpetrator. In this way, the ongoing, perpetual nature of dialectical resolution processes reflected in the group context can be internalized and carried into life beyond treatment. This philosophical theory can promote a self-reflexive and continually evolving and synthesizing stance that allows individuals to respond more effectively in the face of stressors, conflicts, and/or contradictions that previously may have provoked negative thoughts, feelings, and behaviors that contributed to their sexually deviant actions.

Conclusion

The overlap between male victims of childhood sexual abuse and adult sexual offenders creates a complexly integrated clinical population. This population presents with specialized treatment needs that demand an efficacious and informed treatment response. SOST represents a grounded effort to decrease sexually deviant behavior. Augmenting this empirically validated treatment regime with an effective response to the clinical sequelae of childhood sexual victimization can only enhance the efficacy of SOST and reduce the potential incidence of sexual abuse. The VPD model is designed to reinforce the treatment gains of SOST while reducing the negative effects of CSA on adult male victims. Identifying and reconciling the unexamined VPD allows the abused offender to integrate previously unacknowledged or confusing aspects of self that may serve to compromise efforts at relapse prevention. The benefits of the VPD model are captured in the articulated goals to enhance SOST, decrease the psychological distress associated with CSA, and reconcile the victim/perpetrator dialectic; all of which serve the essential purpose of decreasing the incidence and assuaging the effects of sexual victimization.

There are several ways in which this model is limited. Employing a manualized, time-limited format prohibits a more dynamic exploration of essential CSA issues. The brief twelve-week time frame for treatment can force the exclusion of, or superficial attention to, significant clinical issues. A cathartic or abreactive process, seen by many as essential in the treatment of CSA, is not a part of the VPD treatment model. The VPD model, however, represents a preliminary effort at addressing the sequelae of CSA in the lives of sex offenders. It is recommended that additional treatment for sexual abuse issues be pursued when indicated.

Clinical research to explore the treatment efficacy of the VPD model is needed in the future. Outcome findings from a VPD pilot treatment group (Guidry, 1998) showed positive treatment effects with significant decreases in elevated scores on the Traumatic Symptom Inventory (TSI; Briere, 1995). Of particular note was the substantial decrease in scores related to efforts to reduce tension through externalizing behavior. This was a small pilot group and the findings are not generalizable. The results do, however, show promise for the benefit of addressing sexual victimization issues with sexual perpetrators. Additional research on VPD outcome, the impact that addressing victim issues in conjunction with standard sex offenders treatment targets has on lowering recidivism rates, and more details regarding the interaction between CSA and later offending is required to more efficiently and effectively identify the treatment needs of this subpopulation of offenders. Ongoing typological research that includes the presence of CSA as a relevant characteristic to consider for subpopulations of sex offenders will also serve to refine VPD treatment.

The implications of the complex interactional relationship between CSA and adult sexual deviance clearly points to the need for an informed and integrated treatment response. Effectively addressing the clinical phenomenon represented by the interactive manifestation of the psychological sequelae of CSA and the presence of a paraphilic disorder is essential in responding to the impassioned, one-sided, rhetorical public outcry to "end the cycle of sexual abuse." In reality, the VPD is the cycle of abuse. Representing a reprehensible biosocial phenomenon that is derived from multiple sources, sexual abuse, by its very nature, is often self-perpetuating. Stopping the cycle of abuse involves the socioculturally complex task of grasping that in a significant number of cases, the offender and the victim are one and the same. Recognition and reconciliation of this difficult dialectic can empower the development of progressive treatment and cultivate an evolved sociocultural balance between practices of tolerance and transformation.

References

Abel, G. G., & Becker, J. V. (1984). *Treatment manual: The treatment of child molesters.* New York: Columbia University Press.

Abel, G. G., Becker, J. V., Cunninham-Rathner, J., Rouleau, J. L., Kaplan, M., & Reich, J. (1984).

Treatment manual: The treatment of child molesters. Atlanta: Emory University School of Medicine, Department of Psychiatry.

Abel, G. G., Mittelman, M., & Becker, J. V. (1985). Sexual offenders: Results of assessment and recommendation for treatment. In H. H. Ben-Aron, S. I. Huckers, & C. D. Webster (Eds.), *Clinical criminology: Current concepts* (pp. 191–205). Toronto: M. M. Graphics.

Abel, G., Osborn, C., Anthony, D., & Gardos, P. (1992). Current treatments of paraphiliacs. *Annual Review of Sex Research, 3,* 255–290.

Aljazireh, L. (1993). Historical, environmental, and behavioral correlates of sexual offending by male adolescents: A critical review. *Behavioral Sciences and the Law, 11,* 423–440.

Allam, J., Middleton, D., & Browne, K. (1997). Different clients, different needs? Practice issues in community-based treatment for sex offenders. *Criminal Behavior and Mental Health, 7,* 69–84.

American Psychiatic Association. (1994). *Diagnostic and statistical manual of mental disorders* (4th ed.). Washington, DC: Author.

Bagley, C., Wood, M., & Young, L. (1994). Victim to abuser: Mental health and behavioral sequels of child sexual abuse in a community survey of young adult males. *Child Abuse and Neglect, 18(*8), 683–697.

Bauserman, R., & Rind, B. (1997). Psychological correlates of male child and adolescent sexual experiences with adults: A review of the nonclinical literature. *Archives of Sexual Behavior, 26(*2), 105–141.

Becker, J. V. (1988). The effects of child sexual abuse on adolescent sex offenders. In G. E. Wyatt & E. J. Powell (Eds.), *Lasting effects of sexual abuse* (pp. 193–207) . Beverly Hills, CA: Sage.

Beitchman, J. H., Zucker, K. J., Hood, J. E., DaCosta, G. A., Akma, D., & Cassavia, E. (1992). A review of the long-term effects of child sexual abuse. *Child Abuse and Neglect,* 16, 101–117.

Briere, J. (1995). *Traumatic Symptom Inventory (TSI): Professional manual.* Odessa, FL: Psychological Assessment Resources.

Briere, J., Evans, D., Runtz, M., & Wall, T. (1988). Symptomatology in men who were molested as children: A comparison study. *American Journal of Orthopsychiatry, 58*(3), 457–461.

Briere, J., & Runtz, M. (1993). Childhood sexual abuse: Long-term sequelae and implications for psychological assessment. *Journal of Interpersonal Violence, 8*(3), 312–330.

Briere, J., & Smiljanich, K. (1993). *Childhood sexual abuse and subsquent sexual aggression against adult women.* Paper presented at the 101st annual convention of the American Psychological Association, Toronto.

Briggs, F., & Hawkins, R. M. F. (1996). A comparison of the childhood experiences of convicted male child molesters and men who were sexually abused in childhood and claimed to be non-offenders. *Child Abuse and Neglect, 20*(3), 221–233.

Brown, A., & Finkelhor, D. (1986). Impact of child sexual abuse: A review of the research. *Psychological Bulletin, 99*(1), 66–77.

Brownmiller, S. (1975). *Against our will: Men, women and rape.* New York: Simon & Schuster.

Bumby, K. M., & Bumby, N. H. (1997). Adolescent female sex offenders. In B. K. Schwartz & H. R. Cellini (Eds.), *The sex offender: New insights, treatment innovations, and legal developments* (pp. 10-1–10-16). Kingston, NJ: Civic Research Institute.

Burgess, A. W., Hartman, C. R., McCormack, A., & Grant, C. A. (1988). Child victim to juvenile victimizer: Treatment implications. *International Journal of Family Psychiatry, 9*(4), 403–416.

Carrasco, N., & Garza-Louis, D. (1997). Hispanic sex offenders: Cultural characteristics and implications for treatment. In B.K. Schwartz & H. R.Cellini (Eds.), *The sex offender: New insights, treatment innovations, and legal developments* (pp. 13-1–13-10). Kingston, N.J: Civic Research Institute.

Cellini, H. R. (1995). Assessment and treatment of the adolescent sex offender. In B. K. Schwartz & H. R. Cellini (Eds.), *The sex offender: Corrections, treatment, and legal practice* (pp. 6-1–6-12). Kingston, NJ: Civic Research Institute.

Cermak, P., & Molidar, C. (1996). Male victims of child sexual abuse. *Child and & Adolescent Social Work Journal, 13*(5), 385–400.

Coleman, E., & Haaven, J. (2001). Assessment and treatment of intellectually disabled sex offenders. In M. S. Karich & S. Mussack (Eds.), *Handbook of sex offender treatment*. Brandon, VT: Safer Society Program and Press.

Collings, S. J. (1995). The long-term effects of contact and noncontact forms of child sexual abuse in a sample of university men. *Child Abuse and Neglect, 19*(1), 1–6.

Craissati, J., & McClurg, G. (1996). The challenge project: Perpetrators of child sexual abuse in south east London. *Child Abuse and Neglect, 20*(11), 1067–1077.

Dhaliwal, G. K., Gauzas, L., Antonowicz, D. H., & Ross, R. R. (1996). Adult male survivors of childhood sexual abuse: Prevalence, sexual abuse characteristics, and long-term effects. *Clinical Psychology Review, 16*(7), 619–639.

Dhawan, S., & Marshall, W. L. (1996). Sexual abuse histories of sexual offenders. *Sexual Abuse: A Journal of Research and Treatment, 8*(1), 7–15.

Dimock, P. T. (1988). Adult males sexually abused as children. *Journal of Interpersonal Violence, 3*(2), 203–221.

Dube, R., & Herbert, M. (1988). Sexual abuse of children under 12 years of age: A review of 511 cases. *Child Abuse and Neglect, 12*, 321.

Dudek, J. A., Nezu, A. M., & Nezu, C. M. (1997). *From victim to offender: Denial as a mediating variable between past victimization and current sexual deviance.* Paper presented at the 16th annual conference of the Association for the Treatment of Sexual Abusers, Arlington, VA.

Dutton, D. G., & Hart, S. D. (1992). Evidence for long-term, specific effects of childhood abuse and neglect on criminal behavior in men. *International Journal of Offender Therapy and Comparative Criminology, 36*(2), 129–137.

Ertz, D. J. (1997). The American Indian sex offender. In B. K.Schwartz & H. R. Cellini (Eds.), *The sex offender: New insights, treatment innovations, and legal developments* (pp. 14-1–14-12). Kingston, NJ: Civic Research Institute.

Etherington, K. (1995). Adult male survivors of childhood sexual abuse. *Counseling Psychology Quarterly, 8*(3), 233–241.

Finkelhor, D. (1990). Early and long-term effects of child sexual abuse: An update. *Professional Psychologist: Research and Practice, 21*(5), 325–330.

Finkelhor, D., & Browne, A. (1985). The traumatic impact of child sexual abuse: A conceptualization. *American Journal of Orthopsychiatry, 55*(4), 530–541.

Fischer, G. J. (1992). Sex attitudes and prior victimization as predictors of college student sex offenses. *Annals of Sex Research, 5*, 53-60.

Freeman-Longo, R. E. (1986). The impact of sexual victimization on males. *Child Abuse and Neglect, 10*, 411–414.

Freeman-Longo, R. E., Bird, S., Stevenson, W. F., & Fiske, J. A. (1995). *1994 nationwide survey of treatment programs & models: Serving abuse reactive children and adolescent & adult sexual offenders.* Brandon, VT: Safer Society Press.

Freund, K., & Kuban, M. (1994). The basis of the abused abuser theory of pedophilia: A further elaboration of an earlier study. *Archives of Sexual Behavior, 23*(5), 553–563.

Fromuth, M. E., & Burkhart, B. R. (1989). Long-term psychological correlates of childhood sexual abuse in two samples of college men. *Child Abuse and Neglect, 13*, 533–542.

Garland, G. J., & Dougher, M. J. (1990). The abused/abuser hypothesis of child sexual abuse: A critical review of theory and research. In J. R. Feirman (Ed.), *Pedophilia: Biosocial dimensions* (pp. 488–509). New York: Springer-Verlag.

Garland, R. J., & Dougher, M. J. (1991). Motivational intervention in the treatment of sex offenders. In W. R. Miller & S. Rollnick, *Motivational interviewing: Preparing people to change addictive behavior* (pp. 303–313). New York: Guilford Press.

Genuis, M., Thomlison, B., & Bagley, C. (1991). Male victims of child sexual abuse: A brief overview of pertinent findings [Special Issue: Child Sexual Abuse]. *Journal of Child and Youth Care, 6*, 1–6.

Gilgun, J. F., & Reiser, E. (1990). The development of sexual identity among men sexually abused as children. *Journal of Contemporary Human Services, 71*(9), 515–523.

Gordon, M. (1990). Males and females as victims of childhood sexual abuse: An examination of the gender effect. *Journal of Family Violence, 5*(4), 321–332.

Graham, K. R. (1996). The childhood victimization of sex offenders: An underestimated issue. *International Journal of Offender Therapy and Comparative Criminology, 40*(3), 192–203.

Greenberg, D. M., Bradford, J. M. W., & Curry, S. (1993). A comparison of sexual victimization in the childhoods of pedophiles and hebephiles. *Journal of Forensic Sciences, 38,* 432–436.

Groth, A. N. (1979). Sexual trauma in the life histories of rapists and child molesters. *Victimology: An International Journal, 4*(1), 10–16.

Guidry, L. L. (1998). *Addressing the victim/perpetrator dialectic: Treatment for sexually victimized sex offenders.* Doctoral dissertation, Antioch New England Graduate School, Keene, New Hampshire.

Haapasalo, J., & Kankkonen, M. (1997). Self-reported childhood abuse among sex and violent offenders. *Archives of Sexual Behavior, 26*(4), 421–431.

Hanson, R. K., & Slater, S. (1988). Sexual victimization in the history of child sexual abusers: A review. *Annals of Sex Research, 1,* 485–499.

Herman, J. L. (1992). *Trauma and recovery.* New York: Basic Books.

Hindman, J. (1988). Research disputes assumption about child molesters. *National District Attorney's Bulletin, 7*(4), 1–3.

Hunter, J. A. (1991). A comparison of the psychosocial maladjustment of adult males and females sexually molested as children. *Journal of Interpersonal Violence, 6*(2), 205–217.

Hunter, M. (1990). *The sexually abused male: Prevalence, impact, and treatment* (Vol. 1). New York: Lexington Books.

Inderbitzen-Pisaruk, H., Shawchuck, C. R., & Hoir, T.S. (1992). Behavioral characteristics of child victims of sexual abuse: A comparison study. *Journal of Clinical Child Psychology, 21*(1), 14–19.

Johnson, M. K. (1997). Clinical issues in the treatment of geriatric sex offenders. In B. K. Schwartz & H. R. Cellini (Eds.), *The sex offender: New insights, treatment innovations, and legal developments* (pp. 12-1–12-10). Kingston, N.J: Civic Research Institute.

Kendall-Tackett, K. A., Williams, L. M., & Finkelhor, D. (1993). The impact of sexual abuse on children: A review and synthesis of recent empirical studies. *Psychological Bulletin, 113,* 164–180.

Langevin, R., Wright, P. & Handy, L. (1989). Characteristics of sex offenders who were sexually victimized as children. *Annals of Sex Research, 2,* 227–253.

Lew, M. (1990). *Victims no longer: Men recovering from incest and other sexual child abuse.* New York: Harper Collins.

Linehan, M. M. (1993). *Cognitive-behavioral treatment of borderline personality disorder.* New York: Guilford Press.

Lisak, D. (1994). The psychological impact of sexual abuse: Content analysis of interviews with male survivors. *Journal of Traumatic Stress, 7,* 525–548.

Lisak, D. (1995). Integrating a critique of gender in the treatment of male survivors of childhood abuse. *Psychotherapy, 32,* 258–269.

Lisak, D., & Luster, L. (1994). Educational, occupational, and relationship histories of men who were sexually and/or physically abused as children. *Journal of Traumatic Stress, 7,* 507–523.

Longo, R. E. (1982). Sexual learning and experience among adolescent sex offenders. *International Journal of Offender Therapy and Comparative Criminology, 26*(3), 235–241.

Longo, R. E., & Groth, A. N. (1983). Juvenile sexual offenses in the histories of adult rapists and child molesters. *International Journal of Offender Therapy and Comparative Criminology, 27,* 150–155.

Marshall, W. L. (1996a). The sexual offender: Monster, victim, or everyman? *Sexual Abuse: A Journal of Research and Treatment, 8,* 317–335.

Marshall, W. L. (1996b). Assessment, treatment, and theorizing about sex offenders: Developments during the past twenty years and future directions. *Criminal Justice and Behavior, 23,* 162–199.

Marshall, W. L., & Christie, M. M. (1982). The enhancement of social self-esteem. *Canadian Counselor, 16,* 82–89.

Marshall, W. L., & Eccles, A. (1991). Issues in clinical practice with sex offenders. *Journal of Interpersonal Violence, 6*, 68–93.

Marshall, W. L., Jones, R., Ward, T., Johnston, P., & Barbaree, H. E. (1991). Treatment outcome with sex offenders. *Clinical Psychology Review, 11*, 465–485.

Mendel, M. P. (1995). *The male survivor.* Thousand Oaks, CA: Sage.

Miller, D. (1994). *Women who hurt themselves: A book of hope and understanding.* New York: Basic Books.

Miller, D. (1996). Challenging self-harm through transformation of the trauma story. *Sexual Addiction and Compulsivity, 3*(3), 213–227.

Miller, D., & Guidry, L. (2001). *Addictions and trauma recovery: Healing the body, mind and spirit.* New York: Norton.

Miner, M. H., & Crimmins, L. S. (1997). Adolescent sex offenders: Issues of etiology and risk factors. In B. K. Schwartz & H. R. Cellini (Eds.), *The sex offender: New insights, treatment innovations, and legal developments* (pp. 9-1–9-15). Kingston, NJ: Civic Research Institute.

Myers, M. F. (1989). Men sexually assaulted as adults and sexually abused as boys. *Archives of Sexual Behavior, 18*(3), 203–215.

Peters, S. D., Wyatt, G. E., & Finkelhor, D. (1986). Prevalence. In D. Finkelhor (Ed.), *A sourcebook on child sexual abuse* (pp. 15–59). Beverly Hills, CA: Sage.

Pithers, W. D., & Cummings, G. F. (1995). Relapse prevention: A method for enhancing behavioral self-management and external supervision of the sexual aggressor. In B. K. Schwartz & H. R. Cellini (Eds.), *The sex offender: Corrections, treatment, and legal practice* (pp. 20-1–20-32). Kingston, NJ: Civic Research Institute.

Prendergast, W. E. (1991). *Treating sex offenders in correctional institutions and outpatient clinics: A guide to clinical practice.* New York: Haworth Press.

Prentky, R. A., & Burgess, A. W. (1991). Hypothetical biological substrates of a fantasy based drive mechanism for repetitive sexual aggression. In A. W. Burgess (Ed.), *Rape and sexual assault III.* (pp. 235–256). New York: Garland.

Prentky, R. A., & Knight, R. A. (1993). Age of onset of sexual assault: Criminal and life history correlates. In G. C. N. Hall, R. Hirschman, J. R. Graham, & M. S. Zaragoza (Eds.), *Sexual aggression: Issues in etiology, assessment, and treatment* (pp. 43–62). Washington, DC: Taylor & Francis.

Prentky, R. A., Knight, R. A., Sims-Knight, J. E., Straus, H., Rokous, F., & Cerce, D. (1989). Developmental antecedents of sexual aggression. *Development and Psychopathology, 1*, 153–169.

Reinhart, M. A. (1987). Sexually abused boys. *Child Abuse and Neglect, 11*, 229–235.

Renshaw, K. L. (1994). Child molesters: Do those molested as children report larger numbers of victims than those who deny childhood sexual abuse? *Journal of Addictions and Offender Counseling, 15*(1), 24–32.

Roesler, T. A., & McKenzie, N. (1994). Effects of childhood trauma on psychological functioning in adults sexually abused as children. *Journal of Nervous and Mental Disease, 182*(3), 145–150.

Roane, T. H. (1992). Male victims of sexual abuse: A case review within a child protective team. *Child Welfare, 71*(3), 231–239.

Romano, E., & De Luca, R.V. (1996). Characteristics of perpetrators with histories of sexual abuse. *International Journal of Offender Therapy and Comparative Criminology, 40*(2), 147–156.

Romano, E., & De Luca, R. V. (1997). Exploring the relationship between childhood sexual abuse and adult sexual perpetration. *Journal of Family Violence, 12*(1), 85–98.

Rothbaum, B. O. (1997). A controlled study of eye movement desensitization and reprocessing in the treatment of posttraumatic stress disordered sexual assault victims. *Bulletin of the Menninger Clinic, 61*(3), 317–334.

Ryan, G. (1989). Victim to victimizer: Rethinking victim treatment. *Journal of Interpersonal Violence, 4*(3), 325–341.

Ryan, G. (1997). Sexually abusive youth: Defining the problem. In G. Ryan, S. Lane, & A. Rinzler (Eds.), *Juvenile sexual offending: Causes, consequences, and correction* (pp. 3–9). San Francisco: Jossey-Bass.

Ryan, G., Lane, S., & Rinzler, A. (Eds.). (1997). *Juvenile sexual offending: Causes, consequences, and correction.* San Francisco: Jossey-Bass.

Schulte, J. G., Dinwiddie, S. H., Pribor, E., & Yutzy, S. H. (1995). Psychiatric diagnosis of adult male victims of childhood sexual abuse. *Journal of Nervous and Mental Diseases, 183*(2), 111–113.

Schwartz, B. K. (1995). Introduction to the integrative approach. In B. K. Schwartz & H. R. Cellini (Eds), *The sex offender: Corrections, treatment, and legal practice* (pp. 1-1–1-13). Kingston, NJ: Civic Research Institute.

Schwartz, B., & Bergman, J. (1997) Using drama therapy to do personal victimization work with sexual aggressors: A review of the research. In B. K. Schwartz & H. R. Cellini (Eds.), *The sex offender: New insights, treatment innovations, and legal developments* (pp. 20-1–20-23). Kingston, N.J: Civic Research Institute.

Schwartz, B. K., & Cellini, H. R. (Eds.). (1995). *The sex offender: Corrections, treatment, and legal practice.* Kingston, NJ: Civic Research Institute.

Schwartz, M. (1994). Negative impact of sexual abuse on adult male gender: Issues and strategies of intervention. *Child and Adolescent Social Work Journal, 11*(3), 179–194.

Seghorn, T., Prentky, R. A., & Boucher, R. J. (1987). Childhood sexual abuse in the lives of sexually aggressive offenders. *Journal of the American Academy of Child and Adolescent Psychiatry, 26*, 262–267.

Seplar, F. (1990). Victim advocacy and young male victims of sexual abuse: An evolutionary model. In M. Hunter (Ed.), *The sexually abused male: Prevalence, impact, and treatment* (Vol. I, pp. 73–85). New York: Lexington Books.

Shapiro, F. (1989). Eye movement desensitization: A new treatment for post-traumatic stress disorder. *Journal of Behavior Therapy and Experimental Psychiatry, 20*, 211–217.

Shapiro, F. (1995). *Eye movement desensitization and reprocessing: Basic principles, protocols, and procedures.* New York: Guilford Press.

Shapiro, F. (1997). *EMDR: The breakthrough therapy for overcoming anxiety, stress and trauma.* New York: Basic Books.

Struve, J. (1990). Dancing with the patriarchy. In M. Hunter (Ed.), *The sexually abused male: Prevalence, impact and treatment* (Vol. I, pp. 3–45). New York: Lexington Books.

Tharinger, D. (1990). Impact of child sexual abuse on developing sexuality. *Professional Psychology: Research and Practice, 21*(5), 331–337.

Urquiza, A. J., & Capra, M. (1990).The impact of sexual abuse: Initial and long-term effects. In M. Hunter (Ed.), *The sexually abused male: Prevalence, impact, and treatment* (Vol. I, pp. 105–131). New York: Lexington Books.

Urquiza, A. J., & Keating, L. M. (1990). The prevalence of sexual victimization of males. In M. Hunter(Ed.), *The sexually abused male: Prevalence, impact, and treatment* (Vol. I, pp. 89–103). New York: Lexington Books.

Vander Mey, B. (1988). The sexual victimization of male children: A review of previous research. *Child Abuse and Neglect, 12*, 61–72.

van der Kolk, B. A., McFarlane, A. C., & Weiseth, L. (Eds.). (1996). *Traumatic stress: The effects of overwhelming experience on mind, body, and society.* New York: Guilford Press.

Violato, C., & Genuis, M. (1993a). Problems of research in male child sexual abuse. *Journal of Child Sexual Abuse, 2*(3), 33–54.

Violato, C., & Genuis, M. (1993b). Factors which differentiate sexually abused from nonabused males: An exploratory study. *Psychological Reports, 72*, 767–770.

Watkins, B., & Bentovim, A. (1992). The sexual abuse of male children and adolescents: A review of the current research. *Journal of Child Psychology and Psychiatry, 33*, 197–248.

Worling, J. R. (1995). Sexual abuse histories of adolescent male sex offenders: Differences on the basis of the age and gender of their victims. *Journal of Abnormal Psychology, 104*(4), 610–613.

Yates, A. (1982). Children eroticized by incest. *American Journal of Psychiatry, 139*(4), 482–485.

Young, R. E., Bergandi, T. A., & Titus, T. G. (1994). Comparison of the effects of sexual abuse on male and female latency-aged children. *Journal of Interpersonal Violence, 9*(3), 291–306.

Chapter 16

Using Domestic Violence Approaches for Sex Offender Treatment

by Denise Hughes-Conlon, M.S., L.M.H.C.

Overview

The Domestic Abuse Intervention Program stresses that men take full responsibility for their violence. The program uses tools such as the Duluth Power and Control Wheel, and the Duluth Abuse of Children Wheel (Pence & Paymar, 1993) to illustrate tactics that men use to control women and children. These wheels have been useful in helping our sex offender clients identify their use of power and control tactics, their issues with women, and the tactics they have used to keep the secret with their partners and victims. The Duluth Equality Wheel and Nurturing Children Wheel illustrate steps to replace abusive behaviors and have been beneficial in giving the sex offenders new tools to use to enhance their relationships with adults and keep themselves in control when around children. Use of the wheels has given clients specific tools to recognize and change their behaviors. These tools have enhanced their relationships and assisted them in keeping their negative behaviors in check. Most offenders have incorporated aspects from the Power and Control Wheel and the Nurturing Children Wheel into their relapse prevention plan.

This chapter outlines how specific aspects of a batterers program can be adapted for sex offender treatment.

The exercises on responsibility, adapted from *Education Groups for Men Who Batter* (Pence & Paymar, 1993), have been helpful in addressing minimizing, denial, and blaming. The exercise on accountability has been useful in addressing the totality of the abuse and the long-range problems the victims endure. It was adapted from the manual *Safety for Women: Monitoring Batterers Programs* (Hart, 1994). "I" statements adapted from the communications book *Talking Together* (Miller, Nunnally, & Wackman, 1979) continue to enhance the client's development of responsibility and accountability. They have been extremely useful in reducing blaming and denial. It is our premise that offenders not only are responsible for the act of molesting but also have to own the burden of responsibility for broken family relationships, problems in school and at work, difficulties with peers, and other personal problems their victims may experience as a result of the abuse. These exercises are useful in making that premise more clear for offenders.

Introduction

In 1998, after having just completed a batterers group, the Duluth Power and Control Wheel that had been used was still prominently displayed. Several sex offenders came in for their group, noticed the wheel, and began identifying themselves on it. Consequently, we decided to use the wheel that day in group and have been using it, and other domestic violence treatment techniques, ever since. The discovery of penicillin was a similar accident. The mold that grew in a Petri dish was found to be a powerful antibiotic and is commonly used in treatment today. The wheels, in comparison, have been our antibiotics and are now a common yet integral component in our treatment of sex offenders. They have been our penicillin.

We have received an overwhelmingly positive response from our sex offender clients as to how helpful these exercises, adapted from our Batters Intervention Program, have been to them. As a result we have incorporated them into our Sex Offender Treatment Program and believe them to be powerful tools. We have not done research on them as this finding was accidental and from the onset the outcomes have been positive. This information is not meant to be a statistical study. It is meant to be our sharing of information or exercises that we have adapted and used that have been beneficial to the workings of our program.

Responsibility Exercise

This exercise can be written or done orally in group (see Figure 16.1). The offenders are asked to think about all the ways they have blamed or minimized their behavior. Their responses can be put on poster paper throughout the room, and the room can be filled with ways the offenders used to rationalize, minimize, deny, or blame.

This exercise on assuming responsibility is helpful for offenders to recognize the "flags" of their behavior, especially if they hear these same thoughts or notice these same behaviors nearing the surface in the future. Group members begin to notice ways they were blaming or trying to minimize behavior that they had not considered before. Our premise is that the blaming and minimization were the defenses they implemented to keep the abuse going or even to start the abuse. If they hear these in the future these should be flags for them. It brings offenders' thought patterns into the open. It is also helpful for the offenders who are still in denial as they begin to see that their excuses and rationalizations were similar to and used by others. It makes it much more

Figure 16.1
Responsibility Exercise

Responsibility

For change to occur, we have to assume responsibility for our past behavior by acknowledging what we did. This in not easy because we want to hold on to the "But": But she . . . But I was . . . But I only . . .

In this exercise list ways you minimized or denied your sexual abuse and how you blamed your victim or others for what you did

(Use an additional sheet for each victim. Is there a pattern?)

Minimizing : _____

Denying : _____

Blaming : _____

List three steps you can take to accept responsibility for your past use of violence.

1. _____

2. _____

3. _____

---

difficult to attempt to use these rationalizations themselves and makes it easier for them to drop their own denial.

Accountability Exercise

The first part of the accountability exercise (see Figure 16.2) is completed orally in a group setting. The offenders are asked to begin to list the ways that they have sexually abused in the past. Sexual abuse in the domestic arena includes lewd comments, leaving the bathroom door open, brushing up against a breast or penis to see the reaction, walking around the house naked in front of children, using sex as a reward, isolating a person or child so no one else can have her/him, and extends all the way to rape or inserting objects into the vagina or anus.

Discussing sexual abuse in this manner has been helpful to the sex offenders in identifying the progression of the abuse, especially the initial steps. This information allows the clients to recognize their patterns of abuse, their flags, and it facilitates the development of their relapse prevention plans. It is also helpful in setting boundaries if they are to be reunited or are to be around children in the future.

The second half of this exercise is also facilitated in a group setting. Clients are asked to discuss all the ways in which sexual abuse can or may impact the victims. Responses can again be put up around the room or simply discussed. Responses include difficulties in school, difficulties in having normal dating relationships, the difficulties for victims and the nonoffending parents. We have found this to be a very

Figure 16.2
Accountability Exercise

Accountability

To be accountable means to acknowledge and take responsibility for one's actions.

Acknowledgment of Abuse

- I have sexually abused _____ in the following ways. [This includes comments, isolation, etc.]

- I am responsible for all the ramifications of the abuse including financial difficulties, school and peer problems, etc.

List several of the problems that were indirectly caused by the sexual abuse.

_____

_____

_____

---

sobering exercise and one that is helpful in building empathy in the offenders who are out of denial.

"I" Statements

Using "I" statements in our groups is not a specific exercise. It is a tool taught in the first group and we expect the clients to continue to use this throughout their treatment regimen.

Adapted "I" statements help the offenders identify and relate to their own feelings first and help them take responsibility for their own actions.

Upon initial disclosure of their offense "I" statements are introduced to the offenders. It is explained to the offender that he will be asked to use "I" statements throughout treatment and a thorough explanation of what "I" statements are is given. "I" statements are about the person speaking only, and also always include the word "because." The purpose is for offenders to gain insight and information and then to be able to exchange the information with others while holding themselves responsible and accountable for their actions.

For example, "*I* am angry because *I* _____." or "*I* felt _____ because *I* _____," or "*I* did ____." or "*I* did _____ because *I* _____."

This forces the offender to take responsibility for their own actions as opposed to blaming the victims.

We are asking specifically what the person did and not what "she" said or why "she" did not like him, etc. This cuts out a great deal of blaming from the beginning.

Clients are redirected to use "I" statements throughout treatment. If someone slips into blaming and begins to use "she," a simple reminder by the therapist to use "I" turns the client back to what he needs to be addressing in terms of personal accountability. The other group members become very good at redirecting also.

The average length of time of denial in our program is five weeks. When offender are in denial there is a greater concentration on asking them to use "I" statements. This means they cannot use the words "she," "they," "you," etc., only "I." For example, most clients want to say such things as: "she was not doing well at school," "she was a liar," "she was sleeping with others," etc. When they are confronted with "I" statements they cannot use any of those old standbys. They are asked to concentrate strictly on their own behavior, what they did, and what they were feeling. This concentration alleviates many standard excuses and decreases the length of time in denial.

"I" statements are also useful to the clients who are not in denial by helping them identify specifically what they did or felt and why (e.g., "I felt ashamed because I had been abusing my daughter," as opposed to "she was always putting me down").

This tool has been very beneficial in group.

The Duluth Power and Control Wheel

The Duluth Power and Control Wheel (see Figure 16.3) is used on a weekly basis to identify minimizations, blaming, denial, and other attempts to control. Although

Figure 16.3
The Duluth Power and Control Wheel

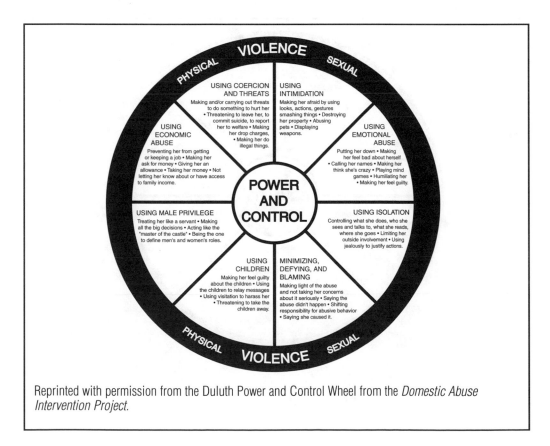

Reprinted with permission from the Duluth Power and Control Wheel from the *Domestic Abuse Intervention Project.*

denial and blaming were confronted on a weekly basis prior to using the wheel it was found that having this visual tool with the explanation of minimizing, denial, and blaming was more effective. Offenders often refer or point to the the Duluth Power and Control Wheel and have incorporated this language into their vocabulary. It is helpful, as most offenders have issues with women and issues of power and control.

The Duluth Power and Control Wheel has been incorporated into several exercises for the sex offenders. The first exercise is simply to pass out the wheel in open discussion and for sex offenders to begin to identify themselves on the wheel in terms of their adult relationships.

The next exercise to follow is one we use by incorporating "I" statements. We ask the offenders to discuss their purposes for using these tactics. What we discovered was that they were using these tactics to keep their partners from discovering the abuse and to make themselves feel better in the same way that batterers do. When a batterer feels badly he begins to blame or abuse in an attempt to make someone else responsible for his behavior. Sexual offenders, to make themselves feel better, use the same tactics. It becomes a vicious cycle.

Figure 16.4
Equality Side of the Duluth Power and Control Wheel

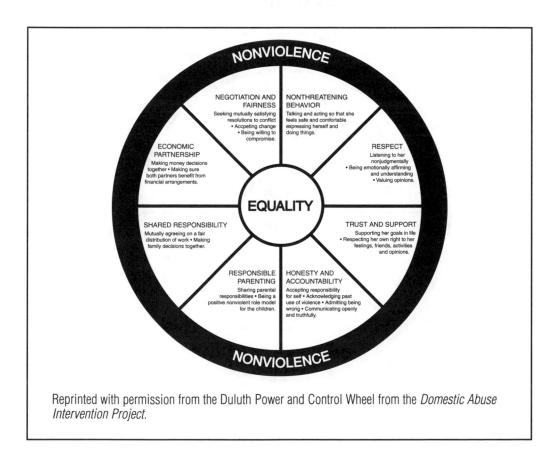

Reprinted with permission from the Duluth Power and Control Wheel from the *Domestic Abuse Intervention Project.*

Once areas of control are identified we spend several sessions addressing the Equality side of the Duluth Power and Control Wheel (see Figure 16.4) and how to actually incorporate its principles into relationships. The incorporation of equality can also be used for nonintimate relationships such as work, friendships, or even group member relationships. Incorporating these skills into their lives has been beneficial in helping sex offenders with their relapse prevention plans and keeping their control issues in constant check.

The Abuse of Children Wheel

Another exercise asks the clients to identify, on the Abuse of Children Wheel (see Figure 16.5), the tactics they used while offending to control their victim. These can be discussed or posted around the room. The result is very sobering.

When this is completed we compare the tactics used when abusing to those identified on the Nurturing Children Wheel (see Figure 16.6) and help identify more pos-

Figure 16.5
Abuse of Children Wheel

Reprinted with permission from the Duluth Power and Control Wheel from the *Domestic Abuse Intervention Project.*

Figure 16.6
Nurturing Children Wheel

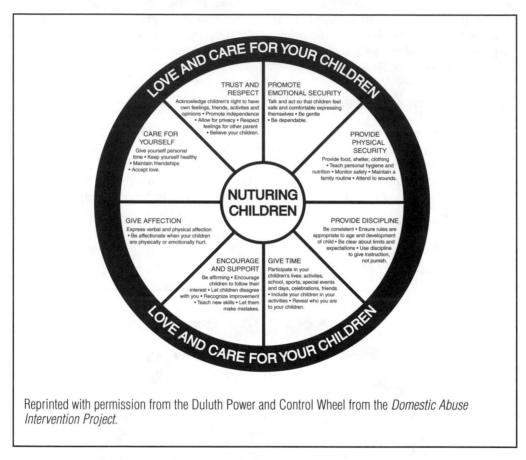

Reprinted with permission from the Duluth Power and Control Wheel from the *Domestic Abuse Intervention Project*.

itive parenting/relationship skills. These skills can also be incorporated into clients' relapse prevention plans to keep their abusive patterns in constant check as many of the tactics identified on the Nurturing Wheel were tactics the sex offenders incorporated into their grooming patterns to gain trust.

Conclusion

Batterers' intervention facilitators have long recognized that sexual abuse is domestic violence. Therapists for sexual offenders have been slower to embrace this idea and the fact that many sexual offenders are also abusive to their partners. It is considered that this abuse stems from their issues with women and their need to keep their partners in the dark about their offending patterns. The tools the batterers' intervention facilitators use to confront denial and enhance responsibility and accountability are straightforward and uncomplicated yet effective. Incorporating them into our sex offender treatment program has given our clients tools that are easy to use and remember. This simplicity has made it easier for our clients to hold themselves accountable on a daily basis. The wheels have become a daily reminder for them of what they need to do to continually work their relapse prevention plans. The wheels are easily incorporated into clients' daily lives, and they work. Using all these tools has been beneficial to the offenders in their communication skills with others and in keeping themselves accountable for all their actions, including the actions that lead up to the abuse, such as their seemingly unimportant decisions. These tools also keep our clients accountable for the abuse perpetrated on their partners to control the partners or keep the partners away from their secrets,, such as their victimizations or their own insecurities. The result: Offenders are the ones practicing these interventions in group and inviting others to use them. It is, in fact, a common occurrence for offenders to openly provide testimony in group about how beneficial these tools have been in their daily lives. Success is often the best reinforcement. Incorporating these tools has definitely contributed to the success of this program.

References

Hart, B. (1988). *Safety for women: Monitoring batterers programs*. Harrisburg: Pennsylvania Coalition Against Domestic Violence.

Miller, S., Nunnally, E. W., & Wackackman, D. B. (1979). *Couple communication, Volume 1: Talking together*. Evergreen, CO: Interpersonal Communications Programs.

Pence, E., & Paymar, M. (1993). *Education groups for men who batter: The Duluth model*. New York: Springer.

Part 5

Adolescent Sex Offenders

In recent years residential treatment programs for troubled adolescents have begun to specialize or have expanded to include programs for youth with sexually inappropriate behavior. This may be, in part, due to willingness on the part of funding sources to finance extended treatment for these individuals. School systems, which fund much of this treatment, may be afraid of returning these young people to the community and are thus willing to provide residential care for years. It is vital to public safety to ensure that only qualified programs be allowed to assume care of these youths.

In his chapter (Chapter 17), Charles Hodges presents a five-step family therapy protocol that can be used to eventually reunite families traumatized by sibling-on-sibling incest. This clearly outlined process takes the therapist from discovery through reunification and includes suggestions for a variety of special problems.

In Chapter 18, Alexis Miranda and Kathleen Davis discuss a variety of theoretical approaches including psychodynamic, object-relations, and victim-to-perpetrator (traumagenic approaches). They review several typologies and then discuss a variety of treatment approaches to sexually inappropriate behaviors as well as comorbid conditions.

Carl Schwartz operates an outpatient treatment program for sexually abusive youths. He has developed a multimedia technique for dealing with dynamic issues, including the offender's feelings about his situation, his victim, and his family. Using projected pictures and photographs, music, and evocative statements the youth is able to connect affectively with this material (see Chapter 19).

Residential treatment programs can do everything right, but everything can be quickly undone if the child is returned to an unsafe, inadequate, or unprepared environment. Bert Harris and Julie Campbell (Chapter 20) have developed the S.A.F.E.R. model, which offers a systematic method for evaluating the child, the family, and the social system prior to reunification. Programs may be pressured into prematurely returning the child in order to save money or because the agent suspects (justified or not) that the program is artificially extended treatment. Using the Sexual Abuse Family Evaluation for Reunification may provide objective criteria for measuring the likelihood of a successful homecoming. Clinically it can assist in identifying areas in need of remediation.

James Yokley expands on the significant subpopulation of youth who act out sexually and also suffer from a variety of other problems. His innovative program trains people to run therapeutic foster homes for this population and then uses a variety of creative approaches to provide intensive outpatient therapy for these juveniles. In Chapter 21, he offers suggestions for recruiting and training foster families and the research on this approach. In Chapter 24, he describes a variety of exercises for developing empathy in this challenging group of adolescents.

To promote the development of quality programs for the sexually abusive child,

Steven Bengis (see Chapter 22) convened a "blue-ribbbon" panel to develop standards for residential care for sexually abusive youth. This panel should prove valuable in establishing minimal standards for health, safety, and treatment conditions. It should also enhance uniformity without stifling creativity.

Staff of residential facilities would do well to read and heed the suggestions presented by Dr. Vicki Agee on building a positive peer culture in residential programs for adolescents who act out sexually. By using the "three R's" (Revising, Relabeling, and Reinforcing), behaviors that can destroy the therapeutic milieu can be remolded (see Chapter 23).

Chapter 17

Family Therapy in Sibling-on-Sibling Sexual Abuse

by Charles E. Hodges, Jr., M.S.W., M.Div.

Overview

In this chapter the author presents a systematic approach to doing family therapy in cases of sibling-on-sibling incest. There are five steps to this approach, and each step identifies treatment goals, participants, treatment focus, and warning signs. Special issues which might be encountered in these situations include dealing with cases in which more than one sibling has been offended against and dealing with parents who may be victims of their child or may have offended against their children.

Introduction

The destructive nature of sibling-on-sibling sexual abuse presents grave consequences for the victim, offender, and other family members if not properly addressed in the context of family therapy (Hodges & Young,1999). It presents unique clinical challenges that differ from sexual offenses committed on family members by non-family members (Harris & Campbell, 1998; Meinig, 1996; Werrbach, 1993; Wiehe, 1997). Parental figures who are entangled in sibling-on-sibling sexual abuse frequently express conflicting feelings toward the siblings. Victims report intense anger at parents for not having protected them or rejecting the offender when the abuse was discovered (Stroud, 1999). Decisions surrounding whether to remove the offending sibling from the home have to be made. There are issues of shame and guilt on the part of the parental figures. The family system frequently exhibits formidable levels of denial and minimization in an unconscious effort to protect the family image. Offenders experience feelings of anger at the victim and rejection by the family. Managing retaliatory impulses by stepparents toward offenders can be volatile and laden with safety concerns. And, the victim may experience guilt for having the offender removed from the home and subtle family pressure to prematurely reconcile with the offender "for the good of the family." Families, however, who have a member sexually abused by a non-family member are in a position of concentrating a greater level of family energy and emotional support for the victim with fewer distractions surrounding loyalty. Feelings of anger and outrage can more singularly be focused on the perpetrator. Concerns surrounding safety considerations and treatment of the victim are clearer. The decision-making process surrounding the interpretation of the abuse and decisions about how to view the attacker are less diffused. And, the potential obstacles for reaching closure surrounding the past egregious event are different when the offender is not a family member.

Introduction to the Five-Step Family Therapy Protocol

The purpose of this chapter is to examine a five-step family therapy protocol that can be used to guide the clinician's work toward healthy reunification in families that have experienced sibling-on-sibling sexual abuse. The five-step family therapy protocol is designed to augment clinical training and experience. It is a dynamic process that is more than a mindless checklist. Family therapy sessions typically begin with nonvictim family members and may culminate in specialized sessions between the offending sibling and the victimized sibling(s) prior to treatment termination. Without clear guidelines and signposts to assess progress in the sessions, the well-meaning clinician can unwittingly do substantial harm by reinforcing distorted family thinking or emotionally retraumatizing the victim. Therefore, the five-step family therapy protocol was developed to promote family healing by encouraging victim recovery, enhancing offender treatment, and developing a new paradigm for future family interactions (Madanes, 1990).

The steps presented here have equal application in community and residential juvenile sexual offender treatment settings (Prendergast, 1991; Steen & Monnette, 1989). But, one must be aware of the differences each setting provides. The residential treatment setting provides built-in safety measures that have added victim protection, increased treatment intensity, behavioral controls, and emotional respite between family sessions that a community setting cannot as easily deliver. Designing safeguards and attentiveness to treatment details are increasingly critical when the sibling offender remains in the home or community with the sibling victim. In addition, the demand for careful monitoring of safety plans, parental supervision, family denial, treatment progress, pressure on victims, and warning signs are especially intense in a community treatment setting.

Considerations Before Using the Five-Step Family Therapy Protocol

Important Terms. The following terms are presented in this chapter to establish a baseline of general understanding among readers as they implement the prescribed steps in family therapy.

Sexual offending is a sexual act that is considered "deviant" if it meets either or both of the prongs of the following definition: "any sexual act that is performed without full informed consent of the other person; and/or any sexual act that is performed on a vulnerable person" (Wieckowski & Hodges, 2000, p. 16).

Family includes those who are tied together through their common biological, legal, cultural, and emotional history and their implied future together (McGoldrick, Gerson, & Shellenbergeret, 1999, p. 7). Family in our context could therefore include extended family members who are living in the home, non-family members who are regularly living in the home, as well as quasi-parental figures who have significant connections to the core family members.

Sibling extends beyond the traditional lines of blood relations or legal confines to include children who live in the same home setting and function as relatives for a significant amount of time with shared parental controls, family rules, and shared resources.

Parental figure is viewed as a biological parent, guardian, or adult who is responsible for the supervision, care, and well-being of siblings in a family unit.

Family reunification is seen as the clinical process of cautiously bringing parental figures, sibling offender, and sibling victim(s) together through the use of the five-step family therapy protocol described in this chapter.

Safety plan is a written plan developed collaboratively by sibling victim(s), parental figures, therapists, and supervising professionals which defines family member roles, boundaries, victim safety supports, detail rules of contact allowed between victim(s) and offender, and consequences if plan expectations are violated. The plan is reviewed with and given to the sibling victim(s) and offender. It is then strictly enforced.

Clinical Tasks. The clinician using the five-step family therapy protocol has a number of broad clinical tasks to manage at all times while working with the family that has experienced sibling-on-sibling sexual abuse. All the tasks emphasize the clinician's responsibility to protect the victim, strengthen the family system, and hold the offender accountable for the abusive actions.

- Ensure the physical and emotional safety of all family members during treatment and transitions to a less structured treatment environment by establishing a collaborative safety plan and enforcement protocol with offender, parental figures, victim, and community resources.

- Create a nonjudgmental atmosphere for the parental figures to assist them in understanding their family's individualized victim and offender dynamics and develop strengthened parental skills.

- Work with the victim's therapist to coordinate reunification sessions, support victim treatment, and establish postsession monitoring and follow-up.

- Educate the family about sexual offending dynamics in general and the offender's specific abuse dynamics.

- Restructure the family unit to strengthen boundaries, clarify roles, and improve communication and interaction patterns.

Family Therapy Treatment Differences. Working with families in this context is similar in some ways to working with other family therapy populations. The therapist will use family assessment tools, facilitate the development of family therapy goals, examine communication and interaction patterns, clarify and strengthen family member roles and boundaries, use therapy experiments, teach parenting skills, initiate termination and transitional steps, and so on. Many standard family therapy theoretical models that teach healthier coping skills, hold people accountable, clarify thinking, support family growth, and change unsafe behaviors will prove helpful in the hands of properly trained and supervised clinicians as they work with this family population (Czech, 1988; Madanes, Keim, & Smelser, 1995).

Some of the general differences to be considered in work with this specialized family treatment population lie in the *timing* of an intervention; managing the significant *risk of harm* to others; the *emphasis* of one intervention versus another; the *degree and pervasiveness* of the individual family member's unhealthy coping behaviors, thoughts, and feeling states; and a *shift in thinking* from a more traditional therapy approach to one of modified roles, techniques, and goals (Wieckowski & Hodges, 2000). Specifically, clinicians using the five-step family therapy protocol find there are limits of confidentiality of material examined in family session due to the need for treatment coordination among multiple treating professionals and mandatory reporting requirements. The family work must always consider at the forefront the level of risk posed by any member's actions to the initial victim and other vulnerable persons available to the offender. Unlike many families that seek out help to manage a family crisis, these families often find themselves as involuntary clients forced by legal and social pressures to enter treatment. The nature of the work itself involves uncomfortable and often embarrassing details surrounding sexual contact, parental responsibility, and family secrets. This work requires a higher level of supportive and constructive confrontation to modify each family member's distorted world view surrounding the abuse to ensure future safety, to accurately interpret the abuse itself, and as a means to encourage positive treatment outcomes. Inevitably, the family work often brings about the disclosures of other family members' abuse. And, there is increased legal liability and involvement in the rigors of an adversarial legal system as family members challenge decisions or try to quash unwanted information or actions generated by the collective treatment process.

The Five-Step Family Therapy Protocol

Each family is different in response to sibling-on-sibling sexual abuse and member composition. In all cases the sexual abuse must be reported and properly evaluated. At the point of entry into the sibling-on-sibling abuse, the family clinician evaluates what parts of the steps in the five-step family therapy protocol may have already taken place, builds on previous efforts, and moves forward in the family work. Parental figures, the sibling victim, and sibling perpetrator are typically the core participants initially involved in the family work. During the course of the work other participants may also include some combination of other sibling victims and nonvictims, the victim's therapist, healthy extended family members, the offender's therapist, and referral sources.

When using the five-step family therapy protocol, a number of possible significant family member dynamics are seen repeatedly across many families and can be found to reoccur during the course of treatment (Sexual Assault Center, 1996). It requires close treatment coordination and collective monitoring between the family therapist and other professionals treating family members to effectively assess, monitor, and confront these possible responses (Breer, 1996; Ryan & Lane, 1997). Some of the most significant dynamics include the following:

- Parental responses wherein parents may:
  — Deny or minimize the abuse details or its seriousness;
  — Blame the other parent for allowing the abuse to have taken place;
  — Express anger and a desire for retaliation against the offending sibling;
  — Abandon one of the siblings;
  — Practice poor boundaries;

— Send mixed messages concerning the significance of the abuse;

— Exhibit emotional ambivalence toward either of the siblings;

— Feel a sense of failure as a parental figure;

— Be reminded of personal abuse;

— Be too unhealthy to participate in family therapy; and

— Learn to protect and maintain a healthy balance in interactions with each sibling.

• Sibling victim's reactions in which the victim may:

— Feel responsible for the abuse experienced;

— Voice anger at parental figures for not providing protection from the abuse;

— Feel guilt for reporting the offending sibling;

— Fear retaliation by the offending sibling or family members;

— Imagine rejection by parental figures;

— Exhibit shame concerning the abuse;

— Express ambivalent feelings toward the abuser;

— Feel responsible for the family intrusion from outside professionals;

— Hold the offender responsible for the abuse;

— Experience jealously toward other siblings who have been able to work through their sibling-on-sibling abuse at a quicker pace;

— Be too unhealthy to participate in family therapy; and

— Reach healthy closure surrounding the abuse.

• Sibling offender's reactions in which the offender may:

— Deny or minimize the abuse itself;

— Continue the abuse or turn to a new victim;

— Try to speed through treatment;

— View self as different from other juvenile offenders;

— Express anger at the reporting sibling;

— Blame the victim for the abuse;

— Seek revenge against the victim;

— Fear rejection by parental figures and others;

— Voice jealousy over real or imagined attention the victim is receiving;

— Exhibit outrage at having to leave the home;

— Be too unhealthy to participate in family therapy; and

— Experience shame and remorse for the offending.

The Five-Step Family Reunification Process

Step One: Report the Abuse and Separate the Sibling Victim and Sibling Offender. When the abuse is discovered, it is desirable to immediately have the offender separated from the victim or removed from the home to a living situation in which there is no access to other potential victims and close supervision is possible. Report the abuse to appropriate authorities and access needed resources. It is important to have all contact between the sibling victim(s) and sibling offender suspended until the depth of the problem is known and safeguards are put in place by the family and professionals. It is prudent to consider all vulnerable family members as either victims or potential victims until a thorough sexual offender investigation has been completed. Typically it is a grave mistake to have the victim removed from the home. To remove the victim may send a signal of rejection to the abused sibling, empower the abusing sibling, and complicate future family therapy efforts.

Goal. Prevent further abuse and barriers to future treatment efforts. A positive sign for future family therapy outcomes during this initial step in treatment includes the reporting of the alleged abuse, the protection of family members, holding the offender accountable, taking the abuse seriously, developing and following initial safety plans, cooperation by family members with outside agencies, and the presence of properly trained professionals to manage the presented dynamics.

Participants. Participants should include healthy parental figures, sibling victim(s), sibling offender, other healthy family members who can provide support, legal representatives, and outside agencies.

Treatment Focus. The focus of treatment during this step is to provide support for all family members, assist the victim in feeling emotionally and physically safe and protected, secure needed medical attention, hold the offender accountable and encourage taking responsibility for his actions, monitor for suicidal or homicidal ideation among family members, support the parental figures in developing a framework to understand the abuse and offending, develop an initial safety plan and share with family members, and establish with the parental figures short-term goals, community resources, and empower them to begin to feel in charge of the crisis.

Warning Signs. Issues that could prevent movement to the next step or complicate future treatment efforts until resolved may include the following:

• Family member may be acting in such a way as to raise safety issues.

• The offender is taking actions that serve to cover up, minimize, or deny the abuse.

• There are indications of noncompliance with initially established safety plan.

• There is resistance to outside resources.

- Family members are not taking the abuse seriously.

- The victim is being blamed;

- The offender is not removed from the house;

- The victim is removed from the house;

- Other family secrets are being protected; and

- Professionals involved are not properly trained to understand and manage the dynamics presented in this type of family case.

Take measures to resolve the warning signs that raise safety concerns and confront presented denial and minimization of the abuse. Proceed to the next step when abuse, offender, and family system evaluations are begun.

Step Two: Complete Evaluations of Family Members. Once the sibling victim is safe and the sibling offender is being properly supervised, the evaluation process can begin (Perry & Orchard, 1992). Evaluations of the abuse and family during this step may include a police investigation, medical assessment and structured abuse interview of victim, sexual offender assessment, psychological tests, and a structured parental interview. It is important that family members be initially informed of the limits of confidentiality due to the need for coordination of treating services of all family members and legal reporting requirements that may have possible consequences. It is critical that the evaluations be conducted by trained professionals who understand sexual abuse and offending dynamics, the law, and family responses to sibling on sibling abuse.

Goal. Determine the appropriateness, treatment amenability, and capacity of each family member to engage in constructive individual and family therapy. Ideally all family members will be able to engage in constructive family therapy surrounding the abuse to some degree during the course of family reunification. In some cases the evaluation conclusions may indicate that a family member may not be ready or ever able to participate in the family therapy. The family member may be emotionally toxic, dangerous, not available, or unwilling to participate; may deny the abuse took place; may be too young; or may have other significant factors that prevent involvement in the family work. The collective evaluations should provide a family picture that outlines the depth of individual needs, barriers to treatment, level of motivation to change, and special needs of each family member to facilitate healing. Based on the conclusions of the evaluations and family member treatment readiness, an overall plan of treatment should be developed with family members and their treating professionals to meet the individual and collective family needs.

Participants. Participants should include healthy parental figures, sibling victim(s), sibling offender, evaluating/treating professionals, and outside agencies.

Treatment Focus. The focus of treatment during this step is to educate family members about the necessity of the evaluations and the benefits of treatment; support the family in not feeling this crisis is unique to them alone; validate family members' feelings; note how each family member is responding to and managing the abuse; consider family strengths and weaknesses, communication and interaction patterns, roles and boundaries, and capacity to respond to available supports; encourage honesty and a willingness to face the situation; establish oneself as a competent treating professional with the necessary experience and training to facilitate the family therapy; begin to develop a working relationship with the family members and other treating professionals; review evaluation results with parental figures and other treating professionals; make necessary referrals; and set initial family therapy appointment.

Warning Signs. Issues that could prevent movement to the next step or complicate future treatment efforts until resolved may include the following:

- There is a lack of cooperation in the evaluation process by family members.

- There are family secrets.

- The safety plan is not being followed.

- Denial and minimization of the abuse continues.

- The victim begins to show signs of isolation and depression.

- The parental figures spend their time fighting among themselves rather than focusing attention on the siblings' needs.

- A parental figure begins to express retaliatory intent toward the offender.

- Abuse details significantly change and conflict with previous information.

- The offending or victim sibling is ostracized from the family.

- The offender becomes physically and verbally assaultive.

- A family member is too unhealthy to participate in constructive treatment.

Take measures to resolve the warning signs that raise safety concerns, confront presented denial and minimization of the abuse, focus family attention on the benefits of treatment, and provide a road map of what to expect during the course of treatment. Proceed to the next step when the sibling offender has begun treatment, a referral has been made for the abused sibling to begin treatment, and the parental figures have committed to the first family therapy session.

Step Three: Begin Family Therapy. The focus of this family work step in the five-step family therapy protocol is to bring the family members together whenever possible as part of a healing process and to support the parallel treatment processes of individual family members outside the family therapy setting. It is not designed to exclusively meet all the complex needs of each individual member. The family therapy setting functions as a laboratory in which new skills learned in individual and family therapies are tested, understanding about abuse and offending information is acquired, family dynamics are restructured, old relationships are redefined, and new family directions are mapped. This is accomplished through the coordination of the family reunification process and close coordination of services with other treatment providers. The family therapy sessions usually take place every two weeks until the sibling offender has completed treatment. This allows the family members time between sessions to work in their own individual therapy on intensely charge material generated in the family session prior to returning to the next family session. When both siblings remain in the home, it will be necessary to have the offender sibling removed if this third step in the protocol is not satisfactorily completed, the safety plan is not followed, the sibling victim is adversely affected, or the offender's treatment is not going well.

Goal. Bring parental figures and offending sibling together in family therapy. A positive outcome would mean that the parental figures begin to feel acceptance and support, understand the offender's offending dynamics and the extent of the sibling abuse, support the offender in treatment, and hold him accountable.

Participants. Participants should include parental figures and the sibling offender. There is no sibling victim(s) involvement at this time. The initial work is with the parental figures and the offending sibling. Other older healthy family members may be brought into the session to support the process after the parental figures have completed the foundational work with the sibling offender.

Treatment Focus. This step typically spans over many sessions. The essential foundational work of this step has to do with the ongoing use of a safety plan; the ability of the parental figures to develop an understanding of the presented sexual abuse and offending dynamics and to clearly hold the offender responsible and exhibit healthy boundaries and role definitions with the siblings; the engagement of the offender in productive treatment; and the forward movement of the abused sibling in individual treatment. During this step the offender will disclose his detailed offending actions, thoughts, and feelings. He will map out his cycle of offending by discussing with his parental figures his means of planning the abuse, maintaining compliance, and covering it up. The parental figures have to be emotionally prepared for the chilling details of the abuse event(s). The clinician must be prepared to work with the intense family member emotions that are sure to come. Ensuring the physical safety of all in attendance is essential. It is critical that the offending sibling be able to progress in treatment to where he is able to understand the depth of the destructive nature of the abuse on the abused sibling and the rest of the family. Maintain close contact with the abused sibling's therapist during this time to exchange disclosed details surrounding the abuse, adequacy and compliance with the safety plan, and the timing of moving to the next step in the family work. Begin to prepare for the next step of sibling contact by educating the parental figures on what to expect. Additional older family members may be brought into the process near the end of this step to show support for the family members and encourage the sibling offender in his treatment.

Warning Signs. Issues that could prevent movement to the next step or complicate future treatment efforts until resolved may include the following:

- Family members want to "speed-up the treatment process."

- Appointments are missed.

- Safety plan is not being followed.

- Offender is threatening the victim or having unsupervised contact.

- Offender is not engaging in productive treatment.

- Offender is complaining about the treatment.

- Offender is trying to make deals to avoid further treatment.

- Victim is having difficulties in individual treatment.

- Victim is having nightmares or demonstrating regressive behaviors.

- Parental figures minimize the abuse.

- Parental figures have poor boundaries and role definition with the siblings.

- Parental figures do not understand the important abuse and offender dynamics present in their family crisis.

Take measures to resolve the warning signs that raise safety concerns and confront presented denial and minimization of the abuse. Proceed to the next step only when the sibling victim and offender have made sufficient progress to be able to tolerate the contact in the family sessions and the parental figures are able to provide the needed support and supervision to each. Closely coordinate the move with other treating professionals.

Step Four: Bring Sibling Victim(s) and Sibling Offender Together in Family Work. This step should not be attempted if step three has not been successfully completed. This is the most critical part of the family reunification work and has the highest level of risk of revictimizing the victim if not managed properly. In some cases the offender may be able to be reintegrated back into the home with the victim when family members have had positive treatment outcomes, parental figures are able to maintain proper levels of support and protection for all members, the offender demonstrates genuine remorse, and the victim acknowledges it was not his or her fault. Reunification in this step may not be possible or desirable if parental figures are in denial about the abuse or prove toxic to the well-being of the victim or offender, treatment steps are skipped or rushed for the sake of "going through the motions," or either the victim or offender demonstrates a poor response to his or her treatment (Counseling & Consultation Services, 1999).

Goal. Safely bring the sibling victim into the family reunification process. Look for the parental figures to develop and practice the skill of protecting the victim while supporting each sibling in treatment and taking charge of managing family interactions; the family reunification supports the treatment of both siblings and the family members develop healthier interaction patterns.

Participants. Participants should include parental figures, sibling victim(s), sibling offender, older supporting family members, and individuals' therapists

Treatment Focus. The function of this step is to begin to bring the victim and offender siblings together in a safe manner that allows for each to practice what they have been learning in their own individual treatment and to develop over time a new paradigm of how the family members will interact in the future. Consult with each sibling's therapist and the parental figures prior to and following each contact to establish session goals and evaluate progress. Empower the sibling victim by talking about the process of the contact prior to and following each session. Develop presession signals for the sibling victim to give if he or she is feeling uncomfortable and wants the sibling offender removed from the session. The work is designed to increase the role of the parental figures in the sessions. The therapist encourages and supports the parental figures in developing increased confidence in their ability to protect the siblings, establish guidelines, enforce rules, and anticipate dynamics that may be presented by each sibling. The sibling victim uses the session to express feelings and thoughts about the offender and the abuse, clearly stating that future abuse will not be allowed to happen again, it was not the sibling victim's fault, and there is a safety plan that will be followed. The sibling offender is given the opportunity to take full responsibility for the abuse, acknowledge the sibling victim's feelings, explain what he has learned in treatment, voice the changes that can be expected in the future, support the safety plan, and encourage reporting if the safety plan details are not followed. The parental figures clearly state support for both siblings; outline knowledge of the sibling offender's cycle, warning signs, high-risk situations, and expectations surrounding future sibling contacts; and voice full support for future consequences if the safety plan is violated.

Warning Signs. Issues that could prevent movement to the next step or complicate future treatment efforts until resolved may include the following:

- Safety plan details are not being enforced.
- Family members may intellectualize the abuse and avoid feelings.
- Offender may try to take control of the sessions.
- Offender attempts to blame the victim.
- Offender becomes sexually aroused.
- Offender distorts the sessions or minimizes the abuse impact.
- Victim could avoid confronting the offender with his or her true feelings.
- Victim has nightmares
- Victim exhibits regressive behaviors
- Victim becomes hostile and threatening.
- Parental figures send mixed signals surrounding their feelings and future expectations.

Take measures to resolve the warning signs that raise safety concerns and look for parental figures' ability and willingness to safely supervise sibling contact, siblings' treating therapists to determine whether they have each proceeded far enough in their individual work to discontinue family sessions. Sibling victim at this point feels safe with parental figures and knows the safety plan details. The abusing sibling knows his cycle, can interrupt his cycle, can identify high-risk situations and avoid them, knows and demonstrates a willingness to use relapse prevention skills, and follows the safety plan.

Step Five: Family Therapy Termination. Lay the early groundwork for this step at the very beginning of the five-step family therapy protocol process. Make referrals as necessary for follow-up services to take over after the completion of the family work. This step in the protocol is the final part of the family reunification effort to promote family healing of sibling-on-sibling sexual abuse by encouraging victim recovery, enhancing offender treatment, and developing a new paradigm for future family interactions. Whenever possible, have the transitional team members who will follow the family participate in a family session to allow each family member to present the work he or she has accomplished, high-risk situations, their interpretation of the abuse, and the details of the safety plan. Work with the family and the transitional professionals in developing future working goals and expectations.

Goal. Review treatment successes, evaluate depth of treatment integration among members, and prepare the family members for family therapy transitioning and termination. A positive outcome in this step would be for the family to follow the safety plan, for the victim to feel safe and empowered to protect him- or herself, for the offender to be able to avoid high-risk situations and prevent relapse, and for parental figures to take the lead in managing their family safely during the termination and transitioning phase of family treatment (National Adolescent Perpetrator Network, 1993).

Participants. Participants should include parental figures, sibling victim(s), sibling offender, older supportive family members, individuals' therapists, and aftercare professionals.

Treatment Focus. The focus of treatment during this step is to review treatment successes and transitional issues; explore the termination fears of each family member; be aware of and gently confront regressive thinking, feelings, or behaviors; explore family therapy termination readiness with each family member; review progress made on initial family treatment goals; establish new transitional goals; discuss offender relapse prevention follow-up services; coordinate the final session with other treating professionals supporting the family; and gain commitment to a three-month follow-up family session.

Warning Signs. Issues that could compromise transition efforts include the following:

- Complaining about transitional expectations;
- Family members lack awareness of regressive behaviors, thinking, or feelings;

- Feeling treatment is over and everything is back to normal;

- Not following the safety plan;

- Not showing up for final family therapy appointments;

- Family members are unable to note high-risk situations to avoid; and

- Family members did not successfully complete their individual therapy.

Take measures to resolve the warning signs that raise safety concerns, to confront treatment regression, to ensure that the family has a realistic plan to meet anticipated concerns surrounding the termination, and to ensure that the follow-up professionals understand the case and have services in place.

Special Areas of Concern

In the course of using the five-step family therapy protocol, there are an unpredictable number of special situations that might arise. Approaches taken to manage these special challenges should always consider victim safety, parental ability to understand how and be willing to protect family members, and holding the offender responsible. A few of the more unsettling commonly seen special challenges are the following:

- *What if there is more than one sibling victim?* This is too often the case. Several guiding principles when working with this family presentation include the following:

  — Treat each sibling victim as an individual who has a common offender and allow all sibling victims to work at their own pace in individual and family work.

  — Consider the different treatment needs based on age, development, gender differences, and abuse characteristics.

  — Never compromise the safety of any sibling victim.

  — Be aware of differing parental responses toward each sibling victim.

  — Support the parental figures in understanding and appreciating the different emerging responses to the abuse by each sibling.

  — Help parental figures and the sibling victims to avoid making destructive comparisons or value judgments concerning each of the victim sibling's responses to the abuse and treatment.

  — Support the family in understanding that inconsistencies in abuse stories may be a function of actual fact, perception of events, or developmental levels.

  — Include each sibling victim in the family therapy process and contact with the offender at his or her own individual pace and when cleared by his or her individual therapist.

- *What if one of the parental figures has also suffered physical or sexual abuse by the offender?* In these cases it is important for the parental figure to also be labeled a victim and be in victim treatment. The parental figure may be able to participate in the family therapy from the beginning if he or she feels safe, is willing to talk about his or her feelings with the offender, can protect him- or herself, has a safety plan in place, and is not being adversely affected by the family work. In such cases the offender may need to be out of the house.

- *What if one of the parental figures is also abusive physically or sexually toward siblings?* Unfortunately this type of family work too often uncovers the reality that one of the parental figures might also be a physical or sexual offender against a family member in the immediate family. When this is discovered it is to be reported, investigated, and steps taken to ensure the safety of all family members. Parental offenders are not to participate in the family therapy process until they have progressed far enough in their own treatment that they are safe and not toxic to the family reunification process. Final clearance to enter sessions is up to the victims' and the offender's therapists.

Conclusion

The five-step family therapy protocol presented provides a guide for clinicians to constructively manage the destructive nature of sibling-on-sibling sexual abuse in the context of family therapy. The framework can be used to augment individual clinical training and experience as decisions have to be made about how to best proceed, family member dynamics to consider, clinical tasks, and cues as to when to discontinue the reunification process or move closer to successful termination. There should always be an emphasis placed on the emotional and physical safety of all family members, especially victims or those who are vulnerable. Family reunification and healing are not always possible in cases of sibling-on-sibling sexual abuse, but following the five-step family therapy protocol presented increases the likelihood of positive family reunification outcomes.

Acknowledgments

It is with great appreciation I acknowledge Adam Young, MSW intern, who participated in the development of the initial work from which this chapter grew and give thanks to the clinical teams at Hanover Juvenile Correctional Center Behavioral Services Unit and The Daybreak Sexual Offender Prevention Program at Poplar Springs Hospital for their support, suggestions, and encouragement as we look together for effective techniques to work with families who are the victims of sexual abuse.

References

Breer, W. (1996). *The adolescent molester.* Springfield, IL: Charles C. Thomas.

Counseling & Consulation Services. (1999). *Protocol for therapeutically tolerated visitation with sex offenders and children.* Johnson City, TN: Author.

Czech, N. (1988). Family therapy with adolescent sex offenders. In J. K. Zeig & S. R. Lankton (Eds.), *Developing Ericksonian therapy: State of the art* (pp. 452–461). New York: Brunner/Mazel.

Harris, B., & Campbell, J. (1998, November 11). *Face to face: A model for therapists to assess readi-*

ness for and provide reunification treatment to juvenile sex offenders and their victims. Paper presented at the conference for the Association for the Treatment for Sexual Abusers, Toronto.

Hodges, C., & Young, A. (1999, September 24). *Healing the juvenile sex offender's family through family reunification.* Paper presented at the conference for the Association for the Treatment for Sexual Abusers, Lake Buena Vista, FL.

Madanes, C. (1990). *Sex, love, and violence: Strategies for transformation.* New York: Norton.

Madanes, C., Keim, J., & Smelser, D. (1995). *The violence of men: New techniques for working with abusive families: A therapy of social action.* San Francisco: Jossey-Bass.

McGoldrick, M., Gerson, R. & Shellenbergeret, S. (1999). *Genograms: Assessment and intervention.* New York: Norton.

Meinig, M. (1996, November 14). *Family therapy protocol.* Paper presented at the conference for the Association for the Treatment for Sexual Abusers, Chicago.

National Adolescent Perpetrator Network. (1993). The revised report from the national task force on juvenile sexual offending. *Juvenile and Family Court Journal, 44,* 4.

Perry, G., & Orchard, J. (1992). *Assessment and treatment of adolescent sex offenders.* Sarasota, FL: Professional Resources Press.

Prendergast, W. E. (1991). *Treating sex offenders in correctional institutions and outpatient clinics: A guide to clinical practice.* New York: Haworth Press.

Ryan, G., Lane, S., & Rinzler, A. (Eds.). (1997). *Juvenile sexual offending: Causes, consequences, and correction.* San Francisco: Jossey-Bass.

Sexual Assault Center of Knoxville, Tennessee. (1999). *Child sexual abuse* [On-line]. Available: http://www.cs.utk.edu/~bartley/sacc/theCenter.html.

Steen, C., & Monnette, B. (1989). *Treating adolescent sexual offenders in the community.* Springfield, IL: Charles C. Thomas.

Stroud, D. (1999). Familial support as perceived by adult victims of childhood sexual abuse. *Sexual Abuse: A Journal of Research and Treatment, 11*(2), 159–175.

Werrbach, G. (1993, November–December). The family reunification role-play. *Child Welfare, 22*(6), 555–567.

Wieckowski, E., & Hodges, C. (2000). *Juvenile sexual offender treatment in community and residential settings: A practical guide for clinicians, administrators, court personnel and direct care staff.* Unpublished manuscript.

Wiehe, V. (1997). *Sibling abuse: Hidden physical, emotional, and sexual trauma.* London, UK: Sage.

Chapter 18

Sexually Abusive Children—Etiological and Treatment Considerations

by Alexis O. Miranda, Ph.D. and Kathleen Davis, M.Ed.

Overview

Not all perpetrators of sexual abuse are adults. Frequently, mental health professionals provide evaluation and clinical services to children who sexually abuse others. Alhough there is clinical and empirical data about sexually aggressive children, few have suggested possible clinical treatment components and their rationale for them. This chapter reviews the plausible etiologies and the correlates of sexual aggression by children to delineate the necessary treatment elements for them.

Introduction

Ample evidence confirms that children are the victims of sexual abuse and that some, in turn, are the perpetrators of it. Some of this evidence has provided information about the dynamics of children's normative and deviant sexual behaviors. Notable in the child sexual victimization literature, for example, are reports such as that of the Task Force on Juvenile Sexual Offenders and Their Victims (1996). This report indicates that children who are younger than age 11 comprise 29% of all forcible rape victims. Other reports echo similar results.

Finkelhor, Hotaling, Lewis, and Smith (1990) in a national survey of 1,200 adults found that 27% of the women and 16% of the men sampled reported sexual abuse victimization in childhood. Surprisingly, the majority of the perpetrators of sexual abuse in the Finkelhor et al. (1990) study are young adolescents or children. Kikuchi's (1995) findings concurred that 20% of all rapes and 30% to 50% of child sexual assaults are committed by young adolescents and children. More recent data (Carter & Van Dalen, 1998) reveals that sibling incest is the most common type of child sexual aggression. Again, the majority of the perpetrators are children.

The pervasiveness of child abuse and the severe and lasting effects for its victims have motivated the consideration of psychological treatment as a viable option for its victims and perpetrators. Many mental health professionals have designed treatment programs for children who display sexually aggressive behaviors (see Araji, 1997). The treatment of children inspires hope within clinical circles because the interventions are implemented at an early stage of development, when rapid and lasting change is achievable. Also, the family, a critical influence in childhood, can be a significant contributor toward the establishment and maintenance of normal sexual functioning in sexually aggressive children (SAC; Corcoran, Miranda, Tenukas-Steblea, & Taylor, 1999).

In this chapter we delineate the characteristics of SAC and the potential etiologies and correlates of the sexually aggressive behaviors that they display. With such background, we describe the factors that may be included by mental health professionals in the treatment of SAC. We lend considerable attention to the sexual reactivity of children whose history includes sexual abuse victimization because we found that it is a common assumption among clinicians that those who are sexually victimized react with sexual aggression toward others.

We adopted the definition of sexually aggressive children offered by Gray and Pithers (1993); that is, SAC are males and females who perpetrate sexual abuse at the age of 12 or before. Also, we adopted the definition of sexual abuse that characterizes it as forced, tricked, or coerced sexual behavior which may include nudity, disrobing, genital exposure, voyeurism, kissing, fondling, masturbation, oral-genital contact, use of pornography, digital penetration, and vaginal or anal intercourse (Friedrich, 1991).

Plausible Etiological Explanations and the Correlates of Sexually Aggressive Behaviors in Children. Like most sexual dynamics, sexual aggression by children is a complex phenomenon. Many theories have partially explained its plausible etiologies and correlates. However, no single theory can be fully credited with the power or comprehensiveness to explain aggressive sexual behaviors displayed by children.

Psychodynamic Theories. Proponents of psychodynamic theory explained that sexual aggression by children follows a distinct pattern. According to Cashwell, Bloss, and McFarland (1995), first, as a victim the child identifies with the aggressor to reduce anxiety. Second, compulsively, the child reexperiences a sexually abusive event in the role of the aggressor in an attempt to gain mastery and power and to counteract the victimization experience. Third, the child reshapes the experience of victimization by perpetrating a sexually aggressive act during a psychological dissociation from the event.

Rasmussen, Burton, and Christopherson (1992), used psychodynamic theory to explain the frequency in which sexual abuse victims abuse others. According to Rasmussen et al. (1992), the transformation from victim to perpetrator of sexual abuse reflects the permeability of the ego boundaries of the SAC and the ease in which these children confuse their personal boundaries with that of others.

Object Relations and Attachment Theories. Object relations theory (Guntrip, 1967) and attachment theory (Bowlby, 1969) propose that children internalize emotion-laden experiences and act in accordance to functional maps derived from interpersonal relationships. Both theories conceptualize the abusive acts of SAC as originating from internalized models of behaviors. Closely approximating the object relations and attachment conceptualizations of sexually aggressive behavior displayed by children, Friedrich (1990) cited Bandura's (1977) ideas to suggest that many SAC act aggressively following exposure to violent sexual behaviors in poorly socialized, punitive homes. Furthermore, Bandura (1977) suggested that continuous reciprocal interactions between behaviors and controlling conditions give rise to opportunities for direct and vicarious learning. In this context, the sexually aggressive acts of children arise from learned or experienced events (Sermabeikian & Martinez, 1994).

Victim-to-Perpetrator Hypothesis

Gil and Johnson (1993) proposed that repetition compulsion explained the commission of sexually aggressive behaviors by children. Similarly, in what may be deemed as the victim-to-perpetrator hypothesis, Knopp (1995), Cantwell (1995), Haugaard and Tilly (1988), Johnson (1988), Briere (1989) and Ryan (1987) asserted that children's sexual aggressive behaviors represent a response to or a reenactment of sexual abuse victimization. There is considerable support for the victim-to-perpetrator hypothesis. For example, Friedrich (1991), and Gray, Busconi, Houchens, and Pithers (1997), found that the younger a child is at the onset of sexually aggressive behavior the more likely that his or her sexual victimization occurred. More important, Friedrich (1991) suggested that sexualized aggressive behaviors exhibited by children frequently constitute a reliable marker for sexual abuse victimization if the sexual behaviors are developmentally inappropriate, frequent, chronic, and persistent.

In the context of developmental inappropriateness, frequency, chronicity, and hardiness of the sexually aggressive behaviors exhibited by SAC, Gray et al. (1997) proposed five criteria for the identification of sexual reactivity: (1) the repetitiveness of the sexually aggressive acts, (2) the unresponsiveness to adult intervention, (3) the criminal nature of the behavior if it were committed by an adult, (4) the occurrence of the behavior across time and situation, and (5) the variety and sophistication of the sexual acts exhibited.

Cunningham and MacFarlane (1996) adapted Finkelhor's (1986) four preconditions to abuse to explain the victim-to-perpetrator hypothesis. Specifically, Cunnigham and MacFarlane (1996) proposed that children's sexualized aggressive behaviors are reactions to the victimization that occurs at a critical period for the development of age-appropriate sexuality. Furthermore, borrowing from psychodynamic theory, Cunnigham and MacFarlane (1996) proposed that the child perpetrator feels mastery and power, over previously felt helplessness and powerlessness experienced as a victim, when able to exert control over the victim.

The traumagenic model explains the victim-to-perpetrator phenomenon. Finkelhor and Browne's (1986) traumagenic dynamics model identified four components of child sexual abuse victimization: (1) traumatic sexualization, (2) betrayal, (3) powerlessness, and (4) stigmatization. The unique characteristics of each abuse incident determines the relative influence of the four aforementioned factors. However, for children a frequent residual effect of sexual abuse victimization is a distortion in the meaning and function of sexual activity (Araji, 1997). Araji (1997) described an adaptation model to sexual abuse victimization that relied on tenets of stress-coping theory (Folkman & Lazarus, 1980). According to Araji, the variability in sexual abuse victimization outcome, including the transformation from victim to perpetrator, is influenced by the victimized child's resilience. Intelligence and overall cognitive abilities, communication skills, peer relationships, academic skills, absence of psychopathology, and familial factors, such as support and the quality of parent-child relationships, are believed to buffer victimized children from the effects of sexual abuse victimization, including sexual abuse reactivity. Furthermore, Araji (1997) suggested that the child's global functioning prior to the abuse; the nature, source, and quality of sexually abusive events; the initial response of the caregivers and other authority figures; and the opportunities and accessibility to treatment all influence the outcome of sexual abuse victimization. Araji's reliance on previctimization stress-coping resources to explain the variability of sexual abuse outcome is congruent with ample empirical evidence that supports the positive effects of children's stress-coping resources to buffer against psychologically taxing events (see Matheny, Aycock, & McCarthy, 1993). Thus, it appears judicious for mental health professionals to consider that resilience may play a critical role in further refining the victim-to-perpetrator framework for children's sexual abuse reactivity.

Empirical Studies of Victim-to-Perpetrator Hypothesis. There are few empirical studies that question the validity of the seemingly inevitable transformation from a victim of sexual abuse to a perpetrator of it. For example, Fedoroff and Pincus (1996) tested three versions of the abuse-to-abuser hypothesis using semistructured interview data from 100 men accused of sexually abusing children. The data revealed partial support for the abuse-to-abuser hypothesis. Specifically, the victim's gender did not correspond to the offender's sexual orientation in nearly 40% of the sample. In addition, there was no association between the offender's abuse age and the age of the victim when the abuse occurred. The frail support for the abuse-to-abuser hypothesis came from the repetition of genital assault perpetrated by the men who were genitally assaulted. That is, men who are genitally assaulted are more likely to genitally assault their victims than men who manually assault.

Pallone and Hennessy (1996) reviewed the studies conducted by Widom and colleagues (Widom, 1989, 1995; Widom & Ames, 1994) about what Widom (1989) terms "the cycle of abuse" (p. 140). Although clear patterns of violence emerge from the data examined by Widom and colleagues, Pallone and Hennessy (1996) suggest that "less than a majority of victims of either abuse or neglect offend criminally, whether as juveniles or as adults" (p. 140). More important, for those children who are neglected or sexually abused, the effects of victimization accelerate offending in their younger years. Moreover, the effect of childhood sexual abuse victimization is negligible in adulthood, which leads Pallone and Hennesy (1996) to assert about Widom's work that "the rate of adult offending among victims of such abuse is slightly lower than the comparable rate among control subjects with no history of abuse or neglect" (p. 151).

A Typology of Sexually Abusive Children. Pithers, Gray, Busconi, and Houchens (1998) suggested that an objectively derived and clinically relevant taxonomy for children with sexual behavioral problems may be the basis for effective treatment interventions to arrest aggressive sexual behaviors. To test the hypothesis that children who exhibit sexually aggressive behaviors do not constitute a homogeneous group, Pithers et al. (1998) used a five-factor cluster analysis that resulted in the differentiation of 127 6- to 12-year-old children into five groups. Interestingly, children's sexual behavior alone was not a significant factor to differentiate among the sexually aggressive, nonsymptomatic, highly traumatized, rule-breaker, and abuse-reactive children. The differences originated from maltreatment histories; objective scores on parent, teacher, and self-report measurements; psychiatric diagnoses; and numerous indices of aggression. The findings suggest that the sexual behaviors of children who sexually aggress are minimally relevant in what differentiates among them. Rather, most of the relevant and statistically significant factors are extrasexual.

Another notable contribution of Pithers et al. (1998) study is the evidence for the efficacy of treatment protocols for the five mutually exclusive groups of children. They concluded that "At least for the highly traumatized children, modified relapse prevention resulted in significantly greater reduction in sexual behaviors relative to the expressive therapy after 16 weeks of a 32-week treatment regimen" (p. 399). Undoubtedly, this study has made a significant contribution to the classification of children who sexually aggress and the design of empirically tested treatment strategies for them. We find that the characteristics of sexually aggressive children, when considered within the context of family functioning, may offer weightier relevance for clinicians to design cogent and effective treatment strategies for these children.

Treatment Implications

Gender. Summit (1988), Porter (1996), and MacFarlane, Cockriel, and Dugan, (1990) noted that male children displayed more sexually aggressive behaviors than did females. Their rationale noted that boys are socialized to externalize behavior; contrarily, girls are taught to internalize them. According to Finkelhor and Russell (1984) and Johnson and Berry (1989), when female children sexually aggress they do so with less violence and coercion than do males. Regardless of gender, however, the sexual behaviors of SAC are in marked contrast to those of children who are not sexually aggressive.

Sexual Behavior. Children engage in a vast array of sexual behaviors as part of typical sexual development (Okami, 1992; Friedrich et al., 1992; Martinson, 1991). The developmental perspective, inclusive of the developmental psychopathology orientation, has been used to differentiate between children's appropriate and inappropriate sexual behaviors. Frequently, the distinction requires the consideration of physical and psychosocial developmental parameters and social standards. At one extreme of the appropriate to inappropriate continuum of sexual behaviors are those behaviors deemed normal, normative, and age-appropriate; at the other extreme are the sexual behaviors of SAC (Araji, 1997; Beitchman, Zucker, Hood, DaCosta, & Akma, 1991; Friedrich, Grambsch, Broughton, Kuiper, & Bielke, 1991; Gil & Johnson, 1993; Miau, 1986).

Friedrich (1988, 1991) suggested that the sexual behaviors of SAC are anomalous based on their deviance from expected psychosexual development stage parameters, are compulsive and resistant to change, and lack the inhibition normally associated with latency. Cunnigham and MacFarlane (1996) deemed the sexual behavior of children normative when they match the behaviors of their cohorts. In addition to the comparison between a child's behavior and that of peers, Cunnigham and MacFarlane urged the examination of the use of coercion, threats, aggression, secrecy, and intent when children display sexual behaviors. It is likely that from their perspective, therefore, the normative sexual play of a child becomes deviant when such behavior involves coercion, verbal or physical aggression, secrecy, and the desire to engage in the sexual activity becomes an obsessive preoccupation. Additionally, the conceptualization of children's deviant sexual behaviors must be sensitive to the concept of compliance and cooperation as part of the broader issue of informed consent.

The Task Force on Juvenile Sexual Offenders and Their Victims (1996) developed criteria to distinguish normative from deviant sexual behavior by addressing the issue of informed consent. Specifically, the criteria included "(1) an understanding of what is proposed based on age, maturity, developmental level, functioning and experience; (2) knowledge of social standards for what is being proposed; (3) awareness of potential consequences and alternatives; (4) assumption that agreements or disagreements will be respected equally; (5) voluntary decisions; and (6) mental competence" (p. 38).

Also, Johnson (1988) showed sensitivity to development in his evaluation of normative versus deviant sexual behavior. Specifically, he included the quality of motivational factors, abuser-to-victim relationship, quality of sexual and nonsexual behaviors displayed, and affect expressed. Furthermore, Johnson (1989) believed that a child's sexual behavior is normal when the motivation for the behavior is curiosity, consent, and mutual interest form the basis of the participants' relationship, the affect is joy, and the behavior is limited to looking and touching. In contrast, deviant sexual behaviors are motivated by bullying, coercion, and the reenactment of past sexual trauma; the relationship between abuser and victim is based on a power differential; the affects from the victim are fear, disgust, shame, and apprehension; and the abuser's motivation is to engage in specific sexual activities with the victim, not sexual exploration.

Johnson (1989) suggested that sexually deviant children could be classified into those who demonstrate sexually reactive behavior, those who engage in extensive mutual sexual behaviors, and those who display sexually aggressive or molesting behaviors. The abnormal sexual behaviors of children are distinguished from the normal ones if they cease at will. Children who display sexually reactive behaviors could not stop at will given that their focus on sexuality was accentuated. Children who engage in extensive mutual sexual behaviors garner a sense of reassurance because of the sexual contact with others. Last, sexually aggressive or molesting children sexualize most contact with others and their sexual behaviors have aggressive, obsessive, and compulsive qualities (Johnson, 1989).

Mental health professionals have been instrumental in the development of criteria to be used in legal proceedings that involve criminal acts committed by juveniles and children. Malamuth (1995) suggested that inappropriate sexual behaviors consist of "sexual offenses that included a power differential between perpetrator and victim (perpetrator has greater age, size, or mental capacity); role differential (perpetrator assumes authority over the child); predatory patterns (perpetrator sets up victim); and elements of coercion (perpetrator uses games, tricks, bribes, threats and/or force)" (p. 2)

Sexually aggressive children perform a wide range of sexual behaviors such as fondling; obsessive masturbation; oral sex; vaginal and anal penetration with fingers, objects, or penis; voyeurism; exhibitionism; and use of pornography. It is usual for SAC to threaten, bribe, or use guilt to prevent disclosure of the abuse by the victims. Many of the behaviors exhibited by SAC have been attributed to manifestations of cognitive and affective dysregulation that may relate to the frequency in which these children receive psychiatric diagnoses that represent behavioral and conduct problems.

Treatment Approaches for Sexually Inappropriate Behaviors

Early in any and all treatment strategies for SAC, attention must be given to the impediments to further sexual aggression. Smets and Cebula (1987) suggest that an indispensable ingredient of SAC treatment is to aim for their appreciation of interpersonal boundaries; to do this it is necessary for SAC to learn the distinction between appropriate and inappropriate sexuality and sexual expressions. It has been our experience that the family is a fundamental influence as children learn about the distinctions between appropriate or inappropriate sexual behaviors.

Pithers, Gray, Cunnigham, and Lane (1993) suggested that SAC treatment must address the separation of sexual arousal from negative situations and affects. Contrarily, Bradford, Motayne, Gretzer, and Pawlak (1995) suggested that to impede escalation of sexually aggressive behavior, treatment needs to focus on the management of anger. Ballester and Pierre (1995) and Sermabeikian and Martinez (1994), suggested that increased control over impulsive behaviors, especially those that are sexualized, is needed to decrease or impede manifestations of abusive sexual behavior by children. Despite the disagreements among the aforementioned authors, the management of sexual aggressive behaviors may be necessary as a precursor to other foci of treatment.

Treatment Approaches for Sexual Abuse Victimization

If a child has been the victim of sexual abuse and has sexually aggressed others, treatment must balance the two concerns (Cashwell et al., 1995). Finkelhor and Browne (1985) suggested that the outcome of sexual victimization is dependent on many pre- and postabuse dynamics. However, in their opinion, the abused child had three options: (1) recovery, (2) self-victimization, or (3) assault. Recovery from the experience of sexual abuse victimization involves working through feelings associated with the trauma and, eventually, resolving and accepting the experience. To do this, attitudinal and cognitive processes related to the abuse must be addressed in treatment.

The role of attitude and cognition in the perpetration of sexual abuse has been extensively documented (Bradford et al., 1995). In treatment, the SAC may be encouraged to identify thoughts that occur before, during, and after a sexual abuse event. The aim is for the SAC to identify triggers, thoughts maintained during an abusive event, and those that follow it. Ultimately, SAC may learn how to identify and circumvent precipitating cognitive cues and environmental stressors that affect their attitude towards potential victims (Ballester & Pierre, 1995; DiGiorgio-Miller, 1994; Pithers et al., 1993; Sermabeikian & Martinez, 1994).

Cognitive distortions such as minimization, justification, or rationalization of sexually abusive behaviors must be confronted in hopes that the child will develop self-regulatory and self-monitoring skills (Bradford et al., 1995). Another focus is for the child to accept responsibility for abusive behavior and to develop empathy for the victim. Pithers et al. (1993) believe that when empathy develops the likelihood of the commission of another sexual offense is lessened.

Psychological and Psychiatric Characteristics

Estimates vary about the number of SAC who may be diagnosed with psychiatric disorders. Goocher (1994) stated that juvenile sexual abuse perpetrators "are now being recognized as a mix of delinquents, conduct-disordered and antisocial personality youth, and youth who are more accurately described as psychiatrically impaired" (p. 247). Gray et al. (1997) found that SAC commonly are diagnosed with conduct disorders (CD), attention deficit/hyperactivity disorder (ADHD), oppositional and defiant disorder (ODD), and adjustment disorder with mixed disturbance of emotions and conduct (AD). Also, Goocher's findings showed that concurrent diagnoses of CD with either ADHD or ODD features are common among SAC. Moreover, when rated by parents and teachers, SAC are characterized by externalizing behaviors (e.g., aggression and disruptiveness), internalizing behaviors (e.g., anxiety, depression, and withdrawal), and sexual problems.

Cunningham and MacFarlane (1996) suggested that SAC suffer from low self-esteem, feelings of inadequacy, vulnerability, and sexual abuse victimization. Furthermore, because of their noncompliance and aggression, SAC are at high risk for peer rejection and academic failure. Sexually aggressive children have been found to lack empathy, reciprocity, and cooperation, all of which are attributed to learned behaviors modeled by family members and peers (Cunningham & MacFarlane, 1996; Friedrich, 1990).

Treatment Approaches for Comorbid Conditions

The co-occurrence of psychiatric and psychological disorders with child sexual aggression led Johnson and Berry (1989) to assert that initial contact with SAC must focus on the comprehensive assessment of all aspects of the children's life. ODD, ADHD, CD, and other disorders warrant careful assessment and the inclusion of medical and psychology personnel in the early stages of the assessment process. Furthermore, if learning disabilities, or other conditions that impede learning, burden the child's successful academic development, school personnel may be encouraged to make accommodations for the child. Also, when appropriate, school personnel must participate to monitor SAC's interactions with other children at school.

It is common for SAC to show aggression and anxiety in a variety of social situations (Bradford et al., 1995). Social, communication, and interpersonal problem-solving skill development may be necessary to counteract social isolation and peer marginalization (DiGiorgio-Miller, 1994; Goocher, 1994). In addition, emphasis on appropriate social interactions must include attention to developmentally appropriate sexual expression (DiGiorgio-Miller, 1994; Sermabeikian & Martinez, 1994).

The Family of the Sexually Abusive Child

Several researchers have studied distinct populations of families that include a sexually abused child to reveal distinct characteristics and family dynamics. For example, it has been suggested that interactions between family members contribute to the sexual climate of the home and that exposure to explicit sexual material is a risk factor for sexual aggression by children (Gray et al., 1997). In addition, Friedrich et al. (1992) noted that "sexual abuse rarely occurs in isolation but rather is associated with greater levels of familial distress and fewer educational and financial resources in the family" (p. 310). Lang and Langevin (1991) suggested that "clinically significant disturbances in father-son relationships" (p. 68) characterize the family life of young, male sexual offenders. In a comparative study of seventy-two SAC and their caregivers, Gray et al. (1997) found that marginal social adjustment within the families is the norm. Violence between the children's parents often escalates to physical violence. Specifically, 61.5% of the 6- to 9- and 42.9% of the 10- to 12-year-olds studied reported having witnessed violence that included hitting, slapping, and shoving between the parents. Families sampled by Gray et al. were characterized by marked sexual interaction among their members. For example, 94% of the victims of the SAC sampled were members of the same family. Moreover, family members exhibit low impulse control, low frustration tolerance, deficient problem-solving skills, and marked social isolation from the community. It is not surprising, therefore, that many SAC exhibit marked impairments in sibling and peer relationships.

In a study of SAC, Friedrich and Luecke (1988) found "profound deficits in variables related to interpersonal functioning" (p. 163). The SAC sampled by Friedrich and Luecke reported frequent rejection by others and tended to act in aggressive, sexualized ways toward their siblings and peers. The families were characterized by longstanding tension between parents and children, which led the authors to conclude that "appropriate parenting was the exception rather than the rule, and this further exacerbated the trauma of sexual abuse, making it more likely for sexually aggressive behavior to occur" (p. 163). In light of the aforementioned evidence about SAC and the families that contain a sexually abused child, counseling programs must be wide in scope to address the multiple needs of the children and their families.

Treatment Approaches With Families of SAC

There is a nearly universal agreement that the treatment of SAC must include the family. However, the inclusion of the family may be one of the most challenging aspects of SAC treatment as many of these families have a multigenerational history of sexual, physical, and substance abuse (Carter & Van Dalen, 1998). It is common for families that have not resolved issues of multigenerational abuse to link the behaviors of the sexually aggressive child to other family difficulties. Cantwell (1995) and Johnson and Berry (1989) suggest that SAC family members frequently blame or ignore the child and feel powerless to intervene to alleviate or impede the aggressive sexual behaviors. Ballester and Pierre (1995) suggest that treatment which involves the family must include attention to the cycles of abuse; interpersonal, communication, and parenting skills; the exploration of gender roles; and the appropriateness of personal boundaries and privacy. In addition, families that include a SAC need connections to support systems to negotiate the requirements of law enforcement, legal, school, and child welfare systems.

Conclusion

The study of the dynamics of sexual behavior in children is in its infancy. Empirical evaluation of the effectiveness of treatments for SAC is nearly absent in the professional literature. Conclusions, such as that of Johnson and Berry (1989) about their program that "very few children have offended while in the program or after graduating" (p. 202) are in grave need of empirical attention. The data reviewed in this chapter led us to delineate the elements that as a minimum seem necessary for mental health professionals to effectively treat SAC.

References

Araji, S. K. (1997). Sexually aggressive children: Coming to understand them. Thousand Oaks, CA: Sage.

Ballester, S., & Pierre, F. (1995). Monster therapy: The use of a metaphor with abuse reactive children. In M. Hunter (Ed.), *Child survivors and perpetrators of sexual abuse: Treatment innovations* (pp. 125–146). Thousand Oaks, CA: Sage.

Bandura, A. J. (1977). *Social learning theory.* Englewood Cliffs, NJ: Prentice-Hall.

Beitchman, J. H., Zucker, K. J., Hood, J. E., DaCosta, G. A., & Akma, D. (1991). A review of the short-term effects of child sexual abuse. *Child Abuse and Neglect, 15*, 537–556.

Bowlby, J. (1969). Disruption of affectional bonds and its effects on behavior. *Canada's Mental Health Supplement, 59*, 12.

Bradford, J. M. W., Motayne, G., Gratzer, T., & Pawlak, A. (1995). Child and adolescent sexual offenders. In G. A. Rekers (Ed.), *Handbook of child and adolescent sexual problems* (pp. 446–475). New York: Lexington Books.

Briere, J. (1989). *Therapy for adults molested as children: Beyond survival.* New York: Springer.

Cantwell, H. B. (1995). Sexually aggressive children and societal response. In M. Hunter (Ed.),

Child survivors and perpetrators of sexual abuse: Treatment innovations (pp. 79–107). Thousand Oaks, CA: Sage.

Carter, G. S., & Van Dalen, A. (1998). Sibling incest: Time limited group as an assessment and treatment planning tool. *Journal of Child and Adolescent Group Therapy, 8*(2), 45–54.

Cashwell, C. S., Bloss, K. K., & McFarland, J. E. (1995). From victim to client: Preventing the cycle of sexual reactivity. *The School Counselor, 42*, 233–238.

Corcoran, C. L., Miranda, A. O., Tenukas-Steblea, K., & Taylor, B. D. (1999). Inclusion of the family in the treatment of juvenile sexual abuse perpetrators. In B. K. Schwartz (Ed.), *The sex offender: Theoretical advances, treating special populations and legal developments* (pp. 17-1–17-9). Kingston, NJ: Civic Research Institute.

Cunningham, C., & McFarlane, K. (1996). *When children abuse: Group treatment strategies for children with impulse control problems.* Brandon, VT: Safer Society Press.

DiGiorgio-Miller, J. (1994). Clinical techniques in the treatment of juvenile sex offenders. *Journal of Offender Rehabilitation, 21*(1–2), 117–126.

Fedoroff, J. P., & Pincus, S. (1996). The genesis of pedophilia: Testing the "abused-to-abuser" hypothesis. *Journal of Offender Rehabilitation, 23*(3–4), 85–102.

Finkelhor, D. (1986). *A sourcebook on child sexual abuse.* Newbury Park, CA: Sage.

Finkelhor, D., & Browne, A. (1986). Initial and long-term effects: A conceptual framework. In D. Finkelhor (Ed.), *A sourcebook on child sexual abuse* (pp. 180–198). Newbury Park, CA: Sage.

Finkelhor, D., Hotaling, G., Lewis, I. A., & Smith, C. (1990). Sexual abuse in a national survey of adult men and women: Prevalence characteristics and risk factors. *Child Abuse and Neglect, 14*, 19–28.

Finkelhor, D., & Russell, D. (1984). How much child sexual abuse is committed by women? In D. Finkelhor (Ed.), *Child sexual abuse: New theory and research* (pp. 171–187). New York: Free Press.

Folkman, S., & Lazarus, R. S. (1980). An analysis of coping in a middle aged community sample. *Journal of Health and Social Behavior, 21*, 219–139.

Friedrich, W. N. (1988). Behavior problems in sexually abused children: An adaptational perspective. In G. E. Wyatt & G. J. Powell (Eds.), *Lasting effects of child sexual abuse* (pp. 171–191). Newbury Park, CA: Sage.

Friedrich, W. N. (1990). Evaluating the child and planning for treatment. In W. N. Friedrich (Ed.), *Psychotherapy of the sexually abused children and their families* (pp. 64–99). New York: Norton.

Friedrich, W. N. (1991). *Casebook of sexual abuse treatment.* New York: Norton.

Friedrich, W. N., Grambsch, P., Broughton, D., Kuiper, J., & Beilke, R. L. (1991). Normative sexual behavior in children. *Pediatrics, 88*, 456–464.

Friedrich, W. N., Grambsch, P., Damon, L., Hewitt, S., Koverola, C., Lang, R., & Wolfe, V. (1992). The child sexual abuse inventory: Normative and clinical comparisons. *Psychological Assessment, 4*, 303–311.

Friedrich, W. N., & Luecke, W. J. (1988). Young school-age sexually aggressive children. *Professional Psychology: Research and Practice, 19*(2), 155–164.

Gil, E., & Johnson, T. C. (1993). *Sexualized children.* Walnut Creek, CA: Launch Press.

Goocher, B. E. (1994). Some comments on the residential treatment of juvenile sex offenders. *Child and Youth Care Forum, 23*(4), 243–250.

Gray, A. S., Busconi, A., Houchens, P., & Pithers, W. D. (1997). Children with sexual behavior problems and their caregivers: Demographics, functioning, and clinical patterns. *Sexual Abuse: A Journal of Research and Treatment, 9*(4), 267–290.

Gray, A. S., & Pithers, W. D. (1993). Relapse prevention with sexually aggressive adolescents. In H. E. Barbaree, W. L. Marshall, & S. M. Hudson (Eds.), *The juvenile sex offender* (pp. 289–320). New York: Guilford Press.

Guntrip, H. (1967). The concept of psychodynamic science. *International Journal of Psycho-Analysis, 48*(1), 32–43.

Haugaard, J. J., & Tilly, C. (1988). Characteristics predicting children's responses to sexual encounters with other children. *Child Abuse and Neglect, 12,* 209–218.

Johnson, T. C. (1988). Children who molest other children: Preliminary findings. *Child Abuse and Neglect, 12,* 219–229.

Johnson, T. C. (1989). Female child perpetrators: Children who molest other children. *Child Abuse and Neglect, 13,* 571–585.

Johnson, T. C., & Berry, C. (1989). Children who molest: A treatment program. *Journal of Interpersonal Violence, 4*(2), 185–203.

Kikuchi, J. J. (1995). When the offender is a child: Identifying and responding to juvenile sexual abuse offenders. In M. Hunter (Ed.), *Child survivors and perpetrators of sexual abuse: Treatment innovations* (pp. 108–124). Thousand Oaks, CA: Sage.

Knopp, F. H. (1995). Building bridges: Working together to understand and prevent sexual abuse. *Sexual Abuse: Journal of Research and Treatment, 7*(3), 231–238.

Lang, R. A., & Langevin, R. (1991). Parent-child relations in offenders who commit violent sexual crimes against children. *Behavioral Science and the Law, 9*(1), 61–71.

MacFarlane, K., Cockriel, K., & Dugan, M. (1990). Treating victims of incest. In R. K. Oates (Ed.), *Understanding and managing child sexual abuse* (pp. 149–177). Sydney, Australia: Harcourt Brace Jovanovich.

Malamuth, N. (1995, October). *A unified developmental theory of sexual aggression: Models in the making.* Paper presented at the 14th annual Research and Treatment Conference of The Association for the Treatment of Sexual Abusers, New Orleans, LA.

Martinson, F. L. (1991). Normal sexual development in infancy and early childhood. In G. D. Ryan & S. L. Lane (Eds.), *Juvenile sexual offending* (pp. 57–82). Lexington, MA: Lexington Books.

Matheny, K. B., Aycock, D. W., & McCarthy, C. J. (1993). Stress in school-aged children and youth. *Educational Psychology Review, 5*(2), 109–134.

Miau, M. (1986). Review of 125 children 6 years of age and under who were sexually abused. *Child Abuse and Neglect, 10,* 223–229.

Okami, P. (1992). Child perpetrators of sexual abuse: The emergence of a problematic deviant category. *Journal of Sex Research, 29*(1), 109–140.

Pallone, N. J., & Hennessey, J. J. (Eds.). (1996). *Tinderbox criminal agression: Neuropsychology, phenominology, demography.* New Brunswick, NJ: Transaction.

Pithers, W. D., Gray, A. S., Busconi, A., & Houchens, P. (1998). Children with sexual behavior problems: Identification of five distinct child types and related treatment considerations. *Child Maltreatment, 8*(4), 384–406.

Pithers, W. D., Gray, A. S., Cunningham, C., & Lane, S. (1993). *From trauma to understanding: A guide for parents of children with sexual behavior problems.* Brandon, VT: Safer Society Program and Press.

Porter, E. (1986). *Treating the young male victim of sexual assault: Issues and intervention strategies.* Orwell, VT: Safer Society Press.

Rasmussen, L. A., Burton, J. E., & Christopherson, B. J. (1992). Precursors to offending and the Trauma Outcome Process in sexually reactive children. *Journal of Child Sexual Abuse, 1*(1), 33–48.

Ryan, G. D. (1987). Juvenile sex offenders: Development and correction. *Child Abuse and Neglect, 11,* 385–395.

Sermabeikian, P., & Martinez, D. (1994). Treatment of adolescent sexual offenders: Theory-based practice. *Child Abuse and Neglect, 18*(11), 969–976.

Smets, A. C., & Cebula, C. M. (1987). A group treatment program for adolescent sex offenders: Five steps toward resolution. *Child Abuse and Neglect, 11,* 247–254.

Summit, R. C. (1988). Hidden victims, hidden pain: Society's avoidance of child sexual abuse. In G. E. Wyatt & G. J. Powell (Eds.), *Lasting effects of child sexual abuse* (pp. 39–60). Newbury Park, CA: Sage.

Task Force on Juvenile Sexual Offenders and Their Victims. (1996). *Juvenile sexual offenders and their victims.* Tallahassee, FL: Author.

Widom, C. S. (1989). Does violence beget violence? A critical examination of the literature: Clarification of publishing history. *Psychological Bulletin, 115*(2), p. 287.

Widom, C. S. (1995, March). *Victims of childhood sexual abuse—Later criminal consequences.* Washington, DC: National Institute of Justice.

Widom, C. S., & Ames, M. A. (1994). Criminal consequences of childhood sexual victimization. *Child Abuse and Neglect, 18*, 303–317.

Chapter 19

Creating Empathic Responses With Adolescent Sex Offenders

by Carl Schwartz, Ph.D., J.D.

Overview

This chapter is designed to provide interested practitioners who work with adolescent sex offenders with a method to increase their ability to strengthen emotional and empathic responses to their clients. The method uses selected images, selected script, and selected music to create emotional responses that have an impact. These images help the offender to become a more direct witness to the betrayals, confusions, and fears that victims often experience.

Introduction

Imagery is one of the most important factors and useful building blocks of our realities. Imagery is probably the most common perceptual ingredient to a mental event. Mental events are the seminal ingredients of self-knowledge. Thoughts consist of pictures, words, sounds and sensations, emotions, and other elements of experience. The usage of imagery to create and enhance client empathy becomes a key strategy to helping clients build better working perceptual systems.

Building New Perceptual Systems

Creating a new perceptual system may well be the foundation for a client's moral system. The client's sense of right and wrong, what is acceptable or inexcusable, must be anchored to feelings so clear that self-centered rationalizations can be detected and challenged. The client's basic emotional instincts must be strong enough to override impulsive, "excitement-oriented" moments. Fantasies of pleasure that may expose victims to potential harm must be responsive to newly developed emotional warnings. This new system is one containing both emotional sensitivity and cognitive clarity: The emotional sensitivity will provide a sense of caution and the cognitive clarity will arouse thinking of potential harm to both client and other.

The challenge to assist clients in learning the skills and capacities to "care" and value the well-being of others is important. This task is necessary both to socially normalize clients and to give them the necessary tools to self-regulate the appetites and passions that inhabit and afflict us all.

Most clinicians are familiar with the difficulty in creating affect in their "offender" clients. Offenders often are conditioned to need the excitements and sexual gratification that come from high-risk behavior. They have not yet developed sufficient capacities to inhibit or manage their needs, drives, and desires. These needs for excitement and immediate emotional gratification will eventually override their abilities to create safe, socially appropriate responses.

The therapeutic challenge is to increase clients' abilities to experience their inhibitory emotions (i.e., anxiety, regret, shame, and sadness) and simultaneously strengthen their social development in order to create a prosocial lifestyle.

Clinicians, by using high-impact images that clients select, can reduce their need to confront and may increase a client's sense of hopefulness regarding change. Defenses that were used to falsely portray client self-respect are reduced. Reasonable amounts of emotional regret are evoked as a part of a larger system of values and beliefs that clients work to develop. This larger system becomes increasingly vital to an offender's growing sense of belonging and participation to both family and community.

Overview of a Session. The session consists of a clinician and client (or any other combination of relevant participants) sitting in a room and viewing the materials outlined herein. The clinician repeats preselected phrases designed to enhance the meaning of each image. The presented images are sequenced in three parts to provide three different broad emotional landscapes: love and belonging; regret, remorse, shame, and guilt; and the anticipation and anxiety of facing readmittance to community and family.

The clinician facilitates a session to help a client increase feelings of love, regret, and hopefulness. The session can focus on all these emotions, or it can be divided so that a client can focus on a particular feeling. The idea is to help establish a new emotionally based moral system. The clinician must use his or her best intuition to guide and shape experiences.

The images chosen, with the client's cooperation, should be as emotionally charged as possible. This high emotional valence factor will allow the client to begin to feel. These feelings help promote a sense of progress. Clients will have previously processed the value in becoming more emotionally responsive. When new emotions become detectable, clients will begin to become eager for more therapeutic encounters. These potential cathartic moments will tend to operate as a beginning form of redemption. The client can view his or her own discomfort as one of the costs to be paid for causing emotional harm. These beginning emotions also help clinicians create other needed understandings. Clients can more easily find themselves understanding a broader emotional palette. These emotions can be useful in increasing a client's sense of self-worth.

Clients sit in front of these images that are prepared as slides or overheads (large formats are helpful). Selected phrases, scripts, and photos are used to enter this new territory of affect and developing values. The client provides music that is associated with these targeted feelings.

The materials needed are as follows:

1. One recent photo of the client, mostly head and face with a serious expression. The photo should reflect thoughtfulness and a serious attitude.

2. One photo of the client's family. The picture must represent family ties and evoke feelings that suggest bonding, yearning to belong, and other useful emotions. Feelings of wanting to belong are the target emotions.

3. One photo or image of one of the victims or someone resembling the victim.

4. A detailed drawing done by the client of his or her sexual wrongdoing. There should be enough detail to stimulate both past sexual memories and the capacity to feel shame. It should both excite and disgust. This is accomplished by evoking the kinds of expressions that reflect the discomfort of the victim.

5. Some photos or images of "normative life" as defined by the therapist and client, including recreational, social, spiritual, scenes, and so on. These images should suggest the client's sense of community.

6. Emotionally evocative music picked by the client that can accompany these imagery sessions and will have a tendency to create appropriate feelings (I use the soundtrack from the move *The Mission*).

Further Comments on Materials and Purpose. The use of the client's own "serious-look picture" helps clients to read into their expression. Clients are required to interpret the measuring of their serious expression. They can begin to assign different concerns that are naturally serious to these sessions. The facilitation is aimed at helping clients to form new, strong cognitions and feelings about the meaning and consequences of their actions. New cognitions and feelings need to be generated by the client, not the clinician. For example, being told that victims hide feelings only becomes useful when a client can "find" these hidden emotions.

Having a client draw a picture of the sexual wrongdoing with sufficient types of detail to evoke both an erotic and a repugnant response is clinically rich. Clients need to be educated and guided through the fear and confusion that may result from their diverse and contradictory responses. Many clients have reported that as their sense of disgust becomes present, their erotic response becomes associated with disgust. They have begun to discover how part of the brain can produce both emotional and sexual messages. The provoking of both types of responses may help a client to more fully discriminate future appropriate responses, both emotional and erotic. The surprise and self consciousness that result from the approximate merger of these two has proven helpful in developing an increased ability for self regulation.

The picture of a client's family must include members who represent a client's "wish to belong." This universal need for affiliation becomes part of the client's expanded emotional palette. After sufficient processing, clients can value feelings of loss, sadness, and vulnerability. Clients may need education and motivation to become involved intimately with their peers. These needs to belong help promote the "relationship building" that is often difficult for the client who is socially fearful. The feelings and desires to find, maintain, and keep a healthy relationship are partly a product of these previous feelings that clients can derive from their own family histories.

Some clients with strongly abusive backgrounds may benefit by focusing on feelings of how they had "wished it had been." Although part of this focus is fictitious, these feelings still represent the emotions of belonging that some day will help these clients establish more stable relationships.

Miscellaneous images of "normalcy" are used to support and to construct future experience. Images from scrapbooks, magazines, or drawings, for example, are useful as props in linking new client-learned responses that can support a client's prosocial lifestyle. These will expand and direct the clients into a wider and more varied lifestyle. Clients will be less likely to reoffend if they meet people and join institutions that are appropriate for their age, background, and interests.

Preparing for an Empathy-Building Session

Prior to beginning empathy-building sessions, the therapist and client should establish a familiarity with several basic beliefs. These beliefs will support the diverse range of challenges that emerge for offenders in their effort to become more responsive and available to treatment goals. Discussions, educational materials, family history, and miscellaneous community involvements are all useful in developing higher-functioning beliefs.

Some of these beliefs include the following:

1. Healing and change processes are difficult and time-consuming. They demand much personal commitment. Journeying into uncertain and unfamiliar areas is necessary to this progress.

2. Staying stuck in deviant beliefs is not inevitable, and changing these conditioned responses and thoughts is feasible. These responses, although sometimes resistant, can evolve into more self-respecting new feelings and behaviors.

3. The therapist will act as a trusted guide and coach throughout the time spent together. The client's therapist has the expertise and background to help chart and create new courses of action. This relationship shall remain free from judgment and will reflect the therapist's best efforts to promote the changes that will reduce known risks.

4. There will be time spent to discover and use newly developed feelings to create a life based on contribution, not retribution. Joining the community "at

large" is a worthy expression of contribution and can reduce alienation and activate feelings of worthiness.

5. Each human being has a right to be respected as a sexual human being, and nonrisky forms of sexual expressions are acceptable. Therapy can support diverse, erotic maps that are based on authentic consent.

6. Part of regaining self-respect is to deepen all feelings for life whether they are joyous or adverse. Emotions are part of feeling alive and their appearance should not be controlled. Numbness is not an acceptable option to learning how to manage one's affect.

7. Time spent in sessions to access, locate, and identify feelings is time well spent. To experience belongingness requires emotion. To know joy is also to know sadness. The world tends to work within the structure of affective opposites.

8. A moral conscience is made up of both the community's accepted values that promote the general well-being and an individual's feelings for his or her own life's interests. Life must be a balance between self and other.

9. Contradiction and conflict are integral parts of human aliveness; knowing how to experience these ever-present puzzles is part of life's mystery.

Preparing a developmentally appropriate client to accept and work with these ideas is necessary to provide a context for empathic work. Searching for and constructing empathic experiences results in the building of a mental and emotional system that can embrace the anomalies of life.

Orchestrating the Session

The therapist should select a number of photos. These images will become more effective for sessions when they are placed in a large format of slides or overheads. A large format is needed to help increase impact. The sessions may be divided into three sections depending on the readiness of the client. The first part of the session will use the image of the client's family. The client is asked to sit in front of this image as music plays. The client has been instructed that the session is designed to help retrieve emotions and that there are no preferred rules or expectations. A relaxation sequence is often helpful in creating a more open and available emotional potential. Clinicians familiar with guided imagery exercises may wish to use them. This helps set the stage for the session.

The client is asked to concentrate in an "open manner" on the images of the family and listen while the clinician speaks. The clinician will speak in a calm, steady, and confident voice. The phrases listed will be spaced and timed according to the clinician's instincts. Following are a few possible phrases:

"I love my family."

"Sometimes things seemed normal."

"Parents protect their children."

"There were some happy times."

"These impulses and thoughts feel dirty."

"My parents love me. I wonder if they know?"

"I wish it wasn't this way."

"What am I about to do?"

These phrases and any other phrases the therapist constructs are introduced to suggest the following types of feelings and beliefs:

1. *"I love my family"*: Everyone can have loving feelings either for or about their family. These emotions are basic for any human being. Difficult upbringings and/or abuse tend not to negate these feelings.

2. *"Sometimes things seem normal"*: In any family, there are times that are memorable and nurturing. No matter how few, they can become the references for building a fuller life. Outside relationships that are healthier do not have to be incompatible with salvaging the "best of the worst."

3. *"Parents protect their children"*: All parents should protect their children. Misuse of social contracts between parents and children—younger and older, richer and poorer, bigger and smaller—all allow abusive exchanges. Childhood should be a time of protected intimacy and exploration. To spoil innocence is to place greed in front of wonder.

4. *"There were some happy times"*: This phrase indicates and supports the idea that humans are resilient and can be capable even under conditions of duress and adversity. Clients with adverse histories can make changes.

5. *"These impulses and thoughts feel dirty"*: Victims carry hidden thoughts that create dirty and difficult feelings.

6. *"My parents love me. I wonder if they know?"*: This phrase suggests that life is contradictory. One can have comforting feelings and suspicious feelings at the same time.

7. *"I wish it wasn't this way"*: Wishing and hoping have not created change. Reverie, daydream, and pretending are not sufficient to develop a safer life style. Need-fulfilling fantasies are not effective substitutes for honest engagements in life. Take time to resolve deeper hidden conflicts.

8. *"What am I about to do?"*: How can one begin to know oneself as someone other than someone who is dangerous. Knowing and sharing one's thoughts and fantasies is helpful to maintain safe behavior.

First Stage. This first stage will help produce feelings of longing, and these yearnings are important to the efficacy and usefulness of our own moral self-doubt. Wanting and desiring to belong are the guideposts back from shame. The therapist can run the gamut from very little intervention to very active intervention. The image of family becomes the symbol of connected living, community values, and valuing others as much as or more than the self. Narcissistic tendencies are trimmed down; reciprocal gestures are massaged open. A therapist during this section can use any combination of materials that may help create these emotional understandings (poetry, letters, stories, articles, tapes, etc.). Of course, the less intervention the better. Clients need time to access, construct, and process their own personal associations. This first part can be repeated in as many variations as necessary until the requisite feelings and sensing have been reported. This would allow the therapist and client to agree that forms of affectional understandings have been evoked.

Second Stage. The client has previously drawn a detailed depiction of his or her sexually inappropriate behavior event, and the therapist and client have previewed the drawing for its ability to cause reactions that span both erotic and regretful responses. As previously mentioned, responses that can span the range from excitatory to inhibitory are clinically useful to shape and orchestrate new responses. This second stage often becomes the emotional "open door" that allows the beginning of the complex development of feelings of regret, shame, and a sense of reparation. Training in psychodrama, gestalt, hypnosis, art therapy, and other forms of process work have been useful in this stage. Clients begin to participate emotionally with both the memory and suggestion of the emotional harm that their behavior caused.

This stage is based on an assumption that the repair and reconciliation process is a matter of emotional restorative justice. To make what is torn whole again is to give back both materially and emotionally. The ability to feel emotional pain becomes the client's aid in feeling some of the victim's hurt. Anguish, guilt, embarrassment, and general emotional dissonance are all part of the suffering with which most of us are acquainted during some parts of our lifetime. No one escapes the pain of failure, the loss of trust, and the anxiety of the unknown. To look directly into a picture drawn by the hand that handed the humiliation to the victim is an important awakening for client moral recognizability. As the client is looking at this image, with the chosen music, the therapist is again stating calmly and confidently phrases that support both the state of mind of the perpetrator and the victim.

Some possibilities include the following:

"I'm scared."

"If I smile, they won't know."

"Please, not me."

"Stop looking at me that way."

"Does anyone know my thoughts?"

"I'll hide, they won't know."

"Stop, it hurts!"

"This feels good, I won't do it again."

"I thought you liked me."

"Please, don't touch me there."

"I hope I don't get caught."

These phrases and any others that the clinician creates are designed to link to the following values and beliefs, which are processed over time to strengthen client abilities to manage conflicts.

1. *"I thought you liked me"; "Stop looking at me that way"*: The victim deeply and truthfully experienced a tear in the fabric of trust that had existed prior to the sexual acting out. This level of betrayal can contaminate future efforts to create intimacy and successful long-term relationships.

2. *"Stop, it hurts"; "I'm scared"*: Fear is somewhat equal to "begging silently that this is all a bad dream." Hoping it goes away has similarities to children's night terrors. The powerlessness and unexplainability are beyond reason. No explaining can ease the fear and avoidance that victims experience.

3. *"Does anyone know my thoughts?"; "If I smile, they won't know"*: Hiding and being deceitful require a fraudulent self to carry out molest behavior. Pretending that life is just fine becomes a habit. Honesty and acceptance are exterminated; the fictitious becomes the norm.

4. *"This feels good, I won't do it again"*: This phrase references an offender's need for pretending that immediate gratification must exist now but need not exist later. Pretending to stop abuse excuses abuse.

The viewing of this drawing of sexual wrongdoing contains all the aspects that can help offenders begin to recognize to what extremes they may be willing to go for their own pleasures. This robbing of another's innocence to help an offender repair his failing sense of competency is another important understanding for a client to endure. History is full of examples of abuse that represent the carnage created by power imbalances. The enslavement of the human spirit by people in privileged positions has existed forever and the offender has entered the shameful halls of this history. The clinical need to reveal the emotional desperation that covets this kind of power is mandatory. The need for "triumph over tragedy" that many offenders temporarily accomplish becomes a challenge for the therapist to uncover. Human feelings of inadequacy are constantly camouflaged through arrogance and indifference.

In this regard, deviancy has a protective function. A perpetrator's awareness of client-induced harm and abuse becomes dominated by a need to restore a sense of a perpetrator's sexual/social adequacy. This illusion of social competency requires secrecy that is held, by fabricating integrity. This shield and its habituated emotional numbness will loosen and crack with careful clinical guidance. Eventually, a client's willingness to experience a high degree of dissonance can assist with inspiring the client's new choices. The discontent with oneself is a key ingredient. Past habitual contentments become punctured by a slowly developing painful awareness of emotional equivacalities. The creation of new and searching questions about the nature of human frailty are seeded. Clients explore personal as well as global understandings of suffering.

The therapist must help clients manage these equivocalities so the anxiety does not shut down and discourage new emotional explorations. The client's ego structure is temporarily disabled in the name of trust, fatigue, hope, and emotional restitution. This becomes a form of symbolic payment for the "return from exile" and back into the community that had been violated. The widening ability of a client to gain acceptance and self-respect becomes a therapeutic goal. The therapist encourages the toleration of emotional equivocality and the anxiety associated with it. This process becomes the hedge against the tendencies for narcissistic comfort. Questions of authenticity and client self-pity must be handled by the therapist as if the client is attempting to give birth to a newborn. This birthing is fraught with pains and hesitancies. All regular and expected thresholds of pain will be suspended. Always remember that clients must deeply value these new awarenesses to be able to internally adjust. A new behavior will tend to extinguish unless a client perceives them as profitable consequences.

Third Stage. The last set of images are those suggestive of a more normal and community-validated lifestyle. These images should represent the client, as he becomes more capable of participating honestly in reciprocal and nondeviant motivated relationships. These images can begin to support the necessary courage and risk taking that the client must endure to make this transition. Much social skill building is needed to help with the necessary confidence to move forward. For clients well established in the community, similar activities must be experienced with a deeper feeling of connectedness and selflessness. Deviant mental activity must be silenced for this feeling of connectedness and selflessness to take place.

Real-life experiences that are available to clients can reinforce a believability of change. Behavioral rehearsals are needed to convince clients of the possibilities of nondeviant alternatives. These options are vast and certainly familiar activities can be helpful. The client and the therapist watch the images with supporting music, using phrases such as the following:

"Am I sure I'm safe?"

"Will people accept you (me)?"

"Can I love others?"

"I have urges sometimes. Should I tell?"

"I hope this lasts."

These type of phrases are designed to expose and process the following kinds of beliefs:

1. *"Am I sure I'm safe?"*: Maintenance may be a lifetime proposition; emotional realities and sexual scripts can interweave at times in a potentially risky manner.

2. *"Will people accept me?"*: Who I trust to know me, as I was and as I am, will challenge my self-confidence. Developing skills of intimacy becomes important as a lifetime goal.

3. *"I have urges sometimes. Should I tell?"*: Urges, risky instincts, and old responses are all part of being alive: balancing and managing these are necessary life skills. Life's anomalies must be channeled creatively.

4. *"Can I love others?"*: Having the courage to learn to love is also part of being

human. Don't hide behind the mask of easy gratification. Commitment to others requires constant renewal.

Conclusion

The foregoing methods will help clients and clinicians to identify important parts of a client's perceptual system. This will help a client develop ability and interest in reforming and forming useful, emotional/cognitive responses. The strengthening of client-affect cognitions systems is instrumental in providing clients with a more developed sense of their own responsibility and "authorship." Responsibility and authorship can sponsor new feelings of adequacy. This newly developing sense of creating one's own story, as it expresses both hope and regret, can foster a stronger feeling of self-esteem. This improved self-worth is valuable for a client's willingness to manage and self-regulate through the many challenging life events that are inevitable. This newly formed feeling of competency helps reduce future inclinations to "act out" because of poorly managed feeling of vulnerability. This then can become a vital part of a client's relapse prevention.

Chapter 20

A Model for Therapists to Assess Readiness for and Provide Reunification Treatment to Juvenile Sex Offenders and Their Victims— The S.A.F.E.R. Model

by Bert Harris, M.A., L.P. and Julie Campbell, M.S.W., L.S.W.

Overview

The professional who treats juvenile sex offenders is faced with a challenge that those treating the adult sex offender need not necessarily deal with—family reunification. Of course, not every juvenile sex offender will end up reunited with his or her family, but this possibility must always be considered. In this chapter, the authors review a process they have developed in evaluating and conducting, when appropriate, this reconciliation.

Introduction

The S.A.F.E.R. (Sexual Abuse Family Evaluation for Reunification) model is a comprehensive clinical guide designed to assist therapists who are treating child sexual abuse victims and/or juvenile sex offenders around the process of family reunification. There is a paucity of literature on family reunification involving juvenile sex offenders and their victims. The S.A.F.E.R. model will begin to fill this void by offering a step-by-step method to assess victim, offender, and family readiness for reunification. Given that sexual abuse treatment requires communication across various systems, each with its own values, methodologies, rules, and beliefs, it is paramount that there is close, honest, and effective dialogue among the systems to ensure the well-being of family members. Knowing how these systems work together and independently of each other is crucial to successful reunification. A specific understanding of the role of both the juvenile justice system and the child welfare system in their intervention in child sexual abuse cases is essential for the therapist treating the juvenile sex offender and the child victim as they work together toward reunification. In addition, a clear understanding of each family's internal dynamics and responses to the intervening systems enables the treating therapist to work toward the optimal conditions of reunification. The S.A.F.E.R. model is designed to help the offender therapist and the victim therapist safeguard the interests of the victim(s), and potential victims, along with helping the offender maintain the gains that indicate readiness for reunification. The model is created with the understanding that reunification is effected by the system(s) that service the family, as well as the family's dynamics.

Levels of Reunification

The S.A.F.E.R. model defines reunification as any level of contact between an offender and his or her victim. For some families, reunification never moves beyond supervised or unsupervised visitation for a variety of reasons. For other families, reunification includes the goal of ultimately having the offender and victim fully reunified and living in the same household. However, it should be noted that even in families that have achieved enough healing for full reunification, the offender and victim are always to be supervised by adults and are never to be left alone together. The S.A.F.E.R. model is applicable to all levels of reunification.

Systemic Influences on Reunification

Numerous systemic difficulties arise in treating outpatient juvenile sex offenders and their victims beginning with the child welfare system response to the offender and to the victim. Because treatment is similar to a mobile, in which each piece has an effect on the other, the systemic responses or lack of responses will have an effect on treatment and reunification. The S.A.F.E.R. model was developed at an outpatient psychiatric center specializing in the treatment of victims of sexual abuse as well as adjudicated and nonadjudicated sex offenders. These treatment populations offer their own set of systemic problems. The S.A.F.E.R. model encourages clinicians to be cognizant of the strengths and weaknesses of the system serving the offender as well as the victim. The S.A.F.E.R. model can be used to indicate when to reunify and when not to do so. At the heart of the model is an interdisciplinary approach among the criminal justice system, the child welfare system, the sex offender treatment provider, and the victim treatment provider. Some of what we have learned through our work with such cases is described. Though sex offenders and victims are both male and female, for ease of discussion, we refer to the offender as "he" and the victim as "she." Further, many sex offenders' and victims' primary caregivers are substitute parents, such as other relatives or foster parents. Again, for ease, we refer to caregivers as the parent(s).

Issues With the Juvenile Justice System

In assessing the system, it is important to understand that the lawyer often tells the adjudicated offender that he has only two options: admit to the charges and remain in the community or plead innocent and risk being sent "away" (i.e., residential placement). This places the juvenile in a situation in which he is encouraged to avoid the more objectionable of the two options. Thus, the juvenile offender may enter treatment under what he interprets as coerced conditions (i.e., he was arm-twisted to admit to all charges). The reality of whether he did everything with which he was charged takes a back seat to feeling "coerced by the system." The offender's parents are also caught in this dynamic. In the initial stages of treatment, it is common for the therapist to hear that their child is innocent and was forced into admission by the courts.

After therapy begins, it is also common to hear offender statements such as "I only said I did it because my lawyer told me I would be put away if I didn't." The impact of such a statement on treatment and reunification is that the offender's retreat into denial goes against the very essence of treatment. Specifically, how does a clinician treat a problem that an offender only said he had because a lawyer advised him to do so? Further, what is the impact of denial on reunification? We use individualized time guidelines for offenders to work through denial. If after a clinically determined period, clients do not relinquish their denial, they are referred back to the court or referral agency. The treatment discharge summary should include a risk assessment and an examination of the reasons why the offender is in denial so that the referral agency can move on with further informed plans for appropriate placement and treatment of the offender. Therapeutically sanctioned reunification should not occur if the offender remains in denial.

Another related problem that begins with the juvenile justice system is plea bargaining. Plea bargaining allows the juvenile offender to admit to a lesser charge (e.g., admitting to a misdemeanor to avoid a felony offense, such as admitting to indecent assault to avoid a rape conviction). In treatment, we tell our youth to tell the truth, yet, often their initial contact with the courts is based on manipulation and negotiated or half-truths. These problems are compounded by the fact that it is also the justice system that has the clout and the power to force the offender into treatment. Thus, when the agency with the power has accepted a half-truth, what motive is there for the offender to state the whole truth?

Fortunately, the client's case manager or officer of the court can have a tremendous impact on the outcome of treatment. The commitment that the offender may have to treatment can be influenced positively or negatively by the leverage of the courts or referral source. It is important that clinicians know how to access and yield this power. We have experienced the most success in working with court and child welfare systems when the probation/parole officer or case managers are part of special units that have training in working with sex offenders. These units are designated as sex offender-specific and provide the court officers/case managers with fundamental knowledge of offending dynamics, an understanding of the reoffense process, the rudimentary process of sex offender treatment efficacy, understanding of victim impact, and factors to consider in supervising sex offenders.

As noted, the role of the juvenile justice system has a significant impact on the offender's denial or admission to the charges or allegations. We assess this impact in terms of risk management and ability to be maintained in the community. For example, as described, an offender may have plea bargained to a misdemeanor so that he is not charged with felony sexual assault, and the courts have agreed to allow him to remain in the community under intensive probation and outpatient juvenile sex offender-specific treatment. Although this may be an optimal disposition for the offender and the court, it can negatively affect treatment and reunification if the offender holds to the belief that he is only in treatment to address what he is charged with rather than the full scope of his offenses. For these reasons, it is essential to make it clear to the offender and the court that the needs and purpose of treatment are often very different from the function of the court in determining a legal disposition of the charges. In treatment, the offender needs to address exactly what he did, not just what he plea-bargained to in court. If reunification does occur, the victim and the family should expect the offender to explain and clarify all of what constituted the sexual assault.

Issues With the Child Welfare System

In addition to understanding how the system responds to the juvenile sex offender, awareness of how the child welfare system responds to the victim and family is also crucial for clinicians when working on victim/offender reunification. The primary function of the child welfare system is to respond to abusive situations quickly to protect minor children. The child welfare social worker must assess the validity of the allegations and the ongoing risk to the identified victim with immediate interventions for safety.

In most instances, this requires a separation in the household in which either the victim or the offender must be moved out of the home. From a clinical point of view, it is always preferable for the offender to be moved to avoid any message of blame or punishment to the victim, and to clearly establish to everyone that the offender is responsible for the abuse and its consequences.

Many events that occur during the stages of initial disclosure will affect the treatment and readiness for reunification. At the point of entry into the child welfare system, the family is in crisis. Family dynamics and loyalty are often significant factors that affect the parent(s)' initial response to the allegations that one of their children, usually an older child, has sexually offended against another child, usually younger. The parent(s) are placed in an immediate bind in their role as parent(s) of both a victim and an offender. For the victim, both the parent(s)' and the offender's initial reaction to the disclosure will greatly affect the victim's internal sense of herself as being responsible for the abuse or not. Often, the offender's threats and/or distortions to the victim during the abuse are either validated or invalidated by the response of others to the disclosure of the sexual abuse. The level of a victim's self-blame is a key factor in assessing the victim's readiness for reunification. The most positive outcome for the victim is to have the offender admit to and take responsibility for the abuse and to have the parent(s) believe, support, and protect the victim immediately. However, denial and minimization are common reactions in the offender and in the parent(s), particularly early on. Further, the parent(s) may face their own scrutiny by the system regarding their functioning as parents, as well as their own personal "adequacy inventory" as they go through a process of self-evaluation. If they are able to believe the allegations, parent(s) are likely to struggle with some level of self-blame and confusion as they try to understand what went wrong in their family. Although this can be a healthy part of treatment and healing, at the point of initial disclosure it often leaves parents feeling overwhelmed with many issues, often with little support for themselves, as well as with too much uncertainty to offer clear support to either the victim or the offender.

The child and family will experience further emotional trauma if the child welfare system determines that foster care placement is the only immediate way to guarantee the victim's safety. This outcome has an impact on the victim, the offender, and the family on many levels around intense feelings of loyalty, blame, abandonment, and guilt. Though out-of-home placement may be the only option to ensure safety in some cases, it is a disruption that strongly affects the prognosis and process of reunification.

Many of the immediate responses of the victim, the offender, and the parent(s) will change after the initial crisis is over. Often, parent(s) who have denied the allegations come to accept the truth and are open to intervention and treatment. However, as described earlier, if the juvenile offender has accepted a plea bargain or has maintained denial, the parent(s) face the challenge of advocating the best outcome for the offender in court while also encouraging the offender to accept responsibility for his offenses, which can be a mixed message. Emotionally, it is usually easier for parents to accept the "plea-bargain version" of the offense. However, this compromises the parent(s) own ability to fully support the child victim and to hold the juvenile offender responsible for the entirety of his offenses. Therefore, clarification of the differences between the role of the court and the function and goals of treatment is essential for the parent(s) as well as for the offender. As with the offender, if parents remain in denial about the sexual abuse, reunification of the victim and the offender is not recommended.

Case Example

The following case example is used throughout our description of the S.A.F.E.R. model. This is an actual case treated over a two-year period and certain details have been changed for confidentiality purposes.

The family has a history of intergenerational incest. Collaboration and communication between the offender and the victim's therapist were essential to the successful reunification of this family. This is a nonadjudicated case. The mother of both the victim and the offender, a single parent, also entered her own treatment at the same agency with a separate therapist, further enhancing collaboration.

The offender (Client A) was a 17-year-old male sexual abuse survivor. He was sexually abused from the ages of 5 to 7 by a paternal uncle. Client A began sexually abusing other children when he was 11 years old. He has had four victims, ages 4 to 7. Client A's victimization was not disclosed until he was 14 years old and in residential treatment for his offending behavior. He spent two and a half years in residential placement. His discharge from placement was considered positive and supportive of reunification. He had fully admitted his offending behavior and had a good grasp of relapse prevention skills. His internal motivation not to reoffend was strong, as was his victim empathy. Lacking in his residential treatment was intensive work on his own victimization. His victimization was addressed in outpatient treatment, which included group, individual, and family therapy with his mother. Client A's outpatient issues that affected reunification were (1) feeling critical and distrustful of the child welfare system, (2) impatience with the slow pace of reunification, (3) anger toward his group residence for placing greater restrictions on him because he was a sex offender, and (4) anger about not being allowed to participate in disciplining his victim who sometimes misbehaved with their mother during reunification visits. During these times, Client A felt that Client B, the victim, was disrespecting their mother and Client A wanted to intervene rather than accept that the role of disciplining Client B belonged only to their mother.

The victim (Client B) was a 9-year-old male who had been sexually abused by his 17-year-old brother (Client A). Client B had been victimized on several occasions by his brother (age 12 at the time) when he was between the ages of 4 and 5. The sexual abuse included fondling and attempted anal penetration. In addition to molesting Client B, Client A also molested a male cousin, from the time he was age 5 until he was age 6. Client A molested both boys at the same time. Further, Client A encouraged the two younger boys to fondle each other. Client B's victimization was disclosed soon after his mother caught Client A, Client B, and their cousin in some play while wearing only their underwear. The mother of Clients A and B found this to be suspicious, and she questioned Client A, who initially denied any sexual activity with either of the boys. However, within a few hours, Client B disclosed that Client A had been touching their cousin sexually, and the same day Client A admitted to sexually abusing their cousin but continued to deny abusing his brother (Client B).

Following the disclosure of the sexual abuse, the mother of Clients A and B became enraged at Client A. She then called the police and child welfare authorities and Client A was immediately removed from the home. Client B did not disclose his own sexual abuse by his brother (Client A) for several weeks. Client B's disclosure was made when his mother discovered him and the cousin engaged in sexual activity after Client A had been removed. As noted, Client A subsequently fully admitted to sexually abusing his brother (Client B) as well as three other victims.

Client B's outpatient treatment issues affecting reunification included (1) strong avoidance of negative affect, (2) the need to seek adult attention by being "good" and either overfunctioning in a parentified manner or entertaining and making jokes to please others, (3) the instability of his home environment due to his mother's recent homelessness and subsequent hospitalizations for depression resulting in Client B's being placed in foster care and with extended family, and (4) feelings of rejection when his brother (Client A) withdrew his affection and positive regard for Client B due to Client B's oppositional behavior toward their mother during reunification visits.

Using the Sexual Abuse Family Evaluation for Reunification

The evaluation for reunification should include an assessment of the service delivery providers that are involved in the family's life as well as the family's ability to reintegrate the offender into the family. The S.A.F.E.R. model provides a qualitative appraisal of the systematic performance in major areas that are critical to the care of the victim, the offender, and the family as a whole (see Figure 20.1).

Figure 20.1
S.A.F.E.R. Model: Sexual Abuse Family Evaluation for Reunification

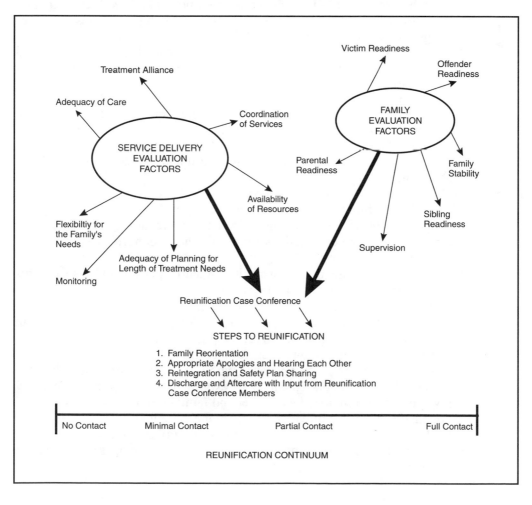

Service Delivery Evaluation Factors. The service delivery evaluation consists of seven factors that are rated along a continuum from inadequate to very adequate (see Appendix 20.1). The offender's therapist and the victim's therapist use the ratings to assess strengths and weaknesses in the delivery of services to the offender and victim. The case example of Client A and Client B is used in Appendix 20.1 as an illustration of how to apply the Service Delivery Provider Ratings. Following are the seven factors with descriptions of how they are defined.

1. *Treatment alliance (for the victim and the offender)*: This is an assessment of how well service delivery providers and the family work together. For example, does family feel that case managers/judicial representatives, child welfare worker, and therapists are on their side, or is an "us vs. them" paradigm operating? Does family feel informed and, when appropriate, consulted about decisions that affect them? Are cultural difference issues understood and addressed?

2. *Coordination of services (for the victim and the offender)*: How well are services coordinated for the offender and for the victim? Does communication occur among professionals in an effective and timely manner? Does the family feel that they receive clear, consistent information among the professionals, or do they get "mixed messages"?

   For the offender: If the offender is being discharged from a residential program, explore the following issues with the primary residential therapist before discharge:

   • Was the offender invested in treatment? Explore quality of the investment.
   • Did the offender sexually act out/victimize while in placement?
   • Was the offender the recipient of any abuse in placement?
   • Assess the offender's overall impulse control and request an actuarial risk assement.
   • How has deviant sexual arousal been assessed and treated?
   • What is the offender's quality of victim emapthy?
   • What are the offender's feelings and wants with regard to reunification?
   • Are the offender's expectations for reunification congruent with the primary therapist's views?
   • Was there any family therapy while in residential placement? If so, did this work address reunification issues?
   • If there has been collaborative family work with the residential therapist and the victim's therapist, obtain authorization so that you can speak with the victim's therapist and start to develop goals together.
   • What does the family want in regard to reunification?
   • Has there been any contact between the victim and the offender while the offender has been in placement? If so, explore the circumstances. This may give you an idea of how the offender and family will respond to limits and boundaries when the offender returns to the community.
   • Do the offender's admissions match the victim(s)' statements?
   • What are the views of the probation officer or case manager with regard to reunification? Are they supportive or pessimistic? Why?

- What has been the family's level of stability since the offender has been away from the home? This will provide information about the capacity of the family to supervise the offender.

For the victim: Assess the victim's/family's experience with the child welfare, medical, and criminal justice systems:

- Did the victim/family experience the child welfare staff as responsive and supportive?
- Was the victim removed from the home? If so, was this handled sensitively for both the victim and the parent(s)?
- Do the victim and the family understand the reasons for the placement?
- If in placement, has the victim been having safe and appropriate contact with the family?
- Was the child victim referred to a medical facility capable of assessing and treating sexual abuse in a timely manner?
- Did the child/family experience the medical exam and staff as helpful and sensitive?
- If a police report was made, were the victim and the family satisfied with their interactions with the police?
- If there was a court hearing involving the victim, was the Court sensitive and helpful regarding the victim's needs and feelings?
- Was the victim referred to an appropriate therapist for treatment quickly?
- Was the victim subjected to repeated interviews by professionals regarding the allegations?
- Were the parent(s) offered supportive counseling for themselves?
- If the offender, victim and/or parent(s) have been in treatment at separate agencies, have the treating clinicians communicated and coordinated together around the needs of the individuals and family?

3. *Flexibility for the family's needs (for the victim and the offender)*: Each family's needs for reunification will not identically match what is offered by various agencies, nor can agencies be infinitely flexible. Is the system of care flexible enough to address the offender, the victim, and the family's needs with regard to reunification?

For the offender: If the offender is in residential treatment and family therapy is indicated:

- Can arrangements be made for visits if the parent(s) do not have transportation?
- Can telephone conferences be held with the family if transportation is not feasible?
- Many families of sexual abusers can be characterized as resistant and will need intensive reaching out before engaging in treatment. How vigorous is outreach to the family?
- If reunification is indicated, are there services available for chaperoning out-of-home visits, in-home visits, and overnight visits if necessary?

For the victim:

- If the victim was removed from the primary home following disclosure, were efforts made to place the child with extended family or close friends?
- If in placement, was visitation and telephone contact with the parent(s) encouraged and arranged in a consistent schedule?
- Were the parent(s)' schedules and financial limitations considered around visitation?
- If the victim was not removed, were in-home services available to the family?

4. *Availability of resources (for the victim, the offender, and the family)*: What is lacking for the victim, the offender and/or the family? Are there resources that are needed but not available (e.g., in-home support services, school-based services, chaperone services, partial hospitalization, residential treatment, psychotropic medication, sexual abuse-specific treatment, diagnostic forensic testing such as the polygraph, Abel Screen or the penile plethysmograph)? What is the major barrier to provision of the needed service(s)?

5. *Adequacy of monitoring (for the victim, the offender, and the family)*: Is there sufficient monitoring of the family and their environment to determine that the victim(s) and the community are safe? If not, why not? Sex offenders should be supervised by probation/parole officers who have received specialized training about sexual offenses. Can the agency provide this kind of supervision? If the offender is not adjudicated, has he been removed from the home? What kind of monitoring is in place?

6. *Adequacy of care (for the victim, the offender, and the family)*: Has the family received sexual abuse-specific treatment by qualified professionals experienced with treating offenders, victims, and their families? Is the offender's risk for re-offending at a level indicating reunification? Are the victim, the offender, and the family ready for reunification?

7. *Adequacy of planning for length of treatment needs (for the victim, the offender, and the family)*: Sexual abuse often occurs in the context of chronic dysfunction in families. This factor looks at preparation for continued care after the sexual abuse issues have been treated. Are there plans in place for care or treatment that addresses the other sources of dysfunction in the family? Are aftercare plans indicated? Many families require additional adjunct treatment such as for drugs/alcohol, parent relationship problems, and so on, in addition to the sexual abuse-specific treatment. Have the providers thought about and assessed this need? Further, if, for example, the family is being treated under a grant, are there plans in place for continuity of care after the grant ends? Without such planning the family may be in danger of returning to conditions that led to the sexual abuse.

Family Evaluation Factors. The S.A.F.E.R. model delineates six factors for family evaluation of readiness for reunification as illustrated in the diagram of the model in Figure 20.1. These six factors include (1) offender readiness, (2) victim readiness, (3) family stability, (4) family supervision, (5) parental readiness, and (6) sibling readiness. Each of these factors must be examined carefully with the needs of both the victim and the offender taken into account. Each of the six family evaluation factors is described herein.

1. *Offender readiness* (also see Appendix 20.2): The S.A.F.E.R. model identifies thirteen variables that affect offender readiness for reunification. These are described in Appendix 20.2. The model recognizes that reunification is a process that may occur along a continuum from not indicated, to minimal contact, to partial contact and, finally, to full contact. Families may also move back and forth along the continuum depending on the course of treatment and their interactions with the other systems that also affect reunification. Such movement back and forth along the continuum may not necessarily mean contraindication for reunification but, rather, that participants are expressing a variety of psychological needs. Of course, if risk for reoffending is an active factor on the continuum, then reunification should be stopped immediately to secure the safety of the potential victim(s). Sex offender treatment is nontraditional in that clinicians also carry the responsibility of community safety along with the responsibility of treating the offender. Therefore, offender readiness for reunification is not assessed solely with regard to reunification with a specific victim but also with regard to the level of risk to all potential victims.

In our case study, Client A was assessed as ready for reunification for the following reasons: (1) He had successfully completed residential sex offense-specific treatment; (2) he showed an adequate ability to handle negative emotional states; (3) his relapse prevention plan was internally motivated; (4) he accepted that, despite his being ready for reunification, other members of the family required further work; (5) he accepted the process of reunification (i.e., the face-to-face contact with his brother would happen slowly with measured and evaluated steps); and (6)the service delivery team supported his readiness for reunification.

2. *Victim readiness* (also see Appendix 20.2): The S.A.F.E.R. model identifies fourteen variables that affect victim readiness for reunification as described in Appendix C. As with offender and family readiness, victim readiness may also occur on a continuum, as described previously. Although reunification can move forward if victims move back and forth on the continuum, reunification should not proceed if the victim is in significant distress about the process. Such distress is likely to manifest itself as regression or a significant change in functioning. If this occurs, it should serve as a signal that must be explored, and the reunification process may need to be slowed down or stopped while the victim's issues are addressed in individual and/or family therapy with the parent(s) but usually not with the offender present. The victim's needs should never be compromised, even if the offender and family are ready to move forward. Further, the therapist must be watchful for either direct or indirect pressure on the victim from the offender and/or family to "hurry up and be ready for reunification."

In our case study, it was determined that Client B was ready for reunification due to the following factors: (1) He was actively engaged in both individual therapy and family therapy with his mother, both of which gave him emotional support around the reunification; (2) his presenting trauma symptoms were largely resolved, and he had developed a repertoire of skills for addressing problems; (3) he was able to tolerate and/or verbalize negative affect in himself and others adequately; (4) his "people-pleasing" behaviors were significantly decreased and he related in age-appropriate ways most of the time; (5) he had returned to his mother's care and his home and school functioning were relatively stable; (6) he no longer blamed himself for his victimization and he held the offender responsible for it; and (7) he verbalized his readiness for reunification and had successfully completed specific sexual trauma work including the completion of his own book about the abuse and a list of feelings and questions he wanted to share with or ask the offender.

3. *Family stability. For the offender*: Family stability is crucial for the offender because without it, he or she has no external boundaries to contain and guide his behavior. When assessing family stability with regard to the offender's readiness for reunification, it is important to understand the circumstances that led to the offense(s). Incest often occurs in a family environment of chaos, blurred roles, parental absences, substance abuse, poor handling of negative emotions, family isolation, past abuse histories, and family secrets. The resolution or at least the healthy management of the factors that led to the youth's sexual offending is essential to maintaining family stability and leading to reunification. Before reunification occurs, it is essential to note how the various family members have responded to treatment as well as their level of acceptance of what the victim and offender report as having occurred. Victim statements and offender admissions should not be minimized or denied by other family participants. Family members' denial of victim and offender reports indicates that further therapy is needed prior to face-to-face sessions between the victim and the offender.

Client A's mother had a history of recent psychiatric hospitalizations. This history had a great impact on reunification because her ability to provide a stable and nurturing home environment was compromised by three hospitalizations over the course of the reunification process. Each time the mother was hospitalized, the face-to-face reunification sessions were put on hold because the victim had to be placed in substitute care until his mother was discharged and had become stable again. Management of the mother's psychiatric illness was handled successfully by having her participate in a partial hospitalization program in addition to continuing her own individual treatment to help her to address reunification issues. The reunification sessions began again after the mother was stabilized.

For the victim: Family stability is equated with safety from further victimization in the home. In addition, family stability is necessary for the victim to be able to handle the stress and anxiety usually experienced during the reunification sessions. If the family and home environment are not stable enough, the reunification is likely to trigger some form of regression in the victim's functioning, as described earlier. The victim needs to have some understanding of what will be different from the past in her family to make reunification safe for her. The victim needs to feel secure that the adults are now aware of what went wrong, how the abuse occurred, and their own role(s) in keeping the victim, the offender, and the family safe.

As noted previously, the mother of both Client A and Client B had a recent history of depression and psychiatric hospitalizations. In addition to the impact this history had on her ability to provide a stable home environment, in response to his mother's illness, Client B would revert back to overfunctioning and trying to meet his mother's emotional needs while also worrying that his "bad" behavior in school and at home had caused his mother's emotional problems. For the victim, following each placement, there was a period of adjustment to returning to live with his mother. During this time, treatment focused on establishing a consistent routine for him with clearly identified parent/child roles and boundaries. Coordination with the mother's individual therapist to support her in strengthening her parenting skills became essential at this point. Further, because the mother was treated individually at the same agency, there were several joint sessions between Client B and his therapist and his mother and her therapist to address the issues together. Treatment also focused on behavior management concerns that emerged as Client B became less parentified and began to test his mother's limits in appropriate yet new ways. As stated previously, reunification sessions began only after Client A and B's mother was stabilized and involved in her own individual therapy and a partial hospitalization program.

4. *Family supervision* (also see Appendix 20.4). *For the offender*: As reunification moves forward along the continuum, more responsibility for supervision is turned over to the parent(s). The parent(s) need to be aware of the specific pattern(s) of the sexual abuse, need to understand the probation and treatment limits/guidelines, and must also have knowledge of the offender's high-risk situations and history of grooming behaviors.

In the case example, first, Client A's therapist met with his mother alone to discuss her feelings and concerns about supervising her son in the home and community. His mother had specific concerns about how Client A managed his anger, particularly around the issue of his involvement in her discipline of the victim. Next, the therapist and Client A met with his mother to discuss her concerns with him and to review his relapse prevention plan. Because anger had been a trigger to the sexual abuse of his victims, Client A's mother's concerns were discussed and alleviated in the context of his relapse prevention plan. The discipline concerns were also addressed, and the victim's therapist also participated in explaining to Client A the importance of his not disciplining his victim.

For the victim: Family supervision is an essential element of reunification readiness as its failure in the past contributed to the victimization. With many victims, a common symptom of sexual abuse is sexual reactivity and sexualized behavior, at times with other children. Therefore, the family is not only responsible for supervising the offender and the victim in their home environment but must also supervise the victim around her own sexualized behavior with others in and/or outside the family. This supervision must be done with a balance of appropriate monitoring without overprotection and with an approach of education and understanding rather than a punitive or blaming response. When handled well, a sexually reactive victim feels secure that her family will provide supportive supervision to help her to feel both safe and assisted in controlling and managing her sexual impulses.

Before reunification sessions began with the offender, Client B participated in several preparatory sessions individually and with his mother. Safety and supervision issues were discussed regarding the upcoming reunification sessions and visits. Client B responded positively to helping to develop a set of guidelines and family rules for safety and supervision for his interactions with his brother/offender. He seemed to feel empowered by the input he gave around his feelings and thoughts about his interactions with the offender. Once sessions and visits began, Client B had no trouble verbalizing his feelings about what he liked and disliked about the sessions and subsequent visits.

5. *Parental readiness. For the offender and the victim* (also see Appendix 20.5): The evaluation of parental readiness for reunification must be made by achieving the most comprehensive understanding of the offender, of the victim, and the family dynamics and circumstances that surrounded the sexual abuse. The parent(s)' perspective and response to treatment must be unwavering in their acceptance that the victim is not responsible for the abuse while also believing in and supporting the offender's recovery. In addition, the parent(s)' need to have addressed the multiple and complex issues that go along with knowing that one of their children has sexually abused another one of their children. Managing their feelings can be challenging, particularly if the parent(s) have their own personal abuse issues that may be triggered. Working through the issues can best be achieved by having their own individual treatment and utilization of parent support groups and psychoeducational classes that are sex offense-specific.

6. *Sibling readiness*: Siblings of the identified victim and offender must be included in the reunification readiness evaluation and treatment if they are or will be living as part of the family. If the same offender also sexually abused other siblings, the S.A.F.E.R. model must be applied to the other sibling victims in the same manner described. Sibling victims must each be viewed separately in terms of their own individual treatment needs and readiness for reunification. When sibling victims share the same offender, it is important for the other family members to respect the needs and time frame of each victim and not expect or pressure siblings to be at the same level of readiness for reunification at the same time.

In such situations, it will be incumbent upon the treatment team to explore when and how to proceed with reunification for each sibling at his or her own pace. In these cases, reunification of the family may occur in segments and may not be fully achieved due to the variable needs of all of the sibling victims.

With regard to nonabused siblings, their feelings and needs around the reunification process also need consideration. Nonabused siblings were affected by the impact of the sexual abuse in their family, and they often have a multitude of feelings related to the abuse and the reunification. Some nonabused siblings may be symptomatic and in need of a segment of their own individual and/or family treatment. Further, siblings believed to be nonabused may in fact have been abused by the offender or by someone else but have not yet disclosed and may be able to disclose in the context of their own treatment. If nonabused siblings will be part of reunification visits, they must also be included in some but not necessarily all the reunification sessions. The timing and level of their involvement will depend on the specific family dynamics of the case.

In our case, there were no other siblings in the family, so sibling treatment was not a component. Unfortunately, the young cousin who was also abused by Client A, was not a part of our treatment due to his parent(s)' denial of the effects of the abuse on their son.

The Reunification Case Conference

As noted in Figure 20.1, the Reunification Case Conference is the component that follows the completion of the Service Delivery Evaluation Factors and the Family Evaluation Factors. The purpose of the Reunification Case Conference is for the service delivery providers to come to a consensus and render a single overall judgment with regard to reunification. Probation/parole officers, therapists, case managers, and other significant members of the service delivery team comprise the conference participants. The offender's and victim's therapists complete the Service Delivery Provider Ratings and also the appropriate family evaluation factor checklists illustrated in Appendices 20.2 through 20.8, which are presented and discussed during the case conference.

These Service Delivery Provider Ratings and Family Evaluation Factors serve as a guide to indicate whether or not reunification is recommended. They can also help to identify areas of strengths and weaknesses regarding the family's overall adjustment and interaction with the service delivery providers. Further, the ratings and the case conference can assist the primary therapists for the victim and the offender in identifying additional areas to be addressed before reunification can occur. The interdisciplinary team's decision and recommendations are communicated to the family by the therapist(s). If the decision of the team is for reunification to begin, the family and therapist(s) move on to the steps to reunification.

The Steps to Reunification

The S.A.F.E.R. model includes four steps in the actual process of family reunification: (1) family reorientation, (2) appropriate apologies and hearing each other, (3) reintegration, and (4) discharge and aftercare (also see Appendix 20.8).

Step 1: Family Reorientation. Once the victim, the offender, and the family have completed their own treatment, the next phase includes combined treatment sessions for the victim, the offender, the parent(s), and the siblings. Ideally, the offender and the victim have not had any contact with each other until the reunification sessions begin. Initially, family reorientation involves separate readiness sessions for the victim and the offender with their parent(s) and their own individual therapist. If the parent(s) are also in their own treatment, they can benefit from some of their own readiness work. During these sessions, each explores his or her thoughts, feelings, hopes, and expectations for the upcoming reunification treatment sessions. It is often important for the therapist(s) to help the individual family members to formulate realistic expectations for their interactions with each other during the initial phases of reunification treatment sessions.

For the face-to-face reunification sessions, it is preferable to have the victim's and the offender's therapists facilitate the sessions together. The sole focus of the initial face-to-face session(s) is to help the family to become reoriented with each other as individuals and as family members. Because in many instances, several months, or even years may have passed since the victim and the offender and possibly other family members have spent time together, the focus needs to begin with ways to reconnect before moving into the "work" of addressing the sexual abuse issues. The initial session should be well planned with a positive atmosphere around the family's ability to come together. The fact that sexual abuse occurred in the family should be verbalized directly and should include some acknowledgment of how hard each person has worked to be ready to begin reunification. This acknowledgment should, however, be offered only as a brief statement of truth and not as the focus of the initial reorientation session.

Spontaneous conversation about what it feels like to see and be with each other should be encouraged. The therapists may need to take the lead in helping the family members to look at the positive things they shared as a family in the past in spite of the abuse. Reminiscing is a good way for the victim and offender, as well as the parent(s), to become reoriented as a family. A shared activity such as a board game or card game about feelings is a useful tool to give the family an enjoyable focus for reconnecting. This is also an opportunity for the therapist(s) to sit back somewhat and observe and comment on the family's interactions.

The reorientation step can be completed in one or several sessions depending on the family's dynamics and the therapist(s)' assessment of their needs and level of comfort with each other. Before this step is completed, the family and the therapists should discuss and plan Step 2. The victim's wishes, if appropriate, should be given precedence when planning the details of the subsequent reunification sessions. For example, the victim should be encouraged to decide where in the room and next to whom she would like to sit and at what point she would like to share her feelings about the abuse (if at all) with the offender and parent(s).

Client A and Client B participated in one reorientation session that included their mother and each of their individual therapists. Prior to the reorientation session, the victim's therapist joined a few of the offender's sessions with his therapist to plan and process how the victim was likely to respond to the sessions. This enabled the offender to anticipate and plan appropriate ways to support his brother (victim) as they reconnected. During the first step, the reorientation session, Client A, Client B, and their mother participated in a family board game while Client A's and Client B's individual therapists observed and supported a positive interaction. Client B decided where each person would sit and asked if he could hug his brother (Client A) if he wanted to. The therapist agreed that his choice to do this would be empowering for him. The reorientation session was very positive for this family, and they spontaneously shared many happy memories as brothers and as a family. The victim and offender each noted how much the other had changed.

Step 2: Appropriate Apologies and Hearing Each Other. The expectation of the offender in this step is to apologize to the victim and read his victim empathy letter to the victim. The offender can be prepared for this step ahead of time by role-play and empty-chair techniques. The victim's therapist can also be engaged in this process by having the offender read his empathy letter to the victim's therapist. This also gives the victim's therapist the opportunity to evaluate the offender's level of empathy and to give any necessary input about the letter on behalf of the victim before it is shared with the victim during the session.

The empathy letter has eight parts and is modeled from the empathy assignment in the Safer Society workbook, *Empathy and Compassionate Action* (Freeman-Longo, Bays, & Bear, 1996): (1) apologize to the victim, (2) take responsibility for the abusive behavior, (3) give a description of behavior with no minimization, (4) acknowledge that the victim has the right to feel whatever she feels, (5) do not to ask the victim for forgiveness, (6) encourage the victim not to blame herself or others for what the offender has done, (7) encourage the victim to get help for the abuse, and (8) close by giving the victim hope for the future and apologize again.

The "hearing each other" step also includes the offender explaining his abusive behavior and being held accountable for the abusive acts. The offender should listen to the feelings of the victim and other family members without being judgmental or defensive. At this point the offender's potential for blaming the victim should be low, but if blaming does occur, it must be confronted and stopped immediately.

After the offender has read the empathy letter, the victim is offered the opportunity to share feelings about the abuse and to ask the offender some specific questions if she chooses to. Most victims need the opportunity to plan this with their own individual therapist. Victims may benefit from writing a letter about their own feelings or making a list of thoughts and feelings to share during a session. It is extremely important that sharing is only offered to the victim as an option, and the victim should not feel pressured to share any thoughts or feelings unless she wants to do so.

The parent(s) should also be encouraged to share their own thoughts and feelings about what it was like for them to have the sexual abuse happen in the family. Again, the parent(s) may benefit from a session to plan this sharing as well. It is important for the therapist(s) to support the parent(s) to be honest about their negative feelings about the abuse and the losses in the family, as well as to share positive feelings of pride around the children's work on the abuse and the healing process.

It is important to remember that although the idea of face-to-face contact between the offender and victim has been discussed and prepared for, the reality of facing each other may be quite different from each person's idea about what it would be like to face each other. The face-to-face contact will be stressful for all involved, and it is important for the therapist(s) to function as teacher, guide, advocate, resource person, crisis manager, and supportive and confrontive clinician(s).

Step 3: Reintegration. Reintegration focuses on the specific details around how the family has changed and healed since the abuse occurred. This step helps the family to look closely at how they will stay healthy and safe around the abuse issues. This step also includes the offender's review of his personal safety plan (also see Appendix 20.6) during a session with his victim and family present. The offender's safety plan should cover relapse prevention, ways to escape and avoid the cycle of offending, identification of warning signs and the high-risk situations for offending, and a description of how the offender will engage the safety plan. In addition, the safety plan for the offender should clearly delineate how his time is structured, who comprises the offender's support system, and how ongoing monitoring will be established. Supervision issues and plans for supervision are also outlined in the safety plan.

In addition to the offender's personal safety plan, the family as a whole should develop a contract about family rules and safety. This is an activity that works well as a joint discussion during a session in which everyone discusses what the family rules will be for safety, supervision of the victim and the offender, privacy, nudity, bathing, physical touching, and sleeping arrangements. Everyone should understand the rules and should sign the contract to indicate an agreement to follow the rules. Appendix 20.7 provides an example of a Family Rules and Safety Contract.

Reintegration also covers a clarification of the steps of contact outside the therapy setting. Because the home is often the place where the offense occurred, it can be packed with emotional memories for the victim, the offender, and the other family members. We feel that it is preferable to have the family meet at a neutral location for their first supervised contact outside the therapy sessions. The victim should be encouraged to choose where she would like the first visit to occur. A professional such as the family's social worker should supervise the initial family contact(s) outside therapy, if possible. Supervision for these meetings needs to be addressed and planned during the prior sessions.

Conjoint family therapy sessions that include the victim, the offender, and the parent(s) with the victim's and offender's therapists should continue, generally on a biweekly schedule, in concurrence with the outside visits that are taking place. During these sessions, the family can process their feelings about the visits and any problems or conflicts can be addressed. The clinical team assesses the family's progress and makes recommendations for decreasing or increasing the visits.

After several face-to-face therapy sessions and the completion of Steps 1, 2, and 3, Client A and Client B participated in their first meeting outside the therapy setting at a restaurant. Their mother and Client A's case manager from his group home supervised this meeting. The case manager acted as a chaperone and participated in a few family sessions prior to being placed in a supervisory role. The visit went well, and we moved to supervised visits within the home. The process of reintegration was discussed in the family sessions as well as in the victim's and the offender's individual therapy sessions. Communication with and feedback to the therapists from the case manager was essential in allowing the process to move along successfully.

Step 4: Discharge and Aftercare. It is not unusual for families to regress and experience separation anxiety when the treatment providers start to discuss discharge and aftercare issues. Regression may indicate that treatment is moving too fast, and the process should be slowed down in order to continue to meet the family's needs. It may also mean that the family has connected so well with the service delivery team that the separation anxiety is a healthy indicator of positive change. If the family is responding well to reunification and things are stable, such regression can be interpreted as fear of not being able to manage their lives without the support and guidance from the familiar treatment providers. The offender and victim therapists should remain central in coordinating with the family and the service providers through this period.

Indicators for discharge include the low risk of the offender for recidivism, the stability of the family, and the adaptive resolution of the sexual abuse trauma by the victim, the offender, and the family as a whole. In addition, the offender and the family should be actively engaging the relapse prevention plan so that the victim will experience an ongoing sense of safety and trust. When preparing for discharge, it is prudent that the therapist(s) set up incremental reductions in contact with the family so that their adjustment to less supervision and therapeutic contact can be monitored. It is important that the therapist(s) continue to engage the other providers in the system so that decisions are not made in a "therapeutic vacuum." The decision for termination from treatment should be reached through communication with the Reunification Case Conference participants. It is important that the individuals and the family are encouraged to contact the treatment providers to seek consultation if any problems regarding the abuse issues arise in the future.

The Reunification Continuum

Gail Ryan and Sandy Lane (1997) describe reunification as moving through various levels from full or partial reentry, to minimal or even no contact. The continuum in Figure 20.1 illustrates these variations. In considering where to place the offender, the victim, and the family along this continuum, it is imperative that the needs of the victim and community safety continue to be placed above the offender's needs or wishes. The factors that place the family along the continuum are extracted from the family's responses to the various services and stages of treatment. Ideally, the stages of treatment should be (1) concurrent individual treatment for the victim, the offender, and the parents; (2) conjoint therapy with the victim and parents; (3) conjoint therapy with the offender and parents; (4) conjoint therapy with the offender, the victim, and the parents; and (5) family reunification sessions.

The reunification continuum is a conceptual framework for therapists to assess the progress of the victim, the offender, and the family with regard to victim and offender contact. There may be disagreement among the service delivery providers about if, when, and how to address reunification. These issues should be discussed in the Reunification Case Conference with a consensus of the best interests of the family with the victim(s)' safety as paramount. Often, the court or other referring agency requires that reunification be a part of the treatment plan. Therapists may disagree with reunification in some cases but still may have little control over whether or not reunification will occur. Therapists often begin with a goal of full contact but after working with the family may ultimately feel that minimal or partial contact is clinically indicated. Minimal contact is defined as face-to-face sessions within the treatment setting. These are used to assess further movement along the continuum. Partial contact means supervised visits outside the therapy setting, and full contact refers to a decrease in supervision outside of the therapy setting leading to the offender's returning to the home. It is important that these steps are assessed at each point by ongoing risk assessment and utilization of the factors that are delineated throughout the S.A.F.E.R. model.

Conclusion

The S.A.F.E.R. model was developed as a guide for therapists working toward family reunification between a juvenile sex offender and his or her victim. The model is based on the treatment experiences of a juvenile offender therapist and a child victim therapist who worked together on family reunification in such cases. In our experience, ongoing collaboration between the two therapists was essential throughout the treatment process in assessing the offender, the victim, and the family regarding readiness for reunification and in facilitating the steps along the reunification process. For families in which one child has sexually abused another, the issues of anger, hurt, betrayal, and guilt can seem insurmountable. We feel that the collaborative work described in the S.A.F.E.R. model offers the families the opportunity to process the complex feelings and issues of the sexual abuse in a supportive and therapeutic context. Further, treatment based on this model provides families with a sense of hope for the future. It also enables families to gain a specific understanding of the issues that contributed to the occurrence of the sexual abuse and provides guidelines for examining and ensuring safety in their family system as they work toward appropriate reunification.

Reference

Freeman-Longo, R., Bays, L., & Bear, E. (1996). *Empathy and compassionate action issues and exercise: A guided workbook for clients in treatment.* Orwell, VT: Safer Society Press.

Porter, E. (1986). *Treating the young male victim of sexual assaultIssues and intervention strategies.* Orwell, VT: Safer Society Press.

Ryan, G., Lane, S., & Rinzler, A. (1997). *Juvenile sex offending: Causes, consequences, and correction.* San Francisco: Jossey-Bass.

Appendix 20.1
Service Delivery Provider Rating Scale

Both the offender therapist and the victim therapist complete this rating scale. Each clinician rates the components of service delivery by placing an "X" along the continuum as shown below using the case example of Client A and Client B. The reason for the rating and problem areas is then briefly described below each continuum.

1. Treatment Alliance Rating:

   For the Offender:

Inadequate	*Adequate Enough*	*Very Adequate*
	X	

Reason for the Rating: (Based on the Case Example) Client A's relationship with his individual therapist is good. Client A is receptive to outpatient treatment. The therapist's relationship with Client A's parent (mother) is good. <u>Problem Area</u>: Client A and his mother have difficulty accessing the child welfare social worker.

   For the Victim:

Inadequate	*Adequate Enough*	*Very Adequate*
	X	

Reason for the Rating: (Based on the Case Example) Client B has developed a positive relationship with the therapist. His mother is also fully engaged in the treatment process.

2. Coordination of Services Rating:

   For the Offender:

Inadequate	*Adequate Enough*	*Very Adequate*
	X	

Reason for the Rating: The therapist was in contact with Client A's residential therapist prior to discharge. The residential therapist supported reunification contingent upon Client A remaining committed to treatment as an outpatient. Client A's outpatient therapist and his victim's therapist have been in close contact and are in agreement on indicators for and the process of reunification. The child welfare social worker is informed of and also agrees with the reunification process.

   For the Victim:

Inadequate	*Adequate Enough*	*Very Adequate*
	X	

Reason for the Rating: The victim's therapist communicated closely with the offender's therapist and his mother's therapist. All of the clinicians are in agreement regarding the process for reunification. <u>Problem Area</u>: Client B's mother has been hospitalized for depression several times lately necessitating foster care and extended family placement for Client B. The child welfare social worker has not followed through with necessary services or plans for the family.

3. Flexibility for the Family's Needs Rating:

For the Offender:

Inadequate	Adequate Enough	Very Adequate
	X	

Reason for the Rating: The Group Home can provide supervision of Client A in the home when the reunification visits occur. The treatment team has adjusted to Client A and B's mother's psychiatric hospitalizations that postpone and prolong the reunification sessions. <u>Problem Area</u>: The Group Home is inflexible about permitting client A to work in the community.

For the Victim:

Inadequate	Adequate Enough	Very Adequate
	X	

Reason for the Rating: The treatment team is very supportive of pacing the reunification process around Client B's needs in consideration of his instability due to placement following his mother's hospitalizations. Client B is living in an adequate foster home that is supportive and flexible about his contact with his mother. The foster mother follows through with the victim's therapy appointments.

4. Availability of Resources Rating:

For the Offender:

Inadequate	Adequate Enough	Very Adequate
	X	

Reason for the Rating: Client A could benefit from being permitted to work in an appropriate job, but his Group Home refuses to grant permission. Other resources are available if needed (e.g. medication, intensive support services, forensic testing, increased community supervision).

For the Victim:

Inadequate	Adequate Enough	Very Adequate
	X	

Reason for the Rating: Client B's mother is connected to an intensive partial hospitalization program and has been stabilized on medication. However, the in-home support services she was given did not work out well due to slow referrals by the child welfare social worker and subsequent turnover of staff at the in-home service agency.

5. Adequacy of Monitoring Rating:

For the Offender:

Inadequate	Adequate Enough	Very Adequate
	X	

Reason for the Rating: Client A has been removed from the home for several years due to his sex-offending behavior. Current monitoring by outpatient treatment and the Group Home is satisfactory.

For the Victim:

Inadequate	Adequate Enough	Very Adequate
	X	

Reason for the Rating: Client B's mother has a strong understanding of the sexual abuse and is vigilant about supervising her son with regard to both his offender (brother) and his own sexually reactive behavior.

6. Adequacy of Care Rating:

For the Offender:

Inadequate	Adequate Enough	Very Adequate
	X	

Reason for the Rating: Client A successfully completed sex-offense-specific residential treatment and is compliant with outpatient treatment. His risk for sexual reoffending is assessed as low. His mother has cooperated with treatment and qualified professionals are providing the treatment.

For the Victim:

Inadequate	Adequate Enough	Very Adequate
	X	

Reason for the Rating: During times when his mother was most stable, Client B has been able to complete a significant amount of direct sexual trauma work. Even when she was hospitalized, Client B's mother stayed in communication with his therapist and urged his temporary caregivers to make sure that he continued to attend all of his therapy appointments. Communication among clinicians continued to be excellent.

7. Adequacy of Planning for the Length of Treatment Needs Rating:

For the Offender:

Inadequate	Adequate Enough	Very Adequate
	X	

Reason for the Rating: The child welfare system has implemented procedures that will allow for Client A to remain under their jurisdiction until he is twenty years old (another three years). Client A will move into a supervised independent living arrangement and will continue with supportive counseling after the completion of sex-offense-specific treatment.

For the Victim:

Inadequate	Adequate Enough	Very Adequate
	X	

Reason for the Rating: Client B has completed specific sexual trauma therapy and almost all of his initial symptoms are resolved. Client B has adjusted to living with an aunt and sees his mother several times weekly. His mother is aware of her current emotional limitations and is realistic about her son's need for stability in her sister's home for the time being. Client B's mother understands that her son can return for additional treatment if necessary in the future.

Appendix 20.2
Checklist for Offender Readiness for Reunification

❑ No denial or minimization of the abuse. No blaming the victim(s).

❑ Has been cleared for visits by service delivery providers (e.g. therapist, judicial system, and child welfare system).

❑ Is stabilized in the community and shows the ability to delay gratification, to manage frustration, and to cope with negative emotional states successfully.

❑ The assessed risk for reoffending is low.

❑ Demonstrates an investment in treatment, a curiosity to understand why he offended, and wants to know how to prevent relapse.

❑ Accepts that together with the therapist(s), the nonoffending parent, and family members will decide if, when, where, and how much reunification will occur. Accepts the supervision plans.

❑ There are no significant differences between the victim statement(s) and the offender admission(s).

❑ If forensic testing such as polygraphs, the Abel Screen, or penile plethsysmography, have been administered, the results do not negatively impact reunification.

❑ Shows willingness to disclose details of his offending to all involved in the family support system.

❑ Has completed victim empathy task and shows genuine remorse. Has an intellectual and emotional understanding of the effects of sexual abuse on the victim(s) and family.

❑ Accepts the possibility that if the relapse prevention plan is not followed, he is at risk to reoffend.

❑ Is not socializing with a delinquent or antisocial peer group. No "I don't care what happens to me" attitude. If client has an Axis II diagnosis of antisocial personality disorder, assess the degree of pychopathy for a reduction in criminal thinking, lifestyle, and behavior.

❑ Has and uses a support system (probation officer, therapist, caseworker, friends, work, significant other). Shows an interest in and has the capacity to maintain intimate relationships.

Appendix 20.3
Checklist for Victim Readiness for Reunification

❑ The victim has completed a course of individual or group treatment focused on the sexual abuse.

❑ The primary symptoms of the sexual abuse have been resolved and home/school functioning is stable.

❑ Has demonstrated a full range of affect and the ability to verbalize his or her own feelings and needs.

❑ Has been able to acknowledge or discuss his/her victimization at some level.

❑   Can identify some feelings about his or her victimization such as sadness, confusion, anger, fear, etc.

❑   Can share some thoughts and/or feelings about the offender.

❑   Expresses some genuine interest in reunification with the offender.

❑   The home environment is stable enough to support treatment/reunification.

❑   Responds well to the emotional support of the family and therapist(s) and can participate in planning sessions prior to reunification.

❑   Clearly understands and can verbalize the rules and boundaries of sexual touching.

❑   Has a healthy sense of self and personal identity (e.g., has friendships with peers; participates in social activities).

❑   Has good refusal skills—the ability to say "No" and assert self in a variety of situations.

❑   Self-blame is absent or minimal and the victim can clearly state that the offender is responsible for the sexual abuse.

❑   Gives appropriate safety responses to possible risky situations involving the offender.

Appendix 20.4
Family Supervision Factors

1. The nonoffending parent(s) are knowledgeable and supportive of the offender's relapse prevention plan including:

    A. The sexual assault cycle

    B. Triggers and high risk situations

    C. Grooming behaviors

    D. Escape and avoidance methods

2. The family's ability to supervise the offender is assessed throughout the duration of treatment. Points of assessment should include the following:

    A. The offender's compliance to the relapse prevention plan.

    B. The supervising parent(s)' degree of collaboration with service delivery providers.

    C. Supervision of contact between the offender and any children.

        i.   The offender should have no responsibility for supervising or disciplining the children.

        ii. The offender should never discuss sexuality with minors.

        iii. The offender is never to engage in horseplay with minors.

        iv. The offender is not to be alone with any children.

        v.   No discussion of the sexual abuse is to occur except in treatment settings.

        vi. No use of alcohol or drugs.

        vii. The offender is not to participate in the physical care or bathing of children.

viii. Depending on their ages, locks should be on all doors so that children can lock their rooms when they want to.

   ix. Any gift giving by the offender to children should be discussed first through the therapy process.

3. Together in treatment sessions, the family completes and signs a detailed contract for safety and boundaries in the home. Such a contract delineates the specific rules for supervision, nudity and privacy, physical affection, etc. (See Appendices 20.5 and 20.6 for examples.)

4. The therapist(s) and service delivery providers need to have knowledge of who is living in the home. Families in which sexual abuse has occurred are often very chaotic with various relatives or friends moving in and out of the house. This may contribute to boundary blurring and changes in family dynamics, which can affect stability.

5. External supervision should be provided by probation/parole officers and others who are knowledgeable about sexual offending behaviors.

Appendix 20.5
Parental Readiness Checklist

❑ The parent(s) are clear about their role in supervising all interactions between the offender and the victim both in and away from the home.

❑ The parent(s) can be both confrontive and nurturing with the offender.

❑ The parent(s) are actively engaged in the process of family recovery. Recovery is not seen as an end point but an ongoing healing process that may be similar to the stages of grief (i.e. denial, depression, anger, bargaining, acceptance, and hope).

❑ The parent(s) are not engaged in the abuse of alcohol or drugs. If in recovery from substance abuse, they are actively engaged in recovery.

❑ The parent(s) are not involved in any criminal activity.

❑ The parent(s) agree to be part of the offender's support system and relapse prevention plan.

❑ The parent(s) can set consistent limits and consequences without abusing their power.

❑ If the parent(s) have a psychiatric illness, they are also stabilized in their own treatment.

❑ The parent(s) have open, honest, and direct communications with each other and can model this in the family.

❑ The parent(s) are able to set and maintain clear and unwavering emotional, sexual, physical, and psychological boundaries.

❑ If intergenerational sexual/physical abuse is present in the family, these issues have been addressed in treatment and have been processed in regard to the current abuse.

❑ The parent(s) are willing to hear sexually deviant information from the offender without being abusive or responding in a way that will isolate the offender.

❑ The parent(s) can support the victim to be assertive about a full range of feelings and needs in relationships with others including the offender, and do not blame the victim for the abuse and disruption of family life.

❑ The parent(s) can negotiate conflicts between the victim and the offender appropriately and without bias toward either child.

Appendix 20.6
Checklist for Offender Safety Plan

❑ The offender's relapse prevention plan is implemented in the home and community.

❑ The offender has identified allies that he/she can go to and discuss feelings, concerns, problems, or worries.

❑ The offender is not to discipline the children.

❑ Warning signs and high-risk situations are acknowledged and understood.

❑ High-risk situations are identified and prevented.

❑ Opportunities for offending are acknowledged and minimized.

❑ Supervision is done only by those who are aware of the family's sexual abuse history and have been taught how to supervise the offender.

❑ Boundaries are respected.

  A. Bathrooms and bedrooms are private. Doors are closed when someone is using the bathroom.

  B. Closed doors mean that someone wants privacy and others should ask permission or knock before entering.

  C. Family members are always clothed in the presence of others.

  D. The offender is not to play games with the children that may lead to sexual behavior (e.g., Catch-A-Girl-Kiss-A-Girl; Doctor; or Simon Says)

Appendix 20.7
Family Rules and Safety Contract (Sample)

1. Keep the bathroom door closed. Keep the bedroom doors closed when you are getting undressed.

2. If a door is closed, knock on the door and wait for an answer before going in.

3. Brothers and sisters will sleep in separate beds and in separate rooms.

4. It is okay to touch your own private parts when you are alone, but do not touch other people's private parts.

5. Everyone can hug each other if both people want a hug. Kissing on the cheek is okay.

6. Brothers and sisters will not kiss each other on the mouth.

7. If someone wants to touch your body in a way that is not okay, say "No," then tell an adult right away.

8. It is not okay to use sexual words or body parts to make jokes such as, "Kiss my butt."

9. If anyone feels uncomfortable about anything at all, tell an adult.

AS SHOWN BY THE SIGNATURES BELOW, EVERYONE IN THE FAMILY AGREES TO FOLLOW THE RULES
WRITTEN ABOVE.

_____   _____

Client A   Client B

_____   _____

Mother   Stepfather

_____

Sister

_____   _____

Psychotherapist   Date of Contract

Appendix 20.8
Steps to Reunification

Step 1: Family Reorientation:

The focus of this step is for the family to reconnect with each other in a positive way.

A. Separate evaluations of the victim(s), the offender, and the parent(s) indicate that face-to-face contact is appropriate.

B. Realistic expectations of the family's interactions with each other are formulated.

C. Face-to-face sessions are well planned with a positive focus around coming together.

D. Ideally, the victim and the offender therapists facilitate the face-to-face sessions together.

E. During the initial session, the family acknowledges that the sexual abuse is a painful truth that required hard work from everyone in order for reunification to begin.

Step 2: Appropriate Apologies and Hearing Each Other:

The focus of this step is an explanation of and accountability for the sexual abuse.

A. The offender is expected to apologize and read the victim empathy letter to his victim.

B. The offender is to listen to the feelings of the victim if the victim is ready to share them, and the offender is to emphasize to the victim that the abuse is not his/her fault.

C. Each family member processes his or her own feelings about the abuse with the offender.

Step 3: Reintegration and Safety Planning:

The focus of this step is to plan for safety for the family's reintegration visits.

A. The offender shares his personal Safety Plan with his victim and the family.

B. Together, the family members develop and sign the Family Rules and Safety Contract.

C. Supervised visits to occur outside of the treatment setting are planned and implemented on a gradual basis while the treatment sessions continue.

D. Gradually, the outside visits increase to unsupervised day visits followed by overnight visits while treatment sessions continue at least biweekly.

Step 4: Discharge and Aftercare:

The focus of this step is to plan the final stage of reunification and discharge from treatment.

A. The victim(s) feel safe and ready for the level of reunification agreed upon for the family.

B. The reunification goals have been achieved.

C. The family has successfully managed an increased level of contact outside of the treatment setting and they are able to supervise themselves safely.

D. The Reunification Case Conference team supports discharge and finalizes the partial or full reunification plan.

E Aftercare plans are in place and are designed to meet the family's needs after discharge.

Chapter 21

The Treatment of Multiple Abuser Youth in Forensic Foster Care— A Social Responsibility Therapy Program Description

by James M. Yokley, Ph.D.

Portions of this chapter were presented at the 16th annual Research and Treatment Conference of the Association for the Treatment of Sexual Abusers in Arlington, Virginia (Yokley, Laraway, & Sprague, 1997). Portions were reproduced from *The Social Responsibility Therapy Work Book: Understanding Abuse Behavior* (Yokley, 1995) as well as *The TASC Program Manual* (Yokley, 1993) with permission from the author. A more detailed description of social responsibility therapy can be found in Yokley (2000).

Overview

This chapter describes the treatment of multiple abuser youth in Forensic Foster Care. Multiple abuser youth exhibit sexually abusive behavior along with other types of abuse that warrant treatment (i.e., physical abuse, property abuse, substance abuse and trust abuse). Forensic Foster Care is a family-based treatment setting for multiple abuser youth whose externalizing behavior can result or has resulted in legal problems. Forensic Foster Care employs social responsibility therapy to help youth control multiple forms of abuse by developing social-emotional maturity as a competing response; developing an understanding of how abusive behavior was acquired, maintained, and generalized; and demonstrating the social responsibility to make restitution. Forensic Foster Care provides another level in the continuum of care between residential and outpatient treatment for multiple abuser youth whose behavior management needs require gradual reentry into the community under supervised conditions when no appropriate family placement exists.

Introduction

Since the foster care population consists primarily of children removed from their homes as the result of neglect or abuse, a brief discussion of this population is warranted. As they get older, children who have been abused or neglected are more likely to perform poorly in school, commit crimes against persons, and experience emotional problems, sexual problems, and substance abuse (Sedney & Brooks, 1984; Starr, MacLean, & Keating, 1991).

Although family functioning moderates the impact of abuse on victims (Brock, Mintz, & Good, 1997), it appears that in general males tend to exhibit more externalizing reactions and are at greater risk for abuse toward others whereas females tend to experience internalizing reactions and are at risk for revictimization. For example, a seven-year foster care follow-up study revealed that physically abused boys were more likely than abused girls to engage in criminal (externalizing) behaviors as adults

(Fanshel, Finch, & Grundy, 1989). Abused boys are more likely than abused girls to identify with the original aggressor and eventually to abuse their spouse and children (Carmen, Reiker, & Mills, 1984). Since the battering of women is associated with more physical aggression toward sons than daughters (Jouriles & Norwood, 1995), the modeling of externalizing behaviors in violent homes may have more of an influence on males than on females. In addition, since viewing self as a victim "is clearly a more difficult identity issue for males than for females in our society" (Cunningham & MacFarlane, 1996, p. 18) seeking relief by "identifying with the aggressor" and physically abusing others after being abused is inherently more likely in males.

This gender split also appears to occur with the impact of sexual abuse. National surveys consistently demonstrate that one in four girls and one in seven boys are sexually maltreated before puberty (Finkelhor, 1984). If both males and females who were molested went on to molestations at the same rate, there would be a great deal more female sex offenders. Despite the fact that almost twice as many child sexual abuse victims are female, most sexual abuse is by males on female children (Faller, 1989; Finkelor, 1979; Russell, 1983; Wyatt, 1985). These data indicate, as many researchers have noted, that males tend to cope with abuse by externalizing their behavior whereas females tend to cope through internalization (MacFarlane, Cockriel, & Dugan, 1990; Summit, 1983). In other words, "boys appear to be more likely to turn their pain into rage and project it outward onto others, while girls typically convert pain into depression and turn it inward on themselves" (Cunningham & MacFarlane, 1996, p. 18).

Therapeutic foster care, like other social service systems, must focus on meeting the needs of the majority of its consumers. Although no single symptom occurs in the majority of abuse victims, sexually and physically abused children frequently manifest internalizing problems such as posttraumatic stress disorder (PTSD), guilt, depression, anxiety, and withdrawal (e.g., Dubner & Motta, 1999; Livingston, 1987; Williamson, Borduin, & Howe, 1991). Dedicating resources for caretaker training and child treatment to the majority of consumers who are young female abuse victims with internalizing problems does not address the treatment and developmental needs of older, externalizing males. Caretaker training and child treatment with generic humanistic counseling or traditional supportive psychotherapy for the elimination of guilt, shame, depression, anxiety, and other internalizing symptoms does not provide the more structured, behavioral interventions needed to help relieve conduct problems, abusive behavior, and other externalizing symptoms.

Traditionally, therapeutic foster care has been in the difficult situation of having to provide for those exhibiting both internalizing and externalizing symptoms with generic therapeutic tools for caretaker training and child treatment. The "therapeutic parent model" was developed by adopting the generic client-centered therapist characteristics considered "necessary and sufficient" (Rogers, 1957) for therapeutic change that were common to all successful therapies regardless of orientation while avoiding the characteristics of abusive parents (Shealy, 1995). Thus in "the therapeutic parent model" youth caretakers were taught to demonstrate acceptance, empathy, and understanding while avoiding hostility, criticism, and mixed messages. Although many of these therapist characteristics that were put forth more than forty years ago (Rogers, 1957) are still considered "necessary," they are no longer considered "sufficient" as therapeutic interventions have now become much more refined and specific. As the result of many advances in psychotherapy evaluation which directly relate to parenting problem children, research reveals that generic training and treatment approaches cannot be equally effective without modification to address specific disorders (e.g., Casey & Berman, 1985). Recent abuse specific treatments that address the internalizing reactions of child victims (e.g., Cohen, Mannarino, Berliner, & Deblinger, 2000) and the externalizing reactions of youth abusers (e.g., Chamberlain & Reid, 1998; Henggeler, Schoenwald, & Pickrel, 1995) are now available for integration into specialized foster care. Forensic Foster Care addresses the needs of externalizing youth with multiple forms of abusive behavior by integrating abuse treatment techniques into their caretaker training and youth treatment plans.

Forensic Foster Care

Forensic medicine applies medical knowledge to legal problems. Forensic Foster Care applies treatment knowledge to foster youth whose externalizing, abusive behavior can result or has resulted in legal problems. Forensic Foster Care fulfills several important system-level treatment needs of youth who have been removed from their homes. First, Forensic Foster Care offers specialized treatment to youth with externalizing problems involving acting out emotions, conduct disorder, and multiple forms of abusive behavior. This is important because the primary focus of existing therapeutic foster care is on treating children who exhibit internalizing problems, including adjustment disorders and other conditions associated with being a victim of abuse or neglect.

Second, this treatment setting offers a less restrictive environment than residential treatment for youth offenders who are not candidates to complete treatment in the outpatient setting due to problems with placement in their family of origin. Third, Forensic Foster Care offers another level in the continuum of care between residential and outpatient treatment for youth abusers whose behavior management needs require gradual reentry into the community under supervised conditions. These youth abusers may now enter a step-down treatment supervision process, progressing from residential treatment to Forensic Foster Care and, finally, to the traditional outpatient setting during family reunification or independent living placement.

Forensic Foster Care program youth are given an opportunity to live in the community in a family setting (i.e., specialized foster home), attend regular school, and receive their treatment as in a functional family with special supervision. There is some evidence that Forensic Foster Care offers a functional family treatment setting that is most conducive to helping youth with a history of behavior that can or has resulted in legal problems. For example, incarcerated boys who were randomly assigned to a Forensic Foster Care program designed to address their special needs ("multidimensional treatment foster care") had significantly fewer criminal referrals and returned to live with relatives more often than did those who received group home care (Chamberlain & Reid, 1998). Thus, Forensic Foster Care is potentially a more cost-effective alternative to continued residential treatment. The Forensic Foster Care program discussed in this chapter, Treatment for Appropriate Social Control (TASC), has been successfully developed, evaluated, and refined over the past seven years. Table 21.1 provides a summary of three basic types of foster care.

The TASC Forensic Foster Care program includes key components associated with foster parent retention. These components include highly specialized parent

Table 21.1
Comparison and Contrast of Three Basic Types of Foster Care

	Regular Foster Care	Therapeutic Foster Care	Forensic Foster Care
Age	66% are under age 13[1]	66% are under age 13[1]	100% are 13 and older
Population served	Primarily serves neglected and dependent children[2] with home environment problems[5]	Primarily serves victims[3] of abuse (most are female) with internalizing[4] and adjustment problems (e.g., PTSD, depression, anxiety, withdrawal)	Exclusively serves youth offenders (most are male) with externalizing, conduct problems (e.g., abusive behavior, dishonesty, defiance, aggression)
Focus	Has strong family support focus	Has strong child support and protection focus	Has strong community protection focus
Clients	Child and parents are the "clients"	Child is the "client"	Youth and community are the "clients"
Treatment	Treatment is optional as needed	Treatment is provided separately from foster care, typically by a general practitioner in weekly Community Mental Health Center visits	Foster parents are an integral part of a treatment team of abuse specialists who provide the therapeutic community treatment approach throughout the week

[1] Benton Foundation (2000).

[2] Neglect is by far the most common form of maltreatment, affects about twice as many children as do physical and sexual abuse (English, 1988). 68% of children removed from the home in California were as the result of neglect (42%) or dependency (caretaker absence or incapacitated, 26%). Little Hoover Commission (1992).

[3] 20% of children removed from the home in California were as the result of physical (12%) or sexual (8%) abuse. Little Hoover Commission (1992).

[4] Sexually and physically abused children frequently manifest internalizing problems such as posttraumatic stress disorder, guilt, depression, anxiety, and withdrawal (e.g., Dubner & Motta, 1999; Livingston, 1987; Williamson et al., 1991). Thus, victim treatment requires interventions that address internalizing symptoms.

[5] Neglected children seem to be less aggressive and more passive than are physically abused children (Green, 1978; Hoffmen-Plotkin & Twentyman, 1984) but have more school performance problems (Eckenrode, Laird, & Doris, 1993; Golden, 2000) making treatment referrals less urgent than in cases where symptoms are externalized through aggressive, abusive behavior.

training (Chamberlain, Moreland, & Reid, 1992; Urquhart,1989) and a team approach where foster parents are integrated into all aspects of youth treatment (Sanchirico, Lau, Jablonka, & Russell, 1998). In addition, a cluster placement model where youth are accepted into more than one foster home at placement admission acts to maximize foster parent support (Urquhart, 1989) and minimize any adverse impact that could be associated with home moves (Proch & Taber, 1985). TASC Forensic Foster Care uses social responsibility therapy to teach youth prosocial alternatives to antisocial abusive behavior.

Simulating a Therapeutic Community Treatment Environment. "It takes a village to raise a child": The high level of structure and positive peer culture are two of a number of important aspects of the highly successful therapeutic community treatment model that matches the needs of youth with abuse behavior problems. Although it is not possible to recreate every aspect of the closed therapeutic community milieu in the open outpatient environment, Forensic Foster Care simulates key aspects of the therapeutic community positive-peer-culture treatment environment. For example, youth are admitted into a foster cluster setting of several foster families who have a shared parenting and activity arrangement, which simulates the extended family milieu of the therapeutic community. The foster family cluster is like the therapeutic community environment in which fellow residents are viewed as "brothers" and "sisters" who must accept their mutual obligation to help each other and hold each other accountable as a family of humans. The therapeutic community discouragement of sexual relationships between residents who are viewed as "brothers" and "sisters" is taken to the next level in Forensic Foster Care, where sexual relationships are viewed as "foster family incest" and are labeled a sex offense relapse.

In therapeutic foster care, different foster families have youth with different types of problems seeing different treatment providers, primarily in different individual therapy sessions. In Forensic Foster Care all the foster families in the forensic foster cluster have youth with the same abusive lifestyle problem seeing the same treatment providers in the same positive-peer-culture group setting exactly as in a residential therapeutic community. The phase system of responsibilities and privileges used in Forensic Foster Care is similar to the highly structured hierarchy of job functions and privileges found in therapeutic communities. The social responsibility therapy focus on developing honesty, trust, loyalty, concern, and responsibility used in Forensic Foster Care is essentially the same as the therapeutic community focus on developing a positive lifestyle. Although therapeutic community learning experiences for abusive lifestyles have traditionally been used in residential settings, these modifications have allowed the use of therapeutic community learning experiences to develop social-emotional maturity and self-control in the outpatient Forensic Foster Care setting.

Treatment Approach: Social Responsiblity Therapy. Forensic Foster Care uses social responsibility therapy (SRT), a treatment approach that addresses abuse by teaching prosocial alternatives to antisocial, abusive behavior. The prosocial/family values focus of SRT make it easily accepted and inherently adaptable for foster parent participation. This abuse behavior treatment has been adapted across the years to accommodate multiple abusers of different age groups in different settings. Multiple abuser youth are youth sex abusers who exhibit more than one type of abuse requiring treatment (i.e., physical, property, substance, and trust abuse in addition to their sexually abusive behavior). Each type of abuse exhibited by these youth involves a maladaptive way for them to assert power, get what they want, and make themselves happy, often at the expense of others. Each type of abuse also involves a pathological level of social-emotional immaturity.

In SRT, abusers develop a socially responsible, positive lifestyle by learning to demonstrate appropriate social behavior control and social-emotional maturity with an emphasis on honesty, trust, loyalty, concern, and responsibility. SRT was designed for individuals who have developed behavioral patterns that are abusive or destructive to themselves and/or others. In SRT, abuse is abuse and it is not sufficient for the abuser to stop sexually abusing others but continue other forms of abuse. SRT targets sexual abuse, physical abuse, property abuse, substance abuse, and trust abuse for relapse prevention directly and through social maturity development. In addition to an expanded treatment focus targeting more than one type of abuse, SRT has expanded the understanding of abusive behavior beyond the typical abuse maintenance cycle provided in most relapse prevention programs to encompass abuse acquisition, maintenance, and generalization.

A final distinction to be made in SRT has to do with avoiding diagnostic labels that diminish the abuser's responsibility for his or her behavior and focusing on the impact of the abuser's behavior. Alcohol and drug treatment divides the seriousness of the problem into two levels by using definitions of abusers (basically, someone whose behavior is excessive but still under his or her willful control) and dependents (or addicts—basically, someone whose behavior is excessive and no longer under his or her willful control). The alcohol and drug treatment concept of addiction is not appropriate for the treatment of individuals whose abuse can or has hurt others. It is too tempting for interpersonal abusers to use a label of addiction as an "I couldn't help it" excuse to avoid responsibility for the impact of their abuse on others. In this respect, one addiction treatment handbook has already categorized those behavioral problems that primarily have an impact on others (e.g., sexual abuse, domestic violence, and the alcohol-affected family) as "socially destructive addictions" (L'Abate, Farrar, & Serritella, 1992).

The important distinctions in SRT are the severity of the behavior and whether the abuser's behavior is primarily harmful to self, harmful to both self and others, or primarily harmful to others. This abuse severity and impact is referred to as the Abuse Behavior Continuum (see Figure 21.1).

Population Targeted for Social Responsibility Therapy: Multiple Abuser Youth.
Most cognitive-behavioral treatments focus on one specific type of abuse behavior (e.g., substance abuse, physical abuse, property abuse, sexual abuse, food abuse, or money abuse). SRT targets multiple forms of abuse behavior.

A brief justification of multiple abuser treatment appears to be warranted given the prevailing focus on the need to provide "offense-specific treatment" for sexual abusers. The basic reason SRT targets multiple forms of abuse is that the referral type of abuse is not usually the only type of abuse, and one type of abuse can trigger another.

Many Abusers Are Multiple Abusers. Youth with sexual behavior problems do not have the specific, entrenched sexual abuse behavior pattern (e.g., specific age, sex, and type of sexual behavior) that adult pedophiles exhibit. They also have not settled on a specific type of abusive behavior to use in externalizing (acting out) their feelings. Thus, various combinations of multiple forms of abusive behavior are quite common in youth sex abusers. Exhibiting multiple forms of abuse in addition to other

Figure 21.1
The Abuse Behavior Continuum: Selected Abuse Examples

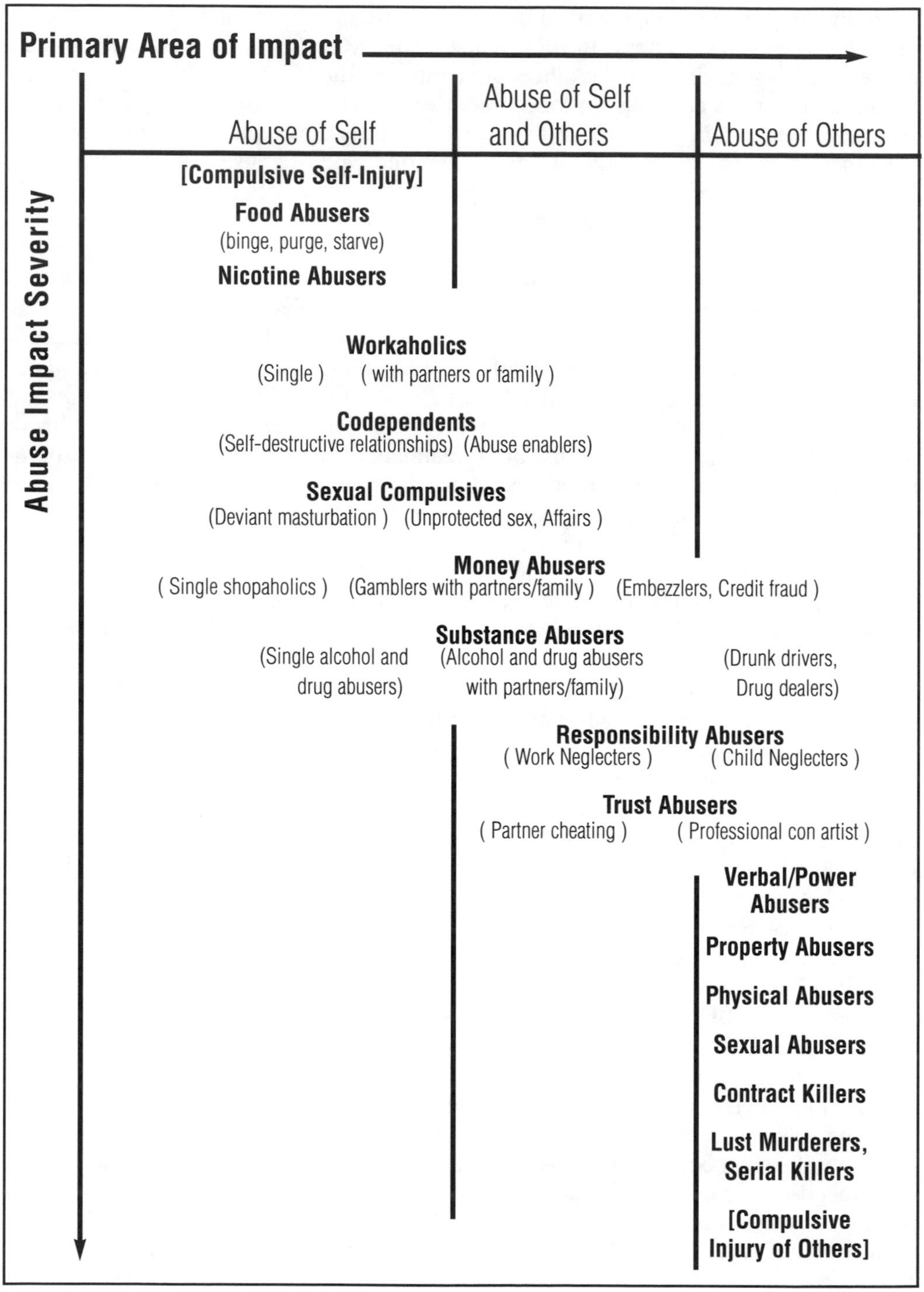

Primary Area of Impact ⟶		
Abuse of Self	Abuse of Self and Others	Abuse of Others

Abuse Impact Severity ↓

[Compulsive Self-Injury]
Food Abusers
(binge, purge, starve)
Nicotine Abusers

Workaholics
(Single)   (with partners or family)

Codependents
(Self-destructive relationships) (Abuse enablers)

Sexual Compulsives
(Deviant masturbation)   (Unprotected sex, Affairs)

Money Abusers
(Single shopaholics)   (Gamblers with partners/family)   (Embezzlers, Credit fraud)

Substance Abusers
(Single alcohol and   (Alcohol and drug abusers   (Drunk drivers,
drug abusers)   with partners/family)   Drug dealers)

Responsibility Abusers
(Work Neglecters)   (Child Neglecters)

Trust Abusers
(Partner cheating)   (Professional con artist)

Verbal/Power Abusers

Property Abusers

Physical Abusers

Sexual Abusers

Contract Killers

Lust Murderers, Serial Killers

[Compulsive Injury of Others]

deviant behaviors (e.g., drug use, vandalism, theft, poor academic performance, sexual precociousness, personal aggression, and disregard for the law) has been demonstrated to be a common phenomenon among adolescents in the research literature (Andrews & Duncan, 1997; Jessor & Jessor, 1977). Adult sexual abusers also frequently commit nonsexual crimes. For example, a meta-analysis of sixty-one treatment studies (predominantly follow-ups) revealed that, on average, the sex offense recidivism rate was 13.4% and the recidivism rate for nonsexual violence was 12.2% (Hanson & Bussière, 1998).

Demographic data from the TASC Forensic Foster Care program revealed that average age was 16, 97% were male, and 72% were Caucasian. The average number of different types of abuse exhibited was 4.5, and 59% exhibited problems at admission with five types of abuse (i.e., sexual abuse, physical abuse, property abuse, substance abuse, and trust abuse). Fifty-three percent were on probation or parole (Yokley & Boettner, 1999).

These Forensic Foster Care abuse behavior data are consistent with other research reports of youth sex offenders which indicates that youth abusers do not limit themselves to exhibiting one specific type of abuse on the Abuse Behavior Continuum (see Figure 21.1; Yokley, 1995). Youth who sexually abuse frequently have histories of other types of abuse and criminal activity. Sex abuser research indicates that 41% to 86% have histories of other types of abuse and criminal activity (Amir, 1971; Awad, Saunders, & Levene, 1984; Becker, Kaplan, Cunningham-Rathner, & Kavoussi, 1986; Fehrenbach, Smith, Monastersky, & Deisher, 1986; Shoor, Speed, & Bartelt, 1966; Van Ness, 1984; Yokley, 1996). Substance abuse between types of interpersonal abusers is roughly the same; for example, sexually abusive, physically abusive, and delinquent juveniles revealed the same level of use and binge pattern in all three groups (Tinklenberg, Murphy, & Murphy, 1981). Because sex offense relapse relates to general criminal behavior as well as specific sexual deviance and sex offenders frequently commit nonsexual crimes (Hanson & Bussière, 1998), comprehensive risk assessment and treatment of sexual abusers needs to address multiple forms of abusive/criminal behavior.

The "Vampire Syndrome" Is Not Always the Case. The "vampire syndrome" (i.e., committing the same type of abuse that was experienced) has been observed in a number of types of abusive behaviors. For example, 19% to 81% of adolescent sexual abusers were previous victims of sexual abuse (Becker et al., 1986; Fehrenbach et al., 1986; Friedrich & Luecke, 1988; Longo, 1982) and 38% of adolescent sex offenders come from homes that evidenced sexual deviation (Awad et al., 1984).

However, the "vampire syndrome" is not always the case. In the "abuse conversion syndrome," trauma from one form of past abuse is converted into any form of abusive behavior that can act to relieve the traumatic stress (i.e., a maladaptive coping reaction to relieve helplessness and increase feelings of power/control). This is seen in adolescent sexual abusers where an estimated 41% to 54% report having been physically abused or neglected (Van Ness, 1984). Child abuse and neglect are strongly related to later substance abuse (Ivanoff, Schilling, Gilbert, & Chen, 1995; Sheridan, 1995). In substance abusers, approximately 44% to 47% were victims of sexual abuse (Cohen & Densen-Gerber, 1982; Glover, Janikowski, & Benshoff, 1995). Being exposed to sexual, physical, or emotional abuse correlates significantly with developing multiple forms of self-abuse (e.g., substance, food, or money abuse) in addition to sexual addiction (Carnes & Delmonico, 1996).

Alcohol impairs judgment, increases the probability of aggression, and disinhibits sexual behavior (e.g., Dermen & Cooper, 1994). Lifetime drinking problems significantly predict current criminal behavior (Greenfield & Weisner, 1995). Crimes most frequently involving alcohol abuse are sexual abuse (34%–75% in four rape studies: Lightfoot & Barbaree, 1993; Scully & Marolla, 1984); physical abuse (20%–80% in twelve wife abuse studies: Carden, 1994); and homicide (19%–83% in ten study reviews: Fendrich, Mackesy-Amiti, Goldstein, Spunt, & Brownstein, 1995). In their review of the literature, Sees and Clark (1993) noted that that abstinence from other substances was enhanced by abstinence from nicotine. Cigarette smoking, in addition to posing its own health risks, is often associated with use of other substances. Continued smoking appears to place abstinent alcohol and drug abusers at elevated risk for relapse. Cross or substitute addictions are conditions associated with (drug/alcohol) relapse (Chiauzzi, 1989; DeLeon, 1997). One report revealed that 19% of those in treatment turned to one new addiction before a full-blown relapse, whereas 43% developed two or more (Chiauzzi, 1989).

In summary, multiple abuser treatment in SRT has a number of advantages for youth sex offenders. In addition to targeting other forms of abuse that can have an adverse impact on the community, result in rearrest, or trigger sex offense relapse through the abstinence violation effect, multiple abuser treatment buffers the damaging effects of labeling. Although labeling may be helpful for those adults who experience some relief at finally being able to identify the condition that has caused them so much difficulty, this is not the case for children whose conditions are still in the formative stages. It is one thing for youth to have to tell their peers that they are in an abuse behavior group and quite another to have to tell them they are in a youth sex offender group. Recent labeling concerns for youth sex offenders have already resulted in changes for the youngest of this population. To avoid unnecessary labeling or stigmatizing of young children, at least one author now refers to preteen sex offenders as "abuse reactive children" (Cunningham & MacFarlane, 1996). Not only does treating "externalizing youth" or "multiple abuser youth" recognize that the referral type of abuse may not be the only type of abuse, but it does not label youth with a specific abuse behavior pattern, which they may not retain later in their adult years.

Multiple Abusers Tend to Exhibit Pathological Social-Emotional Immaturity. Many youth who sexually abuse suffer from "pan-immaturity" in emotional/social adjustment (Fehrenbach et al., 1986; Shoor et al., 1966) and character disorder. Character disordered/antisocial multiple abusers have been described as having serious problems with the following:

- Honesty (i.e., telling blatant or pathological lies: American Psychiatric Association, 1980, 1987, 1994; Buss, 1966; Cleckley, 1976; Hare, 1985; Karpman, 1961);

- Trust (e.g., conning or behaving manipulatively: American Psychiatric Association, 1987, 1994; Hare, 1985; Karpman, 1961);

- Loyalty (e.g., shifting loyalties, inability to form meaningful relationships, inability to sustain relationships: American Psychiatric Association, 1952, 1968, 1980, 1987, 1994; Buss, 1966; Davis & Feldman, 1981; Gray & Hutchison, 1964);

- Concern (i.e., lacks feeling for others; callous to feelings, rights, suffering of others; lacks empathy; self-centered: American Psychiatric Association, 1968, 1987, 1994; Cleckley, 1976; Craft, 1965; Davies & Feldman, 1981; Gray & Hutchison, 1964; Hare, 1985); and

- Responsibility (i.e., irresponsible, unreliable: American Psychiatric Association, 1968, 1980, 1987, 1994; Cleckley, 1976; Davies & Feldman, 1981; Gray & Hutchison, 1964; Hare, 1985).

Pathological social-emotional immaturity is a developmental delay that involves the following:

- Immature, maladaptive social maturity in the form of a prosocial values deficit (e.g., a lack of honesty, trust, loyalty, concern, and responsibility) that impairs the ability to develop positive, healthy relationships; and

- Immature, maladaptive emotional maturity manifest as inadequately developed self-control (e.g., a lack of appropriate social behavior control,[1] emotional control problems including low frustration tolerance,[2] an emotional awareness deficit, and "justifying actions based on feelings") and maladaptive self-image and needs (e.g., low self-efficacy; a control and power obsession; an excessive need for acceptance, excitement, or sensation seeking; authority problem and criminal pride for "getting over" on others; and need to win by intimidation or other opportunistic exploitation that demonstrates a lack of empathy). With respect to peers, criminal pride involves putting dishonest people before honest people. In many cases this involves putting friends before family.

Theoretical Underpinnings of Social Responsibility Therapy. SRT focuses on the development of social and emotional maturity as key factors, which are incompatible with abuse behavior. Teaching clients behaviors/responses that are incompatible with the problem behavior/response dates back to the highly successful behavioral treatment of tension and anxiety by teaching the incompatible response of relaxation (Wolpe, 1995). This theoretical approach—reciprocal inhibition or counterconditioning—is straightforward: Teaching the competing behavior inhibits or blocks the problem behavior. In the case of anxiety, humans simply cannot be tense and relaxed at the same time. Thus, if they are taught to relax as an automatic response (or first line of defense) during tense situations, anxiety attacks are not triggered. This approach was originally used with anxiety and other neurotic problems, and a 90% significant improvement rate was reported (Wolpe, 1958). This approach has also been used successfully with a number of other clinical treatment problems, including inhibiting anger reactions (Hearn & Evans, 1972) and sexual behavior problems such as exhibitionism (Lowenstein, 1973), sexual intercourse genital pain (Haslam, 1965), and frigidity (Chapman, 1968).

It is not possible to exhibit abuse behavior and social-emotional maturity (i.e., prosocial values and appropriate social behavior control) at the same time. Put another way, it is not possible to be an out-of-control abuser while caring about others and controlling one's self. Thus, social-emotional maturity includes important competing responses to abuse behavior that abusers need to learn (i.e., prosocial values and appropriate social behavior control).

SRT teaches youth the prosocial/family values of honesty, trust, loyalty, concern, and responsibility to compete with antisocial abusive behavior. Teaching these family values is necessary to promote family relationships, support, and bonding, which has been found to reduce psychological distress in women and general deviance in men, to produce academic motivation, to reduce substance (marijuana) use in younger adolescents, and to reduce future poor parenting (Andrews & Duncan, 1997; Newcomb, 1997; Newcomb & Loeb, 1999).

In SRT, therapeutic community learning experiences are adapted to the foster cluster treatment group environment and are considered an important part of the intervention tools used to develop social-emotional maturity as well as appropriate social behavior control. Like a number of other sex abuser treatment approaches (e.g., relapse prevention and Twelve-Step groups), therapeutic community learning experiences were also adapted from the substance abuse field. Therapeutic communities have been treating this type of socially immature, irresponsible, acting-out character disorder since 1958 when Synanon began to offer residential treatment to heroin addicts who engaged in multiple forms of abuse and crime (Yablonsky, 1969).

SRT uses therapeutic community learning experiences to address abuse behavior and develop social-emotional maturity for a number of important reasons. First, this approach targets the abusive "criminal lifestyle" characterized by substance abusive, irresponsible (e.g., history of unstable employment), immature (i.e., usually younger) individuals with maladaptive thinking (e.g., procriminal attitudes) and high-risk (i.e., criminal) peer associates (Gendreau, Little, & Goggin, 1996) by developing a competing prosocial lifestyle (DeLeon, 1989).

Second, therapeutic community learning experiences address the special needs of the abuser population. Because socially and emotionally immature abusers are not good vicarious learners and learn best by experience, therapeutic community learning experiences employ experiential treatment approaches that frequently require action on the part of the client.

Third, the therapeutic community approach has solid research support. Significant decreases in criminal involvement after treatment have been demonstrated for both adults and adolescents in the community setting (DeLeon, 1984, 1987; Pompi, 1994) as well as inmates in the corrections setting (e.g., Wexler & Love, 1994).

Fourth, this approach fosters emotional maturity and empathy. Therapeutic community learning experiences get the abuser in touch with the feelings of others, provide role-reversal experiences, and develop emotional expression responding, which satisfies the three-component model of empathy (Feshbach & Feshbach, 1982) found to facilitate prosocial behavior and reduce aggressive behavior (Eisenberg & Miller, 1987; Miller & Eisenberg, 1988).

Fifth, the therapeutic community approach targets a similar population. Both youth referred for therapeutic community substance abuse treatment and those referred for sexual abuse treatment exhibit pathological social-emotional immaturity. This has been documented in the form of immaturity in emotional/social adjustment, a lack of empathy, character disorder, problems delaying gratification, lying, manipulation, and irresponsible acting out (DeLeon, 1989; Fehrenbach et al., 1986; Sgroi, 1982; Shoor et al., 1966).

Social Responsibility Therapy

The three basic treatment components of SRT in Forensic Foster Care involve socially responsible, research-informed treatment procedures and abuse rules with a community safety and security priority. The three basic components are:

1. *Stopping abusive behavior by* developing appropriate social behavior control and social-emotional maturity as competing responses to abusive behavior.

2. *Understanding abusive behavior* by completing an SRT workbook and making a presentation on the Abuse Development Triad (Yokley, 1996) covering how abusive behavior was acquired, maintained, and generalized.

3. *Developing prosocial skills* including emotional restitution to both direct and indirect victims of abuse during victim responsibility training (Yokley, 1990).

After orientation and evaluation where basic assessment and relapse prevention occure during a probation period prior to admission, SRT has three basic phases. During these phases, abuser privileges and community supervision are directly linked to their level of treatment progress, social maturity, and responsibility. The Orientation/Evaluation, Phase 1, Phase 2, Phase 3, and aftercare components in Forensic Foster Care are described in Yokley (1993). These three basic responsibility phases are associated with the aforementioned three treatment components. Figure 21.2 provides a summary of SRT in the TASC Forensic Foster Care program.

Stopping Abusive Behavior. "You're only young once, but you can be immature your whole life." SRT stops abusive behavior by developing appropriate social behavior control and social-emotional maturity as competing responses to abuse

Treatment plans that focus on internal attitude change with the expectation that external behavior change will follow are not appropriate for abuse behavior treatment. Since many abuse behaviors are self-reinforcing, treatment providers have to stop the behavior externally before they can get the client to implement internal behavior change procedures to maintain abuse abstinence. Stopping abusive behavior by developing self-control and social-emotional maturity as competing responses to abuse is accomplished through the following:

- *The use of therapeutic community learning experiences* (i.e., behavioral and social learning through experiential, participant modeling procedures developed by Charles Dietrich, Albert Bandura. and B.F. Skinner).

- *Teaching competing responses to abuse behavior* (i.e., learning incompatible responses and promoting change through cognitive dissonance with procedures developed by Joseph Wolpe and Leon Festinger).

- *Implementing research-informed community safeguards* and abuse behavior rules.

Figure 21.2
Social Responsibility Therapy in the TASC Forensic Foster Care Program

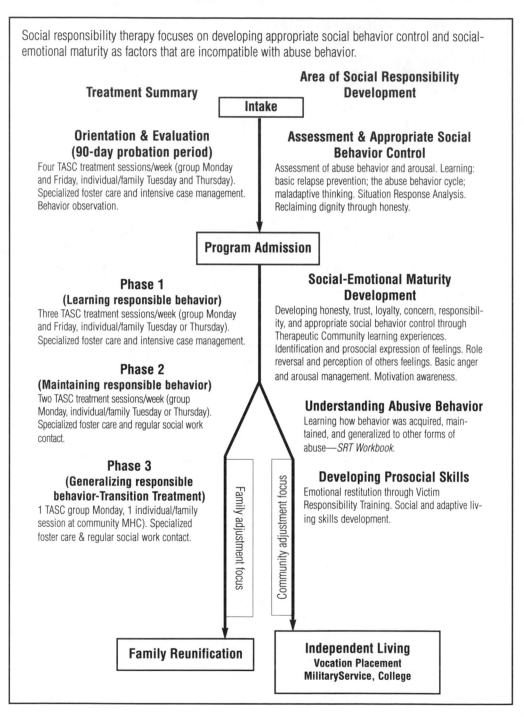

The Use of Therapeutic Community Learning Experiences. Therapeutic community learning experiences aid in tolerance training, treatment motivation enhancement, learning to delay gratification, and other key factors in the development of self-control and social-emotional maturity. Learning to control abuse behavior is the social responsibility of all abusers and the first important component in SRT. This is accomplished by incorporating therapeutic community learning experiences into the treatment regimen along with special parenting skills (i.e., ten three-hour sessions each year) and special supervision methods designed to meet the specific needs of this externalizing, abusive population.

Since there are always advances one can make in the area of social emotional maturity, this treatment component extends throughout the duration of SRT. The basic goal of this treatment component is to block immature, antisocial/abusive, destructive behavior by learning competing mature, prosocial, constructive behavior. Developing social-emotional maturity and appropriate social behavior control is accomplished through the use of therapeutic community learning experiences in conjunction with selected cognitive-behavioral interventions and relapse prevention techniques for abusive behaviors. Therapeutic community learning experiences consist of a combination of natural and logical consequences, which can be viewed as behavior therapy or social learning within the context of a positive peer culture and experiential framework. Since these learning experiences effectively address antisocial, abusive behavior, they serve the purpose of protecting the safety and security of the community while benefiting the abuser (see Yokley, 1999a, 1999b, for a more detailed description of therapeutic community learning experiences).

Teaching Competing Responses to Abuse Behavior. Key factors in the development of self-control and social-emotional maturity include such competing responses as honesty, trust, loyalty, concern, and responsibility. In SRT, these five prosocial competing factors are used to block five types of antisocial abuse behavior (i.e., sexual, physical, property, substance, and trust abuse).

When operationally defined for treatment purposes, some basic examples of social maturity used in treatment goals include the following:

- Being honest enough to hold one's self accountable by disclosing problems that otherwise would not be discovered.

- Trusting others enough to drop criminal pride by sharing real feelings of helplessness, hurt, and inadequacy and allowing the tears that accompany these feelings to be seen in group.

- Being loyal to program rules and what the youth knows is right when peers are pressuring him or her to do otherwise. Pushing past authority problems to make connections with appropriate adults and reestablish positive family loyalty.

- Having enough concern to accept the social responsibility to provide emotional restitution and make amends to direct and indirect victims of abusive behavior. Using confrontation with concern for those who are slipping. Doing things for others when there is nothing to be expected in return. Considering the impact of actions on others as well as their viewpoints and feelings.

• Being responsible enough to take initiative; do tasks at home, school, and work without being told; complete tasks that have been started, making a 100% effort.

When operationally defined for treatment purposes, some basic examples of emotional maturity used in treatment goals include the ability to do the following:

• Identify feelings being experienced; perceive and understand feelings in others (empathy);

• Exhibit adequate frustration tolerance, block justifying an actions based on feelings, and redirect feelings into constructive outlets;

• Form positive social attachments, express love while not mistaking intensity for intimacy, and derive satisfaction out of helping others;

• Push past feelings of tension, anxiety, and insecurity to reach out to others and try new things;

• Delay gratification regarding getting even or acting out;

• Adapt to change and suppress fight-or-flight responses when under stress (i.e., face problems without going AWOL, assaulting, or using drugs/alcohol);

• Consider the future and plan ahead long range;

• Exhibit appropriate social behavior control, which includes knowing how to do the following:

— Recognize and correct maladaptive thinking;

— Recognize and avoid high-risk situations;

— Analyze responses to situations;

— Resolve conflict without physical violence;

— Accept constructive feedback;

— Hold self accountable for own behavior;

— Accept the consequences of behavior without blaming others or acting out feelings (of self-disappointment either for losing control or for getting caught);

— Role-reverse, consider the impact of your behavior on others as well as "do unto others as you would have others do unto you"; and

— Think ahead, play social chess under stress, "If I do this, they'll do that" (i.e., ability to consider immediate consequences of your behavior under pressure).

An important step in the social-emotional maturity development for abusers is to reclaim their dignity through their honesty and to develop appropriate social behavior control through therapeutic community learning experiences. Abusers pass through three important phases on their path to reclaiming dignity through honesty and emotional restitution:

• Phase 1: Abusers pass their first honesty exam, which involves a presentation to their treatment group and significant others (e.g., guardians, relatives, parents, and partners) after passing a polygraph exam on who the victims were and what the abuse did to them.

• Phase 2: Abusers develop an understanding of their abuse behavior and clarify this understanding in a presentation to their treatment group and significant others.

• Phase 3: Abusers clarify their social responsibility for their behavior and apologize to both direct and indirect abuse victims in a supervised session in which all victim questions are answered.

Competing responses to abuse behavior (i.e., honesty, trust, loyalty, concern, and responsibility) are continually improved through the CARE (Computer-Assisted incident Report Evaluation) system which helps identify problem behavior patterns that require therapeutic community learning experience intervention (Yokley & Boettner, 1999).

Implementing Research-Informed Community Safeguards and Abuse Rules. Many children removed from their homes exhibit externalizing disorders involving disruptive behavior (Pilowsky, 1995). Forensic Foster Care directly addresses foster family and community safety concerns (e.g., Horton, 2000; Wilkenson & Baker, 1996) with special safeguards. Since abuse behavior relapse means both harm to others as well as removal of the youth abuser from community treatment, community safety and security are priorities. The TASC Forensic Foster Care program provides twelve basic home safeguards and twelve basic community safety/supervision procedures. Program rules are research-informed and community access is earned on a level system linked to behavior control. State-of-the-art communication, behavior tracking, and supervision technology are employed.

The SRT use of "going to the opposite extreme" with abuse abstinence treatment goals was influenced by the previously discussed research indicating that one type of abuse can trigger another along with the abstinence violation effect literature (Marlatt & Gordon, 1985, 1987). Another influence was an important study in the area of controlled use ("moderation management or harm reduction") versus abuse abstinence by Hall, Havassy, and Wasserman (1989), who followed treated alcoholics, opiate users, and smokers until relapse. These investigators found that abuser relapse was predictable from their self-control goals. Specifically, subjects with the most restrictive absolute abstinence goal were less likely to slip, were less likely to relapse after a slip and had more time between first use and relapse than did subjects with less demanding goals. With respect to setting overall abuse treatment rules policy, these findings tend to indicate the following: "Aim for the stars, fall in the trees, aim for the trees, fall on the ground."

Selection of the therapeutic community philosophy "you have to go to the opposite extreme to meet the median" has defined treatment rules both between and within types of abuse that are listed in the TASC program treatment and community behavior contracts. A few examples follow:

Between types of abuse	*Within types of abuse*	
Don't abuse yourself	Sexual abuse	No pornography
Don't abuse others	Physical abuse	No threats
Don't abuse your treatment	Property abuse	No borrowing
	Substance abuse	No smoking
	Trust abuse	No excuses

Since abuse is self-reinforcing, a critical step in helping abusers develop social-emotional maturity as a competing response to abuse is learning enough emotional constraint to be able to comply with basic supervision, safety, and treatment (e.g, relapse prevention) rules. At this point opinion remains divided on sexual abuser treatment effectiveness, but failure to complete treatment has been found to be a significant predictor of both sexual and nonsexual recidivism (Hanson & Bussière, 1998). The reliable evidence that sexual abusers who attend and cooperate with treatment are less likely to reoffend indicates that treatment programs can contribute to community safety through their ability to supervise and monitor risk (Hanson & Bussière, 1998). Put another way, treatment develops social-emotional maturity and consequent appropriate social behavior control through structure and supervision. Effective supervision is critical to multiple abuser treatment and is "the therapist's best liability insurance."

SRT consists of twelve basic home safeguards and twelve basic community safety procedures that include innovative uses of available communication, behavior tracking, and monitoring technology. Forensic foster home safeguards include youth observation and evaluation procedures, room monitoring, direct communication links with professional staff, and emergency removal procedures. Forensic Foster Care community safety procedures include direct communication links with community youth contacts, viable abuse cycle interruption methods, and containment procedures that limit community access.

Since people do not consistently follow plans if they do not agree, the first safeguard procedure for both the home and community is to get everyone involved to agree on the supervision plans and procedures. Lack of agreement on the supervision plan enables the youth to sabotage supervision efforts by appealing to a team member who does not agree. Thus, all individuals involved with the youth (other youth, therapist, foster parents, caseworker, and parole/probation officer) must sign both the home and the community behavior contracts.

The twelve basic TASC home safeguards are:

Home Safeguard 1: A treatment behavior contract. The contract is signed by the youth, their guardians, treatment providers, and probation/parole officers. The contract details program rules agreed on by all parties. It outlines what is expected of the youth in the home and treatment setting regarding appropriate social behavior control (e.g., no violence, no threats of violence, and staying in control at all times). This includes not abusing others (sexually, physically, verbally), self (using drugs, pornography, going AWOL), or treatment (through denial, negative contracts, hole punching, splitting, assignment refusal). It also includes not entering home or treatment situations that are high risk for abuse (such as unsupervised access to potential victims). Consequences for contract violation are specified and an advanced directive request by the youth to contact authorities to help contain their behavior (if they become a danger to others) is included (Yokley, 1993).

Home Safeguard 2: An incident report behavior management system. Forensic foster parents give the youth the choice of changing their behavior or completing an incident report on themselves. Foster parents give the incident reports to staff who administer therapeutic community learning experiences and behavior consequences based on those reports. This achieves a balance in which foster parents have control over problem behavior but are not the target of revenge for discipline decisions.

Home Safeguard 3: Video/audio tape of abuser treatment sessions. Used for behavior management and youth, foster parent, and probation/parole officer feedback. This safeguard prevents abusers from creating problems between adults that can result in distraction that effects supervision.

Home Safeguard 4: Abuse behavior pattern and arousal assessment. Includes gathering complete records of youth behavior problems in their home and community environments along with contacting past treatment providers for behavior pattern information.

Home Safeguard 5: Regular and random polygraph examination. Clarifies the treatment plan by verifying victim lists and abuser behaviors. In addition, this safeguard prevents unnecessary home moves due to false accusations, promotes child protection in high-risk situations, and reverses past false abuse admissions for secondary gain. For example, some abusers make false admissions to end previous interrogation. Others report trying to continue to look "honest" in treatment and earn privileges by continuing to disclose abuse information, which eventually results in disclosing crimes that were never committed.

Home Safeguard 6: Random drug/alcohol screening. Deters relapse from substance-induced impaired judgment. This is considered important because alcohol impairs judgment, increases the probability of aggression, and disinhibits sexual behavior (Dermen & Cooper, 1994).

Home Safeguard 7: Door alarm. An electronic movement-sensitive door alarm is used during orientation and as needed when relapse signs are exhibited.

Home Safeguard 8: Room baby monitor. A sound-transmitting room baby monitor is used during orientation, when more than one abuser shares a room and as needed when relapse signs are exhibited.

Home Safeguard 9: Random room search. Random searches to check for abuse-related items such as pornography, weapons, and drugs are considered critical to managing abuser behavior.

Home Safeguard 10: Initial and as-needed psychological and psychiatric evaluations. Evaluations to check on emotional stability and help maintain behavior control by providing medical treatment when needed are considered important behavior management safeguards.

Home Safeguard 11: Ability for forensic foster parents to contact staff at all times. Parents receive a wallet contact card with all staff pager, cell phone, e-mail, and fax numbers. Daily parent contact from staff includes reports on abuser behaviors to monitor. E-mail feedback to parents after treatment sessions includes learning experiences to implement for behavior management as well as problems requiring closer observation.

Home Safeguard 12: Emergency placement. Ability to remove youth from the foster home immediately. The TASC program has a respite system involving an immediate transfer to another lower-risk home (e.g., in another school district where the target person does not attend) with group home transfer as a backup procedure to respite.

The twelve basic TASC community safety and security procedures are:

Community Safety Procedure 1: A community behavior contract. The contract is signed by the youth, their guardians, treatment providers, and probation/parole officers. The contract details program rules agreed on by all parties including permission to monitor the youth's behavior in the community and consequences for contract violation (e.g., twenty-four-hour line-of-sight supervision on orientation, total hands-off policy, do not enter community high-risk situations, no contact with victims or potential victims, no baby-sitting, approved associates list, room monitoring, obey the law, respect others' rights of privacy, and no negative contracts) (Yokley, 1993).

Community Safety Procedure 2: A clear list of responsibilities and privileges which limits community access based on behavior. The TASC Forensic Foster Care program uses a three-phase social maturity level system after admission (Yokley, 1993). First there is an orientation/evaluation period, a thirty- to ninety-day probation period prior to admission, during which the youth is restricted to home (room monitor, door alarm, no visitors, uniform). Then:

- Phase 1: Approved school-related supervised activities; approved associates can visit.

- Phase 2: Activities with approved associates added, office visits with appropriate family, office telephone privileges, allowed to get a job, no regular room monitor.

- Phase 3: Overnight visits with appropriate family; foster home telephone use; no door alarm.

Community Safety Procedure 3: Abuse plan/cycle interruption methods. Detention centers are frequently either full or require waiting too long for a juvenile court hearing prior to admission. Moreover, the abuser's out-of-control behavior rarely reflects a mental health problem that makes involuntary hospitalization possible. Thus, the TASC program has implemented abuse-cycle interruption methods such as house arrest, shadowing, and abbreviated boot camp which can be implemented without delay.

Community Safety Procedure 4: A community safety notification system. The legal system continues to wrestle with the issue of under what circumstances mental health professionals and program staff need to notify the community in general and potential victims specifically. Until the courts resolve this issue, the TASC program has instituted a three-step notification procedure summarized as follows: When an abuser enters treatment he has the "green light" in terms of notification, where no disclosure of abuser problems is made to those in contact with the abuser. At the first indication of a loss of appropriate social behavior control, the abuser gets the "yellow light," which involves a partial disclosure of his general behavior control problems. When the abuser is observed in a high-risk situation for relapse or committing high-risk behaviors, he receives the "red light," which involves full disclosure about his abuse behavior problems in meetings with teachers, employers, clergy, or others who have contact with the abuser.

Community Safety Procedure 5: A clergy opinion survey. A survey on sex offenders attending religious services is used to determine the appropriate type of supervision and relapse prevention during religious services (Robinson, Yokley, & Zuzik, 1995).

Community Safety Procedure 6: Pager supervision. The youth receives a pager and only staff/foster parents have the pager number. Whenever the staff/parents page, the youth has fifteen minutes to call back to avoid an incident report and associated consequences for going AWOL.

Community Safety Procedure 7: Shadowing. The abuser is escorted by an adult who is aware of his problem at all times when he is in the community. This procedure has been used successfully to manage the behavior of unruly, abusive youth in alternative schools. There, school administrators have parents of unruly children sign behavior contracts and escort their children in school all day during periods when they exhibit behavior control problems ("Discipline," 1995).

Community Safety Procedure 8: Alternative schooling. Alternative education procedures for abusers who have not graduated from high school such as home instruction, Internet school, day treatment, adult GED classes, and community college courses for high school credit are used as needed given the abuser's behavior pattern and risk level.

Community Safety Procedure 9: An incident report tracking system. An important community safety procedure is to implement a behavior monitoring system that provides objective monitoring of increases in abusive/problem behaviors and decreases in prosocial behavior. The TASC Forensic Foster Care program has established a Computer-Assisted Incident Report Evaluation (CARE) tracking system that provides objective incident report data on current behavior for comparison to past baseline target behavior levels (Yokley & Boettner, 1999). In addition to providing the overall number of incident reports per quarter, this system generates behavior data on the type of abuse, severity, social maturity problem, area where the incidents primarily occur, and intervention impact. Thus, the results of the CARE behavior tracking system allow a behaviorally objective incident report review and behavior pattern "profiling" for community safety decision making.

Community Safety Procedure 10: Gradual supervised community reentry. The safety components of this procedure involve negative peer screening, twenty-four-hour line-of-sight supervision during orientation/evaluation, a "strength" buddy system during Phase 1, and an approved associates list during Phases 2 and 3.

Community Safety Procedure 11: AWOL precautions and deterrent. The traditional AWOL precaution of hospital gown and slippers, although acceptable for other types of abusers, is clearly inappropriate for sexual abusers due to program rules about being completely clothed. In addition, orange prison inmate jumpsuits are too costly. Thus, the TASC program typically uses pajamas or full-length thermal underwear with briefs underneath and slippers during an AWOL risk period. Color digital photographs and descriptions of dangerousness are made up during orientation/evaluation. The descriptions under the photos are assigned to each youth who are told that they are to make up a "Wanted" poster of themselves that is so graphically accurate that the thought of seeing it stapled to community telephone poles would prevent them from even considering running away from treatment. The act of each TASC youth making up his or her own "Wanted" poster description has covert sensitization deterrent qualities that add to this community safety procedure.

Community Safety Procedure 12: AWOL notification plan. Ability to e-mail color digital photographs and descriptions to the local police station upon a youth's going AWOL. Local bus stations, school officials, and other parties who may come in contact with the AWOL youth may also be contacted. Youth who are found and returned typically receive a community risk polygraph on the detailed whereabouts essay they are required to write. They are also escorted by staff to the places they stayed to notify those who harbored them of their situation and the need to contact staff immediately should the youth return requesting a place to stay while AWOL from treatment.

Understanding Abusive Behavior.[3] "If you don't know where you came from you're doomed to return there." A second important component in SRT is understanding how abusive behavior was acquired, maintained, and generalized to other problem areas (Yokley, 1995, 1996). During this treatment component, an SRT workbook is completed, followed by a presentation on the Abuse Development Triad (Yokley, 1995, 1996). The abuse understanding presentation is made in the presence of group members and staff. Involved parties (e.g., probation/parole officers and human services case workers) and significant others (e.g., relatives, parents, and partners) are invited. During this treatment component, the primary contributing factors to abuse behavior are learned in a relapse prevention effort to inhibit further abuse behavior episodes (includes learning cognitive contributors to abuse formulated by Albert Bandura, Samual Yochelson, and Stanton Samenow).

The broad focus on understanding abuse behavior in the Abuse Development Triad expands the knowledge of factors that are important to be aware of or "keep up front" for ongoing relapse prevention. Most sexual abuse treatment programs use understanding the cycle that maintains sexual abuse as the primary focus and framework for their relapse prevention techniques. SRT expands this learning focus by helping multiple abusers understand how their abusive behavior was acquired, maintained, and generalized. The Abuse Development Triad (Yokley, 1995, 1996) involves the chain of events that led up to abuse, the stress-abuse cycle that maintained the abuse, and the anatomy of social maturity problems that set the occasion for abuse to generalize to other areas and that supported multiple forms of abusive behavior (see Figure 21.3).

The Chain of Events That Led to Abuse. The chain of events that led to abuse is a treatment model for understanding how abuse behavior was acquired. This model helps those with abuse behavior problems understand some of the primary contributing factors that led up to their abusive behavior (see Figure 21.3). According to this model: (1) past permanent problems (past trauma, abuse, and other static predisposing historical factors) lead to (2) low self-efficacy (i.e., helplessness, lack of confi-

Figure 21.3
The Abuse Triad: How Abuse Was Acquired, Maintained, and Gerneralized to Other Forms

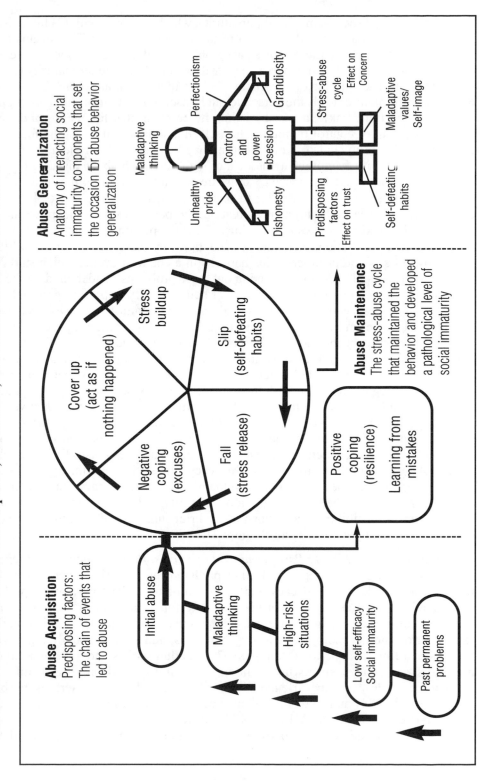

dence/control) and social-emotional immaturity, which combine with (3) high-risk situations and (4) maladaptive thinking to result in abuse behavior. This means that in the first link of the chain, the person's past problems lead him to feel ineffective, powerless or helpless, which stunts personal growth or social-emotional maturity (the second link). The second link of the chain (feeling ineffective and being socially and emotionally immature) leads the person to put himself into situations that are high risk for abuse (the third link). In the third link, he compensates for feeling ineffective, helpless, and out of control by putting himself in a situation in which he feels effective, powerful, and in control. This situation may be one in which the abuser holds a position of authority over others or associates with others who have disadvantages and can be easily controlled. In substance abuse treatment this is sometimes referred to as "associating with inferiors" in order to feel superior, more effective, or less inadequate. Finally, while in the high-risk situation, the person uses maladaptive thinking (the fourth link) which allows him to abuse. Thus the person ends up acting out feelings of anger, frustration, inadequacy, and powerlessness in a manner which is destructive to self and/or others. This happens in a chain of events which starts with having problems and ends up with acting out those problems. Understanding the links in the chain that led up to the abuse behavior helps identify important personal issues that need to be dealt with to improve social-emotional maturity and avoid relapse.

The chain of events that led to abuse is not necessarily linear but is best viewed as a set of primary contributing factors that interact to set the occasion for the initial abuse behavior that warranted a treatment referral. Learning to understand the chain of events that led to abuse helps abusers connect the effect of past permanent problems such as neglect or abuse with their immaturity, low self-efficacy, and tendency to compensate by gravitating toward high-risk situations in which maladaptive thinking is triggered and abusive behavior results. The chain of events helps abusers realize that "there are two things you can't control in life, the past and other people's behavior," which gives them permission to let go of any responsibility they felt for their past permanent problems, low-self efficacy, and social immaturity. At the same time, this model teaches them that developing their self-efficacy through positive accomplishments and their social-emotional maturity by holding themselves accountable is their responsibility now. Following is a brief summary of the links in the chain of events that led to abuse (see also Figure 21.3).

Chain of Events Link 1: Past permanent problems. Past permanent problems are biopsychosocial disadvantages and other predisposing historical factors which set the occasion for low self-efficacy and social immaturity. Past permanent problems include a history of child abuse or neglect; a dysfunctional family; toxic parenting, including absent, disengaged, or enmeshed parents or addicted or criminal parents; removal from home; biological/learning problems; and a dangerous living environment. Regarding dysfunctional families, 67% of adult rapists and 47% of adult child molesters ran away from disruptive homes as youth (Davidson, 1983). Fifty-nine percent of adolescent sex offenders come from families with serious problems (Awad et al., 1984) and 79% of violent juveniles were exposed to extreme family violence (Lewis, Shankok, & Balla, 1979). More than one-third of the mothers and half the fathers of adolescent sex offenders were judged to be rejecting (Awad et al., 1984).

Chain of Events Link 2: Low self-efficacy and social-emotional immaturity. Self-efficacy and perceived control empower persons to be more resistant to pressures or temptations for deviant behavior (Bates & Labouvie, 1995; Hays & Ellickson, 1990; Wills & Shiffman, 1985). Low self-efficacy basically involves feeling incompetent, ineffective, helpless, and hopeless in dealing with life problems, which sets the stage for not being resistant to pressures and temptations. Perceived incompetence can propel a person toward such high-risk situations as involvement with deviant peers, which affords an alternative means of self-enhancement (Wills & Hirky, 1996).

Although previously defined in more detail, social-emotional immaturity basically involves immature, maladaptive social values (e.g., a lack of honesty, trust, loyalty, concern, and responsibility), immature emotional control (e.g., lack of self-control and low frustration tolerance), and maladaptive emotional needs (e.g., for excess control/power, acceptance, and excitement). A sick need for excitement (i.e., sensation seeking or taking physical and social risks for the sake of the experience) is associated with increased adolescent substance use and to a lesser degree other delinquent activities, such as fighting, stealing, destroying property, and trouble with authorities (Bates & Labouvie, 1995; Newcomb & McGee,1991). Youths involved in extensive delinquency show the effects of both social immaturity (feelings of alienation, lack of social closeness) and emotional immature risk taking (Krueger et al., 1994). Social-emotional immaturity has an adverse impact on social behavior as well as achievement (i.e., in school, sports, other extracurricular activities, or even trying to get an after-school job). Low self-efficacy and social-emotional immaturity are logical consequences of past abuse, neglect, dysfunctional families, and toxic parenting. With respect to sexually abusive adolescents, abusive family experiences lead to predictable consequences, including problems with relationships, low self-esteem, and antisocial behavior (Barbaree, Marshall, & McCormick, 1998).

Chain of Events Link 3: High-risk situations. High-risk situations are people, places, or things that disinhibit self-control, trigger abuse behavior, and increase the risk of abuse behavior. It should be noted that what is considered a disinhibitor varies for different types of abuse. For example, interpersonal problems are known disinhibitors for substance abuse and mood-altering substances are known disinhibitors for interpersonal abuse. Entering high-risk situations can involve the need to feel more relaxed or accepted. Entering a high-risk situation may also serve to make those with low-self efficacy feel more effective, competent, or powerful in order to feel "one up" over others, which can set the occasion for abuse. Other reasons for entering a high-risk situation are testing oneself to see whether one can handle the situation and a sick need for excitement or sensation seeking.

An example of a high-risk situation for a sexual abuse episode by a youth with a history of being sexually abused along with a family history of sexual abuse and neglect would be frequently being left home to watch younger siblings whom he resents. Building a deviant sexual arousal pattern by ruminating on and masturbating to deviant sexual fantasies creates another high-risk situation for triggering sexual abuse. A deviant sexual arousal pattern is one of the most consistent predictors of sexually coercive behavior in college students and adults (Prentky & Knight, 1991). Allowing emotional stress to build up by not verbally venting problems of daily living can also create a high-risk situation for sexual abuse. For example, 80% of convicted rapists report a precipitating event involving an upsetting problem of everyday living, 76% of which involved anger over an incident with a wife or girlfriend (Scully & Marolla, 1984). Sexual abusers often report taking comfort in sexual thoughts and behavior when confronted with stressful life events (Cortoni, Heil, & Marshall, 1996).

Chain of Events Link 4: Maladaptive thinking. Maladaptive thinking involves cognitive distortions—including thinking errors; faulty conclusions; biased, inaccurate, or irrational beliefs; false attributions; and affect-impaired perceptions and attitudes—which set the occasion for or allow abuse. Cognitive distortions, biases, and errors are correlates of both adolescent conduct disorder and depression (Kempton, Van Hesselt, Bukstein, & Null, 1994). Cognitive distortions (i.e., attitudes, attributions, thoughts, and irrational beliefs) that mediate emotional arousal and behavior choices are one of the most widely accepted factors in partner aggression (Feldman & Ridley, 1995).

SRT incorporates maladaptive thinking examples from three respected sources. Basic thinking errors from *The Criminal Personality* (Yochelson & Samenow, 1976) are combined with cognitive components from the social learning theory of aggression (Bandura, 1973) along with a set of cognitive distortions designed to help multiple abusers with comorbid depression (Burns, 1980) or pronounced low self-efficacy.

Chain of Events Link 5: Initial abusive behavior. Committing the initial abuse behavior that resulted in a referral is the final link in the chain of events that led to abuse. Initially, the abusive behavior usually artificially increases self-efficacy through external, self-defeating, and antisocial means. According to Ellis (1995), the presence of adversities, neurological anomalies, failures, rejections and stress-overloaded households with easily disturbed relatives leads to deep-seated feelings of worthlessness and hopelessness, more frustration, and low frustration tolerance. This situation, along with old relationships with other addicts, irrational beliefs, and neurotic self-damnation leads the addict to feeling so disturbed that he compulsively compensates through alcohol, drugs, food, gambling, and so on to temporarily allay his disordered thoughts, feelings, and actions (Ellis, 1995). This rational emotive behavior therapy conceptualization of multiple addictions (Ellis, 1995) is similar to the SRT chain of events involving biopsychosocial disadvantages and leading to low self-efficacy and social immaturity, which, combined with maladaptive thinking and high-risk situations, result in abusive behavior.

After committing the initial abuse behavior there is a crossroads where one can use either negative or positive coping, cover it up or open up, let stress build up or use stress management, slip backward or step forward, and fall back into or rise above an abuse behavior pattern. Whether positive or negative coping is used after an abuse behavior episode ultimately determines whether the individual will avoid further problems or enter a cycle of stress and abuse.

The Stress-Abuse Cycle. The stress-abuse cycle is a treatment model to help abusers, their caretakers, and significant others understand how the abuse behavior was maintained. This model helps those with abuse behavior problems understand the components of the cycle that maintained their abusive behavior. Understanding this cycle is considered extremely important in relapse prevention planning as all involved parties need to learn methods to interrupt key components in the cycle of abuse.

Positive vs. Negative Coping: The entrance point to abuse maintenance. The transition from acquisition to maintenance depends on coping. Positive coping (i.e., problem acceptance, honesty, role reversal, and concern) is the more difficult path to take after an initial abuse behavior or episode because problem admission usually brings unwanted consequences. In addition to reclaiming dignity through honesty, trust, loyalty, concern, and responsibility, positive coping develops emotional maturity in the form of the humility, healthy pride, and emotional control needed to hold one's self accountable. Developing social-emotional maturity through positive coping allows better attachments to others as well as decreased life stress, which sets the stage for resilience and slip/lapse avoidance in a positive stress adaptation cycle (see Figure 21.3).

If abusers use negative coping responses to deal with their initial abuse episode, such as denial of the problem or responsibility, they will enter the stress-abuse cycle, which develops social-emotional immaturity, inhibits learning from experience, and sets the stage for other forms of impulsive, destructive, abusive behavior. Abuse relapse typically occurs in a stress-abuse cycle involving the following steps: negative coping, cover-up, stress buildup, slip (lapse), and fall (relapse).

The Stress-Abuse Cycle, Phase 1: Negative coping. Negative coping can happen after a single abuse episode or a period of abuse. Negative coping involves socially and emotionally immature thoughts and behaviors after abusing that avoid dealing with past problems and abuse relapse. During negative coping, abusers hold anything or anyone else responsible for the problem but themselves. They are not honest with themselves about the extent of their abuse problem, the impact of that problem, or even being responsible for the problem. Negative coping involves avoidance of honesty to self and responsibility to others.

Three common types of negative coping include justifying actions based on feelings (e.g., "They deserved it after what they said/did to me"), victim stance/blaming (e.g., "It wasn't my fault"), and minimizing/normalizing (e.g., "I only did it once," "Others have done worse"). Negative coping avoids accepting responsibility, fault, or blame, which justifies cover-up behavior to avoid consequences viewed as unjust.

The Stress-Abuse Cycle, Phase 2: Cover-up. In addition to avoidance of legal consequences, cover-up behavior is also triggered by avoidance of social consequences. Thus, cover-up behavior is supported by unhealthy pride and misplaced priorities which combine to create an image problem in which others' view of the abuser and whether the abuser "wins" the confrontation are more important than the abuser's conduct. During an unhealthy pride cover-up, looking good is more important than doing good. Cover-up tactics are a part of resistance to change and treatment avoidance which contribute to stress buildup, treatment dropout, and relapse.

Cover-up tactics involve trust abuse by misleading others. Three common cover-up tactics are denial, diversion, and division. The most basic form of cover-up is denial. Denial cover-up tactics involve direct misleading by lying and refusing to discuss even the possibility of responsibility for problem behaviors. Denial cover-ups also involve obstruction of honest disclosure, which includes actively attempting to block others from telling the truth about negative behavior by using bribery, threats, or blackmail to tamper with witnesses. On one survey of adults reporting childhood abuse, 47% indicated that an abuser tried to get them to keep the abuse secret (Fish & Scott, 1999).

Diversion cover-up tactics include focusing on personal accomplishments, discussing less serious problems and problems involving others, or setting brushfires to create chaos in order to keep the focus off of oneself. Diversion tactics also involve avoidance of confrontation through word games to mislead others. Diversion word games include omitting key pieces of information (i.e., dishonesty by omission); reframing the situation in a context that makes it look common, normal, socially acceptable, or better; and rephrasing statements to put a positive or less negative light or more positive "spin" on the situation. Diversion cover-up tactics are supported by "acting as if" nothing happened, pretending that everything is normal, and returning to everyday routine.

Cover-up by division basically involves "divide and conquer" damage control strategies. Division involves splitting alliances and playing people against each other so they cannot unite against the abuser. Division creates a communication breakdown so that knowledge about abusive behavior cannot be shared. If abuse behavior information is shared, creating dissention and conflicts prevents others from agreeing or arriving at a consensus about the abuser's problem. Division damage control manipulation involves impression formation techniques, such as fact stacking which misleads others to draw favorable conclusions, and actively developing negative contracts to cover up problems and avoid detection. Energy devoted to cover-up tactics exacerbates inner conflict over reality (i.e., the truth) and public image (i.e., the cover-up) which causes stress to build up.

The Stress-Abuse Cycle, Phase 3: Stress buildup. In stress buildup, worry about cover-up tactics not working and being detected combines with disappointment over getting in trouble and having to cover it up. In some cases, anxiety about caving into abuse urges, along with disappointment over compromising oneself and not being loyal to one's own sense of right and wrong, contributes to stress buildup. Fears of consequences and rejection result. Since responsibility for the behavior has not been accepted, the possibility of consequences is viewed as unjust. Rumination over perceived injustices along with the inability to identify, control, and vent feelings or redirect actions triggered by feelings adds to stress buildup. These stresses are channeled into a preoccupation with injustices, making ongoing problem events and interactions with others less likely to be resolved, which further increases tension and frustration. Cover-up secret keeping blocks open problem solving and sharing with others, which sets up failure and isolation. Stress buildup is a serious violation involving not being loyal to what is right and shifting loyalties from family or positive relationships to negative peers that reinforce denial. This problem results from of the cumulative effect of negative coping and cover-up.

Since stress is cumulative, "if you are not working on the solution, you are part of the problem." Thus, refusal to accept responsibility, lack of effort, and not dealing with feelings are three important factors that further contribute to stress buildup. Not recognizing and dealing with feelings such as anger, boredom, depression, jealousy, rejection, feeling inferior (i.e., put down or "one down"), or feeling out of control (i.e., powerless or helpless) is an antecedent to abuse. One study revealed that negative emotional states precede 35% of all relapses across various addictions (i.e., alcohol, smoking, heroin, gambling, and food; Cummings, Gordon, & Marlatt, 1980). Stress buildup from self-disappointment, anxiety over possible consequences, shifting loyalties, not dealing with feelings, and avoiding the problem lowers self-efficacy and sets the occasion for a slip (or lapse) and consequent fall (or relapse).

The Stress-Abuse Cycle, Phase 4: Slip (or lapse). Slips are relapse antecedents. A slip involves self-defeating thoughts or behaviors which set the stage for giving up self-control and abusing again. A slip is a basic concern violation, which involves not caring enough to keep the abuse problem "up front" or a priority and letting motivation for ongoing relapse prevention planning slip. This includes a lack of effort to look ahead or stay aware of behavior patterns as well as getting lax and allowing oneself to slide back into defeating habits, which sets the stage for relapse. Lack of effort leads to "corner cutting," a form of cheating (trust abuse). Corner cutting characterizes substance abusers who relapse (Rosellini, 1985). Corner cutting is insidious, beginning with "pushing back the line" on self-imposed behavior limits until the threshold of the abstinence violation effect has been reached (e.g., "I've already broken my [sobriety, promise, parole]" so "I might as well go all the way") (Chiauzzi, 1989).

Three common slips or lapses are entering high-risk situations, assertiveness slips, and foresight slips. High-risk situations include people, places, and things that allow or trigger abuse behavior. Assertiveness slips involve a breakdown of refusal skills related to social pressure and the need for acceptance. Social pressure or situations in which the individual experienced direct or indirect pressure from others to violate rules was found to precede 20% of all relapses across various addictions (i.e., alcohol, smoking, heroin, gambling, and food) in one investigation (Cummings et al., 1980). Foresight slips involve both a failure to plan ahead and making apparently irrelevant decisions. Foresight slips include not using high-risk-situation avoidance strategies and not planning ahead with "fantasy fast forward" or "thinking through the drink" to imagine the consequences after indulging in the abusive behavior (Marlatt, 1989).

The Stress-Abuse Cycle, Phase 5: Fall (or relapse). During the fall or relapse phase of the cycle, the abuser has let go of appropriate social behavior control and violated his responsibility to care for self and others by falling back into abusive behavior. Falling back into abuse behavior involves acting out feelings and relieving stress in a manner that is harmful to self and/or others. Three common contributors to a fall or relapse include a maladaptive release of stress buildup, sensation seeking without considering others, and the abstinence violation effect.

When a fall is primarily the result of the abstinence violation effect, maladaptive thinking is the main trigger. The abstinence violation effect involves "all or nothing," perfectionism thinking about recovery and self-control that justifies giving up on oneself after making a mistake during a period of abuse abstinence. In the abstinence violation effect, an individual feels that his abstinence violation mistake or slip has "blown it" and made it impossible for him to regain self-control. The way he reduces internal conflict over this is to redefine himself as a hopeless abuser, addict, or disease victim. This justifies giving up and allowing his behavior to get "out of control" (Marlatt, 1985).

Although it is maladaptive, since abuse behavior acts to artificially boost self-efficacy, that temporary reinforcement increases the probability of repetition. Once a method to boost self-efficacy has been found, other coping strategies are less likely to be tried. Since all coping acts to reduce stress, and the abuser has found a way, he continues to use the negative coping and enters a stress-abuse cycle as opposed to using positive coping and avoiding the cycle. Thus, after taking a fall back into abusive behavior, social-emotional immaturity results in another burst of negative coping to make oneself feel better along with cover-up behavior to avoid consequences, which builds up stress and continues the stress-abuse cycle.

The Anatomy Model of Factors That Support Multiple Forms of Abuse. In SRT, a pathological level of social-emotional immaturity is considered to be a primary contributing factor to the generalization of one type of abuse into other types of abusive behavior as well as a least common denominator that supports multiple forms of abusive behavior. The research literature supports the notion that some factors are associated with the development of more than one type of abusive behavior. For example, in the area of substance abuse, an excessive need for excitement or sensation seeking has been associated with more than one type of substance abuse along with verbal abuse and criminal arrest (e.g., Ball, Carroll, & Rounsaville, 1994; Kasarabada, Anglin, Stark, & Paredes, 2000). A set of common characteristics are said to underlie the development of both a sexual or physical abuse behavior syndrome. This set includes an emotionally impoverished family with dangerous secrets, distorted attachment, and an event that causes the individual to feel out of control (Ryan, 1993). In a study in which adolescent problem gamblers were found to be more at risk of also being problem substance users and vice versa, the authors suggest that these forms of abuse share a common impulse-control deficit origin (Vitaro, Ferland, Jacques, & Ladouceur, 1998).

Behavior problem theory predicts that many forms of adolescent problems and abuse relate to a set of common norm-violating attitudes (e.g., low religiosity, rebelliousness, and disregard for the law) and activities (e.g., drug/alcohol abuse, vandalism, school disciplinary problems, sexual precocity, and aggression) referred to as the general deviance syndrome (McGee & Newcomb,1992), which can differ by setting and severity of deviance (Resnicow, Ross-Gaddy, & Vaughan, 1995). Although sexual offense relapse was best predicted by specific sexual deviance (e.g., deviant sexual interests in children, prior sexual offenses, and deviant victim choices of boys or strangers), general deviance (e.g., antisocial personality disorder and total prior offenses) was also a significant relapse predictor (Hanson & Bussière, 1998). Polydrug problems, property crimes, and poor parenting are associated with a general deviance factor that is maintained in adulthood (Newcomb & Loeb, 1999). Pathological social-emotional immaturity includes the same common characteristics that comprise the "syndrome of social disability" (e.g., problems with relationships, self-esteem, concern/empathy, and antisocial/abusive behavior) observed in adolescent sexual abusers (Barbaree et al.,1998) who, as discussed earlier, frequently exhibit more than one form of abusive behavior.

The abuse anatomy model is consistent with the therapeutic community emphasis on developing a positive lifestyle (DeLeon, 1989), the secondary alcohol recovery tract focus on lifestyle rehabilitation (Zackon, 1986), and the general deviance syndrome research indicating the need to target common abuser norm-violating attitudes (McGee & Newcomb,1992). The anatomy model is useful in helping abusers understand a broad array of characteristics that contribute to pathological social-emotional immaturity and support multiple forms of abusive behavior. It also helps abusers identify overall lifestyle enhancement areas to continue to work on in aftercare in order to improve quality of living and maintain an abuse free lifestyle.

The characteristics of pathological social-emotional immaturity were previously defined and the focus here is on traits, patterns, and factors that support multiple forms of abuse behavior, contribute to a general deviance, and help develop an irresponsible, abusive lifestyle. There are clearly many characteristics associated with social-emotional immaturity and multiple forms of abuse. However, for treatment purposes the categories selected to encompass the anatomy of these characteristics were (1) maladaptive thinking and control-power problems (head and torso), (2) dishonesty and unhealthy pride (right arm), (3) perfectionism and grandiosity (left arm), (4) the chain of events that led to abuse and the self-defeating habits associated with those events (right leg), and (5) the stress-abuse cycle that maintained abuse along with the maladaptive values and self image that are reinforced by that cycle (left leg).

Maladaptive Thinking. It is instructive for abusers to view maladaptive thinking as the head of the abuse anatomy model that controls the type, frequency, and severity of abusive behavior that has been learned. Although most of the examples of maladaptive thinking discussed by Yochelson and Samenow (1976), Bandura (1973), and Burns (1980) will act to support more than one type of abuse behavior, some have a direct effect in generalizing abuse. "Pushing back the line" can link one type of abuse to another. For example, the abuser tells himself, "Since I drank from their liquor cabinet and no one noticed, they won't notice if I take some money off of their dresser." The abstinence violation effect can also link different types of abuse. For example, the abuser reasons, "Since they already told on me for stealing, my parole is violated and I'm going back to jail anyway so I might as well kick their butt." In this portion of SRT, abusers examine how the various forms of their maladaptive thinking have affected their honesty, trust, loyalty, concern, and responsibility.

Control and Power Obsession (CAPO). Abuse behavior involves problems with self-control and the control of others. Because many youth and adult survivors of abuse exhibit a tendency to compensate for past feelings of helpless with maladaptive control responses, the body or torso of this model involves a control and power obsession (CAPO). For example, self-medicating with drugs and alcohol may be used to control unwanted feelings associated with past traumatic memories. Identifying with the aggressor by adopting an overcontrolling relationship style may be used to compensate for past out-of-control feelings around unpredictable parents. Building oneself up by putting others down through sexual molestation may be adopted to compensate for severe helplessness and low-self efficacy resulting from being sexually abused. These control and compensation responses feed the CAPO. Mental health professionals often attribute sexually abusive behavior to power and control problems (e.g., Ward, Connolly, McCormick, & Hudson, 1996). The CAPO is a central component in pathological social-emotional immaturity and the generalization of abuse.

The CAPO results from self-efficacy disequilibrium. When abusers are left feeling helpless, powerless, and devoid of self-efficacy, they compensate by seeking control, power, and feelings of mastery in other areas. Unfortunately, this compensation usually involves identifying with the aggressor and putting someone else down to build themselves up. The escalation of power by violent offenders is viewed as an attempt to compensate for loss of control during their previous trauma/victimization (Maddock, 1995). The maladaptive belief associated with this compensation behavior is "It's better to be an offender than a victim." There is evidence that nonviolent sex offenders also compensate by reenacting past trauma to "take back power" through a repetition compulsion (i.e., prostitution) where they assume a power-and-control role (e.g., Kenny & Lane, 1996).

Dishonesty and Unhealthy Pride. Dishonesty and unhealthy pride can be considered the right arm and fist of abusive behavior because they maintain the veil of secrecy that makes abuse possible. On one survey of adults reporting childhood abuse, 76% indicated there had been a time when no one but themselves and their abusers knew about the abuse (Fish & Scott, 1999). Since abusive relationships are maintained in a secretive environment (Green, 1998), SRT has a "no more secrets policy" where it is everyone's responsibility to confront negative secret-keeping contracts. As expected, dishonesty is associated with "general deviance," including substance abuse, illegal behaviors, risky driving, cheating on tests, and false excuses (Blankenship & Whitley, 2000).

Abuse is covered by dishonesty associated with unhealthy pride. Long-term dishonesty is maintained by an attitude of "it is better to look good than act good," leading to various manipulations to look good and protect unhealthy pride. This is particularly pronounced in child sexual abusers who have a significantly greater fear of negative evaluation than do rapists (Hayashino, Wurtele, & Klebe, 1995). Unhealthy pride blocks one's ability to make amends, apologize, or settle differences and includes blaming others; secret keeping; refusal to admit fault or accept responsibility; qualifying admissions with excuses ("yes but"); justifying actions; refusal to acknowledge feelings of hurt, fear, or anger; and inability to accept criticism. In addition to affecting honesty, unhealthy pride affects image. For example, aggressive youth may act out feelings of inferiority so that they will be viewed as having to be removed from school for bad behavior as opposed to academic inferiority (Symonds, 1978)

Perfectionism and Grandiosity. Another strong arm with a hand in the commission of abusive behavior is perfectionism and grandiosity. Perfectionism is defined as the need to be first, best, perfect, and without any shortcomings, blemishes, or deficiencies. Perfectionism involves unrealistic standards and expectations for self and others. Regarding the chain of events that led to abuse, perfectionism is considered to be one side effect of emotional child neglect (i.e., lack of nurturance, stimulation, encouragement, and protection) along with other problems such as low self-esteem, feelings of inadequacy, and self-destructive behavior (Cook, 1991).

Some forms of perfectionism (e.g., self-oriented) set the person up to quit treatment, give up on himself, and relapse and some forms (e.g., other-oriented perfectionism) set the stage for building oneself up by putting others down. Finally, some forms (e.g., socially prescribed perfectionism) support the need to "excel at any cost," including violating the rights of others to get power and then "conceal at any cost" to protect the perfect public image. Perfectionism is also an important relapse variable that has a negative impact on treatment success. For example, perfectionism has been associated with the negative outcome of cognitive-behavioral, interpersonal, and medical treatment for depression (Blatt, Quinlan, Pilkonas, & Shea, 1995).

Constructing a grandiose self whose maintenance requires profound public respect appears to be an abuser response to avoid a self-esteem crash to a zero state (Yochelson & Samenow, 1976) as the result of condemnation of the abuser's antisocial behavior (Bogg, 1994). The notion that some people use grandiosity, dominance, and a more generalized narcissistic personality style to manage their hostility and maintain a sense of positive regard has received some research support (e.g., Raskin, Novacek, & Hogan, 1991). Thus, grandiosity can combine with CAPO characteristics to set the stage for abusers to displace their anger on others in order to build up their self-esteem. Grandiose overconfidence leads to overestimating the probability of getting away with abuse, which increases the probability of trying.

The Chain of Events and Self-Defeating Habits. The support bases for multiple forms of abusive behavior are the chain of events that led to abuse along with the stress-abuse cycle that maintained it. These two legs are important contributors to the critical deficits in honesty, trust, loyalty, concern, and responsibility that are needed to repeatedly commit abusive behavior. The history of abuse, neglect, dysfunctional family, and toxic parenting found in the chain of events that led to the initial abuse problem is a strong support leg in social-emotional maturity deficits that set the occasion for other forms of abuse. For example, in violent family settings, dishonesty is rewarded by avoiding the severe consequences associated with admitting mistakes. In families in which one adult partner is abusive, the children learn to distrust the other parent's ability to protect them and may believe that the nonoffending parent has no concern for their welfare. In family settings in which child sexual abuse was perpetrated, the concept of loyalty was destroyed. The impact of drugs and alcohol in the dysfunctional family can destroy the concept of responsibility for the child.

The Stress-Abuse Cycle and Maladaptive Self-Image/Values. Each iteration through the stress-abuse cycle directly reinforces the social-emotional immaturity that supports multiple forms of abuse. The successful use of excuses and other negative coping strategies reinforces avoiding responsibility. Dishonesty and distrust are reinforced and expanded through various cover-up techniques. Negative peer loyalty is reinforced by peer support and each relapse or fall back into an abusive behavior episode further erodes concern for self and others.

While eroding basic concern for others, this leg of the abuse anatomy supports the development of maladaptive values and self-image. A common maladaptive value that abusers hold is a form of unhealthy pride called criminal pride. Abusers with criminal pride possess a tough-guy image and view confrontation with concern (i.e., disclosing information about other people's problems to help them) as "snitching." Criminal pride demands loyalty to negative peers who enforce the criminal code of silence (i.e., "snitches get stitches") and brag about criminal abuse. Their exaggerated need for acceptance prevents abusers who state that they can make it on their own and act like they are independent enough to handle whatever problems they encounter (i.e., exhibit "pseudomaturity," Newcomb, 1997) from ever being secure enough to resist negative peer influence. The maladaptive self-image reflects superficial values. For example, looks are valued over loyalty in a partner and image (i.e., how others view the abuser) is valued over actions (i.e., the abuser's conduct).

Developing Prosocial Skills. Developing a number of basic prosocial skills such as assertiveness, empathy, and age-appropriate social interaction ability is considered important for maintaining a mature, socially responsible, positive lifestyle for the abuser. One key prosocial skill that abusers need to develop to help both themselves and others is the ability to demonstrate honesty, trust, loyalty, concern, and responsibility through emotional restitution to both direct and indirect victims of abuse.

Making emotional restitution in a safe, supervised, structured setting is considered a social responsibility of the abuser, which is accomplished during victim responsibility training using the graduated exposure procedure pioneered by Joseph Wolpe (Yokley, 1990).

"Doing the right thing is a lot harder than knowing the right thing": This third important component of SRT includes specific training to help abusers demonstrate social responsibility through emotional restitution to abuse victims and their families in a manner that is therapeutically beneficial to all involved (Yokley, 1990; Yokley & McGuire, 1991). After developing adequate social-emotional maturity as a competing response to abusive behavior as well as learning how their abusive behavior was acquired, maintained, and generalized, a treatment component begins when abusers in recovery interact with survivors of abuse. This treatment component is called victim responsibility training and involves demonstrating social responsibility through emotional restitution.

Victim responsibility training is the final form of emotional restitution made to victims and their significant others by abusers during the course of SRT. During Phase 1 of SRT, it is the abuser's social responsibility to disclose who his victims are so that they may be provided with treatment. It is also the social responsibility of the abuser to provide abuse details to victims' therapists as an aid to their treatment. During Phase 2, abusers assume the social responsibility of developing and understanding their abuse and disclosing how they developed their problem to the families and significant others of their victims. During Phase 3 of SRT, abusers clarify why they were abusive along with other critical information relevant to victim recovery and provide a sincere apology to both the direct and indirect victims of their abuse.

The basic treatment goals of the victim responsibility training are the development of victim impact understanding, victim empathy, and the demonstration of social responsibility by making emotional restitution to both direct and indirect victims of abuse (Yokley, 1990; Yokley & McGuire, 1990, 1991). Chapter 24 (in this volume) describes victim responsibility training in detail.

Forensic Foster Parent Recruiting and Selection, Training, and Retention

Recruiting and Selection. Problems occur whether recruiting forensic foster parents from an existing population of regular or therapeutic foster parents or whether recruiting from the community. Recruiting from populations of existing regular and therapeutic foster parents whose training focus has typically been on elementary-school-age victims requires reeducation and offender-specific training if they are to manage teenage abusers. Past foster parent training focused on child victims can result in treating offenders like victims by trusting without verification, concern without confrontation, and offender enabling, all of which can present community safety hazards. On the other hand, recruiting from the community at large presents an information overload problem related to having to teach new candidates to become effective foster parents while simultaneously training them to deal with serious abuse behaviors.

Thus, recruiting foster parents to take youth who have committed sexually abusive behavior into their homes is predictably difficult. However, some forensic foster family selection characteristics can be offered. With respect to providing an appropriate level of community supervision for youth abusers, four eyes are better than two. With youth abusers, quantity time is more important than quality time. With these youth the most important thing for foster parents to do is be there and be consistent. The importance of supervision by as many adults and extended family members as possible cannot be over emphasized for this population with respect to the issue of community safety and security.

Assertiveness, decisiveness, and enthusiasm are valuable commodities when trading verbal exchanges with resistant multiple-abuser youth. Forensic foster parents must be able to make difficult decisions without delay, be firm in their convictions, and enthusiastic about behavior maintenance or progress. If forensic treatment staff want multiple-abuser youth to learn prosocial values and not compromise them, they need to select foster parents who stick by what they believe to be right even if the treatment staff do not agree with all of the foster parent's values or methods. Abusive youth can be expected to take the victim stance with their human services guardians if they receive firm, consistent discipline. Being able to tolerate criticism helps because in Forensic Foster Care there is no such thing as a perfectly managed case and complaints about parenting decisions are common. The personality profile (i.e., from the 16 Personaltiy Factor Questionnaire) of successful therapeutic foster mothers suggests that self-discipline, maturity, ability to face reality, and enthusiasm, combined with ability to make decisions based on logic, were related to better foster parent functioning (Ray & Horner, 1990).

Tenacity and endurance are important forensic foster parent characteristics. By embroiling the family in conflict, seriously delinquent behavior itself wears down the socialization forces (e.g., supervision and setting limits) that could direct youth into more prosocial patterns of adjustment (Chamberlain & Reid, 1998). Thus, abusive youth need forensic foster parents who model tenacity and endurance while teaching youth to "never give up" and "always finish what you start."

Emotional stability and being well balanced are cornerstones in parenting abusive youth. Both foster parents and staff have to provide mature objection to immature behavior. Part of developing social maturity and appropriate social behavior control is learning to function with rules that set limits on externalizing behavior. This is where father figures with strong leadership traits such as bearing, courage, and dependability can help with authority problems. In this respect, the personality profile of successful therapeutic foster fathers suggests that they are likely to be somewhat more conservative than the norm (Ray & Horner, 1990).

Training. Foster parent training varies by state, but thirty hours of certification training and twenty-four hours of annual continuing education are currently recommended (Foster Family-Based Treatment Association, 1995). In addition to some therapeutic foster parent training in the area of the impact of abuse on victims, offender-specific training is provided. Forensic foster parent training is much more extensive than regular or therapeutic foster parent training and offers actual "on the job" experience where Forensic Foster Care parents are an integral part of the treatment team and are actively involved in ongoing interventions.

In forensic foster parent training, investigative questioning and a focus on teaching concern for others are added to the traditional therapeutic foster parenting emphasis on reflective listening and concern/support for the youth. Conditional behavior based acceptance through "confrontation with concern" and "trust but verify" are substituted for the unconditional positive regard and trust typically promoted in regular or therapeutic foster parent training. Forensic foster parent training uses the "kite analogy of social maturity development." In this analogy, if one provides appropriate, positive resistance and pulls against the kite (i.e., provides consistent confrontation with concern), the kite rises to its maximum potential. If one stands still and does not pull against it but also does not give in (i.e., fails to provide any more structure than was received in the past), the kite maintains its present level. If one gives in, goes in the direction the kite is pulling, or runs after the kite (i.e., "goes along to get along" with the youth), the kite crashes.

Behavior management training in Forensic Foster Care includes how to implement and monitor therapeutic community learning experiences assigned by staff in a shared-parenting discipline arrangement which reduces offender-foster parent conflict. This ongoing, proactive, experiential approach relieves stress buildup, eliminates the need for seclusion/restraint, and has a demonstrated positive impact on developing appropriate social behavior control in youth sex offenders (Yokley, 1999a). The emphasis on prosocial cross-cultural values as competing responses to abusive behavior are consistent with the values and parenting style of most foster parents, are easily accepted, and are easily integrated into ongoing behavior management. What to expect regarding the behavior norms of youth sex offenders in Forensic Foster Care (Yokley & Boettner, 1999) is included in the training. Table 21.2 provides examples of offender-specific training topics in Forensic Foster Care.

Retention. The TASC Forensic Foster Care program includes policies and procedures that are associated with foster parent retention. These empowerment procedures include highly specialized forensic foster parent training and a team approach in which foster parents are integrated into all aspects of youth treatment as well as privy to all communication. A cluster placement model to maximize foster parent support while respecting family diversity and minimizing any adverse impact that could be associated with home moves is an additional empowerment procedure.

Specific, frequent, quality training with relevant content has been identified as a foster parent retention factor (Chamberlain et al., 1992; Denby & Rindfleisch, 1996; Urquhart, 1989). In addition to the mandated sessions for all regular foster parents and on-the-job training during home visits, TASC forensic foster parents receive thirty hours of annual training on topics relating specifically to multiple abusers (see Table 21.2).

The therapeutic community approach used in the TASC Forensic Foster Care program blends paraprofessional and professional staff together in a unified treatment team in which the specialized training and forensic parenting experience of TASC foster parents is respected as a critical aspect of treatment. The research-informed program rules and learning experiences are discussed and accepted by the treatment team (i.e., foster parents, social worker, and psychologist). The intake/placement selection process is inclusive of foster parents. After a screening evaluation by staff, youth abusers have an intake interview during a treatment group where all of the treatment team members (i.e., staff and foster parents) are present and admission requires a majority staff vote as well as acceptance into at least two homes. The treatment team approach effectively addresses the lack of foster parent involvement in types of chil-

Table 21.2
Examples of Offender-Specific Training Topics in Forensic Foster Care

Note: the term "abusive youth" used herein refers to youth exhibiting sexually abusive behavior along with other forms of abuse (i.e., multiple abusers)

- **Abuse reactive children**

  Familiarizes foster parents with the impact of sexual abuse on victims.

- **Introduction to Forensic Foster Care**

  Covers basic types of foster care, overview of offender population and treatment.

- **Characteristics of abusive youth—"The few, the proud, the resistant"**

  Familiarizes foster parents with what to expect in terms of characteristics and behaviors.

- **Understanding abusive youth— "What were they thinking?"**

  Reviews maladaptive thinking (thinking errors, cognitive distortions, attitudes, attributions and irrational beliefs) with brief case examples.

- **Managing the behavior of abusive youth—"Parenting the Impossible 101"**

  Covers behavior management and basic Therapeutic Community learning experiences.

- **Social responsibility therapy for abusive youth**

  Overview of SRT components: Developing social-emotional maturity; Understanding abuse behavior and; Demonstrating social responsibility.

- **Understanding abusive youth: "How did they get these problems?"**

  Provides a more in-depth focus on how youth abusers acquired their behavior problem by reviewing the chain of events that led to offense.

- **Caring for youth with abusive behaviors: Supervision, safety and security**

  Covers basic youth abuser supervision guidelines, twelve basic foster home safeguards, and twelve basic community safety/supervision procedures.

- **The foster parent role in relapse prevention: Interrupting the abuse cycle**

  Provides a more in-depth focus on how abuse behavior is maintained by describing the stress-abuse cycle and the appropriate foster parent response to interrupt it at key points.

- **Television violence**

  Reviews the impact of violent TV and video games on predisposed youth and emphasizes the need for limits and supervision of youth abusers.

- **Stress management for forensic foster parents**

  Covers coping skills to manage stress related to abuse disclosure and problem behavior.

dren placed with them (Denby & Rindfleisch, 1996) as well as service planning (Sanchirico et al., 1998), both of which have been identified as retention factors commonly responsible for foster parent dissatisfaction.

As an integral part of the treatment team, TASC Forensic Foster Care parents are directly connected into the treatment feedback loop. This is accomplished through centralized and as-needed in-home treatment services, daily communication with on-call staff (pagers, cellular telephones, and e-mail), weekly home visits, and brief meetings before or after individual sessions. In addition, forensic foster parents typically sit in during the first ten to fifteen minutes of treatment group sessions to disclose behavior problems and issues that have occurred. E-mail feedback[4] to forensic foster parents on treatment group content, process, and therapeutic community learning experiences that were implemented is provided. The continuity of the TASC Forensic Foster Care program addresses the foster parent retention factor concerning the quantity and quality of agency-foster parent interaction (Urquhart, 1989).

In the TASC Forensic Foster Care program, youth abusers are admitted into a foster cluster of several homes which increases support through shared parenting responsibility and facilitates providing respite visits (i.e., a relationship vacation) during trying times. The foster cluster placement approach makes immediate emergency placement from one home to another easy to accomplish if needed and reduces foster parent burnout associated with keeping a stressful youth simply because there is no other placement for him. Having the youth accepted into more than one family maximizes the probability of getting the basic treatment messages through to them in a different family if they did not get it the first time around (i.e., "It takes a village to raise a child."). The cluster approach enhances foster parent retention by addressing foster parents' expressed need for mutual support among themselves (Urquhart,1989).

Supporting foster parents' discipline decisions and their own house rules with a program policy that respects individual family differences is important. Since teenagers compare responsibilities and privileges at school, they are aware of the diverse differences in family rules. Thus, although the overall treatment program rules are the same for everyone, the rules of the foster homes in the cluster are not standardized and "every house has its own rules." This policy mirrors the real-world environment and teaches the youth to honor diversity by accepting that each setting is different and they must learn to adapt to the rules of each setting they encounter (e.g., home, school, work, and treatment).

Conclusion

Forensic Foster Care provides another level in the continuum of care where multiple-abuser youth can progress through a step-down treatment supervision process from residential to Forensic Foster Care and finally to the traditional outpatient setting during a family reunification or independent living placement. This chapter described innovative techniques and procedures used in a model Forensic Foster Care program for multiple abuser youth whose behavior management needs or family circumstances prevented treatment in their natural family setting. Since a functional family setting is considered most conducive to helping youth with a history of abusive behavior to develop prosocial family values, the family-based setting employed in Forensic Foster Care is considered the treatment setting of choice. Forensic Foster

Care includes key components associated with foster parent retention, a cluster approach to minimize any adverse impact associated with youth home disruption that might occur, and a team approach in which foster parents are integrated into all aspects of youth treatment decision making.

SRT is considered the logical treatment approach for parenting multiple abuser youth as it addresses five basic types of abusive behavior (i.e., sexual abuse, physical abuse, property abuse, substance abuse, and trust abuse) with a therapeutic community approach. SRT teaches social-emotional maturity and cross-cultural values as competing responses to abusive behavior, making it easily accepted and integrated into ongoing behavior management by parents. In addition, SRT helps the youth and their foster parents understand how the abusive behavior was acquired, what maintained it, and how it generalized into other problem areas. Perhaps one of the strong points of SRT is its supervision protocol. Electronic communication, behavior tracking, and monitoring technology are used along with twelve basic foster home safeguards and twelve basic community safety/supervision procedures that target negative peers as well as the multiple-abuser youth. Program evaluation and case study data have demonstrated efficacy with treatment components involving the computer-assisted incident report system (Yokley & Boettner, 1999), the use of therapeutic community learning experiences for behavior management (Yokley, 1999a), and victim responsibility training (Yokley, 1990).

In summary, the treatment of multiple-abuser youth in Forensic Foster Care with SRT combines the logical treatment of choice with the logical setting of choice for this treatment population. Forensic Foster Care is a research-informed treatment approach with treatment component program evaluation and case study data support.

Footnotes

[1] Most criminal abusers lack self-control (Gottfredson & Hirschi, 1990).

[2] Rational emotive behavior therapy (REBT) places an emphasis on abysmal low frustration tolerance as the childish insistence on indulgence that underlies multiple addictions (Ellis, 1995).

[3] This treatment component was originally presented at The 12th annual conference of the National Adolescent Perpetrator Network, Minneapolis, MN (Yokley, 1996).

[4] Only client first names or initials are used to comply with Health Insurance Portability and Accountability Act confidentiality regulations, which cover electronic communications between involved parties.

References

American Psychiatric Association. (1952). *Diagnostic and statistical manual of mental disorders* (1st ed.). Washington, DC: Author.

American Psychiatric Association. (1968). *Diagnostic and statistical manual of mental disorders* (2nd ed.). Washington, DC: Author.

American Psychiatric Association. (1980). *Diagnostic and statistical manual of mental disorders* (3rd ed.). Washington, DC: Author.

American Psychiatric Association. (1987). *Diagnostic and statistical manual of mental disorders* (3rd ed., rev.). Washington, DC: Author.

American Psychiatric Association. (1994). *Diagnostic and statistical manual of mental disorders* (4th ed.). Washington, DC: Author.

Amir, M. (1971). *Patterns of forcible rape*. Chicago: University of Chicago Press.

Andrews, J., & Duncan, S. (1997). Examining the reciprocal relation between academic motivation and substance use: Effects of family relationships, self-esteem, and general deviance. *Journal of Behavioral Medicine, 20*(6) 523–549.

Awad, G., Saunders, E., & Levene, J. (1984). A clinical study of male adolescent sexual offenders. *International Journal of Offender Therapy and Comparative Criminology, 28*, 105–115.

Ball, S., Carroll, K., & Rounsaville, B. (1994). Sensation seeking, substance abuse, and psychopathology in treatment-seeking and community cocaine abusers. *Journal of Consulting and Clinical Psychology, 62*(5), 1053–1057.

Bandura, A. (1973). *Aggression: A social learning analysis*. Englewood Cliffs, NJ: Prentice-Hall.

Barbaree, H., Marshall, W., & McCormick, J. (1998). The development of deviant sexual behaviour among adolescents and its implications for prevention and treatment. *Irish Journal of Psychology, 19*(1), 1–31.

Bates, M., & Labouvie, E. (1995). Personality-environment constellations and alcohol use: A process-oriented study of intraindividual change during adolescence. *Psychology of Addictive Behaviors, 9*(1), 23–35.

Becker, J., Kaplan, M., Cunningham-Rathner, J., & Kavoussi, R. (1986). Characteristics of adolescent incest perpetrators: Preliminary findings. *Journal of Family Violence, 1*, 85–97.

Benton Foundation. (2000). *What you may not know about foster care* [On-line]. Available: www. connectforkids.org.

Blankenship, K., & Whitley, B. (2000). Relation of general deviance to academic dishonesty. *Ethics and Behavior, 10*(1), 1–12.

Blatt, S., Quinlan, D., Pilkonas, P., & Shea, M. (1995). Impact of perfectionism and need for approval on the brief treatment of depression: The National Institute of Mental Health Treatment of Depression Collaborative Research Program revisited. *Journal of Consulting and Clinical Psychology, 63*(1), 125–132.

Bogg, R. (1994, October–December). Psychopathic behavior as perpetual gaming: A synthesis of forensic accounts. *Deviant Behavior, 15*(4), 357–374.

Brock, K., Mintz, L., & Good, G. (1997). Differences among sexually abused and nonabused women from functional and dysfunctional families. *Journal of Counseling Psychology, 44*(4), 425–423.

Burns, D. (1980). *Feeling good: The new mood therapy*. New York: Avon Books.

Buss, A. (1966). *Psychopathology*. New York: Wiley.

Carden, A. (1994). Wife abuse and the wife abuser: Review and recommendations. *The Counseling Psychologist, 22*(4), 539–582.

Carmen, E., Reiker, P., & Mills, T. (1984, March). Victims of violence and psychiatric illness. *American Journal of Psychiatry, 141*(3), 378–383.

Carnes, P., & Delmonico, D. (1996). Childhood abuse and multiple addictions: Research findings in a sample of self-identified sexual addicts. *Sexual Addiction and Compulsivity, 3*(3), 258–268.

Casey, R., & Berman, J. (1985). The outcome of psychotherapy with children. *Psychological Bulletin, 98*, 388–400.

Chamberlain, P., Moreland, S., & Reid, K. (1992, September–October). Enhanced services and stipends for foster parents: Effects on retention rates and outcomes for children. *Child Welfare, 71*(5), 387–401.

Chamberlain, P., & Reid, J. (1998). Comparison of two community alternatives to incarceration for chronic juvenile offenders. *Journal of Consulting and Clinical Psychology, 66*(4), 624–633.

Chapman, J. (1968). Frigidity: Rapid treatment by reciprocal inhibition. *Journal of the American Osteopathic Association, 67*(8), 871–878.

Chiauzzi, E. (1989, December). Breaking the patterns that lead to relapse. *Psychology Today*, pp. 18–19.

Cleckley, H. (1976). *The mask of sanity* (5th ed.). St. Louis, MO: Mosby.

Cohen, F., & Densen-Gerber, J. (1982). A study of the relationship between child abuse and drug addiction in 178 patients: Preliminary results. *Child Abuse and Neglect, 6*(4) 383–387.

Cohen, J., Mannarino, A., Berliner, L., & Deblinger, E. (2000). Trauma focused cognitive behavior therapy: An empirical update. *Journal of Interpersonal Violence, 15*, 1203–1223.

Cook, D. (1991).College students from emotionally neglectful homes. *New Directions for Student Services, 54*, 77–90.

Cortoni, F., Heil, P., & Marshall, W. (1996, November). *Sex as a coping mechanism and its relationship to loneliness and intimacy deficits in sexual offending.* Paper presented at the 15th annual Research and Treatment Conference of the Association for the Treatment of Sexual Abusers, Chicago, IL.

Cummings, C., Gordon, J., & Marlatt, G. A. (1980). Relapse: Strategies of prevention and prediction. In W. R. Miller (Ed.), *The addictive behaviors: Treatment of alcoholism, drug abuse, smoking, and obesity* (pp. 290–321). Oxford, UK: Pergamon Press.

Cunningham, C., & MacFarlane, K. (1996). *When children abuse.* Brandon, VT: Safer Society Press.

Davidson, A. (1983, October). Sexual exploitation of children: A call to action. *Journal of the National Medical Association, 75*(10), 925–927.

Davies, W., & Feldman, P. (1981, April). The diagnosis of psychopathy by forensic specialists. *British Journal of Psychiatry, 138*, 329–331.

DeLeon, G. (1984). *The therapeutic community: Study of effectiveness* (NIDA Research Monograph) (DHHS Publication No. ADM 84–1286). Washington, DC: U.S. Government Printing Office.

DeLeon, G. (1987). Alcohol use among drug abusers: Treatment outcomes in a therapeutic community. *Alcoholism, Clinical and Experimental Research, 11*(5), 430–436.

DeLeon, G. (1989). Psychopathology and substance abuse: What is being learned from research in therapeutic communities. *Journal of Psychoactive Drugs, 21*(2), 177–187.

DeLeon, G. (1997). President's column. *The Addictions Newsletter, 4*(3), 1,6.

Denby, R., & Rindfleisch, N. (1996). African Americans' foster parenting experiences: Research findings and implications for policy and practice. *Children and Youth Services Review, 18*(6) 523–552.

Dermen, K., & Cooper, L. (1994). *Psychology of Addictive Behaviors, 9*, 156.

"Discipline: When is it too much?" (1995, January 20). *48 hours* (for a transcript call 800–777-text and for a videotape copy call 800–338–4847).

Dubner, A., & Motta, R. (1999). Sexually and physically abused foster care children and posttraumatic stress disorder. *Journal of Consulting and Clinical Psychology, 67*(3), 367–373.

Eckenrode, J., Laird, M., & Doris, J. (1993). School performance and disciplinary problems among abused and neglected children. *Developmental Psychology, 29*(1), 53–62.

Eisenberg, N., & Miller,P. A. (1987). The relation of empathy to prosocial and related behaviors. *Psychological Bulletin, 101*, 91–119.

Ellis, A. (1995). Addictive behaviors and personality disorders: A rational emotive behavior therapy approach. *The Addictions Newsletter, 2*(3), 10, 11, 26.

English, D. (1988). The extent and consequences of child maltreatment. *The Future of Children: Protecting Children From Abuse and Neglect, 8*(1), 39–53.

Faller, K. C. (1989). Characteristics of a clinical sample of sexually abused children: How boy and girl victims differ. *Child Abuse and Neglect, 13*, 281–291.

Fanshel, D., Finch, S. J., & Grundy, J. F. (1989, September–October). Foster children in life-course perspective: The Casey Family Program experience. *Child Welfare, 68*(5) 467–478.

Fehrenbach, P. A., Smith, W., Monastersky, C., & Deisher, R. W. (1986). Adolescent sexual offenders: Offender and offense characteristics. *American Journal of Orthopsychiatry, 56*, 225–233.

Feldman, C., & Ridley, C. (1995). The etiology of domestic violence between adult partners. *Clinical Psycholocy Science and Practice, 2*, 317–348.

Fendrich, M., Mackesy-Amiti, M., Goldstein, P., Spunt, B., & Brownstein, H. (1995). Substance involvement among juvenile murderers: Comparisons with older offenders based on interviews with prison inmates. *International Journal of the Addictions, 30*(11), 1363–1382.

Feshbach, N. D., & Feshbach, S. (1982). Empathy training and the regulation of aggression: Potentialities and limitations. *Academic Psychology Bulletin, 4*, 399–413.

Finkelhor, D. (1979). *Sexually victimized children.* New York: Free Press.

Finkelhor, D. (1984). *Child sexual abuse: New theory and research.* New York: Free Press.

Fish, V., & Scott, C. (1999). Childhood abuse recollections in a nonclinical population: Forgetting and secrecy. *Child Abuse and Neglect, 23*(8), 791–802.

Foster Family-Based Treatment Association. (1995, August). *Program standards for treatment foster care* (rev. ed.). Teaneck, NJ: Author.

Friedrich, W. N., & Luecke, W. J. (1988). Young school-age sexually aggressive children. *Professional Psychology: Research and Practice, 19*(2), 155–164.

Gendreau, P., Little, T., & Goggin, C. (1996). A meta-analysis of the predictors of adult offender recidivism: What works! *Criminology, 34,* 575–607.

Glover, N., Janikowski, T., & Benshoff, J. (1995, March–April). The incidence of incest histories among clients receiving substance abuse treatment. *Journal of Counseling and Development, 73*(4), 475–480.

Golden, O. (2000). The federal response to child abuse and neglect. *American Psychologist, 55*(9), 1050–1053.

Gottfredson, M. R., & Hirschi, T. (1990). *A general theory of crime.* Stanford, CA: Stanford University Press.

Gray, K., & Hutchinson, H. (1964). The psychopathic personality: A survey of Canadian psychiatrist's opinions. *Canadian Psychiatric Association Journal, 9,* 452–461.

Green, A. (1978). Dimensions of psychological trauma in abused children. *Journal of the American Academy of Child Psychiatry, 17,* 231–237.

Green, R. (1998). The deadly embrace: An approach to abusive relationships. *Group Analysis, 31*(2) 197–211.

Greenfield, T., & Weisner, C. (1995). Drinking problems and self-reported criminal behavior, arrests and convictions: 1990 US alcohol and 1989 county surveys. *Addiction, 90*(3), 361–373.

Hall, S., Havassy, B., & Wasserman, D. (1989). Commitment to abstinence and acute stress in relapse to alcohol, opiates, and nicotine.*Journal of Consulting and Clinical Psychology, 58*(2), 175–181.

Hanson, K., & Bussière, M. (1998). Predicting relapse: A meta-analysis of sexual offender recidivism studies. *Journal of Consulting and Clinical Psychology, 66*(2), 348–362.

Hare, R. D. (1985). Comparison of procedures for the assessment of psychopathy. *Journal of Consulting and Clinical Psychology, 53,* 7–16.

Haslam, M. (1965). The treatment of psychogenic dyspareunia by reciprocal inhibition. *British Journal of Psychiatry, 111*(472), 280–282.

Hayashino, D., Wurtele, S., & Klebe, K. (1995). Child molesters: An examination of cognitive factors. *Journal of Interpersonal Violence, 10*(1), 106–116.

Hays, R., & Ellickson, P. (1990). How generalizable are adolescents' beliefs about pro-drug pressures and resistance self-efficacy? *Journal of Applied Social Psychology, 20*(4, Pt. 1), 321–340.

Hearn, M., & Evans, D. (1972). Anger and reciprocal inhibition therapy. *Psychological Reports, 30*(3), 943–948.

Henggeler, S., Schoenwald, S., & Pickrel, S. (1995). Multisystemic therapy: Bridging the gap between university- and community-based treatment. *Journal of Consulting and Clinical Psychology, 63*(5), 709–717.

Hoffman-Plotkin, D., & Twentyman, C. T. (1984). A multimodal assessment of behavioral and cognitive deficits in abused and neglected preschoolers. *Child Development, 55,* 794–802).

Horton, J. (2000, February 22). Foster parents shocked by events of tragic night. *Cleveland Plain Dealer* [On-line]. Available: jhorton@plaind.com

Ivanoff, A., Schilling, R. F., Gilbert L., & Chen, D. R. (1995). Correlates of problem drinking among drug-using incarcerated women. *Addictive Behaviors, 20*(3), 359–369.

Jessor, R., & Jessor, S. (1977). *Problem behavior and psychosocial development.* San Diego: Academic Press.

Jouriles, E., & Norwood, W. (1995, March). Physical aggression toward boys and girls in families characterized by the battering of women. *Journal of Family Psychology, 9*(1), 69–78.

Karpman, B. (1961). The structure of neuroses: With special differentials between neurosis, psychosis, homosexuality, alcoholism, psychopathy and criminality. *Archives of Criminal Psychodynamics, 4,* 599–646.

Kasarabada, N., Anglin, M., Stark, E., & Paredes, A. (2000). Cocaine, crime, family history of deviance—Are psychosocial correlates related to these phenomena in male cocaine abusers? *Substance Abuse, 21*(2) 67–78.

Kempton, T., Van Hasselt, V., Bukstein, O., & Null, J. (1994). Cognitive distortions and psychiatric diagnosis in dually diagnosed adolescents. *Journal of the American Academy of Child and Adolescent Psychiatry, 33*(2), 217–222.

Kenny, M., & Lane, R. (1996). Memoirs of a drug-abusing prostitute: Dynamics and treatment considerations in a case of intergenerational child abuse. *Journal of Contemporary Psychotherapy, 26*(4), 361–378

Krueger, R., Schmutte, P., Caspi, A., Moffitt, T., Campbell, K., & Silva, P. (1994). Personality traits are linked to crime among men and women: Evidence from a birth cohort. *Journal of Abnormal Psychology, 103*(2), 328–338.

L'Abate, L., Farrar, J., & Serritella, D. (1992). *Handbook of differential treatments for addictions.* Des Moines, IA: Allyn & Bacon, Longwood Division.

Lewis, A., Shankok, S., & Balla, D. (1979). Perinatal difficulties, head and face trauma of child abuse in the medical histories of seriously delinquent children. *American Journal of Psychiatry, 136,* 419–423.

Lightfoot, L., & Barbaree, H. (1993). The relationship between substance use and abuse and sexual offending in adolescents. In H. E. Barbaree, W. Marshall, & S. Hudson (Eds.), *The juvenile sex offender* (pp. 203–224). New York: Guilford Press.

Little Hoover Commission. (1992, April 9). *Mending our broken children: Restructuring foster care in California.* Sacramento: Commission on California State Government Organization & Economy.

Livingston, R. (1987). Sexually and physically abused children. *Journal of the American Academy of Child and Adolescent Psychiatry, 26,* 413–415.

Longo, R. E. (1982). Sexual learning and experience among adolescent sexual offenders. *International Journal of Offender Therapy and Comparative Criminology, 26*(3), 235–241.

Lowenstein, L. (1973). A case of exhibitionism treated by counter-conditioning. *Adolescence, 8*(30), 213–218

MacFarlane, K., Cockriel, M., & Dugan, M. (1990). Treating young victims of incest. In R. K. Oates (Ed.), *Understanding and managing child sexual abuse* (pp. 149–177). Sydney, Australia: Harcourt Brace Janovich.

Maddock, J. (1995). The perpetrator/victim interaction pattern in sexual assault and abuse. *Nordisk Sexologi, 13*(3), 142–148.

Marlatt, G. (1985). Relapse prevention: Theoretical rationale and overview of the model. In G. Marlatt & J. Gordon (Eds.), *Relapse prevention: Maintenance strategies in addictive behavior change* (pp. 3–70). New York: Guilford Press.

Marlatt, G. (1989). How to handle the PIG: The problem of immediate gratification. In R. Laws (Ed.), *Relapse prevention with sex offenders* (pp. 227–235). New York: Guilford Press.

Marlatt, G., & Gordon, J. (Eds.). (1985). *Relapse prevention: Maintenance strategies in addictive behavior change.* New York: Guilford Press.

Marlatt, G., & Gordon, J. (1987). Abstinence violation effect: Validation of an attributional construct with smoking cessation. *Journal of Consulting and Clinical Psychology, 55*(2) 145–149.

McGee, L., & Newcomb, M. (1992). General deviance syndrome: Expanded hierarchical evaluations at four ages from early adolescence to adulthood. *Journal of Consulting and Clinical Psychology, 60*(5), 766–776.

Miller, P., & Eisenberg, N. (1988). The relation of empathy to aggressive and externalizing/antisocial behavior. *Psychological Bulletin, 103,* 324–344.

Newcomb, M. (1997). General deviance and psychological distress: Impact of family support/bonding over 12 years from adolescence to adulthood. *Criminal Behaviour and Mental Health, 7*(4), 369–400.

Newcomb, M., & Loeb, T. (1999). Poor parenting as an adult problem behavior: General deviance, deviant attitudes, inadequate family support and bonding, or just bad parents? *Journal of Family Psychology, 13*(2), 175–193

Newcomb, M., & McGee, L. (1991). Influence of sensation seeking on general deviance and specific problem: Behaviors from adolescence to young adulthood. *Journal of Personality and Social Psychology, 61*(4), 614–628.

Pilowsky, D. (1995). Psychopathology among children placed in family foster care. *Psychiatric Services, 46*(9), 906–910.

Pithers, W. (1994). Process evaluation of a group therapy component designed to enhance sex offender empathy for sexual abuse survivors. *Behavior Research and Therapy, 32*(5), 565–570.

Pompi, K. (1994). Adolescents in therapeutic communities: Retention and posttreatment outcome. In F. Tims, G. DeLeon, & N. Jainchill (Eds.), *Therapeutic community: Advances in research and application* (NIDA Monograph 144, pp. 128–161) (NIH Publication No. 94–3633). Rockville, MD: National Institute on Drug Abuse Research.

Prentky, R., & Knight, R. (1991). Identifying critical dimensions for discriminating among rapists. *Journal of Consulting and Clinical Psychology, 59*(5), 643–661.

Proch, K., & Taber, M. (1985). Placement disruption: A review of research. *Children and Youth Services Review, 7*(4), 309–320.

Raskin, R., Novacek, J., & Hogan, R. (1991). Narcissistic self-esteem management. *Journal of Personality and Social Psychology, 60*(6), 911–918.

Ray, J., & Horner, W. (1990). Correlates of effective therapeutic foster parenting. *Residential Treatment for Children and Youth, 7*(4), 57–69.

Resnicow, K., Ross-Gaddy, D., & Vaughan, R. (1995). Structure of problem and positive behaviors in African American youths. *Journal of Counsulting and Clinical Psychology, 63*(4), 594–603.

Roberson, G., Yokley, J., & Zuzik, J. (1995, October). *Developing treatment guidelines for sex offender attendance at religious services: A clergy opinion survey.* Paper presented at the 14th annual Research and Treatment Conference of the Association for the Treatment of Sexual Abusers, New Orleans, LA.

Rogers, C. (1957). The necessary and sufficient conditions of therapeutic personality change. *Journal of Consulting Psychology, 21*, 95–103.

Rosellini, G. (1985). *Stinking thinking.* Center City, MN: Hazelden.

Russell, D. E. H. (1983). The incidence and prevalence of intrafamilial and extrafamilial sexual abuse of female children. *Child Abuse and Neglect, 7*, 133–146.

Ryan, G. (1993). Working with perpetrators of sexual abuse and domestic violence. *Pastoral Psychology, 41*(5), 303–319.

Sanchirico, A., Lau, W. J., Jablonka, K., & Russell, S. J. (1998, May). Foster parent involvement in service planning: Does it increase job satisfaction? *Children and Youth Services Review, 20*(4), 325–346.

Scully, D., & Marolla, J. (1984). Convicted repists' vocabulary of motive: Excuses and justifications. *Social Problems, 31*(5).

Sedney, M. A., & Brooks, B. (1984). Factors associated with a history of childhood sexual experience in a nonclinical female population. *Journal of the American Academy of Child Psychiatry, 23*(2), 215–218.

Sees, K.L., & Clark, W. (1993). When to begin smoking cessation in substance abusers. *Journal of Substance Abuse, 10*, 189–195.

Sgroi, S. (1982). *Handbook of clinical intervention in child sexual abuse.* Lexington, MA: Lexington Books.

Shealy, C. (1995). From Boys Town to Oliver Twist: Separating fact from fiction in welfare reform and out-of-home placement of children and youth. *American Psychologist, 50*(8), 565–580.

Sheridan, M. (1995, May). A proposed intergenerational model of substance abuse, family functioning, and abuse/neglect. *Child Abuse and Neglect, 19*(5), 519–530.

Shoor, M., Speed, M., & Bartelt, C. (1966). Syndrome of the adolescent child molester. *American Journal of Psychiatry, 122*, 783–789.

Starr, R. H., Jr., MacLean, D. J., & Keating, D. P. (1991). Life-span developmental outcomes of child maltreatment. In R. H. Starr, Jr. & D. A. Wolfe (Eds.), *The effects of child abuse and neglect: Issues and research* (pp. 1–32). New York: Guilford Press.

Summit, R. C. (1983). The child sexual abuse accommodation syndrome. *Child Abuse and Neglect, 7*, 177–182.

Symonds, M. (1978). The Psychodynamics of Violence-Prone Marriages. *American Journal of Psychoanalysis, 38*, 213–222.

Tinklenberg, J., Murphy, P., & Murphy, P. L. (1981). Drugs and criminal assaults by adolescents: A replication study. *Journal of Psychoactive Drugs, 13*(3), 277–287.

Urquhart, L. (1989). Separation and loss: Assessing the impacts on foster parent retention. *Child and Adolescent Social Work Journal, 6*(3), 193–209.

Van Ness, S. (1984). Rape as instrumental violence: A study of youth offenders. *Journal of Offender Counseling, Services and Rehabilitation, 9*, 161–170.

Vitaro, F., Ferland, F., Jacques, C., & Ladouceur, R. (1998). Gambling, substance use, and impulsivity during adolescence. *Psychology of Addictive Behaviors, 12*(3), 185–194.

Ward, T., Connolly, M., McCormack, J., & Hudson, S. (1996). Social workers' attributions for sexual offending against children. *Journal of Child Sexual Abuse, 5*(3), 39–56.

Wexler, H., & Love, C. (1994). Therapeutic communities in prison. In F. Tims, G. DeLeon, & N Jainchill (Eds.), *Therapeutic community: Advances in research and application* (NIDA Research Monograph 144, pp. 181–208) (NIH Publication No. 94–3633). Rockville, MD: National Institute on Drug Abuse.

Wilkenson, M., & Baker, D. (1996, January 31). Foster mom slain by teen, police say. *The Toledo Blade*, pp. 13–14.

Williamson, J., Borduin, C., & Howe, B. (1991, June). The ecology of adolescent maltreatment: A multilevel examination of adolescent physical abuse, sexual abuse, and neglect. *Journal of Consulting and Clinical Psychology, 59*(3), 449–457.

Wills, T., & Hirky, A. (1996). Coping and substance abuse: A theoretical model and review of the evidence. In M. Zeidner & N. Endler (Eds.), *Handbook of coping: Theory, research, applications* (pp. 279–302). New York: Wiley.

Wills, T., & Shiffman, S. (1985). Coping behavior and its relation to substance use: A conceptual framework. In S. Shiffman & T. A. Wills (Eds.), *Coping and substance use* (pp. 3–24). New York: Academic Press.

Wolpe, J. (1958). *Psychotherapy by reciprocal inhibition.* Stanford: Stanford University Press.

Wolpe, J. (1995). Reciprocal inhibition: Major agent of behavior change. In W. O'Donohue & L. Krasner (Eds.), *Theories of behavior therapy: Exploring behavior change* (pp. 23–57). Washington, DC: American Psychological Association.

Wyatt, G. E. (1985). The sexual abuse of Afro-American and white-American women in childhood. *Child Abuse and Neglect, 9*, 507–519.

Yablonsky, L. (1969). *Synanon: The tunnel back.* Baltimore: Pelican Books.

Yochelson, S., & Samenow, S. (1976). *The criminal personality* (3 vols.). New York: Jason Aronson.

Yokley, J. (1990). The clinical trials model: Victim responsibility training. In J. Yokley (Ed.), *The use of victim-offender communication in the treatment of sexual abuse: Three intervention models* (pp. 69–110). Orwell, VT: Safer Society Press.

Yokley, J. (1993). *Treatment for Appropriate Social Control (TASC) program manual* (rev. 1997, 2000). Available from Clinical and Research Resources, P.O. Box 538 Hudson, Ohio 44236.

Yokley, J. (1995). *Social responsibility therapy work book: Understanding abuse behavior* (rev. 1997, 2000). Available from Clinical and Research Resources, P.O. Box 538 Hudson, Ohio 44236.

Yokley, J. (1996, March). *The development of abuse in youth sex offenders: A conceptual model with treatment Implications.* Paper presented at the 12th annual conference of the National Adolescent Perpetrator Network, Minneapolis, MN.

Yokley, J. (1999a). Using therapeutic community learning experiences with youth sex offenders. In B. Schwartz (Ed.), *The sex offender: Theoretical advances treating special populations and legal developments* (pp. 19-1–19-20). Kingston, NJ: Civic Research Institute.

Yokley, J. (1999b). The application of therapeutic community learning experiences to adult abusers. In B. Schwartz (Ed.), *The sex offender: Theoretical advances treating special populations and legal developments* (pp. 25-1–25-26). Kingston, NJ: Civic Research Institute.

Yokley, J. (2000). *Social responsibility therapy: A positive lifestyle development approach.* Available from Clinical and Research Resources, P.O. Box 538 Hudson, Ohio 44236.

Yokley, J., & Boettner, S. (1999, September). *Behavior norms for outpatient youth sex offenders: Constructing a database for treatment intervention decisions.* Paper presented at the 18th annual Research and Treatment Conference of the Association for the Treatment of Sexual Abusers, Lake Buena Vista, FL.

Yokley, J., Laraway, C., & Sprague, R. (1997, October). *The treatment of youth sex offenders in therapeutic foster care: Social responsibility therapy in the TASC program.* Paper presented at the 16th annual Research and Treatment Conference of the Association for the Treatment of Sexual Abusers, Arlington, VA.

Yokley, J., & McGuire, D. (1990). Introduction to the therapeutic use of victim-offender communication. In J. Yokley (Ed.), *The use of victim-offender communication in the treatment of sexual abuse: Three intervention models* (pp. 7–22). Orwell, VT: Safer Society Press.

Yokley, J., & McGuire, D. (1991, November). *Emotional restitution: The therapeutic use of sex offender communication with victims.* Paper presented at the 10th annual Research and Treatment Conference of the Association for the Treatment of Sexual Abusers, Fort Worth, TX.

Zackon, F. (1986). Lifestyle rehabilitation: The second recovery track. *Alcohol Health and Research World, 11,* 18, 70.

Chapter 22

Standards of Care for Youth in Sex Offense-Specific Residential Programs

by Steven M. Bengis, Ed.D., L.C.S.W.

Overview

The field of juvenile sex offender treatment has expanded dramatically over the past decade. Some of these programs have been specifically developed for this population; however, others have evolved from more generic adolescent treatment programs. In order to insure that this critical treatment reflects the most state-of-the-art approaches, Dr. Bengis along with a number of colleagues have developed a set of standards for residential treatment programs addressing youth with sexually inappropriate behavior.

Introduction

In response to the expanding number of residential treatment centers purporting to treat juvenile sex offenders, the National Offense-Specific Residential Standards Task Force was organized to discuss the establishment of uniform criteria for assessing these programs. This chapter outlines the establishment of the Task Force and discusses the standards.

The Abuse-Specific Field Expands Dramatically

In the last sixteen years, both the research/knowledge base and the number of abuse-specific services for sexually abusive children and adolescents have increased exponentially. In 1982, Fay Honey Knopp had some difficulty identifying nine programs providing specialized residential services (Knopp, 1982). Only ten years later, the Safer Society Foundation conducted a nationwide survey that identified 1,300 adult, adolescent, child abuse-specific services with 300 respondents identifying themselves as providing child and/or adolescent abuse-specific residential services (Safer Society, 1994).

Three Factors Propel This Growth. This residential growth was driven by three converging factors. First, in 1988, the National Task Force on Juvenile Sexual Offending (1988) published its initial findings identifying common assumptions in the adolescent abuse-specific field. This work (updated and reprinted in 1993) provided a growing number of professionals committed to specialized treatment approaches with a respected resource through which to advocate both with their own agencies and with various state institutions for the development of abuse-specific residential services. In addition, the crystalization of perspective and approach represented by the Task Force's work further encouraged providers of existing generic residential programs to modify both their referral criteria and their treatment models to service an abuse-specific population.

Second, the society had started to take more seriously the need to protect children and others from being sexually victimized not only by adults but also by adolescents. This new focus on community safety helped to generate a sense of urgency about the sexually abusing adolescent population that further fueled the creation of resources to safely house, treat, and manage a population that was perceived as high risk or dangerous.

Third, the trend toward managing the costs of health care extended into the mental health/human service sectors. The need for cost containment resulted in the transfer of publicly funded resource allocation to newly created state or private entities. The result was a much closer scrutiny of both the numbers of children and youth placed in costly residential placements and the length of their stay in those same placements. Even in this cost-containment environment, however, due to the perception of risk, sexually abusive youth continued to be placed in residential services. In addition, often, they were allowed to remain there for lengthier periods than were other emotionally disturbed/behaviorally disordered residential populations.

Economics, Increased Consciousness, and Cost Containment Expand Number of Available Abuse-Specific Residential Services. The convergence of professional advocacy for specialization, social concern about risk, and the economic imperative to use costly residential services for only the most needy and/or dangerous clients (and then only for the least amount of time possible) helped fuel the growth of the abuse-specific residential industry. Prior to the Task Force Report, many generic residential programs accepted youth with "sexual behavior problems." Subsequent to the report, these same behavioral problems increasingly were viewed as requiring different treatment approaches Further, concerns about both community safety and risk to other program residents discouraged many service providers from offering services to the sex-abusing population. With an increasing interest in abuse-specific treatment, a decreasing base of residential providers willing to work with these youth, and an increase in providers identifying themselves as offering abuse-specific services (motivated by programmatic and/or economic factors), the numbers of youth placed in "abuse–specific" programs increased and the number of these programs continued to expand.

Expansion of Abuse-Specific Residential Programs Proves Mixed Blessing. The convergence of the previously identified factors proved to be a mixed blessing. On the positive side, although still limited, funding for abuse-specific services expanded. Professionals having long advocated for specialization were in many instances now able to find such services. Service providers desiring to provide the highest quality treatment for this population embraced the perspectives of the National Task Force, modified its treatment models, and invested resources in staff training, specialized consultation, and program development. On the negative side, not all abuse-specific programs provided appropriate or safe care. Certain providers with little appreciation for safety and treatment enhancements saw only the economic potential of a "new market." They enhanced their marketing departments without a concomitant investment in training or program development. Other providers naively announced their willingness to provide abuse-specific residential care prior to developing an understanding of the risks and responsibilities inherent in such a decision. Still other providers, while understanding the safety risks and the need for programmatic enhancements or treatment population shifts, were prevented from making these changes either by "no-eject/no reject" contracts controlled by state agencies or by the absence of state fiscal support for the changes for which they were advocating.

Diagnostic Diversity Further Complicates Safety/Treatment Dilemma

Although economic motivation, naiveté, contracting restrictions, and/or lack of funding contributed to the lack of safety and program quality, an inappropriate mix of client types within individual residential programs further added to the quality dilemma. When the child/adolescent abus-specific field began, a differentiated typology did not yet exist. Any child/adolescent exhibiting sexually inappropriate behavior, regardless of his or her diagnostic profile, was considered in need of an abuse-specific program. Even with expanding resources, the number/types of abuse-specific residential options in any given area generally was severely limited. As the "only game in town" a wide array of diagnostically different clients were often placed in these same programs. Youth with cognitive limitations and learning disabilities, and personality, mental health, hypersexualized/impulsive, and conduct disorders (all of whom committed sexually abusive acts) too often were placed together in a single abuse-specific residence. This client mix proved to be volatile and even the most sophisticated and well-motivated providers found it impossible to safely treat and manage such a diverse population.

States Lack Expertise to Monitor Quality

With the increase in referrals to abuse-specific programs, state licensing authorities inherited responsibility for ensuring program safety and treatment quality. However, these authorities often lacked the knowledge and skill to appropriately evaluate these programs and did not have any objective standards to guide them. In this vacuum, they were forced either to abdicate their evaluative function to the "experts" within the same programs they were overseeing or to use generic standards that did not include any abuse-specific criteria. The lack of agreed-on standards of care left even the most ethical providers and licensing authorities with the daunting tasks of developing appropriate residential models and protecting clients within their programs and the community.

Early Attempts at Developing Quality Standards

The growth in the numbers of youth placed in abuse-specific residential services, the increasing complexity of safely meeting their treatment needs, and concerns about safe/quality services motivated both providers and selected state licensing authorities (which were receiving an increasing number of reports of sexual acting out occurring within abuse-specific programs) to seek professional expertise to either enhance/develop their abuse-specific services or assist them in evaluating the adequacy of the safety and treatment measures being used by these programs.

But the provision of "quality residential services" was an amorphous concept about which even specialists in the sex abuse-specific field were not always in agreement. Even the chosen "experts" had to rely on their own personal perspectives on "quality" and "standards."

Individual Attempts at Standards Creation Leads to Formation of a National Task Force. Examples of such individual standards creation efforts included those by

(1) Cuninggim and Bengis (1991), who constructed a residential evaluation instrument to aid in the program development/evaluation consultations with abuse-specific residential programs in Massachusetts; (2) Jerry Thomas (1986), who developed a similar document for her work in the South; and (3) Bryon Matsuda (1996), who combined some of the foregoing work with his own perspectives to create a formal evaluative instrument for use in Utah. Although these evaluative instruments did provide some level of consistency, they were not identical, comprehensive, or peer reviewed. While inherently limited, these individual efforts did provide some objective framework for programmatic evaluation. More important, they formed the foundation for the national standards effort that was to follow.

Massachusetts Providers Facilitate Creation of a National Task Force to Develop Abuse-Specific Residential Standards. In Massachusetts, the positive experiences of several programs that had been through formal evaluations based on the standards developed by Drs. Bengis and Cuninggim encouraged the attempt to develop national standards. In support of such an effort, the chief executive officers of these programs offered to help subsidize the initial costs of developing national standards. Based on this support, Bengis contacted several national abuse-specific experts whose work had focused significantly on abuse-specific residential care. In addition to Jerry Thomas and Bryon Matsuda, Art Brown from Utah, Rob Freeman-Longo from Vermont, Jonathon Ross from South Carolina, and Ken Singer from New Jersey were consulted. The result of these conversations was the creation of an ad hoc entity committed to developing standards of care for youth in residential abuse-specific programs. After some discussion, the group chose to identify itself as the National Offense-Specific Residential Standards Task Force.

Evolution of National Task Force Work

The evolution of the National Standards project and the rationale for its initiation are most aptly described in the introduction to the recently published *Standards of Care for Youth in Sex Offense-Specific Residential Programs* (National Offense-Specific Residential Standards Task Force, 1999):

> There is a compelling need for coalescing, developing and refining the collective professional expertise of the field to create a model of best standards and practices for the residential treatment of youth with sexual behavior problems. Such collaboratively developed and agreed upon standards are the key to maximizing positive treatment outcomes, reducing the number of victims, and protecting the community. They provide the basic guidelines and template for the most effective, safest, and highest quality residential treatment for youth with sexual behavior problems.
>
> These standards were written: 1) to increase program and professional accountability for sex abuse-specific residential treatment; 2) to provide residential service providers, placement personnel, licensing authorities, parents, and other client advocates with a mechanism for evaluating the quality and appropriateness of sex abuse-specific residential programs; and, 3) to establish a common baseline of safety and competence in abuse-specific residen-

tial care. The authors have worked to maintain programmatic quality and competence while supporting creativity and diversity and recognizing the broad differences among programs in physical site capacities, contracting requirements, licensing and oversight restrictions, and resource availability.

This document has been written for an adolescent population aged thirteen to seventeen years old. While many of the standards and evaluation measures may also apply to younger children and to adults, the document was written and reviewed with an adolescent population in mind. The document should not be used with younger or older populations.

Throughout the document, the evaluation measures allow for variances due to increased or decreased client risk levels. Therefore, the standards are as relevant to shelters and step-down group homes as they are to intensive residential treatment programs. These residential standards represent the best knowledge currently available in the sex abuse-specific field. Should future research and clinical experience alter the assumptions which form the foundation of this work, the authors plan to update the document to reflect this new information. . . . (p. 1)

Together, the group met for the first time in 1996 and defined its mission as follows: "To develop offense-specific standards of practice for residential treatment programs, balancing a commitment to quality and safety with an understanding of the practical realities of administering these programs in a complex and multifaceted service delivery system."

The group members agreed that ultimately treatment programs providing these services should be required to meet specific standards of practice. They decided, however, that a great deal of preliminary work was needed before they discussed whether to form an accrediting body themselves or to pursue the goal through other means. Instead, the early meetings produced the following decisions and objectives.

1. To seek out an advisory board comprised of the top professionals in the offense-specific field to help guide the development of the standards work.

2. To maintain a small working group to maximize productivity.

3. To use current research and existing literature to guide the work whenever possible.

4. To format the document using several sections: A statement of the standard; a rationale for the standard; a definition of relevant terms; and evaluative criteria by which to measure compliance with the standard.

5. To invite wide peer review of the major working drafts of the document prior to dissemination of the final product.

6. To seek approval from the field for the development of standards through a questionnaire and by conducting workshops at national conferences of the Association for the Treatment of Sexual Abusers (ATSA) and the National Adolescent Perpetration Network (NAPN).

7. To share the work during the development stages only with colleagues who were involved in similar standards development efforts at the state level.

8. To seek legal advice regarding standards creation, dissemination, and possible accreditation.

9. To explore the possibility of developing collaborative accreditation procedures through the Joint Commission on Accreditation of Healthcare Organizations (JCAHO) and the Council on Accreditation (COA).

10. To make decisions based upon consensus. (National Offense-Specific Residential Standards Task Force, 1999, p. 4)

Consistent with its stated mission and self-defined mandate, the group started its work by reviewing the standards document created by Bengis and Cuninggim. Early on, the limitations of that document became apparent and various task force members were assigned the task of developing additional standards or altering those already written. At the same time, the Task Force sought to develop an advisory board made up of the most prestigious national experts willing to participate. The National Task Force Advisory Board members, each of whom had agreed to review and comment on working drafts, included Vicki Agee, Ph.D., Judith Becker, Ph.D., Jerry Clark, L.C.S.W., Dave Fowers, M.S.W., John Hunter, Ph.D., Connie Isaac, Bruce Janes, M.S., Saundra Johnson, Gary Lowe, L.C.S.W., Barry Maletzky, M.D., William Murphy, Ph.D., Robert Prentky, Ph.D., Gail Ryan, M.A., Ben Saunders, Ph.D., Joann Schladale, M.S., and Gina Wheeler, M.A.

The Process of Standards Creation by the Task Force

The process of standards development is outlined in the Introduction to the Standards document:

The [Task Force] met in a two-day formal work session for the first time in 1996 and defined the Task Force's mission: To develop offense specific standards of practice for residential treatment programs, balancing a commitment to quality and safety with an understanding of the practical realities of administering these programs in a complex and multifaceted service delivery system.

***

The group began its work by reviewing the initial document created by Drs. Bengis and Cuninggim and by suggesting additional standards. Assignments on the development of individual standards were made according to interest and expertise. Drafts of the standards were reviewed prior to formal meetings and any and all positions were discussed until the Task Force members reached agreement.

When consensus was reached on the initial draft, the advisory board and additional readers were asked to review the document and give input. As anticipated, that input proved invaluable and resulted in a significant re-write of major sections of the document.

During this time, selected members approached Joint Commission on Accreditation of Healthcare Organizations (JCAHO) and the Executive Director of the Council on Accreditation (COA) to explore the possibility of collaboration. On the basis of those discussions, the group decided that a collaborative accrediting venture would not be the most effective way to maintain the integrity of the Standards project. Subsequently, after incorporating comments from the field gathered through questionnaires, the group decided against becoming an accrediting body themselves. Rather, they decided that subsequent to publication of the final document, they would work with state agencies and licensing authorities to encourage them to incorporate the Standards into their own oversight and licensing mandates.

By the Fall of 1998, the working group, now known as the National Sex Offense-Specific Residential Standards Task Force, had: 1) Presented initial drafts of the work at national ATSA and NAPN conferences; 2) completed two document reviews by the advisory board; and, several internal revisions. The Task Force completed a final draft that was prepared for dissemination both over the Internet and by mail to the professional field for peer review. The document appeared on the Internet for three months. Reviewers were asked to complete a questionnaire regarding their views of the document. At a final meeting in February, 1999, the Task Force reviewed these comments and completed the final revision.

Finally the Task Force requested and received a review of the glossary to the Standards by the Center for Sex Offender Management (CSOM). CSOM edited these and made several helpful suggestions that were utilized. CSOM also developed a glossary for general multiagency sex offender intervention that is complimentary to the Standards glossary. In addition, CSOM reviewed the final draft of the Standards and made suggestions for revisions. (National Offense-Specific Residential Standards Task Force, 1999, p. 6)

Specific Standards Developed

The Task Force developed standards in twenty-eight areas organized around four main issues: program-related standards, staff-related standards, residential safety standards, and clinical intervention standards.

Program-Related Standards. This category consists of seven standards:

1. *Commitment of Governing Authority.* The program's governing authority has knowledge of, and is committed to providing, management and resources for quality implementation of an offense-specific program for sexually abusive/ aggressive youth.

2. *Admission and Exclusion Criteria.* The program's admission and exclusion criteria clearly identify the youth that the program can safely manage and effectively treat.

3. *Intake and Informed Consent.* The program has a clear offense-specific intake procedure that includes informed consent.

4. *Least Restrictive Setting.* Each resident has the right to treatment in the least restrictive setting that maximizes resident and community safety.

5. *Victim Rights, Resident Rights, and Community Safety.* The program must

resolve any conflicts between the individual rights of the resident, the rights of victims, and the protection of the community in a manner that is both legally and ethically sound.

6. *Treatment Model.* The program's central treatment model is multi-modal, multi-disciplinary and offense-specific.

7. *Range of Clinical Services.* The program provides a range of clinical services that address both offense-specific and other clinical needs.

Staff-Related Standards. Four standards (Standards 8 through 11) relate to this area.

8. *Staff Qualifications and Competence.* The program employs staff who are qualified and competent to work with sexually abusive/aggressive youth.

9. *Staff Orientation and Training.* The program provides relevant offense-specific orientation and in-service training to all staff.

10. *Staff Communication.* The program uses a comprehensive communication system with a multi-disciplinary team approach.

11. *Staff Supervision.* The program provides regular offense-specific supervision for all staff working directly with residents.

Residential Safety Standards. Six standards (Standards 12 through 17) apply to this category:

12. *Facility Environment.* The facility environment is designed or modified to address the management of offense-specific risks.

13. *Staffing Levels and Patterns.* The program maintains a staff-to-resident ratio and pattern that provide adequate staff supervision.

14. *Prevention of Sexual Contact.* The residential program prohibits and is designed to prevent any consensual or non-consensual sexual contact.

15. *Program Response to Sexual Conduct.* The program has a protocol for addressing sexual contact between residents and/or residents and staff, and follows all state reporting requirements.

16. *Mixed Populations.* A program with mixed treatment populations must demonstrate the ability to safely meet the treatment needs of all residents.

17. *Residential Risk Management.* The residential program mandates that offense-specific criteria be used for risk-management decisions.

Clinical Intervention Standards. Eleven standards (Standards 18 through 28) comprise this category:

18. *Assessment and Evaluation.* The program provides offense-specific assessment of, and evaluation for, each resident.

Figure 22.1
Treatment Model

STANDARD:

The program's central treatment model is multimodal, multidisciplinary and offense-specific.

RATIONALE:

To meet the diverse needs of sexually abusive/ aggressive youth, a program will have to include a wide range of modalities, utilize a variety of theoretical approaches, and be delivered by a competent and well-trained, multidisciplinary team. Then, in order to provide differential diagnosis and treatment for individual residents, the program will need to identify, and consider the impact of, the modalities and theoretical techniques which apply to each resident.

Treatment for sexually abusive/aggressive youth should focus on teaching the skills and abilities necessary for the resident to develop self-control and to manage his/her sexual behavior. This work takes place in various modalities and is integrated into all program components, particularly the direct care interventions.

EVALUATION MEASURES:

1. The treatment model should include an offense-specific program designed to alter those characteristics that support, or are precursors of, offending behavior and should include methods for addressing:

- the development of coping mechanisms necessary to lead a non-offending lifestyle;
- cognitive-behavioral problems related to sexually abusive behaviors;
- relapse prevention;
- deviant arousal, sexual interest, and/or inappropriate fantasies;
- previous victimization history, including post traumatic stress disorder;
- sexual aggression;
- development and demonstration of victim empathy;
- the concept of restitution;
- anger management, assertiveness, interpersonal and communication skills, and observing their implementation;
- precursors to sexual abuse behavior such as the assault cycle, chain, or pattern that may be applied to other behavioral problems;
- cognitive and educational capabilities;
- family needs, issues, and dysfunction;
- integration of the youth back into the community, school, and family;
- positive and healthy sexuality; and
- collateral clinical issues, (e.g., developmental issues, attachment disorders, etc.)

2. There are written assignments and activities that document the youth's movement through the program, including achievement of measurable goals and demonstration of skills. Resident's level of achievement may result in decreased/increased restrictions, supervision and/or privileges.

3. There is a description of services that commits the program to providing specialized treatment to address sexually abusive/aggressive behavior. It is recommended that current research and practice in the field support this description of services.

4. The program provides:

- adequate time for internalizing knowledge in each area identified above;
- written competency-based curricular materials in each area consistent with the cognitive level of the residents; and
- appropriately trained staff to address each treatment model area (see Standards Four and Five).

5. The requisite skills and abilities for program completion are objectively defined and measurable and outlined in the program description.

6. The utilization of innovative approaches not supported by a significant body of research and literature is reviewed and approved by the treatment team and/or management.

7. There are policies and procedures for each treatment modality and method. These are clearly descriptive and identify the multi-disciplinary team member responsible for its delivery.

19. *Treatment Planning.* The program uses comprehensive, offense-specific individual treatment plans for each resident.

20. *Use of Intrusive Methods.* Each resident has the right to be treated using the least intrusive methods necessary to achieve a positive treatment outcome.

21. *Family Involvement.* The program actively encourages and pursues family involvement throughout the treatment process.

22. *Program Milieu.* All treatment components must consider the offense-specific needs of residents and modify policies and procedures accordingly.

23. *Case Management.* The program provides offense-specific case management services.

24. *Multicultural Issues.* The program has policies and procedures to address multicultural issues.

25. *Community Reintegration.* The program develops and implements a systematic community reintegration plan for each resident.

26. *Discharge Criteria.* The program has offense-specific, measurable, and observable discharge criteria.

27. *Aftercare Services.* The program provides, arranges, or advocates for offense-specific aftercare services for each resident.

28. *Evaluating Treatment Effectiveness.* The program evaluates the effectiveness of treatment for each resident.

Standards Format

As explained in the standards document, the format was established to "assist the reader in both interpretation and implementation." As such, in addition to the standard which is a "brief statement that embodies the overall purpose and target area of the standard" the document includes two other elements.

Rationale. The rationale provides more narrative to assist in developing an understanding of the background and intent of the standard.

Evaluation Measures. Each standard provides a list of evaluation measures that gives more detailed guidelines for assessing compliance with, and implementing, the standards. This section is not meant to include all possible measures of compliance.

Figure 22.1 (from National Offense-Specific Residential Standards Task Force, 1999, p. 18) presents a "Treatment Standard" in its entirety.

Conclusion

Since the publication of the Standards, approximately 300 copies have been disseminated. Some abuse-specific residential providers are using the Standards for purposes of self-evaluation, others have requested formal evaluations from experts based on the evaluative criteria contained in the Standards document, and several state agencies, such as the Department of Children and Family Services in New York State (S. M. Bengis, personal communication, 2000) are engaged in a process of modifying the Standards for use in their evaluative/contracting procedures.

As with the National Task Force Report, the Standards document has provided professionals who are advocating for quality services with a valuable and useful resource and State licensing authorities with a reference with which to hold abuse-specific providers accountable. In the words of those who participated in the Standards effort: "It is the hope of each Task Force member that this document will be useful to the field and provide motivation for the improvement of services to this population (National Offense-Specific Residential Standards Task Force, 1999, p. 2).

Initial results point to the success of that stated endeavor.

References

Bengis, S., & Cunningim, P. (1991). *Sex offense specific residential standards.* Unpublished manuscript.

Knopp, F. H. (1982). *Remedial intervention with adolescent sex offenders: Nine program descriptions.* Orwell, VT: Safer Society Press.

Matsuda, B. (1996). *NOJOS evaluation instrument.* Unpublished manuscript.

National Offense-Specific Residential Standards Task Force. (1999). *Standards of care for youth in sex offense-specific residential programs.* Holyoke, MA: NEARI Press.

National Task Force on Juvenile Sexual Offending. (1988). Preliminary report from the National Task Force on Juvenile Sexual Offending. *Juvenile and Family Court Journal, 39,* 2.

National Task Force on Juvenile Sexual Offending. (1993). Preliminary report from the National Task Force on Juvenile Sexual Offending. *Juvenile and Family Court Journal, 44,* 4.

Safer Society. (1994). *Safer Society nationwide survey of sex offender treatment programs.* Brandon, VT: Author.

Thomas, J. (1986). *Plan for treating young sexual offenders in Tennessee.* Nashville, TN: Interdepartmental Coordinating Council, Children's Services Commission.

Chapter 23

Creating a Positive Milieu in Residential Treatment for Adolescent Sexual Abusers

by Vicki MacIntyre Agee, Ph.D.

Overview

Housing a number of behaviorally disordered youths in a residential setting could be a recipe for disaster. What if these peers decide to create an antisocial culture rather than adopting the more prosocial attitudes of the adults who run the facility? After all, it is for exactly such antisocial behavior that these youths are there in the first place. In this chapter, Dr. Agee presents a variety of techniques for encouraging adolescents to develop a positive peer culture.

Introduction

One of the most common mistakes when attempting to implement a residential treatment program for adolescent sexual abusers is allowing program control by a negative milieu. It was once thought that adolescent sexual abusers were not as susceptible to developing an antisocial milieu as were typical juvenile offenders. In spite of their sexual offenses, they were considered to be fairly easy to manage in a residential program. Most of their acting out was covert, so on the surface they appeared generally cooperative. But that has changed, perhaps because of social policies limiting the most restrictive environments to the most disturbed clients. Youths who are sent to residential settings typically have serious conduct problems in addition to their sexual offenses. The aggressive, high-risk offenders in most residential programs now are as prone to defiant, antisocial peer cultures as a population of non-sex offending juvenile offenders. Signs of negative peer milieus includes such behaviors as the following:

- Continual attempts at victimizing others:

    — Sexual acting out
    — Fighting
    — Assaults

- Antisocial or oppositional behaviors toward authority figures

    — Negative subgroups
    — Peers supporting deviant behavior
    — Peers punishing those who show prosocial behaviors

- Contraband: sexually oriented or otherwise

- Peer support for refusal to disclose offenses

- Untidy appearance of unit and residents

- Frequent runaway attempts

- Verbal assaults

    — Insults, name calling
    — Ridicule, taunting
    — Cursing

- Excessive horse play (often sexualized)

- Continual grooming behaviors

— Touching others
— Staring at body parts
— Invading people's personal space
— Removing clothing, exhibiting self
— Sex talk
— Soliciting, plotting

Compounding the difficulty in managing these behaviors is newer evidence that a significant percentage of adolescent sexual abusers have real physical correlates of their disturbing behaviors. A growing body of research shows that a significant percentage of sexual abusers have underlying neurological deficits (Langevin & Watson, 1996). In particular, attention deficit/hyperactivity disorder (ADHD) and other comorbid disorders, are common (Kafka & Prentky, 1994, 1998). Teaching control of negative impulses and prosocial behaviors to youth with normal brain functioning is difficult enough. Changing behavior in youth with neurological impairment is a more formidable task, and one which cannot be done effectively in an antisocial setting.

The effect of grouping negative peers together in itself is highly risky and increases the likelihood that a youth may get worse in a peer-group program. Dishion, McCord, and Pullin (1999) reviewed findings from two studies, which suggested that peer-group interventions increase adolescent problem behavior. The authors describe what they call deviancy training, which is the process of contingent positive reactions to rule-breaking discussions. When youth are reinforced by such behaviors as rapt attention, laughter, obvious excitement, and encouraging comments, the problem behaviors among the peer-group members escalate rapidly. Dishion et al. (1999) conclude that one should avoid congregating high-risk peers together as the result can be iatrogenic.

Of course, Dishion et al. (1999) were studying community programs, and remaining in the community is rarely an option for high-risk adolescent sexual abusers. The herculean challenge in residential settings is to reverse negative peer influences by successfully creating a positive peer milieu. In a positive peer milieu "deviancy training" is confronted and controlled by the same peers who ordinarily would be reinforcing the negative behavior. But there is little question that the process is difficult to establish and maintain.

The movement to create prosocial milieus in treatment settings has a long history and developed from many different roots. Maxwell Jones in 1953 originated the term "therapeutic community," a dramatic contrast to the strict medical model used in psychiatric hospitals. This approach created a whole new movement in the field of mental health treatment. Similarly, in the field of correctional treatment, McCorkle and Bixby (1958) implemented similar techniques with delinquents in New Jersey, calling it guided group interaction. Vorrath and Brendtro (1974, 1985) expanded on the concept and called it positive peer culture.

During subsequent decades, versions of therapeutic community approaches emanated from several different disciplines, including mental health, substance abuse, corrections, education, and social services. The quality of the implementation was as varied. Some felt the approach should not be diluted by adding other components; others combined it with multifaceted treatment programs (Agee, 1979; Gibbs, Potter, & Goldstein, 1995). As would be expected with such a wide range of application, research into effectiveness was spotty. Some studies saw it as an effective approach; others did not. It is not surprising that the research was inconclusive, as the quality of service provision varied widely.

The theory behind milieu approaches is fairly simple. A positive peer milieu approach is not a treatment technique but a team management approach to creating a prosocial environment in which treatment can take place. Unlike a typical institutional model where the youths are disempowered, here they are enlisted as part of the team. Youths, who crave status, respect, and approval from their peers, are given a sense of ownership and responsibility for helping their peers.

Equally important, the positive peer milieu approach dramatically lessens the typical battles with authority that are so characteristic of adolescents in general, and aggressive adolescents in particular. Youth who perceive they are being forced to change are extremely resistant. Resistance decreases when they are considered a significant part of the change process. The positive peer milieu process allows each youth some control, some input, and, most important, the opportunity to see, through the eyes of their peers, that it is in their best interest to change.

Again, the positive peer milieu process takes intense ongoing effort but is far less stressful than ongoing authority battles, crisis management, and deviancy training by peers in a negative milieu. Of course, adolescent sexual abusers typically do not have the social cognitive skills to help themselves, let alone their peers. They need careful guidance from the entire team to ensure that the group culture is a safe, responsible, and helpful one. This chapter describes one approach to creating an effective positive peer milieu in a residential treatment program for adolescent sexual abusers.

Basic Requirements for Positive Peer Milieus

Creating a Safe Environment. The first rule in establishing a positive peer milieu is to ensure that the peers feel safe in the program. The mantra in the field of treatment of sexual abusers, "no more victims," includes victimizing within the program as well as outside. Treating sex offenders is a highly risky endeavor, both for staff and for other clients in the program. Unfortunately, both staff and fellow clients have been victims of sexual assaults in sex offender treatment programs, along with other kinds of victimization. Clearly, in a positive peer milieu, safety and treatment go hand in hand.

In addition to the risk of sexual victimization by their peers, the subtler deviancy training mentioned previously is another huge risk. Controlling the pervasive influence of peers to reinforce deviant behavior requires considerable skill and constant vigilance on the part of the staff. In group therapy, for example, the group members are asked to disclose their offenses, their fears and anxieties, their family problems, and the most intimate details of their troubled lives to each other. What may seem very therapeutic also provides ample opportunities for deviancy training. Peers can subtly, or even obviously, reinforce the deviant behaviors by such actions as rapt attention to prurient details, laughing, allowing excuses, and so on. Also, when group members are asked to confront their peers, they are vulnerable to retaliation, particularly in situations in which they are not being supervised.

To create a safe environment, the first priority is to ensure that residents are never left unattended inside or outside the facility. Line-of-sight supervision must be the standard in the program. Supervision is far more difficult than it is with other client groups, because sexual acting out is so covert. Youths intent on sexual gratification can be amazingly clever and cunning, and human beings attempting to supervise them are fallible. To assist in supervision, many programs use electronic monitoring such as motion detectors and video cameras.

Even with line-of-sight supervision and electronic monitoring, safety cannot occur without the help of the peers themselves. It is not possible, for example, to monitor all peer conversations to ensure that they are not encouraging each other's deviance. There has to be an enforced program norm that when peer support for negative behavior occurs, someone will find out and deal with it. This requires the peers themselves to be a part of the process. Rather than the usual institutional norm of not confronting negative behaviors, in a positive peer milieu, youths are reinforced for doing so. Confronting negative behaviors is reinterpreted for them. Rather than the negative peer interpretation of it as "ratting," it is redefined for them as behavior which responsible people do when others are in danger of harming themselves or others, in other words, as helpful, caring behavior.

Building a Positive Staff Culture. Again, in a positive peer milieu model, the peers are empowered to be responsible for their own peer culture, and the staff's role is to guide them in the process. As mentioned, it is clearly a team management approach—everybody is an important part of the process. In developing an effective team, it is critical that the team members are aware of their own culture and follow their team norms. One of the first steps in team building is the task of agreeing on the staff norms. Following are some examples of norms for effective positive peer milieu staff teams:

- We treat everyone with respect.
- We do not correct another staff member in front of peers.
- We support team decisions, even if we disagree with them.
- We make sure we do not have boundary violations.
- We work together to resist staff splitting.
- We never keep secrets for residents.
- We model responsible behavior.
- We do not reveal personal information about ourselves or about other staff with residents.
- We do not gossip about team members or residents.
- We do not set other staff up against residents.
- We follow the program norms.
- We dress appropriately at all times.
- We honor the code of confidentiality.
- We are not enablers or rescuers.
- We control our anger.

A great deal of the work in establishing the positive staff culture is ensuring that everyone is following the norms. This takes constant open communication and honest feedback, which seems to be much harder to do with fellow staff than with the residents; thus times for giving feedback to each other has to be structured into team meetings.

Following the program norms is equally important to following staff norms. Unfortunately, in many programs, there is a large gap between what the program design is intended to be and what is actually done. Following is an example of how a norms gap appears:

> At Facility X, a rule is that no resident can go on an outing unless he has earned enough points by meeting his goals, and also that he has staff and peer approval. A resident who has not earned the points nor the approval of group, approaches the administrator personally and tells him that his heart will be broken if he can't go on the group outing, He promises to be good the next time. The administrator says, "Okay, but just this once."

This may seem like an unlikely occurrence, but versions of this example happen frequently in residential programs. Naturally, when someone with power makes decisions inconsistent with the structure of the program, it erodes the program effectiveness and disempowers the staff and the peers. The key issue is that the program cannot have traditional institutional management and a positive peer milieu model at the same time. Unfortunately it is not uncommon in programs attempting to develop a positive peer milieu to revert to authoritarian management approaches.

A team management approach does not preclude a hierarchy of management, of course. Clearly, all team members have different roles and responsibilities. The point is that the leaders of the program have to act consistently as the value carriers for the program norms.

A paramount task in a positive peer milieu, as with any effective program, is to build in a process to provide constant monitoring of program standards. A routine quality control process can be readily keyed to the positive peer milieu process while monitoring all the critical components in a comprehensive treatment program for sexual abusers.

The Positive Peer Milieu Process

In a positive peer milieu, staff guide residents to help each other follow the norms. Positive peer milieus are based on norms and the constant sharing and reinforcement of what is expected and why. Again, staff have the daunting responsibility to maintain norms, hold residents accountable for what is expected, and teach them appropriate behavior and thinking. Because the typical youth enters the program in denial, resistant, with poor social skills and little motivation, how do the staff help create a milieu that reinforces the concept that it is in each youth's best interest to change?

There is no easy answer. But the basic concepts involve the same two processes that occur simultaneously in most behavior change programs: (1) guiding the youth to follow prosocial norms and (2) correcting them when they violate norms.

Guiding the Positive Peer Milieu. To address the techniques for guiding in a positive peer milieu, the process can be summarized as reversing, relabeling, and reinforcing.

Reversing. In a positive peer milieu, insistence on accountability is essential to create and maintain motivation to change. All attempts to shift the blame to someone else have to be countered by peers or staff. Most adolescent sexual abusers have been reinforced in the past for various tactics to deny accountability, if by nothing more than escaping without getting consequences. Most of them felt justified in committing their offenses, or they would not have done so. Also, the justification usually includes blaming someone else, parents, friends, society, even the victim. Of course, it is contrary to reason to expect a youth to change behavior he considers someone else's fault.

Although many programs pride themselves on holding residents accountable for their behaviors, in some there is a gap between what is espoused and the overwhelming message the residents perceive. Particularly with offenders who have themselves been victimized in the past, the message the residents may receive inadvertently is that their offense was not a choice but a result of being victims themselves. Again, this lessens the discomfort necessary to be motivated to change. In a positive peer milieu, it is crucial that the peers learn to be responsible for their behavior—to own it. Owning, of course, means that the youth understands that he is accountable for choosing to do the behavior and for the consequences, no matter what happened to him in the past.

Thus, the art of reversing is the art of turning it back on them, as they say in positive peer milieu jargon. The peers are reinforced by the staff to counter any attempts to lay blame externally. Of course, the peers have to be taught to reverse confrontation effectively, even when the excuse for the behavior is convincing. Usually, they are taught labels for the tactics to evade responsibility, such as "minimizing," "victim stance," "attempting to confuse," and "intimidating." Then, they are taught appropriate countering responses (see Figure 23.1 for some examples of a countering tactics to reverse blaming behaviors).

Relabeling. In a positive peer milieu, residents are taught a new language to identify their problems. This is called relabeling. Dr. Deborah Tannen, the linguist, has aptly described the process of why it is necessary to teach new labels in order to shape thinking.

> People who enter psychotherapy . . . soon begin to talk differently, using new words, or, more common and more disconcerting to the uninitiate, using old words in new ways. It is inevitable and important for people who subscribe to a special way of thinking to develop a special way of talking also. For one thing, it establishes a feeling of a common point of view, of rapport, among those who share this way of talking. . . . Also, perhaps most important, a new vocabulary and a new way of talking are tantamount to a new way of looking at the world." (Tannen, 1986, p. 194)

One of the common cognitive deficits in a population of adolescent sexual abusers is being unable to perceive patterns in their behavior. This inability contributes to

Figure 23.1
Countering Tactics to Reverse Blaming Behaviors

Excuse to Evade Responsibilty	Reversal
"What do you expect of someone who was raised by a mother who is a crack addict and a prostitute?"	"Your mother didn't commit your offense. You did."
"I just was playing around with her and only tickled her."	"When you say *just* and *only* you minimize what you really did to your victim."
"I did it because that is what happened to me when I was little."	"What happened to you was not an excuse to hurt someone else."
"I couldn't help it because I was high and didn't know what I was doing."	"You chose to abuse drugs and you chose to do the offense."

repeating the same negative behaviors over and over and not appearing to profit from experience. These behavior patterns result in habitually distorted thinking. Relabeling gives them a new language to describe their thought processes and behaviors and to show them that what they saw as discrete behaviors are really a pattern of behaviors that have contributed to their being in trouble for much of their lives.

Different positive peer milieu programs use a variety of lists of problem behaviors and thinking when they relabel behaviors. Many programs, particularly those with sexual abusers, use some version of thinking errors, originally postulated by Yochelson and Samuelson (1976). The objectives are to teach the youths to identify the thinking errors behind the harmful behaviors (relabeling) and to teach correctives for the thinking errors.

Relabeling has to take place throughout the day. Constant repetition is seen as necessary because so many adolescent sexual abusers have a hard time understanding abstract concepts. And they must learn to look continually at the concept not just the behavior.

> *Example*: Tommy blows up at a staff member and starts cursing him. He says he did it because staff shouldn't tell him what to do.

Of course, this is not an isolated event for Tommy, but a pattern of behaviors reflecting opposition to authority and inability to control anger. The incident could be labeled in a few different ways but would probably be given a thinking error label describing a need to control others, such as power thrust. Relabeling helps the youth understand that each negative incident in his life is not an island to itself. It is connected to the continent of distorted thinking!

After learning to identify the thinking errors, the youth must learn to correct them. Correctives involve teaching prosocial thinking to combat the thinking error. Prosocial skills training has to permeate the program. It takes a long time to learn the many intricacies of acceptable social behavior. It is particularly difficult for youth who may have attention and impulse disorders. Typical prosocial skills modules cover such areas as anger management, victim awareness, values clarification, social skills, independent living skills, and relapse prevention. These classes must be regularly scheduled and proceed as described in the module. Although the principles can be taught in educational modules, practicing the skills must be monitored and shaped in the peer culture.

Correcting thinking errors can also be addressed in individualized treatment plans. For example, if a youth typically demonstrates the thinking error "inability to empathize," treatment plans are designed around completing tasks that can develop empathy.

Reinforcing. The change process is an extraordinarily difficult one. Sexual urges are intense and insistent. This is particularly problematic for youths with impaired prefrontal lobe functioning who have great difficulty in response disinhibition.

It is a constant challenge to convince residents that it is in their best interest to control their sexual impulses and relate to others in a prosocial manner. Teaching them to identify their thought distortions is crucial, as is arousing motivation from feeling discomfort over what they have done. But, it is even more difficult to reinforce them effectively. It requires both concrete and social reinforcers.

In many programs, the residents earn points for prosocial behaviors. They can spend these points at a canteen and/or accumulate them to get privileges and move up levels. The key issue is to make sure the reinforcements are desirable to the residents. Residents' needs and interests are constantly changing. It is a good idea to revise the canteen inventory or the privilege list every six months or so, with input from the peer group on what members would like.

Along with increased privileges, each level has more responsibilities in the peer milieu. To test the durability of the changes under stress, the level design should make it difficult to achieve every promotion. Each level should have explicit tasks to achieve and multiple sources of input before every promotion (e.g. task completions, points accumulated, peer approval, and staff approval). Making the process structured, demanding, and difficult tends to make it more desirable.

Of course, social approval from peers and staff is presumed to be the most effective reinforcement. The highest level in a positive peer milieu program has to have clear status to the lower-level peers. High-status peers have to be seen as role models. Thus, in addition to earning increased privileges, with each promotion, youths earn more respect from peers and staff. At the top level, they are given the status usually reserved for sports stars in a typical high school. This is quite a powerful reinforcement for youths who may once have perceived themselves as society's pariahs. Of course, they have to continuously earn the respect, so any serious norms violation must result in prompt demotion.

While troubled adolescents seem to have considerable talents for reinforcing negative behaviors, they usually do not know how to compliment and praise prosocial behaviors. And with their characteristic egocentricity, it often does not occur to them. Teaching peers to show respect and approval for each other's positive behaviors is an ongoing task for staff. The behavioral approach used is the technique of prompting and fading. Initially staff tells the individual what to say, then, the prompt gets less and less obvious until it fades away. For example, the group leader might begin by saying, "Does the group think they should tell Johnny that he is doing a good job at learning the program?" Later, the group leader could say, "Who has positive feedback for Johnny?"

Staff approval is usually perceived as less important, but that does not mean it is not also imperative. Few people know how to give positive reinforcement well. Approval is only relevant if it is intense, specific, and personal (Andrews & Bonta, 1994). This does not mean "gushing." Approval in a positive peer community is more often done in the form of coach-like encouragement. Excessive praise is often perceived as "babying" by most adolescents and stimulates the natural opposition to authority for this age group, such as, "If adults like it, I hate it!"

In conclusion, giving positive reinforcement for prosocial behaviors is one of the most important and yet one of the most often neglected techniques when establishing a positive peer milieu. It is so important that it should be designated a program standard to be achieved at a high level and measured regularly in the quality control system. Some quality control procedures, for example, have built-in requirements to regularly observe program interactions for sample periods and actually count the ratio of positive to negative reinforcements given by the staff to residents during that time. This would seem an arduous process, but it ensures regular monitoring of whether the standard is being met.

Correcting Norms Violations in the Positive Peer Milieu. A significant part of learning responsible behavior is developing self-discipline. Among other things, becoming a responsible adult necessitates showing respect for authority, controlling impulses, following through on obligations and accepting criticism. Because the majority of the adolescent sexual abusers who are admitted to the residential treatment programs have been out of control for a long time, teaching discipline is an extraordinarily difficult challenge. Many youth have received a great deal of disapproval and harsh consequences in their previous lives to no avail. In the positive peer milieu, the strong reinforcement to youth for choosing to do the "right things" (prosocial behaviors) is paired with strong disapproval and effective consequences for choosing to do the "wrong things" (antisocial behaviors). The beauty of a positive peer milieu approach is that the majority of limit setting is done through the peers—not by the peers but through them.

That is an important distinction—peers do not punish other peers. Rather, they are encouraged to give appropriate social disapproval for violating group norms. Again, this is a powerful negative reinforcement. Most adolescents really care about what a jury of their peers thinks of them. The best part is that the traditional adolescent power struggle between them and adults is sidestepped.

The key is to establish a balance between the staff's responsibilities and the peers' responsibilities. Clearly, adolescent sexual abusers do not have a good record with handling power. In fact, abusing power is a major part of their victimizing of others. With their characteristically weak social cognitions, they have no concept of the many skills it takes to handle leadership appropriately and need ongoing training and guidance from staff.

Following are the usual steps in the behavior management process in a positive peer milieu:

- *Checking.* Checking is another word for giving a prompt. A prompt is intended to build in an early warning system to curb impulsive behavior, particularly important with youths who have problems with prefrontal lobe functioning. The goal is to get the youth himself to identify the thinking error. Youths who are beginning to learn critical self-analysis need a great deal of guidance in identifying their distorted thinking.

    A youth is more likely to attend to prompting if it comes from his peers. The staff's role is to prompt the peers to help the youth identify the thinking errors, and do it in a way that is helpful rather than attacking. The peers are also corrected for failing to prompt their peers. In some programs, for example, the staff checks the whole group for not confronting a norms violation. Checks can be verbal or nonverbal:

    — *Nonverbal check.* When someone sees a resident violating a relatively minor norm, he signals him with a gesture or some other nonverbal sign.

    — *Verbal check.* This is to prompt the person who does not respond to a nonverbal check or whose norms violation is of some concern. Some facilities have the person giving the warning preface the statement with "Check yourself..." This is often preceded with "Can you?" or "Please," followed by "Thank you." Here are some examples:

    "Can you all check yourselves for the noise level in here? Thank you."

    "Check yourself for interrupting. Thank you."

    "Check yourself for getting up from your seat without permission. Thank you."

    "Check yourself for violating others' personal space. Thank you."

- *Confrontation.* If the behavior does not stop after prompting, the next step is usually one of several forms of intervention.

    — *Individual intervention.* The person doing the confronting gives the resident a message that his behavior is violating the norms and that he needs to change his behavior. The key phrases used are:

    "The norm for this is _____."

    "What you need to do is _____."

    "What are your choices right now?"

    — *Huddles or Group Intervention.* In some programs, the high team members request staff (or staff request them) to have a huddle or talk with their peer at this point. The term huddle is a descriptive one for an impromptu, short-term intervention by a small group of peers and staff. A huddle is called during daily living experiences if the following situations occur:

Refusal to follow requests or to respond to checks.

Behavior which is flagrantly disrespectful of others.

The program design explains when and how huddles may be used. Because they disrupt the ongoing program, there may be set times at which huddles may be held or cannot be held. For example, it may be decided that in the school program, behavior management is done by the school's system and huddles are not held during class times. At times at which huddles are allowed, only staff may initiate a huddle. This is an attempt to ensure that the process is not being abused. Any youth may request a huddle, but staff must initiate it. Before initiating it, staff decide and indicate which three or four peers should be in the group. Huddles are conducted standing in a circle. The staff stays with the huddle and guides the process. Ideally, ten minutes would be the longest time for a huddle. During the huddle, the peers are asked to share with the confronted youth how they see his behavior, to try to see his point of view, and to suggest alternative behaviors. At any time during this process if the youth becomes aggressive or refuses to cooperate, he may go to time out. However, he must continue the process when he gets out of time out.

— *Time out.* In some programs, youths are required to go to time out when their behavior persists after they have been prompted. This may occur before or after the previous step, depending on the youth's behavior. Once asked to go, the youth must go quietly. The youth is accompanied by staff, and the other residents are told to step back. If there is resistance, the youth is escorted by the acceptable methods. The time out usually lasts for ten minutes, which starts when the youth is quiet. However, some programs use a graduated time out, such as starting with three minutes, increasing to six, and so on. The time out can occur in any designated area. It can be an empty room, or a marked area of the floor. If it is not in a secluded room, the youth should be directed to turn his back to the group, as youths who are acting out are likely to attempt to enlist other peers by various attention-getting tactics.

• *Consequences.* At this point, if the youth has not responded to the foregoing interventions, more extended consequences go into effect. In most programs, the consequence is usually a level demotion to a restricted status. On the restricted program the youth is not allowed to interact with peers until an individualized behavior contract is completed, including restitution tasks. Privileges are also seriously curtailed.

Consequences must be well defined in the program's behavior management system and then must automatically occur when indicated. Naturally, all consequences must be firm, fair, and consistent. This takes constant work with the staff to monitor how they are implementing the behavior management program. Again, this can be built into the quality control system.

Peer Group Therapy

The key to team management is team meetings. Teams require frequent meetings to work together cooperatively. Similarly, the key to the positive peer milieu is in frequent groups: daily peer group therapy, prosocial skills groups, and huddles. Peers are held responsible for helping each other change, so they need to have ongoing knowledge of each other's problems and progress. The groups provide an opportunity to have concentrated opportunities for peer influence. In groups, the members are able to help each other see through evasive maneuvers such as denial, projection of blame and minimization and are better able reinforce prosocial behaviors.

Traditional approaches to group therapy have been seen to be ineffective with a correctional population. As Andrews and Bonta (1994) state: "Our reading of the literature suggests that these 'insight-oriented,' 'evocative' and 'relationship dependent' approaches to correctional counseling and casework were either ineffective or even criminogenic in their effects. This trend is particularly evident when such unstructured programs are offered to high-risk and/or interpersonally immature cases" (p. 195).

At one time, it was thought that group was group. That is, group leaders chose a theoretical approach and used it universally. There was almost no attempt to match the group structure and process to the unique strengths and deficits of the population. But now we realize that we have to key the approach to the cognitive and social strengths and weakness of the population being treated.

Youthful offenders, including sexual abusers, tend to be impulsive, have difficulty with abstractions, have difficulty adapting to change, have poor verbal receptivity, have low empathy, have poor social skills, and can be easily influenced by negative peers. Positive peer milieu groups are ideal for youths with these deficits because they are structured, frequent, consistent, and peer oriented.

The Group Leaders. The group leader's role is paramount, because he must teach the youth how to be therapeutic—to show concern and caring and to reinforce prosocial behaviors. The group leader teaches, directs, supports, and appears to be always in control. Although there is room for variability in personality style, this is within certain limits. Group leaders who are too laissez-faire (noncommittal or passive) cannot enforce the structure or promote a feeling of safety. Similarly, group leaders who are too authoritarian (controlling, bossy) disempower group members and limit their participation.

A positive peer milieu group requires a group leader who follows a middle ground of being in control but not being controlling. It is important that the leader have an ability to convey "charisma" with youths—someone whose opinion the youths value and whom they would like to impress—which requires someone with obvious self-confidence. As mentioned previously, youths are taking a big risk when they disclose their deepest thoughts, feelings, and bad experiences to their peers. They are also expected to confront violation of norms and negative peers. To do this, they must feel safe. They have to know the group leader has a strong enough personality to control the group so they will not be hurt.

In a way, the group leader has to appear all-knowing, as if nothing the group members say is going to shock him. Somehow, the group leader must convey the impression that he has heard everything and can handle anything. Of course, anyone can still be shocked and no one knows everything, but it is the ability to project this facade that provides comfort to youth who (one often forgets) are still children.

In the positive peer milieu model, the group leader is at the top of the staff treatment team hierarchy. Although there are usually other administrators, it is important that the group leader have major input into the treatment plan of each youth in the group, and major input into what goes on with each group member throughout the program. That gives credibility to the group. Otherwise, it becomes hypocritical to the peer culture. The peers are given the message that they have responsibility for their peers, and that group is the place in which their input is most important, but the work they do in group must be followed up throughout the program. Of course, peers do not make treatment decisions for each other, and they know that staff have final say, but they do think that their input is very important and they are listened to. They count on the group leader to relay their input to other staff. If the group leader is often overruled by some other staff, outside clinician, or administrator, most peers begin to consider group a waste of time. And they look for whoever has the power to attempt to influence that person.

It is very important for groups to have one assigned group leader; in fact, it is a key concept. However, because groups are held each day, neither schedules nor the group leader's stamina allow him to lead all sessions week after week. Therefore, there must be at least two group leaders for each group, and that is one of the main roles of the assistant group leader. When the group leader is present, the assistant group leader takes notes and observes—and only rarely interjects something. Again, the idea is that it is a peer-run group. Two adults talking make it less likely this will happen. The assistant group leader runs group when the group leader is off duty.

The Structure and Process of Peer Group Therapy. The heart of the positive peer milieu is in the daily group counseling sessions. A positive peer milieu group differs from traditional groups in that the peers are held responsible for conducting the group. Because youth enter the program not knowing how to help themselves, let alone help others, this process needs to be guided and shaped. A great deal depends on the skills, perceptiveness, and charisma of the group leader, who acts as a teacher showing the group members how to help each other analyze their thinking patterns and learning alternatives.

The ideal positive peer milieu group size is between eight and twelve members. If possible, the group members should be matched by similar characteristics. For example, they may be divided by personality characteristics, with more vulnerable, immature youths in one group and tougher, more aggressive youths in another. Some programs match by sexual offense history, some by age group. The more similarity the youths have to the other peers, the more rapid the group bonding.

The positive peer milieu group is structured with strong norms or expectations for behavior. To show structure and consistency, the positive peer milieu group is held at the same time every day (five days a week) and it lasts at least an hour and a half. Attendance is mandatory. Once started, the norm is that no one should interrupt group. This structure conveys to the peers the status and importance of the group to the program.

Setting the Agenda. The residents form a circle with their chairs or desks. The group leader sits at one end of the circle. The group leader then directs one or all of the group members to remind the group to recite the group norms. Following is an example of typical group norms.

- We respect the confidentiality of group information.
- We arrive on time and leave on time.
- We stay in group until it is over.
- We sit in a circle, sit up, and pay attention.
- We ask for the agenda on ourselves not others.
- We always look at the person we're talking to.
- We always confront thinking errors.
- We support others when they need encouragement.
- We do not attack anyone, verbally or physically.
- We have no side conversations or subgroups.
- We do not interrupt or dominate the group.
- We do not laugh at people.
- We give honest feedback.
- We never support negative behavior.
- We see things from other people's point of view.
- We don't take offense at helpful criticism.
- We remember our victims.

The group leader then directs one of the residents to start their agenda, and the agenda setting proceeds around the group. It is not an option to ask for the agenda; it is an expectation. The agenda request should be concise and structured to make it easier for the youth who is talking and those who are listening. Abstract concepts and confusing topics are anathema for youth who are easily distracted. Following is an example of a structured agenda request.

My day has been . . .

My thinking errors were . . .

I would like to have the agenda to work on . . .

Whenever possible, the agenda should be on something that is related to the reasons the youth is in the program, or what Andrews and Bonta (1994) refer to as criminogenic behavior, including such broad areas as past victimizing behavior, sexual assault cycles, impulse control, relapse prevention issues, and such specific issues as how ongoing daily behavior is reflecting patterns of distorted thinking. The agenda-setting process should be fairly business-like, so it does not turn into a group session without someone having been chosen for the agenda. When everyone has chosen an agenda, the voting takes place.

To start the voting, the group leader reads out each youth's name and his agenda request and counts the number of hands raised. Group members may vote only once and may vote for themselves. The majority wins. If there is a tie, the group leader chooses which agenda to discuss. The youth with the most votes is awarded the agenda. Using the term "award" helps reinforce the idea that it is considered an honor to be chosen to select the agenda in group. Ideally, the agenda-setting process should take about ten minutes for a group of eight residents.

During Group. The resident who has been awarded group is helped to restate the problem. Then, the group leader asks the group members how they would like to work on the problem. If it is a fairly new group, the group leader can give the group a suggested technique. Because of the low verbal receptivity and impulsivity of most of the youth, action-oriented techniques are preferable, so a role-play, an empty-chair technique, a mirror technique, or doubling are often suggested. If an action technique is used, the group leader acts as director. Throughout the process, the peers are encouraged to give their input. The group leader guides the process by turning it back on group. This involves redirecting questions to the group and teaching members to do most of the talking. Following are examples of typical questions to turn back on group.

> "Do any of the peers know:
>
> . . . what he did to his victim?"
>
> . . . what thinking errors [trigger thoughts, tactics to avoid accountability] he is using here?"
>
> . . . if he is trying to intimidate you?"
>
> . . . why he would think the police [teacher, parent] would pick on him?"
>
> . . . how he tried to manipulate people?"
>
> . . . if he understands the harm he caused his victim?"

Throughout the group, it is also necessary for the group leader to notice whether any group norms are being violated and ask someone to point them out to the violator.

Group should end after solutions are given to the peer who had the agenda, and the peer has made a commitment to make changes.

Processing Group. At the end of group at least ten minutes is spent processing. This is the most important part of group, as this is when the group leader provides positive and/or negative reinforcement to each group member for successive approximations at being a good group member. He encourages the group not to condemn or criticize when identifying residents' problem areas and helps them to reinforce appropriate behaviors.

He does this by going around the circle, peer by peer, giving positive and/or negative feedback.

Example: "Bill, you did very well pointing out thinking errors to Sam."

Or, "Johnny, we would appreciate your input more often and you need to work on following group norms."

The group leader then gives a wrap-up statement to the whole group that sums up the issue of the day or the state of the peer culture.

The group should stay within the time frame designated for group—usually an hour or an hour and a half. It is difficult to finish group in one hour, but because the session is limited to one person's agenda, and because youth with attention deficits can concentrate better for short periods, an hour is acceptable.

The Seed Group

To start a positive peer milieu, whether it is in an existing negative milieu or starting from the beginning in a new program, requires a "seed group." This is a group of cooperative peers who are taught the program well and then "seeded" or divided into two or more new groups. Essentially, the group members are given thorough training in the process, including role playing the behaviors. They are motivated both by giving them a challenge and by some ownership in the process. For example, in a new program, they might have input into the group norms, into the names of the various groups, even into such things as a logo for sweatshirts and "team" colors. A suggested outline of this process follows.

Creating Group Motivation. The group leader challenges the new group by telling the members they are being given the difficult responsibility of making a positive peer milieu. They are told how important it is to have a program that will be able to change them into responsible young men rather than individuals rejected as "perverts" by society. The group leader tells them such things as the following:

- They are founders of the peer community.

- This may be one of the most important things they do in their lives.

- They will make a difference for hundreds of youths in the future, in addition to countless victims.

- They will be able to tell their parents that they not only turned their lives around but also helped start a place where hundreds of kids turned their lives around and stopped victimizing people.

- This is a chance to make their families proud of them and to make amends for hurting people in the past.

- The honor of being the first to reach the highest level of the program is emphasized. They are told that they may be the first high-level peers, but this is not automatic just because they were the first residents. It is emphasized that will take a lot of hard work to be a high-level peer.

Structure of the Seed Group. The seed group meeting is held at the same time as regular group will be held when the program starts. The youths go through a series of training sessions like those described next. The privileges initially are the same as on the entry level in the program. They will go to school, eat meals, attend seed group, and spend the rest of the time studying the program and preparing whatever preparatory paperwork is required for group membership, often an application for group membership. This is a form which includes self-disclosure and setting goals for change. Within a few days, residents who have been doing well are given first-level privileges and start to accumulate points, even though they are not officially on the first level of the program yet. After the seed group training sessions are complete, each peer has to ask for a community group. Community group is designed as an interview/initiation process into the peer culture. There are three tasks for the youth who has community group: reviewing his application for group membership, answering questions to verify his knowledge of the treatment program, and stating his goals for the future. If the resident successfully passes community group, the other residents vote him to the first level of the program. Making it difficult to be promoted is intended to increase the desirability of attaining group membership. There is a great deal of social approval given for completing the process. Along with the increased respect from staff and peers, the youth begins to get the privileges associated with level promotions.

The seed group's training sessions usually take place over three or four weeks before the series of community groups begin and, one by one, youths get promoted to the regular program. Following are some suggested topics for the seed group training sessions. Sessions vary in length and can take several meetings to complete.

- Understanding problem behaviors;
- Positive peer milieu philosophies and program norms;
- Thinking errors and correctives;
- Peer therapy groups, huddles, and prosocial skills groups;
- Level promotions and the behavior management system.

Starting the Positive Peer Community Program. As the seed group training sessions continue, youths are told to begin completing their applications for group membership in order to get ready to request their community group. By this time, they should all be anxious to start the regular program. Community groups are held when new peers enter the existing positive peer culture, or when a youth wants to return to group after being demoted to a discipline level. Because there is no existing positive peer group yet, the seed group itself becomes the community group. As with all groups, the process of community group is quite structured. The youth who sets the agenda goes over his application for group in detail and the group leader guides the other group members to encourage him to follow group norms, to be accountable, and to identify thinking errors. He is especially encouraged to direct his talk to peers and not to staff as would be done in a traditional group. After the youth has gone over his group application, he is asked questions on the program. If he answers most of them and has done an adequate job of owning his past behaviors, he is promoted to the first level of the program. If not, he is sent back to the seed group until he is ready to try again.

When the majority of seed group members have completed their community group and have been promoted to the first level, the regular program begins. It is pointless to do such intense training of the residents without following it up with ongoing mentoring by staff. Staff not only have to be good mentors but must be firm with behavior management and must faithfully follow the structure of the program from the beginning.

Taking Over an Existing Negative Peer Culture. Reversing an existing negative peer culture is a difficult process that requires careful strategic planning. There may be a great deal of resistance from the existing peer culture. Negative peers like to be in control and oppose having their control removed. Thus it is important to prepare action plans for what do when various scenarios of resistance occur. It is particularly important to review the plan for handling group disturbances.

The first step in the action plan involves identifying those youth who are being positive even in the middle of a negative peer culture and choosing them to be the seed group. The second step is usually shutting down the existing program. That means demoting every youth who has been acting out negatively to a restricted level. Usually, this is preceded by a warning informing the youth that the program is going to change after a certain date and that their behavior until that time will determine their level in the program. Then, when the date for starting the positive peer milieu arrives, the peers who have been selected for the seed group are brought together and the rest are demoted until their behavior improves. The positive peers remain on whatever level of the program they had been on in the previous program and continue to get whatever privileges they had been having. The seed group goes through the aforementioned sessions, adapted based on what they should already know. For example, if the same behavior management system will be used, they just go over it briefly to be reminded of how it is supposed to work

Meanwhile, the negative peers are strictly on a structured, basic, and rather uninteresting program, lacking privileges or reinforcements. It is important to protect the positive peers from the negative group and keep them separate as much as possible. The change to a positive peer culture will occur only if the new positive group is both protected and empowered by staff, because the negative peer leaders will do their best to regain control. The message given to each negative peer on the restricted level is that when his behavior is consistently cooperative (measured by behavior scores or staff opinion), he may apply to be a member of the new positive peer group. Until then, he is out of group. This reinforces the concept that peer group membership is a privilege. And again, being out of group means he is out of all the positive aspects of the program also, such as recreation (other than basic exercise) and other privileges.

As each negative peer shows improved behavior and fills out his application for group membership, a community group is scheduled with the seed group. Even though the youth may have completed a similar form when he started the program, he is asked to do it again because he clearly had not been working in the program. The message is that he needs to start over.

It is often best to separate the strongest negative leader from his strongest followers and bring the latter into community groups first. Sometimes, however, the negative leader perceives the inevitability of change very quickly and capitulates, at least on the surface. Bringing him into the group at that time may be a strategic move if the newly developed positive peer group is empowered enough to keep him from taking over leadership.

When all the youths are off of the basic level, the program must still be supervised extremely closely and prompt demotions must occur for negative behaviors. The negative peers will attempt to reestablish their subgroup as soon as possible. Part of the ongoing staff strategic planning must involve closely observing the peers to monitor for signs of reemergence of the negative peer culture and to intervene.

Conclusion

Establishing a positive peer culture takes the concerted continuous effort of the entire staff, but it is far preferable to the damage that can be done by a negative peer culture. It is highly unlikely that effective behavior change can take place in a setting where peers are reinforcing antisocial behaviors.

Brendtro and Ness (1982) described some of the things that go wrong with the positive peer milieu approach. One of the most common mistakes is to allow abuse of confrontation, either staff-peer or peer-peer. This often occurs when individuals are empowered to confront others, but given no training and ongoing mentoring in how to do it in a positive, helpful manner. The approach is a powerful behavior management tool that can be used irresponsibly by staff as well as peers. In some programs, for example, staff would use peers to carry out discipline, which is exceedingly inappropriate and destructive.

Another problem in some positive peer milieu programs was the lack of parental involvement in the treatment process. As the peers were empowered, the parents were disempowered. Family involvement was minimized. Usually, the family already feels helpless and anxious. It is a terrible blow to a family to have a child who is labeled a sexual abuser. Excluding them from the treatment process continues the disempowerment and more or less guarantees future difficulties when their son returns home. Effective treatment programs, of course, include the family as part of the team. In fact, the quality and quantity of family involvement in the program are often the most important predictors of treatment success.

Another major problem in implementation of a positive peer milieu was one that Brendtro and Ness (1982) referred to as purist rigidity. Some positive peer milieu model programs had no room for flexibility, creativity, or change. The field of treatment of sexual abusers is experiencing what is almost a knowledge explosion. So much excellent research is going on that it is completely unrealistic for any treatment program to remain static. Effective program administrators must stay current with the literature and schedule an annual program review to make sure the program is evolving to meet the changing needs of the clients and new developments in the field. Again, the positive peer milieu approach is the milieu in which the treatment takes place; it is not the treatment program. The positive peer milieu should be the structure underlying a dynamic, flexible, and changing program.

Reversing negative peer influence in a residential treatment program for adolescent sexual abusers is a difficult and ongoing process, but it is a necessary condition to providing effective treatment.

References

Agee, V. L. (1979). *Treatment of the violent incorrigible adolescent.* Lexington, MA: Lexington Books.

Andrews, D. A., & Bonta, J. (1994). *The psychology of criminal conduct.* Cincinnati, OH: Anderson Press.

Brendtro, L. K., & Ness, A. E. (1982). Perspectives on peer group treatment: The use and abuse of Guided Group Interaction/Positive Peer Culture. *Children and Youth Services Review, 4,* 307–324.

Dishion, T. J., McCord, J., & Poulin, F. (1999, September). When interventions harm: Peer groups and problem behavior. *American Psychologist, 54,* 755–764.

Gibbs, J. C., Potter, G. B., & Goldstein, A. P. (1995). *The equip program: Teaching youth to think and act responsibly through a peer-helping approach.* Champaign, IL: Research Press

Jones, M. (1953). *The therapeutic community.* New York: Basic Books.

Kafka, M. P., & Prentky, R. A. (1994). Preliminary observations of DSM III-R Axis I comorbidity in men with paraphilias and paraphilia related disorders. *Journal of Clinical Psychiatry, 55,* 481–487.

Kafka, M. P., & Prentky, R. A. (1998). Attention deficit hyperactivity disorder in males with paraphilias and paraphilia-related disorders: A comorbidity study. *Journal of Clinical Psychiatry, 59,* 388–396.

Langevin, R., & Watson, R. J. (1996). Major factors in the assessment of paraphilics and sex offenders. *Journal of Offender Rehabilitation, 23*(3 & 4), 39–70.

McCorkle, E., & Bixby, F. L. (1958). *The Highfields story.* New York: Holt.

Tannen, D. (1986). *That's not what I meant.* New York: Ballantine.

Vorrath, H. H., & Brendtro, L. K. (1974). *Positive peer culture* (1st ed.). Chicago: Aldine.

Vorrath, H. H., & Brendtro, L. K. (1985). *Positive peer culture* (2nd ed.). Hawthorne, NY: Aldine.

Yochelson, S., & Samenow, S. E. (1976). *The criminal personality: Vol. 1. A profile for change.* New York: Jason Aronson.

Chapter 24

Demonstrating Social Responsibility Through Emotional Restitution— Victim Responsibility Training

by James M. Yokley, Ph.D.

Overview

Victim empathy development components and apology/clarification sessions are common procedures in sexual abuser treatment, with 91% of child, youth, and adult programs reporting the use of a victim empathy component in their treatment and 73% using victim apologies (Freeman-Longo, Bird, Stevenson, & Fiske, 1994). Despite their prevalence, there is a paucity of research-informed clinical protocols and evaluation research regarding these procedures in the literature.

This chapter describes victim responsibility training (VRT), a research-informed treatment protocol with the basic treatment goals of helping abusers develop an understanding of the impact of abuse on victims and victim empathy and demonstrate social responsibility by making emotional restitution during apology/clarification sessions to abuse survivors.[1] VRT is an important component of social responsibility therapy for individuals with abuse behavior problems. VRT begins after abusers have developed a track record of appropriate social behavior control and involves demonstrating social responsibility through emotional restitution to abuse victims and their families in a manner that is therapeutically beneficial to all parties involved.

Introduction

Genuine emotional restitution cannot be made to abuse survivors without an adequate level of understanding of the impact of abuse on victims and victim empathy. Having problems with empathy for others "is the hallmark of the perpetrator of child sexual abuse" and "simplifies abuse of power because failure to perceive the negative consequences of exploitation of the victim diminishes or even eliminates guilt for the perpetrator" (Sgroi, 1982, p. 253). When compared to nonoffenders, sexual abusers of children have been found to be deficient in victim empathy, perspective taking, intimacy, and self-esteem (Fisher, Beech, & Browne, 1999; Hanson & Scott, 1995; Marshall, 1993). The sex abuser's empathy deficit is considered to be important in the development and maintenance of the deviant behavior (Marshall, Hudson, Jones, & Fernandez, 1995). Thus, developing victim empathy is considered imperative to relapse prevention and is a key component for sex abuser programs to achieve maximum effectiveness (Ryan, 1997; Pithers, 1999; Schwartz, 1994).

The empathy, perspective-taking, and role reversal deficits exhibited by sexual abusers appear to be responsive to treatment. For example, increased empathetic skills were revealed by one process evaluation of a group treatment component using cognitive, affective, and behavioral procedures designed to enhance abusers' empathy for sexual abuse survivors (Pithers, 1994). In addition, specialized treatment has been shown to enhance abusers' empathy for victims and to eliminate the contextual empathy deficit that was evident during abuse precursive moods (Pithers, 1999).

Empathy deficits may be more person specific than was previously thought (Marshall et al., 1995), and general empathy in sexual abusers of children may not be directly related to empathy for their victims (Fisher et al., 1999). Thus, VRT components focus specifically on victim empathy not general empathy, general perspective taking, or generic role reversal ability. Since the first four components of VRT in this treatment description are specific to teaching sexual abusers to understand survivors of sexual abuse, the news articles, victim letters, and videos used in VRT[2] pertain to sexual abuse. These materials must be substituted with abuse-specific information if the VRT approach is to be effectively applied with multiple abusers referred for treatment of other forms of abuse (e.g., physical abuse, such as domestic violence, or alcohol abuse.

The VRT emotional restitution mandate, a specific explanation about why the victim-understanding information components are being provided, along with when abusers will be held accountable for making emotional restitution to their victims and how they will be evaluated, is consistent with the transfer of training research. Specifically, the three "signals" that have been demonstrated to influence organizational trainees' intentions to apply what they have learned occur when trainees (1) received relevant information before the training program, (2) recognized that they would be held accountable for learning, and (3) perceived training as mandatory (Baldwin & Magjuka, 1991).

VRT consists of eight consecutive cognitive-behavioral interventions on two separate levels. The first level involves abusers assuming their social responsibility to learn the impact of their behavior and to develop victim empathy so that they can demonstrate their social responsibility to make genuine emotional restitution during the second level. VRT uses research-informed clinical procedures to address the basic factors that can act to block abusers from adequately demonstrating their social responsibility to learn victim impact information on Level 1 and make genuine emotional restitution during Level 2. Although theoretical benefits to victims and offenders are expected (Yokley & McGuire, 1990), this portion of social responsibility therapy[3] incorporates psychological testing to monitor victims who participate in impact groups and apology sessions with abusers.

Victim Responsibility Training Level 1: Developing Victim Impact Understanding

Level 1 of VRT was designed to help the abuser learn to understand the victim's thoughts and feelings. The understanding, perspective-taking procedures, and group discussions used in Level 1 of this process are typically referred to as victim empathy training in sex abuser treatment (Knopp, 1982). In addition to relapse prevention with sexually abusive youth, comprehension of the victim's experience of sexual abuse is relevant to the youth's victims of abuse as well as the abuser's own past victimization (Ryan, 1997).

There is more than one theory about what causes empathy problems. According to Marshall (1993), poor attachment bonds between the child who is to become a sexual abuser and his[4] parents lead to low self-confidence, poor social skills, and a lack of empathy for others, which is reinforced during puberty by maladaptive social messages. Maladaptive social messages that exacerbate empathy problems emphasize power and control over others, objectify others as instruments of sexual pleasure, and deny the need for social skills as well as compassion for others, which feeds the emotional loneliness that breeds aggression and selfishness (Marshall, 1993).

The abuser's lack of empathy or appropriate prosocial thoughts toward his victims could also represent an affective avoidance response. P. Thomas of the sex abuser therapy program at Echo Glen Children's Center, Snoqualmie, Washington, has stated that based on his experience "adolescent sex abusers do not so much lack empathy for their victims as avoid it . . . because of the considerable anxiety and guilt it elicits" (Knopp, 1982, p. 98). Empathic distress caused by emotional overarousal may create an aversive state, which exceeds an individual's subjective distress tolerance. When this tolerance is exceeded, cognitive functions that impede empathy and decrease the probability of prosocial action may occur. For example, the distressed person may become self-focused and preoccupied with the aversive state or make a causal attribution such as blaming the victim to reduce his level of discomfort (Palmer, 1989). Maladaptive self-statements which rationalize, justify, or minimize the effects that abusers have on others are thought to contribute to this deficit (Knopp, 1982). Inaccurate perceptions and faulty attributions that blame the abuser's behavior on others or attribute that behavior to external factors are also considered to be contributing factors. Thus from this perspective, distress related to experiencing empathy triggers maladaptive thinking which relieves the discomfort by blaming, minimizing, and justifying to avoid or block the emotional distress.

Whether the abuser's empathy deficit is the result of a developmental delay related to poor parental attachments or an affective avoidance response, stimulus overload can trigger maladaptive thinking and shut down the abuser's ability to learn the victim impact information presented in Level 1 of VRT. Thus, a graduated exposure approach to this victim understanding, impact, and empathy development level is warranted to maximize the probability of successful completion. Graduated exposure pioneered by Joseph Wolpe (1958, 1995) as a part of his systematic desensitization treatment prevents stimulus overload and avoidance responses by gradually exposing the client to increasing levels of the target condition. This procedure is the treatment approach of choice when tension, anxiety, stimulus overload, anger, defensiveness, shutting down, and other avoidance defenses are predicted.

To modify the maladaptive self-statements and cognitive distortions that abusers hold regarding their abusive behavior that impairs empathy development, abuser programs use a variety of victim impact/understanding interventions. In addition to group process techniques, these interventions include bibliotherapy (i.e., articles about or letters by victims), live or videotaped psychoeducational presentations (i.e., in which victims or victims' therapists speak about the abuse), or various types of role playing (Knopp, 1984). Ross and Loss (1988) have recommended different forms of the first three types of VRT Level 1 victim understanding interventions.

The four victim understanding interventions in Level 1 of VRT are presented in a hierarchy of increasing cognitive/affective impact on the abuser in an attempt to prevent stimulus overload and affective avoidance responses through maladaptive thinking. This procedure is conducted in group therapy sessions in which abusers are gradually exposed to the anxiety/guilt-eliciting subject of the impact of their behavior on their victims. This form of graded *in vivo* exposure can be referred to as *in vivo* group flooding (i.e., the gradual increase in group exposure to the distressing stimulus with escape response prevention). Both exposure and flooding techniques are considered readily adaptable for group use on clients with similar fear and avoidance responses (Emmelkamp, 1982; Michelson, 1985).

After the completion of each of the four interventions on Level 1, all abusers rate the effects of that intervention on a twenty-two-item abuser impact questionnaire (Yokley, 1990). The first twenty-one questions involve impact ratings. For example each abuser would respond to the impact question "How much general anxiety or fear did you experience during this learning experience?" by marking a 5-point scale which ranges from "none" to "a great deal" of impact. Question number 22 asks the abusers to "Please comment on what affected you most about this learning experience." Completion of the impact questionnaires on all four Level 1 interventions is followed by group discussions of abuser reactions to the interventions where response modeling, feedback, and verbal reinforcement are employed. During these discussions, prosocial responses are verbally praised while maladaptive thinking and inappropriate affective responses are confronted by both therapists and positive peer models. Figure 24.1 provides a summary of the VRT Level 1 interventions.

Intervention 1: Victim News Articles on Abuse Impact. In the first VRT intervention, all abusers receive a bibliotherapy reading assignment of newspaper articles about the impact of sexual abuse on victims. The articles describe the types of thoughts and feelings victims experience and how their trauma is often revived by news of sexual assaults. One article describes the specific trauma suffered by a victim of a serial rapist who was not charged because he was caught after the statute of limitations on his crime was exceeded. After reading the articles, all abusers complete their impact questionnaires, discuss what they have learned in a group session, and receive a graded homework assignment, which involves answering six questions based on the articles.

Intervention 2: Letters Written by Victims on Abuse Impact. The second intervention involves a bibliotherapy procedure whereby the abusers hear actual letters written by victims about their abuse. Several letters written by victims are read to the abuser groups by their therapists. The first letter is the least emotional most general one, and it is followed by more serious and specific letters. A student who describes how sexual abuse makes victims feel and addresses all abusers in general wrote the first letter. The following letter was written by a teenage female incest victim in treatment at a local agency victim's program. That letter expresses her specific feelings directly toward the stepfather who abused her and begins with "Dear Rick, I hate your guts." That same incest victim wrote another letter to her unassertive, enabling mother expressing her specific feelings directly toward the mother. This letter also gets right to the point and begins with "Dear Terri, You always asked me what it was you were doing wrong in raising your children, well now I'm going to tell you . . . ." After reading the letters, all abusers complete their impact questionnaires, discuss what they have learned in a group session, and receive another six-question graded homework assignment.

Intervention 3: Victim Videotape on Abuse Impact. In the third intervention, abusers observe an emotional videotape documenting the impact of sexual abuse on real-life victims. Regarding the use of victim videotapes to educate abusers, a television documentary of a victim-abuser reconciliation group has been produced which uses a tape of five actual victims of different crimes to help incarcerated individuals visualize what they have done to others (Pollak, 1990).

In the videotape used,[5] four real-life survivors of sexual abuse (two males and two females) discussed the actual abuse they suffered and their thoughts and feelings about being abused as well as some of the coping mechanisms they employed. The first victim, who was molested by both her father and grandfather, makes a statement that is considered of particular importance to the preparation of abusers for responsible behavior toward their victims. Specifically she states:

> My grandfather died before I had the chance to go back and confront him about what he did to me. I determined that I wasn't going to let that happen with my father. . . . It was real important to give him back his burden. I needed something from him. I needed him to say "I did it and I'm sorry" and to really recognize what he had done to me.

Figure 24.1
Victim Responsibility Training Summary

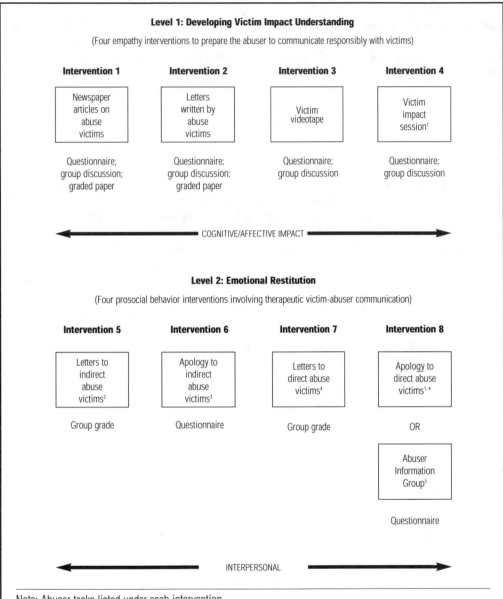

Note: Abuser tasks listed under each intervention

1. Victim's emotional state (i.e., test measures of depression, anxiety, anger, external control) is evaluated before and after contact with the abuser.

2. Telephone feedback on victim impact is gathered after this intervention.

3. Impact questionnaire on the apology/clarification letter and session is given to indirect victim.

4. Impact questionnaires are given to victim and his/her therapist after this intervention.

5. Both victim's and abuser's emotional state is evaluated before and after group contact with each other.

After watching the victim videotape, all abusers complete their impact questionnaires and discuss what they have learned in a group session.

Intervention 4: Victim Impact Group. Transfer of training research indicates that elements of the posttraining environment can encourage or block the application of new skills and knowledge (Baldwin & Ford, 1988). Thus, victim or offender treatment environments not supportive of victim-offender meetings can block the offender's ability to make emotional restitution even if the abuser has internalized the training and can express himself in a socially responsible, empathic manner. This makes it important for abuser treatment staff to work closely with the victims' therapists or advocates and victims prior to all interventions involving therapeutic victim-offender communication. In VRT, this means careful planning, discussion, and interaction with victims' therapists prior to Intervention 4, 6, and 8 as well as a careful review and discussion of victim "What I want to know" lists in abuser groups prior to any offender information group for abuse survivors.

In the Intervention 4 victim impact group, an unrelated sexual abuse victim (or victims) discloses the impact of sexual abuse on her life in a face-to-face session with the sexual abusers while sitting between the victim's and abuser's therapists. The victim impact group used in Intervention 4 is similar to the victim impact panels used by Mothers Against Drunk Drivers to confront drunk driving offenders. Although parents of those killed by drunk driving offenders are overcome by grief, they also suffer the helplessness and powerlessness that sex abuse victims experience, which is associated with not being able to control the situation.

No previous data are available on the benefits of victim impact groups for sexual abuse victims and their abusers. However, in a related intervention Newbauer and Hess (1994) have indicated that conjoint group treatment for youth sex abusers and survivors with the goals of increased abuse understanding and victim empathy helps abusers learn to identify and confront distortions in language and incongruities in behavior. In addition, Lord (1989) reports that this intervention is valuable for both victims of drunk driving and the offenders. According to Lord (1989), victims serving on an impact panel experience the following:

- A decrease in affective distress after telling their story;

- A positive feeling of increased personal strength after the emotionally draining panel; and

- A belief that they may be preventing the victimization of others.

Victim impact panels are reported as valuable in helping abusers move beyond focusing on their own consequences to considering the pain that their behavior has caused others and breaking down their problem denial. Impact panels have also been reported to imprint cognitive imagery of real people suffering which can be recalled when reoffending is being considered and thus can help change abuser behavior. In a controlled study of the victim impact panel presentations on "hard core" drunk drivers, significant positive attitude shifts and changes in behavioral intentions were revealed (Badovinac, 1994). Specifically, drunk driving offenders were more likely to agree that planning ahead, taking precautions (e.g., using taxis or designated drivers), and imposing limits on alcohol consumption by drivers at bars was important. In addition, a prosocial attitude in the form of the desire to prevent others from driving impaired appeared to be increased by the panel presentations.

One victim-abuser reconciliation group which was established in the largest prison in the free world at Vacaville, California, brought abusers "face to face with victims so that they could face and free themselves" (Pollak, 1990). This group used the victim impact panel approach whereby victims come into the prison and speak directly to the abusers about their victimization as well as the impact of the crime on their lives. At the time of the report, the group had met once a week for the past eighteen months and among the first to meet the abusers were three victims of brutal rape. One of the victims stated her belief that "you have to put faces on the victims and you have to put faces on the abusers before anything can change" (Pollak, 1990). One of the abusers confirmed this belief by stating, "When I started thinking about this person's parents, their mother and father and how I would feel if it would have been my dad or my sister or somebody close to me like that, it made me want to cry, it really hurt me deep inside and made me want to think of doing something to repay it" (Pollak, 1990). That abuser was expressing the socially responsible motivation to make emotional restitution that VRT hopes to instill.

In the victim impact session employed in VRT Intervention 4, volunteer survivors of sexual abuse from a local agency's victim treatment program address the abuser group. These survivors describe the sexual abuse committed against them and give direct feedback to the abusers on the specific impact that sexual abuse has had on their lives. The survivors may then ask the abusers to disclose their offenses, clarify why they felt they offended, and request answers to other questions in areas they want to clarify. Thus, in addition to the goal of developing abusers' understanding of the impact of their abuse behavior, this intervention also has the goal of helping victims decrease their emotional distress by getting answers about abusers' thoughts and behaviors. It is hoped that these answers may empower the survivors with knowledge of abusers that they can apply to their recovery.

The victim impact group is the first real opportunity for abuser treatment staff to observe socially responsible behavior in the actual presence of a victim. During the victim impact group, a therapist sits on both sides of the survivors so that no abuse survivor is sitting next to an abuser in the group, and a video camera is placed behind the victims and focused on the abusers. Other victim safeguards include discussing responsible and appropriate behavior toward the survivors conducting the impact group and signing a ten-item behavior contract which specifies the expected abuser behaviors toward the survivors before, during, and after the session (Yokley, 1990). Abusers attending the impact session must have reached a level where they understand their social responsibility obligation to make emotional restitution and to answer any questions they are asked by members of the victim impact panel in an open, honest, concerned, and responsible manner.

The primary purpose of the victim impact group is to change the abuser's thoughts, feelings, and behaviors while observing and evaluating abusers in an environment similar to what they will experience during the apology/clarification sessions with their actual victims of abuse. However, victim protection from adverse emotional impact receives equal attention and care. To monitor the victim volunteers for possible adverse impact as the result of meeting with abusers, victims are administered psychological tests before and after they address the abuser group. Test measures of depression, anxiety, and anger along with a locus-of-control scale are typically administered.

In addition to psychological testing, all survivor volunteers who participate in the victim impact group receive a follow-up questionnaire (Yokley, 1990) to tap the subjective impact of the group on the victims in other areas. After attending the victim impact group, all abusers complete their impact questionnaires and discuss what they have learned in a group session. Although some victim-abuser interaction occurred, because abusers were instructed to speak only when spoken to, Figure 24.1 does not label this intervention "interpersonal."

Victim Responsibility Training Level 2: Emotional Restitution

It has been argued that for sex abuser programs to achieve maximum effectiveness, an integrated approach needs to be taken which includes, among other things, making amends to those damaged directly or indirectly by destructive behavior (Schwartz, 1994). The second level of VRT consists of four prosocial behavior interventions (i.e., Interventions 5 through 8) in which abusers demonstrate their social responsibility to make emotional restitution to both direct and indirect victims of their abusive behavior for the burden they have placed on them. Since abusive behavior often leaves victims feeling guilty and culpable, the abusers make emotional restitution through attempting to relieve some of the emotional burden they have inflicted. This is done by a series of letters and sessions that clarify the abusers' responsibility for their behavior along with the manipulations used to make victims feel culpable and thus less likely to disclose the abusers' behavior to others.

As mentioned previously, high levels of empathic/emotional arousal may lead to distress, which triggers maladaptive thinking (e.g., blaming, minimizing, and justifying) and impedes the abuser's ability to make genuine emotional restitution. Thus, in Level 2 of VRT, a graduated exposure to an emotional restitution intervention hierarchy is used to address this issue. In addition, the interventions are structured to promote transfer of training and further maximize the probability of a favorable outcome.

The structure and format of the emotional restitution training interventions in Level 2 of VRT is consistent with the transfer of training research on training task and abuser ability problems that can interfere with applying what has been learned. The effectiveness of a training procedure has been found to be a function of the similarity of the training task to the target task and the student's level of general ability (Goska & Ackerman, 1996; Sullivan, 1964). While students with a wide range of general reasoning ability can benefit from near-transfer training (i.e., where training and target situations are nearly the same), those of higher ability generally do better applying what they learned in more distant-transfer training than those of lower ability (Goska & Ackerman, 1996; Sullivan, 1964). In VRT, except for the person receiving the apology/clarification, the designated "training" components (i.e., an apology/clarification letter and session for emotional restitution to an indirect abuse victim) are exactly the same as the target components (i.e., the same procedures for emotional restitution to a direct abuse victim). Since the VRT training and target tasks are nearly the same, transfer of training should be maximized even for abusers of lower ability.

In addition to learning information that is relevant to the task or responsibility that must be completed, transfer of training from the learning environment to the target setting requires practice, modeling, and suggestions to build the level of self-efficacy (mastery) needed for implementation (e.g., Carroll, 1993). Thus, role playing, behavior rehearsal, performance feedback, and verbal praise move the abuser along a graduated sequence of four prosocial behavior interventions culminating in abusers demonstrating their social responsibility to make emotional restitution to their direct victim of abuse in an apology/clarification session. Since the first two interventions involve family or significant others close to the direct victim, these are considered the "training" interventions which prepare abusers for the target interventions with their actual direct victim(s) of abuse. If learning from one setting or problem is to be generalized to another actual "teaching to transfer" is considered important (Gladstone, 1989). "Teaching to transfer" occurs during group sessions in which the apology/clarification letters are presented by the abusers to their group, whose members play the role of victims asking questions about issues they may want clarified. The victim role assumed by the group members has the added advantage of developing the prospective-taking component of empathy. Since the social support system appears to play a central role in the transfer of training (Tracey, Tannenbaum, & Kavanagh, 1995), a cohesive abuser group along with strong treatment provider support is critical.

Victim safeguards are an important part of Level 2 of VRT. During this portion of treatment, behavioral observation of what the abuser has learned, videotape monitoring of the offender, psychological testing of victims who attend sessions with the abuser, and self-report of victims are used to monitor victim-abuser therapeutic interactions for possible adverse emotional impact.

Intervention 5: Apology/Clarification Letter to Indirect Abuse Victim. In the fifth intervention, abusers use what they learned about the impact of sexual abuse and victim empathy in the previous four interventions to write an apology/clarification letter(s) to individuals other than their direct victim(s) who have also been affected by their abuse. These are usually the parents, caretakers, significant others, or family of the direct victim of abuse. Family members (especially parents of direct victims) often experience feelings of anxiety, guilt, or shame over the victimization. Thus, in most cases at least one family member can be defined as an indirect victim of the abuser's crime. At least one family member (preferably a parent or adult) who has not sexually offended or been sexually victimized is designated as an indirect victim for this intervention.

Intervention 5 is structured to serve the dual purposes of preventing abuser emotional stimulus overload while benefiting the indirect victim by providing an initial nonthreatening form of emotional restitution that supplies "preview" information. This preview decreases victim apprehension about what can be expected to be disclosed in the actual apology session. Writing an emotional restitution letter is considered important because going into an emotional restitution session with the indirect victim without any preparation could create emotional stimulus overload, trigger defensiveness, and shut down the abuser's ability to make genuine emotional restitution. Presenting that letter to the treatment group serves as a "dry run" training session during which group members can help prepare abusers for potential victim questions. Preparation by the abuser group helps the other abusers in the group with their role reversal and perspective-taking skills. In addition to gradually introducing abusers to the emotional restitution process through letter writing to prevent stimulus overload, this intervention also acts as an initial emotional restitution action designed to benefit the abuse victim.

After the abuser has demonstrated his commitment to make emotional restitution by writing an apology/clarification letter and reading that letter to his treatment group, a group feedback session is conducted. The letter is discussed and the abuser uses questions and feedback from peers as well as staff to make victim-sensitive revisions along with further honest disclosures. After this feedback session, each member in the group gives the abuser presenting the letter a grade, the average is computed, and a group grade is assigned. The abuser revises and resubmits his letter to the group until he receives a group grade of "B" or above. When the letter is completed with a satisfactory grade by the abuser group, the indirect victim (and the family therapist if applicable) is contacted by telephone, informed of the apology/clarification letter, and given the option whether to have it mailed. If the indirect victim chooses to receive the apology/clarification letter, it is sent. A two-page brief review of what is known about why youth molest is included to help family members in their struggle to understand and cope with the abuser's behavior.

Several days after the apology/clarification letter is sent, the indirect victim is again contacted by telephone and asked if he or she found the letter to be sincere and helpful. The impact of the letter is discussed with the indirect victim and the decision of whether to schedule an apology/clarification session with the abuser is made. If the apology/clarification letter is judged sincere and helpful by both the indirect victim and the abuser's therapist, the abuser is allowed to apologize to the indirect victim in person.

Intervention 6: Apology/Clarification Session for Indirect Abuse Victim. The sixth intervention involves a personal apology and clarification of the abuser's problem and reasons for their abuse by the abuser to his indirect victim(s). Given that family members may continue to be upset or even outraged at the abuser's behavior despite the length of time that has passed since the abuse was committed, some degree of abuser stress inoculation is warranted prior to the indirect victim apology/clarification session.

Intervention 6 serves three basic purposes: addressing indirect victim issues, abuser preparation for the direct victim session, and acting as a direct victim emotional safeguard. With respect to indirect victim issues experienced by the victim's family and significant others, this intervention is important for clarification and closure on unresolved issues related to the abuser's behavior. The indirect victim apology session is the second opportunity for abuser treatment staff to observe socially responsible behavior in the actual presence of a victim. This intervention is also the designated "training" apology/clarification session in which a behavioral observation of how the abuser handles an apology/clarification session is conducted. The videotape review and performance feedback of the indirect victim session is considered critical in preparation for the direct apology/clarification session. Finally, the feedback from this intervention is critical to ensuring emotional security for the direct victim during the upcoming apology session. The appropriateness of the abuser's behavior during this session will be evaluated and used to determine whether the abuser will be allowed to write a letter to his direct victim(s) and again in deciding whether to hold a session with the direct victim.

To minimize anxiety for the abuser and victim, as the content of the indirect victim letter is familiar territory most likely to be at least somewhat comfortable both for the abuser and the indirect victim(s), the abuser begins the session by reading the letter he sent to his indirect victim. However, the indirect victim apology/clarification session can be started by family or significant others who are anxious to express themselves, speaking up with questions, concerns, or statements of their feelings. The indirect victim apology/clarification sessions are typically held in the abuser treatment facility with a video camera behind the indirect victim(s) and focused on the abuser. Since this VRT training task and the direct victim session target task are nearly the same, transfer of training should be maximized even for abusers of lower ability.

After the apology/clarification session with his indirect victim, the abuser completes an abuser impact questionnaire (Yokley, 1990). At this time, indirect victims are asked to complete a follow-up questionnaire on the impact that the apology/clarification letter and the apology/clarification session had on them (Yokley, 1990). If the abuser's apology/clarification session behavior with the indirect victim is judged appropriate and helpful by both the indirect victim and the abuser's therapist, the abuser is allowed to write an apology/clarification letter to an actual direct victim of his abuse. Corrective performance feedback from the indirect victim session along with verbal reinforcement of positive points are given before the abuser has any contact with his actual victim(s).

If the abuser's behavior is not socially responsible, sincere, and appropriate in terms of making emotional restitution to the indirect victim(s), the abuser is not allowed to write or have any contact of any form with any direct victim and must undergo additional treatment. If the indirect victim and the abuser's therapist disagree on the abuser's behavioral indicators of readiness to make emotional restitution to his direct victim, the indirect victim's feedback is carefully reviewed for use in further abuser treatment. Under these circumstances, the abuser is not allowed to proceed in writing to his direct victim until both the indirect victim and the therapist consider it appropriate. If indicated, indirect victims may receive a referral for therapy to help them deal with both past unresolved issues as well as the present decision to recommend for or against an apology/clarification session with the abuser and any direct victim.

Intervention 7: Apology/Clarification Letter to Direct Abuse Victim. In the seventh intervention, abusers who handled their indirect victim apology/clarification session responsibly use the skills developed during the previous six interventions to write their actual victims an apology/clarification letter. Apology/clarification letters are also used in the *Hope & Recovery: Twelve Step Guide for Healing from Compulsive Sexual Behavior* (1987). Step nine of this guide requires abusers to make direct amends to their victims whenever possible, except when to do so would injure the victims or others. The guide further states:

> Whenever we felt uncertain about whether or not direct amends would harm certain people further . . . first we wrote letters to these people stating that we realized we'd harmed them and we were making efforts to change our behav-

ior and improve ourselves. . . . Next, we called these people to ask if they would be willing to share with us their reactions to the letters that they had received from us. If people were not open to sharing their reactions and feelings with us, we did not pursue the issue further with them" (p. 58).

The difference between the aforementioned twelve step approach and VRT basically involves the preparation interventions, graduated exposure, transfer of training techniques, and multiple victim safety measures.

Like the previous apology/clarification letter intervention, Intervention 7 is also structured to serve the dual purposes of preventing abuser emotional stimulus over load while benefiting the victim through information to decrease victim apprehension about what can be expected to be disclosed in the actual apology session. As mentioned earlier, writing an emotional restitution letter is important in preventing emotional stimulus overload, which could shut down the abuser's ability to make genuine emotional restitution. The presentation of the letter to the treatment group functions as a training session and the process of group members helping prepare the abuser for potential victim questions is a therapeutic perspective-taking exercise for the rest of the group. In addition to graduated abuser exposure to emotional restitution, this intervention is also an emotional restitution act designed to benefit the abuse victim.

The apology/clarification letter to the direct victim is discussed and modified in a feedback loop with the abuser group in the same manner as the letter to the indirect victim in Intervention 5. Abuser letters that receive high group grades and verbal praise from the group include socially responsible content such as full acceptance of responsibility for the crime along with acknowledgement that getting reported or arrested was needed and helpful. Letters that include expressions of genuine sorrow for specific emotional/physical damage done and appropriate feelings of shame or self-disgust are also verbally praised and receive good group grades.

After the direct victim apology/clarification letter is completed and receives a satisfactory grade of "B" or above from the abuser group, the victim's therapist is contacted by telephone and informed that the apology/clarification letter is being mailed to the therapist. The decision regarding whether to give the apology/clarification letter to the victim is left up to the victim's therapist. If the victim's therapist feels that the victim is ready to receive the letter and/or that the letter will be therapeutic, that therapist will present and process the letter in his or her therapy sessions with the victim. In cases in which the apology/clarification letter is given to the victim, the impact of that letter is evaluated from two follow-up questionnaires that were enclosed with the apology/clarification letter. The victim completes one of these questionnaires and the victim's therapist completes the other. Except for title changes, these questionnaires are the same as those used in Intervention 6 to gather impact information on the indirect victim apology session (Yokley, 1990). If both the victim's therapist (i.e., with input from the victim) and the abuser's therapist judge the apology/clarification letter sincere and helpful, the abuser is allowed to apologize to the victim in a therapy session. Every attempt is made to include both the abuser's therapist and the victim's therapist in the actual apology/clarification session.

Intervention 8: Apology/Clarification Session for Direct Abuse Victim. The eighth and final intervention involves a personal apology and clarification of the abuser's problem and reasons for his abuse by the abuser to the direct victim(s) of their abuse. Given that this type of session can be emotionally charged, some degree of abuser stress inoculation is warranted. The primary purpose of Intervention 8 is for abusers to demonstrate social responsibility by making emotional restitution to the direct victim(s) of their abuse. This intervention is considered important for the victim in terms of providing help with clarification and closure on unresolved issues related to the abuser's behavior.

Apology sessions to direct victims are used by the twelve step program for compulsive sexual behavior which requires abusers to make direct amends to their victims whenever it is possible, when it is not likely to injure others and when the victim agrees to a meeting (*Hope & Recovery*, 1987). In those cases, the twelve step guide indicates: "We selected a neutral meeting place—in other words, a place that would not bring back feelings of shame about our acting-out behaviors or in any way tempt us to resume those behaviors" (*Hope & Recovery*, 1987, p. 58). In VRT, there is more of a focus on demonstrating social responsibility to others; every attempt is made to schedule the victim-abuser meeting in the office of the victim's therapist or another safe and secure environment for the victim. If the victim's primary caretaker, therapist, or advocate believes that a direct apology/clarification session would be traumatic as opposed to a clarification-closure healing experience or if the victim declines the apology/clarification session, the abuser still has the social responsibility to make emotional restitution. In this situation, the abuser is asked to conduct an abuser information group for members of a victim treatment group.

To minimize abuser and victim anxiety, the abuser begins the session by reading the letter he sent to his direct victim. However, it is important to support the needs of the victims to start this session if the victims are anxious to express themselves with questions, concerns, or feelings. Like the victim impact group, the direct victim apology/clarification session is held in an environment familiar to the victim with a video camera behind the victims and focused on the abusers. When an apology/ clarification session is scheduled, the direct victim is carefully monitored for the possibility of any adverse emotional impact. As described in Intervention 4, one week before and after the apology/clarification session, direct victims are asked to complete psychological tests to monitor their emotional state, typically with test measures of depression, anxiety, anger, and external locus of control.

The impact of the victim apology/clarification session is also evaluated from follow-up questionnaires distributed to both the victim and the victim's therapist (Yokley, 1990). The abuser receives corrective performance feedback from the direct victim session along with verbal reinforcement of positive points. In Intervention 8, if any clinically significant adverse emotional impact is detected by any of the test measures employed or on the apology/clarification session follow-up questionnaire, the abuser's therapist contacts the victim's therapist immediately. During this contact, the abuser's therapist may recommend that (1) all victim-abuser communication and/or contact including supervised visits be stopped and (2) the victim begin immediate psychotherapy sessions to reduce the stress associated with the abuser contact. After Intervention 8, the abuser completes another abuser impact questionnaire (Yokley, 1990). Figure 24.1 outlines the VRT Level 2 interventions.

To date, there has been no adverse impact reported from the direct victim apology/ clarification sessions. However, if indicated, by the psychological testing and clinical observations of the therapists present, direct victims may receive therapy sessions to help them deal with unresolved stressful issues that were brought up during the apology/clarification session. The VRT training has thus far been successful in preventing inappropriate behaviors from abusers toward victims in joint sessions. If at any time during Level 2 of VRT the abuser's behavior is not considered socially responsible, sincere, and appropriate, the abuser receives more information on victim safety rules and must undergo additional treatment.

Not all direct or indirect abuse survivors and/or their therapists feel that the apology/clarification letters are sincere and helpful. In addition, not all are ready to receive an apology/clarification from the abuser even if they or their therapists believe it would be beneficial. To decrease the stress associated with making the apology/clarification session decision, direct victims are informed that if they choose not to participate in an apology/clarification session now, they retain the right to schedule a session at any time in the future. In this situation, although the abuser has been excused from his apology/clarification by the victim, he is not excused from his responsibility to demonstrate a prosocial, helpful behavior toward one or more victims. In this situation, the abuser must first sign a behavior contract to apologize to the victim when that victim and his or her therapist feel that the victim is ready. Second, since the abuser may not be present at the future time that the victim and his or her therapist request an apology/clarification session, the abuser must make a victim videotape apology/clarification for the victim and his or her therapist to use at any time in the future that they request it. Finally, the abuser must prepare himself to conduct an abuser information group for victims in a local treatment center during which the abuser reads his apology/clarification letter, apologizes for his behavior, and answers any questions asked by the victims about which they are concerned.

In an abuser information group, arrangements are made with a local victim treatment group for two or three abusers who are unable to apologize and clarify important issues to their victims to address the victim therapy group. The members of the victim group decide whether to meet with the abusers and a separate victim group time is scheduled so that those victim members who choose not to meet with the abusers do not miss their regularly scheduled group. For the victims, the purpose of the abuser information group is to be able to ask questions, express feelings, confront fears in a safe environment, and move toward regaining a sense of mastery and control through awareness and understanding.

The primary purpose of the abuser information group is for the abusers to demonstrate socially responsible behavior toward victims by providing information that may be helpful in bringing closure to their understanding of why they were abused. This involves abusers taking full responsibility for their behavior, explaining to the best of their ability how they developed and maintained their abusive behavior, and answering any questions that victims ask. To provide a positive peer participant model, an abuser who has successfully apologized to his victim is typically included in the abuser information group. As in the victim impact group, there are abuser and victim therapists in attendance. These therapists sit between the victims and abusers so that no victim is sitting next to an abuser.

Prior to the abuser information group, information that the victims want to know from the abusers is gathered using a brief one-page "Things I Want To Know" questionnaire (Yokley, 1990). Like the victim impact group, the abuser information group is held in a victim treatment center with a video camera behind the victims and focused on the abusers. As described in the aforementioned victim impact group and the direct victim apology/clarification session procedure, one week before and after the victim-abuser session tests, tests to monitor emotional state (i.e., typically measures of depression, anxiety, anger, and external locus of control) are administered to all victim participants. However, because there typically has been no designated training session for the abuser information group (i.e., most who conduct this group were declined sessions with their indirect abuse victims), test measures of abuser emotional state are also administered. In addition to emotional state measures, all victims receive a "Thoughts and Feelings Questionnaire" and all abusers receive an abuser impact questionnaire (Yokley, 1990) to tap the subjective impact of the group on its participants in other areas.

Conclusion

Despite the fact that victim empathy development components and apology/clarification sessions are common procedures in sexual abuser treatment programs, research-informed clinical protocols and evaluation research of these procedures are almost nonexistent in the literature. This chapter described victim responsibility training, a research-informed treatment protocol designed to help abusers develop victim impact understanding and victim empathy and demonstrate social responsibility by making emotional restitution to abuse survivors. Although this treatment component is based on principles that make it useful with multiple forms of abuse, the description in this chapter focused on sexual abuse. As a part of social responsibility therapy, VRT has a strong victim safety and security focus where videotaped sessions are backed up with psychological testing and exit interviews to guard against adverse impact from any victim-offender communication. To date, there has been no adverse impact revealed by psychological testing or reported by the victims and offenders participating in the communication procedures involved in VRT. Subjective benefits are routinely reported by victims in the form of decreased feelings of anxiety, anger and depression.

Footnotes

---

[1] In this treatment component description, the terms "victim" and "survivor" are used interchangeably with equal respect to those who have suffered abuse.

[2] A case example, copies of questionnaires, and other materials used in victim responsibility training are provided in Yokley (1990). Portions and aspects of this treatment component were presented at the Ohio Coalition for the Treatment of Adolescent Sex Offenders Conference, Columbus (Yokley, 1989), the 10th annual Research and Treatment Conference of the Association for the Treatment of Sexual Abusers, Fort Worth, Texas (Yokley & McGuire, 1991), and the 13th annual Research and Treatment Conference of the Association for the Treatment of Sexual Abusers, San Francisco, California (Yokley & Tener, 1994). Portions were reproduced from The *TASC Program Manual* (Yokley, 1993), *The Social Responsibility Therapy Work Book: Understanding Abuse Behavior* (Yokley, 1995), and *Social Responsibility Therapy: A Positive Lifestyle Development Approach* (Yokley, 2000) with permission from the author.

[3] Social responsibility therapy is described in detail in Chapter 21 of this volume.

[4] The masculine gender is used in this chapter because at this time, the majority of sex offenders are male; however, a proportion of such offenders are female and VRT applies to female offenders as well.

⁵ The videotape was "Surviving Sexual Abuse," which can be obtained from the University of California Extension Media Center, 2176 Shattuck Avenue, Berkeley, CA 94704.

References

Badovinac, K. (1994). The effects of victim impact panels on attitudes and intentions regarding impaired driving. *Journal of Alcohol and Drug Education, 39*(3), 113–118.

Baldwin, T., & Ford, J. (1988). Transfer of training: A review and directions for future research. *Personnel Psychology, 41*, 63–105.

Baldwin, T. T., & Magjuka, R. J. (1991). Organizational training and signals of importance: Linking pretraining perceptions to intentions to transfer. *Human Resource Development Quarterly, 2*, 25–36.

Carroll, J. (1993). Theory to practice: Self-efficacy related to transfer of learning as an example of theory-based instructional design. *Journal of Adult Education, 22*(1), 37–43.

Emmelkamp, P. (1982). Exposure in vivo treatments. In A. Goldstein & D. Chamberless (Eds.), *Agoraphobia: Multiple perspectives on theory and treatment.* New York: Wiley.

Fisher, D., Beech, A., & Browne, K. (1999). Comparison of sex offenders to nonoffenders on selected psychological measures. *International Journal of Offender Therapy and Comparative Criminology, 43*(4), 473–491.

Freeman-Longo, R. E., Bird, S., Stevenson, W. F., & Fiske, J. A. (1995). *1994 nationwide survey of treatment programs & models: Serving abuse reactive children and adolescent & adult sexual offenders.* Brandon, VT: Safer Society Press.

Gladstone, R. (1989). Teaching for transfer versus formal discipline. *American Psychologist, 44*(8), 1159–1159.

Goska, R., & Ackerman, P. (1996). An aptitude-treatment interaction approach to transfer within training. *Journal of Educational Psychology, 88*(2), 249–259.

Hanson, R., & Scott, H. (1995, October). Assessing perspective-taking among sexual offenders, nonsexual criminals, and nonoffenders. *Sexual Abuse: Journal of Research & Treatment, 7*(4), 259–277.

Hope & recovery: A twelve step guide for healing from compulsive sexual behavior. (1987). Minneapolis, MN: CompCare.

Knopp, F. H. (1982). *Remedial intervention in adolescent sex offenses: Nine program descriptions.* Orwell, VT: Safer Society Press.

Knopp, F. H. (1984). *Retraining adult sex abusers: Methods and models.* Orwell, VT: Safer Society Press.

Lord, J. (1989). *Victim impact panels: A creative sentencing approach.* Hurst, TX: Mothers Against Drunk Driving.

Marshall, W. L. (1993). The role of attachments, intimacy and loneliness in the etiology and maintenance of sexual offending. *Sexual and Marital Therapy, 8*, 109–121.

Marshall, W., Hudson, S., Jones, R., & Fernandez, Y. (1995). Empathy in sex offenders. *Clinical Psychology Review, 15*(2), 99–113.

Michelson, M. (1985). Flooding. In A. Bellak & M. Herson (Eds.), *Dictionary of behavior therapy techniques.* New York: Pergamon Press.

Newbauer, J., & Hess, S. (1994). Treating sex offenders and survivors conjointly: Gender issues with adolescent boys. *Journal for Specialists in Group Work, 19*(2), 129–135.

Palmer, R. (1989, April). *Empathy: Frankly my dear, I don't give a damn.* Paper presented at the Ohio Coalition for the Treatment of Adolescent Sex Abusers Conference, Columbus.

Pithers, W. (1994). Process evaluation of a group therapy component designed to enhance sex offenders' empathy for sexual abuse survivors. *Behaviour Research and Therapy, 32*(5), 565–570.

Pithers, W. (1999), Empathy: Definition, enhancement, and relevance to the treatment of sexual abusers. *Journal of Interpersonal Violence, 14*(3), 257–284.

Pollak, M. [Field Producer]. (1990). *The reporters* [television documentary]. STF Productions.

Ross, J., & Loss, P. (1988). *Psychoeducational curriculum for the adolescent sex abuser.* Unpublished manuscript.

Ryan, G. (1997). Consequences for the victim of sexual abuse. In G. Ryan, S. Lane, & A. Rinzler (Eds.), *Juvenile sexual offending: Causes, consequences, and correction.* (pp. 157–167). San Francisco: Jossey-Bass.

Schwartz, M. (1994). The Masters and Johnson treatment program for sex offenders: Intimacy, empathy and trauma resolution. *Sexual Addiction and Compulsivity, 1*(3), 261–277.

Sgroi, S. (1982). *Handbook of clinical intervention in child sexual abuse.* Lexington, MA: Lexington Books.

Sullivan, A. M. (1964). *The relation between intelligence and transfer.* Unpublished doctoral dissertation, McGill University, Montreal.

Tracey, J., Tannenbaum, S., & Kavanagh, M. (1995). Applying trained skills on the job: The importance of the work environment. *Journal of Applied Psychology, 80*(2), 239–252.

Wolpe, J. (1958). *Psychotherapy by reciprocal inhibition.* Stanford, CA: Stanford University Press.

Wolpe, J. (1995). Reciprocal inhibition: Major agent of behavior change. In W. O'Donohue & L. Krasner (Eds.), *Theories of behavior therapy: Exploring behavior change* (pp. 23–57). Washington, DC: American Psychological Association.

Yokley, J. (1989, April). *An evaluation of four procedures used to develop victim empathy in youth sex offenders.* Proceedings of the Ohio Coalition for the Treatment of Adolescent Sex Offenders Conference, Columbus, OH.

Yokley, J. (1990). The clinical trials model: Victim responsibility training. In J. Yokley (Ed.), *The use of victim-offender communication in the treatment of sexual abuse: Three intervention models* (pp. 69–110). Orwell, VT: Safer Society Press.

Yokley, J. (1993). Treatment for Appropriate Social Control (TASC) program manual (rev. 1997, 2000). Available from Clinical and Research Resources, P.O. Box 538 Hudson, OH 44236.

Yokley, J. (1995). *Social responsibility therapy work book: Understanding abuse behavior* (rev. 1997, 2000). Available from Clinical and Research Resources, P.O. Box 538 Hudson, OH 44236.

Yokley, J. (2000). *Social responsibility therapy: A positive lifestyle development approach.* Available from Clinical and Research Resources, P.O. Box 538 Hudson, OH 44236.

Yokley, J., & McGuire, D. (1990). Introduction to the therapeutic use of victim-offender communication. In J. Yokley (Ed.), *The use of victim-offender communication in the treatment of sexual abuse: Three intervention models* (pp. 7–22). Orwell, VT: Safer Society Press.

Yokley, J., & McGuire, D. (1991, November). *Emotional restitution: The therapeutic use of sex offender communication with victims.* Paper presented at the 10th annual Research and Treatment Conference of the Association for the Treatment of Sexual Abusers, Fort Worth, TX.

Yokley, J., & Tener, R. (1994, November). *The victim conducted impact group for sex offenders.* Paper presented at the 13th annual Research and Treatment Conference of the Association for the Treatment of Sexual Abusers, San Francisco.

Part 6

Emerging Populations

The treatment of sex offenders began with adults who were either committed or incarcerated. It expanded to offenders in the community, either on probation or parole. However, by 1980 there was a nearly equal number of adolescent and adult programs. Between 1992 and 1994, 390 programs identified themselves as treating sexually reactive children. Specialized programs for female adolescent and adults with sexually inappropriate behavior have grown slowly since the 1980s. Therapists are beginning to specialize in subgroups such as those dually diagnosed with psychiatric disabilities. In this section, three authors describe treatments for subgroups that have previously received little attention.

Family therapy has always been a key component of adolescent sex offender treatment. Some adult treatment programs have offered treatment or support groups to non-offending spouses. Gayle Christensen and Heather Reu (Chapter 25) write about the assessment and treatment of the nonoffending parent of the adolescent with sexually inappropriate behavior. Clearly these individuals initially feel overwhelmed by the revelation of their child's behavior and the subsequent encounters with the criminal justice system. They may feel blamed by professionals in the system, including therapists evaluating and treating their child. There may be few support people with whom they can share their feelings of betrayal, loss, and confusion. These authors discuss how therapists can assist such individuals in dealing with their trauma so that they can become effective supports for their children.

Timothy Foley (Chapter 26) discusses a group that is receiving a great deal of attention. Technological advancement has created a new brand of sexual offenders: the Internet offenders. These individuals come to the attention of authorities for two main reasons, either they have attempted to groom children through chat rooms or they have downloaded and/or distributed child pornography. Who are these individuals? Are they all pedophiles? Are they otherwise law-abiding citizens with no evidence of deviant sexual arousal except that they are interested in child pornography? Heated debates are raging around these issues. Foley treats a large number of these individuals and, in his chapter, writes of his research on this subgroup.

Another newly emerging group of potential patients is the product of laws regarding sexual harassment that have evolved over the past several decades. Between 1991 and 1999, complaints of gender harassment increased 40 to 60%. Some 42% of females complain that they have been subject to significant sexual harassment. Yet sexual harassment is a civil right violation—not a criminal offense. Offenders may have to pay damages but will not be incarcerated or placed on probation. They also cannot be mandated into treatment. Thus a pattern of abusing females that may differ only in degree from sexual assault may continue. Erin Oksol, in Chapter 27, discusses the similarities between the offender and the harasser with implications for treatment.

Chapter 25

Assessment and Treatment of the Nonoffending Parent for the Benefit of the Victim—A Dynamic Continuum of Reaction and Response

by Gayle E. Christensen, L.C.S.W., B.C.D. and Heather Cramer Reu, L.C.S.W.

Overview

Treatment of the nonoffending parent in families in which incest has occurred is difficult for professionals. The last decade has shown an increase in the availability of research and theory focused on the treatment of sex offenders and sexual abuse victims, but the experience of the nonoffending parent in cases of incest has not been documented as fully. In addition, well-defined paradigms have not been developed to assess their experience and formulate an appropriate treatment plan. This chapter presents information on a manner in which concerned professionals should conceptualize the reactions, strengths, and needs of the nonoffending parents in cases of intrafamilial sexual abuse. It also sets the stage for appropriate treatment interventions aimed at strengthening the protective capacity of nonoffending parents and developing their ability to provide an environment of healing for the sexual abuse victim.

The experience of the nonoffending parent is dramatically different in several important domains from the experience of parents whose children have been sexually abused by an extrafamilial sex offender. Treatment of this group is complex for involved professionals, whether mental health professionals or child protection workers. It is difficult due to the puzzling behavior that is often exhibited by the nonoffending parent upon disclosure. Clinicians are then faced with the task of developing treatment plans and therapeutic responses to this often confusing and surprising behavior. Most professionals believe that a protective and supportive response is in the child's best interest and would be expected of any "good" parent. Treatment of the nonoffending parent is a challenge to therapeutic skills and stirs up personal feelings for the professional who is committed to working with abused children.

Introduction

In cases of incest, the vast majority of nonoffending parents are the mothers of children who have been sexually violated by a member of their own family. Historically, these mothers have been viewed as having some level of culpability in the sexual abuse and have been treated as such. The perpetration of sexual abuse on a child is a nightmare few parents are equipped to handle, but when the perpetrator of such a crime is the partner or spouse of the nonoffending parent, the ramifications of such an act on her life are profound. Though there are instances in which the nonoffending parent in intrafamilial sexual abuse is a father, this scenario is a rarity in the professional literature, with the majority of work being focused on the nonoffending parent in cases of incest perpetrated by male family members. Because the phenomenon of a maternal nonoffending parent is far more universal in the experience of mental health professionals and child protection workers, this chapter addresses the experience of the mothers of the victims of incest.

Immediate Reactions and Contact With Professionals at First Disclosure

The notion of an unsupportive mother has been historically presented in the literature. Mothers have typically been portrayed as unwilling or unable to be supportive or protective, as responding inadequately once the incest has been disclosed, as believing their daughters seduced the fathers, or as refusing to believe the disclosures (DeYoung, 1994). DeYoung (1994) looked at a group of mothers whose daughters had been victims of paternal incest. They were asked to describe their immediate emotional reaction to the disclosure of the incest. It was found that there was less collusion and disbelief of the allegations than had been historically represented, and that the immediate reactions of the nonoffending parents were described with terms such as "shocked," "enraged," "numb," "dumbstruck," "panic-stricken," "disgusted," "anxiety-ridden," and "terrified." Other researchers have found similar emotional reactions by the nonoffending parent to the disclosure of child sexual assault (Fong & Walsh-Bowers, 1998; Newberger, Gremy, Waternaux, & Newberger, 1993). Emotional reactions of this type can lead to feelings of immobilization, and immobilization can lead to ineffectual action. These nonoffending parents have often needed some time alone before they could take action.

Healing and recovery in the lives of nonoffending parents, and thus in their children's lives, are linked to their ability to feel and be empowered in a system that they often perceive as controlling, demeaning, and judgmental. There is often pressure on the nonoffending parent to respond appropriately immediately upon disclosure. Although this would be the ideal situation, an appropriate response is sometimes delayed. The goal of all members of the treatment team should be to assist the nonoffending parent in becoming part of the team of support people that is being assembled for the victim. It is important to realize that this is a process, not an event. Even nonoffending parents who believe and support their sexually abused child will still need to be educated on the impact of the abuse on the victim if they are going to be well prepared for the aftermath of abuse and the overall impact of their child's disclosure. By the time the family has gone through the investigation, interviews by Child Protective Services (CPS), court proceedings, conversations with relatives and friends, and various other events, they often report feeling alienated and judged by others.

The Reactions of Professionals to the Nonoffending Parent

In many cases, the first professionals to have contact with the nonoffending parent in intrafamilial sexual abuse cases are professionals involved in CPS. The degree of training and preparation that these workers have had for dealing with intrafamilial sexual abuse cases may vary drastically from one locale to the other. It has been posited that in such cases, lacking relevant descriptive information about the unique dynamics involved, CPS workers must rely on their own beliefs and attitudes about sexual abuse and incest when becoming involved with families after such a disclosure (Deitz & Craft, 1980). Unfortunately, there are times when relying on one's own attitudes and beliefs can have a negative impact on the initial interactions that professionals have with the nonoffending parents. Professionals who lack understanding or education about the dynamics in families in which incest has occurred may be ill equipped to respond to the initial crisis following disclosure. When the nonoffending parent does not respond according to expectations, the result from professionals is often rejection, anger, or frustration toward her (Hindman, 1989).

In a qualitative analysis of the nonoffending mothers in incest cases (Fong & Walsh-Bowers, 1998), one study participant reported, "The perpetrator is innocent until proven guilty, but the mother is guilty until proven innocent" (p. 34). This sentiment is explored in an article by Womack, Miller, & Lassiter (1999), which reported that only a small percentage of professionals assigned full responsibility for sexual abuse to the offender. An overwhelming majority assigned partial blame to the mother, victim, and society. Other professionals either believed that mothers could have prevented the sexual abuse, were silent partners in the abuse, or believed that they could not adequately protect their children.

Professionals Hold Definite Expectations for Nonoffending Parents

Society and professionals have expectations of the nonoffending parent that mirror our feelings about child sexual abuse. Generally, the expectation is that the nonoffending parent will respond with support and belief, demonstrating the compassion that is felt for the child who has been molested. When the nonoffending parent does not respond in the expected way, professionals are likely to be dismayed or angered at a range of other responses that may include disbelief, blame, indifference, anger, withdrawal, or distraction with seemingly unimportant issues. Also fundamental in the formation of this response by professionals is the belief that the "good mother" has complete knowledge about what is happening in her family, has the strength and power to put a stop to anything that is not appropriate, and intuitively has the capacity and resources to know how to handle difficult matters (Breckenridge & Baldry, 1997).

In some cases, the reaction of professionals to the nonoffending parent's response may exacerbate the emotional crisis, making it even more difficult for the nonoffending parent to respond appropriately. It is critical for all professionals who come in contact with a nonoffending parent early in the disclosure process to remember that this is a stage of acute crisis. Professionals are not likely to judge a family member for reacting emotionally to the news that another family member has been injured in an accident or diagnosed with a life-changing illness. We would not be surprised when a person who loses his or her house to a fire responds with anger, blame, or disbelief. Consider the context for most nonoffending parents: They may get up and go to work thinking that their children are safe, their spouse is trustworthy, their finances are in some order, and their family problems are manageable. A typical disclosure at school, which prompts investigation and a phone call to the nonoffending parent to come to the police station or advocacy center, changes in a conversation all the things she has believed about her life. To fully accept and comprehend the sexual abuse disclosure means that none of these things are true. The child was not safe, even in his or her own home; the spouse is not trustworthy; financial disaster often is at hand; and the person has suddenly become, in fact, a single parent for the foreseeable future.

Most people have limited information about victims (even those who are victims themselves). The behavior of victims, while living under the cloak of secrecy, does not often fit with the expectations of those who are not familiar with the consequences of child sexual abuse. An abused child may not exhibit symptoms, and the behavior of the nonsymptomatic child does not make sense to the parent who was just told that her child reported that the abuse has been occurring for the last two years. Thus the responses of these nonoffending parents do not always meet the expectations of professionals. Because there is incongruency between the expected response and the actual response, close to 30% of nonoffending mothers lose custody of their children for at least some period (Massat & Lundy, 1998).

Nonoffending parents (in this case, mothers), when interviewed about their experience regarding interactions with professionals, often feel that they are left alone to deal with the aftermath of the sexual abuse disclosure. They report feeling discounted and misunderstood when dealing with authorities and helping professionals (Fong & Walsh Bowers, 1998).

Dynamic Continuum of Response and Reaction

It has been helpful to view the reactions, responses, and processes of the nonoffending parent with regard to the disclosure of intrafamilial sexual abuse as being on a dynamic continuum. Understanding their responses throughout the process of disclosure, treatment, and potential reunification is critical for working with the nonoffending parent and facilitating familial change and victim healing. In the same way that there is no reliable profile of the sex offender, there is no reliable profile of the nonoffending parent. Stereotypical beliefs about nonoffending parents include that they are victims themselves, passive victims of the controlling offender, inadequate parents, and must have known something was going on and have been in denial. Often these beliefs are not accurate.

Nonoffending parents are best understood in terms of where they are functioning at the present time. This requires an understanding that they will most often move across a continuum of responses, depending on the influences that they encounter, the emotional and practical issues with which they must cope, and the time that has passed from the point of disclosure.

On one end of the continuum is the nonoffending parent who believes the disclosure and is supportive of the child. These are the people who professionals are most able to understand, and who offend them least. These nonoffending parents immediately believe their children, respond with compassion and concern, and are immediately available as a resource for the child. On the other end of the continuum is the nonoffending parent who was either involved in the abuse or was aware of the abuse and colluded with the offender to hide it. This end of the continuum does not include parents who reacted poorly upon disclosure, or who discovered the abuse and believed they had intervened and stopped it. Some nonoffending parents may have intervened in ways that they naively believed would put an end to the sexual abuse. They may have talked to a trusted clergy member or confronted the offender, believing that these interventions would be effective. Handling intrafamilial sexual abuse is something for which most nonoffending parents have no preparation; consequently, they may not know the most appropriate interventions. Rather than fault them for this, professionals should recognize that even if ineffective means were chosen, there is a desire and an attempt on the part of the nonoffending parent to be protective of their children.

During the first months following disclosure and upon entry into treatment, most nonoffending parents are not in a static position; rather, they are constantly moving along the continuum either toward supporting and believing their child or away from being a helpful resource for the child. A variety of influences move them across this continuum, including feelings of fear, confusion, guilt, and betrayal. This movement is also influenced by the behavior of the offender. The offender has become practiced at deceitful manipulation and control and will exercise these behaviors in an attempt to get his needs met or to control the nonoffending parent. Furthermore, the victim's behavior may be confusing or frustrating during this time, further exacerbating the crisis for his or her parent.

Characteristics of Victim Contribute to the Response

One of the factors that can affect where the nonoffending parent is on this dynamic continuum of responses is the severity and intrusiveness of the sexual abuse that took place and the age of the child abused. Mothers of adolescent daughters were at greatest risk for being nonprotective. Maternal belief of the disclosure and support for the sexually abused teenager may be undermined by the mother's anger about other problems the adolescent may be exhibiting. Some may feel that the teenagers "know better," implying that they agreed to the sexual encounter (Heriot, 1996). In addition, mothers of children whose sexual abuse involved penetration may have had difficulty believing their children and may be at increased risk of being nonprotective. Typically, the more severe the abuse, the less supportive the reaction (Heriot, 1996).

Goals for Treating the Nonoffending Parent

The goal of treatment should be to assist nonoffending parents in moving toward a position on the continuum where they will be protective and can provide the victim with the support and belief that will help reduce trauma. In dealing with the nonoffending parent who is frightened and confused, providing information and support on practical matters such as financial concerns, child care, and transportation will often move her in the desired direction. Once the initial fear and shock of the disclosure have passed, nonoffending parents are often anxious to learn what they can do to reduce trauma and help their child to feel safe and to recover from the sexual abuse. Once they get to this point, they will often respond to information and accept opportunities to process their own feelings of betrayal and guilt and to receive education on the needs of traumatized children.

Nonoffending parents who believe but minimize the abuse or the impact of the abuse are often attempting, through defensive thinking, to manage their own feelings and fears about their responsibilities. Their ability to move along the continuum to a position of a more appropriate response will help to assess whether they are ultimately a resource for the victim or whether they will remain entrenched in denial in order to preserve the relationship with the offender. Many nonoffending parents who take a position of minimization are ultimately able to recognize the impact and extent of the sexual abuse. Others are moving on the continuum toward more entrenched denial and alignment with the offender.

Supportive Avoidance of Premature Decision Making

One of the salient issues connected to nonoffending parents' positions on this dynamic continuum is related to their belief that involved professionals want them to make decisions with regard to their relationship with the offender. Early in the treatment process, nonoffending parents will not be in a position emotionally to make decisions related to termination of a relationship with the offender, or to immediately contemplate divorce or reunification. In fact, professionals should give nonoffending parents the message that they should not be making those decisions early in the process; rather, they should be given "permission" to experience the ambivalent feelings and reactions they may be having. Though the language of "giving permission" may appear paternalistic, it is quite important and may, in fact, be empowering. Many nonoffending parents feel pressured by professionals, family members, and friends to make such decisions quickly. Even the process of coming to a decision about the potential for a future relationship with the offender is dynamic. Nonoffending parents should be expected to vacillate numerous times on the decision about whether to continue or end the relationship with the offender. Treating professionals who take a stand on this issue often allow the nonoffending parent and the offender to align with one another against the "system" that is trying to "break up the family." This sort of alignment against CPS or the treatment program shuts down the process for the nonoffending parent, who may need time to sort through feelings about her needs and the needs of her child.

Dealing With Denial

A nonoffending parent who denies that sexual abuse occurred and who blames the victim for false reporting is often the most difficult to assess in terms of her ability to become a resource for her children. A nonoffending parent who reacts with blame and anger upon the initial disclosure often offends professionals and, in fact, may not be able to provide care for the victim in the initial stages of treatment due to the potential for further trauma for the child. However, professionals must remember that the potential for movement along the continuum of responses is much more indicative of the parent's ability to become a resource for the child than is the initial reaction. In fact, the initial reaction may reflect the ongoing behavior of the offender as much as it does the potential of the nonoffending parent to become a resource for the victim. It is not uncommon for offenders in treatment to describe the ways in which they have created dynamics within the family system so that nonoffending parents have a difficult time believing disclosures of sexual abuse. One offender in treatment described that he made it a point to be outraged at learning of someone abusing a child, knowing that if his victims told their mother, she would be less likely to believe them.

As Hindman (1998) has explained, the nonoffending parent who continues to disbelieve her child's disclosure of sexual abuse, in spite of all evidence to the contrary, must eventually be seen as responsible for continuing to contribute to the trauma to the child. This responsibility, however, should not be confused with an assignment of culpability to the nonoffending parent for the sexually abusive act itself. Those who are able to move toward a position of believing and supporting may need to make considerable effort to repair damage that has been done to their relationships with the victim(s) by the initial response to the disclosure.

Assessment of Family Dynamics

All treatment work should begin with a through assessment of family dynamics. Salient issues to include in this assessment are strengths, needs, the costs and effects of the sexual abuse disclosure on the family, information about the families of origin, the relationship history of the nonoffending parent, and the influence of the offender. It is important in treatment planning to realize not only the commonalties present in families that have experienced paternal incest but also the unique strengths that are often present in individuals and families. Professionals must also recognize that denial is a defense that serves the psychological function of attempting to maintain self-esteem. It will be through recognizing and using strengths and acknowledging the role of denial that we will be most effective in developing treatment interventions that will increase the support and protection of the child who has been victimized. The following factors must be considered in a comprehensive assessment of the nonoffending parent in intrafamilial sexual abuse cases.

Strengths. The identification of individual and family strengths allows professionals to engage in strength-based treatment planning. Unfortunately, there is often a tendency for helping professionals to focus on the sometimes glaring deficits that are present in the families of intrafamilial sex offenders. This tendency can be compounded by the disparity between the nonoffending parent's initial reaction to disclosure and the expectations of the professionals. It is a rare occurrence for a nonoffending parent to present without any strengths. Some of the facts that should be considered include the following: the quality of relationships between family members, the ability of the nonoffending parent to reach out to and use outside resources, the availability of kinship and extended family resources, the spiritual/religious affiliations and connections of the family, and the nonoffending parent's attitudes toward being an effective parent. Identification of strengths in these areas, to be included in treatment planning, will lead to better outcomes for the primary goal of providing support for the victimized child.

Reporting Costs and Areas of Need. When assessing ways in which to intervene with families that have experienced incest, professionals should be aware of a number of dynamics that affect not only the experience of the family prior to disclosure but also how the nonoffending parent will be able to respond throughout the treatment process. The term "reporting costs," coined by Massat and Lundy (1998), is one model in which to conceptualize and define the changes and losses that the nonoffending parent in intrafamilial sexual abuse cases experiences. The authors specified four areas in which nonoffending parents experience loss or change: relational, financial, vocational, and residential. All areas should be considered when developing treatment plans with nonoffending parents because many experience significant relationship losses, increased dependence on government programs, employment disruption, and changes in residence following the disclosure of paternal incest (Massat & Lundy, 1998). Often, the families of intrafamilial sex offenders experience sudden financial hardship (Fong & Walsh-Bowers, 1998), as the offender must move from the family residence and set up a separate household in order to maintain a safe environment for the victim and other children. One significant way of reducing the reporting cost to the victim and the nonoffending parent is to remove the offender from the household rather than the victim. In many ways it is important to assist the nonoffending parent in maintaining the family home once the offender has been removed.

Feelings of Loss and Betrayal. Many nonoffending parents in paternal incest cases report feeling a sense of loss and rejection, as well as isolation following the disclosure of incest. Even if the relationship the nonoffending parent had with the offender was abusive and controlling, the nonoffending parent often perceives the ending of the relationship as a major loss (Massat & Lundy, 1998). If the nonoffending parent has not made a decision to end the relationship with the offender, she must still confront her feelings of helplessness and depression (Fong, 1998) that follow this type of betrayal. Other nonoffending parents report that they experience difficulty with sexual intimacy (Fong & Walsh-Bowers, 1998) following the disclosure of intrafamilial sexual abuse. Many nonoffending parents also report feelings of anger and guilt. The feelings that the nonoffending parent has toward the offender can vary greatly from anger to alignment, strong emotion to ambivalence, particularly in the early stages of disclosure and treatment planning. Often well-meaning but busy professionals focus on important tasks such as protective concerns and how the nonoffending parent will keep her children from having contact with the offender and forget to ask the simple questions such as, "What has this been like for you?" and "What would be helpful to you during this time?" Even a few minutes spent assessing the subjective experiences of the nonoffending parent will greatly aid in developing a therapeutic relationship between this parent and the helping professionals.

In addition to validating the emotional experiences of the nonoffending parent, attention to practical issues such as child care, maintaining jobs, financial management, and transportation can be essential in reducing the sense of crisis. This will allow the nonoffending parent to return her focus to the needs of the victim.

History of the Nonoffending Parent. The family-of-origin issues and history that the nonoffending parent brings to the table are important to assess and consider when developing intervention plans. Family history affects the attitudes, beliefs, and, therefore, behavior of nonoffending parents in their efforts to protect and promote healing for their children. When the family histories of nonoffending parents are considered, professionals should not be surprised to find that these parents were witness to or victims of abuses of power in their families of origin. Although not a universal commonality, many mothers of abused children have themselves been victims of childhood sexual abuse (Hagood, 1991). Adults who were sexually abused as children, particularly if they received little or no treatment, often have a poor understanding of sexual intimacy (Hindman, 1989). Other nonoffending parents were often victims of emotional or physical abuse or witnessed their own mothers subjected to abuse. Such a history can influence the beliefs a parent may have about choices and options. One such example is that of a nonoffending parent who grew up in a household in which all family members tiptoed around a physically aggressive parent. She is less likely then to consider herself as having the right to defend herself from an angry, controlling offender.

In addition to experiencing abuses of power in their families of origins, it is not uncommon for the nonoffending parents in cases of paternal incest to have experienced abuses of power in their adult relationships. DeYoung (1994) found that many women whose children had been victims of incest described personal histories of physical, sexual, and/or emotional abuse by their husbands. Our clinical experience confirms, anecdotally, that many nonoffending parents have experienced repeated abuses of power in adult relationships, if not by the identified offender then in past relationships.

The Influence of the Offender on the Nonoffending Parent

It is rare to find incestuous acts occurring out of impulse, despite the initial claims by sex offenders. There is consistently a period during which the offender has tricked, bribed, manipulated, and groomed the child. In addition to using such strategies to gain the compliance of the child victim, the offender has developed and employed similar strategies to control the family system, including the nonoffending parent. It is not surprising, then, that the reactions that nonoffending parents have toward the occurrence of paternal incest sometimes parallel those of the victims (Deitz & Craft, 1980; Strand, 1990). The influence that incest offenders have on nonoffending parents and family dynamics is enormous. Consider the following case:

> A nonoffending parent, a mother, was informed in a therapist's office of a disclosure that had occurred in therapy. Both the therapist and the CPS worker were impressed with the mother's ability to respond to her daughter's needs. She was very clear that her child was the priority, and that she would always be protective and understanding about what the child had been through. However, when the mother went home to move the offender (also the child's father) out of the house, his influence was powerful. Her next response was to call the CPS worker and demand that this lying child be removed from her house.

Offenders often describe in treatment the great efforts they have made to discredit the child and to introduce doubt in the nonoffending parent's mind. Some have identified elaborate schemes designed to create relationship schisms between the victim and the nonoffending parent. This sometimes takes the form of turning the nonoffending parent against the child by presenting the child in negative terms, focusing on inappropriate behaviors exhibited by the child, or introducing "evidence" of the child's general dishonesty and untrustworthiness. In essence, the offender influences the nonoffending parent via manipulation and lies to align with himself against the victim.

Sometimes the offender uses his influence to set up an alignment with the child victim against the nonoffending parent. In this scenario, the offender acts in such a manner as to "split" the nonoffending parent and the child, thus creating a wedge (Hindman, 1998) in the relationship. The offender may give special treatment to the victim, providing the child with gifts, preferential treatment, or privileges that the child may not get from the nonoffending parent. In addition, the offender might stick up for the child or "defend" the child from the disciplinary strategies of the nonoffending parent. This dynamic not only aligns the offender with the child victim but also negates the positive and appropriate influence that the nonoffending parent may have on the child. When the nonoffending parent's positive influence is disrupted by the manipulative efforts of the offender, the victim may not be able to see the parent as a protective resource. Therefore, the offender's influence not only gains him increased access to the victim but also maintains the secrecy of the sexual abuse.

The influence offenders have not only on the victim but also on the nonoffending parent is enormous. Again, it is important to emphasize that the nonoffending parent's initial reaction to the disclosure of the sexual abuse may be a greater reflection of the influence of the offender rather than the potential the parent has to be a resource for the child victim. In many cases, the efforts of the offender in maintaining secrecy and in grooming the victim have existed for years. When this influence has resulted in a negative or antagonistic relationship between the victim and the nonoffending parent, professionals should expect to witness an initial reaction from the nonoffending parent that is less than supportive of the victim, or even nonbelieving of the disclosure. This is exactly the reaction the offender has been cultivating for a lengthy period. Therefore, a critical piece of the assessment should be focused on the ways in which the offender has influenced family members, including any nonabused siblings. Treatment plans should be developed that provide an opportunity to mend broken relationships, disintegrate inappropriate alignments, and remove the "wedges" in relationships between the nonoffending parent and other family members.

Setting the Stage for Treatment

Developing the Victim Support Team. As previously noted, the subjective experience that many nonoffending parents report having with child protection workers and therapeutic staff is less than helpful. The combination of the nonoffending parent's immediate reaction and the expectations of the professionals can serve the unintended function of creating an unfortunate "us and them" dynamic. Again, the ultimate goal of all professionals should be the process of getting the nonoffending parent onto the team of support people who are being assembled for the victim. The first contact with the nonoffending parent is crucial and presents an important opportunity to intervene.

Responding to the Nonoffending Parent in Emotional Crisis. Given the powerful emotional reactions that can follow the disclosure of incest, it is unfortunate that the nonoffending parent's potential for protection and support of the victim is judged at that moment of crisis. This is a dangerous and potentially damaging practice. The danger of such a practice involves the potential inaccuracy of assessing an individual based on her initial reaction to an emotional crisis. As noted previously, the first contact with the nonoffending parent is crucial and presents an opportunity to begin the treatment process and to intervene in a potent way. Few would argue that the disclosure of sexual abuse by an intimate partner with your child creates a moment of acute emotional crisis. In the first hours, days, and weeks following such a disclosure, it is critical for all helping professionals to remain sensitive and to be aware of the emotional crisis that is unfolding for the nonoffending parent. Nonoffending parents often report that it is of great importance that professionals respond in a way that indicates that they will provide help in this crisis and are willing to listen to the account of the nonoffending parent's experiences.

Professionals must be willing to take the time and listen to the experiences of these nonoffending parents. They should be able to provide immediate assistance in primary areas of need. Many nonoffending parents report that their vocational opportunities are affected by the disclosure of sexual abuse. They find it necessary to take frequent time off from their jobs in order to coordinate interviews, court dates, and therapy appointments. Helping professionals should also work hard to assist in coordinating these necessary obligations in such a way as to minimize as much as possible the disruption in the daily life of the nonoffending parent. Parents who believe that they are being misunderstood by a "system" insensitive to their needs are ultimately going to be less able to provide emotionally for their child.

If the first experiences the nonoffending parent has with helping professionals are overwhelmingly negative, the ability to create a therapeutic alliance with that parent will be much more difficult. In fact, the more a nonoffending parent feels alienated and blamed by the child protection system, the less likely it will be that she will become a positive and appropriate resource in the healing process for the victim. In many unfortunate cases, the only issue on which the victim and nonoffending parent agree and align together is their intensely negative beliefs and feelings about the child protection and criminal justice systems. When this dynamic becomes more powerful than the influence of the therapeutic system, any potential benefits for the family are negated.

What Are the Goals? The goal of treatment for the nonoffending parent should be to promote the development of resources for the victim, for other affected children, and for the parent. Hindman's (1989) work on identifying the factors that intensify trauma for the victims of incest cites disastrous disclosure as a major traumatic factor for the victim. The term "disastrous disclosure" pertains in part to the reaction of the nonoffending parent following disclosure. The victims, and other children in the household, are increasingly reliant on the remaining parent when the offender is arrested and/or removed from the home. Because of the previously noted influences that the offender has had on the relationship between the victim and the nonoffending parent, the nonabusive parent may not be an immediately appropriate resource for the child in need. Therefore, the primary goal of treatment is to increase the functioning of the nonoffending parent in such a manner so that she will become an increasingly appropriate and stable resource.

When the nonoffending parent has a number of significant deficits, amelioration of those deficits is also a primary goal. Massat and Lundy (1998) observed that the most troubled parents had children who were in the greatest distress. An unstable and out-of-control nonoffending parent has little capacity to provide stability for children in need. The inability to protect children from harm is associated with self-blame and shame (Massat & Lundy, 1998), and therefore resolution of these feelings is critical in assisting the nonoffending parent to become appropriately supportive and protective.

Assessing and Understanding the Usefulness of Defensive Thinking Patterns

The concept of cognitive distortions, also referred to as "thinking errors" or "criminal thinking" (Samenow, 1984), should be familiar to any professional who has worked with sex offenders. These cognitive distortions are the thinking patterns employed by sex offenders as they attempt to justify their offenses and the continuation of offense behavior patterns and, ultimately, attempt to explain their offensive behavior after disclosure. Simply put, these cognitive distortions allow the sex offender to justify the sexually abusive behaviors and live with himself after behaving in a manner that has violated the rights and boundaries of an innocent child.

A similar process of cognitively distorted thinking can be observed in nonoffending parents following the disclosure of the sexual abuse of their children. Cognitive distortions often occur due to an attempt to avoid feeling responsible for any role in the sexually abusive and secretive family dynamics, or to avoid facing difficult feelings. It is critical to note, however, that this process of distorted thinking serves a different function for the nonoffending parent than for the offender. The nonoffending parent is typically trying to cope with the traumatic news of disclosure whereas offenders are pursuing their own selfish needs. Rather than justifying and maintaining abusive behavior, this process of distorted thinking serves to defend the nonoffending parent from the harsh realities and impact of sexual abuse on the lives of the victim and other family members. It is helpful to distinguish this distorted thinking from that of the sexual offender by referring to these thinking patterns as "defensive thinking" rather than criminal thinking.

Defensive thinking patterns may initially provide the "anchor" that keeps the nonoffending parent afloat during the period of emotional upheaval that surrounds and follows the disclosure of sexual abuse. Defensive thinking patterns can include: denial that the offense has occurred or that it will have a significant impact on their children; blaming self or others for the offender's behavior; making excuses for the offender's abusive behavior; justifying continued contact between the offender and the victim; and in many cases viewing the offender as a victim, particularly of the criminal justice system.

Defensive thinking is an understandable first response to the shock of disclosure of sexual abuse within the family. It functions in three ways. First, the defensive thinking functions to manage the overwhelming and confusing feelings the nonoffending parent will likely experience on disclosure. Second, defensive thinking is an attempt to sort out the overwhelming sense of responsibility the nonoffending parent may believe she has for the abuse of her child. Third, defensive thinking arises from concern for the well-being of the offender, who may be seen as a victim of the system's response to the disclosure. This thinking may be exacerbated by the reactions of others who may expect the immediate exclusion of the offender from the family.

Denial of the traumatic effects of sexual abuse on the victim, or the wish to believe that the abuse could not have happened, may be an attempt to deal with overwhelming feelings of guilt, fear, or shame. When the nonoffending parent is employing defensive thinking, comments such as "It wasn't so bad, at least he didn't have intercourse with you," or " The courts are really making it tough on your dad," are not conducive to creating an environment of safety and support. Professionals need to assist nonoffending parents in restructuring their patterns of defensive thinking. The victim needs to begin to feel support and belief as quickly as possible to minimize the negative effects of sexual abuse. Although the statements made by nonoffending parents who are using defensive thinking may be offensive to those who work with victims, it is important to understand this concept in order to effectively intervene. Helping nonoffending parents to identify and understand their defensive thinking will help them to reexamine their initial response to disclosure and can enable them to move from an initial damaging response to one of support of and belief in the victim.

Treatment Interventions

Group Therapy. One of the most effective treatment interventions for the nonoffending parent in intrafamilial sexual abuse cases is group therapy. Nonoffending parents report that meeting with other mothers who were contending with the same circumstances helped reduce their sense of segregation and provided opportunities to find applicable solutions (Fong & Walsh-Bowers, 1998). Providing multiple opportunities for the nonoffending parent to interact with others in her situation may enhance recovery. Groups provide an opportunity for belonging, the reduction of isolation, and the development of new social relationships and support and provide hope and promote new skill acquisition (Womack et al., 1999). Many nonoffending parents will be able to reduce their sense of isolation and alienation by interacting with other parents. Most report that they looked for help from both informal and formal sources (Fong & Walsh-Bowers, 1998), and the development of relationships with others who were experiencing similar circumstances was important. The positive influence of other nonoffending parents, particularly in the gentle confrontation of defensive thinking, can have more impact, and be more effective, than the influence of treatment professionals alone.

Any clinical practice that treats more than one case of incest will find that group treatment is an effective approach. Groups of nonoffending parents not only can share support and decrease isolation but also can confront the distortions and denial in parents who have just begun the adjustment to the changes and realities with which they are faced. There is a great deal of power in having another parent describe her process of acceptance to a parent who is still in some level of denial. In addition, the support offered in groups by other parents who have had the same experience is significant in offsetting the attempts by offenders to promote denial and to isolate and control the nonoffending parent.

Making Restitution. Treatment for the nonoffending parents in incest cases should include a mechanism by which the parent can "make amends" to the child for any disastrous responses to disclosure of the sexual abuse. Restitution-focused therapy is common for sex offenders in intrafamilial cases, but the concept of the nonoffending parent accepting responsibility for inappropriate responses is less often applied in treatment. Borrowing many concepts from the clarification that offenders provide to victims (Hindman, 1989), nonoffending parents may make restitution to the victim by acknowledging the harm their initial response may have caused the victim and identifying the response that the victim actually deserved. Typically, when the nonoffending parent is able to restructure her defensive thinking patterns and correctly identify the negative influence of the offender in the family's dynamics, she experiences a great deal of remorse, pain, and shame. This remorse and regret can have a negative impact on her ability to provide stability and an environment of healing for her children. Therefore, helping the nonoffending parent "repair the damage" can be some of the most powerful and important work done with the victims of incest.

Conclusion

To effectively treat the nonoffending parent and ensure benefit to the victims of incest, professionals need to consider of a number of issues. To avoid alienating families from the treatment process, professionals must develop an awareness of their personal attitudes toward nonoffending parents and work toward understanding the unique stresses and thought patterns that affect these individuals. The reactions and responses of nonoffending parents can be seen in terms of a dynamic continuum, and treatment strategies strive to move these nonoffending parents along the continuum toward responses that benefit the victim. Treatment interventions should be grounded in a comprehensive assessment of the family and should take into account the unique impact of a disclosure of intrafamilial sexual abuse on the nonoffending parent. The professional must be particularly aware of the influence of the offender on the nonoffending parent. Ultimately, professionals must work toward assisting the nonoffending parent in becoming a vital part of the victim's support team and in attempting to repair any damage that may have been done by initial responses to the disclosure. When interventions with a nonoffending parent are effective, not only is she empowered to assert and provide for her own needs but she is far more capable of providing appropriate protection and support for her children.

References

Breckenridge, J., & Baldry, E. (1997). Workers dealing with mother blame in child sexual assault cases. *Journal of Child Sexual Abuse, 6*(1), 65–80.

Deitz, C., & Craft, H. (1980). Family dynamics of incest: A new perspective. *Social Casework, 61*, 602–609.

DeYoung, M. (1994). Immediate maternal reactions to the disclosure or discovery of incest. *Journal of Family Violence, 9*(1), 21–33.

Fong, J., & Walsh-Bowers, R. (1998). Voices of the blamed: Mothers' responsiveness to father-daughter incest. *Journal of Family Social Work, 3*(1), 25–41.

Hagood, M. (1991). Group art therapy with the mothers of sexually abused children. *The Arts in Psychotherapy, 18*, 17–27.

Heriot, J. (1996). Maternal protectiveness following the disclosure of intrafamilial child sexual abuse. *Journal of Interpersonal Violence, 11*(2), 181–194.

Hindman, J. (1989). *Just before dawn.* Ontario, OR: AlexAndria Associates.

Massat, C. R., & Lundy, M. (1998). "Reporting costs" to nonoffending parents in cases of intrafamilial child sexual abuse. *Child Welfare, 40*(4), 371–388.

Newberger, C. M., Gremy, I. B., Waternaux, C. M., & Newberger, E. H. (1993). Mother of sexually abused children: Trauma and repair in longitudinal perspective. *American Journal of Orthopsychiatry, 63*, 92-102.

Samenow, S. E. (1984). *Inside the criminal mind.* New York: Random House.

Strand, V. (1990). Treatment of mothers in the incest family: The beginning phase. *Clinical Social Work Journal, 18*(4), 353–366.

Womack, M. E., Miller, G., & Lassiter, P. (1999). Helping mothers in incestuous families: An empathic approach. *Women and Therapy, 22*(4), 17–35.

Chapter 26

Forensic Assessment of Internet Child Pornography Offenders

by Timothy P. Foley, Ph.D.

Overview

This chapter surveys aspects of the law, child pornography, sexual fantasy, and deviant behaviors. Psychometric data from psychological evaluations of a group of convicted child pornographers are used to aid in understanding and describing the motivations of this group. A taxonomy is proposed based on this data.

Introduction

Little is known about the extent, effects, or availability of child pornography. Likewise, the link between sexual fantasy and subsequent deviant behaviors has not been empirically established. Since the advent of widespread Internet access, child pornography has become accessible, cheap, and anonymous. Law enforcement has used the same Internet tool to investigate and prosecute hundreds of individuals caught downloading, and thus possessing, pornographic images of children.

What Is Legal and What Is Illegal on the Internet?

Before describing the legal implications of Internet child pornography, a review of what is legal and illegal on the Internet may be useful and instructive. It is likely that many individuals incorrectly assume that pornography freely downloaded from a news group or chat room is either legal or will not be vigorously prosecuted. There are no prominent warnings concerning the legality of pornography found on these venues. Many may assume that their Internet connection is confidential and that their carrier sanctions the material found on its server. Ironically, net service providers have statutory immunity from liability for illegal pornographic postings although their customers do not (Communications Decency Act of 1996). Following is an outline of what is legal and not legal, on the Internet. It should be noted that pay sites often warn that some pornography may be illegal in the downloaded locale. In those instances, the consumer is surrendering anonymity and made aware of the legal limits related to his or her Internet behavior before downloading.

Kenneth V. Lanning (1998) of the FBI writes that illegal sexual activity involving the use of computers, and the focus of law enforcement investigations, includes (1) producing or possessing child pornography, (2) uploading and downloading child pornography, and (3) soliciting sex with "children."

He continues that sexual activity involving the use of computers that is "usually legal" includes (1) validating sexually deviant behaviors and interests; (2) reinforcing deviant arousal patterns; (3) storing and sharing sexual fantasies; (4) lying about one's age and identity; (5) collecting adult erotica that is not obscene; (6) disseminating "indecent" material, talking dirty, providing sexual instructions, "cyber-sex," etc.; and (7) injecting oneself into the "problem" of computer exploitation of children to rationalize one's interests.

Based on this outline, downloading and storing child pornography are no different legally than possessing a hard copy of a magazine, film, or videotape. Collecting and storing adult pornography is legal but subject to local regulation.

Internet Child Pornography and the Law

United States v. McBroom (1998) contains tragic elements of an individual's life, as well as one story indicative of the cultural impact of the Internet. Kenneth McBroom was an attorney, a reported victim of sexual abuse, an abuser of drugs and alcohol, and compulsively driven to download child pornography from the Internet, even while knowing that his behavior was being scrutinized by federal authorities. Kenneth McBroom pled guilty to, and was convicted of, one count of possession of child pornography in violation of 18 U.S.C. § 2252(a)(4). McBroom requested a downward departure pursuant to Federal Sentencing Guideline 5K2.13 on the grounds that he suffered from a significantly reduced mental capacity. The Court found that McBroom was able, at the time of the offense, to absorb information in the usual way and to exercise the power of reason, thus denying his motion. His case was appealed and the Court was instructed to broaden the sentencing criteria to consider that he suffered from a "volitional impairment which impaired him from controlling his behavior or conforming it to the law." The Federal Sentencing Guidelines were amended to define "significantly reduced mental capacity" as "a significantly impaired ability to (A) understand the wrongfulness of the behavior comprising the offense or to exercise the power of reason; or (B) control behavior that the defendant knows is wrongful." The revised guidelines also instructed that the amount of the departure should be congruent with the extent of the impairment. In short, the new Federal Sentencing Guideline now includes a volitional prong which may be used to depart from minimum sentences mandated by the law.

Background to *United States v. McBroom*

Background information concerning McBroom and the circumstances of his case is contained in the public record. It shows that in late 1994, McBroom bought a personal computer for work-related activities and "soon discovered the Internet." At that time, most service providers charged an hourly access fee. In following years, access was charged on a monthly basis and at a much lower rate for heavy users. Prior to purchasing his computer, McBroom had cycled through several drug and alcohol rehabilitation programs and bought, and then destroyed, reams of print pornography. At times, he incurred astronomical phone bills for phone sex connections. He reported being amazed by the "wealth of pornography available on the Internet" and types he had never seen before, including child pornography, bestiality, masochism, bondage, and every imaginable sexual fetish.

According to federal investigators, approximately 25% of the images McBroom received constituted child pornography, and the remainder were within the limits of the law. McBroom, in explaining his compulsive behavior, relayed that "every time I turned the computer on there were hundreds of new pictures depicting all sorts of pornography. . . . When I wasn't sitting at the computer looking at this stuff, I was thinking about looking at it, I thought nothing of spending three consecutive hours at the computer at a single sitting." There were no allegations that McBroom had sexual contact with children, bought or sold illegal pornography, or attempted to contact a child. He was granted a downward departure on the basis of his "reduced mental capacity" and his "extraordinary" rehabilitation efforts and was sentenced, under the amended guidelines, for eight to fourteen months in federal custody. The Court explained that the "criminal justice system has long meted out lower sentences to persons, who although not technically insane are not in full command of their actions" (*McBroom*, 991 F. Supp. at 450).

The essence of the Court ruling was that although McBroom knew and understood that his behavior was illegal, he was unable to control his behavior. The Court added that there is "strong need to deter behavior that exploits children" (*McBroom*, 991 F. Supp. at 449) and explained that the law was imposed "not only because of the harm to the children who were abused and photographed in the depictions for which the offender is punished, but also because of the harm these photographs will likely cause to other children—by encouraging viewers to engage in the abusive conduct depicted" (*McBroom*, 991 F. Supp. at 449). Thus, the Court inferred that viewing child pornography leads to and validates child molestation. The literature concerning this inference is surveyed later in this chapter, as well as the powerful influence that the Internet has on some individuals.

The Internet, Technology, and Pornography

Apart from dramatic impact of *McBroom*, it comes as no surprise that the Internet plays an increasingly important role in our daily lives. Membership in America Online has increased ninety-seven-fold from June 1992 to June 1999. It is reported that 350 new members are added per hour and that plans are to double membership and increase the time a subscriber spends online from a current average of fifty-two minutes per day to at least three hours. User time spent online translates to increased AOL advertising revenues in the millions of dollars (Kanaley, 1999).

It should also come as no surprise that a significant portion of the Internet content is devoted to pornography. Several authors (Cooper, 1998; Freeman-Longo & Blanchard, 1998) report that pornograpy is the Internet's most frequently searched topic. Heavy Internet usage by men has been related to increased exposure to pornography and several indices of psychological distress (Cooper, Scherer, Boies, & Gordon, 1999). Both male and female users who report compulsive use of the Internet are more likely to spend a considerable amount of that time in chat rooms (Cooper et al., 1999). Young (1996) identified three psychological variables underlying computer-mediated communication: social support, sexual fulfillment, and creating a persona. In other words, the individual is able to find company, gratify sexual needs, and freely fantasize whatever he or she wishes. Other studies link depression, sexual compulsivity, and sensation-seeking behaviors as related to excessive use of the Internet (Young & Rogers, 1998). Young (1996) found that Internet "addicts" were online an average of thirty-eight hours per week for nonacademic and nonprofessional purposes. Not surprisingly, spending large amounts of time on the Internet may be related to a host of psychological difficulties if only stemming from social isolation (Leiblum, 1997).

Internet pornography ranges from the relatively innocuous soft-core types to the most abhorrent presentations featuring barely imaginable combinations of behaviors.

Satiation is not limited by expense, availability, or diversity of pornographic sources, as described by Mr. McBroom.

Notes on the History of Pornography

The growth of Internet pornography parallels in many ways the early history of pornography. Pornography's sixteenth-century emergence is linked to the development of print technology and "vast social processes which brought about the modern world" (Hunt, 1996). Cited developments were "the growth of cities, and with them, an audience of literate readers; the development of new kinds of experience, especial ly privatization of belongings; and the splitting off of sexuality from the rest of life in an urban, capitalist, industrial, and middle-class world" (Marcus, 1974, p. 282), not unlike our own current computer information revolution. As technology developed, and became cheaper and more available, print pornography became more accessible and anonymously circulated to a wider audience. In the same way the Internet as well as computers have become widely available, cheap, and easy to use. As noted earlier, current net service providers' revenues come more from advertising and less from user fees. It is now possible for individuals to work, play, shop, and form all sorts of relationships without losing sight of their computer screen.

Child Pornography

Child pornography was legally circulated in the late 1960s in at least two European-based magazines. Distribution was limited in the United States by logistics and stiff legal sanctions. Dissemination was also limited by expense, consistent with inherent legal risk to the seller as well as to the buyer. Most of the child pornography freely available on the Internet today was produced from 1969 to 1979 when Danish laws did not prohibit any form of pornography from being consumed or produced (O'Toole, 1998). Around the same time, a Dutch magazine was published from home-made images, sent to the magazine, which continue to be scanned onto chat rooms and news groups dedicated to child pornography. It is likely that this is the major source of pornographic child depictions, along with some naturalist images, which continue to be circulated. Naturalist images are depictions of nudist camps and beaches where nudity is permitted. It is often reported that little new child pornography is currently being produced and widely distributed, although a recent influx from Russian sources is mentioned. Danish laws concerning child pornography were tightened in the late 1970s, and by 1985 it was illegal around the world. Several home-based magazines continued and, ironically, the U.S. government maintained the only U.S.-produced magazine of child pornography with a seized magazine used to entrap suspected pedophiles. Laws were necessitated, and enforced, primarily to protect exploited children. There were also concerns that child pornography paralleled and incited child molestation. All this is not to mention the violation of cultural taboos associated with childhood sexuality.

There are media reports (Shannon, 1998) which describe worldwide child pornography rings and sophisticated encryption techniques used to frustrate law enforcement. One such group, Wonderland, required its estimated 200 international members to possess a minimum of 10,000 pornographic images of children stored on their computer for membership. In 1996, members of the Orchid Club reportedly conspired to sexually molest five girls ages 4 to 10 and trade sexually explicit pictures of them on the Internet. Widespread circulation of newly produced child pornography is, however, rare, costly, and illegal everywhere.

Anonymity, easy availability, and only the cost of a modem and computer appear to have facilitated access among otherwise disinterested individuals. The deviant appetite of the fixated pedophile or preferential child molester is unlikely to have been altered to a great degree by this technological development. Widely distributed images scanned from dated print sources are unlikely to have an appeal to those already in possession of those materials. It is illogical to suppose that expensive pornography would be freely distributed to Internet users for their private use.

Assumptions of the Government

In 1994, the federal government initiated a campaign, Innocent Images, to curb the pornographic exploitation of children over the Internet. As of March 10, 1999, the FBI claimed that more than 329 arrests and 184 convictions had been realized by this program (Hearing of the Commerce, Justice, State, and Judiciary Subcommittee of the Senate Appropriations Committee, March 10, 1998). The FBI director testified that there were 684 active pending cases and seven of those cases were "travelers cases," which were described as attempts to contact a child or minor over the Internet for "illicit sexual purposes." Several assumptions about consumers of child pornography, from a 1995 FBI conference concerning this campaign, were mentioned in an archival search warrant:

1. Preferential child molesters/collectors and child pornographers receive sexual gratification, stimulation and satisfaction from actual physical contact with children and from fantasies they may have viewing children engaged in photographs or other visual media or from literature describing such activity.

2. They collect sexually explicit or suggestive materials (hardcore and soft-core pornography, whether of adults and or children, and child erotica) consisting of photographs, magazines, motion pictures, video tapes, books, slides and/or drawings or other visual media that they use for their own sexual arousal and gratification. Further, they commonly use this type of sexually explicit material to lower the inhibitions of children they are attempting to seduce, or arouse the selected child partner, and to demonstrate the desired sexual acts.

3. Child pornographers, and preferential child molesters/collectors, almost always maintain and possess their material (pictures, films, videotapes, magazines, negatives, photographs, correspondence, mailing lists, books, tape recordings, child erotica etc.) in the privacy of their homes or some other secure location for many years.

4. In addition, they often correspond and/or meet others to share information and materials; rarely destroy correspondence from other preferential child molesters/collectors and child pornographers; conceal such correspondence as they do their sexually explicit material; and often maintain lists of names, address-

es, and telephone numbers of individuals with whom they have been in contact and who share the same interests in child pornography.

5. Preferential child molesters/collectors and child pornographers who collect sexually oriented pictures of minors are not without their child pornography and/or child erotica for any prolonged time period. This behavior has been documented by law enforcement officers involved in the investigation of child pornography throughout the United States.

The federal government seems to have concluded that all consumers of child pornography are pedophiles and exclusively prefer sexual contact with children over adults. Second, the pedophilic consumer has an insatiable thirst for child pornography which parallels the physical molestation of children. In other words, pedophilia is equated with child molestation. No such association, however, is implied by the diagnosis of pedophilia (302.2), according to the fourth edition of *Diagnostic and Statistical Manual of Mental Disorders* (DSM-IV; American Psychiatric Association, 1994). The diagnostic criteria detail that "over a period of at least 6 months, recurrent, intense sexually arousing fantasies, sexual urges, or behaviors involving sexual activity with a prepubescent child or children (usually age 13 or younger)" (p. 528) must have occurred. The criteria also state that "the fantasies, sexual urges, or behaviors cause clinically significant distress or impairment in social, occupational, or other important areas of functioning." The diagnosis of pedophilia does not require child molestation. Marshall (1997) writes that he could find "no clear evidence of recurrent urges or fantasies in almost 60% of our non-familial child molesters and in over 75% of incest offenders. Apparently, recurrent urges and fantasies are not diagnostic of all chid molesters" (p. 161). Basically, the literature indicates that not all pedophiles are child molesters, and not all child molesters are pedophiles.

Pedophiles, Child Molesters, and Pornography

The literature on sexual offenders is consistent on few points. Predictive psychological test profiles have yet to be established. Given the heterogeneity of offenders, it is not surprising that the typical offender has not been found. The Internet offender however appears to be more homogeneous than other offender groups at least in terms of demographic variables. Commonality is driven by socioeconomic, educational, technological interest, expertise, and pornographic exposure variables. A prime difficulty in investigating contact sexual offenders is that the majority of their offenses are unreported, undiscovered, and not adjudicated. The role of pornography in their offense cycles in similarly unclear.

The literature shows that child pornography is used by some offenders for a variety of purposes. Along with feeding deviant fantasy, it may be used to disinhibit potential victims by pornographic exposure. Illicit pornography is often hypothesized to play a role in the escalation toward child molestation. It is well-known that sexual fantasies are nearly universally experienced by men and women and can affect later sexual behavior as well as reflect past experience (see Leitenberg & Henning, 1995). In fantasy, one can imagine anything one likes, however unrealistic, without experiencing embarrassment or rejection or societal and legal restrictions. Some authors

(Abel & Blanchard, 1974) consider sexual fantasies as fundamental in the commission of sexual offenses such as exhibitionism, rape, and child sexual abuse. Conversely, a lack of sexual fantasies, or excessive guilt about them, may contribute to sexual dysfunction (Cado & Leitenberg, 1990; Zimmer, Borchardt, & Fischle, 1983). In general, fantasies can be used to stimulate sexual arousal, but the reverse pathway is also possible (i.e., arousal can stimulate fantasies). Most sexual fantasies appear to be deliberate patterns of thought designed to stimulate or enhance pleasurable sexual feelings, regardless of whether the fantasies involve reminiscing about past sexual experiences, imagining anticipated future sexual activity, engaging in wishful thinking, or having daydreams that are exciting to imagine without any desire to put them into practice. In short, the term "sexual fantasy" refers to almost any mental imagery that is sexually arousing or erotic to the individual. The essential element of a deliberate sexual fantasy is the ability to control in imagination exactly what takes place. Even reminiscences of past events can be altered so that only particularly exciting aspects are recalled or enhanced. It is usually thought that sexual fantasies begin occurring on a regular basis during early adolescence, concurrent with a general increase in sex drive and sexual arousal. Retrospective studies (Gold & Gold, 1991) suggest that the mean ages at which adults recall experiencing their first sexual fantasy are approximately 11 to 13. There appear to be four overarching sexual fantasy content categories for both men and women: (1) conventional intimate sexual imagery with past, present, or imaginary lovers who usually are known to the person; (2) scenes demonstrating sexual power and irresistibility (including seduction scenes, multiple partners, etc.); (3) scenes involving somewhat varied or "forbidden" sexual imagery (different settings, positions, practices, questionable partners, etc.); and (4) submission-dominance scenes in which some physical force or sadomasochistic imagery is involved or implied.

It is widely accepted that child molesters, rapists, and other sexual offenders have a vast array of motivations for their behavior. If anything is certain, it is that no credible profile which reliably predicts sexual offending behaviors is known. Some authors (Abel & Blanchard, 1974) posit that sex offenders are more sexually aroused by stimuli associated with the sexual offense (e.g., thoughts of rape or of sex with a child) than by stimuli associated with mutually consenting sexual activity; as a result, it is assumed they are more likely to fantasize about and to engage in the deviant sexual behavior. The underlying hypothesis of this position appears to be that deviant arousal increases the likelihood of deviant fantasy, which in turn increases the likelihood of deviant behavior, at least for sex offenders. There is some evidence to support the hypothesis that some sexual offenders engage in deviant sexual fantasies differentially than nonoffenders. In one outpatient study, Laws (1988) showed that nearly all pedophiles admitted to being exposed to adult erotica at least once in their lives but relatively few admitted to ever having been exposed to any type of child pornography (9.1%). The author went on to conclude that "pornography use plays a role in the commission of a small percentage of child molestation cases."

Of course, an association between past fantasy and past behavior does not necessarily mean that the fantasy caused the behavior to occur. Some research (Pithers, Beal, Armstrong, & Petty, 1989) shows that deviant fantasizing was an immediate precursor of child molestation in only 51% of offenders, although it is likely that deviant fantasies are underreported. Marshall (1997) finds that sexual fantasizing about children is far more of a risk factor once offending has commenced, rather than before. Moreover, there is no evidence that sexual fantasies, by themselves are either a sufficient or a necessary condition for committing a sexual offense. Many men who have never committed a sexual offense have fantasies of forcing sex on someone. The range is from a low of 13% (Hunt, 1974) to a high of 54% (Grendlinger & Byrne, 1987) and the mean percentage across seven studies is 31% (Arndt, Foehl, & Good, 1985; Crepault & Couture, 1980; Grendlinger & Byrne, 1987; Hunt, 1974; Miller & Simon, 1980; Person, Terestman, Myers, Goldberg, & Salvadori, 1989; Sue, 1979). In nonoffender samples of men (Grendlinger & Byre, 1987) such fantasies accounted for only 6.57% of the variance in any type of past coercive sexual behavior, and Gold and Clegg (1990) did not find any significant association. Even fantasies about sex with children, and arousal to sexual imagery of children, do not by themselves indicate that someone is a child molester or has a strong potential to be a child molester. For example, in an anonymous survey (Briere & Runtz, 1989), the authors found that 21% of male undergraduate students endorsed the statement that "little children sometimes attract me sexually," and 9% of the students admitted having sexual fantasies about children. Fedora et al. (1992) report that 18% of their controls showed sexual arousal to children in their study. None of these individuals, however, said that they had molested children. Crepault and Couture (1980) reported that 61% of their adult male sample said they had experienced a sexual fantasy in which they "sexually initiated a young girl." Templeman and Stinnett (1991) found that 17% of male college students admitted recently experiencing a sexual thought about having sex with girls under age 15 (5% with girls under 12). Given the widespread cultural taboos in this area, one might expect that the percentages are greater than would be expected. Finally, nearly 20% of nonoffender control samples show arousal to imagery of prepubescent children in plethysmography studies (Barbaree & Marshall, 1989; Fedora et al., 1992). In summary, sex offenders often report that they have sexual fantasies related to their offense. However, these kinds of fantasies are also not uncommon in people who have never acted on them. Therefore, unless the boundary between fantasy and behavior has been crossed, or other risk factors for committing a sexual offense are evident, occasional experiences of fantasies such as these are not by themselves signals of imminent danger. Deviant sexual fantasies may be predictive of later offending among groups of known sex offenders but not strongly predictive when applied to the nonoffending population at large.

Current Study

Forensic psychological evaluations were performed on a consecutively drawn group of individuals referred as a result of illegal behaviors involving child pornography. These offenses involved downloading from child pornography chat rooms and/or ordering videotaped child pornography catalogues through the mail. Referral sources were defense attorneys, federal public defenders, federal probation officers, and psychologists seeking specialized evaluations for these kinds of offenses. All the evaluations were used in the sentencing phase of the judicial process.

Demographics. All the members of the group ($N = 22$), except one, were Caucasian, educated ($X = 14.75$, $SD = 2.04$), and between the ages of 26 and 55 ($X = 39.68$, SD

= 10.17). The majority (68%) were heterosexual and either living with a significant other (25%) or married (31.2%) while 43% lived alone. Three members (13.6%) were bisexual and two (9%) identified themselves as homosexual. One member disclaimed any sexual orientation or interest. All the offenses occurred at home, except for one. Several members of the group mentioned that they visited pornographic Internet sites occasionally while at work.

Sexual Offense Histories. Three individuals (13.6%) had been charged with or admitted to sexual contact offenses. Five (22.7%) had been charged with, or admitted to, attempting a sexual contact with a minor. In only one of the cases was there evidence that the offender communicated on a regular basis with a group of child pornographers over the Internet.

It is interesting to note that over the past several years more than 100 evaluations of convicted incest and extrafamilial child molesters were conducted and child pornography was not mentioned in any of those cases. This finding seems to delineate these two groups, at least in this sample. It is likely that other groups of child pornographers do have substantial histories of child molestation, as is discussed later in this chapter.

Sexual Exploitation History of the Pornographer. Eleven of the twenty-two individuals (50%) reported that they had been sexually exploited or coerced as a young teenager or as a child. Only one of the offenders identified himself as a victim of sexual abuse. Most of the incidents occurred with older siblings or friends. The sexually coerced individuals often portrayed their early sexualization as an "honor" or without lasting identifiable impact. None of the individuals reported treatment for posttraumatic stress disorder symptoms either before or after their arrest.

Depending on the definition of what constitutes child sexual abuse, Hanson and Slater (1988) found from their review of the literature that anywhere from 0% to 67% of child molesters reported themselves to be childhood victims. Dhawan and Marshall (1996) attempted to correct for a potential self-report bias and found that 50% of incarcerated child molesters reported being sexually abused as children whereas only 20% of incarcerated non-sex offenders reported such abuse.

Psychological Testing

Psychological evaluations consisted of a number of tests which were not administered to all participants in all the evaluations. The referral question dictated the number, type, and extent of the psychological testing.

Rorschach Test (Comprehensive System). The Rorschach Test using Exner's Comprehensive System was administered to thirteen members of the sample. The test was scored by the author with assistance from the Rorschach Interpretive Assistance Program (RIAP). All the protocols were valid and interpretively useful. Number of responses ranged from fourteen to thirty ($X = 22.46$, $SD = 5.48$) and there were no card rejections. Fourteen responses is considered the minimum number for a valid profile (Exner, 1988) and nonpatient adults provide between seventeen and twenty-seven responses (Exner, 1986).

A number of variables mentioned in the Multitrait Forensic Assessment Approach

(MFRAA; Foley & Prentky, 1998) are discussed in this section. Briefly, traits that are commonly mentioned in the sex offender literature are noted. Many Rorschach variables are categorical rather than continuous, and the means of these variables may not have a particular significance.

Narcissism. A majority of the records (61.5%) contained a reflection response and the mean for the sample was 1.0 ($X = 1.0$, $SD = 1.08$). Typically, only 7% of nonpatient adults provide a reflection response (Weiner, 1998). Individuals who give a reflection response are typically self-centered individuals who have an inflated sense of their importance and an exalted estimate of their attributes. They tend to be selfish, arrogant persons who assign higher priority to their own needs and interests than to those of others and are rarely drawn to acts of helpfulness and generosity that entail self-sacrifice (Weiner, 1998). The number of reflection responses does not constitute the extent of narcissism. Rather, the existence of a reflection-coded response serves as evidence of the trait.

It is interesting to note the mean reflection response for non-sexually victimized individuals was .5 ($X = .5$, $SD = .54$) and the mean for sexually victimized individuals was 1.42 ($X = 1.42$, $SD = 1.27$). Thus, as would be expected, it appears that sexually victimized individuals may be more likely to experience narcissistic traits than non-sexually abused individuals.

Abuse of Fantasy. Abuse of fantasy entails a predilection to avoid responsibilities by excessively escaping via mental imagery. This Rorschach variable is indicated when coding for passive human movement is greater than the coding for active human movement (Ma < Mp). People who abuse fantasy attempt to deal with situations in their lives not by thinking through what they could or should do about them but instead by imagining how other people or fortuitous events will make their decisions and solve their problems for them (Weiner, 1998). The mean scores for passive human movement ($X = 2.84$, $SD = 1.95$) were greater than for active human movement ($X = 1.46$, $SD = 1.19$), which is indicative of the abuse of fantasy which might be expected in a group of individuals who have been apprehended for their use of pornography. Immoderate solo consumption of pornography entails avoidance of meaningful contact with others at the very least. It is also likely that a frustrated search for intimacy invites a sexualized investment in depictions of power and control involving children.

Perceiving Events Realistically. One of the goals of fantasy fortified by pornography is to distort reality in order that the person has more perceived control over real and imagined sexual restraints. The Distorted Form variable (X-%) is an indication of whether the individual is perceiving their experience realistically. This sample universally demonstrated this proclivity with a range of .18 to .43 ($X = .27$, $SD = .07$) The mean for X-% is .07 among adult nonpatients. When the Distorted Form variable exceeds .15 it is likely that the person perceives events incorrectly, forms mistaken impressions of themselves, misinterprets the actions and intentions of others, fails to anticipate the consequences of their own actions, and misconstrues what constitutes appropriate behavior (Weiner, 1998).

It is likely that misperceptions precede the onset of excessive exposure to child pornography. It may also be hypothesized that excessive pornographic exposure adds to the tendency for perceptual distortion (Malamuth, 1981; Zillman & Bryant, 1984). Many of this sample shared that they did not, over time, perceive the sexual depictions of vulnerable children as real children. Some offered that their fantasies involved imagining themselves as children, and as part of the pornographic scene. Anecdotally, these types of cognitive distortions are often found in child molesters as well. In other words, the offender rationalizes his or her behavior by believing, or attempting to get others to believe, that the child was not really a child.

Another dimension of perceptual distortion is captured by the Rorschach Lambda variable. Individuals with high scores (Lambda > 1.00) are hypothesized (Weiner, 1998) to have problems in the balance of their focus of attention. High Lambda individuals tend to lead their lives as if they have blinders on, looking straight ahead but rarely to the right or left. This deficit leads to a psychological tunnel vision and overooking nuances of social and interpersonal situations. The mean score for Lambda in this sample were slightly below the cutoff ($X = .93$, $SD = .67$) while 46.1% of the sample had scores above the cutoff. The range was from .21 to 2.83. These results indicate that the child pornographer is more likely than other adults to perceptually distort stimuli through a narrow lens that invites unconventional responding.

Anger. Unmanaged anger is often associated with sexually inappropriate behaviors. Manifest and latent anger interferes with the establishment of mature interpersonal relationships and inhibits meaningful affective exchanges. It may promote avoidance of others as well as others' avoidance of the individual. When the number of Space responses in a protocol exceeds two, there is likely a generalized oppositional tendency that goes beyond adaptive autonomy and is associated with pervasive feelings of anger or resentment. A findings of S > 2 is uncommon at all ages and usually identifies a personality liability that interferes with pleasurable affective experience (Weiner, 1998). Individuals with an S elevation typically harbor more than ordinary amounts of anger and resentment toward people and situations in their lives that they regard as unfairly failing to meet their needs or posing obstacles to their goals. Exner (1986) writes that as the S variable increases above 3 it is more than likely a stable personality characteristic exists. The mean for this sample exceeds Exner's limit ($X = 3.46$, $SD = 2.02$) with a range from 0 to 7. Because all the individuals had been arrested, and some of them had been incarcerated, some of this score may reflect aversive feelings related to those experiences.

Individuals with anger problems may be more likely to seek out sexual imagery that does not evoke oppositional reactions. In other words, depictions of children, particularly at a distance, may promote a sense of simple and uncomplicated interaction that is sexually reinforced in pornographic stimuli. Depictions of adults may be a cue for disappointment, unwanted relationship complexity, demands, and past failures. The individual may seek in pornographic fantasy what has not yet failed in reality.

Negative Affective Experiences. It has been hypothesized that individuals who invest in viewing child pornography are affectively isolated, depressed, and inadequate in terms of social skills. The mean scores for the Exner Isolation Index ($X = .15$, $SD = .15$) do not show evidence of this trait. This finding is contrary to the previously mentioned research concerning psychological indices of excessive Internet use. In general, individuals who score > .33 tend to avoid social interaction or have deficient opportunities for interpersonal contact. At the same time, the majority of the protocols (69.2%) had no Texture response. In contrast, only 11% of nonpatient protocols (Exner, 1986) were absent of this response coding. The absence of T indicates deficits in ability to form close attachments with others. It is also likely that when such individuals form attachments they are with like others. T-less protocols are typical among inpatient depressives (57%) and character disorders (72%). Gacono and Meloy (1994) report that it is quite characteristic among those with antisocial personality disorders.

This sample of individuals may have initiated relationships with others who had similarly low needs for depth of relationship. The relationship may be built on convenience, children, or finances. These individuals prefer to have others in their vicinity but not too closely or for too long. This profile was demonstrated in offenders who were married with children and, for all appearances, enjoyed good relationships. The search for child pornography may be explained as filling a void created by vacated adult entanglements. There may also be a sense that these individuals are damaged and have little to offer in a psychologically intimate adult relationship. Rorschach coding for MORBID is given when the perception is damaged, destroyed, or defective in some way. It is interpreted as related to a damaged sense of self with accompanying deficits in relating. The mean MOR for this sample ($X = 1.66$, SD) was greater than for nonpatient adults ($X = .70$, $SD = .94$). This hypothesis is strengthened by the finding of an affective ratio of less than .5 for this sample ($X = .46$, $SD = .17$). Scores below .5 reportedly (Weiner, 1998) only occur in 7% of adult samples and indicate an aversion to situations involving expressions of feelings and, consequently, maladaptive emotional withdrawal.

Minnesota Multiphasic Personality Inventory. The Minnesota Multiphasic Personality Inventory (MMPI) was administered in fifteen of the twenty-two cases included in this sample. Seven of the fifteen profiles (46.4%) had psychopathic deviate scores above T = 70 ($X = 63.1$, $SD = 10.08$) which is a strong indicator of a rebellious, antisocial approach to others and the environment. Only one of the clinically significant psychopathic deviate scores also was elevated for mania, which is an indication of acting-out potential. Seven of the profiles (46.4%) had depression scales above T = 70 (X = 62.0, $SD = 13.36$), but it is difficult to determine whether depression preceded the index offense or came as a result. None of the social introversion scales were clinically significant ($X = 53.4$, SD 10.7) which is counterintuitive but consistent with the previously mentioned Isolation Index scores from the Rorschach.

The MMPI results suggest that this sample is relatively free from thought disorders or severe Axis I diagnosis. This finding is supported by the generally high level of functioning found in this sample. It should be noted that the Rorschach is better suited to measuring aspects of psychological style and the MMPI is better suited to determining the presence of psychopathology.

Abel Screening

The Abel Screening is a computer-driven assessment of sexual interest. The individual previews and rates a series of 160 slides of clothed men, women, children, fetish items, and sadomasochistic scenes for sexual attractiveness. Outside the person's awareness, the length of time each slide is viewed is measured, grouped, and compared with overall mean responses times for the individual. Z-scores are provided for twenty-two categories by age, gender, race, and several experimental categories (i.e. voyeuristic scenes and fetish items). The results indicate deviant sexual interest and a ranking of the individual sexual interests. Individuals are hypothesized to look longest at images that most attractive to them (Abel, Huffman, Warberg, & Holland, 1998).

All the protocols were valid and interpretively useful. None of the individuals reported being aware of the covert measure of response latency used as an objective measure of sexual interest. Five of fifteen (33.3%) protocols were indicative of a sexual interest in children. None of the protocols were indicative of sadomasochistic interests involving adults. None of the slides depict a pairing of children and violent scenes.

It is likely that the five protocols showing sexual interest in children are related to amount of exposure to child pornography. The available data do not allow a test of this hypothesis at this time. All these individuals had been sexually victimized as children.

This finding supports the contention that the majority of the individuals were not primarily motivated by pedophilic interest. It should be recalled that few of the individuals were found guilty of child molestation and there were no indications of attempts to contact children or take on the persona of a child in sexually oriented chat rooms. Nonetheless, it is difficult to ascertain why so few of the individuals who were entertaining sexual depictions of children and ostensibly reinforcing with masturbation did not have more measured pedophilic interest. It could be that they did not experience the Abel slides as arousing because they are not particularly provocative or pornographically depicted. In other words, sexualized children may not be viewed as real children, as mentioned earlier. They may also have avoided looking at images of children given the nature of the examination, although this possibility seems remote given previous studies concerning pedophilic dissimulation on this test (Abel et al., 1998). Many of the offenders denied masturbating to the child pornographic depictions and maintained that they were primarily motivated by curiosity and taboo or that they collected the images because they were there, would be available for future trading, or some other reason. As previously mentioned, child pornography, compared to pornography at large, is rather rare and thus carries an intrinsic value. Many of the individuals may also be characterized as hoarders of images that had no value to them or interest to them.

A Taxonomic Attempt

The data collected in this study preclude strong conclusions concerning a taxonomy for individuals charged with possession of child pornography. Only one of the cases involved an individual who had been arrested on more than one occasion for possession of child pornography.

Mastery. As previously reported, 50% of the individuals report being sexually coerced by an older individual when they were children. Most of those reporting early sexualization were arrested for downloading child pornography that approximated their age at the time of sexualization. It is hypothesized that one motive for downloading child pornography, reminiscent of their own victimization, was to master associated ambivalent thoughts and feelings. Confused thoughts and feelings may ensue from an experience that may have been in part pleasurable but disconcerting at the same time. None of the examined individuals labeled themselves "sexual abuse victims," although those reporting sexualization had clear memories of the event.

In other words, the offenders were motivated to return to the scene of the crime and in doing so committed a crime themselves. Some of the offenders expressed a life-long "fascination with incest" which motivated their pursuit of child pornography. Others recalled their primary sexualization as quite pleasant and not matched in subsequent experiences. The child pornographic search may be for the perfect image that matches the template of the initial sexual experience. In these cases, a compulsive approach to the search may be employed. Still others relayed that they were more sexually active during childhood than as adolescents or adults.

The literature provides some support for this taxonomic hypothesis. McGuire, Carlisle, and Young (1965) found that stimuli that are initially associated with sexual arousal can acquire even greater arousal properties if they are later imagined during masturbation or during other sexually arousing activities leading to orgasm. The fantasy is then elaborated on and altered in various ways during repeated masturbatory episodes. The elements of the fantasy that are most arousing are retained, and the elements that are not arousing are discarded. New elements can be incorporated into the fantasy if they are found to be arousing, and new experiences can lead to new fantasies or can reinforce earlier ones. Eventually, particular fantasies can become entrenched as a result of being repeatedly reinforced by the pleasurable sensations of sexual arousal and orgasm during masturbation and sexual activity with a partner.

Rebellious/Angry. This category reflects those individuals who appear to have been attracted in part by the taboo associated with child pornography. In other words, they felt as if they were getting away with something and the illegality of the behavior contributed to the reinforcement value. This grouping may also tap those who became habituated to adult pornography and sought to defeat boredom with the novelty of child pornography.

Disorganized. This category reflects those who appear to have downloaded as much freely available pornography as possible. Some of the investigations showed that the child pornography was mixed with a variety of materials and that there was little or no attempt at organizing it. In these cases, there was no clear evidence that most of the materials were ever viewed, although the individual was certainly aware that child pornography existed on his computer. Two members of this taxonomy contended that they wished to infiltrate the computers of other child pornographers and were collecting depictions for that end.

Pedophilic/Child Molester/Traveler. Individuals who comprise this category are thought to entertain pedophilic or deviant sexual interests over a long period. They are more likely to have a history of paraphilic interests and behaviors. Evidence of an antisocial personality disorder and sexual preoccupation is often found during examination. These types of individuals are more likely than not to have formed few adult relationships over the course of their life.

Conclusion

This small sample of psychological evaluations of individuals charged with down-loading child pornography does not support the reported assumptions of the federal government that guide the pursuit of many offenders. It seems clear that a relatively small clique of individuals produce and view child pornography while exercising extreme caution in their activities. Individuals discussed in this chapter who freely download child sexual depictions from news groups and chat rooms likely differ at least in terms of child molestation histories.

The individuals in this sample primarily appear to be angry, rebellious, and given to abuse of fantasy. They are likely to distort perceptions of themselves and others which increases the likelihood of unconventional, asocial behaviors. Some appear to be narcissistic and have problems in forming deep, meaningful relationships with others. As a group they are less socially isolated than would be expected.

The MMPI, as a measure of gross psychopathology, was generally indicative of depression and antisocial attitudes. The Rorschach, which is attuned to determining personality style over pathology, was indicative of an anger, narcissism, and misperceptions of self and others.

There are indications that this group of offenders may differ in some respects from the universe of child pornography offenders. Those receiving longer sentences which reflect histories of child molestation may not have been referred for assessment. It is also likely that a proportion of this sample deny a history of child molestation or their offenses have not been discovered for a variety of reasons.

A fundamental question for future inquiry is, How do individuals come to enjoy and pursue depictions that involve the sexual victimization of children and minors, no matter how remote? Does anonymously viewing pornographic images lead to a shaping phenomenon which undermines empathic concerns which would make these sort of materials aversive? Do individuals who have a propensity for pedophilic interests gravitate to this sort of pornography and only later act out with contact offenses? These and other questions remain.

Reference

Abel, G. G., & Blanchard, E. B. (1974). The role of fantasy in the treatment of sexual deviations. *Archives of General Psychiatry, 30*, 467–475.

Abel, G. G., Huffman, J., Warberg, B. W., & Holland, C. L. (1998, Spring). Visual reaction time and plethysmography as measures of sexual interest in child molesters. *Sexual Abuse: A Journal of Research and Treatment, 10*(2), 81–85.

American Psychiatric Association. (1994). *Diagnostic and statistical manual of mental disorders* (4th ed.). Washington, DC: Author.

Arndt, W. B., Foehl, J. C., & Good, F. E. (1985). Specific fantasy themes: A multidimensional study. *Journal of Personality and Social Psychology, 48*, 472–480.

Barbaree, H. E., & Marshall, W. L. (1989). Erectile responses among heterosexual child molesters, father-daughter incest offenders, and matched nonoffenders: Five distinct age preference profiles. *Canadian Journal of Behavioral Sciences, 21*, 70–82.

Briere, J., & Runtz, M. (1989). University males' sexual interest in children: Predicting potential indices of "pedophilia" in a non-forensic sample. *Child Abuse and Neglect, 13*, 65–75.

Cado, S., & Leitenberg, H. (1990). Guild reactions to sexual fantasies during intercourse. *Archives of Sexual Behavior, 19*, 49–63.

Cooper, A. (1998). Sexuality and the internet: Surfing into the new millennium. *CyberPsychology and Behavior, 1*, 181–187.

Cooper, A., Scherer, C. R., Boies, S. C., & Gordon, B. L. (1999). Sexuality on the Internet: From sexual exploration to pathological expression. *Professional Pschology: Research and Practice, 30*(2).

Crepault, C., & Couture, M. (1980). Men's erotic fantasies. *Archives of Sexual Behavior, 9*, 565–581.

Dhawan, S., & Marshall, W. L. (1996). Sexual abuses offenders. *Sexual Abuse: A Journal of Research and Treatment, 8*, 7–15.

Exner, J. E. (1986). *The Rorschach: A comprehensive system* (Vol. 1, 2nd ed.). New York: Wiley.

Fedora, O., Reddon, J. R., Morrison, J. W., Fedora, S. K., Pascoe, H., & Yendall, L. T. (1992). Sadism and other paraphilias in normal controls and aggressive and nonaggressive sex offenders. *Archives of Sexual Behavior, 21*, 1–15.

Foley, T. P., & Prentky, R. A. (1998). *Multitrait multimethod forensic assessment approach.* Paper presented at the 17th annual Research and Treatment Conference of the Association for the Treatment of Sexual Abusers, Vancouver.

Freeman-Longo, R. E., & Blanchard, G. T. (1998). *Sexual abuse in America: Epidemic of the 21st century.* Brandon, VT: Safer Society Press.

Gacono, C. B., & Meloy, J. R. (1994). *Rorschach assessment of aggressive and psychopathic personalities.* Hillsdale, NJ: Erlbaum.

Gold, S. R., & Clegg, C. L. (1990). Sexual fantasies of college students with coercive experiences and coercive attitudes. *Journal of Interpersonal Violence, 5*, 464–473.

Gold, S. R., & Gold, R. G. (1991). Gender differences in first sexual fantasies. *Journal of Sex Education and Therapy, 17*, 207–216.

Grendlinger, V., & Byrne, D. (1987). Coercive sexual fantasies of college men as predictors of self-reported likelihood to rape and overt sexual aggression. *Journal of Sex Research, 23*, 1–11.

Hanson, R. K., & Slater, S. (1988). Sexual victimization in the history of sexual abusers: A review. *Annals of Sex Research, 1*, 485–499.

Hunt, L. (1996). *The invention of pornography: Obscenity and the origins of modernity, 1500–1800.* New York: Zone Books.

Hunt, M. (1974). *Sexual behavior in the 1970s.* New York: Dell Books.

Kanaley, R. (1999, July 25). How much bigger can AOL really get? *Philadelphia Inquirer.*

Lanning, K. V. (1998). Cyber pedophiles: Behavioral perspective. *The APSAC Advisor, 11*(4), 12–18.

Laws, D. R. (1988). *Use of pornography by pedophiles.* Unpublished raw data.

Leiblum, S. R. (1997). Sex and the Net: Clinical implications. *Journal of Sex Education and Therapy, 22*, 21–28.

Leitenberg, H., & Henning, K. (1995). Sexual fantasy. *Psychological Bulletin, 117*(3), 469–496.

Malamuth, N. M. (1981). Rape fantasies as a function of exposure to violent sexual stimuli. *Archives of Sexual Behavior, 10*, 33–47.

Marcus, S. (1974). *The other Victorians: A study of sexuality and poronography in mid-nineteenth century England.* New York: Basic Books.

Marshall, W. L. (1997) Pedophilia: Psychopathology and theory: In D. R. Laws & W. O'Donohue, (Eds.), *Sexual deviance: Theory, assessment, and treatment* (pp. 152–174). New York: Guilford Press.

McGuire, R. J., Carlisle, J. M., & Young, B. G. (1965). Sexual deviation as conditioned behavior. *Behavior Research and Therapy, 2*, 185–190.

Miller, P. Y., & Simon, W. (1980). The development of sexuality in adolescence. In J. Abelson (Ed.), *Adolescent psychology* (pp. 383–407). New York: Wiley.

Murrin, M. A., & Laws, D. R. (1990). The influence of pornography on sexual crimes. In W. L. Marshall, D. R. Laws, & H. E. Barbaree (Eds.), *Handbook of sexual assault: Issues, theories, and treatment of the offender* (pp. 73–89). New York: Guilford Press.

O'Toole, L. (1998). *Pornocopia: Porn, sex, technology, and desire.* London: Serpent's Tail.

Person, E., Terestman, N., Myers, W., Goldberg, E., & Salvadori, C. (1989). Gender differences in sexual behaviors and fantasies in a college population. *Journal of Sex and Marital Therapy, 15*, 187–198.

Shannon, E. (1998, September 14). Main Street monsters. *Time, 152*(11), 59.

Pithers, W. D., Beal, L. S., Armstrong, J., & Petty, J. (1989). Identification of risk factors through clinical interviews and analysis of records. In D. R. Laws (Ed.), *Relapse prevention with sex offenders* (pp. 77–87). New York: Guilford Press.

Sue, D. (1979). Erotic fantasies of college students during coitus. *Journal of Sex Research, 15*, 299–305.

Templeman, T. L., & Stinnett, R. D. (1991). Pattern of sexual arousal and history in a "normal" sample of young men. *Archives of Sexual Behavior, 20*, 137–150.

Weiner, I. B. (1998). *Principles of Rorschach interpretation.* Mahwah, NJ: Erlbaum.

Young, K. S. (1996, August). *Internet addiction: The emergence of a new clinical disorder.* Paper presented at the 104th annual convention of the American Psychological Association, Toronto.

Young, K. S., & Rogers, R. C. (1998). The relationship between depression and Internet addiction. *CyberPsychology and Behavior, 1*, 25–28.

Zillman, D., & Bryant, J. (1984). Effects of massive exposure to pornography. In N. M. Malamuth & E. Donnerstein (Eds.), *Pornography and sexual aggression* (pp. 115–141). Orlando, FL: Academic Press.

Zimmer, D., Borchardt, E., & Fischle, C. (1983). Sexual fantasies of sexually distressed and nondistressed men and women: An empirical comparison. *Journal of Sex and Marital Therapy, 9*, 38–50.

Chapter 27

Sexual Harassment as Sexual Abuse

by Erin M. Oksol, M.A., Kirk A. Brunswig, M.S. and William T. O'Donohue, Ph.D.

Overview

This chapter makes the case that sexual harassment is a form of sexual abuse. There is much we already know about a female's risk for sexual abuse outside the workplace. We know that females experience a high risk for sexual abuse as children (Salter, 1993) and for rape as adults (Russell, 1984). Unfortunately, within the workplace, a great number of women also are at high risk for another form of sexual abuse: sexual harassment. The authors of this chapter demonstrate that because sexual harassment hurts people and is sexual in nature, sexually harassing behaviors constitute another form of sexual abuse.

Introduction

In this chapter we provide a brief review of the published literature on sexual harassment. We also provide information concerning the definition and types of sexual harassment, sexual harassment law, epidemiological data, and treatment and prevention issues. We describe the effects and consequences of sexual harassment and discuss suggestions for future research in this area.

Sexual Harassment as Sexual Abuse

Though few agree on the definition of sexual harassment, most definitions agree that sexual harassment is unwelcome and inappropriate behavior of a sexual nature. Existing research indicates that sexual harassment is a frequent form of sexual victimization of women, even more common than rape. For example, Till (1980) has identified five types of sexual harassment, one of which is sexual assault—nonconsensual sexual conduct obtained by threat or use of force. Many researchers and clinicians have likened the psychological effects of being sexually harassed to those of someone who has been raped. Also, many similarities exist between the symptoms experienced by sexual harassment victims and those experienced by victims of other types of sexual assault.

The Beginnings of Sexual Harassment Law

Legal definitions of sexual harassment are typically narrow and evolve from a series of case rulings, appellate decisions, and definitions provided from regulatory agencies such as the Equal Employment Opportunity Commission (EEOC; O'Donohue, Downs, & Yeater, 1998). Interestingly, when the 1964 Civil Rights Act (i.e., Title VII) was passed, there was no explicit mention of sexual harassment in the statute. The first efforts to bring sexual harassment claims under Title VII failed because they were seen by the courts as maters of interpersonal conflict (Goodman-Delahunty, 1999). The first reported sexual harassment claim was *Williams v. Saxbe* (1976), a case in which the court ruled that Title VII had been violated when a supervisor retaliated against an employee who had refused his sexual advances.

Typologies of Sexual Harassment

Quid Pro Quo. In common language, quid pro quo sexual harassment means "this for that." Most commonly, employment benefits are exchanged for sexual favors. Quid pro quo harassment might include advancement, hiring, or compensatory gain contingent upon sexual interactions. It can also include demotion, firing, or financial loss contingent upon the withholding of sexual interactions. In sexual harassment court cases involving quid pro quo harassment, the plaintiff must demonstrate that (1) she is qualified to otherwise receive the job benefit(s), and (2) these job benefits were withheld or altered because she was sexually harassed.

Hostile Environment. The second and more common form of sexual harassment involves the creation of a hostile work environment. Conte (1997) provides these examples of hostile environment harassment: offensive or explicit signs, calendars, literature, photographs, graffiti, and verbal conduct. Thus, an offensive environment can be created by verbal or nonverbal behaviors.

The legal elements of hostile workplace sexual harassment differ from those of a quid pro quo claim in that employers, supervisors, and employees could create a hostile work environment without the threat of losing job benefits if the harassing behavior unreasonably altered the work conditions and created an abusive working environment. Claims of hostile environment sexual harassment challenge "workplace practices, rather than tangible job benefits, and consist of verbal or physical conduct of a sexual nature" (Conte, 1997, pp. 51–52). A work environment can be offensive when sexist signs, cartoons, pinups, calendars, literature, or photos are displayed. In *Danna v. New York Telephone Co.* (1990) the courts ruled that offensive graffiti may demean and intimidate an employee and affect her job performance.

A hostile work environment is typically experienced by many employees in addition to the complainant. It can take many forms and, interestingly, offensive conduct need not be sexual in nature to contribute to a hostile work environment. Other examples of how an employer could alter working conditions include denigrating or embarrassing the employee in front of other coworkers, monitoring her work more closely than others, picking on her, threatening her job security, or giving her different work assignments or less desirable physical facilities (Conte, 1997).

Although quid pro quo sexual harassment can only be committed by someone with authority (e.g., employer and supervisor), a hostile work environment can be created by employers, supervisors, coworkers, customers, or clients. Hostile work environments are also more ambiguous in terms of whether or not an employer or supervisor is acting within his or her job description. Justice Thurgood Marshall noted that a supervisor's responsibilities do not only include hiring, firing, and disciplining employees but extend to the supervision of the day-to-day work environment and ensuring that the workplace is a safe and productive environment for all employees. Justice Marshall concluded that "there was no reason why abuse of the latter authority should have different consequences than abuse of the former" (cited in Conte, 1997, p. 54).

Fitzgerald, Swan, and Magley (1997) further divided hostile environment harassment into two components: gender harassment and unwanted sexual attention. Gender harassment is not directed at sexual cooperation but, instead, is intended to demean, denigrate, or insult the victim, or a category of victims. For example, sexual epithets, gestures, slurs toward members of a gender, and pornographic material would fall under the heading of gender harassment.

Unwanted sexual attention can include verbal and nonverbal behaviors (Fitzgerald et al., 1997). Whereas quid pro quo harassment involves the offer of an exchange of gain for sexual acts, unwanted sexual attention is the introduction of unwanted sexual requests without promises of benefits or withholding of punishment. Fitzgerald et al. (1997) combine gender harassment and unwanted sexual attention for behaviors legally considered hostile environment harassment, while naming quid pro quo harassment as sexual coercion.

Legal Definitions. The courts and regulatory agencies such as the EEOC have attempted to provide a legal definition to help decrease the ambiguity regarding hostile environment sexual harassment claims. The most recent and legal standard and the one with the most impact was first set forth by the U.S. Supreme Court in *Meritor Savings Bank v. Vinson* (1986) where it was decided that to be actionable, sexual harassment must be "sufficiently severe or pervasive to alter the conditions of the plaintiff's employment and create an abusive working environment" (p. 67). Because of the definition's vagueness and need for subjective interpretation by either the officiating body or the victim, in several sexual harassment cases the courts have allowed expert testimony to establish what behaviors in the workplace meet the standard.

The legal definition of sexual harassment most commonly used in the courts was offered by the EEOC, the federal agency responsible for enforcing the antidiscrimination laws, in 1980. The EEOC's guidelines define sexual harassment as follows:

> Unwelcome sexual advances, requests for sexual favors, and other verbal or physical conduct of a sexual nature constitute sexual harassment when (1) submission to such conduct is made either explicitly or implicitly a term or condition of an individual's employment, (2) submission to or rejection of such conduct by an individual is used as the basis for employment decisions affecting such individual, or (3) such conduct has the purpose or effect or unreasonably interfering with an individual's work performance or creating an intimidating, hostile, or offensive working environment. (29 C.F.R. §1604.11(f) (2000))

Reasonable Person and Reasonable Woman Standards of Sexual Harassment. Many courts have simply relied on the "reasonable person" standard to help demarcate sexual harassment (*Rabidue v. Osceola Refining Co.*, 1986/1987; *Radtke v. Everett*, 1993). In *Harris v. Forklift Systems, Inc.* (1993), the Supreme Court said that the conduct (behaviors) under consideration must be sufficiently severe or pervasive to create an objectively hostile or abusive work environment—an environment that a reasonable person would find hostile or abusive. Since 1991, that reasonable person standard has been adopted to a "reasonable woman" standard. In the landmark case, *Ellison v. Brady* (1991), the Court of Appeals for the Ninth Circuit held that a female plaintiff states a prima facie case of hostile environment when she alleges conduct which a reasonable woman would consider sufficiently severe or pervasive to alter the conditions of employment and create an abusive working environment (cited in Gutek & O'Connor, 1995).

Defining Sexual Harassment: Problems With Perceptions. One of the greatest problems in dealing with sexual harassment allegations is that what one may consider a clear instance of sexual harassment, another may see as innocuous.

In contrast to legal definitions of sexual harassment, psychological definitions focus on the victim's experience or perception of the sexually harassing behavior. Fitzgerald et al. (1997) provide a definition of sexual harassment as "an unwanted sex-related behavior at work that is appraised by the recipient as offensive, exceeding her resources or threatening her well-being" (p. 20). They propose that the victim's perception of the potentially sexually harassing incident depends on stimulus factors (the behavior itself), contextual factors (the environment or organization in which the behavior takes place), and individual factors.

Factors That Influence Perceptions of Sexual Harassment

Pryor's "person X situation" model of sexual harassment (Pryor, LaVite, & Stoller, 1993) attempts to answer the question, "What characteristics of potential sexual harassment victims and sexually harassing incidents influence one's perception of sexual harassment and how?" As Pryor's model suggests that situational and individual factors both contribute to the incidence of sexual harassment, we suggest these factors also contribute to perceptions of sexually harassing behaviors. Based on what Pryor's model suggests, then, we would assert that the reasonable woman (and person) weighs multiple variables when determining whether that behavior meets her own personal criteria for sexual harassment. Judgments of sexually harassing behaviors are the result, then, of an interaction between characteristics of the individual making the appraisal and the environmental setting in which the behavior is appraised.

Age. Reilly, Carpenter, Dull, and Bartlett (1982, cited in Pryor, 1987) found that when social-sexual behaviors are performed by older married actors, they are viewed as more harassing than the same behaviors performed by younger single actors. Baker, Terpestra, and Cutler (1987) examined the sexual harassment perceptions of 409 state government employees in the western United States, and found that older workers perceived most incidents to be more harassing than did younger workers. One can imagine how age could influence one's perception of social-sexual behaviors. Due to cohort effects, maturation, and life-stage interests, a woman in her 20s may interpret sexual behaviors remarkably differently from her 60-year-old female coworker. Likewise, the age difference between the target and the instigator of sexual behavior may influence perceptions. For example, a 20-year-old women may view a sexual comment made by a 20-year-old attractive coworker of the opposite sex as flirtation and, hence, welcome the behavioral advance, whereas the same behavior made by a 55-year-old coworker may be interpreted as unwelcome, interfering, and inappropriate. Young individuals who are single and socially active may have codes of conduct that are more accepting of sexually oriented behaviors (e.g., requesting dates). Furthermore, younger persons have probably experienced sexual harassment less simply because of their relative youth and limited work experience. As they grow older and come into contact with harassing situations, they experience the negative outcomes of such behavior, and, thus, their perceptions may change to be less accepting of behaviors that were, at one time, acceptable

Gender. Gender is one of the most common variables examined in studies regarding perceptions of sexual harassment. Typically, the findings indicate that women perceive more types of behaviors to be sexual harassment than do men (Baker et al., 1987). Also, the sexual advances of a woman to a man are seen as less likely and also less harassing than the same advances of a man to a woman (Gutek, Morasch, & Cohen, 1983). No empirical studies have investigated the effects of same-sex sexual harassment. One can easily imagine a scenario in which a heterosexual male receives sexual comments from a female coworker and perceives it as a "come-on," whereas the same sexual comments coming from another male may be perceived as sexual harassment. A possible theoretical generalization is that the extent to which the person is seen as a sexually desirable partner contributes to the labeling of a behavior as sexual harassment.

History of Victimization. Generally speaking, persons with a past history of sexual harassment rate significantly more scenarios as sexual harassment than do those respondents with no history of sexual harassment (Terpestra & Baker, 1987). Participants who have life histories involving sexual harassment may have experienced some of the many negative consequences of being the victim of sexual harassment and, as a result, may have become less tolerant of such behavior and more likely to recognize potential sexually harassing behaviors as just that.

Repeated Pattern of Behavior. An interesting aspect of sexual harassment that has been studied is the repetitious quality of the sexual harassment. What has emerged from studies investigating this variable is the general notion that a pattern of behaviors is an important aspect of sexual harassment. Findings show that ratings of harassment are generally higher when the harasser behaved consistently toward the target over time (Pryor, 1987).

Status. The status (i.e., power) of the harasser has been shown to influence perceptions of sexual harassment (Gutek et al., 1983; Reilly et al., cited in Pryor, 1987). A survey by Gutek et al. (1983) examined power imbalance in incidents of harassment. They found that the more power an actor is perceived as having over a victim, the more likely that the behavior will be seen as sexually harassing. Interestingly, research indicates that perpetrators of sexual harassment in the workplace are much more likely to be peers or coworkers than persons with explicit power over the victim (Gutek et al., 1983).

Incidence and Prevalence. Determining the frequency at which sexual harassment occurs is difficult as it is based solely on self-report measures. The prevalence of sexual harassment, then, is at best the percentage of women who self-report being the victim of sexual harassment. Given this, many studies have been conducted which sample groups of women and ask them whether they have ever been sexually harassed. The research literature to date indicates that sexual harassment is a common form of sexual abuse, which may affect nearly 50% of all women who have at one time been employed and approximately 30% of women who have attended a four-year college (Adams, Kottke, & Padgitt, 1983; Gutek et al., 1980).

Gender-based discrimination complaints account for approximately 30% of the discrimination claims filed each year with the EEOC. Statistics on types of gender-based employment discrimination charges filed with the EEOC reflect a steady increase in the number and proportion of sexual harassment claims filed from 1991 through the present. In 1991, for example, 40% (6,883 sexual harassment charges out of a total of 17.672 gender claims) were filed, and by the end of the year 1999, sexual harassment claims accounted for 64% of the gender claims (15,222 out of a total of 23,907 gender-based claims) (Goodman-Delahunty, 1999).

The first large-scale study of sexual harassment was conducted by the United States Merit Systems Protection Board (USMSPB, 1981). This study included a sample of 23,964 federal workers. Results indicated that 42% of females reported being the victim of sexual harassment. Gutek (1985) reported a slightly higher rate (53%) of sexual harassment in a sample of employed women living in Los Angeles.

Many American women have experienced sexual harassment, with estimates ranging from one-third to three-fourths of employed women (Gruber, 1990, 1997). The topic of sexual harassment, although not new to the workplace, has been increasingly in the spotlight with such public cases as those involving Supreme Court nominee Clarence Thomas and Anita Hill as well the case of former President William Clinton and Paula Jones.

Research conducted in this domain to date has focused almost exclusively on normative and descriptive analyses. Among the areas adequately addressed are the types and definitions of sexual harassment, responses to sexual harassment, and the effects of sexual harassment on the victim. In Fitzgerald's (1993) review of the issues presented in research on sexual harassment, she reports that approximately one-third of women experienced unwanted verbal remarks, one-fourth of women experienced unwanted touching, and roughly one in ten women had been coerced for sexual contact. In the development of the Sexual Experiences Questionnaire, the most often used measure in sexual harassment research, Fitzgerald et al. (1988; Fitzgerald, Gelfand, & Drasgow, 1995) found that roughly one-third of women reported experiencing gender harassment (defined below) while approximately 16% had experienced "seductive sexual approaches" from supervisors.

The few experimental studies exploring sexual harassment have been limited to evaluations of the effectiveness of prevention programs (Grundman, O'Donohue, & Peterson, 1997).

Effects and Consequences of Sexual Harassment

Sexual harassment affects the victim, the harasser, and the organization. Whereas the direct costs of litigation and liability can be quantified quite easily, the effect on the organizational climate and workplace productivity as well as the psychological impact is not as easily assessed.

The research that has been conducted has focused primarily on the effects for the individual victim, although we have some information about the negative effects that an organization sustains. The majority of the sexual harassment outcomes research falls into one of four categories: work-related effects, legal effects, psychological effects, and health-related effects. Despite the fact that most of these studies have been descriptive in nature, rather than involving hypothesis testing based on some theory, knowing what these consequences are is of the utmost importance. First, understanding the effects of sexual harassment might better enable victims to receive the care or services they need after being sexually harassed. Second, understanding sexual harassment outcomes can affect the quality and accuracy of educational efforts directed toward preventing sexual harassment. Third, dispelling false assumptions surrounding the "typical" sexual harassment victim might be an important means to affect and increase the quality of coworker relationships. Fourth, an understanding of the effects of sexual harassment could greatly influence sexual harassment legislation, better serving the needs of victims (Dansky & Kilpatrick, 1997).

Work-Related Effects. Victims of sexual harassment may experience a number of negative job-related outcomes. Some of these include decreased job satisfaction, decreased motivation, interrupted careers, decreased morale, increased absenteeism, lower productivity, and impaired interpersonal relationships with coworkers and employers (Dansky & Kilpatrick, 1997). Some argue that there are more subtle effects of sexual harassment on job performance. For example, sexual harassment, as seen as a form of sexual discrimination, may interfere with a women's informal social interactions with coworkers. The negative effect, then, is that sometimes such interactions provide the "inside scoop" necessary for influencing promotions, raises, and other desirable outcomes.

Psychological Effects. In a study conducted by Loy and Stewart (1984), 75% of the women surveyed reported symptoms of emotional distress due to being sexually harassed. The symptoms most often mentioned included nervousness, irritability, uncontrolled anger, and uncontrolled crying. Another finding in this study was the more serious the harassment, the greater likelihood of personal distress.

In a study conducted by Salisbury, Ginorio, Remick, and Stringer (1986), investigating the effects of sexual harassment, the authors described a typical sequence of reactions that sexual harassment victims experience. First, victims often are confused and blame themselves, believing the harassment will stop. If and when the harassment worsens, they feel helpless and out of control. Next they feel anxious and fearful, feeling "paranoid" and fearing for their career and economic self-sufficiency. Their general work performance and self-esteem also typically are adversely affected. If the woman accepts her victim status, more often than not her anxiety turns to anger and depression. Last, they are faced with their disappointment as they deal with disloyalty from coworkers, their employer, the courts, and perhaps federal or state agencies.

Sexual Harassment as Related to Posttraumatic Stress Disorder. Research studies looking at the psychological effects of sexual harassment have shown that approximately 10% of sexual harassment victims meet criteria for posttraumatic stress disorder (PTSD). Glomb, Munson, Hulin, Bergman, and Drasgow (1999) found that sexual harassment victims endorsed more PTSD symptoms as measured by ten items on the Symptoms Checklist-1990-Revised (SCL-90-R) compared to persons who have not been sexually harassed (Derogatis, 1977). Some have advocated for the use of a PTSD model to help understand the psychological effects of sexual harassment. This suggestion is based on the reports by sexual harassment victims that they experience flashbacks, sleep disturbances, and emotional numbing as a consequence of being harassed (Gutek & Koss, 1993; Koss, 1990).

Avina and O'Donohue (in press) have argued that many forms of sexual harassment meet several of the diagnostic criteria for PTSD. In particular, they argue that sexual harassment meets PTSD Criterion A of DSM-IV (the person has been exposed to a traumatic event in which . . . the person experienced, witnessed, or was confronted with an event or events that involved actual or threatened death or serious injury, or a physical threat to the physical integrity of self or others) (American Psychiatric Association, 1994). They argue that sexual harassment meets this criterion for the following reasons: sexual harassment poses a financial threat to the individual's standard of living, it violates one's personal values regarding personal boundaries, and it can create a state of fear and learned helplessness concerning others' potential of sexually assaultive behavior at work.

Hamilton and colleagues have argued that some sexual harassment victims suffer from a "posttrauma syndrome," experiencing symptoms that include depression (Gutek, 1985; Paludi & Barickman, 1991), increased fear of crime (Junger, 1987), anxiety and fear about rape (Holgate, 1989; Murphy, 1986), decreased self-esteem and self-confidence (Benson & Thompson, 1982; Gruber & Bjorn, 1986), and difficulties with interpersonal relationships, anger, and increased irritability (Gutek, 1985; Loy & Stewart, 1984; Paludi & Barickman, 1991).

Dansky and Kilpatrick (1997) conducted a national study by the Crime Victims Research and Treatment Center at the Medical University of South Carolina. Their results suggest that the lifetime risk of PTSD or major depression is significantly higher among sexual harassment victims than among women who report never being sexually harassed. They found that one in ten sexual harassment victims had current PTSD and one in five had current depression. At the time of the study, then, 10% of the victims of sexual harassment were experiencing PTSD symptoms. This finding illustrates the long-term negative effects of sexual harassment, as the average amount of time that had elapsed since the actual sexual harassment incident was eleven years.

In summary, it is clear that sexual harassment is a form of sexual abuse. Sexually harassing behaviors are sexual in nature, many sexual harassment victims experience PTSD symptoms, sexual harassment hurts those who experience it, and as we describe later in this chapter, sexual harassers could conceivably be treated with the same treatment that other sexual offenders, such as rapists, receive.

Coping Strategies. Dansky and Kilpatrick (1997) describe those coping strategies that are most typically adopted by victims of sexual harassment. The most common victim response is to ignore, or attempt to ignore, the harassment. When ignoring does not work, Dansky and Kilpatrick report that the victims then tend to attempt to manage the harassment by redirecting conversations, avoiding the harasser, or even leaving the environment altogether (e.g., quitting the job, dropping the class, or transferring schools). Examples of the explanations victims offer for indirect responses are

self-blame for harasser's behavior, ignorance of remediatory options, severe consequences to harasser, and helplessness. These indirect attempts to address the harassment are often unsuccessful and sometimes result in an escalation of the harassment
(Rabinowitz, 1990).

Legal Effects. Conte (1997) and Burns (1995) provide thorough analyses of the legal
issues surrounding sexual harassment. Conte states that a company assumes liability
when it engages in the negligent hiring, retention, or supervision of someone known
to sexually harass. Thus, if one is fired from an executive job for sexual harassment,
future employers may be held liable for any future misconduct of this individual. This
legal finding results in a hidden cost of sexual harassment: the cost of training this
individual, plus the cost of finding a replacement, if that is possible. Burns (1995) provides an interesting analysis of employer liability. She states:

> [The] prevailing rule is that an employer is liable for the acts of its agents
> when they were acting within the scope of their authority; accordingly, where
> a supervisor uses his supervisory powers to make a sexual demand on some-
> one under his authority, the employer is liable (*Meritor*, 1986). Where the
> conduct did not directly involve the abuse of authority, the employer may be
> liable for the acts of its employees (supervisory and non supervisory), and
> perhaps others as well, where the employer knew or should have known of the
> conduct and failed to take prompt and effective remedial action (*Henson*,
> 1985; *Meritor*, 1986). In many potential instances of alleged sexual harass-
> ment, the employer might avoid liability by developing strategies to prevent
> sexual harassment and to remedy it when it occurs. (pp. 204–205)

Thus, prevention and remediation are two areas in which employers can reduce
their liability and expenses.

Health-Related Effects. Several researchers have documented a variety of somatic
complaints experienced by sexual harassment victims. Some of these negative health
consequences include gastrointestinal disturbance, dental-related problems,
headaches, sleep disturbances, fatigue, nausea, weight loss, and loss of appetite (as
cited in Dansky & Kilpatrick, 1997). In an archival study conducted by Crull (1982),
case materials from 262 women who claimed to have been sexually harassed were
gathered. Crull's group of subjects reported harmful stress reactions that were categorized as affecting physical health, among others. Some 63% of the women who
answered the questionnaires identified physical symptoms that were a consequence of
being harassed, most commonly tiredness, headaches, and nausea.

Organizational Costs. The economic costs of sexual harassment have been quantified in several reports. Excluding the cost of litigation, Wagner (1992) estimates that
for Fortune 500 companies, the annual per-company cost of sexual harassment was
$6.7 million. Increases in sick days, medical claims, job turnover, and retraining
inflate the cost of sexual harassment. The USMSPB (1981) reported a job turnover
rate of 10%. This turnover results in the need for recruiting, hiring, and training new
personnel, which adds to the cost (Gosselin, 1986). In the follow-up to the USMSPB's
first report, it was estimated that sexual harassment costs the federal government more
than a $250 million over a two-year period (USMSPB, 1987).

Effects on the Harasser. Although not discussed in the empirical literature, there are a few reports of the effects of sexual harassment on those found to have harassed. Most of these documented effects are the loss of financial resources as a result of the harassment. The loss of income, familial difficulties including separation or divorce, and a difficulty in procuring employment commensurate with experience and education are all additional effects of harassment experienced by the harasser.

Successful Interventions for Sexual Harassers: Do They Exist?

The Sexual Harasser: What We Know. The legal definition of sexual harassment is not, by nature, gender specific, but in practice, sexual harassment is most often perpetrated by men and experienced by women, Almost every survey constructed to date has found that the most common perpetrator of sexual harassment is male and the most common victim female (Culbertson, Rosenfeld, Booth-Kewley, & Magnusson, 1992; Culbertson, Rosenfeld, & Newel, 1993; Fitzgerald et al., 1988; Martindale, 1992).

There is minimal data on those who sexually harass. However, recent steps have been taken to develop a self-report instrument for the assessment of incidence and prevalence of sexual harassment behaviors, from the harasser's self-report (O'Donohue, Fitzgerald, & Brunswig, 1999). What data exist in this area relate to analog studies of constructs such as sexual harassment proclivity and the likelihood to sexually harass (Bartling & Eisenman, 1993; Bingham & Burleson, 1996; Pryor, 1987).

Although treatments have been developed for victims and offenders of other sexual offenses (Laws & O'Donohue, 1997), to date, no studies have described the development and validation of a treatment for sexual harassers. With a lack of treatments for harassers, employers are often left with a single remediatory option: disciplining the harasser (unpaid leave of absence, terminating the harasser, etc.). This proves problematic for two reasons. First, it cannot be realistically expected that the harasser will forever remain in isolation from society. Second, the general problem of relapse with sexual offenders suggests that just disciplining those who sexually misbehave is not effective. The view of relying solely on discipline as a relapse prevention approach is not based on a psychologically sophisticated model of this kind of offending. Finally, some employers mandate that sexual harassers receive therapy. However, currently there is no evidence that any therapies are effective for this population. A review of the literature indicates a need for a treatment for sexual harassers (O'Donohue, 1997).

What Can Be Done With Sexual Harassers? Conte (1995) presents several of the effects of sexual harassment and hints at the outcome for the harasser. Typically, the harasser is provided the option of therapy, termination of the employment contract, or some other disciplinary measure. Although no treatment has been validated for the treatment of sexual harassers (O'Donohue, 1997) it can be a better option than firing the employee, leaving the maladaptive behavior in the harasser's repertoire, ready for the next victim, albeit in another setting. Moreover, there is no evidence that other disciplinary measures, such as leave without pay, are effective "treatments." Furthermore, there are some instances in which firing the employee would not be an appropriate solution (e.g., in a family-owned small business). Were the owner of a mom-and-pop shoestore found liable for sexual harassment, the owner would most likely not choose to fire himself. Another example would be that of a uniquely qualified individual who is an irreplaceable asset to a corporation. If this person were found liable of sexual harassment, it is unlikely he or she would be fired. On the other hand, companies can be left with the options of firing the harasser, in a sense, passing the buck to the next unfortunate company and its staff; retaining the harasser and not providing any treatment; or providing the harasser with the option of a treatment which has not been shown to be efficacious for the reduction and/or hopeful elimination of the sexually harassing behaviors.

Laws and O'Donohue (1997) recently edited a book that presented successful treatments for a variety of sexual misbehaviors (e.g., sexual assault, fetishism, exhibitionism, and voyeurism). The common theme throughout their book is that relapse prevention (RP) has been shown to be an efficacious approach to the treatment of a variety of sexual misbehaviors. The similarities between sexual abuse and sexual harassment are discussed in the next section.

Working from the premise that sexual harassment is a form of sexual misbehavior, it follows that treatments shown efficacious for other forms sexual misbehaviors are adaptable to sexual harassment. The RP model originally developed by Marlatt and Gordon (1980) was used as a maintenance program for such behaviors as alcohol and drug abuse, overeating, and cigarette smoking. The RP model was modified for work with sexual offenders. RP and harm reduction (HR) have been consistently demonstrated as efficacious treatments for sexual abusers (cf. Laws, 1989; Laws & O'Donohue, 1997). For his work with sexual offenders, Laws (1989) defines RP as follows:

> . . . a self-control program designed to teach individuals who are trying to change their behavior how to anticipate and cope with the problems of relapse. In very general terms, relapse refers to a breakdown or failure in a person's attempt to change or modify any target behavior. The RP program focuses on enabling the person to prevent relapse and thereby maintain the newly adopted behavior pattern. Based on social cognitive principles RP has a psychoeducational thrust that combines behavioral skill-training procedures with cognitive intervention techniques. (p. 2)

Sexual Offending and Sexual Harassment. There are several important similarities between sexual harassment and sexual offending which support the adaptation of the RP model to sexual harassers. First and foremost, they both are essentially problems of self-control. Second, sexual harassers may be more likely to sexually harass certain people in certain situations; thus an analysis of high-risk situations is appropriate. Third, cognitive distortions are important to both as is the problem of immediate gratification (PIG). Fourth, both sexual harassment and sexual offending result in significant victimization of another individual and thus are priorities to control appropriately. Furthermore, there is an element of fantasy to sexual harassment (Sandberg & Marlatt, 1989). Finally, another similarity between sexual harassment and sexual abuse is seen in the definitions of lapses and relapses. In both sexual harassment and sexual abuse, a lapse can be defined as engaging in behavior-related fantasy, willful elaboration, a formulation of a plan of action, or the undesired behavior. A relapse would be the overt undesired behavior.

There are differences between sexual harassers and sexual abusers that dictate the need for some modifications of the RP model for work with sexual harassers. First, whereas the majority of sexual harassment cases adjudicated are done so in civil actions, the majority of sexual abuse cases are adjudicated in criminal courts (Conte, 1997). Thus, some of the contingencies in place in correctional settings do not exist in the treatment of sexual harassers. For example, there is a reduced likelihood of court-ordered treatment, sentence reduction for completion of treatment, probation and parole supervision, and inpatient control in an outpatient treatment program for sexual harassers. For sexual harassers, treatment is outpatient, whereas for sexual offenders, treatment often takes place in prisons.

Thus, it appears that treatments shown to be efficacious for sexual-offending populations are promising foundations from which to build a treatment for sexual harassers. Given the concerns expressed by Laws (1995) and the aforementioned differences between sexual offenders and sexual harassers, a modified adaptation of the RP model is appropriate for the treatment of sexual harassment.

The literature on the treatment of sexual offenders indicates several areas of concern when working with sexually offending populations. First among these is the offender's motivation (Laws, 1989). An unmotivated client is unlikely to participate or succeed in this program. In addition, a client denying his offense is also unlikely to participate successfully (Maletzky, 1997). O'Donohue and Letourneau (1993) describe a group treatment plan design to shift clients from denial to admittance.

The Research Agenda

Sexual harassment in organizations is a real and important problem that must be addressed. Behavioral scientists can play a role in developing research that helps establish the prevalence of the phenomenon, helps determine important relationships between sexual harassment and other variables, and helps determine the most effective treatment for sexual harassers.

Using Surveys to Assess Sexual Harassment: Problems and Solutions. As a means to establish the extent of sexual harassment, organizations and researchers have used surveys to estimate the number and percentages of women who perceive sexual harassment as well as to determine the effects of harassment. The effects of these surveys have been revealing and results have been presented throughout this chapter. However, there are problems and issues associated with using survey methodologies that can affect the estimates of prevalence they provide. It is not the purpose of this chapter to explain these problems in depth, but interested readers are directed to read more about these issues in Arvey and Cavanaugh's (1995) article in the *Journal of Social Issues*. In summary, the authors suggest that survey research includes problems with respect to the definition of sexual harassment, response sets, the use of retrospective self-report measures, sample selection bias, validity and reliability, and generalizability.

Arvey and Cavanaugh (1995) make six recommendations in terms of conducting survey research to assess sexual harassment: (1) develop precise definitions of sexual harassment, using actual behaviors as examples, (2) limit time periods of interest to twelve months or less, (3) pay attention to the psychometric properties of the surveys, (4) refrain from labeling particular kinds of behaviors as sexual harassment and, instead, seek information concerning what behaviors have actually occurred, (5) review databases for potential sample biases, and (6) acknowledge biases when they exist.

Most survey research studies of sexual harassment have ignored the issue of how individuals themselves define sexual harassment, asking subjects instead to respond to a definition provided to them or simply responding "yes" or "no" regarding whether they see a certain behavior or vignette as constituting "sexual harassment" (Arvey & Cavanaugh, 1995; Frazier, Cochran, & Olson, 1995l; Powell, 1986). To prevent possible contamination of research results, future research could provide the respondent with the opportunity to judge various behaviors on the three definitional criteria set forth by the EEOC. Specifically, after each scenario or behavior described, the respondent could answer "yes" or "no" to the following questions:

1. Would you find the above behavior unwanted or unwelcome?

2. Would you feel that the above behavior has the purpose or effect of unreasonably interfering with your work performance?

3. Would you feel that the above behavior creates a hostile, offensive, intimidating work environment?

A third response choice of "Pattern" could also be included. Endorsing "pattern" would indicate that the scenario would deserve a "yes" response if the behavior occurred more than one time. The response choice of "pattern" could theoretically both increase the reality of the scenarios and decrease the ambiguity often inherent in single incident scenarios. The concern here is to make research studies of perceptual differences in sexual harassment as relevant to actual court cases as possible. Most sexual harassment cases that find their way to the courts are based on recurring harassing behavior (Gutek & O'Connor, 1995). Many studies have unknowingly distorted the impact of judgments of harassment in actual cases because they often use single incidents of ambiguous behavior rather than patterns of behavior that are on the whole, more objectionable.

Attractiveness of the Sexual Harasser. Attractiveness of the potential harasser is a contextual variable that has yet to be studied as an important aspect influencing perceptions of sexual harassment. One could compare responses to potentially sexually harassing scenarios involving an attractive coworker to those involving an unattractive coworker. Interestingly, a person's attractiveness has been studied extensively by social psychologists in other content areas. A plethora of desirable qualities and consequences such as intelligence (Landy & Sigall, cited in Hatfield & Sprecher, 1986), popularity in schoolchildren (Adams and Adams & Cohen, cited in Hatfield & Sprecher, 1986), obtaining more positive social attention from others (Baracos & Black, cited in Hatfield & Sprecher, 1986), likelihood to be hired by an employer (Dipboye, Fromkin, & Wiback, cited in Hatfield & Sprecher, 1986), and so on are more likely to be attributed to attractive individuals than to unattractive individuals. In general, exposure to physically attractive others has been found to lead to a state of positive affect in the observer (Byrne & Clore, 1970; Byrne, London, & Reeves, 1968). It is conceivable that attractiveness of the harasser might influence perceptions of sexual harassment, with attractive coworkers being perceived as generally less harassing than unattractive coworkers.

Psychometry and Methodology. Welsh (1999) and Brunswig, Oksol, and Bowers (2000) have outlined the problematic state of affairs in the psychometry of sexual harassment. These authors point to the need for clear demonstrations of the validity and reliability of the measures used in sexual harassment research across broad populations. In addition, Welsh (1999) directs research toward longitudinal data, while Brunswig et al. (2000) review the need for measures with predictive validity in sexual harassment research.

Other Types of Sexual Harassment. Others areas needing research are the behaviors of sexual harassers (Brunswig et al., 2000), the sexual harassment of men, and same-sex harassment (Berdahl, Magley, & Waldo, 1996; Stockdale, Visio, & Batra, 1999; cf. Welsh, 1999). We also know very little concerning the usual outcomes for those found responsible for sexual harassment at their workplace. What are the most effective therapeutic approaches for remediating these problematic behaviors? Several of these needs can be met when we move away from theories evaluated with structural equations modeling and factor analysis and move toward principle-based theories that inform theory-based intervention and prevention programs.

Conclusion

In 1976, the first sexual harassment case was heard. Since that time, sexual harassment has become an issue about which every employee and employer should be aware. Women and men who experience this type of discrimination suffer symptoms not unlike those of rape victims. Their offenders share many of the dynamics of other types of individuals who sexually abuse others. Emerging treatments may be able to intervene in what would otherwise be a continuing cycle of abuse.

References

Adams, J. W., Kottke, J. L., & Padgitt, J. S. (1983). Sexual harassment of university students. *Journal of College Student Personnel, 24*, 484–490.

American Psychiatric Association. (1994). *Diagnostic and statistical manual of mental disorders* (4th ed.). Washington, DC: Author.

Arvey, R. D., & Cavanaugh, M. A. (1995). Using surveys to assess the prevalence of sexual harassment: Some methodological problems. *Journal of Social Issues, 51*(1), 39–52.

Avina, C., & O'Donohue, W. T. (in press). Sexual harassment and PTSD: Is sexual harassment a diagnosable trauma? *Journal of Traumatic Stress.*

Baker, D. D., Terpestra, D. E., & Cutler, B. D. (1987). Perceptions of sexual harassment: A re-examination of gender differences. *The Journal of Psychology, 124*(4), 409–416.

Bartling, C. A., & Eisenman, R. (1993). Sexual harassment proclivities in men and women. *Bulletin of the Psychonomic Society, 31*, 189–192.

Benson, D. J., & Thompson, G. E. (1982). Sexual harassment on a university campus: The confluence of authority relations, sexual interest, and gender stratification. *Social Problems, 29*, 236–251.

Berdahl, J. L., Magley, V. J., & Waldo, C. R. (1996). The sexual harassment of men? Exploring the concept with theory and data. *Psychology of Women Quarterly, 20*, 527–547.

Bingham, S. G., & Burleson, B. R. (1996). The development of a sexual harassment proclivity scale: Construct validation and relationship to communication competence. *Communication Quarterly, 44*(3), 308– 325.

Brunswig, K. A., Oksol, E. M., & Bowers, A. H. (2000). *A review of the measurement and assessment of sexual harassment and sexual harassment-related phenomena.* Poster presented at the 19th annual meeting of the Association for the Treatment of Sexual Abusers, San Diego.

Burns, S. E. (1995). Issues in workplace sexual harassment law and related social science research. *Journal of Social Issues, 51*, 193–207.

Byrne, D., & Clore, G. L. (1970). A reinforcement-affect model of evaluative responses. *Personality: An International Journal, 1*, 103–128.

Byrne, D., London, O., & Reeves, K. (1968). The effects of physical attractiveness, sex, and attitude on interpersonal attraction. *Journal of Personality, 36*, 259–271.

Conte, A. (1997). Legal theories of sexual harassment. In W. T. O'Donohue (Ed.), *Sexual harassment: Theory, research, and treatment* (pp. 50–83). Needham Heights, MA: Allyn & Bacon.

Crull, P. (1982). Stress effects of sexual harassment on the job: Implications for counseling. *American Journal of Orthopsychiatry, 52*, 539–544.

Culbertson, A. L., Rosenfeld, P., Booth-Kewley, S., & Magnusson, P. (1992). *Assessment of sexual harassment in the Navy: Results of the 1989 Navy-wide survey.* San Diego, CA: Navy Personnel Research and Development Center.

Culbertson, A. L., Rosenfeld, P., & Newel, C. E. (1993). *Sexual harassment in the active duty Navy. Assessment of sexual harassment in the Navy: Results of the 1989 Navy-wide survey.* San Diego, CA: Navy Personnel Research and Development Center.

Danna v. New York Telephone Co., 752 F. Supp. 594 (S.D.N.Y. 1990).

Dansky, B. S., & Kilpatrick, D. G. (1997). Effects of sexual harassment. In W. T. O'Donohue (Ed.), *Sexual harassment: Theory, research, and treatment* (pp. 152–174). Needham Heights, MA: Allyn & Bacon.

Derogatis, L. R. (1977). *The SCL-90-R manual I: Scoring administration and procedures for the SCL-90-R.* Baltimore: Clinical Psychometrics.

Ellison v. Brady, 924 F.2d 872 (9th Cir. 1991).

Equal Employment Opportunity Commission. (1980). *Discriminations because of sex under Title VII of the Civil Rights Act of 1964, as amended, adoption of interim interpretive guidelines.* 45 Fed. Reg. 25024–23025.

Fitzgerald, L. F. (1993). Sexual harassment: Violence against women in the workplace. *American Psychologist, 48*(10), 1070–1076.

Fitzgerald, L. F., Gelfand, M. J., & Drasgow, M. J., (1995). Measuring sexual harassment: Theoretical and psychometric advances. *Basic and Applied Social Psychology, 17*(4), 425–445.

Fitzgerald, L. F., Shullman, S. L., Bailey, N., Richards, M., Swecker, J., Gold, Y., Ormerod, M., & Weiztmand, L. (1988). The incidence and dimensions of sexual harassment in the academia and the workplace. *Journal of Vocational Behavior, 32*, 152–175.

Fitzgerald, L. F., Swan, S., & Magley, V. J. (1997). But was it really sexual harassment? Legal, behavioral, and psychological definitions of the workplace victimization of women. In W. T. O'Donohue (Ed.), *Sexual harassment: Theory, research, and treatment* (pp. 5–28). Needham Heights, MA: Allyn & Bacon.

Frazier, P. A., Cochran, C. C., & Olson, A. M. (1995). Social science research on lay definitions of sex harassment. *Journal of Social Issues, 51*(1), 21–37.

Glomb, T. M., Munson, L. J., Hulin, C. L., Bergman, M. E., & Drasgow, F. (1999). Structural equation models of sexual harassment: Longitudinal explorations and cross-sectional generalizations. *Journal of Applied Psychology, 84*(1), 14–28.

Goodman-Delahunty, J. (1999). Pragmatic support for the reasonable victim standard in hostile workplace sexual harassment cases. *Psychology, Public Policy, and Law, 5*(3), 519–555.

Gosselin, H. L. (1986). Sexual harassment on the job: Psychological, social and economic repercussions. *Canadian Mental Health, 32*, 21–24.

Gruber, J. E. (1990). Methodological problems and policy implications in sexual harassment research. *Population Research and Policy Review, 9*, 235–254.

Gruber, J. E. (1997). An epidemiology of sexual harassment: Evidence from North America and Europe. In W. T. O'Donohue (Ed.), *Sexual harassment: Theory, research, and treatment* (pp. 84–98). Needham Heights, MA: Allyn & Bacon.

Gruber, J. E., & Bjorn, L. (1986). Women's responses to sexual harassment: An analysis of sociocultural, organization, and personal resource models. *Social Science Quarterly, 67*, 815–826.

Grundman, E. O., O'Donohue, W. T., & Peterson, S. H. (1997). The prevention of sexual harassment. In W. T. O'Donohue (Ed.), *Sexual harassment. Theory, research, and treatment* (pp. 175–184). Needham Heights, MA: Allyn & Bacon.

Gutek, B. A. (1985). Sex and the workplace: *The impact of sexual behavior and harassment on women, men, and organizations.* San Francisco: Jossey-Bass.

Gutek, B. A., & Koss, M. P. (1993). Changed women and changed organizations: Consequences of and coping with sexual harassment. *Journal of Vocational Behavior, 42*, 28–48.

Gutek, B. A., Morasch, B., & Cohen, A. G. (1983). Interpreting social-sexual behavior in a work setting. *Journal of Vocational Behavior, 22*, 30–48.

Gutek, B. A., Nakamura, C. Y., Gahart, M., Handschumacher, I., & Russell, D. (1980). Sexuality and the workplace. *Basic and Applied Social Psychology, 1*, 255–265.

Gutek, B. A., & O'Connor, M. (1995). The empirical basis for the reasonable woman standard. *Journal of Social Issues, 51*(1), 151–166.

Hamilton, J. A., Alagna, S. W., King, L. S., & Lloyd, C. (1987). The emotional consequences of gender-based abuse in the workplace: New counseling programs for sex discrimination. *Women and Therapy, 6*, 155–182.c

Harris v. Forklift Systems, Inc., 126 L. Ed. 2d 295 (1993).

Hatfield, E., & Sprecher, S. (1986). Measuring passionate love in intimate relationships. *Journal of Adolescence, 9* (4), 383–410.

Holgate, A. (1989). Sexual harassment as a determinant of women's fear of rape. *Australian Journal of Sex, Marriage, and the Family, 10*, 21–28.

Junger, M. (1987). Women's experiences of sexual harassment. *British Journal of Criminology, 27*, 358–383.

Koss, M. P. (1990). Changed lives: The psychological impact of sexual harassment. In M. Paludi (Ed.), *Ivory power: Sex and gender harassment in academia* (pp. 73-92). Albany: State University of New York Press.

Laws, D. R. (Ed.). (1989). *Relapse prevention with sex offenders.* New York: Guilford Press.

Laws, D. R. (1995). A theory of relapse prevention. In W. O'Donohue & L. Krasner (Eds.), *Theories of behavior therapy: Exploring behavior change* (pp. 445–476). Washington DC: American Psychological Association.

Laws, D. R., & O'Donohue, W. (1997). Introduction. In D. R. Laws & W. O'Donohue (Eds.), *Sexual deviance* (pp. 1–21). New York: Guilford Press.

Loy, P. H., & Stewart, L. P. (1984). The extent and effects of the sexual harassment of working women. *Sociological Focus, 17*, 31–43.

Maletzky, B. M. (1997). Exhibitionism: Assessment and treatment. In D. R. Laws & W. O'Donohue (Eds.), *Sexual deviance* (pp. 40–74). New York: Guilford Press.

Marlatt, G. A., & Gordon, J. R. (1980). Determinants of relapse: Implications for the maintenance of behavior change. *British Journal of Addiction, 79*, 261–273.

Martindale, M. (1992). Sexual harassment in the military: 1988. *Sociological Practice Review, 2*, 200–216.

McMullin, R. E. (1986). *Handbook of cognitive therapy techniques.* New York: Norton.

Meritor Savings Bank v. Vinson, 106 S. Ct. 2399 (1986).

O'Donohue, W. T. (1997). Introduction. In W. O'Donohue (Ed.), *Sexual harassment: Theory, research and practice* (pp. 1–4). Boston: Allyn & Bacon.

O'Donohue, W., Fitzgerald, L., & Brunswig, K. A. (1999). *A Self-Report Sexual Harassment Inventory.* Paper presented at the 18th annual meeting of the Association for the Treatment of Sexual Abusers, Orlando, FL.

O'Donohue, W. T., & Letourneau, E. (1993). A brief group treatment for the modification of denial in child sexual abusers: Outcome and follow-up. *Child Abuse and Neglect, 17*, 299–304.

Paludi, M. A., & Barickman, R. B. (1991). *Academic and workplace sexual harassment: A manual of resources.* Albany: State University of New York Press.

Pithers, W. D., Beal, L. S., Armstrong, J., & Petty, J. (1989). Identification of risk factors through clinical interviews and analysis of risk factors. In D. R. Laws (Ed.), *Relapse prevention with sex offenders* (pp. 77–87). New York: Guilford Press.

Powell, G. N. (1986). Effects of sex role identity and sex on definitions of sexual harassment. *Sex Roles, 14*(1–2), 9–19.

Pryor, J. B. (1987). Sexual harassment proclivities in men. *Sex Roles, 17*(5–6), 269–290.

Rabinowitz, V. C. (1990). Coping with sexual harassment. In M. Paludi (Ed.), *Ivory power: Sexual harassment on campus* (pp. 199–213). Albany: State University of New York Press.

Salisbury, J., Ginorio, A. B., Remick, H., & Stringer, D. M. (1986). Counseling victims of sexual harassment. *Psychotherapy, 23*, 316–324.

Sandberg, G. G., & Marlatt, G. A. (1989). Relapse fantasies. In D. R. Laws (Ed.), *Relapse prevention with sex offenders* (pp. 147–152). New York: Guilford Press.

Stockdale, M. S., Visio, M., & Batra, L. (1999). The sexual harassment of men: Evidence for a broader theory of sexual harassment and sex discrimination. *Psychology, Public Policy, and Law, 5*(3), 630–644.

Till, F. J. (1980). *Sexual harassment: A report on the sexual harassment of students.* Washington, D.C. National Advisory Council on Women's Educational Programs.

United States Merit Systems Protection Board. (1981). *Sexual harassment of federal workers: Is it a problem?* Washington, DC: U.S. Government Printing Office.

United States Merit Systems Protection Board. (1987). *Sexual harassment of federal workers: An update.* Washington, DC: U.S. Government Printing Office.

Wagner, E. J. (1992). *Sexual harassment in the workplace: How to prevent, investigate and resolve problems in your organization.* New York: AMACOM.

Welsh, S. (1999). Gender and sexual harassment. *Annual Review of Sociology, 25*, 169–190.

Williams v. Saxbe, 413 F. Supp. 654, 657 (D.D.C. 1976).

Appendix A

Bibliography

Abel, G. (1989). Paraphilias. In H. Kaplan & B. Sadock (Eds.), *Comprehensive textbook of psychiatry* (5th ed., pp. 1069–1085). Philadelphia: Williams & Wilkins.

Abel, G. G., & Becker, J. V. (1984). *Treatment manual: The treatment of child molesters.* New York: Columbia University Press.

Abel, G. G., Becker, J. V., Cunninham-Rathner, J., Rouleau, J. L., Kaplan, M., & Reich, J. (1984). *Treatment manual: The treatment of child molesters.* Atlanta: Emory University School of Medicine, Department of Psychiatry.

Abel, G. G., & Blanchard, E. B. (1974). The role of fantasy in the treatment of sexual deviations. *Archives of General Psychiatry, 30,* 467–475.

Abel, G. G., Huffman, J., Warberg, B. W., & Holland, C. L. (1998, Spring). Visual reaction time and plethysmography as measures of sexual interest in child molesters. *Sexual Abuse: A Journal of Research and Treatment, 10*(2), 81–85.

Abel, G. G., Mittelman, M., & Becker, J. V. (1985). Sexual offenders: Results of assessment and recommendation for treatment. In H. H. Ben-Aron, S. I. Huckers, & C. D. Webster (Eds.), *Clinical criminology: Current concepts* (pp. 191–205). Toronto: M. M. Graphics.

Abel, G., & Osborn, C. (1992). The paraphilias: The extent and nature of sexually deviant and criminal behavior. *Psychiatric Clinics of North America, 15,* 675–687.

Abel, G., Osborn, C., Anthony, D., & Gardos, P. (1992). Current treatments of paraphiliacs. *Annual Review of Sex Research, 3,* 255–290.

Adams, J. W., Kottke, J. L., & Padgitt, J. S. (1983). Sexual harassment of university students. *Journal of College Student Personnel, 24,* 484–490.

Agee, V. L. (1979). *Treatment of the violent incorrigible adolescent.* Lexington, MA: Lexington Books.

Ainsworth, M. D. S. (1989). Attachments beyond infancy. *American Psychologist, 44,* 709–716.

Ainsworth, M. D. S., Blehar, M. C., Waters, E., & Walls, S. (1978). *Patterns of attachment: A psychological study of the Strange Situation.* Hillsdale, NJ: Erlbaum.

Alexander, J. F., Barton, C., Schiavo, S., & Parsons, B. V. (1976). Systems-behavioral intervention with families of delinquents: Therapist characteristics, family behavior and outcome. *Journal of Consulting and Clinical Psychology, 44,* 656–664.

Alexander, M. A. (1999). Sexual offender treatment efficacy revisited. *Sexual Abuse: A Journal of Research and Treatment, 11*(2), 101–116.

Alexander, P. (1992). Application of attachment theory to the study of sexual abuse. *Journal of Consulting and Clinical Psychology, 60*, 185–195.

Aljazireh, L. (1993). Historical, environmental, and behavioral correlates of sexual offending by male adolescents: A critical review. *Behavioral Sciences and the Law, 11*, 423–440.

Allam, J., Middleton, D., & Browne, K. (1997). Different clients, different needs? Practice issues in community-based treatment for sex offenders. *Criminal Behavior and Mental Health, 7*, 69–84.

Allen, M., D'Alessio, D., & Brezgel, K. (1995). A meta-analysis summarizing the effects of pornography. II: Aggression after exposure. *Human Communication Research, 22*, 258–283.

American Group Psychotherapy Association. (1991). *Guidelines for group psychotherapy practice.* New York: Author.

American Psychiatric Association. (1952). *Diagnostic and statistical manual of mental disorders* (1st ed.). Washington, DC: Author.

American Psychiatric Association. (1968). *Diagnostic and statistical manual of mental disorders* (2nd ed.). Washington, DC: Author.

American Psychiatric Association. (1980). *Diagnostic and statistical manual of mental disorders* (3rd ed.). Washington, DC: Author.

American Psychiatric Association. (1987). *Diagnostic and statistical manual of mental disorders* (3rd ed., rev.). Washington, DC: Author.

American Psychiatric Association. (1994). *Diagnostic and statistical manual of mental disorders* (4th ed.). Washington, DC: Author

American Psychiatric Association Task Force on Sexually Dangerous Offenders. (1999). *Dangerous sex offenders: A task force report of the American Psychiatric Association.* Washington, DC: Author.

Amir, M. (1971). *Patterns of forcible rape.* Chicago: University of Chicago Press.

Andrews, D. A., & Bonta, J. (1994). *The psychology of criminal conduct.* Cincinnati, OH: Anderson Press.

Andrews, D. A., & Bonta, J. (1995). *LSI-R: The Level of Service Inventory—Revised.* Toronto: Multi-Health Systems.

Andrews, D. A., & Bonta, J. (1998). *The psychology of criminal conduct* (2nd ed.). Cincinnati, OH: Anderson Press.

Andrews, J., & Duncan, S. (1997). Examining the reciprocal relation between academic motivation and substance use: Effects of family relationships, self-esteem, and general deviance. *Journal of Behavioral Medicine, 20*(6) 523–549.

Annis, H. M., & Chan, D. (1983). The differential treatment model: Empirical evidence from a personality typology of adult offenders. *Criminal Justice and Behavior, 10*, 159–173.

Araji, S. K. (1997). Sexually aggressive children: Coming to understand them. Thousand Oaks, CA: Sage.

Arndt, W. B., Foehl, J. C., & Good, F. E. (1985). Specific fantasy themes: A multidimensional study. *Journal of Personality and Social Psychology, 48*, 472–480.

Arvey, R. D., & Cavanaugh, M. A. (1995). Using surveys to assess the prevalence of sexual harassment: Some methodological problems. *Journal of Social Issues, 51*(1), 39–52.

Ashby, J. D., Ford, D. H., Guerney, B. G., & Guerney, L. F. (1957). Effects on clients of a reflective and leading type of psychotherapy. *Psychological Monographs, 453*, 71.

Aspinwall, L. G., & Taylor, S. E. (1992). Modeling cognitive adaptation: A longitudinal investigation of the impact of individual differences and coping on college adjustment and performance. *Journal of Personality and Social Psychology, 63,* 989–1003.

Association for the Treatment of Sexual Abusers. (1997). *Ethical standards and principles for the management of sexual abusers.* Beaverton, OR: Author.

Avina, C., & O'Donohue, W. T. (in press). Sexual harassment and PTSD: Is sexual harassment a diagnosable trauma? *Journal of Traumatic Stress.*

Awad, G.A., & Saunders, E. B. (1991). Male adolescent sexual assaulters. *Journal of Interpersonal Violence, 6,* 446–460.

Awad, G., Saunders, E., & Levene, J. (1984). A clinical study of male adolescent sexual offenders. *International Journal of Offender Therapy and Comparative Criminology, 28,* 105–115.

Babitsky, S., Mangraviti, J. J., & Todd, C. J. (2000). *The comprehensive forensic services manual: The essential resources for all experts.* Falmouth, MA: SEAK.

Badovinac, K. (1994). The effects of victim impact panels on attitudes and intentions regarding impaired driving. *Journal of Alcohol and Drug Education, 39*(3), 113–118.

Bagley, C., Wood, M., & Young, L.

(1994). Victim to abuser: Mental health and behavioral sequels of child sexual abuse in a community survey of young adult males. *Child Abuse and Neglect, 18*(8), 683–697.

Baker, D. D., Terpestra, D. E., & Cutler, B. D. (1987). Perceptions of sexual harassment: A re-examination of gender differences. *The Journal of Psychology, 124*(4), 409–416.

Baldwin, T., & Ford, J. (1988). Transfer of training: A review and directions for future research. *Personnel Psychology, 41,* 63–105.

Baldwin, T. T., & Magjuka, R. J. (1991). Organizational training and signals of importance: Linking pretraining perceptions to intentions to transfer. *Human Resource Development Quarterly, 2,* 25–36.

Ball, S., Carroll, K., & Rounsaville, B. (1994). Sensation seeking, substance abuse, and psychopathology in treatment-seeking and community cocaine abusers. *Journal of Consulting and Clinical Psychology, 62*(5), 1053–1057.

Ballester, S., & Pierre, F. (1995). Monster therapy: The use of a metaphor with abuse reactive children. In M. Hunter (Ed.), *Child survivors and perpetrators of sexual abuse: Treatment innovations* (pp. 125–146). Thousand Oaks, CA: Sage.

Bancroft, J., Tennent, G., Loucas, K., & Cass, J. (1974). The control of deviant sexual behaviour by drugs. I. Behavioural changes following oestrogens and anti-androgens. *British Journal of Psychiatry, 125,* 310–315.

Bandura, A. (1973). *Aggression: A social learning analysis.* Englewood Cliffs, NJ: Prentice-Hall.

Bandura, A. (1977). Self-efficacy:

Toward a unifying theory of behavioral change. *Psychological Review, 84,* 191–215.

Bandura, A. J. (1977). *Social learning theory.* Englewood Cliffs, NJ: Prentice-Hall.

Bandura, A. (1978). Social learning theory of aggression. *Journal of Communication, 28,* 12–29.

Bandura, A. (1986). *Social foundations of thought and action: A social cognitive theory.* Englewood Cliffs, NJ: Prentice-Hall.

Bandura, A., Lipsher, D. H., & Miller, P. E. (1960). Psychotherapists' approach-avoidance reactions to patients' expressions of hostility. *Journal of Consulting Psychology, 24,* 1–8.

Bandura, A., O'Leary, A., Taylor, C. B., Gauthier, J., & Gossard, D. (1987). Perceived self-efficacy and pain control: Opioid and nonopioid mediators. *Journal of Personality and Social Psychology, 53,* 563–571.

Barbaree, H. E., & Marshall, W. L. (1989). Erectile responses among heterosexual child molesters, father-daughter incest offenders, and matched nonoffenders: Five distinct age preference profiles. *Canadian Journal of Behavioral Sciences, 21,* 70–82.

Barbaree, H., Marshall, W., & McCormick, J. (1998). The development of deviant sexual behaviour among adolescents and its implications for prevention and treatment. *Irish Journal of Psychology, 19*(1), 1–31.

Barbaree, H. E., & Seto, M. C. (1998). *The ongoing follow-up of sex offenders treated at the Warkworth Sexual Behaviour Clinic: Research report.* Toronto: Centre for Addiction and Mental Health.

Barbaree, H. E., Seto, M. C., Langton, C., & Peacock, E. (2001). Evaluating the predictive accuracy of six risk assessment instruments for adult sex offenders. *Criminal Justice and Behavior, 28*(4), 490–521.

Barkman, M., & Shapiro, D. A. (1986). Counselor verbal response modes and experienced empathy. *Journal of Counseling Psychology, 33,* 3–10.

Baron, D. P., & Unger, H. R. (1977). A clinical trial of cyproterone acetate for sexual deviancy. *New Zealand Medical Journal, 85,* 366–369.

Bartling, C. A., & Eisenman, R. (1993). Sexual harassment proclivities in men and women. *Bulletin of the Psychonomic Society, 31,* 189–192.

Bartholomew, A. A. (1968). A long-acting phenothiazine as a possible agent to control deviant sexual behavior. *American Journal of Psychiatry, 124,* 917–923.

Bartholomew, K. (1990). Avoidance of intimacy: An attachment perspective. *Journal of Social and Personal Relationships, 7,* 147–178.

Bartholomew, K., & Horowitz, L. M. (1991). Attachment styles among young adults: A test of a four-category model. *Journal of Personality and Social Psychology, 61,* 226–244.

Bartholomew, K., & Shaver, P. R. (1998). Methods of assessing adult attachment: Do they converge? In J. A. Simpson & W. S. Rholes (Eds.), *Attachment theory and close relationships* (pp. 25–45). New York: Guilford Press.

Bártová, D., Hajnová, R., Náhunek, K., & Svestka, J. (1979). Comparative study of prophylactic lithium and diethylstilbestrol in sexual deviants.

Activitas Nervosa Superior (Praha), 21, 163–164.

Bártová, D., Buresová, A., Hajnová, R., Náhunek, K., & Svestka, J. (1984). Comparison of oxyprothepine deconoate, lithium and cyproteron acetate in deviant sexual behaviour. *Activitas Nervosa Superior, 26,* 278.

Bates, M., & Labouvie, E. (1995) Personality-environment constellations and alcohol use: A process-oriented study of intraindividual change during adolescence. *Psychology of Addictive Behaviors, 9*(1), 23–35.

Bauserman, R., & Rind, B. (1997). Psychological correlates of male child and adolescent sexual experiences with adults: A review of the nonclinical literature. *Archives of Sexual Behavior, 26*(2), 105–141.

Beck, A. (1981). Developmental characteristics of the system forming process. In J. E. Durkin (Ed.), *Living groups: Group psychology and general systems theory* (pp. 316–322). New York: Brunner/Mazel.

Beck, A. T., Rush, P. J., Shaw, B. F., & Emery, G. (1979). *Cognitive therapy for depression.* New York: Guilford Press.

Becker, J. V. (1988). The effects of child sexual abuse on adolescent sex offenders. In G. E. Wyatt & E. J. Powell (Eds.), *Lasting effects of sexual abuse* (pp. 193–207) . Beverly Hills, CA: Sage.

Becker, J. V. (1994). Offenders: Characteristics and treatment. *The Future of Children: Sexual Abuse of Children, 4,* 176–197.

Becker, J., Kaplan, M., Cunningham-Rathner, J., & Kavoussi, R. (1986). Characteristics of adolescent incest per-

petrators: Preliminary findings. *Journal of Family Violence, 1,* 85–97.

Becker, J. V., Kaplan, M. S., Tenke, C. E., & Tartaglini, A. (1991). The incidence of depressive symptomatology in juvenile sex offenders with a history of abuse. *Child Abuse and Neglect, 15,* 531–536.

Becker, J. V., & Murphy, W. D. (1998). What we know and do not know about assessing and treating sex offenders. *Psychology, Public Policy, and Law, 4*(1–2), 116–137.

Beech, A., & Fordham, A. S. (1997). Therapeutic climate of sexual offender treatment programs. *Sexual Abuse: A Journal of Research and Treatment, 9,* 219–237.

Beitchman, J. H., Zucker, K. J., Hood, J. E., DaCosta, G. A., & Akma, D. (1991). A review of the short-term effects of child sexual abuse. *Child Abuse and Neglect, 15,* 537–556.

Beitchman, J. H., Zucker, K. J., Hood, J. E., DaCosta, G. A., Akma, D., & Cassavia, E. (1992). A review of the long-term effects of child sexual abuse. *Child Abuse and Neglect,* 16, 101–117.

Bell, M. (1995). *Bell Object Relations and Reality Testing Inventory manual.* Los Angeles: Western Psychological Services.

Bell, M., Billington, R., & Becker, B. (1986). A scale for the assessment of object relations: Reliability, validity, and factorial invariance. *Journal of Clinical Psychology, 42,* 733–741.

Bemporad, J. R. (1980). Review of object relations theory in light of cognitive development. *Journal of the American Academy of Psychoanalysis, 8,* 57–75.

Benassi, V. A., Sweeney, P. D., &

Dufour, C. L. (1988). Is there a relation between locus of control orientation and depression? *Journal of Abnormal Psychology, 97,* 357–336.

Bennun, I., Hahlweg, K., Schindler, L., & Langlotz, M. (1986). Therapist's and client's perceptions in behavior therapy: The development and cross-cultural analysis of an assessment instrument. *British Journal of Clinical Psychology, 25,* 275–283.

Benoit, J. L., & Kennedy, W. A. (1992). The abuse history of male adolescent sex offenders. *Journal of Interpersonal Violence, 7,* 543–548.

Benson, D. J., & Thompson, G. E. (1982). Sexual harassment on a university campus: The confluence of authority relations, sexual interest, and gender stratification. *Social Problems, 29,* 236–251.

Benton Foundation. (2000). *What you may not know about foster care* [Online]. Available: www.connectforkids.org.

Berdahl, J. L., Magley, V. J., & Waldo, C. R. (1996). The sexual harassment of men? Exploring the concept with theory and data. *Psychology of Women Quarterly, 20,* 527–547.

Berlin, F., Malin, H., & Thomas, K. (1995). Nonpedophiliac and nontransvestic paraphilias. In G. Gabbard (Ed.), *Treatment of psychiatric disorders* (pp. 1941–1958). Washington, DC: American Psychiatric Press.

Berlin, F. S., & Coyle, G. S. (1981). Sexual deviation syndromes [clinical conference]. *Johns Hopkins Medical Journal, 149,* 119–125.

Berlin, F. S., & Meinecke, C. F. (1981). Treatment of sex offenders with antiandrogenic medication: Conceptualization,

review of treatment modalities, and preliminary findings. *American Journal of Psychiatry, 138,* 601–607.

Berliner, L., & Elliot, D. M. (1996). Sexual abuse of children. In J. Briere, L. Berliner, J. A. Bulkley, C. Jenny, & T. Reid (Eds.), *The APSAC handbook on child maltreament* (pp. 51–71). Thousand Oaks, CA: Sage.

Berner, W., Brownstone, G., & Sluga, W. (1983). The cyproteronacetat treatment of sexual offenders. *Neuroscience and Biobehavioral Review, 7,* 441–443.

Bernstein, D. P., & Fink, L. (1998). *Childhood Trauma Questionnaire: A retrospective self-report manual.* San Antonio, TX: Psychological Corporation.

Bernstein, D. P., Fink, L., Handelsman, L., Foote, J., Lovejoy, M., Wenzel, K., Sapareto, E., & Ruggiero, J. (1994). Initial reliability and validity of a new retrospective measure of child abuse and neglect. *American Journal of Psychiatry, 151,* 1132–1136.

Beutler, L. E., Pollack, S., & Jobe, A. M. (1978). "Acceptance," values and therapeutic change. *Journal of Consulting and Clinical Psychology, 46,* 198–199.

Bingham, S. G., & Burleson, B. R. (1996). The development of a sexual harassment proclivity scale: Construct validation and relationship to communication competence. *Communication Quarterly, 44*(3), 308– 325.

Black, C. A., & DeBlassie, R. R. (1993). Sexual abuse in male children and adolescents: Indicators, effects and treatments. *Adolescence, 28,* 123–133.

Black, D., Kehrberg, L., Flumerfelt, D., & Schlosser, S. (1997). Characteristics of 36 subjects reporting compulsive sexual behavior. *American Journal of Psychiatry, 154*, 243–249.

Blanchard, G. (1998). *The difficult connection:Therapeutic relationship with sex offenders* (rev.). Brandon, VT: Safer Society Press.

Blankenship, K., & Whitley, B. (2000). Relation of general deviance to academic dishonesty. *Ethics and Behavior, 10*(1), 1–12.

Blatt, S., Quinlan, D., Pilkonas, P., & Shea, M. (1995). Impact of perfectionism and need for approval on the brief treatment of depression: The National Institute of Mental Health Treatment of Depression Collaborative Research Program revisited. *Journal of Consulting and Clinical Psychology, 63*(1), 125–132.

Blatt, S. J., Wiseman, H., Prince-Gibson, E., & Gatt, C. (1991). Object representations and change in clinical functioning. *Psychotherapy, 28*, 273–283.

Blay, S. L., Ferraz, M. P., & Calil, H. M. (1982). Lithium-induced male sexual impairment: Two case reports. *Journal of Clinical Psychiatry, 43*, 497–8.

Blumer, D., & Migeon, C. (1975). Hormone and hormonal agents in the treatment of aggression. *Journal of Nervous and Mental Disorders, 160*, 127–137.

Boer, D. P., Hart, S. D., Kropp, P. R., & Webster, C. D. (1997). *Manual for the Sexual Violence Risk—20: Professional guidelines for assessing risk of sexual violence.* Burnaby, British Columbia: The Mental Health, Law, & Policy Institute, Simon Fraser University.

Boer, D. P., Wilson, R. J., Gauthier, C. M., & Hart, S. D. (1997). Assessing risk of sexual violence: Guidelines for clinical practice. In C. D. Webster & M. A.

Jackson (Eds.), *Impulsivity: Theory, assessment, and treatment (*pp. 326–342). New York: Guilford Press.

Bogg, R. (1994, October–December). Psychopathic behavior as perpetual gaming: A synthesis of forensic accounts. *Deviant Behavior, 15*(4), 357–374.

Bourgeois, J. A., & Klein, M. (1996). Risperidone and fluoxetine in the treatment of pedophilia with comorbid dysthymia [letter]. *Journal of Clinical Psychopharmacology, 16*, 257–258.

Bowlby, J. (1944). Forty-four juvenile thieves: Their characters and home-life (II). *International Journal of Psycho-Analysis, 25*, 107–128

Bowlby, J. (1969). Disruption of affectional bonds and its effects on behavior. *Canada's Mental Health Supplement, 59*, 12.

Bowlby, J. (1976). Human personality development in an ethological light. In G. Serban & A. Kling (Eds.), *Animal models in human psychobiology* (pp. 27–36). New York: Plenum.

Braaten, E. B., Otto, S., & Handelsman, M. (1993). What do people want to know about psychotherapy? *Psychotherapy, 30*, 565–570.

Bradford, J. M., & McLean, D. (1984). Sexual offenders, violence and testosterone: A clinical study. *Canadian Journal of Psychiatry, 29*, 335–343.

Bradford, J. M., & Pawlak, A. (1987). Sadistic homosexual pedophilia: Treatment with cyproterone acetate—A single case study. *Canadian Journal of Psychiatry, 32*, 22–30.

Bradford, J. M., & Pawlak, A. (1993a). Double-blind placebo crossover study of cyproterone acetate in the treatment of the paraphilias. *Archives of Sexual Behavior, 22*, 383–402.

Bradford, J. M., & Pawlak, A. (1993b). Effects of cyproterone acetate on sexual arousal patterns of pedophiles. *Archives of Sexual Behavior, 22*, 629–41.

Bradford, J., & Wiseman, R. (1995). *An open pilot study of sertraline in the treatment of outpatients with pedophilia.* Paper presented at the annual meeting of the American Psychiatric Association, Miami, FL.

Breckenridge, J., & Baldry, E. (1997). Workers dealing with mother blame in child sexual assault cases. *Journal of Child Sexual Abuse, 6*(1), 65–80.

Breer, W. (1996). *The adolescent molester.* Springfield, IL: Charles C. Thomas.

Brendtro, L., Brokenleg, M., & Van Bockern, S. (1990). *Reclaiming youth at risk: Our hope for the future.* Bloomington, IN: National Education Service.

Brendtro, L. K., & Ness, A. E. (1982). Perspectives on peer group treatment: The use and abuse of Guided Group Interaction/Positive Peer Culture. *Children and Youth Services Review, 4*, 307–324.

Bretherton, I. (1985). Attachment theory: Retrospect and prospect. *Monographs of the Society for Research in Child Development, 50*, 3–35.

Briere, J. (1989). *Therapy for adults molested as children: Beyond survival.* New York: Springer.

Briere, J. (1995). *Traumatic Symptom Inventory (TSI): Professional manual.* Odessa, FL: Psychological Assessment Resources.

Briere, J. N., & Elliott, D. M. (1994). Immediate and long-term impacts of child sexual abuse. *Sexual Abuse of Children: The Future of Children, 4*(2), 54–69.

Briere, J., Evans, D., Runtz, M., & Wall, T. (1988). Symptomatology in men who were molested as children: A comparison study. *American Journal of Orthopsychiatry, 58*(3), 457–461.

Briere, J., & Runtz, M. (1989). University males' sexual interest in children: Predicting potential indices of "pedophilia" in a non-forensic sample. *Child Abuse and Neglect, 13*, 65–75.

Briere, J., & Runtz, M. (1993). Childhood sexual abuse: Long-term sequelae and implications for psychological assessment. *Journal of Interpersonal Violence, 8*(3), 312–330.

Briere, J., & Smiljanich, K. (1993). *Childhood sexual abuse and subsquent sexual aggression against adult women.* Paper presented at the 101st annual convention of the American Psychological Association, Toronto.

Briggs, F., & Hawkins, R. M. F. (1996). A comparison of the childhood experiences of convicted male child molesters and men who were sexually abused in childhood and claimed to be non-offenders. *Child Abuse and Neglect, 20*(3), 221–233.

Broadhurst, R. G., & Maller, R.A. (1992). The recidivism of sex offenders in the Western Australian prison population. *British Journal of Criminology, 32*(1), 54–80.

Brock, K., Mintz, L., & Good, G. (1997). Differences among sexually abused and nonabused women from functional and dysfunctional families. *Journal of Counseling Psychology, 44*(4), 425–423.

Brown, A., & Finkelhor, D. (1986). Impact of child sexual abuse: A review of the research. *Psychological Bulletin, 99*(1), 66–77.

Brownmiller, S. (1975). *Against our will: Men, women and rape.* New York: Simon & Schuster.

Brunink, S., & Schroeder, H. E. (1979). Verbal therapeutic behavior of expert psychoanalytically oriented, Gestalt and behavior therapists. *Journal of Consulting and Clinical Psychology, 47*, 567–574.

Brunswig, K. A., Oksol, E. M., & Bowers, A. H. (2000). *A review of the measurement and assessment of sexual harassment and sexual harassment-related phenomena.* Poster presented at the 19th annual meeting of the Association for the Treatment of Sexual Abusers, San Diego.

Bumby, K. M., & Bumby, N. H. (1997). Adolescent female sex offenders. In B. K. Schwartz & H. R. Cellini (Eds.), *The sex offender: New insights, treatment innovations, and legal developments* (pp. 10-1–10-16). Kingston, NJ: Civic Research Institute.

Bumby, K. M., Marshall, W. L., & Langton, C. M. (1999). Shame and guilt, and their relevance for sexual offender treatment. In B. K. Schwartz (Ed.), *The sex offender: Theoretical advances, treating special populations, and legal developments* (pp. 5-1–5-12). Kingston, NJ: Civic Research Institute.

Buresová, A., Bártová, D., & Svestka, J. (1990). Comparison of pharmacotherapeutic procedures in the treatment of sexual deviant behaviour. *Activitas Nervosa Superior(Praha), 32*, 299–301.

Burgess, A. W., Hartman, C. R., McCormack, A., & Grant, C. A. (1988). Child victim to juvenile victimizer: Treatment implications. *International Journal of Family Psychiatry, 9*(4), 403–416.

Burns, D. (1980). *Feeling good: The new mood therapy.* New York: Avon Books.

Burns, D. D., & Auerbach, A. (1996). Therapeutic empathy in cognitive-behavioral therapy: Does it really make a difference? In P. Salkovskis (Ed.), *Frontiers of cognitive therapy* (pp. 135–164). New York: Guilford Press.

Burns, D. D., & Nolen Hocksema, S. (1992). Therapeutic empathy and recovery from depression in cognitive-behavioral therapy: A structural equation model. *Journal of Consulting and Clinical Psychology, 59*, 305–311.

Burns, S. E. (1995). Issues in workplace sexual harassment law and related social science research. *Journal of Social Issues, 51*, 193–207.

Burtenshaw, R. P. (1997, August). An ethnic comparison of the ranked value of Yalom's therapeutic factors among chemically dependent incarcerated adult males in group psychotherapy. *Dissertation Abstracts International, 58*(2-A).

Burton, D., Burton, D., Smith-Darden, J., Levins, J., Fiske, J., & Longo, R. E. (2000). *1996 nationwide survey of treatment programs & models: Serving abuse reactive children and adolescent & adult sexual offenders.* Brandon, VT: Safer Society Press.

Buss, A. (1966). *Psychopathology.* New York: Wiley.

Byrne, D., & Clore, G. L. (1970). A reinforcement-affect model of evaluative responses. *Personality: An International Journal, 1*, 103–128.

Byrne, D., London, O., & Reeves, K. (1968). The effects of physical attractiveness, sex, and attitude on interpersonal attraction. *Journal of Personality, 36*, 259–271.

Cado, S., & Leitenberg, H. (1990). Guilt reactions to sexual fantasies during intercourse. *Archives of Sexual Behavior, 19*, 49–63.

Camp, B. H., & Thyer, B. S. (1993). Treatment of adolescent sex offenders: A review of empirical research. *Journal of Applied Social Sciences, 17,* 191–206.

Cantor, B. J. (1997). *The role of the expert witness in a court trial (a guide for the expert witness).* Belmont, MA: Civil Evidence Photography Seminars.

Cantwell, H. B. (1995). Sexually aggressive children and societal response. In M. Hunter (Ed.), *Child survivors and perpetrators of sexual abuse: Treatment innovations* (pp. 79–107). Thousand Oaks, CA: Sage.

Carden, A. (1994). Wife abuse and the wife abuser: Review and recommendations. *The Counseling Psychologist, 22*(4), 539–582.

Carich, M. A. (1999). In defense of the assault cycle: A commentary. *Sexual Abuse: A Journal of Research and Treatment, 11*(3), 249–251.

Carey, C. H., & McGrath, R. J. (1989). Coping with urges and cravings. In R. Laws (Ed.), *Relapse prevention with sex offenders* (pp. 188–196). New York: Guilford Press.

Carmen, E., Reiker, P., & Mills, T. (1984, March). Victims of violence and psychiatric illness. *American Journal of Psychiatry, 141*(3), 378–383.

Carnes, P., & Delmonico, D. (1996). Childhood abuse and multiple addictions: Research findings in a sample of self-identified sexual addicts. *Sexual Addiction and Compulsivity, 3*(3), 258–268.

Carrasco, N., & Garza-Louis, D. (1997). Hispanic sex offenders: Cultural characteristics and implications for treatment. In B. K. Schwartz & H. R.Cellini (Eds.), *The sex offender: New insights, treatment innovations, and legal developments* (pp. 13-1– 13-10). Kingston, NJ: Civic Research Institute.

Carroll, J. (1993). Theory to practice: Self-efficacy related to transfer of learning as an example of theory-based instructional design. *Journal of Adult Education, 22*(1), 37–43.

Carter, G. S., & Van Dalen, A. (1998). Sibling incest: Time limited group as an assessment and treatment planning tool. *Journal of Child and Adolescent Group Therapy, 8*(2), 45–54.

Casals-Ariet, C., & Cullen, K. (1993). Exhibitionism treated with clomipramine [letter; comment]. *American Journal of Psychiatry, 150*, 1273–1274.

Casey, R., & Berman, J. (1985). The outcome of psychotherapy with children. *Psychological Bulletin, 98*, 388–400.

Cashwell, C. S., Bloss, K. K., & McFarland, J. E. (1995). From victim to client: Preventing the cycle of sexual reactivity. *The School Counselor, 42*, 233–238.

Cellini, H. R. (1995). Assessment and treatment of the adolescent sex offender. In B. K. Schwartz & H. R. Cellini (Eds.), *The sex offender: Corrections, treatment, and legal practice* (pp. 6-1– 6-12). Kingston, NJ: Civic Research Institute.

Center for Sex Offender Management. (1999). *Understanding juvenile sexual offending behavior: Emerging research, treatment approaches and management practices.* Silver Spring, MD: Center for Sex Offender Management.

Cermak, P., & Molidar, C. (1996). Male victims of child sexual abuse. *Child and & Adolescent Social Work Journal, 13*(5), 385–400.

Cesnik, J., & Coleman, E. (1989). Use of lithium carbonate in the treatment of autoerotic asphyxia. *American Journal of Psychotherapy, 43*, 277–286.

Chamberlain, P., Moreland, S., & Reid, K. (1992, September–October). Enhanced services and stipends for foster parents: Effects on retention rates and outcomes for children. *Child Welfare, 71*(5), 387–401.

Chamberlain, P., & Reid, J. (1998). Comparison of two community alternatives to incarceration for chronic juvenile offenders. *Journal of Consulting and Clinical Psychology, 66*(4), 624–633.

Chapman, J. (1968). Frigidity: Rapid treatment by reciprocal inhibition. *Journal of the American Osteopathic Association, 67*(8), 871–878.

Charlton, P. F. C., & Thompson, J. A. (1996). Ways of coping with psychological distress. *British Journal of Clinical Psychology, 35,* 517–530.

Chiauzzi, E. (1989, December). Breaking the patterns that lead to relapse. *Psychology Today*, pp. 18–19.

Chorn, R., & Parekh, A. (1997). Adolescent sexual offenders: A self-psychological perspective. *American Journal of Psychiatry, 51*, 210–228.

Christenson, G. A., Popkin, M. K., Mackenzie, T. B., & Realmuto, G. M. (1991). Lithium treatment of chronic hair pulling. *Journal of Clinical Psychiatry, 52*, 116–120.

Cleckley, H. (1976). *The mask of sanity* (5th ed.). St. Louis, MO: Mosby.

Cohen, F., & Densen-Gerber, J. (1982). A study of the relationship between child abuse and drug addiction in 178 patients: Preliminary results. *Child Abuse and Neglect, 6*(4) 383–387.

Cohen, J., Mannarino, A., Berliner, L., & Deblinger, E. (2000). Trauma focused cognitive behavior therapy: An empirical update. *Journal of Interpersonal Violence, 15*, 1203–1223.

Cole, P. M., & Putnam, F. W. (1992). Effect of incest on self and social functioning: A developmental psychophathology perspective. *Journal of Consulting and Clinical Psychology, 60*, 174–184.

Coleman, E., Dwyer, S. M., Abel, G., Berner, W., Breiling, J., Hindman, J., Honey-Knopp, F., Langevin, R., & Pfafflin, F. (1995). The treatment of adult sex offenders: Standards of care. *Journal of Offender Rehabilitation, 23(*3–4), 5–11.

Coleman, E., Gratzer, T., Nesvacil, L., & Raymond, N. C. (2000). Nefazodone and the treatment of nonparaphilic compulsive sexual behavior: a retrospective study. *Journal of Clinical Psychiatry, 61*, 282–284.

Coleman, E., & Haaven, J. (2001). Assessment and treatment of intellectually disabled sex offenders. In M. S. Karich & S. Mussack (Eds.), *Handbook of sex offender treatment*. Brandon, VT: Safer Society Program and Press.

Collings, S. J. (1995). The long-term effects of contact and noncontact forms of child sexual abuse in a sample of university men. *Child Abuse and Neglect, 19*(1), 1–6.

Conte, J. R. (1988). The effects of sexual

abuse on children: Results of a research project. *Annals of the New York Academy of Sciences*, 528, 310–326.

Cook, D. (1991).College students from emotionally neglectful homes. *New Directions for Student Services, 54*, 77–90.

Cooley, E. J., & Lajoy, R. (1980). Therapeutic relationship and improvements as perceived by clients and therapists. *Journal of Clinical Psychology, 36*, 562–570.

Cooper, A. J. (1981). A placebo-controlled trial of the antiandrogen cyproterone acetate in deviant hypersexuality. *Comprehensive Psychiatry, 22*, 458–465.

Cooper, A. J. (1987). Medroxyprogesterone acetate (MPA) treatment of sexual acting out in men suffering from dementia. *Journal of Clinical Psychiatry, 48*, 368–370.

Cooper, A. (1998). Sexuality and the internet: Surfing into the new millennium. *CyberPsychology and Behavior, 1*, 181–187.

Cooper, A. J., & Cernovsky, Z. Z. (1994). Comparison of cyproterone acetate (CPA) and leuprolide acetate (LHRH agonist) in a chronic pedophile: A clinical case study. *Biological Psychiatry, 36*, 269–271.

Cooper, A. J., Cernovsky, Z., & Magnus, R. V. (1992). The long-term use of cyproterone acetate in pedophilia: A case study. *Journal of Sex and Marital Therapy, 18*, 292–302.

Cooper, A. J., Ismail, A. A., Phanjoo, A. L., & Love, D. L. (1972). Antiandrogen (cyproterone acetate) therapy in deviant hypersexuality. *British Journal of Psychiatry, 120*, 59–63.

Cooper, A. J., Sandhu, S., Losztyn, S., & Cernovsky, Z. (1992). A double-blind

placebo controlled trial of medroxyprogesterone acetate and cyproterone acetate with seven pedophiles. *Canadian Journal of Psychiatry, 37*, 687–93.

Cooper, A., Scherer, C. R., Boies, S. C., & Gordon, B. L. (1999). Sexuality on the Internet: From sexual exploration to pathological expression. *Professional Pschology: Research and Practice, 30*(2).

Cooper, C. L., Murphy, W. D., & Haynes, M. R. (1996). Characteristics of abused and nonabused adolescent sexual offenders. *Sexual Abuse: A Journal of Research and Treatment, 8*, 105–119.

Corcoran, C. L., Miranda, A. O., Tenukas-Steblea, K., & Taylor, B. D. (1999). Inclusion of the family in the treatment of juvenile sexual abuse perpetrators. In B. K. Schwartz (Ed.), *The sex offender: Theoretical advances, treating special populations and legal developments* (pp. 17-1–17-9). Kingston, NJ: Civic Research Institute.

Cordoba, O. A., & Chapel, J. L. (1983). Medroxyprogesterone acetate antiandrogen treatment of hypersexuality in a pedophiliac sex offender. *American Journal of Psychiatry, 140*, 1036–1039.

Corrigan, J. D., Dell, D. M., Lewis, K. N., & Schmidt, L. D. (1980). Counseling as a social influence process: A review. *Journal of Counseling Psychology Monograph, 27*, 395–441.

Cortoni, F. A. (1998). *The relationship between attachment styles, coping, the use of sex as a coping mechanism, and juvenile sexual history in sexual offenders.* Unpublished doctoral dissertation, Queen's University, Kingston, Ontario.

Cortoni, F., Heil, P., & Marshall, W. (1996, November). *Sex as a coping mechanism and its relationship to loneliness and intimacy deficits in sexual offending.* Paper presented at the 15th annual Research and Treatment Conference of the Association for the Treatment of Sexual Abusers, Chicago.

Cortoni, F. A., Looman, J. A., & Anderson, D. (1999). *Locus of control and coping in sexual offenders.* Paper presented at the 18th annual Research and Treatment Conference of the Association for the Treatment of Sexual Abusers, Orlando, FL.

Cortoni, F. A., & Marshall, W. L. (1995). *Childhood attachments, juvenile sexual history and adult coping skills in sex offenders.* Paper presented at the 14th annual Research and Treatment Conference of the Association for the Treatment of Sexual Abusers, New Orleans.

Cortoni, F. A., & Marshall, W. L. (1996). *Juvenile sexual history, sex and coping strategies: A comparison of sexual and violent offenders.* Paper presented at the International Congress of Psychology, Montreal.

Cortoni, F. A., & Marshall, W. L. (1998). *The relationship between attachment and coping in sexual offenders.* Paper presented at the 17th annual Research and Treatment Conference of the Association for the Treatment of Sexual Abusers, Vancouver.

Cortoni, F. A., & Marshall, W. L. (2001). Sex as a coping strategy and its relationship to juvenile sexual history and intimacy in sexual offenders. *Sexual Abuse: A Journal of Research and Treatment, 13,* 27–44.

Councilman, E. F., & Gans, J. S. (1999). The missed session in psychodynamic group psychotherapy. *International Journal of Group Psychotherapy, 49*(1), 71–86.

Counseling & Consultation Services. (1999). *Protocol for therapeutically tolerated visitation with sex offenders and children.* Johnson City, TN: Author.

Cox, P. D., Ilfield, Jr., F., Ilfield, B. S., & Brennan, C. (2000). Group therapy program development: Administrator collaboration in new practice settings. *International Journal of Group Psychotherapy, 50*(1), 3–24.

Craissati, J., & McClurg, G. (1996). The challenge project: Perpetrators of child sexual abuse in south east London. *Child Abuse and Neglect, 20*(11), 1067–1077.

Crenshaw, T., & Goldberg, J. (1996). *Sexual pharmacology.* New York: Norton.

Crepault, C., & Couture, M. (1980). Men's erotic fantasies. *Archives of Sexual Behavior, 9,* 565–581.

Croughan, J., Saghir, M., Cohne, R., & Robins, E. (1981). A comparison of treated and untreated male cross-dressers. *Archives of Sexual Behavior, 10,* 515–528.

Crull, P. (1982). Stress effects of sexual harassment on the job: Implications for counseling. *American Journal of Orthopsychiatry, 52,* 539–544.

Culbertson, A. L., Rosenfeld, P., Booth-Kewley, S., & Magnusson, P. (1992). *Assessment of sexual harassment in the Navy: Results of the 1989 Navy-wide survey.* San Diego, CA: Navy Personnel Research and Development Center.

Culbertson, A. L., Rosenfeld, P., & Newel, C. E. (1993). *Sexual harassment in the active duty Navy. Assessment of sexual harassment in the Navy: Results of the 1989 Navy-wide survey.* San Diego, CA: Navy Personnel Research and Development Center.

Cullari, S. (1996). *Treatment resistance: A guide for practitioners.* Boston: Allyn & Bacon.

Cummings, C., Gordon, J., & Marlatt, G. A. (1980). Relapse: Strategies of prevention and prediction. In W. R. Miller (Ed.), *The addictive behaviors: Treatment of alcoholism, drug abuse, smoking, and obesity* (pp. 290–321). Oxford, UK: Pergamon Press.

Cunningham, C., & McFarlane, K. (1996). *When children abuse: Group treatment strategies for children with impulse control problems.* Brandon, VT: Safer Society Press.

Curtis, J.M. (1982). The effect of therapist self-disclosure on patient's perceptions of empathy, competence, and trust in an analogue psychotherapeutic interaction. *Psychotherapy: Theory, Research, and Practice, 19*, 54–62.

Czech, N. (1988). Family therapy with adolescent sex offenders. In J. K. Zeig & S. R. Lankton (Eds.), *Developing Ericksonian therapy: State of the art* (pp. 452–461). New York: Brunner/Mazel.

Dansky, B. S., & Kilpatrick, D. G. (1997). Effects of sexual harassment. In W. T. O'Donohue (Ed.), *Sexual harassment: Theory, research, and treatment* (pp. 152–174). Needham Heights, MA: Allyn & Bacon.

Darke, J. L. (1990). Sexual aggression—Achieving power through humiliation. In W. L. Marshall, D. R. Laws, & H. E. Barbaree (Eds.), *Handbook of sexual assault* (pp. 55–72). New York: Plenum.

Davidson, A. (1983, October). Sexual exploitation of children: A call to action. *Journal of the National Medical Association, 75*(10), 925–927.

Davidson, J., Kwan, M., & Greenleaf, W. (1982). Hormonal replacement and sex-uality. *Clinical Endocrinology and Metabolism, 11*, 599.

Davies, T. S. (1974). Cyproterone acetate for male hypersexuality. *Journal of Internal Medicine Research, 2*, 159–163.

Davies, W., & Feldman, P. (1981, April). The diagnosis of psychopathy by forensic specialists. *British Journal of Psychiatry, 138*, 329–331.

Davis, G. E., & Leitenberg, H. (1987). Adolescent sex offenders. *Psychological Bulletin, 101*, 417–427.

Deberdt, R. (1971). [Benperidol (R4584) in the treatment of sexual offenders]. *Acta Psychiatrica Belgique, 11*, 396–413.

Deitz, C., & Craft, H. (1980). Family dynamics of incest: A new perspective. *Social Casework, 61*, 602–609.

DeLeon, G. (1984). *The therapeutic community: Study of effectiveness* (NIDA Research Monograph) (DHHS Publication No. ADM 84–1286). Washington, DC: U.S. Government Printing Office.

DeLeon, G. (1987). Alcohol use among drug abusers: Treatment outcomes in a therapeutic community. *Alcoholism, Clinical and Experimental Research, 11*(5), 430–436.

DeLeon, G. (1989). Psychopathology and substance abuse: What is being learned from research in therapeutic communities. *Journal of Psychoactive Drugs, 21*(2), 177–187.

DeLeon, G. (1997). President's column. *The Addictions Newsletter, 4*(3), 1,6.

Dembo, P., Deitke, M., la Voie, L., & Borders, S. (1987). Physical abuse, sexual victimization and illicit drug use: A structural analysis among high risk adolescents. *Journal of Adolescence, 10,* 13–34.

Denby, R., & Rindfleisch, N. (1996). African Americans' foster parenting experiences: Research findings and implications for policy and practice. *Children and Youth Services Review, 18*(6) 523–552.

Dermen, K., & Cooper, I. (1994) *Psychology of Addictive Behaviors, 9,* 156.

Derogatis, L. R. (1977). *The SCL-90-R manual I: Scoring administration and procedures for the SCL-90-R.* Baltimore: Clinical Psychometrics.

Development Services Group. (2000). *Understanding treatment and accountability in juvenile sex offending: Results and recommendations from an OJJDP Focus Group.* Paper prepared for Office of Juvenile Justice and Delinquency Prevention Training and Technical Assistance Division, Bethesda, MD 20814.

DeYoung, M. (1994). Immediate maternal reactions to the disclosure or discovery of incest. *Journal of Family Violence, 9*(1), 21–33.

Dhaliwal, G. K., Gauzas, L., Antonowicz, D. H., & Ross, R. R. (1996). Adult male survivors of childhood sexual abuse: Prevalence, sexual abuse characteristics, and long-term effects. *Clinical Psychology Review, 16*(7), 619–639.

Dhawan, S., & Marshall, W. L. (1996). Sexual abuse histories of sexual offenders. *Sexual Abuse: A Journal of Research and Treatment, 8*(1), 7–15.

Dickey, R. (1992). The management of a case of treatment-resistant paraphilia with a long-acting LHRH agonist. *Canadian Journal of Psychiatry, 37,* 567–569.

Dies, R. (1986). Practical theoretical, and empirical foundations for group psychotherapy. In A. Francis & R. Hales (Eds.), *The American Psychiatric Association annual review* (Vol. 5; pp. 659–677). Washington, DC: American Psychiatric Press.

Dietz, P. E., Hazelwood, R. R., & Warren, J. (1990). The sexually sadistic criminal and his offenses. *Bulletin of the American Academy of Psychiatry and Law, 18,* 163–178.

DiGiorgio-Miller, J. (1994). Clinical techniques in the treatment of juvenile sex offenders. *Journal of Offender Rehabilitation, 21*(1–2), 117–126.

Dimock, P. T. (1988). Adult males sexually abused as children. *Journal of Interpersonal Violence, 3*(2), 203–221.

"Discipline: When is it too much?" (1995, January 20). *48 hours* (for a transcript call 800–777-text and for a videotape copy call 800–338–4847).

Dishion, T. J., McCord, J., & Poulin, F. (1999, September). When interventions harm: Peer groups and problem behavior. *American Psychologist, 54,* 755–764.

Donnerstein, E., & Malamuth, N. (1997). Pornography: Its consequences on the observer. In L. B. Schlesinger & E. Revitch (Eds.), *Sexual dynamics of anti-social behavior* (2nd ed., pp. 30–49). Springfield, IL: Charles C. Thomas.

Doren, D. (1999). *Using and testifying about sex offender risk instrumentation.* Paper presented at 1999 annual conference of the Association for the Treatment of Sex offenders.

Doren, D. (1999, September). *A comprehensive comparison of risk assessment instruments to determine their rel-*

ative value within civil commitment evaluations. Paper presented at the 18th annual Research and Treatment Conference of the Association for the Treatment of Sexual Abusers in Lake Buena Vista, FL.

Doren, D. (2000, November). *Being accurate about the accuracy of commonly used risk assessment instruments.* Paper presented at the 19th annual Research and Treatment Conference of the Association for the Treatment of Sexual Abusers, San Diego, CA.

Doren, D. M., & Roberts, C. F. (1998, October). *The proper use and interpretation of actuarial instruments in assessing recidivism risk.* Paper presented at the 17th annual Research and Treatment Conference of the Association for the Treatment of Sexual Abusers, Vancouver.

Doster, J. A., & Nesbitt, J. E. (1979). Psychotherapy and self-disclosure. In G. J. Chelune (Ed.), *Self-disclosure* (pp. 177–224). San Francisco: Jossey-Bass.

Dua, P. S. (1970). Comparison of the effects of behaviourally oriented action and psychotherapy re-education on introversion-extroversion, emotionality, and internal-external control. *Journal of Counseling Psychology, 19,* 253–260.

Dube, R., & Herbert, M. (1988). Sexual abuse of children under 12 years of age: A review of 511 cases. *Child Abuse and Neglect, 12,* 321.

Dubner, A., & Motta, R. (1999). Sexually and physically abused foster care children and posttraumatic stress disorder. *Journal of Consulting and Clinical Psychology, 67*(3), 367–373.

Dudek, J. A., Nezu, A. M., & Nezu, C. M. (1997). *From victim to offender: Denial as a mediating variable between past victimization and current sexual deviance.* Paper presented at the 16th annual conference of the Association for the Treatment of Sexual Abusers, Arlington, VA.

Dutton, D. G., & Hart, S. D. (1992). Evidence for long-term, specific effects of childhood abuse and neglect on criminal behavior in men. *International Journal of Offender Therapy and Comparative Criminology, 36*(2), 129–137.

D'Zurilla, T. J., & Goldfried, M. R. (1971). Problem-solving and behavior modification. *Journal of Abnormal Psychology, 78,* 107–126.

Eccles, A., & Marshall, W. L. (1999). Relapse prevention. In W. L. Marshall, D. Anderson, & Y. Fernandez (Eds.), *Cognitive behavioural treatment of sexual offenders* (pp. 127–146). London: Wiley.

Eckenrode, J., Laird, M., & Doris, J. (1993). School performance and disciplinary problems among abused and neglected children. *Developmental Psychology, 29*(1), 53–62.

Egan, G. (1998). *The skilled helper: A problem-management approach to helping.* Pacific Grove, CA: Brooks/Cole.

Eisenberg, N., & Miller, P. A. (1987). The relation of empathy to prosocial and related behaviors. *Psychological Bulletin, 101,* 91–119.

Ellerby, L. A. (1999, September 24). *Holistic approach to treating sexual abusers.* Workshop at the 18th annual conference of the Association for the Treatment of Sexual Abusers, Lake Buena Vista, FL.

Elliot, D. M., & Briere, J. (1995). Posttraumatic stress associated with delayed recall of sexual abuse: A general population study. *Journal of Traumatic Stress Studies, 8*, 629–648.

Elliot, R. (1986). Interpersonal process recall as a psychotherapeutic process research method. In L. L. Greenberg & W. M. Pinsof (Eds.), *The psychotherapeutic process: A research handbook* (pp. 503–507). New York: Guilford Press.

Elliot, R., Barker, C. B., Caskey, N., & Pistrang, N. (1982). Differential helpfulness of counselor verbal response modes. *Journal of Counseling Psychology, 29*, 354–361.

Ellis, A. (1995). Addictive behaviors and personality disorders: A rational emotive behavior therapy approach. *The Addictions Newsletter, 2*(3), 10, 11, 26.

Emmelkamp, P. (1982). Exposure in vivo treatments. In A. Goldstein & D. Chamberless (Eds.), *Agoraphobia: Multiple perspectives on theory and treatment.* New York: Wiley.

Endler, N. S., & Parker, J. D. A. (1999). *Coping Inventory for Stressful Situations: Manual* (2nd ed.). Toronto: Multi-Health Systems.

English, D. (1988). The extent and consequences of child maltreatment. *The Future of Children: Protecting Children From Abuse and Neglect, 8*(1), 39–53.

Epperson, D. L., Kaul, J. D., Huot, S. J., Hesselton, D., Alexander, W., & Goldman, R. (1999). *Minnesota Sex Offender Screening Tool—Revised (MnSOST-R): Development, performance, and recommended risk level cut scores* [On-line]. Available: http://psych-server.iastate.edu/faculty/epperson/MnSOST-R.htm.

Equal Employment Opportunity Commission. (1980). *Discriminations because of sex under Title VII of the Civil Rights Act of 1964, as amended, adoption of interim interpretive guidelines.* 45 Fed. Reg. 25024–23025.

Erickson, M. F,. & Egeland, B. (1996). Child neglect. In J. Briere, L. Berliner, J. A. Bulkley, C. Jenny, & T. Reid (Eds.), *The APSAC handbook on child maltreatment* (pp. 4–20). Thousand Oaks, CA: Sage.

Erikson, E. (1950). *Childhood and society.* New York: Norton.

Ertz, D. J. (1997). The American Indian sex offender. In B. K.Schwartz & H. R. Cellini (Eds.), *The sex offender: New insights, treatment innovations, and legal developments* (pp. 14-1–14-12). Kingston, NJ: Civic Research Institute.

Etherington, K. (1995). Adult male survivors of childhood sexual abuse. *Counseling Psychology Quarterly, 8*(3), 233–241.

Exner, J. E. (1986). *The Rorschach: A comprehensive system* (Vol. 1, 2nd ed.). New York: Wiley.

Faller, K. C. (1989). Characteristics of a clinical sample of sexually abused children: How boy and girl victims differ. *Child Abuse and Neglect, 13*, 281–291.

Famularo, R., Kinscheff, R., Fenton, T., & Bolduc, S. M. (1990). Child maltreatment histories among runaway and delinquent children. *Clinical Pediatrics, 29*, 713- 718.

Fanshel, D., Finch, S. J., & Grundy, J. F. (1989, September–October). Foster children in life-course perspective: The Casey Family Program experience. *Child Welfare, 68*(5) 467–478.

Fedora, O., Reddon, J. R., Morrison, J. W., Fedora, S. K., Pascoe, H., & Yendall, L. T. (1992). Sadism and other paraphilias in normal controls and aggressive and nonaggressive sex offenders.

Archives of Sexual Behavior, 21, 1–15.

Fedoroff, J. P. (1988). Buspirone hydrochloride in the treatment of trans-vestic fetishism [see comments]. *Journal of Clinical Psychiatry, 49,* 408–409.

Fedoroff, J. P. (1992). Buspirone hydrochloride in the treatment of an atypical paraphilia. *Archives of Sexual Behavior, 21,* 401–406.

Federoff, J. (1993). Serotonergic drug treatment of deviant sexual interests. *Annals of Sex Research, 6,* 105–121.

Fedoroff, J. (1995). Antiandrogens vs. serotoninergic medications in the treat-ment of sex offenders: A preliminary compliance study. *Canadian Journal of Human Sexuality, 4,* 111–122.

Fedoroff, J. P., & Pincus, S. (1996). The genesis of pedophilia: Testing the "abused-to-abuser" hypothesis. *Journal of Offender Rehabilitation, 23*(3–4), 85–102.

Fedoroff, J., Winser-Carlson, R., Dean, S., & Berlin, F. (1992). Medroxy-proges-terone acetate in treatment of paraphilic sexual disorders. *Journal of Offender Rehabalitation, 18,* 109–123.

Feeney, J. A. (1995). Adult attachment, coping style and health locus of control as predictors of health behavior. *Australian Journal of Psychology, 47,* 171–177.

Feeney, J. A., Noller, P., & Hanrahan, M. (1994). Assessing adult attachment. In M. B. Sperling & W. H. Berman (Eds.), *Attachment in adults: Clinical and developmental perspectives* (pp. 128–152). New York: Guilford Press.

Fehrenbach, P. A., Smith, W., Monastersky, C., & Deisher, R. W. (1986). Adolescent sexual offenders: Offender and offense characteristics.

American Journal of Orthopsychiatry, 56, 225–233.

Feldman, C., & Ridley, C. (1995). The etiology of domestic violence between adult partners. *Clinical Psycholocy Science and Practice, 2,* 317–348.

Fendrich, M., Mackesy-Amiti, M., Goldstein, P., Spunt, B., & Brownstein, H. (1995). Substance involvement among juvenile murderers: Comparisons with older offenders based on interviews with prison inmates. *International Journal of the Addictions, 30*(11), 1363–1382.

Ferguson, G. E., Eidelson, R. J., & Witt, P. H. (n.d.). *RRAS validity study* [On-line]. Available: http://inpsyte.asarian-host.org/njrras.htm.

Fernandez, H. H., & Durso, R. (1998). Clozapine for dopaminergic-induced paraphilias in Parkinson's disease. *Movement Disorders, 13,* 597–598.

Fernandez, Y. M., & Marshall, W. L. (2000). Contextual issues in relapse prevention treatment. In D. R. Laws, S. M. Hudson, & T. Ward (Eds.), *Remaking relapse prevention with sex offenders* (pp. 225–235) New York: Guilford Press.

W. L. (1999, September). *The reliable identification of therapist features in the treatment of sexual offenders.* Paper pre-sented at the 18th annual Research and Treatment Conference of the Association for the Treatment of Sexual Abusers, Orlando, FL.

Feshbach, N. D., & Feshbach, S. (1982). Empathy training and the regulation of a ggression: Potentialities and limitations. *Academic Psychology Bulletin, 4,* 399–413.

Field, L. H. (1973). Benperidol in the treatment of sexual offenders. *Medical*

Science and Law, 13, 195–196.

Findley, M. J., & Cooper, H. M. (1983). Locus of control and academic achievement: A literature review. *Journal of Personality and Social Psychology, 44*, 419–427.

Finkelhor, D. (1984). *Child sexual abuse: New theory and research.* New York: Free Press

Finkelhor, D. (1986). *A sourcebook on child sexual abuse.* Newbury Park, CA: Sage.

Finkelhor, D. (1990). Early and long-term effects of child sexual abuse: An update. *Professional Psychologist: Research and Practice, 21*(5), 325–330.

Finkelhor, D. (1994). Current information on the scope and nature of child sexual abuse. *Sexual Abuse of Children: The Future of Children, 4*(2), 31–69.

Finkelhor, D., & Browne, A. (1986). Initial and long-term effects: A conceptual framework. In D. Finkelhor (Ed.), *A sourcebook on child sexual abuse* (pp. 180–198). Newbury Park, CA: Sage.

Finkelhor, D., & Browne, A. (1985). The traumatic impact of child sexual abuse: A conceptualization. *American Journal of Orthopsychiatry, 55*(4), 530–541.

Finkelhor, D., Hotaling, G., Lewis, I. A., & Smith, C. (1990). Sexual abuse in a national survey of adult men and women: Prevalence, characteristics and risk factors. *Child Abuse and Neglect, 14*, 19–28.

Finkelhor, D., & Russell, D. (1984). How much child sexual abuse is committed by women? In D. Finkelhor (Ed.), *Child sexual abuse: New theory and research* (pp. 171–187). New York: Free Press.

Fischer, G. J. (1992). Sex attitudes and prior victimization as predictors of college student sex offenses. *Annals of Sex Research, 5*, 53-60.

Fish, V., & Scott, C. (1999). Childhood abuse recollections in a nonclinical population: Forgetting and secrecy. *Child Abuse and Neglect, 23*(8), 791–802.

Fish-Murray, C., Koby, E., & van der Kolk, B. A. (1987). Evolving ideas: The effect of abuse on children's thought. In B. A. van der Kolk (Ed.), *Psychological trauma* (pp. 89–110). Washington, DC: American Psychiatric Press.

Fisher, D., & Beech, A. R. (1999). Current practice in Britain with sexual offenders. *Journal of Interpersonal Violence, 14*(3), 240–256.

Fisher, D., Beech, A., & Browne, K. (1999). Comparison of sex offenders to nonoffenders on selected psychological measures. *International Journal of Offender Therapy and Comparative Criminology, 43*(4), 473–491.

Fitzgerald, L. F. (1993). Sexual harassment: Violence against women in the workplace. *American Psychologist, 48*(10), 1070–1076.

Fitzgerald, L. F., Gelfand, M. J., & Drasgow, M. J., (1995). Measuring sexual harassment: Theoretical and psychometric advances. *Basic and Applied Social Psychology, 17*(4), 425–445.

Fitzgerald, L. F., Shullman, S. L., Bailey, N., Richards, M., Swecker, J., Gold, Y., Ormerod, M., & Weiztmand, L. (1988). The incidence and dimensions of sexual harassment in the academia and the workplace. *Journal of Vocational Behavior, 32*, 152–175.

Fitzgerald, L. F., Swan, S., & Magley, V. J. (1997). But was it really sexual harassment? Legal, behavioral, and psychological definitions of the workplace victimization of women. In W. T.

O'Donohue (Ed.), *Sexual harassment: Theory, research, and treatment* (pp. 5–28). Needham Heights, MA: Allyn & Bacon.

Flammer, A. (1995). Developmental analysis of control beliefs. In A. Bandura (Ed.), *Self-efficacy in changing societies* (pp. 69–113). Melbourne, Australia: Cambridge University Press.

Foley, T. P., & Prentky, R. A. (1998). *Multitrait multimethod forensic assessment approach.* Paper presented at the 17th annual Research and Treatment Conference of the Association for the Treatment of Sexual Abusers, Vancouver.

Folkman, S. (1984). Personal control and stress and coping processes: A theoretical analysis. *Journal of Personality and Social Psychology, 46,* 839–852.

Folkman, S. (1992). Making the case for coping. In B. N. Carpenter (Ed.), *Personal coping: Theory, research, and application* (pp. 31–46). Westport, CT: Praeger.

Folkman, S., & Lazarus, R. S. (1980). An analysis of coping in a middle aged community sample. *Journal of Health and Social Behavior, 21,* 219–139.

Fonagy, P. (1994). Mental representations from an intergenerational cognitive science perspective. *Infant Mental Health Journal, 15,* 57–68.

Fong, J., & Walsh-Bowers, R. (1998). Voices of the blamed: Mothers' responsiveness to father-daughter incest. *Journal of Family Social Work, 3*(1), 25–41.

Ford, J. (1978). Therapeutic relationship in behavior therapy: An empirical analysis. *Journal of Consulting and Clinical Psychology, 46,* 1302–1314.

Ford, M. E., & Linney J. A. (1995). Comparative analysis of juvenile sexual offenders, violent non-sexual offenders, and status offenders. *Journal of Interpersonal Violence, 10,* 56–70.

Foster Family-Based Treatment Association. (1995, August). *Program standards for treatment foster care* (rev. ed.). Teaneck, NJ: Author.

Foulds, M. L. (1971). Changes in locus of control internal-external control. *Comparative Group Studies, 2,* 293–300.

Fowler, C., Burns, S. R., & Roehl, J. E. (1983). The role of group therapy in incest counseling. *International Journal of Family Therapy, 5*(2), 127–135.

Fraley, R. C., & Waller, N. G. (1998). Adult attachment patterns: A test of the typological model. In J. A. Simpson & W. S. Rholes (Eds.), *Attachment theory and close relationships* (pp. 77–114). New York: Guilford Press.

Frank, J. D. (1971). Therapeutic factors in psychotherapy. *American Journal of Psychotherapy, 25,* 350–361.

Frank, J. D. (1973). *Persuasion and healing* (2nd ed.). Baltimore: John Hopkins University Press.

Frankl, V .E. (1978). *The unheard cry for meaning: Psychotherapy and humanism.* New York: Simon & Schuster.

Frazier, P. A., Cochran, C. C., & Olson, A. M. (1995). Social science research on lay definitions of sex harassment. *Journal of Social Issues, 51*(1), 21–37.

Free, N. K, Green, B. L., Grace, M. D., Chernas, L. A., & Whitman, R. M. (1985). Empathy and outcome in brief, focal dynamic therapy. *American Journal of Psychiatry, 142,* 917–921.

Freeman-Longo, R. E. (1986). The

impact of sexual victimization on males. *Child Abuse and Neglect, 10,* 411–414.

Freeman-Longo, R. E.   , Bird, S., Stevenson, W. F., & Fiske, J. A. (1995). *1994 nationwide survey of treatment programs & models: Serving abuse reactive children and adolescent & adult sexual offenders.* Brandon, VT: Safer Society Press.

Freeman-Longo, R. E., & Blanchard, G. T. (1998). *Sexual abuse in America: Epidemic of the 21st century.* Brandon, VT: Safer Society Press.

Freeman-Longo, R. E., & Knopp, H. F. (1992). State-of-the-art sex offender treatment: Outcome and issues. *Annals of Sex Research, 5*(3), 141–160.

Freeman-Longo, R. E., & Pithers, W. D. (1992). *A structured approach to preventing relapse.* Brandon, VT: Safer Society Press.

Freund, K., & Kuban, M. (1994). The basis of the abused abuser theory of pedophilia: A further elaboration of an earlier study. *Archives of Sexual Behavior, 23*(5), 553–563.

Frey, C. (1987). Mini-marathon group sessions with incest offenders. *Social Work, 32*(4), 534–535.

Friedrich, W. N. (1988). Behavior problems in sexually abused children: An adaptational perspective. In G. E. Wyatt & G. J. Powell (Eds.), *Lasting effects of child sexual abuse* (pp. 171–191). Newbury Park, CA: Sage.

Friedrich, W. N. (1990). Evaluating the child and planning for treatment. In W. N. Friedrich (Ed.), *Psychotherapy of the sexually abused children and their families* (pp. 64–99). New York: Norton.

Friedrich, W. N. (1991). *Casebook of sexual abuse treatment.* New York: Norton.

Friedrich, W. N. (1998). Behavioral manifestations of child sexual abuse. *Child Abuse and Neglect, 17,* 523–531.

Friedrich, W. N., Grambsch, P., Broughton, D., Kuiper, J., & Beilke, R. L. (1991). Normative sexual behavior in children. *Pediatrics, 88,* 456–464.

Friedrich, W. N., Grambsch, P., Damon, L., Hewitt, S., Koverola, C., Lang, R., & Wolfe, V. (1992). The child sexual abuse inventory: Normative and clinical comparisons. *Psychological Assessment, 4,* 303–311.

Friedrich, W. N., & Luecke, W. J. (1988). Young school-age sexually aggressive children. *Professional Psychology: Research and Practice, 19*(2), 155–164.

Fromuth, M. E., & Burkhart, B. R. (1989). Long-term psychological correlates of childhood sexual abuse in two samples of college men. *Child Abuse and Neglect, 13,* 533–542.

Fuller, F., & Hill, C. E. (1985). Counselor and helper perceptions of counselor intentions in relation to outcome in a single counseling session. *Journal of Counseling Psychology, 32,* 329–338.

Furby, L., Weinrott, M. R., & Blackshaw, L. (1989). Sex offender recidivism: A review. *Psychological Bulletin, 105,* 3–30.

Gacono, C. B., & Meloy, J. R. (1994). *Rorschach assessment of aggressive and psychopathic personalities.* Hillsdale, NJ: Erlbaum.

Gagne, P. (1981). Treatment of sex offenders with medroxyprogesterone acetate. *American Journal of Psychiatry, 138,* 644–646.

Galli, V., McElroy, S., Soutullo, C., Kizer, D., Raute, N., Keck, P., & McConville, B. (1999). The psychiatric diagnoses of twenty-two adolescents who have sexually molested other children. *Comprehensive Psychiatry, 40*, 85–88.

Galli, V. B., Raute, N. J., McConville, B. J., & McElroy, S. L. (1998). An adolescent male with multiple paraphilias successfully treated with fluoxetine. *Journal of Child and Adolescent Psychopharmacology, 8*, 195–197.

Ganzarain, R., & Buchele, B.J. (1990). Incest perpetrators in group therapy: A psychodynamic perspective. *Bulletin of the Menninger Clinic, 54*(3), 295–310.

Garfield, S., & Bergin, A. (Eds.). (1986). *Handbook of psychotherapy and behavior change.* New York: Wiley.

Gardner, H. (1983). *Frames of mind: The theory of multiple intelligences.* New York: Basic Books

Garland, G. J., & Dougher, M. J. (1990). The abused/abuser hypothesis of child sexual abuse: A critical review of theory and research. In J. R. Feirman (Ed.), *Pedophilia: Biosocial dimensions* (pp. 488–509). New York: Springer-Verlag.

Garland, R. J., & Dougher, M. J. (1991). Motivational intervention in the treatment of sex offenders. In W. R. Miller & S. Rollnick, *Motivational interviewing: Preparing people to change addictive behavior* (pp. 303–313). New York: Guilford Press.

Gediman, H. K. (1991, Fall). Seduction trauma: Complemental intrapsychic and interpersonal perspectives on fantasy and reality. *Psychoanalytic Psychology, 8*(4), 381–401.

Gendreau, P. (1998, October 18). *Correctional programs that work.* Paper presented at the annual conference of the Association for the Treatment of Sexual Abusers, Vancouver.

Gendreau, P., Little, T., & Goggin, C. (1996). A meta-analysis of the predictors of adult offender recidivism: What works! *Criminology, 34*, 575–607.

Genuis, M., Thomlison, B., & Bagley, C. (1991). Male victims of child sexual abuse: A brief overview of pertinent findings [Special Issue: Child Sexual Abuse]. *Journal of Child and Youth Care,, 6*, 1–6.

Gerber, P. N. (1990). Victims becoming offenders: A study of ambiguities. In M. Hunter (Ed.), *The sexually abused male* (Vol. 1, pp. 153–175). Lexington, MA: Lexington Books.

Gibbs, J. C., Potter, G. B., & Goldstein, A. P. (1995). *The equip program: Teaching youth to think and act responsibly through a peer-helping approach.* Champaign, IL: Research Press

Gijs, L., & Gooren, L. (1996). Hormonal and psychopharmacological interventions in the treatment of paraphilias: An update. *Journal of Sex Research, 33*, 273–290.

Gil, E., & Johnson, T. C. (1993). *Sexualized children.* Walnut Creek, CA: Launch Press.

Gilgun, J. F., & Reiser, E. (1990). The development of sexual identity among men sexually abused as children. *Journal of Contemporary Human Services, 71*(9), 515–523.

Gillis, J. S., & Jessor, R. (1970). Effects of brief psychotherapy on belief in internal control: An exploratory study. *Psychotherapy: Theory, Research and Practice, 7*, 135–137.

Gladstone, R. (1989). Teaching for transfer versus formal discipline. *American Psychologist, 44*(8), 1159–1159.

Glicken, V. K., & Glicken, M. D. (1982). The utilization of locus of control theory in treatment. *Indian Journal of Social Work, 43,* 173–185.

Glomb, T. M., Munson, L. J., Hulin, C. L., Bergman, M. E., & Drasgow, F. (1999). Structural equation models of sexual harassment: Longitudinal explorations and cross-sectional generalizations. *Journal of Applied Psychology, 84*(1), 14–28.

Glover, N., Janikowski, T., & Benshoff, J. (1995, March–April). The incidence of incest histories among clients receiving substance abuse treatment. *Journal of Counseling and Development, 73*(4), 475–480.

Gold, S. R., & Clegg, C. L. (1990). Sexual fantasies of college students with coercive experiences and coercive attitudes. *Journal of Interpersonal Violence, 5,* 464–473.

Gold, S. R., & Gold, R. G. (1991). Gender differences in first sexual fantasies. *Journal of Sex Education and Therapy, 17,* 207–216.

Goldberg, R. L., & Buongiorno, P. A. (1982). The use of carbamazepine for the treatment of paraphilias in a brain damaged patient. *International Journal of Psychiatry and Medicine, 12,* 275–279.

Golden, O. (2000). The federal response to child abuse and neglect. *American Psychologist, 55*(9), 1050–1053.

Goleman, D. (1995). *Emotional intelligence: Why it can matter more than IQ.* New York: Bantam Books.

Goocher, B. E. (1994). Some comments on the residential treatment of juvenile sex offenders. *Child and Youth Care Forum, 23*(4), 243–250.

Goodman-Delahunty, J. (1999). Pragmatic support for the reasonable victim standard in hostile workplace sexual harassment cases. *Psychology, Public Policy, and Law, 5*(3), 519–555.

Goodman, W. K., McDougle, C. J., & Price, L. H. (1992). Pharmacotherapy of obsessive compulsive disorder. *Journal of Clinical Psychiatry, 53*(Suppl.), 29 37.

Gordon, M. (1990). Males and females as victims of childhood sexual abuse: An examination of the gender effect. *Journal of Family Violence, 5*(4), 321–332.

Goska, R., & Ackerman, P. (1996). An aptitude-treatment interaction approach to transfer within training. *Journal of Educational Psychology, 88*(2), 249–259.

Gosselin, H. L. (1986). Sexual harassment on the job: Psychological, social and economic repercussions. *Canadian Mental Health, 32,* 21–24.

Gottesman, H. G., & Schubert, D. S. (1993). Low-dose oral medroxyprogesterone acetate in the management of the paraphilias. *Journal of Clinical Psychiatry, 54,* 182–188.

Gottfredson, M. R., & Hirschi, T. (1990). *A general theory of crime.* Stanford, CA: Stanford University Press.

Gordon, A., & Nicholaichuk, T. (1996). Applying the risk principle to sex offender treatment. *Forum on Corrections Research, 8*(2), 36–38.

Gordon, A., & Porporino, F. J. (1990). *Managing the treatment of sexual offenders: A Canadian perspective* (Research Report No. B-05). Ottawa: Correctional Service of Canada.

Graham, K. R. (1996). The childhood victimization of sex offenders: An underestimated issue. *International Journal of Offender Therapy and Comparative Criminology, 40*(3), 192–203.

Grann, M., Belfrage, H., & Tengström, A. (2001). Actuarial assessment of risk for violence: Predictive validity of the VRAG and historical part of the HCR-20. *Criminal Justice and Behavior, 27,* 97–114.

Gray, A. S., Busconi, A., Houchens, P., & Pithers, W. D. (1997). Children with sexual behavior problems and their caregivers: Demographics, functioning, and clinical patterns. *Sexual Abuse: A Journal of Research and Treatment, 9*(4), 267–290.

Gray, A. S., & Pithers, W. D. (1993). Relapse prevention with sexually aggressive adolescents. In H. E. Barbaree, W. L. Marshall, & S. M. Hudson (Eds.), *The juvenile sex offender* (pp. 289–320). New York: Guilford Press.

Gray, K., & Hutchinson, H. (1964). The psychopathic personality: A survey of Canadian psychiatrist's opinions. *Canadian Psychiatric Association Journal, 9*, 452–461.

Green, A. (1978). Dimensions of psychological trauma in abused children. *Journal of the American Academy of Child Psychiatry, 17*, 231–237.

Green, R. (1998). The deadly embrace: An approach to abusive relationships. *Group Analysis, 31*(2) 197–211.

Greenberg, D., & Bradford, J. (1997). Treatment of paraphilic disorders: A review of the role of selective serotonin reuptake inhibitors. *Sexual Abuse: A Journal of Research and Treatment, 9*, 349–360.

Greenberg, D. M., Bradford, J. M. W., &

Curry, S. (1993). A comparison of sexual victimization in the childhoods of pedophiles and hebephiles. *Journal of Forensic Sciences, 38,* 432–436.

Greenberg, D. M., Bradford, J. M., Curry, S., & O'Rourke, A. (1996a). A comparison of treatment of paraphilias with three serotonin reuptake inhibitors: A retrospective study. *Bulletin of the American Academy of Psychiatry and Law, 24*, 525–532.

Greenberg, D., Bradford, J., Curry, S., & O'Rourke, A. (1996b). *A controlled study of the treatment of paraphilia disorders with selective serotonin reuptake inhibitors.* Paper presented at the annual meeting of the Canadian Academy of Psychiatry and the Law, Tremblay, Quebec.

Greenfield, T., & Weisner, C. (1995). Drinking problems and self-reported criminal behavior, arrests and convictions: 1990 US alcohol and 1989 county surveys. *Addiction, 90*(3), 361–373.

Grendlinger, V., & Byrne, D. (1987). Coercive sexual fantasies of college men as predictors of self-reported likelihood to rape and overt sexual aggression. *Journal of Sex Research, 23*, 1–11.

Gretton, H. M., McBride, M., Hare, R. D., O'Shaugnessy, R., & Kumka, G. (2001). Psychopathy and recidivism in adolescent sex offenders. *Criminal Justice and Behavior, 28*(4), 427–449.

Griffin, D. W., & Bartholomew, K. (1994). The metaphysics of measurement: The case of adult attachment. In K. Bartholomew & D. Perlman (Eds.), *Advances in personal relationships* (Vol. 5, pp. 17–52). London: Jessica Kingsley.

Griffin, J. E., & Wilson, J. D. (1998). Disorders of the testes and male reproductive tract. In J. D. Wilson, D. W. Foster, H. M. Kronenberg, & P. R.

Larsen (Eds.), *Williams textbook of endocrinology* (9th ed., pp. 819–875). Philadelphia: Saunders.

Grossman, L. S., & Cavanaugh, J. L., Jr. (1990). Psychopathology and denial in alleged sex offenders. *Journal of Nervous and Mental Disorders, 178*, 739–744.

Grossman, L. S., Martis, B., & Fichtner, C. G. (1999). Are sex offenders treatable? A research review. *Psychiatric Services, 50*(3), 349–361.

Groth, A. N. (1979). Sexual trauma in the life histories of rapists and child molesters. *Victimology: An International Journal, 4*(1), 10–16.

Grove, W. M., & Meehl, P. E. (1996). Comparative efficiency of informal (subjective, impressionistic) and formal (mechanical, algorithmic) prediction procedures: The clinical-statistical controversy. *Psychology, Public Policy, and Law, 2*, 293–323.

Grove, W. M., Zald, D. H., Lebow, B. S., Snitz, B. E., & Nelson, C. (2000). Clinical versus mechanical prediction: A meta-analysis. *Psychological Assessment, 12*(1), 19–30.

Gruber, J. E. (1990). Methodological problems and policy implications in sexual harassment research. *Population Research and Policy Review, 9*, 235–254.

Gruber, J. E. (1997). An epidemiology of sexual harassment: Evidence from North America and Europe. In W. T. O'Donohue (Ed.), *Sexual harassment: Theory, research, and treatment* (pp. 84–98). Needham Heights, MA: Allyn & Bacon.

Gruber, J. E., & Bjorn, L. (1986). Women's responses to sexual harassment: An analysis of sociocultural, organization, and personal resource models. *Social Science Quarterly, 67*, 815–826.

Grubin, D., & Wingate, S. (1996). Sexual offence recidivism: Prediction versus understanding. *Criminal Behaviour and Mental Health, 6*, 349–359.

Grundman, E. O., O'Donohue, W. T., & Peterson, S. H. (1997). The prevention of sexual harassment. In W. T. O'Donohue (Ed.), *Sexual harassment: Theory, research, and treatment* (pp. 175–184). Needham Heights, MA: Allyn & Bacon.

Guidry, L. L. (1998). *Addressing the victim/perpetrator dialectic: Treatment for sexually victimized sex offenders.* Doctoral dissertation, Antioch New England Graduate School, Keene, New Hampshire.

Guntrip, H. (1967). The concept of psychodynamic science. *International Journal of Psycho-Analysis, 48*(1), 32–43.

Gutek, B. A. (1985). Sex and the workplace: *The impact of sexual behavior and harassment on women, men, and organizations.* San Francisco: Jossey-Bass.

Gutek, B. A., & Koss, M. P. (1993). Changed women and changed organizations: Consequences of and coping with sexual harassment. *Journal of Vocational Behavior, 42*, 28–48.

Gutek, B. A., Morasch, B., & Cohen, A. G. (1983). Interpreting social-sexual behavior in a work setting. *Journal of Vocational Behavior, 22*, 30–48.

Gutek, B. A., Nakamura, C. Y., Gahart, M., Handschumacher, I., & Russell, D. (1980). Sexuality and the workplace. *Basic and Applied Social Psychology, 1*, 255–265.

Gutek, B. A., & O'Connor, M. (1995). The empirical basis for the reasonable woman standard. *Journal of Social Issues, 51*(1), 151–166.

Haapasalo, J., & Kankkonen, M. (1997). Self-reported childhood abuse among sex and violent offenders. *Archives of Sexual Behavior, 26*(4), 421–431.

Hagood, M. (1991). Group art therapy with the mothers of sexually abused children. *The Arts in Psychotherapy, 18*, 17–27.

Hall, G. C. N. (1995). Sexual offender recidivism revisited: A meta-analysis of recent treatment studies. *Journal of Consulting and Clinical Psychology, 63*, 802–809.

Hall, G. C. N. (1996). *Theory-based assessment, treatment, and prevention of sexual aggression.* New York: Oxford University Press.

Hall, S., Havassy, B., & Wasserman, D. (1989). Commitment to abstinence and acute stress in relapse to alcohol, opiates, and nicotine.*Journal of Consulting and Clinical Psychology, 58*(2), 175–181.

Hamilton, J. A., Alagna, S. W., King, L. S., & Lloyd, C. (1987). The emotional consequences of gender-based abuse in the workplace: New counseling programs for sex discrimination. *Women and Therapy, 6*, 155–182.c

Hanson, R. K. (1997). How to know what works with sexual offenders. *Sexual Abuse: A Journal of Research and Treatment, 9*, 129–145.

Hanson, R. K. (1997). *The development of a brief Actuarial Risk Scale for Sexual Offense Recidivism* (User Report 97–04). Ottawa: Department of the Solicitor General of Canada.

Hanson, R. K. (1998). What do we know about sex offender risk assessment? *Psychology, Public Policy, and the Law, 4*(1/2) 50–72.

Hanson, R. K. (2000). *The effectiveness of treatment for sexual offenders: Report of the ATSA collaborative data research committee.* Paper presented at the 19th annual Research and Treatment Conference, San Diego.

Hanson, R. K. (2000). What is so special about relapse prevention? In D. R. Laws, S. M. Hudson, & T. Ward (Eds.), *Remaking relapse prevention with sex offenders: A sourcebook* (pp. 27–38). Thousand Oaks, CA: Sage.

Hanson, R. K., & Bussière, M. T. (1998). Predicting relapse: A meta-analysis of sexual offender recidivism studies. *Journal of Consulting and Clinical Psychology, 66*(2), 348–362.

Hanson, R. K., & Harris, A. (1999). *Where should we intervene? Dynamic predictors of sex offense recidivism.* Ottawa: Corrections Research, Solicitor General of Canada.

Hanson, R. K., & Harris, A. (2000). *The Sex Offender Needs Assessment Rating (SONAR): A method for measuring change in risk levels* (User Report 2000-1). Ottawa: Solicitor General of Canada.

Hanson, R. K., & Nicholaichuk, T. P. (2000). A cautionary note regarding Nicholaichuk, et al. (2000). *Sexual Abuse: A Journal of Research and Treatment*, 12, 289–293.

Hanson, R., & Scott, H. (1995, October). Assessing perspective-taking among sexual offenders, nonsexual criminals, and nonoffenders. *Sexual Abuse: Journal of Research & Treatment, 7*(4), 259–277.

Hanson, R. K., & Slater, S. (1988).

Sexual victimization in the history of child sexual abusers: A review. *Annals of Sex Research, 1*, 485–499.

Hanson, R. K., Steffy, R. A., & Gauthier, R. (1993). Long-term recidivism of child molesters. *Journal of Consulting and Clinical Psychology, 61*, 646–652.

Hanson, R. K., & Thornton, D. (1999). Improving risk assessments for sex offenders: A comparison of three actuarial scales. *Law and Human Behavior, 24*(1), 119–136.

Hanson, R. K., & Thornton, D. (1999). *Static-99: Improving actuarial risk assessments for sex offenders* (User Report No. 99-02). Ottawa: Solicitor General of Canada.

Hare, R. D. (1985). Comparison of procedures for the assessment of psychopathy. *Journal of Consulting and Clinical Psychology, 53*, 7–16.

Hare, R. D. (1991). *The Hare PCL-R Rating Booklet.* North Tonowanda, NY: Multi-Health Systems.

Hare, R. D. (1991). *The Hare Psychopathy Checklist—Revised.* North Tonowanda, NY: Multi-Health Systems.

Hare, R. D. (1996). Psychopathy: A clinical construct whose time has come. *Criminal Justice and Behaviour, 23*, 25–54.

Harlow, H. F. (1958). The nature of love. *American Psychologist, 13*, 673–685.

Harris, B., & Campbell, J. (1998, November 11). *Face to face: A model for therapists to assess readiness for and provide reunification treatment to juvenile sex offenders and their victims.* Paper presented at the conference for the Association for the Treatment of Sexual Abusers, Toronto.

Harris, G. T., Rice, M. E., Quinsey, V.

L., Lalumière, M. L., Boer, D., & Lang, C. (2001). *A multisite comparison of actuarial risk instruments for sex offenders.* Manuscript submitted for publication.

Hart, B. (1988). *Safety for women: Monitoring batterers programs.* Harrisburg: Pennsylvania Coalition Against Domestic Violence.

Hart, S. D., Kropp, P. R., & Hare, R. D. (1988). Performance of male psychopaths following conditional release from prison. *Journal of Consulting and Clinical Psychology, 56*, 227–232.

Haslam, M. (1965). The treatment of psychogenic dyspareunia by reciprocal inhibition. *British Journal of Psychiatry, 111*(472), 280–282.

Hatfield, E., & Sprecher, S. (1986). Measuring passionate love in intimate relationships. *Journal of Adolescence, 9* (4), 383–410.

Haugaard, J. J., & Tilly, C. (1988). Characteristics predicting children's responses to sexual encounters with other children. *Child Abuse and Neglect, 12*, 209–218.

Haviland, M. G., Sonne, J. L., & Woods, L. R. (1995). Beyond post-traumatic stress disorder: Object relations and reality testing disturbances in physically and sexually abused adolescents. *Journal of the American Academy of Child and Adolescent Psychiatry, 34*, 1054–1059.

Hayashino, D., Wurtele, S., & Klebe, K. (1995). Child molesters: An examination of cognitive factors. *Journal of Interpersonal Violence, 10*(1), 106–116.

Haynes, A. K., Yates, P. M., Nicholaichuk, T., Gu, D., & Bolton, R. (2000, June). *Sexual deviancy, risk, and recidivism: The relationship between deviant arousal, the Rapid Risk*

Assessment for Sexual Offence Recidivism (RRASOR) and sexual recidivism. Paper presented at annual convention of the Canadian Psychological Association, Ottawa.

Hays, R., & Ellickson, P. (1990). How generalizable are adolescents' beliefs about pro-drug pressures and resistance self-efficacy? *Journal of Applied Social Psychology, 20*(4, Pt 1), 321–340.

Hazan, C., & Shaver, P. (1987). Romantic love conceptualized as an attachment process. *Journal of Personality and Social Psychology, 52,* 511–524.

Hearn, M., & Evans, D. (1972). Anger and reciprocal inhibition therapy. *Psychological Reports, 30*(3), 943–948.

Heim, N., & Hursch, C. J. (1979). Castration for sex offenders: Treatment or punishment? A review and critique of recent European literature. *Archives of Sexual Behavior, 8,* 281–304.

Henggeler, S., Schoenwald, S., & Pickrel, S. (1995). Multisystemic therapy: Bridging the gap between university- and community-based treatment. *Journal of Consulting and Clinical Psychology, 63*(5), 709–717.

Henn, F., Herjanic, M., & Vanderpearl, R. (1976). Forensic psychiatry: Profiles of two types of sex offenders. *American Journal of Psychiatry, 133,* 694–696.

Henry, F., & McMahon, P. (2000, May 16). *What survivors of child sexual abuse told us about the people who abuse them.* Poster presented at the National Sexual Violence Prevention Conference, Dallas, TX.

Heriot, J. (1996). Maternal protectiveness following the disclosure of intrafamilial child sexual abuse. *Journal of Interpersonal Violence, 11*(2), 181–194.

Heppner, P. P., & Claiborn, C. D. (1989). Social influence research in counseling: A review and critique. *Journal of Counseling Psychology, 36,* 365–387.

Heppner, P. P., & Dixon, D. N. (1981). A review of the interpersonal influence process in counseling. *Personnel and Guidance Journal, 59,* 542–550.

Heppner, P. P., & Heesacker, M. (1982). Interpersonal influence process in real-life counseling: Investigating client perceptions, counselor experience level, and counselor power over time. *Journal of Counseling Psychology, 29,* 215–223.

Heppner, P. P., & Heesacker, M. (1983). Perceived counselor characteristics, client expectations, and client satisfaction with counseling. *Journal of Counseling Psychology, 30,* 31–39.

Herman, J. L. (1992). *Trauma and recovery.* New York: Basic Books.

Hewitt, P. L., & Flett, G. L. (1996). Personality traits and the coping process. In M. Zeidner & N. S. Endler (Eds.), *Handbook of coping: Theory, research, applications* (pp. 410–433). New York: Wiley.

Hill, C. E., Carter, J. A., & O'Farrell, M. K. (1983). A case study of the process and outcome of time-limited counseling. *Journal of Counseling Psychology, 30,* 3–18.

Hill, C. E., Helms, J. E., Tichenor, V., Spiegal, S. B., O'Grady, K. E., & Perry, E. S. (1988). Effects of therapist response modes in brief psychotherapy. *Journal of Counseling Psychology, 35,* 222–233.

Hindman, J. (1988). Research disputes assumption about child molesters. *National District Attorney's Bulletin, 7*(4), 1–3.

Hindman, J. (1989). *Just before dawn.* Ontario, OR: AlexAndria Associates.

Hodges, C., & Young, A. (1999, September 24). *Healing the juvenile sex offender's family through family reunification.* Paper presented at the conference for the Association for the Treatment of Sexual Abusers, Lake Buena Vista, FL.

Hodgins, S. (1992). Mental disorder, intellectual deficiency, and crime. Evidence from a birth cohort. *Archives of General Psychiatry, 49*, 476–483.

Hodgins, S. (1998). Epidemiological investigations of the associations between major mental disorders and crime: Methodological limitations and validity of the conclusions. *Social Psychiatry and Psychiatric Epidemiology, 33*(Suppl. 1), S29–S37.

Hodgins, S., Mednick, S. A., Brennan, P. A., Schulsinger, F., & Engberg, M. (1996). Mental disorder and crime. Evidence from a Danish birth cohort. *Archives of General Psychiatry, 53*, 489–496.

Hoffman-Plotkin, D., & Twentyman, C. T. (1984). A multimodal assessment of behavioral and cognitive deficits in abused and neglected preschoolers. *Child Development, 55*, 794–802).

Holgate, A. (1989). Sexual harassment as a determinant of women's fear of rape. *Australian Journal of Sex, Marriage, and the Family, 10*, 21–28.

Holohan, C. J., Moos, R. H., & Schaeffer, J. A. (1996). Coping, stress resistance, and growth: Conceptualizing adaptive functioning. In M. Zeidner & N. S. Endler (Eds.), *Handbook of coping: Theory, research, applications* (pp. 410–433). New York: Wiley.

Hope & recovery: A twelve step guide for healing from compulsive sexual behavior. (1987). Minneapolis, MN: CompCare.

Horner, K. L. (1996). Locus of control, neuroticism, and stressors: Combined influences on reported physical illness. *Personality and Individual Differences, 21*, 195–204.

Horton, J. (2000, February 22). Foster parents shocked by events of tragic night. *Cleveland Plain Dealer* [On-line]. Available: jhorton@plaind.com.

Horvath, A. O. (2000). The therapeutic relationship: From transference to alliance. *Journal of Clinical Psychology, 56*, 163–173.

Horvath, A. O., & Symonds, B. D. (1991). Relation between working alliance and outcome in psychotherapy: A meta-analysis. *Journal of Counseling Psychology, 38*, 139–149.

Hucker, S., Langevin, R., & Bain, J. (1988). A double blind trial of sex drive reducing medication in pedophiles. *Annals of Sex Research, 1*, 227–242.

Hudson, S. M., & Ward, T. (1997). Intimacy, loneliness, and attachment style in sexual offenders. *Journal of Interpersonal Violence, 12*, 323–339.

Hughes, D. A. (1997). *Facilitating developmental attachment.* Northvale, NJ: Jason Aronson.

Hunt, L. (1996). *The invention of pornography: Obscenity and the origins of modernity, 1500–1800.* New York: Zone Books.

Hunt, M. (1974). *Sexual behavior in the 1970s.* New York: Dell Books.

Hunter, J. A. (1991). A comparison of the psychosocial maladjustment of adult males and females sexually molested as children. *Journal of Interpersonal Violence, 6*(2), 205–217.

Hunter, M. (1990). *The sexually abused male: Prevalence, impact, and treatment* (Vol. 1). New York: Lexington Books.

Inderbitzen-Pisaruk, H., Shawchuck, C. R., & Hoir, T.S. (1992). Behavioral characteristics of child victims of sexual abuse: A comparison study. *Journal of Clinical Child Psychology, 21*(1), 14–19.

Ivanoff, A., Schilling, R. F., Gilbert L., & Chen, D. R. (1995). Correlates of problem drinking among drug-using incarcerated women. *Addictive Behaviors, 20*(3), 359–369.

Jessor, R., & Jessor, S. (1977). *Problem behavior and psychosocial development.* San Diego: Academic Press.

Johnson, M. K. (1997). Clinical issues in the treatment of geriatric sex offenders. In B. K. Schwartz & H. R. Cellini (Eds.), *The sex offender: New insights, treatment innovations, and legal developments* (pp. 12-1–12-10). Kingston, N.J: Civic Research Institute.

Johnson, T. C. (1988). Children who molest other children: Preliminary findings. *Child Abuse and Neglect, 12,* 219–229.

Johnson, T. C. (1989). Female child perpetrators: Children who molest other children. *Child Abuse and Neglect, 13,* 571–585.

Johnson, T. C., & Berry, C. (1989). Children who molest: A treatment program. *Journal of Interpersonal Violence, 4*(2), 185–203.

Johnson, V. E. (1973). *I'll quit tomorrow.* New York: Harper & Row.

Jones, M. (1953). *The therapeutic community.* New York: Basic Books.

Jourard, S. M., & Jaffe, P. E. (1970). Influence of an interviewer's self-disclosure on the self-disclosure behavior of interviewees. *Journal of Counseling Psychology, 17,* 252–257.

Jouriles, E., & Norwood, W. (1995, March). Physical aggression toward boys and girls in families characterized by the battering of women. *Journal of Family Psychology, 9*(1), 69–78.

Junger, M. (1987). Women's experiences of sexual harassment. *British Journal of Criminology, 27,* 358–383.

Kafka, M. (1991). Successful antidepressant treatment of nonparaphilic sexual additions and paraphilias in men. *Journal of Clinical Psychiatry, 52,* 60–65.

Kafka, M. P. (1991). Successful treatment of paraphilic coercive disorder (a rapist) with fluoxetine hydrochloride. *British Journal of Psychiatry, 158,* 844–847.

Kafka, M. P. (1994). Paraphilia-related disorders—Common, neglected, and misunderstood. *Harvard Review of Psychiatry, 2,* 39–42.

Kafka, M. (1994). Sertraline pharmacotherapy for paraphilias and paraphilia-related disorders: An open trial. *Annals of Clinical Psychiatry, 6,* 189–195.

Kafka, M. (1995). Sexual impulsivity. In E. Hollander & D. Stein (Eds.), *Impulsivity and aggression* (pp. 201–228). New York: Wiley.

Kafka, M. P., & Hennen, J. (2000). Psychostimulant augmentation during treatment with selective serotonin reuptake inhibitors in men with paraphilias and paraphilia-related disorders: A case series. *Journal of Clinical Psychiatry, 61,* 664–70.

Kafka, M. P., & Prentky, R. (1992). Fluoxetine treatment of nonparaphilic sexual addictions and paraphilias in men. *Journal of Clinical Psychiatry, 53,* 351–358.

Kafka, M. P., & Prentky, R. A. (1994). Preliminary observations of DSM III-R Axis I comorbidity in men with paraphilias and paraphilia related disorders. *Journal of Clinical Psychiatry, 55,* 481–487.

Kafka, M. P., & Prentky, R. A. (1998). Attention deficit hyperactivity disorder in males with paraphilias and paraphilia-related disorders: A comorbidity study. *Journal of Clinical Psychiatry, 59,* 388–396.

Kamm, I. (1965). Control of sexual hyperactivity with thioridazine. *American Journal of Psychiatry, 121,* 922–923.

Kanaley, R. (1999, July 25). How much bigger can AOL really get? *Philadelphia Inquirer.*

Kanfer, F. H., & Goldstein, A. P. (1991). *Helping people change.* New York: Pergamon Press.

Karpman, B. (1961). The structure of neuroses: With special differentials between neurosis, psychosis, homosexuality, alcoholism, psychopathy and criminality. *Archives of Criminal Psychodynamics, 4,* 599–646.

Kasarabada, N., Anglin, M., Stark, E., & Paredes, A. (2000). Cocaine, crime, family history of deviance—Are psychosocial correlates related to these phenomena in male cocaine abusers? *Substance Abuse, 21*(2) 67–78.

Kaufman, G. (1980). *Shame: The power of caring.* Cambridge, MA: Schenkman.

Kavoussi, R. J., Kaplan, M., & Becker, J. V. (1988). Psychiatric diagnoses in adolescent sex offenders. *Journal of the American Academy of Child and Adolescent Psychiatry, 27,* 241–243.

Kear-Colwell, J., & Pollock, P. (1997). Motivation or confrontation: Which approach to the child sex offender? *Criminal Justice and Behavior, 24,* 20–33.

Keijsers, G. P. J., Schapp, C. P. D. R., & Hoogduin, C. A. L. (2000). The impact of interpersonal patient and therapist behavior on outcome in cognitive-behavior therapy. *Behavior Modification, 24,* 264–297.

Keijsers, G. P. J., Schapp, C. P. D. R., Hoogduin, C. A. L., & Lammers, M. W. (1995). Patient-therapist interaction in the behavioral treatment of panic disorder with agoraphobia. *Behavior Modification, 19,* 491–517.

Kempton, T., Van Hasselt, V., Bukstein, O., & Null, J. (1994). Cognitive distortions and psychiatric diagnosis in dually diagnosed adolescents. *Journal of the American Academy of Child and Adolescent Psychiatry, 33*(2), 217–222.

Kendall, P. C., Moses Jr., J. A., & Finch, A. J. (1980). Impulsivity and persistence in adult inpatient "impulse" offenders. *Journal of Clinical Psychology, 36,* 363–365.

Kendall, P. C., & Wilcox, L. E. (1980). Cognitive behavioral treatment for impulsivity: Concrete versus conceptual training in non-self-controlled problem children. *Journal of Consulting and Clinical Psychology, 48,* 80–91.

Kendall-Tackett, K. A., Williams, L. M., & Finkelhor, D. (1993). The impact of sexual abuse on children: A review and synthesis of recent empirical studies. *Psychological Bulletin, 113,* 164–180.

Kenny, M., & Lane, R. (1996). Memoirs of a drug-abusing prostitute: Dynamics and treatment considerations in a case of intergenerational child abuse. *Journal of*

Contemporary Psychotherapy, 26(4), 361–378

Kernberg, O. F. (1976). *Object-relations theory and clinical psychoanalysis.* New York: Jason Aronson.

Kiersch, T. A. (1990). Treatment of sex offenders with Depo-Provera. *Bulletin of the American Academy of Psychiatry and Law, 18*, 179–187.

Kikuchi, J. J. (1995). When the offender is a child: Identifying and responding to juvenile sexual abuse offenders. In M. Hunter (Ed.), *Child survivors and perpetrators of sexual abuse: Treatment innovations* (pp. 108–124). Thousand Oaks, CA: Sage.

Kilpatrick, J. (1996, November). *From the mouths of victims: What victimization surveys tell us about sexual assault and sex offenders.* Paper presented at the 15th annual Research and Treatment Conference of the Association for the Treatment of Sexual Abusers, Chicago.

Kleinke, C. L. (1994). *Common principles of psychotherapy.* Pacific Grove, CA: Brooks/Cole.

Knight, R. (1999, September). *Unified theory of sexual coercion.* Paper presented at the 18th annual Research and Treatment Conference of the Association for the Treatment of Sexual Abusers in Buena Vista, FL.

Knopp, F. H. (1982). *Remedial intervention with adolescent sex offenders: Nine program descriptions.* Orwell, VT: Safer Society Press.

Knopp, F. H. (1984). *Retraining adult sex abusers: Methods and models.* Orwell, VT: Safer Society Press.

Knopp, F. H. (1995). Building bridges: Working together to understand and prevent sexual abuse. *Sexual Abuse:*

Journal of Research and Treatment, 7(3), 231–238.

Knopp, F. H., Freeman-Longo, R. E., & Stevenson, W. F. (1993). *Nationwide survey of juvenile & adult sex offender treatment programs & models, 1992.* Orwell, VT: Safer Society Press.

Knopp, F. H., Rosenberg, J., & Stevenson, W. F. (1986). *Report on nationwide survey of juvenile and adult sex-offender treatment programs and providers, 1986.* Orwell, VT: Safer Society Press.

Knopp, F. H., & Stevenson, W. F. (1989). *Nationwide survey of juvenile & adult sex-offender treatment programs & models, 1988.* Orwell, VT: Safer Society Press.

Kobayashi, J., Sales, B. D., Becker, J. V., Figueredo, A. J., & Kaplan, M. S. (1995). Perceived parental deviance, parent-child bonding, child abuse and child sexual aggression. *Sexual Abuse: A Journal of Research and Treatment, 7,* 25–44.

Kohut, H. (1990). The role of empathy in psychoanalytic cure. In R. Langs (Ed.), *Classics in psychoanalytic techniques* (rev. ed., pp. 463–473). Northvale, NJ: Aronson.

Kolko, D. J. (1996). Child physical abuse. In J. Briere, L. Berliner, J. A. Bulkley, C. Jenny, & T. Reid (Eds.), *The APSAC handbook on child maltreament* (pp. 21–50). Thousand Oaks, CA: Sage.

Kornreich, C., Den Dulk, A., Verbanck, P., & Pelc, I. (1995). Fluoxetine treatment of compulsive masturbation in a schizophrenic patient [letter]. *Journal of Clinical Psychiatry, 56,* 334.

Koss, M. P. (1990). Changed lives: The psychological impact of sexual harassment. In M. Paludi (Ed.), *Ivory power:*

Sex and gender harassment in academia (pp. 73-92). Albany: State University of New York Press.

Koss, M. P., & Burkhart, B. R. (1989). The long-term impact of rape: A conceptual model and implications for treatment. *Psychology of Women Quarterly, 13*, 133–147.

Kotin, J., Wilbert, D. E., Vorburg, D., & Soldinger, S. M. (1976). Thioridazine and sexual dysfunction. *American Journal of Psychiatry, 133*, 82–85.

Kottler, J. A., Sexton, T. L., & Whiston, S. C. (1994). *The heart of healing: Relationship in therapy.* San Francisco: Jossey-Bass.

Kravitz, H. M., Haywood, T. W., Kelly, J., Wahlstrom, C., Liles, S., & Cavanaugh, J. L., Jr. (1995). Medroxyprogesterone treatment for paraphiliacs. *Bulletin of the American Academy of Psychiatry and Law, 23*, 19–33.

Kravitz, H. M., Haywood, T. W., Kelly, J., Liles, S., & Cavanaugh, J. L., Jr. (1996). Medroxyprogesterone and paraphiles: Do testosterone levels matter? *Bulletin of the American Academy of Psychiatry and Law, 24*, 73–83.

Krueger, R., Schmutte, P., Caspi, A., Moffitt, T., Campbell, K., & Silva, P. (1994). Personality traits are linked to crime among men and women: Evidence from a birth cohort. *Journal of Abnormal Psychology, 103*(2), 328–338.

Kruesi, M., Fine, S., Vallrdares, L., Phillips, R., & Rapoport, J. (1992). Paraphilias: A double-blind crossover comparison of clomipramine versus desipramine. *Archives of Sexual Behavior, 21*, 587–593.

Kwan, M., Greenleaf, W. J., Mann, J.,

Crapo, L., & Davidson, J. M. (1983). The nature of androgen action on male sexuality: A combined laboratory–self-report study on hypogonadal men. *Journal of Clinical Endocrinology and Metabolism, 57*, 557–562.

L'Abate, L., Farrar, J., & Serritella, D. (1992). *Handbook of differential treatments for addictions.* Des Moines, IA: Allyn & Bacon, Longwood Division.

Lambert, M. J. (1989). The individual therapist's contribution to psychotherapy process and outcome. *Clinical Psychology Review, 9*, 469–485.

Lang, R. A., & Langevin, R. (1991). Parent-child relations in offenders who commit violent sexual crimes against children. *Behavioral Science and the Law, 9*(1), 61–71.

Langevin, R., Bain, J., Wortzman, S., Hucker, S., Dickey, R., & Wright, P. (1988). Sexual sadism: Brain, blood and behavior. *Annals of New York Academy of Science, 528*, 163–171.

Langevin, R., Paitch, D., Hucker, S., Newman, S., & Ramsay, G. (1979). The effects of assertiveness training, provera, and sex of therapist in the treatment of genital exhibitionism. *Journal of Behavior Therapy and Experimental Psychiatry, 10*, 275–282.

Langevin, R., & Watson, R. J. (1996). Major factors in the assessment of paraphilics and sex offenders. *Journal of Offender Rehabilitation, 23*(3 & 4), 39–70.

Langevin, R., Wright, P. & Handy, L. (1989). Characteristics of sex offenders who were sexually victimized as children. *Annals of Sex Research, 2*, 227–253.

Langston, C. A. (1994). Capitalizing on and coping with daily-life events:

Expressive responses to positive events. *Journal of Personality and Social Psychology, 67,* 1112–1125.

Lanning, K. V. (1998). Cyber pedophiles: Behavioral perspective. *The APSAC Advisor, 11*(4), 12–18.

Laschet, U., & Laschet, L. (1971). Psychopharmacotherapy of sexual offenders with cyproterone acetate. *Pharmakopsychiatrie Neuropsychopharmakolgic, 4,* 99–104.

Laws, D. R. (1988). *Use of pornography by pedophiles.* Unpublished raw data.

Laws, D. R. (Ed.). (1989). *Relapse prevention with sex offenders.* New York: Guilford Press.

Laws, D. R. (1995). A theory of relapse prevention. In W. O'Donohue & L. Krasner (Eds.), *Theories of behavior therapy: Exploring behavior change* (pp. 445–474). Washington DC: American Psychological Association.

Laws, D. R., Hudson, S. M., & Ward, T. (Eds.). (2000). *Remaking relapse prevention with sex offenders: A sourcebook.* Thousand Oaks, CA: Sage.

Laws, D. R., & O'Donohue, W. (1997). Introduction. In D. R. Laws & W. O'Donohue (Eds.), *Sexual deviance* (pp. 1–21). New York: Guilford Press.

Lazarus, R. S. (1966). *Psychological stress and the coping process.* New York: McGraw-Hill.

Lazarus, R. S., & Folkman, S. (1984). *Stress, appraisal, and coping.* New York: Springer.

LeBon, G. (1920). *The crowd: A study of the popular mind.* New York: Fisher Unwin.

Lefcourt, H. M. (1976). *Locus of control: Current trends in theory and research.* Hillsdale, NJ: Erlbaum.

Lefcourt, H. M. (1981). *Research with the locus of control construct* (Vol. 1). New York: Academic Press.

Lefcourt, H. M. (1992). Perceived control, personal effectiveness, and emotional states. In B. N. Carpenter (Ed.), *Personal coping: Theory, research, and application* (pp. 111–131). Westport, CT: Praeger.

Lehne, G. (1984–1986). Brain damage and paraphilia: Treated with medroxyprogesterone acetate. *Sexuality and Disability, 7,* 145–158.

Leiblum, S. R. (1997). Sex and the Net: Clinical implications. *Journal of Sex Education and Therapy, 22,* 21–28.

Leitenberg, H., & Henning, K. (1995). Sexual fantasy. *Psychological Bulletin, 117*(3), 469–496.

Lemmon, J. H. (1996). The effect of child maltreatment on juvenile delinquency among a cohort of low-income urban males. *Dissertation Abstracts International, 58*(02), 0587A.

Leo, R. J., & Kim, K. Y. (1995). Clomipramine treatment of paraphilias in elderly demented patients. *Journal of Geriatric Psychiatry and Neurolology, 8,* 123–124.

Lew, M. (1990). *Victims no longer: Men recovering from incest and other sexual child abuse.* New York: Harper Collins.

Lewis, A., Shankok, S., & Balla, D. (1979). Perinatal difficulties, head and face trauma of child abuse in the medical histories of seriously delinquent children. *American Journal of Psychiatry, 136,* 419–423.

Lewis, D. O., Shankok, S. S., & Pincus, J. H. (1979). Juvenile male sexual assaulters. *American Journal of Psychiatry, 136,* 1194–1196.

Lightfoot, L., & Barbaree, H. (1993). The relationship between substance use and abuse and sexual offending in adolescents. In H. E. Barbaree, W. Marshall, & S. Hudson (Eds.), *The juvenile sex offender* (pp. 203–224). New York: Guilford Press.

Linehan, M. M. (1993). *Cognitive-behavioral treatment of borderline personality disorder.* New York: Guilford Press.

Lisak, D. (1994). The psychological impact of sexual abuse: Content analysis of interviews with male survivors. *Journal of Traumatic Stress, 7,* 525–548.

Lisak, D. (1995). Integrating a critique of gender in the treatment of male survivors of childhood abuse. *Psychotherapy, 32,* 258–269.

Lisak, D., & Luster, L. (1994). Educational, occupational, and relationship histories of men who were sexually and/or physically abused as children. *Journal of Traumatic Stress, 7,* 507–523.

Litt, M. D. (1988). Cognitive mediators of stressful experiences: Self-efficacy and perceived control. *Cognitive Therapy and Research, 12,* 241–260.

Little Hoover Commission. (1992, April 9). *Mending our broken children: Restructuring foster care in California.* Sacramento: Commission on California State Government Organization & Economy.

Livingston, R. (1987). Sexually and physically abused children. *Journal of the American Academy of Child and Adolescent Psychiatry, 26,* 413–415.

Llewelyn, S. P., & Hume, W. I. (1979). The patient's view of therapy. *British Journal of Medical Psychology, 52,* 29–35.

Long, L., & Cope, C. (1980). Curative factors in a male felony offender group. *Small Group Behavior, 11,* 389–398.

Longo, R. E. (1982). Sexual learning and experience among adolescent sexual offenders. *International Journal of Offender Therapy and Comparative Criminology, 26*(3), 235–241.

Longo, R. E. (2000, April 6). *Revisiting Megan's law and sex offender registration: Prevention or problem* [On-line]. Available: http://www.appa-net.org.)

Longo, R. E. (2001). *Paths to wellness.* Holyoke, MA: NEARI Press.

Longo, R. E., & Groth, A. N. (1983). Juvenile sexual offenses in the histories of adult rapists and child molesters. *International Journal of Offender Therapy and Comparative Criminology, 27,* 150–155.

Lord, J. (1989). *Victim impact panels: A creative sentencing approach.* Hurst, TX: Mothers Against Drunk Driving.

Lowenstein, L. (1973). A case of exhibitionism treated by counter-conditioning. *Adolescence, 8*(30), 213–218

Loy, P. H., & Stewart, L. P. (1984). The extent and effects of the sexual harassment of working women. *Sociological Focus, 17,* 31–43.

Lu, L., & Chen, C. S. (1996). Correlates of coping behaviours: Internal and external resources. *Counselling Psychology Quartely, 9,* 297–307.

Luborsky, L. (1984). *Principles of psychoanalytic psychotherapy: A manual for supportive/expressive treatment.* New York: Basic Books.

Luborsky, L., McLellan, T., Woody, G. E., O'Brien, C. P., & Auerbach, A. (1985). Therapist success and its determinants. *Archives of General Psychiatry, 42,* 602–611.

Lykken, D. T. (1995). *The antisocial personality.* Hillsdale, NJ: Erlbaum.

MacDevitt, J. W., & Stanislaw, C. (1987). Curative factors in male felony offender groups. *Small Group Behavior, 18*(1), 72–81.

MacFarlane, K., Cockriel, M., & Dugan, M. (1990). Treating young victims of incest. In R. K. Oates (Ed.), *Understanding and managing child sexual abuse* (pp. 149–177). Sydney: Harcourt Brace Janovich.

MacKenzie, K. R. (1983) The clinical application of a group climate measure. In R. R. Dies & K. R. MacKenzie (Eds.), *Advances in group pychotherapy: Integrating research and practice* (pp. 159–170). New York: International Universities Press.

MacKenzie, K. R., & Tschuschke, V. (1993). Relatedness, group work, and outcome in long-term inpatient psychotherapy groups. *Journal of Psychotherapy Practice and Research, 2,* 147–156.

MacKnight, C., & Rojas-Fernandez, C. (2000). Quetiapine for sexually inappropriate behavior in dementia [letter]. *Journal of the American Geriatric Society, 48,* 707.

MacMillan, H., Fleming, J., & Trocme, N. (1997). Prevalence of child physical and sexual abuse in the community. Results from the Ontario Health Supplement. *Journal of the American Medical Association, 278,* 131–135.

Madanes, C. (1990). *Sex, love, and violence: Strategies for transformation.* New York: Norton.

Madanes, C., Keim, J., & Smelser, D. (1995). *The violence of men: New techniques for working with abusive families: A therapy of social action.* San Francisco: Jossey-Bass.

Maddock, J. (1995). The perpetrator/victim interaction pattern in sexual assault and abuse. *Nordisk Sexologi, 13*(3), 142–148.

Mahoney, M. J. (1974). *Cognition and behavior modification.* Cambridge, MA: Ballinger.

Main, M. (1996). Introduction to the special section on attachment and psychopathology II: Overview of the field of attachment. *Journal of Consulting and Clinical Psychology, 64,* 237–243.

Malamuth, N. M. (1981). Rape fantasies as a function of exposure to violent sexual stimuli. *Archives of Sexual Behavior, 10,* 33–47.

Malamuth, N. (1995, October). *A unified developmental theory of sexual aggression: Models in the making.* Paper presented at the 14th annual Research and Treatment Conference of The Association for the Treatment of Sexual Abusers, New Orleans.

Maletzky, B. M. (1997). Exhibitionism: Assessment and treatment. In D. R. Laws & W. O'Donohue (Eds.), *Sexual deviance* (pp. 40–74). New York: Guilford Press.

Maletzky, B. M. (1998). Defining our field II: Cycles, chains, and assorted misnomers. *Sexual Abuse: A Journal of Research and Treatment, 10*(1), 1–3.

Maletzky, B. M. (1999). Groups of one. *Sexual Abuse: A Journal of Research and Treatment, 11*(3), 179–181.

Mann, R. (1998, October). *Relapse prevention? Is that the bit where they told me all the things I couldn't do anymore?* Paper presented at the 17th annual Research and Treatment Conference of the Association for the Treatment of Sexual Abusers, Vancouver.

Mann, R. E. (2000). Managing resistance and rebellion in relapse prevention intervention. In D. R. Laws, S. M. Hudson, & T. Ward (Eds.), *Remaking relapse prevention with sex offenders: A sourcebook* (pp. 187–200). Thousand Oaks, CA: Sage.

Marcus, S. (1974). *The other Victorians: A study of sexuality and poronography in mid-nineteenth century England.* New York: Basic Books.

Marlatt, G. (1985). Relapse prevention: Theoretical rationale and overview of the model. In G. Marlatt & J. Gordon (Eds.), *Relapse prevention: Maintenance strategies in addictive behavior change* (pp. 3–70). New York: Guilford Press.

Marlatt, G. (1989). How to handle the PIG: The problem of immediate gratification. In R. Laws (Ed.), *Relapse prevention with sex offenders* (pp. 227–235). New York: Guilford Press.

Marlatt, G. A., & Gordon, J. R. (1980). Determinants of relapse: Implications for the maintenance of behavior change. *British Journal of Addiction, 79,* 261–273.

Marlatt, G., & Gordon, J. (Eds.). (1985). *Relapse prevention: Maintenance strategies in addictive behavior change.* New York: Guilford Press.

Marlatt, G., & Gordon, J. (1987). Abstinence violation effect: Validation of an attributional construct with smoking cessation. *Journal of Consulting and Clinical Psychology, 55*(2) 145–149.

Marques, J. K., Day, D. M., Nelson, C., & Miner, M. H. (1989). The sex offender treatment and evaluation project: California's relapse prevention program.

In D. R. Laws (Ed.), *Relapse prevention with sex offenders* (pp. 247–267). New York: Guilford Press.

Marshall, W. L. (1993). The role of attachments, intimacy and loneliness in the etiology and maintenance of sexual offending. *Sexual and Marital Therapy, 8,* 109–121.

Marshall, W. L. (1994). Treatment effects on denial and minimization in incarcerated sex offenders. *Behaviour Research and Therapy, 5,* 559–564.

Marshall, W. L. (1996). Assessment, treatment, and theorizing about sex offenders: Developments during the past twenty years and future directions. *Criminal Justice and Behavior, 23,* 162–199.

Marshall, W. L. (1996). The sexual offender: Monster, victim or everyman? *Sexual Abuse: A Journal of Research and Treatment, 8,* 317–335.

Marshall, W. L. (1997) Pedophilia: Psychopathology and theory: In D. R. Laws & W. O'Donohue, (Eds.), *Sexual deviance: Theory, assessment, and treatment* (pp. 152–174). New York: Guilford Press.

Marshall, W. L., & Anderson, D. (2000). Do relapse prevention components enhance treatment effectiveness? In D. R. Laws, S. M. Hudson, & T. Ward (Eds.), *Remaking relapse prevention with sex offenders: A sourcebook* (pp. 39–55). Thousand Oaks, CA: Sage.

Marshall, W. L., Anderson, D., & Champagne, F. (1996). Self-esteem and its relationship to sexual offending. *Psychology, Crime and Law, 3,* 81–106.

Marshall, W. L., Anderson, D., & Fernandez, Y. M. (1999). *Cognitive behavioral treatment of sexual offenders.* London: Wiley.

Marshall, W. L., & Barbaree, H. E. (1990). An integrated theory of the etiology of sexual offending. In W. L. Marshall, D. R. Laws, & H. E. Barbaree (Eds.), *Handbook of sexual assault: Issues, theories and treatment of the offender* (pp. 257–275). New York: Plenum.

Marshall, W. L., & Barbaree, H. E. (1990). Outcome of comprehensive cognitive behavioral treatment program. In W. L. Marshall, D. R. Laws, & H. E. Barbaree (Eds.), *Handbook of sexual assault: Issues, theories and treatment of the offender* (pp. 257–275). New York: Plenum.

Marshall, W. L., & Christie, M. M. (1982). The enhancement of social self-esteem. *Canadian Counselor, 16,* 82–89.

Marshall, W. L., Cripps, E., Anderson, D., & Cortoni, F. A. (1999). Self-esteem and coping strategies in child molesters. *Journal of Interpersonal Violence, 14,* 955–962.

Marshall, W. L., & Eccles, A. (1991). Issues in clinical practice with sex offenders. *Journal of Interpersonal Violence, 6,* 68–93.

Marshall, W. L., Hudson, S. M., & Hodkinson, S. (1993). The importance of attachment bonds in the development of juvenile sex offending. In H. E. Barbaree, W. L. Marshall, & S. M. Hudson (Eds.), *The juvenile sex offender* (pp. 164–181). New York: Guilford Press.

Marshall, W., Hudson, S., Jones, R., & Fernandez, Y. (1995). Empathy in sex offenders. *Clinical Psychology Review, 15*(2), 99–113.

Marshall, W. L., Jones, R., Ward, T. Johnson, P., & Barbaree, H. E. (1991). Treatment outcome with sex offenders. *Clinical Psychology Review, 11,* 465–485.

Marshall, W. L., & Marshall, L. E. (2000). The origins of sexual offending. *Trauma, Violence, and Abuse: A Review Journal, 1,* 250–263.

Marshall, W. L., Mulloy, R., & Serran, G. A. (1999). T*he identification of treatment-facilitative behaviors enacted by sexual offender therapists.* Unpublished manuscript, Queen's University, Kingston, Ontario.

Marshall, W. L., & Pithers, W. D. (1994). A reconsideration of treatment outcome with sex offenders. *Criminal Justice and Behavior, 21*(1), 10–27.

Marshall, W. L., & Serran, G. (2000). Improving the effectiveness of sexual offender treatment. *Trauma, Violence & Abuse: A Review Journal, 1,* 203–222.

Marshall, W. L., Serran, G. A., & Cortoni, F. A. (2000). Childhood attachment, sexual abuse, and the relationship to adult coping in child molesters. *Sexual Abuse: A Journal of Research and Treatment, 12,* 17–26.

Marshall, W. L., & Mazzucco, A. (1995). Self-esteem and parental attachment in child molesters. *Sexual Abuse: A Journal of Research and Treatment, 7,* 279–285.

Martin, D. J., Garske, J. P., & Davis, M. K. (2000). Relation of the therapeutic alliance with outcome and other variables: A meta-analytic review. *Journal of Consulting and Clinical Psychology, 68,* 438–450.

Martindale, M. (1992). Sexual harassment in the military: 1988. *Sociological Practice Review, 2,* 200–216.

Martinson, F. L. (1991). Normal sexual development in infancy and early childhood. In G. D. Ryan & S. L. Lane

(Eds.), *Juvenile sexual offending* (pp. 57–82). Lexington, MA: Lexington Books.

Marzuk, P. M. (1996). Violence, crime, and mental illness. How strong a link? [editorial]. *Archives of General Psychiatry, 53*, 481–486.

Massat, C. R., & Lundy, M. (1998). "Reporting costs" to nonoffending parents in cases of intrafamilial child sexual abuse. *Child Welfare, 40*(4), 371–388.

Matheny, K. B., Aycock, D. W., & McCarthy, C. J. (1993). Stress in school-aged children and youth. *Educational Psychology Review, 5*(2), 109–134.

Mathews, A. M. (1976). Imaginal flooding and exposure to real phobic situations: Treatment outcome with agoraphobic patients. *British Journal of Psychiatry, 129*, 362–371.

Matsuda, B. (1996). *NOJOS evaluation instrument.* Unpublished manuscript.

McConaghy, N., Blaszczynski, A., & Kidson, W. (1988). Treatment of sex offenders with imaginal desensitization and/or medroxyprogesterone. *Acta Psychiatrica Scandinavica, 77*, 199–206.

McCorkle, E., & Bixby, F. L. (1958). *The Highfields story.* New York: Holt.

McDougall, W. (1920). *The group mind.* New York: Putnam.

McElroy, S. (2000). *Psychopathology and pharmacotherapy of sexually aggressive offenders.* Paper presented at the annual meeting of the American Psychiatric Association, Chicago.

McElroy, S., Keck, P., Hudson, J., Phillips, K., & Strakowski, S. (1996). Are impulse control disorders related to bipolar disorder? *Comprehensive Psychiatry, 37*, 229–240.

McElroy, S., Soutullo, C., Taylor, P., Nelson, E., Beckman, D., & Keck, P. (1998). *Psychiatric features of 30 sex offenders.* Paper presented at the annual meeting of the American Psychiatric Association, Toronto.

McElroy, S., Soutullo, C., Taylor, P., Nelson, E., Beckman, D., Strakowski, S., & Keck, P. (1999). Psychiatric features of 36 persons convicted of sexual offenses. *Journal of Clinical Psychiatry, 60*, 414–420.

McGee, L., & Newcomb, M. (1992). General deviance syndrome: Expanded hierarchical evaluations at four ages from early adolescence to adulthood. *Journal of Consulting and Clinical Psychology, 60*(5), 766–776.

McGoldrick, M., Gerson, R. & Shellenbergeret, S. (1999). *Genograms: Assessment and intervention.* New York: Norton.

McGrath, R. J., Cumming, G., Livingston, J. A., & Hoke, S. E. (2000, November). *The Vermont treatment program for sexual aggressors: An evaluation of a prison-based treatment program.* Poster presentation at the 19th annual Research and Treatment Conference of the Association for the Treatment of Sexual Abusers, San Diego, CA.

McGrath, R. J., Hoke, S. E., & Vojtisek, J. E. (1998). Cognitive-behavioral treatment of sex offenders. *Criminal Justice and Behavior, 25*(2), 203–225.

McGuire, R. J., Carlisle, J. M., & Young, B. G. (1965). Sexual deviation as conditioned behavior. *Behavior Research and Therapy, 2*, 185–190.

McIntosh, E. G., & Matthews, C. O. (1992). Use of direct coping resources in dealing with jealousy. *Psychological Reports, 70*, 1037–1038.

McLeod, J. (1990). The client's experience of counseling and psychotherapy: A review of the research literature. In D. Mearns & W. Dryden (Eds.), *Experiences of counseling in action* (pp. 66–79). London: Sage.

McMullin, R. E. (1986). *Handbook of cognitive therapy techniques.* New York: Norton.

Meco, G., Falachi, P., & Casacchia, M. (1985). Neuroendocrine effects of haloperidol decanoate in patients with chronic schizophrenia. In D. Kemali & G. Ragagni (Eds.), *Chronic treatments in neuropsychiatry* (pp. 89–93). New York: Raven Press.

Meinig, M. (1996, November 14). *Family therapy protocol.* Paper presented at the conference for the Association for the Treatment of Sexual Abusers, Chicago.

Melton, G. B., Petrila, J., Poythress, N. G., & Slobogin, C. (1987). *Psychological evaluations for the courts.* New York: Guilford Press.

Mendel, M. P. (1995). *The male survivor.* Thousand Oaks, CA: Sage.

Mercy, J. (1999). Having new eyes: Viewing child sexual abuse as a public health problem. *Sexual Abuse: A Journal of Research and Treatment, 11*(4), 317–322.

Meyer, W. J. D., Cole, C., & Emory, E. (1992). Depo provera treatment for sex offending behavior: An evaluation of outcome. *Bulletin of the American Academy of Psychiatry and Law, 20*, 249–259.

Miau, M. (1986). Review of 125 children 6 years of age and under who were sexually abused. *Child Abuse and Neglect, 10*, 223–229.

Michelson, M. (1985). Flooding. In A. Bellak & M. Herson (Eds.), *Dictionary of behavior therapy techniques.* New York: Pergamon Press.

Miller, D. (1994). *Women who hurt themselves: A book of hope and understanding.* New York: Basic Books.

Miller, D. (1996). Challenging self-harm through transformation of the trauma story. *Sexual Addiction and Compulsivity, 3*(3), 213–227.

Miller, D., & Guidry, L. (2001). *Addictions and trauma recovery: Healing the body, mind and spirit.* New York: Norton.

Miller, P., & Eisenberg, N. (1988). The relation of empathy to aggressive and externalizing/antisocial behavior. *Psychological Bulletin, 103*, 324–344.

Miller, P. Y., & Simon, W. (1980). The development of sexuality in adolescence. In J. Abelson (Ed.), *Adolescent psychology* (pp. 383–407). New York: Wiley.

Miller, S., Nunnally, E. W., & Wackackman, D. B. (1979). *Couple communication, Volume 1: Talking together.* Evergreen, CO: Interpersonal Communications Programs.

Miller, W. R. (1983). Motivational interviewing with problem drinkers. *Behavioral Psychotherapy, 1*, 147–172.

Miller, W. R., & Rollnick, S. (1991). *Motivational interviewing: Preparing people to change addictive behavior.* New York: Guilford Press.

Miller, W. R., & Sovereign, R. G. (1989). The check-up: A model for early intervention in addictive behaviors. In T. Loberg, W. R. Miller, P. E. Nathan, & G. A. Marlatt (Eds.), *Addictive behaviors: Prevention and early intervention* (pp. 219–231). Amsterdam: Swets & Zeitlinger.

Miller, W. R., Taylor, C. A., & West, J. C. (1980). Focused versus broad-spectrum behavior therapy for problem drinkers. *Journal of Consulting and Clinical Psychology, 48*, 590–601.

Miner, M. H. (2000). Competency-based assessment. In D. R. Laws, S. M. Hudson, & T. Ward (Eds.), *Remaking relapse prevention with sex offenders: A sourcebook* (pp. 213–224). Thousand Oaks, CA: Sage.

Miner, M. H., & Crimmins, L. S. (1997). Adolescent sex offenders: Issues of etiology and risk factors. In B. K. Schwartz & H. R.Cellini (Eds.), *The sex offender: New insights, treatment innovations, and legal developments* (pp. 9-1–9-15). Kingston, NJ: Civic Research Institute.

Miner, M. H., Day, D. M., & Nafpaktitis, M. K. (1989). Assessment of coping skills: Development of a Situational Competency Test. In D. R. Laws (Ed.), *Relapse prevention with sex offenders* (pp. 127–136). New York: Guilford Press.

Miner, M. H., Marques, J. K., Day, D. M., & Nelson, C. (1990). Impact of relapse prevention in treating sex offenders: Preliminary findings. *Annals of Sex Research, 3*, 165–185.

Monahan, J., & Steadman, H. (1994). *Violence and mental disorder: Developments in risk assessment.* Chicago: University of Chicago Press.

Money, J. (1987). Treatment guidelines: Antiandrogen and counseling of paraphilic sex offenders. *Journal of Sex and Marital Therapy, 13*, 219–223.

Money, J., & Bennett, R. (1981). Post adolescent paraphilic sex offenders: Antiandrogenic and counseling therapy follow up. *International Journal of Mental Health, 10*, 122–133.

Money, J., Wiedeking, C., Walker, P. A., & Gain, D. (1976). Combined antiandrogenic and counseling program for treatment of 46, XY and 47, XYY sex offenders. In E. J. Sachar (Ed.), *Hormones, behavior, and psychopathology* (pp. 105–20). New York: Raven Press.

Moos, R. (1994). *Group Environment Scale: A social climate scale.* Palo Alto, CA: Consulting Psychologists Press.

Morgan, R., Luborsky, L., Crits-Christoph, P., Curtis, H., & Solomon, J. (1982). Predicting the outcome of psychotherapy by the Penn Helping Alliance Rating Method. *Archives of General Psychiatry, 39*, 397–402.

Morgan, R. D., Winterowd, C. L., & Ferrell, S. W. (1999). A national survey of group psychotherapy services in correctional facilities. *Professional Psychology: Research and Practice, 30*(6), 600–606.

Morris, R. J., & Suckerman, K. R. (1974). Therapist warmth as a factor in automated systematic desensitization. *Journal of Consulting and Clinical Psychology, 42*, 244–250.

Morrison, T., Erooga, M., & Beckett, R. (1994). *Sexual offending against children: Assessment and treatment of male abusers.* London and New York: Routledge.

Motiuk, L., & Belcourt, R. (1996). Profiling the Canadian federal sex offender population. Research in brief. *Forum on Corrections Research, 8*(2), 3–7.

Murphy, P. M., Cramer, D., & Lillie, F. J. (1984). The relationship between curative factors perceived by patients in their psychotherapy and treatment outcome: An exploratory study. *British Journal of Medical Psychology, 57*, 187–192.

Murrin, M. A., & Laws, D. R. (1990). The influence of pornography on sexual crimes. In W. L. Marshall, D. R. Laws, & H. E. Barbaree (Eds.), *Handbook of sexual assault: Issues, theories, and treatment of the offender* (pp. 73–89). New York: Guilford Press.

Myers, B. A. (1991). Treatment of sexual offenses by persons with developmental disabilities. *American Journal of Mental Retardation, 95*, 563–569.

Myers, M. F. (1989). Men sexually assaulted as adults and sexually abused as boys. *Archives of Sexual Behavior, 18*(3), 203–215.

National Adolescent Perpetrator Network. (1993). The revised report from the national task force on juvenile sexual offending. *Juvenile and Family Court Journal, 44*, 4.

National Offense-Specific Residential Standards Task Force. (1999). *Standards of care for youth in sex offense-specific residential programs.* Holyoke, MA: NEARI Press.

National Survey of Treatment Programs and Models. (1994). Brandon, VT: Safer Society Program and Press.

National Task Force on Juvenile Sexual Offending. (1988). Preliminary report from the National Task Force on Juvenile Sexual Offending. *Juvenile and Family Court Journal, 39*, 2.

National Task Force on Juvenile Sexual Offending. (1993). Preliminary report from the National Task Force on Juvenile Sexual Offending. *Juvenile and Family Court Journal, 44*, 4.

Neidigh, L., & Tomiko, R. (1991). The coping strategies of child sexual abusers. *Journal of Sex Education and Therapy, 17,* 103–110.

Nelson, E., Brusman, L., Holcomb, J.,

Soutullo, C., Beckman, D., Welge, J., Kuppili, N., & McElroy, S. (2000). Divalproex sodium in sex offenders with bipolar disorder and comorbid paraphilias. *Journal of Affective Disorders, 64*, 249–255.

Newbauer, J., & Hess, S. (1994). Treating sex offenders and survivors conjointly: Gender issues with adolescent boys. *Journal for Specialists in Group Work, 19*(2), 129–135.

Newberger, C. M., Gremy, I. B., Waternaux, C. M., & Newberger, E. H. (1993). Mother of sexually abused children: Trauma and repair in longitudinal perspective. *American Journal of Orthopsychiatry, 63*, 92-102.

Newcomb, M. (1997). General deviance and psychological distress: Impact of family support/bonding over 12 years from adolescence to adulthood. *Criminal Behaviour and Mental Health, 7*(4), 369–400.

Newcomb, M., & Loeb, T. (1999). Poor parenting as an adult problem behavior: General deviance, deviant attitudes, inadequate family support and bonding, or just bad parents? *Journal of Family Psychology, 13*(2), 175–193

Newcomb, M., & McGee, L. (1991). Influence of sensation seeking on general deviance and specific problem: Behaviors from adolescence to young adulthood. *Journal of Personality and Social Psychology, 61*(4), 614–628.

Nicholaichuk, T. P. (1996). Sex offender treatment priority: An illustration of the risk/need principle. *Forum on Corrections Research, 8*(2), 30–32.

Nicholaichuk, T. P., Gordon, A., Gu, D., & Wong, S. (2000). Outcome of an institutional sexual offender treatment program: A comparison between treated &

matched untreated offenders. *Sexual Abuse: A Journal of Research and Treatment, 12*(2), 139–153.

Nicholaichuk, T., Templeman, R., & Gu, D. (1999, May). *Empirically based screening for sex offender risk.* Paper presented at the Conference of the Correctional Services of Canada, Ottawa.

Nigg, J. T., Silk, K. R., Westen, D., Lohr, N., Gold, L. J., Ogata, S., & Goodrich, S. (1991). Object representations in the early memories of sexually abused borderline patients. *American Journal of Psychiatry, 148*, 864–869.

O'Donohue, W. T. (1997). Introduction. In W. O'Donohue (Ed.), *Sexual harassment: Theory, research and practice* (pp. 1–4). Boston: Allyn & Bacon.

O'Donohue, W., Fitzgerald, L., & Brunswig, K. A. (1999). *A Self-Report Sexual Harassment Inventory.* Paper presented at the 18th annual meeting of the Association for the Treatment of Sexual Abusers, Orlando, FL.

O'Donohue, W. T., & Letourneau, E. (1993). A brief group treatment for the modification of denial in child sexual abusers: Outcome and follow-up. *Child Abuse and Neglect, 17*, 299–304.

Okami, P. (1992). Child perpetrators of sexual abuse: The emergence of a problematic deviant category. *Journal of Sex Research, 29*(1), 109–140.

Orlinsky, D. E., & Howard, K. I. (1986). Process and outcome in psychotherapy. In S. L. Garfield & A. E. Bergin (Eds.), *Handbook of psychotherapy and behavior change* (3rd ed., pp. 311–384). New York: Wiley.

Ornduff, S. R., & Kelsey, R. M. (1996). Object relations of sexually and physically abused female children: A TAT analysis. *Journal of Personality Assessment, 66*, 91–105.

Ortmann, J. (1980). The treatment of sexual offenders: Castration and antihormone therapy. *International Journal of Law and Psychiatry, 3*, 443–451.

O'Toole, L. (1998). *Pornocopia: Porn, sex, technology, and desire.* London: Serpent's Tail.

Oxford English Dictionary (2nd ed.). (1989). Oxford, UK: Clarendon Press.

Packard, W. S., & Rosner, R. (1985). Psychiatric evaluations of sexual offenders. *Journal of Forensic Science, 30*, 715–720.

Pallone, N. J., & Hennessey, J. J. (Eds.). (1996). *Tinderbox criminal agression: Neuropsychology, phenominology, demography.* New Brunswick, NJ: Transaction.

Palmer, R. (1989, April). *Empathy: Frankly my dear, I don't give a damn.* Paper presented at the Ohio Coalition for the Treatment of Adolescent Sex Abusers Conference, Columbus.

Palmer, R., & Childers, T. (1999). The grand alliance—Probation officer and therapist. In B. K. Schwartz (Ed.), *The sex offender: Theoretical advances, treating a special population and legal developments* (pp. 12-1–12-7), Kingston, NJ: Civic Research Institute.

Paludi, M. A., & Barickman, R. B. (1991). *Academic and workplace sexual harassment: A manual of resources.* Albany: State University of New York Press.

Parker, J. D. A., & Endler, N. S. (1992). Coping with coping assessment: A critical review. *European Journal of Personality, 6,* 321–344.

Parker, J. D. A., & Endler, N. S. (1996).

Coping and defense: A historical overview. In M. Zeidner & N. S. Endler (Eds.), *Handbook of coping: Theory, research, applictions* (pp. 3–23). New York: Wiley.

Parkes, K. R. (1986). Coping in stressful episodes: The role of individual differences, environmental factors, and situational characteristics. *Journal of Personality and Social Psychology, 51,* 1277–1292.

Pearson, H., Marshall, W., Barbaree, H., & Southmayd, S. (1992). Treatment of a compulsive paraphiliac with buspirone. *Annals of Sex Research, 5,* 239–246.

Pearson, H. J. (1990). Paraphilias, impulse control, and serotonin [letter; comment]. *Journal of Clinical Psychopharmacology, 10,* 233.

Pence, E., & Paymar, M. (1993). *Education groups for men who batter: The Duluth model.* New York: Springer.

Perilstein, R. D., Lipper, S., & Friedman, L. J. (1991). Three cases of paraphilias responsive to fluoxetine treatment. *Journal of Clinical Psychiatry, 52,* 169–170.

Perry, G., & Orchard, J. (1992). *Assessment and treatment of adolescent sex offenders.* Sarasota, FL: Professional Resources Press.

Person, E., Terestman, N., Myers, W., Goldberg, E., & Salvadori, C. (1989). Gender differences in sexual behaviors and fantasies in a college population. *Journal of Sex and Marital Therapy, 15,* 187–198.

Peters, S. D., Wyatt, G. E., & Finkelhor, D. (1986). Prevalence. In D. Finkelhor (Ed.), *A sourcebook on child sexual abuse* (pp. 15–59). Beverly Hills, CA: Sage.

Pilowsky, D. (1995). Psychopathology among children placed in family foster care. *Psychiatric Services, 46*(9), 906–910.

Pinta, E. R. (1978). Treatment of obsessive homosexual pedophilic fantasies with medroxyprogesterone acetate. *Biological Psychiatry, 13,* 369–373.

Pithers, W. D. (1990). Relapse prevention with sexual aggressors: A method for maintaining therapeutic change and enhancing external supervision. In W. L. Marshall, D. R. Laws, & H. E. Barbaree (Eds.), *Handbook of sexual assault: Issues, theories, and treatment of the offender* (pp. 363–385). New York: Plenum.

Pithers, W. D. (1993). Treatment of rapists: Reinterpretation of early outcome data and exploratory constructs to enhance therapeutic efficacy. In G. C. N. Hall & R. Hirschman (Eds.), *Sexual aggression: Issues in etiology, assessment, and treatment* [Series in Applied Psychology: Social Issues and Questions] (pp. 167–196). Washington, DC: Taylor & Francis.

Pithers, W. D. (1994). Process evaluation of group therapy component designed to enhance sex offender empathy for sexual abuse survivors. *Behavior Research and Therapy, 32*(5), 565–570.

Pithers, W. (1999), Empathy: Definition, enhancement, and relevance to the treatment of sexual abusers. *Journal of Interpersonal Violence, 14*(3), 257–284.

Pithers, W. D., Beal, L. S., Armstrong, J., & Petty, J. (1989). Identification of risk factors through clinical interviews and analysis of records. In D. R. Laws (Ed.), *Relapse prevention with sex offenders* (pp. 77–87). New York: Guilford Press.

Pithers, W. D., & Cumming, G. F. (1989). Can relapse be prevented? Initial outcome data from the Vermont

Treatment Program for Sexual Aggressors. In D. R. Laws (Ed.), *Relapse prevention with sex offenders* (pp. 313–325). New York: Guilford Press.

Pithers, W. D., & Cummings, G. F. (1995). Relapse prevention: A method for enhancing behavioral self-management and external supervision of the sexual aggressor. In B. K. Schwartz & H. R. Cellini (Eds.), *The sex offender: Corrections, treatment, and legal practice* (pp. 20-1–20-32). Kingston, NJ: Civic Research Institute.

Pithers, W. D., Gray, A. S., Busconi, A., & Houchens, P. (1998). Children with sexual behavior problems: Identification of five distinct child types and related treatment considerations. *Child Maltreatment, 8*(4), 384–406.

Pollak, M. [Field Producer]. (1990). *The reporters* [television documentary]. STF Productions.

Polvi, N. (1999). *The prediction of violence in pretrial forensic patients: The relative efficacy of statistical versus clinical predictions of dangerousness.* Unpublished doctoral dissertation, Simon Fraser University Department of Psychology.

Pompi, K. (1994). Adolescents in therapeutic communities: Retention and post-treatment outcome. In F. Tims, G. DeLeon, & N. Jainchill (Eds.), *Therapeutic community: Advances in research and application* (NIDA Monograph 144, pp. 128–161) (NIH Publication No. 94–3633). Rockville, MD: National Institute on Drug Abuse Research.

Porter, E. (1986). *Treating the young male victim of sexual assault: Issues and intervention strategies.* Orwell, VT: Safer Society Press.

Powell, G. N. (1986). Effects of sex role identity and sex on definitions of sexual harassment. *Sex Roles, 14*(1–2), 9–19.

Prendergast, W. E. (1991). *Treating sex offenders in correctional institutions and outpatient clinics: A guide to clinical practice.* New York: Haworth Press.

Prentky, R. A., & Burgess, A. W. (1991). Hypothetical biological substrates of a fantasy based drive mechanism for repetitive sexual aggression. In A. W. Burgess (Ed.), *Rape and sexual assault III.* (pp. 235–256). New York: Garland.

Prentky, R. A., & Burgess, A. W. (2000). *Forensic management of sexual offenders.* New York: Kluwer Academic/Plenum.

Prentky, R., & Edmunds, S.B. (1997). *Assessing sexual abuse: A resource guide for practitioners.* Brandon, VT: Safer Society Press.

Prentky, R.A., Harris, B., Frizzell, K., & Righthand, S. (2000). An actuarial procedure for assessing risk with juvenile sex offenders. *Sexual Abuse: A Journal of Research and Treatment, 12*(2), 71–87.

Prentky, R., & Knight, R. (1991). Identifying critical dimensions for discriminating among rapists. *Journal of Consulting and Clinical Psychology, 59*(5), 643–661.

Prentky, R. A., & Knight, R. A. (1993). Age of onset of sexual assault: Criminal and life history correlates. In G. C. N. Hall, R. Hirschman, J. R. Graham, & M. S. Zaragoza (Eds.), *Sexual aggression: Issues in etiology, assessment, and treatment* (pp. 43–62). Washington, DC: Taylor & Francis.

Prentky, R. A., Knight, R. A., Sims-Knight, J. E., Straus, H., Rokous, F., & Cerce, D. (1989). Developmental antecedents of sexual aggression. *Development and Psychopathology, 1,* 153–169.

Prentky, R. A., Lee, A. E. S., Knight, R. A., & Cerce, D. (1997). Recidivism rates among child molesters and rapists: A methodological analysis. *Law and Human Behavior, 21*(6), 635–659.

Proch, K., & Taber, M. (1985). Placement disruption: A review of research. *Children and Youth Services Review, 7*(4), 309–320.

Proctor, E. K., & Rosen, A. (1983). Structure therapy: A conceptual analysis. *Psychotherapy, 20,* 202–207.

Pryor, J. B. (1987). Sexual harassment proclivities in men. *Sex Roles, 17*(5–6), 269–290.

Pryor, S. (1996). *Object relations in severe trauma.* London: Jason Aronson.

Quackenbush, R. (2000). *The assessment of sex offenders in Ireland and the Irish Sex Offender Risk Tool.* Unpublished manuscript.

Quinsey, V. L., Harris, G. T., Rice, M. E., & Cormier, C. A. (1998). *Violent offenders: Appraising and managing risk.* Washington, DC: American Psychological Association.

Quinsey, V. L., Harris, G. T., Rice, M. E., & Lalumiere, M. (1993). Assessing the treatment efficacy in outcome studies of sex offenders. *Journal of Interpersonal Violence, 8*(4), 512–523.

Quinsey, V. L., Khanna, A., & Malcolm, P. B. (1998). A retrospective evaluation of the regional treatment centre sex offender treatment program. *Journal of Interpersonal Violence, 13*(5), 621–644.

Quinsey, V. L., & Lalumiere, M. (1996). *Assessment of sexual offenders against children.* Thousand Oaks, CA: Sage.

Rabavilas, A. D., Boulougouris, I. C., & Perissaki, C. (1979). Therapist qualities related to outcome with exposure in vivo in neurotic patients. *Journal of Behavior Therapy and Experimental Psychiatry, 10,* 293–294.

Rabinowitz, V. C. (1990). Coping with sexual harassment. In M. Paludi (Ed.), *Ivory power: Sexual harassment on campus* (pp. 199–213). Albany: State University of New York Press.

Raboch, J., Cerna, H., & Zemek, P. (1984). Sexual aggressivity and androgens. *British Journal of Psychiatry, 151,* 398–400.

Rapee, R. M., Craske, M. G., Brown, T. A., & Barlow, D. H. (1996). Measurement of perceived control over anxiety-related events. *Behavior Therapy, 27,* 279–293.

Raskin, R., Novacek, J., & Hogan, R. (1991). Narcissistic self-esteem management. *Journal of Personality and Social Psychology, 60*(6), 911–918.

Rasmussen, L. A., Burton, J. E., & Christopherson, B. J. (1992). Precursors to offending and the Trauma Outcome Process in sexually reactive children. *Journal of Child Sexual Abuse, 1*(1), 33–48.

Ray, J., & Horner, W. (1990). Correlates of effective therapeutic foster parenting. *Residential Treatment for Children and Youth, 7*(4), 57–69.

Raymond, N. C., Coleman, E., Ohlerking, F., Christenson, G. A., & Miner, M. (1999). Psychiatric comorbidity in pedophilic sex offenders. *American Journal of Psychiatry, 156,* 786–788.

Reinhart, M. A. (1987). Sexually abused boys. *Child Abuse and Neglect, 11,* 229–235.

Renshaw, K. L. (1994). Child molesters: Do those molested as children report larger numbers of victims than those who deny childhood sexual abuse? *Journal of Addictions and Offender Counseling, 15*(1), 24–32.

Resnicow, K., Ross-Gaddy, D., & Vaughan, R. (1995). Structure of problem and positive behaviors in African American youths. *Journal of Counsulting and Clinical Psychology, 63*(4), 594–603.

Rice, M. E., & Harris, G. T. (1997). Cross-validation and extension of the violence risk appraisal guide for child molesters and rapists. *Law and Human Behavior, 21*(2), 231–241.

Rice, M. E., & Harris, G. T. (1999, May). A multi-site follow-up study of sex offenders: The predictive accuracy of risk prediction instruments. Paper presented at the 3rd annual Forensic Psychiatry Program Research Day, University of Toronto, Penetanguishene, Ontario.

Rice, M. E., Harris, G. T., & Cormier, C. A. (1992). An evaluation of a maximum security therapeutic community for psychopaths and other mentally disordered offenders. *Law and Human Behavior, 16*(4), 399–412.

Rice, M. E., Harris, G. T., & Quinsey, V. L. (1990). A follow-up of rapists assessed in a maximum security psychiatric facility. *Journal of Interpersonal Violence, 5*, 435–448.

Rice, M. E., Quinsey, V. L., & Harris, G. T. (1991). Sexual recidivism among child molesters released from a maximum security psychiatric institution. *Journal of Consulting and Clinical Psychology, 3*, 381–386.

Rich, S. S., & Ovsiew, F. (1994). Leuprolide acetate for exhibitionism in Huntington's disease. *Movement Disorders, 9*, 353–357.

Richer, M., & Crismon, M. L. (1993). Pharmacotherapy of sexual offenders. *Annals of Pharmacotherapy, 27*, 316–320.

Roane, T. H. (1992). Male victims of sexual abuse: A case review within a child protective team. *Child Welfare, 71*(3), 231–239.

Roberson, G., Yokley, J., & Zuzik, J. (1995, October). *Developing treatment guidelines for sex offender attendance at religious services: A clergy opinion survey.* Paper presented at the 14th annual Research and Treatment Conference of the Association for the Treatment of Sexual Abusers, New Orleans.

Roesler, T. A., & McKenzie, N. (1994). Effects of childhood trauma on psychological functioning in adults sexually abused as children. *Journal of Nervous and Mental Disease, 182*(3), 145–150.

Rogers, C. R. (1957). The necessary and sufficient conditions of therapeutic personality change. *Journal of Consulting Psychology, 21*, 95–103.

Rogers, C. R. (1961). *On becoming a person.* Boston: Houghton-Mifflin.

Rogers, C. R. (1975). Empathic: An unappreciated way of being. *Counseling Psychologists, 5*, 2–10.

Rogers, C. R. (1980). *A way of being.* Boston: Houghton-Mifflin.

Romano, E., & De Luca, R.V. (1996). Characteristics of perpetrators with histories of sexual abuse. *International Journal of Offender Therapy and Comparative Criminology, 40*(2), 147–156.

Romano, E., & De Luca, R. V. (1997). Exploring the relationship between childhood sexual abuse and adult sexual perpetration. *Journal of Family Violence, 12*(1), 85–98.

Rosellini, G. (1985). *Stinking thinking.* Center City, MN: Hazelden.

Rösler, A., & Witztum, E. (1998). Treatment of men with paraphilia with a long-acting analogue of gonadotropin-releasing hormone *New England Journal of Medicine, 338,* 416–422.

Rösler, A., & Witztum, E. (2000). Pharmacotherapy of paraphilias in the next millennium. *Behavioral Science and Law, 18,* 43–56.

Ross, L. A., Bland, W. P., Ruskin, P., & Bacher, N. (1987). Antiandrogen treatment of aberrant sexual activity [letter]. *American Journal of Psychiatry, 144,* 1511.

Ross, J., & Loss, P. (1988). *Psychoeducational curriculum for the adolescent sex abuser.* Unpublished manuscript.

Ross, R. (1996). *Return to the teaching.* Toronto: Penguin Books.

Rothbaum, B. O. (1997). A controlled study of eye movement desensitization and reprocessing in the treatment of posttraumatic stress disordered sexual assault victims. *Bulletin of the Menninger Clinic, 61*(3), 317–334.

Rotter, J. B. (1954). *Social learning and clinical psychology.* Englewood Cliffs, NJ: Prentice-Hall, 1954.

Rotter, J. B. (1966). Generalized expectancies for internal versus external control of reinforcement. *Psychological Monographs, 80,* 1–28.

Rotter, J. B. (1978). Generalized expectancies for problem solving psy-

chotherapy. *Cognitive Therapy and Research, 2,* 1–10.

Rotter, J. B., Chance, J., & Phares, E. J. (Eds.). (1972). *Applications of a social learning theory of personality.* New York: Holt, Rinehart & Winston.

Rousseau, L., Couture, M., Dupont, A., Labrie, F., & Couture, N. (1990). Effect of combined androgen blockade with an LHRH agonist and flutamide in one severe case of male exhibitionism. *Canadian Journal of Psychiatry, 35,* 338–341.

Rubenstein, E. B., & Engel, N. L. (1996). Successful treatment of transvestic fetishism with sertraline and lithium [letter]. *Journal of Clinical Psychiatry, 57,* 92.

Rubinow, D. R., & Schmidt, P. J. (1996). Androgens, brain, and behavior. *American Journal of Psychiatry, 153,* 974–984.

Russell, D. E. H. (1983). The incidence and prevalence of intrafamilial and extrafamilial sexual abuse of female children. *Child Abuse and Neglect, 7,* 133–146.

Rutan, J. S., & Stone, W. N. (1993). *Psychodynamic group psychotherapy* (2nd ed.). New York: Guilford Press.

Ryan, G. D. (1987). Juvenile sex offenders: Development and correction. *Child Abuse and Neglect, 11,* 385–395.

Ryan, G. (1989). Victim to victimizer. *Journal of Interpersonal Violence, 4*(3), 325–341.

Ryan, G. (1993). Working with perpetrators of sexual abuse and domestic violence. *Pastoral Psychology, 41*(5), 303–319.

Ryan, G. (1997). Consequences for the victim of sexual abuse. In G. Ryan, S.

Lane, & A. Rinzler (Eds.), *Juvenile sexual offending: Causes, consequences, and correction* (pp. 157–167). San Francisco: Jossey-Bass.

Ryan, G. (1997). Sexually abusive youth: Defining the problem. In G. Ryan, S. Lane, & A. Rinzler (Eds.), *Juvenile sexual offending: Causes, consequenses, and correction* (pp. 3–9). San Francisco: Jossey-Bass.

Ryan, G., & Associates. (1999). *Web of meaning: A developmental-contextual approach in sexual abuse treatment.* Brandon, VT: Safer Society Press.

Ryan, G., Lane, S., & Rinzler, A. (Eds.). (1997). *Juvenile sex offending: Causes, consequenses, and correction.* San Francisco: Jossey-Bass.

Ryan, G., Miyoshi, T. J., Metzner, J. L., Krugman, R. D., & Fryer, G. E. (1996). Trends in a national sample of sexually abusive youth. *Journal of the American Academy of Child and Adolescent Psychiatry, 35*, 17–25.

Ryan, V. L., & Gizynski, M. N. (1971). Behavior therapy in retrospect: Patient's feelings about their behavior therapies. *Journal of Consulting and Clinical Psychology, 37*, 1–9.

Safer Society. (1994). *Safer Society nationwide survey of sex offender treatment programs.* Brandon, VT: Author.

Safran, J. D., & Muran, J. C. (Eds.). (1995). The therapeutic alliance [Special issue]. *Session: Psychotherapy in Practice, 1*(1). (Reissued as millenial issue, February 2000)

Safran, J. D., & Segal. Z. V. (1990). *Interpersonal process in cognitive therapy.* New York: Basic Books.

Salisbury, J., Ginorio, A. B., Remick, H., & Stringer, D. M. (1986). Counseling victims of sexual harassment. *Psychotherapy, 23*, 316–324.

Samenow, S. E. (1984). *Inside the criminal mind.* New York: Random House.

Sanchirico, A., Lau, W. J., Jablonka, K., & Russell, S. J. (1998, May). Foster parent involvement in service planning: Does it increase job satisfaction? *Children and Youth Services Review, 20*(4), 325–346.

Sandberg, G. G., & Marlatt, G. A. (1989). Relapse fantasies. In D. R. Laws (Ed.), *Relapse prevention with sex offenders* (pp. 147–152). New York: Guilford Press.

Sandler, J. (Ed.). (1987). *Projection, identification, projective identification.* Madison, CT: International Universities Press.

Sandyk, R. (1988). Naltrexone suppresses abnormal sexual behavior in Tourette's syndrome. *International Journal of Neuroscience, 43*, 107–110.

Saunders, B. E., Kilpatrick, D. G., Hanson, R. F., Resnick, H. S., & Walker, M. E. (1999). Prevalence, case characteristics, and long-term psychological correlates of child rape among women: A national survey. *Child Maltreatment, 4*(3), 187–200.

Saunders, E., Awad, G. A., & White, G. (1986). Male adolescent sexual offenders: The offender and the offense. *Canadian Journal of Psychiatry, 31*, 542–549.

Saunders, S. M. (1999). Clients' assessment of the affective environment of the psychotherapy session: Relationship to session quality and treatment effectiveness. *Journal of Clinical Psychology, 55*, 597–605.

Schapp, C., Bennun, I., Schindler, L., &

Hoogduin, K. (1993). *The therapeutic relationship in behavioral psychotherapy*. Chichester, UK: Wiley.

Scharfe, E., & Bartholomew, K. (1994). Reliability and stability of adult attachment patterns. *Personal Relationships, 1*, 23–43.

Scheidlinger, S. (2000). The group psychotherapy movement at the millennium: some historical perspectives. *International Journal of Group Psychotherapy, 50*(3), 315–339.

Schiavi, R. C., & Segraves, R. T. (1995). The biology of sexual function. *Psychiatric Clinics of North America, 18*, 7–23.

Schiller, G., & Marques, J. (n.d.). *The California Actuarial Risk Assessment Tables (CARAT) for rapists and child molesters*. Unpublished manuscript, California Department of Mental Health.

Schindler, L., Hohenberger-Sieber, E., & Halweg, K. (1989). Observing client-therapist interaction in behavior therapy: Development and first application of an observational system. *British Journal of Clinical Psychology, 28*, 213–226.

Schmahl, D. P., Lichtenstein, E., & Harris, D. E. (1972). Successful treatment of habitual smokers with warm, smoky air and rapid smoking. *Journal of Consulting and Clinical Psychology, 38*, 105–111.

Schneider, E. L. (1990, October). The effects of brief psychotherapy on the level of patient's object relations. *Dissertations Abstracts International, 51*(4-A), 1391.

Schram, D. D., Milloy, C. D., & Rowe, W. E. (1991). *Juvenile sex offenders: A follow-up study of reoffense behavior*. Research funded by the Washington State Institute for Public Policy.

Schulte, J. G., Dinwiddie, S. H., Pribor, E., & Yutzy, S. H. (1995). Psychiatric diagnosis of adult male victims of childhood sexual abuse. *Journal of Nervous and Mental Diseases, 183*(2), 111–113.

Schwartz, B. K. (1988). Interpersonal techniques in treating adult sex offenders. In *A practitioners guide to treating the incarcerated male sex offender*. Washington, DC: U.S. Department of Justice, National Institute of Corrections.

Schwartz, B. K. (1995). Group therapy. In B. K. Schwartz & H. R. Cellini (Eds.), *The sex offender: Corrections, treatment and legal practice* (pp. 14-1–14-16). Kingston, NJ: Civic Research Institute.

Schwartz, B. K. (1995). Introduction to the integrative approach. In B. K. Schwartz & H. R. Cellini (Eds), *The sex offender: Corrections, treatment, and legal practice* (pp. 1-1–1-13). Kingston, NJ: Civic Research Institute.

Schwartz, B. K. (1995). Theories of sex offenses. In B. K. Schwartz & H. R. Cellini (Eds.), *The sex offender: Corrections, treatment and legal practice* (Vol. 1, pp. 2-1–2-32). Kingston, NJ: Civic Research Institute.

Schwartz, B., & Bergman, J. (1997) Using drama therapy to do personal victimization work with sexual aggressors: A review of the research. In B. K. Schwartz & H. R. Cellini (Eds.), *The sex offender: New insights, treatment innovations, and legal developments* (pp. 20-1–20-23). Kingston, N.J: Civic Research Institute.

Schwartz, B. K., & Cellini, H. R. (Eds.). (1995). *The sex offender: Corrections, treatment, and legal practice*. Kingston, NJ: Civic Research Institute.

Schwartz, M. (1994). Negative impact of

sexual abuse on adult male gender: Issues and strategies of intervention. *Child and Adolescent Social Work Journal, 11*(3), 179–194.

Schwartz, M. (1994). The Masters and Johnson treatment program for sex offenders: Intimacy, empathy and trauma resolution. *Sexual Addiction and Compulsivity, 1*(3), 261–277.

Scully, D., & Marolla, J. (1984). Convicted repists' vocabulary of motive: Excuses and justifications. *Social Problems, 31*(5).

Sedney, M. A., & Brooks, B. (1984). Factors associated with a history of childhood sexual experience in a non-clinical female population. *Journal of the American Academy of Child Psychiatry, 23*(2), 215–218.

Sees, K.L., & Clark, W. (1993). When to begin smoking cessation in substance abusers. *Journal of Substance Abuse, 10,* 189–195.

Seghorn, T. K., Prentky, R. A., & Boucher, R. J. (1987). Childhood sexual abuse in the lives of sexually aggressive offenders. *Journal of the American Academy of Child and Adolescent Psychiatry, 26,* 262–267.

Segraves, R. (1988). Hormones and libido. In S. Leblum & R. Rosen (Eds.), *Sexual desire disorders* (pp. 271–312). New York: Guilford Press.

Seidman, B., Marshall, W. L., Hudson, S. M., & Robertson, P. J. (1994). An examination of intimacy and loneliness in sex offenders. *Journal of Interpersonal Violence, 9,* 518–534.

Seplar, F. (1990). Victim advocacy and young male victims of sexual abuse: An evolutionary model. In M. Hunter (Ed.), *The sexually abused male: Prevalence, impact, and treatment* (Vol. I, pp. 73–85). New York: Lexington Books.

Serin, R. C. (1996). Violent recidivism in criminal psychopaths. *Law and Human Behaviour, 20,* 207–217.

Serin, R. C., Mailloux, D. L., & Malcolm, P. B. (2001). Psychopathy, deviant sexual arousal and recidivism among sexual offenders. *Journal of Interpersonal Violence, 16*(3), 234–246.

Serin, R. C., Peters, R. D., & Barbaree, H. E. (1990). Predictors of psychopathy and release outcome in a criminal population. *Psychological Assessment: A Journal of Consulting and Clinical Psychology, 2,* 419–422.

Sermabeikian, P., & Martinez, D. (1994). Treatment of adolescent sexual offenders: Theory-based practice. *Child Abuse and Neglect, 18*(11), 969–976.

Sexual Assault Center of Knoxville, Tennessee. (1999). *Child sexual abuse* [On-line]. Available: http://www.cs.utk.edu/~bartley/sacc/theCenter.html.

Sgroi, S. (1982). *Handbook of clinical intervention in child sexual abuse.* Lexington, MA: Lexington Books.

Shannon, E. (1998, September 14). Main Street monsters. *Time, 152*(11), 51.

Shapiro, F. (1989). Eye movement desensitization: A new treatment for post-traumatic stress disorder. *Journal of Behavior Therapy and Experimental Psychiatry, 20,* 211–217.

Shapiro, F. (1995). *Eye movement desensitization and reprocessing: Basic principles, protocols, and procedures.* New York: Guilford Press.

Shapiro, F. (1997). *EMDR: The breakthrough therapy for overcoming anxiety, stress and trauma.* New York: Basic Books.

Shealy, C. (1995). From Boys Town to Oliver Twist: Separating fact from fiction in welfare reform and out-of-home placement of children and youth. *American Psychologist, 50*(8), 565–580.

Sheridan, M. (1995, May). A proposed intergenerational model of substance abuse, family functioning, and abuse/neglect. *Child Abuse and Neglect, 19*(5), 519–530.

Shields, W. (2000). Hope and the inclination to be troublesome: Winnicott and the treatment of character disorder in group therapy. *International Journal of Group Psychotherapy, 50*(1), 87–103.

Shoor, M., Speed, M., & Bartelt, C. (1966). Syndrome of the adolescent child molester. *American Journal of Psychiatry, 122*, 783–789.

Siassi, I. (1982). Lithium treatment of impulsive behavior in children. *Journal of Clinical Psychiatry, 43*, 482–484.

Siegal, D. (2000). *Toward an interpersonal neurobiology of the developing mind: Attachment relationships, mindsight, and neural integration.* Paper presented at the 19th annual treatment and research conference of the Association for the Treatment of Sexual Abusers, San Diego.

Sjöstedt, G., & Långström, N. (in press). Assessment of risk for criminal recidivism among rapists in Sweden: A comparison of different procedures. *Psychology, Crime, and Law.*

Skakkebaek, N. E., Bancroft, J., Davidson, D. W., & Warner, P. (1981). Androgen replacement with oral testosterone undecanoate in hypogonadal men: A double-blind controlled study. *Clinical Endocrinology (Oxford), 14*, 49–61.

Sloane, R. B., Staples, F. R., Cristol, A. H., Yorkston, N. J., & Whipple, K. (1975). *Psychotherapy versus behavior therapy.* Cambridge, MA: Harvard University Press.

Sloane, R. B., Staples, F .R., Whipple, K., & Cristol, A. H. (1977). Patients' attitude toward behavior therapy and psychotherapy. *American Journal of Psychiatry, 134*, 134–137.

Smets, A. C., & Cebula, C. M. (1987). A group treatment program for adolescent sex offenders: Five steps toward resolution. *Child Abuse and Neglect, 11*, 247–254.

Solomon, Z., Mikulincer, M., & Avitzur, E. (1988). Coping, locus of control, social support, and combat-related post traumatic stress disorder: A prospective study. *Journal of Personality and Social Psychology, 55*, 279–285.

Smallbone, S. W. (1998). *The role of attachment insecurity in the development of sexual offending behaviour.* Unpublished doctoral dissertation, Griffith University, Brisbane, Queensland, Australia.

Smallbone, S. W., & Dadds, M. R. (1998). *Attachment and coercive behaviour.* Unpublished report. Griffith University, Brisbane, Queensland, Australia.

Smith, R. E. (1970). Changes in locus of control as a function of life crisis resolution. *Journal of Abnormal Psychology, 75*, 328–332.

Smith, R. (1995). Sex offender treatment program planning and implementation. In B. K. Schwartz & H. R. Cellini (Eds.), *The sex offender: Corrections, treatment and legal practice* (pp. 7-1–7-13). Kingston, NJ: Civic Research Institute.

Spaccarelli, S., Bowden, B., Coatsworth, J. D., & Kim, S. (1997). Psychosocial correlates of male sexual aggression in a chronic delinquent sample. *Criminal Justice and Behavior, 24*, 71–95.

Spodak, M., Falck, Z., & Rappeport, J. (1978). The hormonal treatment of paraphilias with depo provera. *Criminal Justice and Behavior, 5*, 304–313.

Starr, R. H., Jr., MacLean, D. J., & Keating, D. P. (1991). Life-span developmental outcomes of child maltreatment. In R. H. Starr, Jr. & D. A. Wolfe (Eds.), *The effects of child abuse and neglect: Issues and research* (pp. 1–32). New York: Guilford Press.

Steen, C., & Monnette, B. (1989). *Treating adolescent sexual offenders in the community.* Springfield, IL: Charles C. Thomas.

Stein, D. J., Hollander, E., Anthony, D. T., Schneier, F. R., Fallon, B. A., Liebowitz, M. R., & Klein, D. F. (1992). Serotonergic medications for sexual obsessions, sexual addictions, and paraphilias. *Journal of Clinical Psychiatry, 53*, 267–271.

Stein, E., & Brown, J. D. (1991). Group therapy in a forensic setting. *Canadian Journal of Psychiatry, 36*(10), 718–722.

Stern, D. N. (1985). *The interpersonal world of the infant.* New York: Basic Books.

Stierlin, H. (1970). The function of "inner objects." *International Journal of Psychoanalysis, 51*, 321–329.

Stockdale, M. S., Visio, M., & Batra, L. (1999). The sexual harassment of men: Evidence for a broader theory of sexual harassment and sex discrimination. *Psychology, Public Policy, and Law, 5*(3), 630–644.

Strand, V. (1990). Treatment of mothers in the incest family: The beginning phase. *Clinical Social Work Journal, 18*(4), 353–366.

Strickland, B. R. (1978). Internal-external expectancies and health-related behaviors. *Journal of Consulting and Clinical Psychology, 46,* 1192–1211.

Stroud, D. (1999). Familial support as perceived by adult victims of childhood sexual abuse. *Sexual Abuse: A Journal of Research and Treatment, 11*(2), 159–175.

Strupp, H. H. (1982). The outcome problem in psychotherapy: Contemporary perspectives. In J. H. Harvey & M. M. Parks (Eds.), *The master lecture series: Psychotherapy research and behavior change* (Vol. 1, pp. 43–71). Washington, DC: American Psychological Association.

Struve, J. (1990). Dancing with the patriarchy. In M. Hunter (Ed.), *The sexually abused male: Prevalence, impact and treatment* (Vol. I, pp. 3–45). New York: Lexington Books.

Sue, D. (1979). Erotic fantasies of college students during coitus. *Journal of Sex Research, 15*, 299–305.

Sullivan, A. M. (1964). *The relation between intelligence and transfer.* Unpublished doctoral dissertation, McGill University, Montreal.

Summit, R. C. (1983). The child sexual abuse accommodation syndrome. *Child Abuse and Neglect, 7*, 177–182.

Summit, R. C. (1988). Hidden victims, hidden pain: Society's avoidance of child sexual abuse. In G. E. Wyatt & G. J. Powell (Eds.), *Lasting effects of child sexual abuse* (pp. 39–60). Newbury Park, CA: Sage.

Swanson, J. (1993). Alcohol abuse, mental disorder, and violent behavior. An epidemiologic inquiry. *Alcohol Health Research World, 17*, 123–132.

Swanson, J. W., Holzer, C. E. D., Ganju, V. K., & Jono, R. T. (1990). Violence and psychiatric disorder in the community: Evidence from the Epidemiologic Catchment Area surveys. *Hospital and Community Psychiatry, 41*, 761–770.

Sweet, A. A. (1984). The therapeutic relationship in behavior therapy. *Clinical Psychology Review, 4*, 253–272.

Symonds, M. (1978). The Psychodynamics of Violence-Prone Marriages. *American Journal of Psychoanalysis, 38*, 213–222.

Tanghe, A., & Vereecken, J. (1970). Some experiences with a new neuroleptic: Benperidol. *Encephale, 59*, 479–485.

Tannen, D. (1986). *That's not what I meant.* New York: Ballantine.

Task Force on Juvenile Sexual Offenders and Their Victims. (1996). *Juvenile sexual offenders and their victims.* Tallahassee, FL: Author.

Templeman, T. L., & Stinnett, R. D. (1991). Pattern of sexual arousal and history in a "normal" sample of young men. *Archives of Sexual Behavior, 20*, 137–150.

Tennent, G., Bancroft, J., & Cass, J. (1974). The control of deviant sexual behavior by drugs: A double-blind controlled study of benperidol, chlorpromazine, and placebo. *Archives of Sexual Behavior, 3*, 261–271.

Tharinger, D. (1990). Impact of child sexual abuse on developing sexuality. *Professional Psychology: Research and Practice, 21*(5), 331–337.

Thibaut, F., Cordier, B., & Kuhn, J. M. (1993). Effect of a long-lasting gonadotrophin hormone-releasing hormone agonist in six cases of severe male paraphilia. *Acta Psychiatrica Scandinavica, 87*, 445–450.

Tiihonen, J., Isohanni, M., Rasanen, P., Koiranen, M., & Moring, J. (1997). Specific major mental disorders and criminality: A 26-year prospective study of the 1966 northern Finland birth cohort. *American Journal of Psychiatry, 154*, 840–845.

Till, F. J. (1980). *Sexual harassment: A report on the sexual harassment of students.* Washington, D.C. National Advisory Council on Women's Educational Programs.

Tillitski, C. (1990). A meta-analysis of estimated effect sizes for group vs., individual vs. control treatments. *International Journal of Group Psychotherapy, 40*, 215–224.

Tinklenberg, J., Murphy, P., & Murphy, P. L. (1981). Drugs and criminal assaults by adolescents: A replication study. *Journal of Psychoactive Drugs, 13*(3), 277–287.

Torres, A. R., & Cerqueira, A. T. (1993). Exhibitionism treated with clomipramine [letter; comment]. *American Journal of Psychiatry, 150*, 1274.

Tracey, J., Tannenbaum, S., & Kavanagh, M. (1995). Applying trained skills on the job: The importance of the work environment. *Journal of Applied Psychology, 80*(2), 239–252.

Truscott, D. (1993). Adolescent offenders: Comparison for sexual, violent, and property offences. *Psychological Reports, 73*, 657–658.

Tuckman, B. W. (1965). Developmental sequence in small groups. *Psychological Bulletin, 63*, 384–399.

U.S. Bureau of Justice Statistics. (1996). *Criminal victimization in the United*

States: A National Crime Victimization Survey Report, 1993. Washington, DC: Author.

United States Merit Systems Protection Board. (1981). *Sexual harassment of federal workers: Is it a problem?* Washington, DC: U. S. Government Printing Office.

United States Merit Systems Protection Board. (1987). *Sexual harassment of federal workers: An update.* Washington, DC: U. S. Government Printing Office.

Urquiza, A. J., & Capra, M. (1990).The impact of sexual abuse: Initial and long-term effects. In M. Hunter (Ed.), *The sexually abused male: Prevalence, impact, and treatment* (Vol. I, pp. 105–131). New York: Lexington Books.

Urquiza, A. J., & Keating, L. M. (1990). The prevalence of sexual victimization of males. In M. Hunter(Ed.), *The sexually abused male: Prevalence, impact, and treatment* (Vol. I, pp. 89–103). New York: Lexington Books.

Urquhart, L. (1989). Separation and loss: Assessing the impacts on foster parent retention. *Child and Adolescent Social Work Journal, 6*(3), 193–209.

van der Kolk, B. A., & Fisler, R. E. (1994). Childhood abuse and neglect and loss of self-regulation. *Bulletin of the Menninger Clinic, 58*, 145–168.

van der Kolk, B. A., McFarlane, A. C., & Weiseth, L. (Eds.). (1996). *Traumatic stress: The effects of overwhelming experience on mind, body, and society.* New York: Guilford Press.

Vander Mey, B. (1988). The sexual victimization of male children: A review of previous research. *Child Abuse and Neglect, 12*, 61–72.

Van Moffaert, M. (1976). Social reintegration of sexual delinquents by a combination of psychotherapy and anti-androgen treatment. *Acta Psychiatrica Scandinavica, 53*, 29–34.

van Naerssen, A. (1991). Man-boy lovers: Assessment, counseling, and psychotherapy. *Journal of Homosexuality, 20*, 175–187.

Van Ness, S. (1984). Rape as instrumental violence: A study of youth offenders. *Journal of Offender Counseling, Services and Rehabilitation, 9*, 161–170.

van Zessen, G. (1991). A model for group counseling with male pedophiles. *Journal of Homosexuality, 20*, 189–198.

Veenhuizen, A., Van Strien, D., & Cohen-Kettenis, P. (1992). The combined psychotherapeutic and lithium carbonate treatment of an adolescent with exhibitionism and indecent assault. *Journal of Psychology and Human Sexuality, 5*, 53–64.

Vinarova, E., Uhlir, O., Stika, L., & Vinar, O. (1972). Side effects of lithium administration. *Activitas Nervosa Superior, 14*, 105–107.

Violato, C., & Genuis, M. (1993a). Problems of research in male child sexual abuse. *Journal of Child Sexual Abuse, 2*(3), 33–54.

Violato, C., & Genuis, M. (1993b). Factors which differentiate sexually abused from nonabused males: An exploratory study. *Psychological Reports, 72*, 767–770.

Virkkunen, M. (1976). The pedophilic offender with antisocial character. *Acta Psychiatrica Scandinavica, 53*, 401–405.

Vitaro, F., Ferland, F., Jacques, C., & Ladouceur, R. (1998). Gambling, substance use, and impulsivity during adolescence. *Psychology of Addictive Behaviors, 12*(3), 185–194.

Vizard, E., Monck, E., & Misch, P. (1995). Child and adolescent sex abuse perpetrators: A review of the research literature. *Journal of Child Psychology and Psychiatry, 36,* 731–756.

Volavka, J. (1999). The neurobiology of violence: An update. *Journal of Neuropsychiatry and Clinical Neuroscience, 11,* 307–314.

Vorrath, H. H., & Brendtro, L. K. (1974). *Positive peer culture* (1st ed.). Chicago: Aldine.

Vorrath, H. H., & Brendtro, L. K. (1985). *Positive peer culture* (2nd ed.). Hawthorne, NY: Aldine.

Wagner, E. J. (1992). *Sexual harassment in the workplace: How to prevent, investigate and resolve problems in your organization.* New York: AMACOM.

Wålinder, J. (1965). Transvestism, definition and evidence in favor of occasional derivation from cerebral dysfunction. *International Journal of Neuropsychiatry, 1,* 567–573.

Ward, N. (1975). Successful lithium treatment of transvestism associated with manic-depression. *Journal of Nervous and Mental Disorders, 161,* 204–206.

Ward, T., Connolly, M., McCormack, J., & Hudson, S. (1996). Social workers' attributions for sexual offending against children. *Journal of Child Sexual Abuse, 5*(3), 39–56.

Ward, T., & Hudson, S. M. (1996). Relapse prevention: A critical analysis. *Sexual Abuse: A Journal of Research and Treatment, 8*(3), 177–200.

Ward, T,. & Hudson, S. M. (1998). A model of the relapse process in sexual offenders. *Journal of Interpersonal Violence, 13,* 400–425.

Ward, T., & Hudson, S. M. (2000). A self-regulation model of relapse prevention. In D. R. Laws, S. M. Hudson, & T. Ward (Eds.), *Remaking relapse prevention with sex offenders: A sourcebook* (pp. 79–101). Thousand Oaks, CA: Sage.

Ward, T., & Hudson, S. M. (2000). Sexual offenders' implicit planning: A conceptual model. *Sexual Abuse: A Journal of Research and Treatment, 12,* 189–202.

Ward, T., Hudson, S. M., & Marshall, W. L. (1995). Cognitive distortions and affective deficits in sexual offenders: A cognitive deconstructionist approach. *Sexual Abuse: A Journal of Research and Treatment, 7,* 67–83.

Ward, T., Hudson, S. M., & Marshall, W. L. (1996). Attachment style in sex offenders: A preliminary study. *Journal of Sex Research, 33,* 17–26.

Ward, T., Hudson, S. M., Marshall, W. L., & Siegert, R. (1995). Attachment style and intimacy deficits in sex offenders: A theoretical framework. *Sexual Abuse: A Journal of Research and Treatment, 7,* 317–335.

Watkins, B., & Bentovin, A. (1992). The sexual abuse of male children and adolescents: A review of current research. *Journal of Child Psychology and Psychiatry, 33,* 197–248.

Wauchope, B. A., & Straus, M. A. (1990). Physical punishment and physical abuse of American children: Incidence rates by age, gender, and occupational class. In M. A. Straus & R. J. Gelles (Eds.), *Physical violence in American families: Risk factors and adaptations to violence in 8,145 families* (pp. 133–148). New Brunswick, NJ: Transaction.

Wawrose, F. E., & Sisto, T. M. (1992).

Clomipramine and a case of exhibition-ism [letter]. *American Journal of Psychiatry, 149*, 843.

Way, I. F., & Balthazor, T. J. (1990). *A manual for structured group treatment with adolescent sexual offenders.* Notre Dame, IN: Jalice.

Webster, C. D., Douglas, K. S., Eaves, S. D., & Hart, S. D. (1997). Assessing risk of violence to others. In C. D. Webster & M. A. Jackson (Eds.), *Impulsivity: Theory, assessment and treatment* (pp. 251–277). New York: Guilford Press.

Webster, C. D., Harris, G. T., Rice, M. E., Cormier, C., & Quinsey, V. L. (1994). *The Violence Prediction Scheme: Assessing dangerousness in high risk men.* Toronto: Centre of Criminology, University of Toronto.

Wege, J. W., & Moller, A. T. (1995). Effectiveness of a problem solving train-ing program. *Psychological Reports, 76*, 507–514.

Weiner, B. (1986). An attributional theo-ry of motivation and emotion. New York: Springer.

Weiner, I. B. (1998). *Principles of Rorschach interpretation.* Mahwah, NJ: Erlbaum.

Welsh, S. (1999). Gender and sexual harassment. *Annual Review of Sociology, 25*, 169–190.

Werrbach, G. (1993, November–December). The family reunification role-play. *Child Welfare, 22*(6), 555–567.

Westen, D. (1995). *Social Cognition and Object Relations Scale: Q-Sort for Projective Stories (SCORS-Q).* Un-published manuscript, Cambridge Hospital and Harvard University Medical School, Department of Psychiatry.

Westen, D., Silk, K. R., Lohr, N., & Kerber, K (1985). *Object relations and social cognition: TAT scoring manual.* Unpublished manuscript, University of Michigan, Ann Arbor.

Westen, D., Klempster, J., Ruffins, S., Silverman, M., Lifton, N., & Boekamp, J. (1991). Object relations in childhood and adolescence: The development of working representations. *Journal of Consulting and Clinical Psychology, 59*, 400–409.

Wexler, H., & Love, C. (1994). Therapeutic communities in prison. In F. Tims, G. DeLeon, & N Jainchill (Eds.), *Therapeutic community: Advances in research and application* (NIDA Research Monograph 144, pp. 181–208) (NIH Publication No. 94–3633). Rockville, MD: National Institute on Drug Abuse.

Widom, C. S. (1989). Does violence beget violence? A critical examination of the literature: Clarification of publish-ing history. *Psychological Bulletin, 115*(2), p. 287.

Widom, C. S. (1995, March). *Victims of childhood sexual abuse—Later criminal consequences.* Washington, DC: National Institute of Justice.

Widom, C. S., & Ames, M. A. (1994). Criminal consequences of childhood sexual victimization. *Child Abuse and Neglect, 18*, 303–317.

Wieckowski, E., & Hodges, C. (2000). *Juvenile sexual offender treatment in community and residential settings: A practical guide for clinicians, adminis-trators, court personnel and direct care staff.* Unpublished manuscript.

Wiehe, V. (1997). *Sibling abuse: Hidden physical, emotional, and sexual trauma.* London, UK: Sage.

Wilkenson, M., & Baker, D. (1996, January 31). Foster mom slain by teen, police say. *The Toledo Blade,* pp. 13–14.

Williamson, J., Borduin, C., & Howe, B. (1991, June). The ecology of adolescent maltreatment: A multilevel examination of adolescent physical abuse, sexual abuse, and neglect. *Journal of Consulting and Clinical Psychology, 59*(3), 449–457.

Wills, T., & Hirky, A. (1996). Coping and substance abuse: A theoretical model and review of the evidence. In M. Zeidner & N. Endler (Eds.), *Handbook of coping: Theory, research, applications* (pp. 279–302). New York: Wiley.

Wills, T., & Shiffman, S. (1985). Coping behavior and its relation to substance use: A conceptual framework. In S. Shiffman & T. A. Wills (Eds.), *Coping and substance use* (pp. 3–24). New York: Academic Press.

Wincze, J. P., Bansal, S., & Malamud, M. (1986). Effects of medroxyprogesterone acetate on subjective arousal, arousal to erotic stimulation, and nocturnal penile tumescence in male sex offenders. *Archives of Sexual Behavior, 15,* 293–305.

Wiseman, S. V., McAuley, J. W., Freidenberg, G. R., & Freidenberg, D. L. (2000). Hypersexuality in patients with dementia; possible response to cimetidine. *Neurology, 54,* 2024.

Witt, P. H., DelRusso, J., Oppenheim, J., & Ferguson, G. (1996). Sex offender risk assessment and the law. *Journal of Psychiatry and Law, 24,* 343–377.

Wolf, S. C., Conte, J. R., Engel-Meinig, M. (1998). Assessment and treatment of sex offenders in a community setting. In L. E. A. Walker (Ed.), *Handbook on sexual abuse* (pp. 365–383). New York: Springer.

Wolpe, J. (1958). *Psychotherapy by reciprocal inhibition.* Stanford, CA: Stanford University Press.

Wolpe, J. (1995). Reciprocal inhibition: Major agent of behavior change. In W. O'Donohue & L. Krasner (Eds.), *Theories of behavior therapy: Exploring behavior change* (pp. 23–57). Washington, DC: American Psychological Association.

Womack, M. E., Miller, G., & Lassiter, P. (1999). Helping mothers in incestuous families: An empathic approach. *Women and Therapy, 22*(4), 17–35.

Wong, S., Olver, M., Wilde, S., Nicholaichuk, T., & Gordon, A. (2000, June). *Violence Risk Scale (VRS) and the Violence Risk Scale—Sex Offender Version (VRS-SO).* Paper presented at the annual convention of the Canadian Psychological Association, Ottawa, Ontario.

Wong, S., Templeman, R., Gu, D., Andre, G., & Leis, T. (1996). *Criminal Career Profile: A quantitative index of past violent convictions.* Saskatoon, Canada: Correctional Service of Canada.

Worling, J. R. (1995). Sexual abuse histories of adolescent male sex offenders: Differences on the basis of the age and gender of their victims. *Journal of Abnormal Psychology, 104,* 610- 613.

Worling, J. R. (1995). Adolescent sex offenders against females: Differences based on the age of their victims. *International Journal of Offender Therapy and Comparative Criminology, 39,* 276–293.

Worling, J. R. (1995). Sexual abuse histories of adolescent male sex offenders: Differences on the basis of the age and gender of their victims. *Journal of Abnormal Psychology, 104*(4), 610–613.

Worling, J. R. (2000). *Personality-based typology of adolescent male sexual offenders: Differences in recidivism rates, victim-selection characteristics, and personal victimization histories.* Unpublished manuscript.

Worling, J. R., & Curwen, T. (1998). *Adolescent sexual offender project: A 10-year follow-up study.* Toronto: SAFE-T Program and Ontario Ministry of Community and Social Services.

Worling, J. R., & Curwen, T. (2000). *The "ERASOR": Estimate of Risk of Adolescent Sexual Offense Recidivism (version 1.2).* Toronto: SAFE-T Program.

Wyatt, G. E. (1985). The sexual abuse of Afro-American and white-American women in childhood. *Child Abuse and Neglect, 9,* 507–519.

Yablonsky, L. (1969). *Synanon: The tunnel back.* Baltimore: Pelican Books.

Yalom, I. D. (1980). *Existential psychotherapy.* New York: Basic Books.

Yalom, I. (1995). *The theory and practice of group psychotherapy* (4th ed.). New York: Basic Books.

Yates, A. (1982). Children eroticized by incest. *American Journal of Psychiatry, 139*(4), 482–485.

Yates, P. M., Goguen, B. C., & Nicholaichuk, T. P. (2000). *National sex offender treatment: Volume II. Moderate intensity treatment.* Ottawa, Canada: Correctional Services of Canada.

Yates, P. M., & Nicholaichuk, T. (1998). *The relationship between Criminal Career Profile, psychopathy, and treatment outcome in the Clearwater sex offender program.* Paper presented at the annual conference of the Canadian Psychological Association, Edmonton, Alberta.

Yochelson, S., & Samenow, S. (1976). *The criminal personality* (3 vols.). New York: Jason Aronson.

Yochelson, S., & Samenow, S. E. (1976). *The criminal personality: Vol. 1. A profile for change.* New York: Jason Aronson.

Yokley, J. (1989, April). *An evaluation of four procedures used to develop victim empathy in youth sex offenders.* Proceedings of the Ohio Coalition for the Treatment of Adolescent Sex Offenders Conference, Columbus, OH.

Yokley, J. (1990). The clinical trials model: Victim responsibility training. In J. Yokley (Ed.), *The use of victim-offender communication in the treatment of sexual abuse: Three intervention models* (pp. 69–110). Orwell, VT: Safer Society Press.

Yokley, J. (1993). *Treatment for Appropriate Social Control (TASC) program manual* (rev. 1997, 2000). Available from Clinical and Research Resources, P.O. Box 538 Hudson, OH 44236.

Yokley, J. (1995). *Social responsibility therapy work book: Understanding abuse behavior* (rev. 1997, 2000). Available from Clinical and Research Resources, P.O. Box 538 Hudson, OH 44236.

Yokley, J. (1996, March). *The development of abuse in youth sex offenders: A conceptual model with treatment Implications.* Paper presented at the 12th annual conference of the National Adolescent Perpetrator Network, Minneapolis.

Yokley, J. (1999). Using therapeutic community learning experiences with youth sex offenders. In B. Schwartz (Ed.), *The sex offender:Theoretical advances treating special populations and legal developments* (pp. 19-1–19-20). Kingston, NJ: Civic Research Institute.

Yokley, J. (1999). The application of therapeutic community learning experiences to adult abusers. In B. Schwartz (Ed.), *The sex offender:Theoretical advances treating special populations and legal developments* (pp. 25-1–25-26). Kingston, NJ: Civic Research Institute.

Yokley, J. (2000). *Social responsibility therapy: A positive lifestyle development approach.* Available from Clinical and Research Resources, P.O. Box 538 Hudson, OH 44236.

Yokley, J., & Boettner, S. (1999, September). *Behavior norms for outpatient youth sex offenders: Constructing a database for treatment intervention decisions.* Paper presented at the 18th annual Research and Treatment Conference of the Association for the Treatment of Sexual Abusers, Lake Buena Vista, FL.

Yokley, J., Laraway, C., & Sprague, R. (1997, October). *The treatment of youth sex offenders in therapeutic foster care: Social responsibility therapy in the TASC program.* Paper presented at the 16th annual Research and Treatment Conference of the Association for the Treatment of Sexual Abusers, Arlington, VA.

Yokley, J., & McGuire, D. (1990). Introduction to the therapeutic use of victim-offender communication. In J. Yokley (Ed.), *The use of victim-offender communication in the treatment of sexual abuse: Three intervention models* (pp. 7–22). Orwell, VT: Safer Society Press.

Yokley, J., & McGuire, D. (1991, November). *Emotional restitution: The therapeutic use of sex offender commu-nication with victims.* Paper presented at the 10th annual Research and Treatment Conference of the Association for the Treatment of Sexual Abusers, Fort Worth, TX.

Yokley, J., & Tener, R. (1994, November). *The victim conducted impact group for sex offenders.* Paper presented at the 13th annual Research and Treatment Conference of the Association for the Treatment of Sexual Abusers, San Francisco.

Young, K. S. (1996, August). *Internet addiction:The emergence of a new clinical disorder.* Paper presented at the 104th annual convention of the American Psychological Association, Toronto.

Young, K. S., & Rogers, R. C. (1998). The relationship between depression and Internet addiction. *CyberPsychology and Behavior, 1*, 25–28.

Young, R. E., Bergandi, T. A., & Titus, T. G. (1994). Comparison of the effects of sexual abuse on male and female latency-aged children. *Journal of Interpersonal Violence, 9*(3), 291–306.

Zackon, F. (1986). Lifestyle rehabilitation: The second recovery track. *Alcohol Health and Research World, 11*, 18, 70.

Zamble, E., & Quinsey, V. L. (1997). *The criminal recidivism process.* Cambridge, UK: Cambridge University Press.

Zbytovsky, J. (1993). Haloperidol decanoate (Janssen) in the treatment of sexual deviations. *Cesko-Slovenská Psychiàtre, 89*, 15–17.

Zgourides, G., Monto, M., & Harris, R. (1997). Correlates of adolescent male sexual offense: Prior adult sexual contact, sexual attitudes, and use of sexually explicit materials. *International Journal* of *Offender Therapy and Comparative Criminology, 41*, 272–283.

Zillman, D., & Bryant, J. (1984). Effects of massive exposure to pornography. In N. M. Malamuth & E. Donnerstein (Eds.), *Pornography and sexual aggression* (pp. 115–141). Orlando, FL: Academic Press.

Zimmer, D., Borchardt, E., & Fischle, C. (1983). Sexual fantasies of sexually distressed and nondistressed men and women: An empirical comparison.

Journal of Sex and Marital Therapy, 9, 38–50.

Zohar, J., Kaplan, Z., & Benjamin, J. (1994). Compulsive exhibitionism successfully treated with fluvoxamine: A controlled case study. *Journal of Clinical Psychiatry, 55*, 86–88.

Zubenko, G. S., George, A. W., Soloff, P. H., & Schulz, P. (1987). Sexual practices among patients with borderline personality disorder. *American Journal of Psychiatry, 144*, 748–752.

Appendix B

Table of Figures and Tables

Figures

Tables

Index

[References are to pages.]

[References are to pages.]

[References are to pages.]

[References are to pages.]

[References are to pages.]

[References are to pages.]

[References are to pages.]

[References are to pages.]

[References are to pages.]

[References are to pages.]

[References are to pages.]

[References are to pages.]

[References are to pages.]

[References are to pages.]

THE SEX OFFENDER

[References are to pages.]

[References are to pages.]